CW00954366

Scribe Publications
J.M. COETZEE

For Santa

J.M. COETZEE

A life in writing

J.C. Kannemeyer

Translated by Michiel Heyns

SCRIBE
Melbourne · London

Scribe Publications Pty Ltd
18–20 Edward St, Brunswick, Victoria 3056, Australia
50A Kingsway Place, Sans Walk, London, EC1R 0LU, United Kingdom

Published in Australia and New Zealand by Scribe 2012
Published in the United Kingdom by Scribe 2013

This edition published by arrangement with Uitgeverij Cossee, Amsterdam

Typeset in 10.25/14 pt ITC New Baskerville
Original text design by Etienne van Duyker, Cape Town
Printed and bound in the UK by TJ International Ltd,
Padstow, Cornwall

National Library of Australia Cataloguing-in-Publication entry

Kannemeyer, John Christoffel.

J.M. Coetzee : a life in writing / J.C. Kannemeyer.

9781922070081 (hbk.)

1. Coetzee, J.M., 1940-
2. Authors, South African–20th century–Biography.
3 Authors, Australian–20th century–Biography.
4. Fiction–Male authors–Biography.

A823.3

scribepublications.com.au
scribepublications.co.uk

Contents

V
Australia (2002–)

INDICES

Preface

I

The research for this biography of J.M. Coetzee began in July 2008 with a rereading of his published work and a preliminary investigation of the secondary literature. I was fully aware that I was dealing with a renowned author, a central figure in English studies at universities worldwide. About 500 M.A. and doctoral dissertations on his work have been completed while new books on his novels are appearing all the time in various languages.[1] In September 2008 I worked my way through some of this abundance of studies on Coetzee in the National English Literary Museum (NELM) in Grahamstown. In March 2009 I visited Coetzee in Adelaide, Australia, where I interviewed him extensively for two weeks. With the help of an assistant, I acquired copies of the vast collection of documents to which he had granted me access, and explored those of his manuscripts still in his keeping. For further information I was able to contact people with whom Coetzee had put me in touch. I started writing the manuscript on 1 January 2010. While writing, I continued researching, and in April 2010 I visited the Houghton Library at Harvard, where most of Coetzee's manuscripts were then lodged.[2] The final draft of the manuscript was completed in September 2011.

When I arrived in Adelaide in March 2009 to interview Coetzee, he told me that his major concern was that the biography should be factually correct. He would in no way interfere with my interpretation of the data.

From the outset Coetzee cooperated unstintingly and even enthusiastically. He answered all my questions succinctly and pertinently, but did not want to be drawn into speculations and opinions, especially not on interpretations of his work. Even when I asked him which critics he felt had most nearly approached saying something fundamental about his work, he adroitly redirected the question, avoiding a reply. Questions on sensitive topics—such as the estrangement and divorce from his wife, Philippa Jubber; the death of their son, Nicolas; and the illness of his daughter, Gisela—he answered in detail, succinctly, directly, and as objectively as possible, however unsettling the facts.

II

The significance of biographical information in dealing with a writer like J.M. Coetzee is a moot point. In her 1990 introduction to a bibliography of his writings, Teresa Dovey, the author of *The Novels of J.M. Coetzee*, states that in dealing with somebody like Coetzee personal biography is of lesser importance.[3] This statement is approvingly quoted by David Attwell, a prominent expert on Coetzee's work, in *J.M. Coetzee: South Africa and the Politics of Writing* (1993).[4]

Dovey and Attwell made these pronouncements before the publication of the triptych of autobiographical works initiated by *Boyhood* (1997) and followed by *Youth* (2002) and *Summertime* (2009). But even before publication of this trilogy, researchers might have discerned autobiographical moments in Coetzee's work. In his very first novel, *Dusklands* (1974), for instance, he makes play with his ancestors and with his own history. Eugene Dawn, in 'The Vietnam Project', reports to a man named Coetzee; and in 'The Narrative of Jacobus Coetzee', the 'translator', 'J.M. Coetzee,' adds an afterword by his 'father' to the 'original' narrative of his eighteenth-century forbear. If they had known, also, how the Coetzee family farm, Voëlfontein, sporadically formed the background to the author's second novel, *In the Heart of the Country* (1976), they could have found autobiographical traces there as well.

Up to the publication of *Boyhood* the autobiographical element in Coetzee's fiction was under-appreciated, but by 2005, with the first two parts of the trilogy published, Derek Attridge could say about the autobiographical context of Coetzee's writings: 'Coetzee's biographers, when they draw their connections between the life and the fiction, will have a mass of material to work with: even with the small amount of biographical information that is currently in the public domain it is clear that the novels are woven out of personal experiences and obsessions.'[5]

Coetzee himself on more than one occasion commented on autobiography as a genre, and chose it as the subject of his inaugural professorial address at the University of Cape Town.[6] According to him, all the writings of an author, including his literary criticism, are autobiographical, since he often comments on traditions with which he aligns himself or from which he consciously diverges, and on writers who have 'influenced' him or whose work speaks to him with particular urgency. When a writer commits himself to recording his own life, he selects from a whole reservoir of memories. Autobiography, as Coetzee puts it in one of his interviews with David Attwell, 'is a kind of self-writing in which you are constrained to respect the facts of your history. But which facts? All the facts? No. All the facts are too many facts. You choose the facts insofar as they fall in with your evolving purpose.'[7]

For Coetzee, then, the question of selection is crucial in auto-biographical writing. Even when he is being absolutely faithful to the facts, the author makes a selection from the many facts at his disposal, so that the relation between a true biography and a fictional biography is by no means as clear-cut as one might think. That's why Coetzee tells Attwell: 'All autobiography is storytelling, all writing is autobiography.'[8] It is not the aim of the artist to reproduce reality faithfully, but to use and process reality. Through ordering and selecting, the artist arrives at a more complete truth than the historian, who is bound by facts. An autobiography is, in truth, as Martin van Amerongen says, not a verifiable curriculum vitae, but an interpretation, sometimes even a complete, self-sufficient work of art with its own laws and criteria.[9] Indeed, James Olney claims that 'the autobiographer half discovers, half creates a deeper design and truth than adherence to historical and factual truth could ever make claim to.'[10]

With the publication of *Boyhood, Youth* and *Summertime*, the autobiographical element in Coetzee's work became more conspicuous, but also in some respects more deceptive. In pronouncements on *Boyhood* and *Youth* Coetzee stressed that the books were fictionalised autobiographies, though he may have exaggerated the fictional aspects of the first two books. The factual details of Coetzee's life correspond to a large degree with their rendering in *Boyhood* and *Youth,* even though the experiences of the boy and the young man are recounted from maturity by a distanced narrator. In my account of Coetzee's childhood I have allowed myself a certain liberty in regarding *Boyhood*, particularly, as based for the most part on verifiable facts. I have done so after visiting the family farm Voëlfontein several times and following conversations with Coetzee's relatives. The most elusive of the autobiographies, from an historical point of view, is *Summertime,* where the character Sophie rightly says to the prospective biographer: 'What Coetzee writes there cannot be trusted, not as a factual record—not because he was a liar, but because he was a fictioneer.'[11] In *Summertime* Coetzee rearranges the historical record with a view to arriving at a deeper account of the truth.

Any biographer of Coetzee would have to take careful account of this uncommon relation between fact and fiction, and of his relativising and elusive narrative strategies. He would have to consider the writer's evident shying away from authorial responsibility, and be wary of appropriating *Summertime,* in particular, to his project. Even in a work like *Diary of a Bad Year,* the narrative strategy does not allow the reader invariably to ascribe the pronouncements of the fictionalised writer to the author J.M. Coetzee. In an essay on Joseph Frank's comprehensive biography of Dostoevsky, it is clear that Coetzee prizes the Russian writer precisely for his execution of what he calls the dialogical novel. 'A fully dialogical novel,' Coetzee writes in *Stranger Shores,* 'is one in which there is no dominating central authorial consciousness, and therefore no claim to truth or authority, only competing voices and discourses.'[12] It is this narrative strategy that Coetzee adopts in a major part of his oeuvre.

Coetzee could thus, with Roland Barthes, assert that the birth of the reader must occur at the cost of the death of the author.[13] Keats's concept of the chameleon writer, in essence identityless and bereft of fixed opinions or ideas, has never, to my knowledge, been taken to such extremes as in the case of Coetzee. This, too, complicates the task of the biographer, however seductive the challenge of capturing the life of such a writer.

A Coetzee biography, however, need not draw its meaning primarily from the light it sheds on the author's creative output, or from its relevance to literary criticism. The life story of this writer with his exceptional achievements is valuable in its own right, and his extraordinary novels stimulate an interest in him as a person. That he uses autobiographical elements in his work does not in itself justify a biography, even though the special creative game he plays with the autobiography could lead to an engrossing relation between biographer and author, or between the biographer and the author's work. The biographer is, of course, peculiarly prone to the perils of the 'biographical fallacy', the distortion of the meaning of the novels through biographical projections. He has to guard against being misled by the writer's creative reworking of the facts of his own life; he must not take fictions for truths, but needs to search for true facts outside or beyond the novels.

If he can do this, he can report on the life in writing, the way through the world that the author, as both a writer and a human being, has made for himself. This is where the biographer's task differs most from that of the novelist, and from this the biography derives the authority of such truth as is in its power to convey.

III

In writing this biography I am indebted in the first place to J.M. Coetzee, who readily granted me interviews and made available to me documents in his possession. During the writing, he responded by e-mail to my queries of a factual nature. He said he wanted the facts in the book to be correct, but that he would leave the interpretation of the data in my hands entirely. He did not wish to see the manuscript before publication. Quotations from documents in his possession are made with his permission. For quotations from other sources (letters and unpublished manuscripts) of which he holds the copyright, his permission was sought in every instance. I would like to thank his publishers for permission, granted through Coetzee's mediation, to quote from his published work. Acknowledgement of Coetzee's copyright appears on the colophon. I am grateful to the Houghton Library at Harvard University for making the Coetzee manuscripts and photocopies available to me. Since my visit in April 2010, these documents have been transferred to the University of Texas at Austin, and are now permanently lodged in the Harry Ransom Humanities Research Centre at Austin. I am grateful to the University of Texas for permission to reproduce a photographic copy of a page from the manuscript of *Dusklands* and to use fragments from this and other manuscripts.

Through Coetzee, I made the acquaintance of his partner, Dorothy Driver, and conducted a fruitful interview with her. She arranged for Jeremy Schwerdt, a student at a tertiary institute in Adelaide and the son of one of her colleagues, to photocopy the enormous number of documents in Coetzee's possession.

Lynette Märki of Tamboerskloof in Cape Town, a cousin of Coetzee's, put me in touch with other members of the Coetzee family, and besides providing me with documents and photographs in her possession, arranged for me to conduct an interview in Mowbray with Coetzee's daughter, Gisela. In Beaufort West I had a conversation with Sylvia Coetzee, J.M. Coetzee's favourite aunt, the widow of his father's brother Son. I was able on several occasions to visit the beautiful farm Voëlfontein, near Leeu-Gamka, which belonged to Coetzee's grandfather and features in *Boyhood* and *Summertime*. The present owner, Gerald Coetzee, a cousin of Coetzee's, showed me around the farm and pointed out places that feature in the books. Stefan Wehmeyer of Cape Town kindly made available to me his extensive documentation of Coetzee's maternal ancestors. This was supplemented by the research done by Pieter Hugo and Gerhard Geldenhuys. From the Fransie Pienaar Museum in Prince Albert I received, through the mediation of Lydia Barrella, information on Gerrit Maxwell Coetzee, grandfather of the writer. The Laingsburg Tourist Office provided helpful information on Voëlfontein and the adjacent town, Merweville.

At St Joseph's Marist College in Rondebosch I interviewed the principal, Hugh Finn, and perused the school annuals covering the period of Coetzee's attendance. The UCT Manuscripts and Archives, with the help of Guillaume Brümmer, who dealt direct with the university administration, provided information on the courses taught in the Department of English during the years 1957–1961 and the years when Coetzee was employed at UCT; also on the results of his two children, both of whom had been students there. The National English Literary Museum, in particular Ann Torlesse and her colleagues, made a large number of photocopies available to me and on two occasions welcomed me as a researcher. In the Cape Archives I was able, with the help of Erica le Roux, to track down motions of the Cape Division of the Supreme Court relating to the career of Jack Coetzee, the writer's father. With the help of Deon Knobel, professor emeritus in forensic medicine at UCT, and later also of an attorney friend, Gustav Pienaar, I gained access to the police records relating to Nicolas, Coetzee's son, who died when he had barely turned twenty-three. I was fortunate to be able to discuss some medical matters with Kay (J.C.) de Villiers, a prominent neurosurgeon and former professor at UCT. Howard Wolf, a former colleague of Coetzee's at the State University of New York at Buffalo, kindly, with the help of Peter Nelson, put at my disposal a number of letters to him from Coetzee, lodged in the library of Amherst College.

In Stellenbosch, Marina Brink of the Documentation Centre of the J.S. Gericke Library replied promptly to my queries, and Mimi Seyffert, also of the Centre, copied the many photographs of Coetzee for me electronically. The name of the owner or host institution appears with the photos reproduced in this biography. In the National Library in Cape Town I had access to volumes of newspapers and periodicals not available in Stellenbosch.

My friend Jan van der Vegt—biographer of Hans Andreus, A. Roland Holst and Hendrik de Vries—kindly provided me with numerous articles and reviews relating to Coetzee in Dutch newspapers and journals. I exchanged views on several occasions with Hermann Giliomee, who from the start showed great interest in this project. Jerzy Koch, professor in Dutch and Afrikaans in Wroclaw, Poland, read and commented on some of the chapters. Etienne Britz commented in detail on each chapter and from time to time offered suggestions that obliged me to revise and rewrite. My friend Anton Naudé also expertly read the manuscript and offered stimulating observations. Michiel Heyns, who did the English translation, with his meticulous exploration of my manuscript, pointed out typing and transcription errors, problems of syntax, etc. At a late stage David Attwell and Derek Attridge offered incisive commentary based upon their immense knowledge of Coetzee, of which I availed myself gratefully. My sincerest thanks to all these people and institutions.

I would also like to express my thanks to the following people who all provided me with information through interviews, telephone conversations or by e-mail: Peter Bergsma, Frans Bulhof, Maxwell Coetzee, Eva Cossée, Jonathan V. Crewe, Jackie Dent, Jonty Driver, Rodney Edgecombe, Kruger Geldenhuys, Ian Glenn, Carol Goosen, Agnes Heinrich, Marilyn Honikman (formerly Kirkwood), R. Howard, Daniel Hutchinson, Manju Jaidka, Christine Jeannett, Ekin Kensch, John Kensch, Paul Kloppers, Lionel Knight, Peter Knox-Shaw, Catherine Lauga du Plessis, Marina le Roux, Jonathan Lear, Lesley Marx, Peter McDonald, Jane Parry, Chris and Sandra Perold, Lisa Perold, Karel Schoeman, Stan Silcock, Jane Smith, Nic Stathakis, Billy Steele, Wilma Stockenström, D.P. van Velden, David Welsh and Hermann Wittenberg.

For my work on this project I received financial aid from Het Jan Marais Nationale Fonds, the L.W. Hiemstra Trust, Anfasa (the Academic and Non-fiction Authors' Association of South Africa), the Van Ewijck Foundation and the National Research Foundation (NRF). All opinions, findings and conclusions in this biography are mine and are not attributable to the NRF. Arnold van Zyl, at the time vice-rector research at the University of Stellenbosch, displayed great interest in the project and on two occasions made grants from his discretionary fund.

I am grateful for the interest of Ton Vosloo, chairman, and Koos Bekker, chief executive officer of Naspers. It was thanks to their involvement and the generous support of Naspers that an adequate budget was made available for this extensive project. Hannes van Zyl, without any financial benefit to himself, kindly took charge, within the confines of the budget, of the editing and design. By relieving me of negotiations with publishers and my international agent, he enabled me to attend to the research and writing free from administrative cares. His commentary was one of the most penetrating and meaningful critiques I have ever had on my work. Where I have disregarded his suggestions, this must be ascribed to my obstinacy alone. To all these bodies and people, also, my warmest thanks.

IV

This biography is not a psychological study of the man J.M. Coetzee. Psychological details in a biography can seldom lay any real claim to reliability; years of reading of life histories have made me wary of playing the psychiatrist. I am inclined to agree with Wim Hazeu, writing in his biography of Simon Vestdijk:

> A biographer with a literary, poetic, journalistic, documentary and dramaturgical background should be wary of assuming the psychiatrist's chair and starting to psychologise. That is not his subject. If he does so anyway, he joins the band of charlatans.[14]

In writing this biography, I was once again plagued by the doubt that besets biographers—whether it is ever possible to create a satisfying and convincing portrait of a subject, even in a comprehensive study. Many creative writers are, not without reason, sceptical about the value of such a report, and question the sense of all biographical writing. I nevertheless believe that the biographer need not end up in a state of complete epistemological impotence. As long as he can accept with equanimity how limited and relative his perception of another person is, there may still be some point to studying an extensive collection of documents such as those relating to Coetzee. At the very least, the biographer can make available facts that were not previously in the public domain, and with modesty and reticence may yet contribute something to an understanding of what it is to be human.

J.C. Kannemeyer
University of Stellenbosch

I

ORIGINS, EARLY YEARS AND FIRST WRITINGS

(1940–1961)

CHAPTER 1

'THE LABYRINTH OF MY HISTORY': ANCESTRY AND ROOTS

I

J.M. Coetzee's reference, in 2003, to a small 'critical industry'[1] that had sprung up in the previous decade around his fictional writer Elizabeth Costello could be seen as a possibly ironic allusion to the massive industry generated by his novels, an industry producing some of the most insightful and penetrating literary criticism in the field of English studies. Despite this close and comprehensive exploration of his work, it is remarkable, in surfing websites dedicated to J.M. Coetzee, or consulting random biographical sketches, how many half-truths and blatant falsehoods one comes across.[2] The claim that Coetzee was born as John Michael Coetzee, but later changed his middle name to Maxwell,[3] is an example of misinformation that persists and sometimes even affects the interpretation of the novels.[4]

Coetzee's birth certificate states unequivocally that he was born on 9 February 1940 as John Maxwell Coetzee in the Mowbray Nursing Home in Cape Town. The 'usual place of residence' of his parents is indicated as Victoria West in the Great Karoo, and the profession of his father, Zacharias Coetzee, as attorney, so that it would seem that his parents—or his mother, at any rate—had travelled to Cape Town for the confinement. His mother's full name is given as Vera Hildred Wehmeyer. What is not mentioned is that she was a primary-school teacher.

The founding ancestors of Coetzee came to the Cape from the Netherlands. The *Vereenighde Oostindische G'octrooijeerde Compagnie* (VOC) (United East Indian Chartered Company) established a 'halfway post' between the Netherlands and the East where ships could replenish their supplies on the long voyage. This is the historical situation to which Coetzee alludes in the introduction to *White Writing* (1988), his first collection of critical essays, dealing specifically with the 'culture of letters' in South Africa. He writes:

In 1652 a European settlement was planted at the tip of the African continent, at the Cape of Good Hope. It was set there for a specific and limited purpose: to provide fresh produce to East Indiamen trading between the Netherlands and Asia. [...] For the next century and a half [...] the company tried [...] to discourage the spread of settlement into the interior, to hold the colony to what it had originally been planned as: a trading post, a garden.⁵

Among the Dutch who settled in the Cape as early as the seventeenth century, was Dirk Couché, who later wrote his family name as Coetsé.⁶ Couché⁷ established the farm Coetzenburg on the banks of the Eerste River in Stellenbosch and later also acquired Assegai Bosch in the adjacent Jonkershoek. On the original title deed of Coetzenburg, dating from the decade 1682–1692, Johannes Mulder, the town's first *landdrost* (magistrate) and surveyor, made a small sketch of the simple first homestead on the farm, with a cosy plume of smoke twirling from the chimney.⁸ Couché became a leading citizen of Stellenbosch — he was elected first as deacon and later as elder in the church, and in 1687 as a member of the *heemraad* (village council). By 1706 he was the commander of the Stellenbosch infantry, with the rank of captain. He probably had a hand in the struggle against the unpopular W.A. van der Stel, who succeeded his father as governor of the colony in 1699, but was recalled to Amsterdam by the Here XVII (Lords Seventeen) in 1707 on account of his dictatorial style of management, self-aggrandisement and nepotism. Couché's involvement in this affair can be deduced from the fact that the couple in their joint will of 1714 appointed Adam Tas, one of the leaders of the resistance against Van der Stel, as one of two guardians of their under-aged children.⁹

In 1721 Coetzenburg passed to Dirk's son Gerrit, baptised in the Cape in 1683, who in 1722 married Susanna Loefke (later spelt Lubbe) of the Netherlands. Coetzenburg remained in Gerrit's possession until 1753, when the farm was transferred to the *Colonie* (town council) of Stellenbosch.

The eldest son of the succeeding three generations, like the eldest son of the patriarch, would repeatedly bear the name Gerrit, after the Dutch Gerard, which was to become the dominant first name in the J.M. Coetzee line of the Coetzees.¹⁰ While the son of the patriarch still spelt his family name Coetsé, from the third and fourth generations on it increasingly became Coetzee, the spelling that succeeding generations in South Africa would mostly adopt.

A fascinating figure from the third generation of Coetzees at the Cape was Jacobus Coetsé, a son of Johannes Hendrik Coetsé and Anna Elizabeth Paal.[11] He was the first free burgher adventurous enough to explore the unknown interior on his own. The policy of Simon van der Stel, commander and later governor from 1679 to 1699, was to confine the original refreshment station at the Cape to a small farming colony, to settle the burghers in the immediate vicinity of the Cape no further away than Stellenbosch, Paarl and Franschhoek, and to discourage expansion into the interior. In *White Writing* J.M. Coetzee writes:

> The Dutch East India Company, which ran the settlement, had little interest in the hinterland of the Cape, which, report said, was barren, inhospitable, and sparsely peopled by primitive Hottentots and Bushmen. Interest waned further when exploring parties failed to find any workable mineral deposits.[12]

This policy of the VOC, however, was applied half-heartedly and was in any case unsuccessful, because Van der Stel's son and successor, W.A. van der Stel, governor from 1699 to 1707, strongly encouraged cattle farming. This prompted farmers to penetrate further and further into the interior, producing a new type of nomad, who learned to love the open spaces and was physically and psychologically equipped to deal with the hardships of a pioneering life. Thus, though the Coetzee patriarch and most of his ten children preferred to stay in the relatively tranquil surroundings of the Cape, some of his descendants were soon to show signs of the restless trekking of the emerging Afrikaner nation, in moving into the interior, at first towards the Northwest and later to Sutherland in the Roggeveld and Graaff Reinet in the Great Karoo.

Two of the first to leave the cosy basin of the Cape were the patriarch's fourth and fifth sons, Johannes Hendrik and Cornelius respectively. Both acquired, in terms of the VOC's system of loan farms, grazing rights for their cattle near the present Piketberg, where the VOC by 1670 had established the northernmost military outpost of the Colony at the foot of the later Piekenierskloof Pass, to defend the Dutch colonists against the raids of the Khoikhoi on the other side of the mountain. On the death of Cornelius, his widow married Johann Heinrich Lange, but in 1758 the farm was taken over by Johannes Hendrik's sixth son, Jacobus, who, as a young child, had moved to this then border territory of the Colony with his parents, brothers and sisters.

Jacobus, born in 1730, married to Maria Margaretha Cloete in 1754 and deceased between 1810 and 1816, was a bit of an adventurer and daredevil.[13] In 1760, with the blessing of Governor Rijk Tulbagh, he left on an expedition into uncharted territory north of the later Piekenierskloof.[14] Functionaries of the VOC had undertaken journeys into this territory between 1660 and 1664 to trade with the indigenous people, and to look for the legendary domain of Monomotapa and the golden city Vigita Magna, but it was not until 1683 that Oloff Bergh got as far north as the Copper Mountains in Namaqualand, a feat repeated by Simon van der Stel in 1685.

Jacobus Coetsé, as he was known, travelled even further, to the Great River, originally the Gariep and later the Orange River, and as far as the south of what is now Namibia. He saw many giraffes, an animal then unknown at the Cape. He also discovered many plant species and named the camel thorn, because he noticed that the giraffes (*kameelperde*, literally camel horses) liked to eat the highest leaves of this tree. He was probably the first white person to penetrate so far into this region. After his return he attended the annual weapons show at Stellenbosch, where his account of his journey caused a sensation. He was persuaded to have his experiences put to paper by the political secretary at the Castle of Good Hope. On the strength of the information supplied by Coetsé—in particular that he had heard of, without encountering, the Damrokwas, a people described as yellow in colour, long-haired and wearing linen clothes—Governor Rijk Tulbagh gave permission in 1761 for Hendrik Hop, accompanied by Jacobus Coetsé as guide and interpreter, to undertake an official expedition along the same route.

The '*Relaas*' (Narrative) of Jacobus Coetsé was duly put in writing by the political secretary, and signed by Coetsé with a cross, from which one deduces that he was illiterate. This is strange, since his grandfather as a *heemraad* (village councillor) was a prominent inhabitant of Stellenbosch and could certainly read and write. The grandson's illiteracy can probably be ascribed to his leaving the relatively cultured Cape at an early age, and to the lack of proper teachers at the outpost. He was also someone who revelled in nature, the open air and the adventure of discovering new territories. Thus Jacobus Coetsé is clearly not a literary forbear of the later prominent author. Indeed, as the son of Johannes Hendrik Coetsé, he is descended from a different line to that of J.M. Coetzee.

When J.M. Coetzee was working in the UK and later studying in the US, he had the opportunity to read, in the British Library and in the well-stocked library of the University of Texas at Austin, the reports of the early travellers in Southern Africa. In Austin he came across the '*Relaas*' of Jacobus Coetsé, and found the story so fascinating that he used it as a source, adapted and skilfully transmuted into a pseudo-documentary, for 'The Narrative of Jacobus Coetzee', the second part of his first novel, *Dusklands* (1974). In the 'Afterword', presented by J.M. Coetzee as the work of his fictional father, the historian Dr S.J. Coetzee, the '*Relaas*' is referred to as the product of 'a Castle hack',[15] a rank-and-file secretary of the VOC, a pen-pusher who had to write down Jacobus's account, and in the official style of the time restricted himself to dry-as-dust facts, as imitated in the 'Appendix', which is given the appearance of an authentic document. That dramatic tale of power hunger and violence that the hack writer in the castle did *not* write down, thus becomes the actual matter of 'The Narrative of Jacobus Coetzee', which in reality is a rewriting of the original '*Relaas*', with the emphasis on what 'really' happened.

When, before the publication of *Dusklands*, J.M. Coetzee was asked by his publisher, Peter Randall of Ravan Press, to provide some biographical details for publicity purposes, he was reluctant to comply. 'As for my family background,' he wrote to Randall in a letter of 17 January 1974, 'I am one of the 10, 000 Coetzees, and what is there to be said about them except that Jacobus Coetzee begat them all?' From this assertion, which Randall, against Coetzee's inclination, used on the dust cover of *Dusklands*, it seems that the writer was unaware of the true place of Jacobus Coetsé in the family tree of the Coetzees, and that he regarded him as a direct forbear. Perhaps, as a cultural descendant of the family in South Africa, he saw himself, like the character Jacobus Coetzee in *Dusklands*, as 'a tool in the hands of history'.[16]

II

The eldest son of Frederik Laurens Johannes Coetzee and his wife, Elizabeth Agnes Mills, was Gerrit Maxwell Coetzee, the grandfather of the writer. He was born on 19 November 1868 in Hopefield, and married Mary Ann Fuller, born in Scotland in 1870. This marriage brought an infusion of British influence into the Coetzee line, even though Mary

Ann was not the grandmother of J.M. Coetzee. Two daughters born from the marriage died young, but a son and a daughter survived: Irene Linda (1899–1990) and Stanley Maxwell Buller (1901–1985). Two months after Stanley's birth, in 1902, his mother died, at the youthful age of thirty-two, probably of complications with the confinement. Gerrit Maxwell Coetzee got married for the second time in 1905, this time to Magdalena Catherina (Lenie) de Beer, who was born in 1884 in Prince Albert and died at an advanced age in Cape Town in 1978.

The De Beers, to whom the Coetzees were connected through this marriage, were a prominent family in Prince Albert.[17] Their farm Kweekvallei at the foot of the Great Swartberg was visited in February 1804 by the traveller Hinrich Lichtenstein, accompanied by General J.W. Janssens, the Governor of the short-lived Batavian Rule at the Cape from 1802 to 1806. De Beer commandeered the entire white population, about twenty people, to parade with guns at their arrival, while his eldest children played recorders, and the Batavian flag flew over the house. He served the guests an excellent meal and Lichtenstein took some of De Beer's wines back to Europe with him. In spite of this cordial reception, Lichtenstein found De Beer a vain, conceited fellow. In the English translation of his *Travels in South Africa* he writes:

> The principal features of his character were vanity, bigotry and a love of domination, accompanied by a certain querulousness, and political fanaticism. [...] [H]e prided himself not a little upon it, as shewing how much wiser he was than his neighbours, and looked down with a sort of contempt upon them. [...] He asserted, as is very common among his countrymen, that Africa would be the most fertile and blessed country upon the globe, would produce every thing, if the peasants were less idle and stupid. As a proof of this, he cited his own experience in the fertility of his place, on which he dilated so warmly.[18]

Samuel de Beer named two of his children after French generals: Bonaparte and Moreau. He was overjoyed when the Cape, through the Peace of Amiens, once again passed into Dutch hands, since Holland had been an ally of France in the war against England. It is curious that the Coetzee family, who later would have such strong pro-British sentiments and in the twentieth century would look askance at ascendant Afrikaner nationalism, should have married into a family with such an anti-British ancestor. A later descendant, Zacharias (Zaag) Johannes Hendricus de Beer, born in 1858, was a more moderate man, and a businessman, owning two stores in Prince Albert, and for twenty-five years served as deacon, elder and secretary in the church, besides serving on the town council. He was the father of Lenie de Beer, who married Gerrit Maxwell Coetzee. His wife was Magdalena Maria le Roux, the daughter of Gabriel Jacobus le Roux, who was an ancestor of the writer Etienne Leroux, known for, among other novels, *Sewe Dae by die Silbersteins* (1962). There is thus, however tenuously, a family connection between two of South Africa's principal novelists.

Lenie studied the piano, organ and violin in Stellenbosch in the early twentieth century, and remained an excellent pianist into her nineties. In her old age she told her children and grandchildren about her father's trading post on the Swartberg, during the construction of the impressive Swartberg Pass road, which was opened in 1886. One day, as a little girl, she was on the mountain with him, when a storm started brewing, and one of the convicts working on the pass had to carry her into the town. In the family there was a silver spoon, a gift from Thomas Bain, the master builder of the Swartberg Pass and other mountain pass roads—the 'colossus of roads', as Patricia Storrar[19] calls him. During the Boer War, at the age of sixteen, Lenie was placed under house arrest because she had dared to play the Transvaal national anthem in the presence of British soldiers during a 'sing-song'.[20]

The name Maxwell, which enters the Coetzee family through Gert Maxwell, did not descend through the Coetzee line. It would be tempting to imagine that it was passed down through the family of Elizabeth Agnes Mills, Gerrit Maxwell's mother, who had married his father, Frederik Laurens Johannes Coetzee. But there is no Maxwell to be found in the Mills family register. In a letter from an unknown correspondent written on an unknown date to the mother of J.M. Coetzee, and of which only a fragment survives,[21] the author states that Maxwell 'was not a family name, but a friend [of Frederik Laurens Johannes Coetzee] who was a partner of the old firm Maxwell and Earp in Cape Town'. This firm had originally been run by John Eben Maxwell, but by the end of the nineteenth century it was being managed by his widow with her son Robert Miller Maxwell (1862–1935), in partnership with Edward John Earp. They traded mainly in cutlery and hardware, which probably included blacksmith's tools.[22] Frederik Laurens Johannes Coetzee was such a close friend of the Maxwells that he christened his son Gerrit Maxwell.

Gerrit Maxwell grew up in Aurora, near Velddrif on the Cape West Coast, but later moved, with his parents and ten younger siblings, to Ceres.[23] Among his brothers there were two bookkeepers, a postmaster and a bank manager, all of them upright citizens, respectable rather than illustrious. Gerrit Maxwell was the exception, a highly successful businessman and farmer, and an eminent man in his part of the world. He presumably left school after Standard VII, probably because of the financial need occasioned by his father's sequestration, and as a stripling left for the Karoo. At first he made a living as a transport driver, and then opened a small grocery shop on Koup station near Laingsburg. Later he became an assistant in a shop in Laingsburg belonging to one Fuller, whose daughter became his first wife. By the time she died, he was the owner of a shop and butchery in Laingsburg, as well as the hotel and the butchery in Fraserburg Road (the later Leeu-Gamka), which were run by his two unmarried sisters. In the liquidation and distribution account of the estate of his first wife, several items suggest that Gerrit Maxwell had significant dealings with the firm of Maxwell & Earp.[24] He must, like his father, have had an exceptionally close friendship with Robert Miller Maxwell, because he requested his children always to include the name Maxwell in the names of their firstborn sons. The nature of this friendship is not known, but it was evidently so close that all Frederik's sons and grandsons respected his request.

After his marriage to Lenie de Beer, fifteen years his junior, Gerrit, or Gert as he was known, remained living in Laingsburg, where their first three children were born, and where he served as mayor in 1907–1908.[25] On Saturdays he often travelled by train to nearby Matjiesfontein, where the young Scotsman, Jimmy Logan, ran a splendid hotel, frequented by streams of travellers en route by ox wagon, horse cart, coach or train to the riches of the Kimberley diamond fields. Logan developed his village into a beautiful Victorian health and holiday resort for Europeans with chest complaints, for which the dry Karoo air promised a cure. Cecil John Rhodes, prominent Cape politicians and several members of the British aristocracy were regular visitors, and Olive Schreiner, author of the internationally famous *The Story of an African Farm* (1883), stayed there for a while and repeatedly returned for visits. Her important book *Thoughts on South Africa* (written in 1896 but published posthumously in 1923) was conceived here. During the Boer War a large horse provision camp with 10 000 troops and 20 000 horses was established outside Matjiesfontein, and part of the hotel was converted to a convalescent hospital for British officers, with the little central turret used as an armed lookout against possible enemy attacks.

As an avid cricketer, Gert enjoyed taking part in the matches that Logan, also an enthusiast, arranged at Matjiesfontein on Saturdays. Even his wife, Lenie, was an ardent participant, taking up a position on the pitch known, according to legend, as 'suicide point'. Logan spared no expense to advance the cause of cricket in South Africa. He once invited the MCC, the English cricket team, to South Africa, and included Gert in his local team.[26]

When one of Gert's sisters, who had helped run the hotel and butchery, got married, Gert and Lenie moved to Fraserburg Road (Leeu-Gamka) with their children. There the family acquired its first motor car, a BSA, and for fun they would all race a train on the Kruidrivier-Leeu-Gamka road at the dizzying speed of fifteen miles an hour. In 1916 Gert bought the farm Vogelfontein, known in the family as Voëlfontein, and in 1919 moved there with his household. With his many business concerns, Gert was by then a well-to-do man, and besides his sheep, farmed fruit on a large scale. He was a regular valuator for the Land Bank, and was for more than thirty years a judge of cart horses and mules at agricultural shows, from Rosebank and Goodwood in the Cape to Worcester and Swellendam. During his years on Voëlfontein he served on the town council of nearby Merweville. He and his wife donated the pulpit of the Dutch Reformed Church in this town.[27]

The family farm, which today belongs to Gerald Coetzee, a cousin of J.M. Coetzee's, was originally 14 130 morgen (about 30 000 acres/12 thousand hectare) in area, and is about 30 kilometres from Leeu-Gamka. Here Gert had a beautifully spacious homestead built, complete with a Cape Dutch gable. Every year the extended family, sometimes up to forty people, would gather from all over for Christmas or Easter, the number of attendees increasing every year with the expanding families. There was much laughter and banter and shared recollection on the broad stoep, with its view over the bright Karoo, the bougainvillea to one side and the orange orchard right in front. For the men this was a time to hunt wild birds or small antelope in the early morning. The attic was a source of secrets and discoveries for the grandchildren. There were beds in almost every room of the house, or mattresses and folding cots, with some of the children sleeping on the long stoep or even on the back of pickup trucks.[28] In the spacious kitchen Lenie, later assisted by her daughters and daughters-in-law and numerous farm women, served morning coffee with delicious pastries, and cooked large meals for the visitors. Above the farmhouse was the dam, and the children could swim in the fountain, which was always specially cleaned for these visits. Close to the farmyard were the kraal walls, up to two feet thick. Many of the children and grandchildren had inherited Gert and Lenie's musical aptitude, and almost all of them loved sport. During these family gatherings, the sons as well as the daughters would play cricket, with the rest of the family watching from the wide stoep.

Some of the younger children born from Gert and Lenie's marriage were first taught on the farm by their half-sister Irene, a trained teacher, and then continued their education in Prince Albert, where they could stay with Grandfather and Grandmother De Beer. In the 1930s they could also stay with Gert and Lenie, who had settled in Prince Albert after the farm was taken over by two of the sons, Stanley (from Gert's first marriage) and Gerald (known as Son). From September 1935 to September 1941 Gert was the mayor of Prince Albert.[29] For their secondary education the older children were sent to Cape schools: the girls to Wynberg Girls' High, the boys to Paarl Boys' High.

Gert was an Anglophile. Half English and besotted with cricket, he always remained a strong *Sap* (United Party voter) and a Smuts supporter, and it is odd that he married an offspring of the De Beer family, staunch supporters of the National Party in the twentieth century, and participants in the inauguration of the Voortrekker Monument in Pretoria in 1949. Gert and Lenie's home language was Afrikaans, although they both spoke English well, thanks to their English-language schooling, which was common practice in the Cape Colony of the nineteenth century.

Gert died on 21 June 1946 on Voëlfontein at the age of 77. In the graveyard his tomb with its marble headstone dominates the other graves, all of them earlier inhabitants of the farm. On the stone is the date of his death and his age, with this inscription: '*In liefdevolle herinnering aan my dierbare eggenoot Gert Maxwell Coetzee. En daar sal geen nag meer wees nie.*' ('In loving memory of my beloved husband Gert Maxwell Coetzee. And there shall be no night there.') The last sentence — from Revelation 21:25 and 22:5 — is called into question by Gert's grandson's later description of the surroundings of the graveyard in the merciless aridity of the Great Karoo: 'Whatever dies here dies firmly and finally:

its flesh is picked off by the ants, its bones are bleached by the sun, and that is that. From the earth comes a deep silence, so deep that it could almost be a hum.'[30] Grandson John was just over six years old at the time of Gert's death, and would carry with him the memory of 'a stooped, grouchy old man with a bristly chin.[31] This well-to-do and well-dressed grandfather was known as the *boordjie-boer*[32] (collar-and-tie farmer); in the words of the grandson:

> His grandfather, the one with the gentlemanly pretensions, once owned not only the farm and a half-share in the hotel and general dealer's store at Fraserburg Road, but a house in Merweville with a flagpole in front of it on which he hoisted the Union Jack on the King's birthday.[33]

His sons, according to this source, called him *'n Ware ou jintlman en 'n ware ou jingo!* ('A true old gentleman and a true old jingo!'), words which they maintained should by rights have been inscribed on his headstone. John's mother, who at times had strained relations with her in-laws, responded to such mockery by scornfully pointing out how scared the old man's sons had been of him: 'You were afraid to light a cigarette in front of him, even when you were grown men.'[34] As John's cousin Margot tells it in *Summertime*, with its engrossing blend of fact and fiction:

> After the midday meal [...] the whole house would freeze into silence: Grandpa was having his nap. Even at that age she was surprised to see how fear of the old man could make grown people creep about like mice. Yet without that old man she would not be here, nor would John [...] a man who started out as a *smous*, a hawker peddling cotton prints and pots and pans and patent medicines to countryfolk, then when he had saved up enough money bought a share in a hotel, then sold the hotel and bought land and settled down as of all things a gentleman horse-breeder and sheep-farmer.[35]

Compared with this doughty old man, Margot maintains, the other Coetzee men were '*slapgatte*':[36]

> While their father thundered and roared and made them quake in their boots, their mother tiptoed around like a mouse. The result

was that when they went out into the world they lacked all fibre, lacked backbone, lacked belief in themselves, lacked courage. [...]

What made the Coetzees so easygoing and therefore so *gesellig*, such good company, was precisely their preference for the easiest available path; and their *geselligheid* was precisely what made the Christmas get-togethers such fun. They never quarrelled, never squabbled among themselves. [...] [T]heir children went out into the world expecting the world to be just another slap, *gesellige* place, Voëlfontein writ large. And behold, it was not![37]

III

From Gert and Lenie's union ten children were born: Leonore (Lynne); Constance (Connie); Gerald Zacharias (Son or Sonny), who would carry on the farming on Voëlfontein; Zacharias (Jack); Janet Agnes (Girlie), who would marry Joshua Joubert Olivier and live on a farm in the Williston district; Agnes Elizabeth; Joy; Alfred Kenneth (Bubbles); Alan Hubert and James Mills. Bubbles farmed in the Williston district and was known for his dry humour, and Alan often wrote witty letters to the press. With one exception, all Gert's children, the two from his first marriage and nine out of the ten from his second, were cultural Afrikaners in the sense that Afrikaans was their home language.

The exception was John's father, Zacharias (later called Zach or Jack), who was born on 29 September 1912 in Prince Albert and died in Cape Town on 30 June 1988. He was named after his maternal grandfather and his great-grandfather De Beer. As a young boy he passionately wanted to become a sailor, navigate strange seas and visit exotic lands, but his father would have none of that.[38] His cherishing of such ideals suggests that he was something of a romantic dreamer, a wild offshoot of the Coetzee family tree. But instead of setting sail for the great unknown, he served as an articled clerk with a firm of attorneys in Caledon, and, after a brief period in Cape Town, opened his own practice in Victoria West. There he met Vera Hildred Marie Wehmeyer, daughter of Piet and Louisa Wehmeyer of the farm Oude Wolwekraal in the Uniondale district. Vera was born on 2 September 1904 in Uniondale and died on 6 March 1985 in Cape Town. Although she spoke Afrikaans well, she spoke English to her children, probably under the influence of her mother, Louisa, who on account of a childhood in the US favoured English. After matriculating, Vera completed a one-year course in primary education at the University of Cape Town before starting to teach in Victoria West. There she and Jack met and fell in love. They were married in 1936. By the time their children were born, English had been established as their home language. From the birth certificate of their eldest son, John, it appears that in the year of their marriage Jack was twenty-four and Vera thirty-two—a difference of eight years, hardly the norm at the time.[39]

According to J.M. Coetzee,[40] his mother told him that Louisa had a life-long cultural aversion to Afrikaners, and raised her children in English, a language she had acquired during her American childhood, along with the German of her parents. Thus she gave her children English names: Roland, Winifred, Ellen, Vera, Norman, Lancelot. Even so, she and her children must also, in the predominantly Afrikaans area of Uniondale, have had a proper knowledge of Afrikaans. What is surprising, is that Piet Wehmeyer was one of the founder members of the National Party in Uniondale. In spite of his wife's strong aversion, he must have had many friends in the town's Afrikaans community. Probably the couple agreed to disagree on the subject of politics, which was not uncommon among Afrikaners in the first half of the twentieth century.

The Wehmeyers of South Africa are not a huge clan. Gottlieb the younger (of the third generation) was the most prominent of the South African family, and is mentioned in Dalene Matthee's novel *Fiela se Kind* (*Fiela's Child*). A census taker turns up to write down the names of Fiela and her family and to establish who the land belongs to on which she lives: 'It's my ground. My father and grandfathers spent their lives working for the Wehmeyers. You could say they worked themselves to death for the Wehmeyers. After the old man's death these twelve morgen from Oude Wolwekraal were put on the name of my late father, the will and all are with Mister Cairncross in town in Uniondale.'[41]

IV

The marriage of Piet Wehmeyer (1864–1931) and Louisa du Biel (1873–1928) provided the children of Jack and Vera Coetzee with a fascinating forefather, but one whose eccentric behaviour inclines one to doubt his sanity. Louisa was the daughter of one Balcer Dubyl, who later changed his name to Balthazar du Biel. He was born in 1844 in the village of Schwarswald in the province of Posen in Poland and died in Stellenbosch in 1923. As a young boy, he herded his father's cattle, and was prone to having visions. In one such vision he was instructed to go and preach the gospel to the heathens. He submitted his documents to the Rhenish Mission Society in Barmen, who ordained him as a missionary. Towards the end of 1868 he was sent to South Africa, where in 1870 he married Anna Louisa Brecher, the daughter of a Moravian missionary. Du Biel served as a missionary in Berseba and Keetmanshoop in the then German Southwest Africa, but left for the United States in 1872, where he preached among the Evangelical Germans, moving about constantly, at one stage living in Bloomington, Illinois. In 1881 he returned to South Africa on the recommendation of his father-in-law, Ferdinand Brecher, as assistant to an elderly missionary of the Rhenish Mission Society in Namaqualand. After only nine months in this position he turned to the Dutch Reformed Church, in which he served as an elementary-school teacher and assistant preacher in Uniondale. Eight months later he severed all ecclesiastical ties and took to the world of business, going about the Mossel Bay area as a *smous* (pedlar).

Du Biel and Anna Louisa had six children. Louisa Amalia was born in Petersburg in the district of Menard, Illinois, in 1873, and died in Uniondale in 1928. Through her marriage to Piet Wehmeyer she would become the grandmother of J.M. Coetzee.

Balthazar du Biel was the first recorded writer among John Coetzee's ancestors. The cousin Margot in *Summertime* is close to the truth when she tells the prospective biographer that the author's 'oddness', meaning his talent, was not derived from the Coetzees, but from his mother's side of the family, 'from the Meyers or whatever the name was, the Meyers from the Eastern Cape. Meyer or Meier or Meiring'.[42] Jacobus Coetzee's '*Relaas*' was the product of an unimaginative scribe in the Castle in the Cape, and the Coetzee family in South Africa is, with notable exceptions such as Ampie and Christoffel Coetzee, not known for its writing talent.[43] Balthazar du Biel, on the other hand, was the author of two 'spiritual' books. After his death his daughter Anna, or Annie as she was known, translated these books from German into Afrikaans, adapted and abridged by her brother Albert: *Deur 'n gevaarlike krankheid tot ewige genesing* (1934) (Through a dangerous malady to eternal healing) and *'n Ewebeeld en stroom musiek* (1941) (A likeness and a stream of music). These books are based on Du Biel's diary.[44] The published work speaks of a troubled spirit whose many visions beset his life's path with care and obstacles. When great-aunt Annie, who was John's godmother, fell in her Rosebank flat and broke her hip, he, his mother and his brother visited her in hospital. In the store-room of her flat, Coetzee writes in *Boyhood*, they found piles of old newspapers, paper intended for packaging books and hundreds of copies of *Deur 'n gevaarlike krankheid tot ewige genesing* that had remained unsold. John tried reading the book, but found it boring. 'No sooner has Balthazar du Biel got under way with the story of his boyhood in Germany,' he recounts in *Boyhood*, 'than he interrupts it with long reports of lights in the sky and voices speaking to him out of the heavens.'[45] Nor does his portrait inspire affection: 'In the photograph in Aunt Annie's bedroom Balthazar du Biel has grim, staring eyes and a tight, harsh mouth. Beside him his wife looks tired and cross.'[46] 'Was Aunt Annie's father mad?', John asks his mother. 'Yes, I suppose he was mad,' she replies. In all probability, she continues, Aunt Annie consented to the translation for fear of him. 'He was a terrible old German, terribly cruel and autocratic. All his children were afraid of him.'[47] It has been argued that bipolar disorder and psychosis on the one hand and artistic talent on the other often occur together in families, and that the psychosis predominates and leads to instability when the artistic impulses are not allowed a proper outlet.[48] In the case of Balthazar du Biel it produced a pernicious religious mania and a couple of unreadable books, and some of his descendants in reaction against this became a-religious. In the case of John Coetzee, the artistic talent was given free rein, in keeping with the not uncommon phenomenon that exceptional talent in the arts is preceded in a family line by mediocre practitioners.

This is true also of one of Balthazar's children, his son Johann Albert Ernst, who under the name of Albert du Biel achieved modest fame in the 1920s as a writer of Afrikaans novels. Albert was taught to read and write by his parents and did not have much formal education. In 1928, with the help of some collaborators, he started a small publishing firm in Paarl, which published the magazine *Die Boereblad*, with articles in English and Afrikaans, and also some of Du Biel's books. In the depression of the 1930s the journal went bankrupt.

Albert Du Biel became acquainted with written Afrikaans only at the age of fifteen, when he read some of the stories and poems in S.J. du Toit's periodical *Ons Klyntji*. Although some of his first writings were in English, his novels and tales were in Afrikaans and were intended to provide instructive Afrikaans reading matter for young people.[49] As stated in the advertisement for the series *Oor berg en vlakte*, he wanted the main characters in his works to set an example of 'clean and strong' living to young people; and his stories were meant to make pleasant reading and have an 'educational and ennobling' effect on the reader.[50] In keeping with this aim, his novels are constantly interrupted by a didactic narrator who delivers homilies that stop the story in its tracks, as also happens when he fills in the historical background for the reader. To keep the attention of a reading public for whom books in their own language were still a novelty, he employed, in *Die misdade van die vaders*, the tried and trusted recipe of a romantic intrigue and a star-crossed love with a happy ending, interwoven with the nineteenth-century history of the Boers on the Eastern border on the eve of the Great Trek. Contributing to the romantic atmosphere is the sporadic appearance of a mysterious nocturnal horseman who defends the farmers against the attacks of black tribes—a 'skilful Afrikanerisation,' as P.C. Schoonees puts it,[51] 'of the Medieval knight errant'.

Also, in employing the figure of a patriarch and land-owner who provides a livelihood for a number of *bywoners* (tenant farmers) on his farm, Du Biel's novels follow a typical pattern of the early Afrikaans novel. The stories he collected in *Die verraaier* are set against the background of the Boer War, but are more particularly located in the vicinity of Oudtshoorn at the time of the Cape rebellion and the traitors to the 'Boer cause'. Apart from that, some of the stories feature young blades who come courting young maidens, and lives that are spoilt by parents who foist their daughter upon a much older but richer man, rather than allow her to marry the love of her life. To read, now, a mother's reproach to her daughter for rejecting a rich suitor is to understand something of the economic realities governing such decisions at the time, even though to a modern ear the reproach sounds naïve: 'If you marry Klaas, you'll be able to eat white bread all your life, and slaughter from your own kraal.'[52]

Nowadays Albert du Biel is left unread, except by specialists interested in the historical aspects of his work. According to *Boyhood*, the youthful John Coetzee, with his mother's permission, removed *Die misdade van die vaders* and *Kain* from his aunt's flat. *Die misdade van die vaders* he tried to read, but found it so boring that he got no further than page 10. His mother, so she informs him, did read one of her uncle's books years ago, but can't remember anything about it. The novels, she says, 'are very old-fashioned. People don't read books like that any more.'[53]

And yet Du Biel's work is important for Coetzee's later development. *Die misdade van die vaders*, however ludicrously the crimes of the ancestors are contrived, addresses a theme central to the Coetzee oeuvre: the misdeeds and transgressions of a single person that are visited upon the children, who have to live with that disgrace. In the work of Sarah Gertrude Millin, whom Coetzee in *White Writing* calls the most important South African novelist between Olive Schreiner and Nadine Gordimer (although neglected nowadays because of her morally repulsive treatment of race), the dominant theme is the crimes of the fathers as a form of degeneracy, whereby succeeding generations are infected with a 'legacy of evil'.[54] 'Blood, Taint, Flaw, Degeneration,' Coetzee calls the process in his essay on Millin.[55]

In Coetzee the theme of the interconnectedness of generations is treated very differently than in Millin or Albert du Biel. Although Du Biel is also intrigued by the motifs of degeneration and hereditary sin, in his case it is seen as punishment and admonition from a Judaeo-Christian perspective, as also in other writers with their tales of the degeneration of dynasties on the great farms. Even so, it is tempting to wonder whether Du Biel, for all his clumsiness, may not have unconsciously provided Coetzee with a theme he would explore at several levels and in several facets, personally as well as nationally, to culminate in his great novel *Disgrace* (1999). As early as his first book, *Dusklands*, the character Eugene Dawn wants, with the doctors treating him, 'to pick our slow way through the labyrinth of my history', the multitude of generations preceding him, so that he may at last know what sins of the fathers he is guilty of. At the end of 'The Vietnam Project', the first part of *Dusklands*, he has 'high hopes of finding whose fault I am'.[56]

Chapter 2

Childhood

I

When John Coetzee was born in Mowbray in Cape Town on 9 February 1940, the Second World War had been under way for a few months. There had been few military manoeuvres in Europe after the German invasion of Poland, but the picture would soon change dramatically with the German occupation of Denmark and Norway, followed by the invasion of Holland, Belgium and Luxembourg, the bombing of Rotterdam, the fall of France and the rescue of British troops trapped on the beaches of Dunkirk.

Among Coetzee's papers there is a sheet of paper on which he has noted all the places where, as his mother told him, he lived in the first few years of his life. It shows what an exceptionally nomadic existence the young mother led. For the first three months after John's birth in 1940, he and his parents lived in Victoria West in the Great Karoo. For the next seven months they settled in Warrenton in the Northern Cape, a small town about 75 kilometres north of Kimberley. From December 1940 to January 1941 Vera and John stayed with Vera's eldest sister, Winnie, in Mowbray, Cape Town. Then they moved to Prince Albert for two months. Vera rented a room from a friend she had met during her year at university, who ran the grocery shop in the village with her husband. After this the family moved to Johannesburg, where Vera and John, and initially Jack as well, lived in a flat. Here the couple's second son, David Keith Coetzee, was born on 8 April 1943, after Jack's departure for the war. When John was four and a half years old, Vera and her two sons stayed in Prince Albert again for a while, and then moved to Voëlfontein to stay with her parents-in-law. For ten months in 1944 and 1945 they found cheap accommodation in a beach hut in Plettenberg Bay, after which they spent another two months on Voëlfontein and two months with Jack's sister Girlie and her husband on the farm Skipperskloof near Williston. Although Vera did not always get along with her in-laws, she was very fond of her sister-in-law Girlie and her husband, Joubert Olivier, whom she admired. He had studied medicine in Scotland, but had to abandon his studies when the world-wide depression left his parents unable to support him. In spite of this, he qualified in dentistry, and installed an electrical generator on Skipperskloof.

The many removals suggest dire financial straits, which relates to Jack Coetzee. According to Gerald Coetzee, the present owner of Voëlfontein and the cousin of the writer, Jack was an excellent attorney, who could perform brilliantly in court.[1] With his neat clothing and well-groomed look, he made a good impression and got on well with people. At first he was employed by the firm Gird & Guthrie in Cape Town, but on 18 July 1936 he opened a practice in Victoria West, where as a newcomer he had to compete with old, established firms. Irregularities started cropping up in his practice, such as his failure to register an antenuptial contract, or to pay recovered debts into a client's account. He wrote cheques that bounced, and on several occasions omitted to reply to urgent letters and writs of demand. Very soon, on 25 May 1940, he left Victoria West, heavily in debt, and settled as an attorney in Warrenton—without informing the Law Society of the Cape of Good Hope of the change, as the profession requires. He started practising anew, but got virtually no work. He closed his office in March 1941 and left the town, once again with debts he could not meet. It transpired that virtually all funds had been withdrawn from his trust account, but that he had continued to write cheques against this account, knowing that the bank would refuse payment.

The Law Society was obliged to take action against him. In a letter to the Society dated 28 February 1941, written while he was still living in Warrenton, Jack says that he has not been able to make a living in the town, that his wife and child 'have been in dire need', that he is without any prospect of work, and that he is considering joining the South African forces who, as their contribution to the war effort, were fighting in North Africa. He continues: 'I have gone through very hard times since commencing business here, but I have at all times tried to keep high the honour of the profession to which I belong.' This letter failed to impress the Society, and he was struck off the roll of attorneys on 10 November 1941. The Society would normally have acted against him on behalf of the creditors, and a court case could have resulted in a prison sentence. However, his father interceded and paid large sums of money to keep him out of trouble and out of jail.[2] After this Jack,

Vera and John moved to Johannesburg, where from April 1941 to April 1942 he was employed as a bookkeeper by Gerrie Pieterse's Motors at 17 Rissik Street, and from May 1942 in the same capacity by Electrolux of South Africa. On 28 July 1942, he quit this position, joined the Union Defence Force and went to war in North Africa, the Middle East and later Italy.[3]

Why did Jack Coetzee join up as a soldier, given that he was leaving his wife and child in direst poverty, and that she was pregnant before his departure? A story John heard later was that one could not be prosecuted if you enlisted in the defence force.[4] This was true, because in a state of war all kinds of moratoriums are put in place, giving the government of the day the power to intercede in normal legal procedures if deemed necessary. In terms of the War Measures Act No 13 of 1940, the government indemnified soldiers engaged in active service on foreign soil against legal action for the duration of the war. If indeed Jack Coetzee made use of this moratorium to avoid prosecution it would also imply that he had further debts of which his father was unaware, and which he was hoping to escape.

The result of Jack's action was that in three years Vera moved six times, first with John, as he was to recount in *Boyhood*, and later also with David. While they were living in the flat in Johannesburg, Vera had a part-time job—John would remember later[5] that he was placed in a crèche during the day. Is it from this time or even earlier that John was to recall, as his first memory, his mother's white breasts? 'He suspects he must have hurt them when he was a baby, beaten them with his fists, otherwise she would not now deny them to him so pointedly, she who denies him nothing else.'[6] Another early memory dates from this time. He is leaning out of the window of their flat at dusk, and sees a car hit a small dog: 'With its hind legs paralysed, the dog drags itself away, squealing with pain. No doubt it will die; but at this point he is snatched away from the window.'[7]

From shortly before David's birth to some time after, Vera had to give up her job, and fell back on cheap accommodation wherever she could find it, or on the hospitality of friends and family. She and her children had to survive on the £6 that Jack contributed from his lance-corporal's pay, supplemented with £2 from the Governor-General's Distress Fund.[8] Of Prince Albert at the foot of the Great Swartberg, where they stayed in a rented room for an initial two months and later for another month, John could later remember 'only the whine of mosquitoes in the long hot nights and his mother walking to and fro in her petticoat, sweat standing out on her skin, […] trying to soothe his baby brother, forever crying; and days of terrible boredom spent behind closed shutters sheltering from the sun.'⁹ Besides this description in *Boyhood*, these days may also figure in Mrs Curren's recollections of her childhood in *Age of Iron* (1990): 'When I think back to my own childhood I remember only long sun-struck afternoons, the smell of dust under avenues of eucalyptus, the quiet rustle of water in roadside furrows, the lulling of doves.'¹⁰ Another early memory suggested by *Boyhood* may date from a bus trip with his mother over the Swartberg Pass between Prince Albert and Oudtshoorn, when he released a sweet wrapper from the bus window and watched it fluttering away: 'He thinks all the time of the scrap of paper, alone in all that vastness, that he abandoned when he should not have abandoned it. One day he must go back to the Swartberg Pass and find it and rescue it. That is his duty: he may not die until he has done it.'¹¹ One notes the realisation of his responsibility not only to *find* the paper one day, but to *rescue* it.

Vera at this time felt very strongly that her parents-in-law on Voël-fontein could do more to help her and her children, but the expected invitation to the farm did not arrive immediately. When it finally turned up, and they spent four months on the farm, she had the impression that they were not welcome, mainly on account of what she interpreted as Lenie Coetzee's opposition to the visit.¹² For that reason she and her children sought shelter in Plettenberg Bay in one of the prefabricated huts that were let to holidaymakers in summer, but that for the rest of the year mostly stood empty. This is where they were in June 1945 when the war ended, because John could recall the thanksgiving service held in one of the churches.¹³

The constant removals left Vera and her children very much dependent on each other's company and they became very close. When they were old enough, she told them of her early experiences and her life before she married Jack. As a child she sometimes went on holiday to Plettenberg Bay with her parents. The family would travel there by ox wagon, and along the way camp next to the road. This is a detail that recurs in Coetzee's novel *Age of Iron*.¹⁴ As a young girl, accompanied by her brother Norman, Vera went on a tour of Europe with a group of hockey and tennis players. In her album there were beautiful photos of Scotland and its capital Edinburgh, Norway with its fjords, the Swiss Alps, Germany and the Rhine.¹⁵ In this album John's father also puts in an appearance 'with his dapper little moustache and his cocky look'.[16] From his mother's stories he gathered how happy she had been in Victoria West before her marriage.

While Vera and her two sons were moving from place to place trying to exist on her husband's meagre contribution, Jack was at the front in North Africa and the Middle East with the South African forces. Under the command of the prime minister, General Jan Smuts, they played an important part in recapturing Abyssinia and in the battles of Tobruk and El Alamein. When Mussolini fell, the South African forces helped with the clearing-up in Italy, and Jack got to know Italian opera by attending many performances. During the war, probably while they were in Italy, one of Jack's comrades died, and he wrote his only extant poem: an obituary in a lofty elegiac tone and the somewhat archaic English traditionally reserved for this kind of poetry.[17]

When the war ended in 1945, Jack returned with the South African forces and rejoined his family. John was very proud of his father's war service, unaware of the events preceding it. It was not clear to him why Jack had never advanced beyond the rank of lance-corporal, and in conversation with his friends he tended to omit the 'lance'. He liked paging through his father's album, so different to his mother's European album, looking at the South Africans in khaki uniforms against the backdrop of the Egyptian pyramids or the devastated Italian cities. From overheard conversations, he recounts in *Boyhood*, he learnt that his mother regarded the Germans as the best people on earth, but that the terrible Hitler had caused them much hardship. When her brother Norman came to visit, he disagreed, saying that, on the contrary, Hitler had restored the dignity of the Germans. ' "The Germans didn't want to fight against the South Africans," says Norman. "They like the South Africans. If it hadn't been for Smuts we would never have gone to war against Germany. Smuts was a *skelm*. He sold us to the British." '[18]

When his father wanted to rile his mother, in their late-night quarrels in the kitchen, he taunted her about her brother who had not joined up, but marched with the Ossewabrandwag instead. ' "That's a lie!" she maintains angrily. "Norman was not in the Ossewabrandwag. [...]" '[19] These disagreements made John aware of a greater world outside the immediate circle of family, and of events potentially affecting all people on earth. He liked the political arguments between Jack, Vera and Norman:

He enjoys the heat and passion, the reckless things they say. He is
surprised that his father [...] is the one he agrees with: that the
English were good and the Germans bad, that Smuts was good and
the Nats are bad.[20]

It is clear that even at this early stage John felt ambivalence towards
his father, although Jack had for quite a few years been only a great
absence in his life, an unknown entity. When reading a memoir, one
bears in mind that it transcribes impressions and memories differing in
time from the actual experience; even so, this burgeoning feeling is very
evocatively expressed in *Boyhood*:

His father likes the United Party, his father likes cricket and
rugby, yet he does not like his father. He does not understand this
contradiction, but has no interest in understanding it. Even before
he knew his father, that is to say, before his father returned from
the war, he had decided he was not going to like him. In a sense,
therefore, the dislike is an abstract one: he does not want to have
a father, or at least does not want a father who stays in the same
house.[21]

He was very fond of his mother, on the other hand, a woman known
among the Coetzees as an intelligent, humble person with an overwhelming love of her two sons, for whom she would have sacrificed
everything.[22] 'He cannot imagine her dying,' John writes in *Boyhood*.
'She is the firmest thing in his life. She is the rock on which he stands.
Without her he would be nothing.'[23] From early on in his life John
realised that his father occupied a subservient position in the home: to
him 'the husband is no more than an appendage, a contributor to the
economy as a paying lodger might be. [...]As long as he can remember
he has had a sense of himself as prince of the house, and of his mother
as his dubious promoter and anxious protector.'[24]

Vera's all-absorbing love once led her brother-in-law to remark: 'You
really should leave some of the protection to the Man Up There.'[25] John
at times rebelled against this suffocating solicitude and withdrew into
himself, to create a distance from his mother.

II

On his father's return the family initially lived in a military camp in Pollsmoor near False Bay in Greater Cape Town. With the influx of returning soldiers after the war there was a tremendous shortage of housing in the urban centres, and the waiting list for homes was endless. The government had temporary settlements erected for the soldiers and their families, and Pollsmoor was one such settlement. It comprised prefabricated huts, showers and toilets, a recreation hall and a school for the younger children from Sub A to Standard Three.[26] The family moved into this settlement at the beginning of 1946, and John received his first schooling at the Pollsmoor Primary School. In his first report, dated 21 June 1946, he is commended for his command of language and his very satisfactory progress—so satisfactory that at the beginning of the second semester of 1946 he was transferred to Sub B. Eventually this transfer would be detrimental to his school career, because in high school, at the onset of puberty, he would lag behind his classmates physically. This would hamper his prowess at sport, even though he was from an early age an accomplished cricketer. It would also intensify the feeling of being an outsider, which was already a part of him. In the same year, Jack was appointed as controller in charge of housing for returning soldiers. Before the end of the year the family was able to move into a rented house at 8 Liesbeeck Way in Rosebank near the University of Cape Town. In front of the house was a big old oak for John to climb. He later nostalgically remembered 'the house with the big overgrown garden and the observatory with the domed roof and the two cellars'.[27] This is the house where his mother took in lodgers, including Trevelyan, about whom Coetzee would write in *Boyhood*.[28]

To help her with the housekeeping Vera arranged with her sister Winnie in Stellenbosch for a seven-year-old coloured boy named Eddie, from Ida's Valley on the outskirts of the town, to come and work for them. He would receive free board and lodging and his mother £2.10.0 a month. After two months Eddie ran away, but Trevelyan found him in the bushes next to the Liesbeeck River and gave him a flogging with a leather belt.[29] This was the first time the young John saw how harshly white adults could treat a coloured boy. This was the boy with whom he had wrestled on the lawn in front of their house and who had taught him to ride the bicycle that he had bought second-hand for five pounds for his eighth birthday.[30] What would happen to Eddie when he returned to Ida's Valley he did not know, but if he had to credit his mother's forebodings, Eddie would probably start smoking cigarette butts and later take to drink and drugs. 'Will he ever escape from Eddie? If they passed each other in the street one day, would Eddie, despite all his drinking and dagga-smoking, despite all the jail and all the hardening, recognize him and stop and shout "*Jou moer*!"'[31]

The move to Rosebank meant that John could transfer to the Rosebank Junior School, which he attended until April 1949. The school's sports grounds formed part of the Rondebosch Common in the heart of suburban Rondebosch, next to Rosebank. Here John took part in athletics and the long-jump, and in 1948, at the age of eight, won the running-backwards race.[32] A fellow-pupil at the school was Nic Stathakis, who became a close friend when John was six and would share his years at high school and the University of Cape Town. They have kept contact ever since, even when Stathakis married a Swiss woman and settled in Switzerland.[33] They played cricket together at the Coetzee house, though Stathakis was more interested in rugby. Stathakis remembers the steaming cups of hot Milo that Vera made them on cold winter's days and the delicious sweet-potato dishes that came from her kitchen.[34]

In Rosebank Junior School John was consistently the best in his class. In June 1947 he achieved an aggregate of 92.5 per cent, and his class teacher commented on his report card: 'John has done excellent work in all subjects and well deserves his position at the top of the class.' At the beginning of 1947 he won a prize in the junior division of an essay competition set by the South African Broadcasting Corporation. His essay, of which the text has not been preserved, was entitled 'What I did in the holidays.' How highly developed his imagination already was, is evident from another essay, of which part has been preserved, 'The man-eating tiger of Patna'. According to his last report card from this school, dated 4 April 1949, he achieved a mark of 319 out of 350 in the exams. 'Excellent work throughout!' his class teacher commented in the report. His mother, who had been a teacher herself, saw to it that John and David were exposed to books from an early age. She bought them comic books, so that they could connect pictures and words. Later she bought them as a reference source a set of *The Children's Encyclopaedia*, which was found in many homes in the English-speaking world at the time. Arthur Mee was the chief editor, assisted by many experts in their field.

The set comprised eight volumes, each containing various sections, such as nature, the Earth, countries of the world, prominent people, Biblical tales, famous books and writers, etc. These books aimed to make the learning process interesting and enjoyable, to shape character and to inculcate a sense of duty. John often, when he was too ill to go to school, would summon his mother to bring him one of the 'green books'.[35]

Radical change was taking place in South Africa. Smuts and his United Party had had a comfortable majority in parliament; but in the elections on 26 May 1948 there was a surprising swing to D.F. Malan's National Party and their ally, N.C. Havenga's Afrikaner Party, with 70 and 9 seats respectively, defeating the United Party with 65 and its ally, the Labour Party, with 6 seats. This victory could be ascribed to a delimitation of constituencies benefiting rural seats, because in reality the National Party and the Afrikaner Party combined received 100 000 fewer votes than the total of the United and Labour parties. In retrospect analysts ascribed the swing to the right to the unpopularity of the liberal Jan Hofmeyr, the deputy prime minister and likely successor to Smuts, who possibly alienated conservative supporters of the United Party. Smuts's impatience with local affairs and his pursuit of South Africa's international interests also upset those voters with more provincial mindsets. Whatever the reason for it, the majority of South Africans were stunned by this result.[36]

With the National Party in power, South Africa assumed a course directly contrary to that of post-war Western Europe, where individual freedom was cherished. In the face of the emergence of independent African states and the increasing criticism of South Africa in the United Nations, a solidarity and sense of a common fate developed among Nationalist Afrikaners, reinforced by the unifying functions of language, culture and religion, and ritually celebrated at nationalistic rallies (*volksfeeste*) seeking to draw inspiration from the past.

Shortly after Dr Malan took office, the government enacted a series of laws to enforce the policy of apartheid. In 1949 marriages between people of different races or colours were prohibited by law, and in 1950 the Immorality Act outlawed sexual intercourse between people of different races. The Group Areas Development Act and related legislation in the 1950s established residential apartheid in urban areas. To suppress unrest under black and coloured people and to prohibit the activity of black 'agitators', the Suppression of Communism Act was passed in 1950, banning the Communist Party and criminalising the promotion of communist doctrines. The most controversial legislation in the 1950s was the act, forced through parliament in 1951, placing enfranchised coloured people on a separate voters' roll. When the Appeal Court declared this strategy invalid, the government solved the constitutional crisis by appointing more judges to the Appeal Court and attaining the required two-thirds majority in parliament by enlarging the Senate. This ruse gave the government what it wanted—the coloured people were placed on a separate voters' roll in 1956—but its handling of the affair created doubts, especially among intellectuals, about the integrity and reliability of what had until then been considered by most white people as a democratic regime.

With the publication in 1988 of his volume of essays, *White Writing*, Coetzee would comment on this change of government and its effects on South Africa. He writes:

> A measure of the power of the repression that came after 1945 is given by the fact that in South Africa, where a party with Nazi sympathisers in high positions was elected to office in 1948 and set about a program of racial legislation whose precursor if not model was the legislation of Nazi Germany, political prudence dictated that the rationale for race classification, race separation and race dominance should not be couched in terms of eugenics and biological destiny. In fact the public language of the National Party in South Africa has undergone Byzantine elaboration since 1945 to keep from voicing the key opposition— *über* versus *unter*—that was uttered with such confidence by Nazism in its heyday.[37]

In spite of the election defeat, Jack Coetzee, like his brothers and sisters, remained faithful to the United Party, which after Hofmeyr's death in 1949 and Smuts's in 1950, suffered a loss of direction, due to a lack of strong leadership.

With the resettlement of the soldiers accomplished, Jack's post as Controller of Letting was declared redundant and abolished. Thus, when Coetzee writes in *Boyhood*, much later, that his father lost his job because he was a United Party supporter,[38] he is reproducing rumours and a child's interpretation of them. In truth, there was no further need for a controller of letting. The abolition of the post had no connection with the change of government.

Jack Coetzee, unemployed for the second time in his life, found

a position fairly soon as a bookkeeper with Wolf Heller's Standard
Canners & Packers in Worcester, a sizeable town in the Breede River
Valley, about 110 kilometres from Cape Town. Founded in 1820 by the
British governor Lord Charles Somerset, it had established itself by the
1940s and '50s as an important commercial centre.

John had to leave behind his friends in Rosebank and the school
where he had been so happy. At the beginning of May 1949, when he
was in Standard Three, he went to the local Primary School for Boys
in Worcester. It was a parallel-medium school offering classes in both
English and Afrikaans.

III

In Worcester, Jack and Vera and their two sons moved into a new house
in a housing project on the outskirts of the town, between the railway
line and the national road to the north. All the houses were built to a
uniform pattern, though not totally identical. The streets were named
after trees, but the trees themselves were lacking, John notes in *Boyhood*.
The Coetzees lived on a large plot at 12 Poplar Avenue in Reunion Park,
as the new extension was called. A wire fence separated them from their
neighbours. In the backyard of every house there was a toilet and a room
intended for a servant, but the Coetzees did not employ one. They had a
chicken run with three chickens, but Vera's attempt at chicken-farming
failed when the chickens developed swellings on their legs due to the
rainy weather, and stopped laying.[39] When the neighbourhood dogs got
into the chicken run and bit the chickens, she sewed up the lesions with
needle and thread, but the hens developed maggots and started rotting
slowly from inside.[40] She acquired a bicycle to do the shopping because,
as she made clear to her family, she didn't want to be a prisoner in the
house.[41] To the delight of her family, however, her cycling was extremely
inept, and one day the bicycle was simply gone, without any explanation.
The memory of his mother on the bicycle stayed with John, as an early
image of her desire for freedom.[42]

The move to Worcester brought the family one huge advantage: they
were now only slightly more than 300 kilometres from Voëlfontein, the
Coetzee family farm, which had, after the death of Grandfather Coetzee
in 1946, passed to his sons Stanley and Gerald (Son). Although John's
mother had also grown up on a farm, Oude Wolwekraal in the Uniondale

district, it had played no part in his life. As a child he frequently visited the farm Skipperskloof of his Aunt Girlie and her husband, Joubert Olivier, near Williston, but the farm that would play a central role in his life was Voëlfontein, which he often visited up to about his twelfth year and where he spent long holidays. The farms in his parents' background, he felt, distinguished him from his school-fellows. 'Through the farms,' Coetzee writes in *Boyhood*, 'he is rooted in the past; through the farms he has substance.'[43] This consciousness of his roots was crucial to his development and his later extended essays on the '*plaasroman*' (farm novel), a concept that he established in his critical work, and that was to gain currency in both Afrikaans and English literary criticism.

John would later recall the family gatherings over Christmas and Easter when, as he puts it in *Summertime*, 'they were children roaming the veld as free as wild animals'.[44] On the great stoep of the farmstead, as depicted in *Boyhood*, the uncles would, with 'a note of nostalgia and pleasurable fear,' recollect 'their schoolmasters and their schoolmasters' canes' and 'cold winter mornings when the cane would raise blue weals on their buttocks.'[45] On his first visit to Voëlfontein, when he was four or five and his brother a baby, John played with the coloured boys. All of a sudden he became aware that he was able to speak Afrikaans fluently, without pauses for reflection. By the time he was at school in Worcester, he drank in the atmosphere on the farm greedily, liking the good-natured mixture of Afrikaans and English in which the uncles conversed with each other. When he first came on holiday to the farm, there were still horses, donkeys, cows and calves, pigs, ducks, nanny-goats and bearded billy goats, and some hens and a rooster that crowed to greet the rising sun. After the grandfather's death the farmyard declined until nothing remained except the sheep with their golden fleece.

In the 1950s the high wool prices brought the farmers wealth, new cars and long seaside holidays—a prosperity they did not share with their labourers. The only crop sown in those days was lucerne. Of the orchard only the orange grove remained, yielding the sweetest navels every year. Sometimes on the stoep after the afternoon nap, over cups of tea, the uncles talked about their father, the 'gentleman farmer' who 'kept a carriage and pair, who grew corn on the lands below the dam which he threshed and ground himself'.[46] In a corner of the stoep, in the shadow of the bougainvillea, hung a canvas water bottle that remained cool in the heat, like the meat hanging in the dark of the store-room without rotting, and the pumpkins on the roof that could

withstand the scorching heat and stay fresh.[47] *Boyhood* suggests that John
deliberately drank little water, which would stand him in good stead,
he thought, if he got lost in the veld: 'He wants to be a creature of the
desert, this desert, like a lizard.'[48] Here, in the allure of a naked, barren
earth, without adornment or embellishment, may perhaps be found one
inspiration for the mature Coetzee's sparse prose style with its sparing
use of words.[49]

Apart from the uncles and aunts on Voëlfontein. John also got to
know the coloured labourers [50]. There were two coloured families on the
farm, each with their own house. Near the dam wall there was another
house, now roofless, which used to be inhabited by Outa Jaap: 'Outa
Jaap was on the farm before his grandfather; he himself remembers
Outa Jaap only as a very old man with milky-white, sightless eyeballs
and toothless gums and knotted hands.' Everyone who had known him
when he was younger remembered him with respect. Oupa Jaap dated
from a time before jackal-proof fences, when the shepherd had to take
his sheep for grazing to distant camps and guard them for weeks on
end. He belonged to a previous generation and had been completely
a part of the farm, even though his grandfather had been the owner.
'Outa Jaap came with it, knew more about it, about sheep, veld, weather,
than the newcomer would ever know. That was why Outa Jaap had to be
deferred to; that is why there is no question of getting rid of Outa Jaap's
son Ros, now in his middle years, though he is not a particularly good
workman, unreliable and prone to get things wrong.' That was why Ros
would stay on the farm and die there. 'Freek, the other hired man, is
younger and more energetic than Ros, quicker on the uptake and more
dependable. Nevertheless, he is not of the farm: it is understood that he
will not necessarily stay.'[51]

John was struck by the correctness and formality of relations between
his Uncle Son and his labourers. Every morning he conferred with the
two men about the day's task. He did not issue orders, but suggested
tasks that had to be executed. They discussed it, with long gaps in the
conversation. Then, suddenly, the matter was settled, and with the words
'Well then, we'll get going now, baas Sonnie,' they would take their leave.[52]
The same would happen in the kitchen, where Ros's wife, Tryn, and
Lientjie, his daughter from a previous marriage, worked. They arrived at
breakfast time and left after lunch, the main meal of the day. They were
both shy, but he heard them talking in low voices, 'the soft, comforting
gossip of women, stories passed from ear to ear to ear, till not only the

farm but the village at Fraserburg Road and the location outside the village are covered by the stories, and all the other farms of the district too: a soft white web of gossip spun over past and present.'[53] Freek had a bicycle and a guitar, and sometimes sat in his room playing. On Saturday afternoons he cycled to the location at Fraserburg Road, where he stayed until Sunday evening.[54] Although he was a hired man and could depart at any time, Freek, John thought—squatting on his haunches and gazing out over the veld with his pipe in his mouth—belonged to the Karoo more truly than the Coetzees: 'The Karoo is Freek's country, his home; the Coetzees, drinking tea and gossiping on the farmhouse stoep, are like swallows, seasonal, here today, gone tomorrow, or even like sparrows, chirping, lightfooted, short-lived.'[55]

One of the great pleasures the farm provided John was the hunting, *Boyhood* suggests. When he visited the farm, an old .22 taking a single cartridge was borrowed from the neighbours for his use, even if he shot nothing more than frogs and mousebirds in the orchards. 'Yet never does he live more intensely than in the early mornings when he and his father set off with their guns up the drybed of the Boesmansrivier in search of game: steenbok, duiker, hares, and, on the bare slopes of the hills, korhaan.'[56] They always went hunting in the early morning. In the afternoons, they often travelled in his uncle's Studebaker, with Uncle Son driving, his father in the passenger seat, and he and Ros in the dickey seat. It was his privilege to jump out and open the farm gates. Sometimes, too, they went hunting by night, but he thought the blinding light of the bulala lamp was unfair to the buck being hunted. What he enjoyed during the day, besides the adventure of the hunt, was the silence when they stopped, 'always the landscape enclosing them, the beloved landscape of ochre and grey and fawn and olive-green'.[57] He grew so attached to this landscape that he yearned always to live in the Karoo:

> Is there no way of living in the Karoo—the only place in the world where he wants to be—as he wants to live: without belonging to a family? [...] There is not enough time in a single life to know all of Voëlfontein, know its every stone and bush. No time can be enough when one loves a place with such devouring love. [...] Yet Voëlfontein has its mysteries too, mysteries that belong not to the night and shadow but to hot afternoons when mirages dance on the horizon and the very air sings in his ears.[58]

On Fridays, when a sheep was slaughtered for the farm people, John liked going with Ros and Freek to pick the animal and take it to the slaughtering place behind the shed, out of sight of the house. 'Freek holds down the legs while Ros, with his harmless-looking little pocket-knife, cuts its throat, and then both men hold tight as the animal kicks and struggles and coughs while its lifeblood gushes out. He continues to watch as Ros flays the still warm body and hangs the carcase from the syringa tree and splits it open and tugs the insides out into a basin.' He also looked on when Ros castrated the lambs and cut the tails.[59] He watched Son's every action, and was fascinated by his uncle's knowledge of sheep. He liked eating the meat, and looked forward to the ringing of the bell for lunch, 'and the huge repast it announces: dishes of roast potatoes, yellow rice with raisins, sweet potatoes with caramel sauce, pumpkin with brown sugar and soft bread-cubes, sweet-and-sour beans, beetroot salad, and, at the centre, in pride of place, a great platter of mutton with gravy to pour over it.'[60]

Yet, after seeing the sheep being slaughtered, he shied away from raw meat, avoiding butcher shops back in Worcester. 'Sometimes when he is among the sheep—when they have been rounded up to be dipped, and are penned tight and cannot get away,' he writes in *Boyhood*:

> he wants to whisper to them, warn them of what lies in store. But then in their yellow eyes he catches a glimpse of something that silences him: a resignation, a foreknowledge not only of what happens to sheep at the hands of Ros behind the shed, but of what awaits them at the end of the long, thirsty ride to Cape Town on the transport lorry. They know it all, down to the finest detail, and yet they submit. They have calculated the price and are prepared to pay it—the price of being on earth, the price of being alive.[61]

In September, in spring, the shearers arrived on their bicycles. A fat wether would be slaughtered for them, and they would move into the old shed, and start shearing the sheep the next morning. John would be woken up by the sound of hooves and the smell of coffee in the kitchen. 'By first light he is outside, dressed, too excited to eat. He is given a task. He has charge of a tin mug full of dried beans. Each time a shearer finishes a sheep, and releases it with a slap on the hindquarters, [...] the shearer may take a bean from the mug.'[62]

According to *Boyhood*, his cousin Agnes of Skipperskloof was also there. Together they watched the shearers racing to see who worked the fastest. By the evening of the second day the work was done, and every shearer was paid according to his number of beans. The bales of wool were carted away in a big lorry. 'Every year the shearers come, every year there is this adventure and excitement':[63]

> The farm is greater than any of them. The farm exists from eternity to eternity. When they are all dead, when even the farmhouse has fallen into ruin like the kraals on the hillside, the farm will still be here.[64]

Of all the places John came to know, Voëlfontein was the one that, from early childhood, he loved most:

> he loves every stone of it, every bush, every blade of grass, loves the birds that give it its name, birds that as dusk falls gather in their thousands in the trees around the fountain, calling to each other, murmuring, ruffling their feathers, settling for the night. It is not conceivable that another person could love the farm as he does.[65]

When he dies, the young John thinks in *Boyhood*, he would like to be buried on the farm, or, if he is cremated, have his ashes scattered there.[66]

Love of the farm permeated his life, but it had a dark side, because as the son of Jack and Vera, rather than of Son and Sylvia, he would never have a permanent abode on the farm:

> He must go to the farm because there is no place on earth he loves more or can imagine loving more. [...]Yet since as far back as he can remember this love has had an edge of pain. He may visit the farm but he will never live there. The farm is not his home; he will never be more than a guest, an uneasy guest.[67]

He did not feel at home on the farm, or in the company of his admired uncle:

> Uncle Son always treats him kindly, yet he knows he does not really like him. How does he know? By the uneasy look in Son's eyes when he is around, the forced tone in his voice. If Son really liked him, he

would be as free and offhand with him as he is with Ros and Freek. Instead, Son is careful always to speak English to him, even though he speaks Afrikaans back. It has become a point of honour with both of them; they do not know how to get out of the trap.[68]

John's sense of his uncle's dislike may well have been no more than youthful diffidence, because the strong attraction he felt towards his uncle is unlikely to have been one-sided. This attraction is evident from his declaration in *Boyhood* that 'If he had a choice between Son and his own father as a father, he would choose Son.'[69] Years later, on 13 August 1979, when he was visiting the US and was informed by his wife, Philippa, of the death of Son, he wrote a letter to Son's widow, Sylvia:[70]

It has come as a shock to me. I knew that he had been in hospital, but I had no idea that it was as serious as this.

I know you and the children, and indeed the whole family, must be heartbroken. I cannot tell you how sad it has made me feel, even though the news has taken so long to reach me here. Uncle Son was one of the finest, kindest, most generous people in the whole world. Everyone thought this of him. During the time that we lived in the Leeu-Gamka district[71] I learned that everyone who knew him liked and respected him. He seemed to be a man completely without enemies.

I am truly sorry that I could not pay my respects last week. My thoughts are with you and Gerald and Valmé.

During the holidays on Voëlfontein John got to know his cousin Agnes of Skipperskloof, and together they roamed the veld barefoot. They developed an affinity for each other: 'Agnes occupies a place in his life that he does not yet understand.'[72] In his conversations with her he was franker than with anybody else. He was attracted both to her physical presence and to her readiness to enter into large subjects of speculation:

Being with her is different from being with his school friends. It has something to do with her softness, her readiness to listen, but also with her slim brown legs, her bare feet, the way she dances from stone to stone. He is clever, he is top of his class; she is reputed to be clever too; they roam around talking about things that the grown-ups would shake their heads over: whether the universe had a beginning; what lies beyond Pluto, the dark planet; where God is, if he exists.

Why is it that he can speak so easily to Agnes? Is it because she is a girl? To whatever comes from him she seems to answer without reserve, softly, readily. She is his first cousin, therefore they cannot fall in love and get married. In a way that is a relief: he is free to be friends with her, open his heart to her. But is he in love with her nevertheless? Is this love—this easy generosity, this sense of being understood at last, of not having to pretend?[73]

John felt at once limited and liberated by the fact that it was his cousin who initiated him into a realm of intimacy, femininity, sensual beauty and kindred concerns that could be love. The inevitable tension between the norms prohibiting a close relationship between family members and Agnes's readiness to follow and reply to John's intellectual explorations created a balance that suited the young boy and enabled him to relax. In Coetzee's fiction this theme of love relationships with women, of sex and beauty, as presaged by the passage from *Boyhood*, was to become a complex theme, full of questions, problems and dangers, always subject to revision and reconsideration.

IV

When the family moved to Worcester in 1949, John was for the first time exposed to a predominantly Afrikaans-speaking community. On the school playground and in the streets, he encountered Afrikaans in all its registers, including the crude and obscene language current among schoolboys. Before the move to Worcester he had learnt Afrikaans during school holidays on Voëlfontein from the coloured boys and from his cousins who couldn't speak English fluently. Two of the cousins, Agnes and Lynette, whose English was better, spoke, like the Coetzees of his father's generation, an Afrikaans riddled with English words, a macaronic speech 'lighter, airier than the Afrikaans they study at school, which is weighed down with idioms that are supposed to come from the *volksmond*, but seem to come only from the Great Trek, lumpish, nonsensical idioms about wagons and cattle and cattle-harness.'[74]

John himself found, as a child, that he became another person when speaking Afrikaans, because the language had an appealing simplicity.[75] Although he had an Afrikaans surname, he was convinced he would not pass for an Afrikaner: 'The range of Afrikaans he commands is thin and bodiless; there is a whole dense world of slang and allusion commanded by real Afrikaans boys—of which obscenity is only a part—to which he has no access.'[76] What he did not like was the subservient form of address of his cousins, with its repetition of 'Mammie' and 'Pappie', without the use of pronouns ('*Mammie moet 'n kombers oor Mammie se knieë trek*'—Mommy should cover Mommy's knees with a rug), and the kind of 'civilised' concern that urged Afrikaners to enquire rhetorically after each other's welfare. He sometimes reacted with impatience to this kind of conversation, which branded him within the family as rude, asocial and eccentric.

In the history taught at school, he was sceptical about the distinction drawn between good and less good or downright bad historical figures:

> Although, in examinations, he gives the correct answers to the history questions, he does not know, in a way that satisfies his heart, why Jan van Riebeeck and Simon van der Stel were so good while Lord Charles Somerset was so bad. Nor does he like the leaders of the Great Trek as he is supposed to, except perhaps for Piet Retief, who was murdered after Dingaan tricked him into leaving his gun outside the kraal. Andries Pretorius and Gerrit Maritz and the others sound like the teachers in the high school or like Afrikaners on the radio: angry and obdurate and full of menaces and talk about God.[77]

He despised the subservient, uncritical mentality of Afrikaans children belonging to the Voortrekker youth movement and the way in which their religiosity and patriotism were vented at gatherings in the school hall when a minister of religion came to address them. Something of this can be found in Mrs Curren's reminiscences of her youth in *Age of Iron*:

> What, after all, gave birth to the age of iron but the age of granite? Did we not have Voortrekkers, generation after generation of Voortrekkers, grim-faced, tight-lipped Afrikaner children, marching, singing their patriotic hymns, saluting their flag, vowing to die for their fatherland? *Ons sal lewe, ons sal sterwe.* Are there not still white

zealots preaching the old regime of discipline, work, obedience, self-sacrifice, a regime of death, to children some too young to tie their own shoelaces? What a nightmare from beginning to end! The spirit of Geneva triumphant in Africa. Calvin, black-robed, thin-blooded, forever cold, rubbing his hands in the after-world, smiling his wintry smile.[78]

South Africa, he concluded, was a county without heroes, except perhaps for Wolraad Woltemade[79], who in the eighteenth century had had the courage to rescue sailors from the stormy waters of Table Bay, only to drown with his horse. And then South Africa acquired another hero. On 31 May 1950, the 23-year-old Vic Toweel fought Manuel Ortiz of the US in Johannesburg for the world bantamweight title, and beat him convincingly on points.[80] With his father, John listened to the broadcast commentary: 'In the last round,' he writes in *Boyhood*,

> Toweel, bleeding and exhausted, hurls himself at his opponent. Ortiz reels; the crowd goes wild, the commentator's voice is hoarse with shouting. The judges announce their decision: South Africa's Viccie Toweel is the new champion of the world. He and his father shout with elation and embrace each other. He does not know how to express his joy. Impulsively he grips his father's hair, tugs with all his might. His father starts back, looks at him oddly.[81]

Whatever John did at school, he kept from his mother.[82] Everything he wanted or liked, had to be turned into a secret. This secretiveness was partly a reaction to his mother's blind, self-sacrificing love of him and his brother[83], which made him close himself off from her: 'He begins to think of himself as one of those spiders that live in a hole in the ground with a trapdoor. Always the spider has to be scuttling back into its hole, closing the trapdoor behind it, shutting out the world, hiding.'[84] He also became aware of something lacking in his family. Unlike other boys, he and David were not given beatings.[85] Also, they wore shoes every day, whereas most of their friends turned up at school barefoot.[86] Unlike other Worcester children, they did not go to church, and they addressed their parents by their first names, even calling Vera by her pet name of Dinny.[87] This caused raised eyebrows at Voëlfontein, and a distrust of Vera's bizarre pedagogical methods. His father seemed strange to John. He was an attorney, he had been a soldier in the war and had played rugby in Cape Town. In Worcester he played cricket; he was a bowler, not a batsman.[88] But there was a problem:

> [I]n each case there is an embarrassing qualification. He is an attorney but no longer practices. He was a soldier but only a lance-corporal. He played rugby, but only for Gardens second team, and Gardens are a joke, they always come bottom of the Grand Challenge league. And now he plays cricket, but for the Worcester second team, which no one bothers to watch.[89]

Once a classmate walked in through the open door of their home and found John lying on his back under a chair. Asked what he was doing, John replied: 'Thinking. I like thinking.'[90]

> Soon everyone in his class knew about it: the new boy was odd, he wasn't normal. From that mistake he has learned to be more prudent. Part of being prudent is always to tell less rather than more.[91]

Because in his own family, as in the family of both his parents, religion played no part, John, when asked, stated his religion as Roman Catholic.[92] This made him a bit of an outsider in a community in which most boys' parents were members of the Dutch Reformed Church, and in which religion was important. What he did not divulge to his fellows was that, unlike them, he favoured the Russians over the Americans. He had learnt about the Russians from photographs in a three-volume history of the Second World War belonging to his father,[93] the soldiers in their white ski uniforms making a great impression on him. Unlike his schoolfellows, he had a great admiration for everything Russian,[94] even for the 'stern but fatherly Field-Marshal Stalin, the greatest and most far-sighted strategist of the war'.[95]

During his three years at school in Worcester, John, always of slender build, grew into an athletic and attractive young boy, cycling to school every morning on the Smiths-BSA that he had bought in Rosebank before his departure.[96] With this bicycle, and especially with the daily trip to school, he started a special relationship with this form of transport. Coetzee has ever since enjoyed cycling, taking part annually in cycle races, and sometimes travelling abroad to cycle long distances with a friend or his daughter. 'There is nothing', he writes, to match the elation of riding a bicycle, of leaning over and swooping through the curves [...] the half-mile from Reunion Park to the railway crossing, then the mile on the quiet road alongside the railway line. Summer mornings are the best. Water murmurs in the roadside furrows, doves coo in the bluegum trees; now and then there is an eddy of warm air to warn of the wind that will blow later in the day, chasing gusts of fine red clay-dust before it.[97]

With his mother he went to buy his Boy Scout uniform—a felt hat, a badge to fix to the hat, shorts and stockings, a leather belt, green shoulder-tabs and green stocking-flashes. He attended the meetings, took the exams and went on a camp, during which they had to swim in the Breede River, even though he had not had any swimming lessons. He almost drowned and regarded his rescue as a providential granting of a second life.[98] The sport that he was most interested in, and that was to fascinate him ever after, was cricket. *Boyhood* demonstrates this fascination. When, with the bat, he for the first time assumed the lone position against his opponents, he realised that everybody was against him and was plotting to cut short his joy before the wickets, with nobody to protect him:

> Cricket is not a game. It is the truth of life. If it is, as the books say, a test of character, then it is a test he sees no way of passing yet does not know how to dodge. At the wicket the secret that he manages to cover up elsewhere is relentlessly probed and exposed. 'Let us see what you are made of,' says the ball as it whistles and tumbles through the air toward him. Blindly, confusedly, he pushes the bat forward, too soon or too late. Past the bat, past the pads the ball finds its way. He is bowled, he has failed the test, he has been found out, there is nothing to do but hide his tears, cover his face, trudge back to the commiserating, politely schooled applause of the other boys.[99]

At home John sometimes tossed a cricket ball in the backyard, but devoted most of his energy to his collections of stamps, tin soldiers and cards of Australian cricketers, English footballers and cars of the world. To get the cards, he had to buy packets of cigarettes made of nougat and icing sugar, with pink-painted tips. He also spent hours with his Meccano set.[100] On a birthday, he was given ten shillings to take a few friends to the Globe Café for banana splits or chocolate fudge sundaes. The occasion was spoilt for him, though, by a group of coloured children in ragged clothes who peered through the window at them enjoying their ice cream. He felt empathy with these children who did not have the same privileges:

> On the faces of these children he sees none of the hatred which, he is prepared to acknowledge, he and his friends deserve for having so much money while they are penniless. On the contrary, they are like children at a circus, drinking in the sight, utterly absorbed, missing nothing.[101]

He went to the movies every Saturday, even though the films no longer gripped him as they had in Cape Town. He could not understand why Errol Flynn was regarded as a good actor, when he looked the same in every role. He found it difficult to believe in Tarzan, because there was a different actor in the role every time. He often listened to the radio. He had outgrown *The Children's Corner*, but liked listening to *Superman* every day at 5.00pm and to *Mandrake the Magician* at 5.30pm. His favourite story was *The Snow Goose* by Paul Gallico. *Treasure Island* by R.L. Stevenson, of which he owned a copy, was dramatised on radio, but he preferred *The Swiss Family Robinson* by Johann David Wyss, a tale about a family shipwrecked on the East Indian Islands on their way to Port Jackson in Australia. John owned an attractive copy with pretty colour plates, and was entranced by the illustrations of the ship the family built from the wreckage to transport all their animals home with them, like Noah and his ark. 'The only thing that puzzles him is why, when they are so snug and happy on the island, they have to leave at all.'[102]

In Worcester, John discovered, the wind blew almost constantly. His mother had to buy a vacuum cleaner to keep the floors dust-free. There were also lots of ants, flies and fleas. Although he was healthy and full of energy, he seemed always to have a cold. He often woke up with a sore throat, and sneezed incessantly, which made him stay in bed. His father thought he was malingering, but his mother kept him from school. A day in bed was a chance to read. He read fast, and sometimes his mother had to go to the library twice a week to take out books for him: two on her name and two on his.[103] He read all the Enid Blyton mystery adventures, all the Hardy Boys and all the Biggles. He loved the tales of the French Foreign Legion by P.C. Wren. When his father asked him who the greatest writer on earth was, he proposed P.C. Wren. When Jack nominated Shakespeare instead, John thought that if his father liked Shakespeare, Shakespeare had to be bad.[104] He nevertheless started reading Shakespeare in a yellowing edition with tattered margins to find out why people praised him so highly. He read *Titus Andronicus* and *Coriolanus* on account of their Roman names, but skipped the long monologues, as he skipped descriptions of nature in his library books.[105]

His father also owned the poems of Wordsworth and Keats, and his mother had an edition of Rupert Brooke. These books were on the mantelpiece in their sitting room along with Shakespeare, *The Story of San Michele* in a leather binding, and *Country Doctor* by A.J. Cronin, a novella about the Scottish Dr Finlay who practised in the fictitious town of Tannochbrae. He tried twice to read *The Story of San Michele* by the Swedish physician Axel Munthe, but got bored.[106] His father tried to interest him in Wordsworth, but he declined with bad grace, and his father gave up. He suspected that his father's so-called interest in poetry was pure pretension. He could believe his mother's story that she had to go and hide in the attic with her poetry book to escape her sisters' teasing; but he could not believe that as a boy his father had really read poetry, because nowadays he read nothing but the newspaper. Besides, he skimmed through the paper to get to the crossword puzzle.[107] His mother venerated Shakespeare and thought *Macbeth* was his greatest drama. He found it puzzling that, though his mother could not help him with his Standard Four homework, her English was impeccable, especially in writing.[108]

Apart from *The Swiss Family Robinson*, John owned a copy of Reginald Pound's *Scott of the Antarctic*, the history of the explorer who reached the South Pole on 17 January 1912, only to find that he had been beaten to it by Roald Amundsen's Norwegian expedition. On the journey back Scott and four of his comrades died of hunger, exhaustion and the violence of the fierce winter. John also browsed the volumes of Arthur Mee's *Children's Encyclopaedia*, in particular Part 10, the index, full of factual information. He found the pictures beautiful, especially the photos of marble sculptures: 'Smooth, slim marble girls fill his erotic dreams.'[109] As he was charmed on Voëlfontein by Agnes's beauty, he now found some of the boys at school very attractive, especially the Afrikaans boys with their tight shorts and slender, tanned legs:

Beauty and desire: he is disturbed by the feelings that the legs of
these boys, blank and perfect and inexpressive, create in him. What
is there that can be done with legs beyond devouring them with
one's eyes? [...]

Of all the secrets that set him apart, this may in the end be the
worst. Among all these boys he is the only one in whom this dark
erotic current runs; among all this innocence and normality, he is
the only one who desires.[110]

With all this reading and these influences, John extended his range,
in spite of the countrified limits of Worcester, and continued the
achievements of Rosebank at his new school. At first it did seem as if the
move had adversely affected him. From the first two reports of 1949 it
appears that, though the teachers were quite satisfied with his work and
regarded him as well-mannered, he had lost his customary first place in
class. By the last report of 1949 he had moved up to fifth in class, but
from 1950 onwards he maintained the first place, except once when he
was absent from school for fifteen days on account of flu, and fell back to
second place. He consistently averaged 89 per cent or more. His work was
repeatedly described as exceptionally satisfactory. 'He is a very pleasant
boy and a conscientious worker,' Mr G. Gouws, his class teacher, noted in
the report of March 1951.

At the age of twelve John had started to realise that his family and
some of the extended family were not exactly what passed for as 'ordinary'
people. He became aware, for instance, of the Coetzee habit of mixing
languages. Whereas most of his male and female cousins, unlike their
parents, spoke a pure Afrikaans and little English, Agnes spoke the same
mixture of English and Afrikaans as the older generation. The Afrikaans
spoken by his uncles and aunts at the annual gatherings on the farm
was not what he heard in Worcester. 'My background,' Coetzee has said
in an interview, 'is very mixed. I can't remember anyone in my father's
family producing an Afrikaans sentence without an English word in it,
and vice versa.'[111]

The Coetzees of his father's generation were Afrikaners without
any hotheaded nationalistic tendencies, unlike the parents of his
schoolmates. The Coetzees were pre-1948 Afrikaners. After 1948,
amid a proliferation of nationalist festivals, Afrikaner identity acquired
a political and ideological charge, and people like his parents were
vilified from the pulpit as traitors. Coetzee was a child from an Afrikaans

background attending English-medium classes at a time of rampant Afrikaner nationalism, when one discriminatory law after the other was passed. There was even some talk of legislation to prevent people with an Afrikaans background from sending their children to English-language schools, but this never materialised. By the age of twelve John had developed a strong sense of social marginality.[112] 'By the time we moved to Worcester, in 1948,' he wrote in 2008, 'being Afrikaans was a hot political issue. As someone neither English enough nor Afrikaans enough, I was deeply marked by the culture wars of those days.'[113]

This feeling of alienation was partly a result of Jack and Vera's cultural backgrounds. Both came from a milieu and an era when Afrikaans was despised as a kitchen language and education tended to be conducted in English. Jack's English was excellent, though he spoke with a strong Afrikaans accent. His Afrikaans vocabulary was limited. He completed the *Cape Times* crossword puzzle every day, paging around in the *Pocket Oxford Dictionary* for assistance,[114] but John doubted whether he would be up to doing the *Die Burger*'s puzzle. John never saw him reading an Afrikaans book, whereas he did know a certain number of 'high' English literary classics such as Shakespeare and Wordsworth, and could quote from them. His mother's English was even better than his father's. Although her education was limited, and included only a year's training at university,[115] her command of English grammar was near-faultless. She spoke Afrikaans with a good accent, but her vocabulary was sparse, and, like his father, she never read an Afrikaans book.

John Coetzee thus had, from a relatively early age, an awareness of the twofold nature of his origins and a measure of ambivalence towards English and Afrikaans He would react to this in various ways at different stages of his life and in various novels. But reminiscing about his youth in 2008, he expressed his appreciation for the good English he had learnt in Worcester from his parents and teachers:

> From them, from the teachers of my early years, many of whom came from a similar background, and from my reading, I learned what I think was very good English. For example, from Mr Gouws, my Standard Five teacher in Worcester, I learned intricacies of English grammar beyond the ken of university students today. Yet Mr Gouws spoke Afrikaans at home and did not have a university degree. Most of my cousins on my father's side are, culturally speaking, Afrikaners. All my cousins on my mother's side, with one

exception, are 'English'. Until I moved to the city at the age of twelve, my social intercourse was more with extended family than with friends (a pattern that no longer survives).[116]

And in an interview with David Attwell in 1992 he spoke warmly of the beautiful and wonderful things he had experienced in his youth:

I too had a childhood that—in parts—seems more entrancing and miraculous as I grow older. Perhaps that is how most of us come to see our childhood selves: with a gathering sense of wonder that there could once have been such an innocent world, and that we ourselves could have been at the heart of that innocence. It's a good thing that we should grow fond of the selves we once were—I wouldn't want to denounce that for a moment. The child is father to the man: we should not be too strict with our child selves, we should have the grace to forgive them for setting us on the paths that led us to become the people we are. Nevertheless, we can't wallow in comfortable wonderment at our past. We must see what the child, still befuddled from his travels, still trailing his clouds of glory, could not see. We—or at least some of us, enough of us—must look at the past with a cruel enough eye to see what it was that made that joy and innocence possible. Forgivingness but also unflinchingness: that is the mixture I have in mind, if it is attainable. First the unflinchingness, then the forgivingness.[117]

V

At the end of 1951 the Coetzees returned to Cape Town. As an accountant, Jack Coetzee knew that the finances of his employer, Wolf Heller, and his firm, Standard Canners & Packers, were at a low ebb, and that his future with the firm was not secure. Therefore he tried to be reinstated as an attorney.

In the documentation submitted to the Law Society of the Cape of Good Hope, he writes that he had been discharged from the army on 20 February 1946, and that he had then served as Controller of Letting in Cape Town. He had resigned in December 1948 and accepted employment with Standard Packers & Canners in Worcester. With his application he included two references testifying to his diligence, honesty, sober habits and his 'ability and tact in dealing with members of the public'.

Since all the debts incurred earlier had been discharged, and none of his clients had suffered any loss, the Law Society was well disposed towards the application. He was re-admitted to the attorney's roll on 13 March 1950.[118] Jack Coetzee probably first had to earn the money required to open his own practice, because the family moved to Cape Town only at the end of 1951, enabling John and David to commence their schooling there at the start of the new school year.

CHAPTER 3

ST JOSEPH'S MARIST COLLEGE, 1952–1956

I

When Jack Coetzee returned to the legal profession in Cape Town, he left Worcester in December 1951 to rent a house for his family and establish an office for his practice. Vera stayed behind to pack their possessions and found a contractor for the move at a bargain price.[1]

Jack found a house in Plumstead at £25, instead of the meagre £12 a month they had paid in Worcester. Plumstead is a southern suburb of Cape Town towards False Bay, more prosperous than nearby Ottery to the east, but considerably less upscale than Constantia to the west. The house was on the outer boundary of Plumstead in Evremond Road, where all of the houses, as in Reunion Park in Worcester, had been newly built, with picture windows and parquet floors.[2] The plots on the other side of the street had not yet been built on, and harboured vagrants and tramps drinking methylated spirits. Rumour had it that a dead baby had once been found there in a paper bag. Later the family moved to Milford Road, immediately parallel to Evremond Road.[3] Eventually they settled down in Camp Ground Road in Rondebosch, a much more sought-after area, closer to the city centre and to Goodwood, where Jack would have his first practice.

In the urban environment of Plumstead John found he could no longer cycle as freely as in Worcester. He had lost interest in his stamp collection and Meccano set, but kept his passion for cricket and played ceaselessly with a ball on the front stoep, goading the neighbours to complain to his mother.[4] In Rondebosch John developed into a competent photographer and acquired a small camera, firmly convinced it was intended for espionage. He converted a spare room into a darkroom to develop his photographs.[5] Nic Stathakis, the friend who had been at school with him in Rosebank, now re-entered his life. Stathakis could recall, many years later, how they had between classes mischievously taken photos in secret of teachers and schoolfellows, and how they had one day almost blinded themselves by experimenting for hours in the darkroom with sparks between two live wires.[6] John kept his interest in photography for many years. When studying at the University of Cape Town, he acquired a better quality camera that he used for many years. In his novel *Slow Man* (2006), the protagonist—Paul Rayment, also a skilled photographer, with a valuable collection of photographs—tends to trust photos more than words, because, as soon as they leave the darkroom, they are fixed, unchangeable:

> The camera, with its power of taking in light and turning it into substance, has always seemed to him more a metaphysical than a mechanical device. His first real job was as a darkroom technician; his greatest pleasure was always in darkroom work. As the ghostly image emerged beneath the surface of the liquid, as veins of darkness on the paper began to knit together and grow visible, he would sometimes experience a little shiver of ecstasy, as though he were present at the day of creation.[7]

When John's family moved to Cape Town in 1952, he was not yet twelve. He had to go to Standard Six, which up to then had been a part of primary school, but in that year was moved to high school. Thanks to Vera's brother Lance, who was in education, Vera and John were granted an interview at the highly regarded Rondebosch Boys' High School. In spite of his good results in Worcester, he was not accepted. He was placed on the waiting list of two other schools, without success.[8] The last resort was St Joseph's Marist College, a private school connected with the Roman Catholic Church:

> What is being brought home to them, to him and his mother, is that [...] St Joseph's caters for, if not the lowest class, then the second-lowest. Her failure to get him into a better school leaves his mother bitter [...]
>
> The real English do not go to a school like St Joseph's. But on the streets of Rondebosch, on their way to and from their own schools, he can see them every day, can admire their straight blond hair and golden skins, their clothes that are never too small or too large, their quiet confidence.[9]

This passage may be a deliberate attempt to isolate and marginalise the desubjectified John of *Boyhood*. Rondebosch Boys' High was then, as now, a sought-after government school, and Bishops, the Diocesan College, also in Rondebosch, was an expensive private institution where the pupils, besides a good education, enjoyed all kinds of added advantages, comparable with those at a British public school. But St Joseph's was not some second-rate school, as this passage would suggest. Its teachers worked hard to give of their best in the South African context of the time.

Most of the teachers were members of the Marist order, men who with their 'black cassocks and white starched stocks' held an aura of mystery for John.[10] The college is one of five Marist Catholic schools in South Africa and was established in 1918 in Belmont Park in Rondebosch. It is part of a farm dating back to the early eighteenth century. In 1909 it was one of the places where, in the presence of the then Transvaal prime minister, Louis Botha, and J.C. Smuts, at the time the colonial secretary of the Transvaal, a first concept was drawn up, preceding the National Convention that led to the formation of the Union of South Africa in 1910.

In the years that John attended St Joseph's College, it was a boys' school, drawing pupils from beyond South Africa's borders. Although aimed at children from Roman Catholic homes, it from the start also accommodated other religions and cultural backgrounds.[11] In the South Africa of the 1950s racial segregation was practised by law in schools, but John could later remember that in his 'white' school there were nevertheless one or two coloured Catholic boys from the South West Africa of the time (now Namibia). However, in the light of the government's prohibition, this was not the school's official policy. The admission of these boys would have happened tacitly, with the school authorities turning a blind eye.[12]

At first, while they were living in Plumstead, John had a half-an-hour walk from their house in Evremond Road to the station, followed by a fifteen-minute train trip to Rondebosch station, which was a five-minute walk from the school. To provide for delays, he had to leave home at 7.30am to get to the school before the 8.30am start; but for fear of being late, he usually left at 7.00am.[13] When they moved to Camp Ground Road in Rondebosch, he was a stone's throw from the school. This allowed him to take part in more extra-mural activities at St Joseph's. With its large contingent of foreign teachers and its Roman Catholic tenets, St Joseph's was in many respects an island apart, indifferent to

South African conditions. Nevertheless, one of the teachers organised a bus for the pupils to attend the 1952 Van Riebeeck Festival, the tricentennial celebration of the arrival of the Dutch colonists, held on the then largely vacant Foreshore. John later recalled the nationalistic zeal and religious rhetoric of the day:

> When he was twelve he was herded into a bus full of schoolchildren and driven to Adderley Street, where they were given paper orange-white-and-blue flags and told to wave them as the parade of floats passed by (Jan van Riebeeck and his wife in sober burgher dress; Voortrekkers with muskets; portly Paul Kruger). Three hundred years of history, three hundred years of Christian civilization at the tip of Africa, said the politicians in their speeches: to the Lord let us give thanks.[14]

At school John was a dedicated sportsman. But because he had been promoted in his first school year from Sub A to Sub B, he was younger than his classmates, and usually played for teams that were one or even two years lower than theirs. Although he was not overly interested in rugby, he played prop for the under-13 team, only to find that St Joseph's regularly lost all their matches against other schools. By sheer dedication he developed into a fine cricketer, and in his matric year played for the school's first team.[15] In his 2001 introduction to the Penguin edition of Robert Musil's *The Confusions of Young Törless*, Coetzee wrote about Musil in terms that make one wonder whether he wasn't also thinking of himself in his St Joseph's years: 'Younger and smaller than his classmates at school, [Musil] cultivated a physical toughness that he maintained throughout his life.'[16] In 1953, in Standard Seven, John wrote an article for the annual, the *St Joseph's College Magazine*, under the heading 'Ye olde history of Crickete', which was evidently based on thorough research. A notable feature is the economical use of words, later to become so characteristic of his prose style. 'The game of cricket', he opens his article,

> is founded on the earliest known type of game, that of Bat and Ball. This game, which has been played since people have started to play games in their leisure hours, simply consists of hitting a stone, or some similar object with a branch of a tree or a stick. As simple a game as this has now developed into one of the most scientific

sports, and is followed by a large number of 'fans', playing and non-playing.[17]

The fact that John was younger than his classmates hampered his social development. When confronted with a problem, physical or intellectual, his instinct was to bottle up his emotions. He was an outsider who often did not share in the fun and games of his classmates. In the college annual of 1956, where each of the matrics is summed up in a single phrase, John is characterised by the declaration 'I refuse to Rock and Roll.' Apart from the social marginalisation John experienced on account of his reserved nature, there was a political marginalisation stemming from the Coetzees' support of the United Party, though this would not have been an issue at St Joseph's. John's undemonstrative manner did not preclude an early empathy with his fellow-beings. Nic Stathakis remembered him in 2008 as a youth with a strong sympathy with others, especially with the underprivileged:

> One small example is fixed in my memory. In Cape Town in the Fifties the suburban trains going down the Peninsula to the suburbs would stand at Cape Town station with the whites-only section at the buffer or concourse end. The non-white coaches were way down at the end of the platform. While still schoolboys John once told me that one of the saddest things he had seen was a large black woman weighed down with shopping bags sweatily running/shuffling down the platform to get to the non-white section in time, the departure whistle already having been blown. Entering the first coach (whites only) and walking through the train as would be done in any normal country, was out of the question.[18]

After the budding awareness of his cousin Agnes's physical beauty on Voëlfontein and the tight shorts and tanned legs of the Afrikaans boys in Worcester, adolescence brought John a sexual awakening. At St Joseph's he was regarded as an a-sexual wimp[19] — unjustly, as is clear from *Boyhood* and its abundant evidence of an interest in the beauty of the body and the role of sexuality in his life. In her bottom drawer his mother had a book titled *Ideal Marriage*,[20] with pictures of the sex organs. When he took the book to school to show his friends, it caused a sensation, but John's reaction was quite clinical — 'inserting the male organ into the vagina sounds like an enema'.[21]

He became friendly with Theo Stavropoulos,[22] a Greek boy reputed to be homosexual, though John refused to believe the rumours. He was attracted to Theo's appearance: 'He likes the look of Theo, likes his fine skin and his high colouring and his impeccable haircuts and the suave way he wears his clothes.'[23] Theo's father was rich and owned a factory. He and his brothers were brought to school in the morning in a black Buick, often by a chauffeur in a black uniform. John was invited to their home and was overwhelmed by the opulence at the meal. He glimpsed Theo's father fleetingly and met his mother, but an elder sister was 'so beautiful, so expensively educated, so marriageable, that she is not allowed to be exposed to the gaze of Theo's friends'.[24]

John seemed driven to be top of the class at all costs, perhaps so that he would not seem younger than his classmates. But at St Joseph's he came across, for the first time in his school career, a formidable opponent—Oliver Matter, a Swiss boy who before John's arrival had been regarded as the brightest pupil in the class. They took turns to come first in individual tests, but then Oliver stopped attending school. After a month's absence, Brother Gabriel announced that Oliver was in hospital with leukaemia, and that everyone should pray for him. Oliver died in hospital. 'It is with deep regret,' the *St Joseph's College Magazine* of 1953 states, 'that we have to record the sudden passing of Master R.O. Matter on August 13th. Oliver, who came to the College in 1949, was a boy of a quiet disposition, friendly and very popular. His conduct in class and in the general life of the College was excellent, and both teachers and boys esteemed him for his sterling qualities. As a student he showed outstanding ability and great promise, having gained one first and two second places in the general Standard Six examinations held last December for all Marist schools in South Africa.' In *Boyhood*, the third-person protagonist reacts according to his own priorities: 'The threat has receded. He breathes more easily; but the old pleasure in coming first is spoiled.'[25] The somewhat unappealing glimpse this affords into the ambitions of the young John is softened by the honesty of the adult author, capable, in 1997, of writing so soberly, however unfavourably to himself, about his own feelings or lack thereof.

In the years at St Joseph's, John, for a variety of reasons, no longer visited the family farm, the place he recognised early in his life as 'his place of origin'.[26] In adolescence he was enrolled as a nominal Protestant in a Catholic school, with Greek and Jewish friends, and rampant nationalism calling the tune countrywide. 'All of this,' he writes in *Doubling the*

Point, 'confirms his (quite accurate) sense of being outside a culture that at this moment in history is confidently setting about enforcing itself as the core culture of the land.'[27] Increasingly, John Coetzee became persuaded that as an outsider he had no connection with the world around him.

II

Whereas in Worcester John had posed as a Roman Catholic, he now found himself in a Roman Catholic school, as a nominal Protestant but from an areligious home. The brothers slept in a wing of the school, waking up at four in the morning to pray, after which they sat down to a meagre meal. Few of them had English as their first language, and English lessons were left in the hands of a Catholic layman, Terence Whelan, an Irishman who hated the English: 'He is supposed to read the Gospel of St Luke with them. Instead they hear over and over again about Parnell and Roger Casement and the perfidy of the English.'[28] Whelan set essays on boring subjects in which John could not feign an interest. Whelan's method of teaching Shakespeare's *Julius Caesar* was to assign the boys various roles and have them read them aloud in class.

Brother Augustine, or Gussie as he was called by the pupils,[29] taught John several subjects in the lower standards, including mathematics and science. In John's matric year Brother Augustine taught English and coached the first cricket team. On first meeting John, in Standard Six, Brother Augustine found him rather puny and shy, probably because he was about eighteen months younger than the rest of the class. In the higher standards he was physically stronger but still reserved. Even so, the other boys did not look down on him or bully him, because he was in every respect their intellectual superior. About the essays John wrote in his matric year, Brother Augustine has written:

> In his Matric year, as his English teacher, I gave John's class an essay a
> week making use of a marking system in which each individual would
> have had to see to his own corrections and possible improvement in
> expression. John's contribution was outstanding, and his clarity of
> thought and use of the language improved weekly to such an extent
> that in September of that year I sent a copy of one of his essays to

the Joint Matriculation Examination Board enquiring whether his work would be properly evaluated under the examination marking system. The essay was returned with the comment 'If this pupil does not obtain a distinction in English, then ask for a remark.' As things turned out John came out as top student in English in the 1956 Joint Board Examination. [...] In all my career as a teacher I never met a pupil with the ability to express himself as lucidly and meaningfully as John was able. He might have written with an economy of words – but the message spoke volumes! [30]

John's classmate Billy Steele in later years recalled Brother Augustine one day turning up with a newspaper photo of a black boy with a bicycle and a candle about which they had to write an essay. From John's essay, in which he imagined the stolen bicycle and the candle as the boy's sole possessions, Steele could years later recall a sentence verbatim that had impressed him: 'The mathematical moth flying in ever decreasing circles to its own destruction.' [31]

Brother Augustine adopted an at the time novel way of instructing English literature, derived from I.A. Richards. He taught the boys to concentrate on the 'sense, intention, feeling and tone' in a poem. [32] Their poetry setwork book was *The Living Tradition*, an anthology of English poetry from 1340 to 1940, compiled by T. Tyfield and K.R. Nicol. In their introduction they declare:

> It should be stated categorically that poetry is not a sensitive plant, unable to endure the gales of modern life. Like all forms of art it seeks to interpret life, and as long as men and women exist on earth the poet will have a function to perform in society. [...] At the same time, no growth exists without roots and the living tradition has been traced from Chaucer to Alan Rook. [33]

Through the chronologically arranged poems, John became acquainted with the tradition of English poetry, and the eminent figures of the twentieth century, such as William Butler Yeats, T.S. Eliot and W.H. Auden. He was particularly taken with T.S. Eliot's 'Preludes', with their Modernist imagery, stripped of romantic embellishment.

John noticed, however, that many of his contemporaries seemed rather bored with having to read and study poetry. In *Diary of a Bad Year*, with the covert and laconic humour that characterises Coetzee's late work in particular, there is a passage that could be taken as direct autobiography:

> As a child I [...] was convinced that the boredom endemic among my contemporaries was a sign of their higher nature, that it expressed a tacit judgment on whatever it was that bored them, and therefore that whatever bored them should be looked down on for failing to meet their legitimate human needs. So when my schoolfellows were bored by poetry, for instance, I concluded that poetry itself was at fault, that my own absorption in poetry was deviant, culpable, and above all immature.
>
> In reasoning thus I was abetted by much of the literary criticism of the day, which said that the modern age (meaning the twentieth century) demanded poetry of a new, modern cast that would break decisively with the past, in particular with the poetry of the Victorians. To the truly modern poet nothing could be more retrograde and therefore more contemptible than a liking for Tennyson.
>
> The fact that my classmates were bored by Tennyson proved to me, if proof were needed, that they were the authentic if unconscious bearers of the new, modern sensibility. Through them the Zeitgeist pronounced its stern judgment on the Victorian age, and on Tennyson in particular. As for the troublesome fact that my classmates were equally bored (to say nothing of being baffled) by T.S. Eliot, this was to be explained by a lingering effeteness in Eliot, a failure on his part to measure up to their brusque masculine standards.
>
> It did not occur to me that my classmates found poetry boring—as they found all their subjects boring—because they could not concentrate.[34]

At St Joseph's John did consistently well, though he was bored with subjects like history and geography, which required memorising a plethora of facts. He always came first in his class. In Standards Six and Seven he achieved an aggregate of 85 per cent and 86 per cent, and in the higher classes maintained this standard, scoring high marks in especially English and mathematics. He passed both the Junior and the Senior Certificate in the First Class. In December 1953 he came first in the exams administered countrywide at Marist Brothers Colleges. In 1955 he qualified for a bursary on the grounds of his Junior Certificate results, and he earned a total of £10 for the exams in June and at the end of the year. He was the only boy in the school who in 1956, quite voluntarily, wrote and passed the bilingualism exam of the South African Academy for Arts and Sciences.

In spite of his academic prowess, *Boyhood* suggests that John did not always enjoy school. In Worcester he used to go to school with a mixture of dread and excitement: 'In Cape Town, in contrast, he soon feels that he is wasting his time. School is no longer a place where great passions are aired. It is a shrunken little world, a more or less benign prison [...]. Cape Town is not making him cleverer, it is making him stupider. The realization causes panic to well up in him. Whoever he truly is, whoever the true "I" is that ought to be rising out of the ashes of his childhood, is not being allowed to be born, is being kept puny and stunted.'[35]

When, years later, in 1981, he was asked in an interview how his school career had shaped him, he answered: 'I had what I regard as a poor education in all respects. But then everyone around me was getting a poor education.'[36] Fundamental to this extremely negative assessment is the conviction that would in time become central to Coetzee's mindset, namely that pupils and students in the colonies, in contrast with the metropolis, received an inferior education. In a letter of 17 January 1974 to Peter Randall, his first publisher, who had requested biographical information for the cover text of *In the Heart of the Country*, Coetzee replied that he was in two minds as to whether he should provide the information. With a touch of exaggeration he writes: 'A few words about my schooling, for example, make me a player in the English-South African game of social typing and can even be read as a compliment to those monsters of sadism who ruled over my life for eleven years.'

Coetzee also still harboured ambivalence towards Afrikaners and their place in his ancestry. The Afrikaners were the pioneers who, with the Great Trek, the victory at Majuba and the Anglo-Boer War, had achieved a certain epic and heroic dimension. By contrast, the English-speaking South Africans, with their 'home' expatriate mentality, had initially not experienced the heroic element to the same extent, not to mention the epic. Then again, the young boy was aware of the horrors of apartheid being perpetrated after the election of 1948, with the series of discriminatory laws being passed in parliament. Shortly after the Nationalist victory, he had been transplanted to an environment heady with the euphoria of nationalism. Now, in Cape Town, with parents

having access to neither Afrikaans nor English society, he found himself
in a school that to some extent stood outside the South African reality.
All this reinforced his sense of marginalisation, of being at a cultural
and social disadvantage.

He also felt ambivalent towards the Afrikaans language. To an
enquiry regarding his relation to his bilingual origins, he replied in
2008:

> I had a divided attitude toward Afrikaans from 1948 until the 1960s.
> At school in Cape Town I was good at Afrikaans as a school subject.
> I was the only boy in my Matric year who took and passed the
> bilingualism examination of the Akademie. I was never ashamed of
> being 'good' at Afrikaans. But the thought did not cross my mind
> of reading Afrikaans magazines and books for pleasure. I did not
> think of myself as an Afrikaner (though it was difficult for me to
> think of myself as 'English' either): I did not question the National
> Party's definition of what was needed to be an Afrikaner, and was
> proud I did not meet that definition.[37]

III

Paging through the school magazines published during Coetzee's years
at St Joseph's Marist College, one finds that few contributions by him
appear there. To an enquiry made on 20 October 2008, he replied:
'I have no unpublished poems from those early years and don't think
there are any.'[38]

The only extant poem by Coetzee published in the *St Joseph's College
Magazine* is the long 'In the Beginning', a poem of 147 lines, which he
described in the subtitle as 'An Account of the Creation according to
the Legends of Greece and Rome'. It seems hardly credible that this
ambitious poem was the only poem that Coetzee wrote during his school
years. One suspects that his other juvenilia were not preserved. In *Youth*
he states that he used to write Keatsian sonnets, an infatuation he later
abjured. Even at school T.S. Eliot revealed to him an impersonal type of
poetry that soon led him to abandon his Keatsian phase. 'Keats is like
watermelon,' he writes in *Youth*, 'soft and sweet and crimson, whereas
poetry should be hard and clear like a flame. Reading half a dozen
pages of Keats is like yielding to seduction.'[39] Later the works of Ezra

Pound would teach him to distrust the easy sentiment of the Romantics and the Victorians.[40]

'In the Beginning' appeared in the school magazine of 1956, and was announced as the winner in the poetry section of the Cape Town Eisteddfod, the first of many times that one of Coetzee's works would be awarded a prize.[41]

For a youthful poet, 'In the Beginning' embodies a vast vision, impressively realised, showing promise. With this poem, Coetzee, probably unconsciously, indicates the Western cultural and literary tradition to which he sees his work as belonging.

John was starting to cultivate other interests. When he turned fifteen, he nagged his parents for music lessons, and his mother bought a piano. He had ambitions to become a great musician, but the step-by-step method of instruction bored him and the lessons were not a success.[42] He did not, however, lose interest in music. Nic Stathakis recalled, many years later, how furiously they started reading and immersing themselves in classical music. 'From 15, or maybe earlier,' Stathakis writes in a letter of 27 October 2008,[43] 'with John leading, and another boy of Greek extraction called Tony (now deceased)[44] and myself following, we were deep into 19th and early 20th century European literature, especially the Russians, and, especially John and Tony, into English and modern Greek poetry. We would be mesmerized by classical music, Beethoven and Bach. John taught himself to play Bach on the piano. I was left way behind in this department but was infected with an abiding love of classical music.'

This sensitivity to music led the youthful John to one of the most significant experiences of his school career. It is an intense and illuminating experience he was to refer to in 1991 in his lecture 'What is a Classic?', delivered in Graz, Austria.[45]

One Sunday afternoon in 1955, when he was fifteen, while loitering in the backyard of their home in Rondebosch, bored and at a loose end, he heard music coming from the house next door. He was transfixed, and listened breathlessly, feeling the music speak to him as never before. What he was listening to was a recording of a harpsichord rendering of Bach's *Wohltemperierte Klavier*, a title he came to know only later when he was more knowledgeable about 'classical music'.

The house next door was home to a floating population of students; the student listening to Bach must have moved on or lost interest in Bach, because Coetzee never heard the piece again. Apart from his grandmother, who had played the piano, Coetzee did not stem from a musical line, and the schools he attended offered no tuition in music. In the colonies, in any case, classical music was often regarded as the refuge of 'sissies'. At home they had up to then never had a musical instrument or a record player. After hearing the Bach, he nagged his mother to let him take music lessons and mastered works like Beethoven's *Moonlight Sonata* and Schubert's B-flat Major sonata. He taught himself to read music and borrowed many records from the Provincial Library to listen to with his friends Nick and Theo.

The Bach afternoon was a revelation to Coetzee. For the first time he experienced the impact of a classic. At that moment he subconsciously made a symbolic choice for himself. He writes about that choice:

> The question I put to myself, somewhat crudely, is this: is there some non-vacuous sense in which I can say that the spirit of Bach was speaking to me across the ages, across the seas, putting before me certain ideals; or was what was really going on at that moment that I was symbolically electing high European culture, and command of the codes of that culture, as a route that would take me out of my class position in white South African society and ultimately out of what I must have felt, in terms however obscure or mystified, as an historical dead end—a road that would culminate (again symbolically) with me on a platform in Europe addressing a cosmopolitan audience on Bach.[46]

In his lecture in Graz, Coetzee explains how it is possible for classical works to have an impact on people over centuries. Sentimental or romantic explanations are inadequate. Classical works define themselves within history, often as symbolic texts within political and cultural movements, and eventually continue as texts that obtain new meaning through robust criticism. Historical understanding, also of the history of the classic, is understanding of the past as a shaping force upon the present.

It is, Coetzee argues, possible to experience classic art in a disinterested, and in a sense impersonal, aesthetic manner. At the same time his yet unconscious decision, that afternoon, to align himself with a European canon and tradition, was also a decision that he would not get stuck in a small corner of provincial South Africa, but that he would enter the greater world of the metropolis. He became determined to escape from the periphery to the epicentre; to escape colonial restriction and become part of the mainstream of Western civilisation.

IV

There was another reason why he wanted to escape the enclave in which he was living[47] and find a capsule in which to live.[48]

Vera was teaching again to sustain the family until Jack's practice in Goodwood could establish itself and start generating an income. At first the enterprise seemed to flourish. Jack appointed a typist and a clerk, he helped people draw up their wills and he lent out money. But the practice was making no money. Jack seemed to be cultivating the company of bar cronies, and spending his money on them. He indulged in an atmosphere of extravagant bonhomie, in which he spent large sums in large gestures, and consumed large quantities of alcohol. When things did not go according to plan, he closed his practice and opened a second in Wynberg, but ran it for only a few months. 'Jack is like a child when it comes to money,' Vera exclaimed in despair.[49] Eventually it transpired that he had again withdrawn money illegally from a trust account. The Law Society of the Cape of Good Hope found that he had not followed the prescribed regulations in his accounting. There were no details regarding deposits made into his trust account, and he had neglected to issue receipts for deposits. Included in the money misappropriated were transfers on property transactions and monthly rentals.

Jack was now unemployed, plunging the family into a chronic financial predicament. He left home at seven in the morning, ostensibly to look for a job, but returned an hour or so later when everybody had left home, as John discovered one day when he stayed home from school. Jack would then put on his pyjamas and get into bed with the *Cape Times* crossword, a bottle of brandy and a jug of water. Before the rest of the household returned at two, he'd go to his club in Wynberg, where he dined and spent the night drinking. Sometimes he came home after midnight, his two sons eavesdropping in dismay on a 'flurry of heated whispering' in the bedroom.[50]

For the second time in his life Jack was facing the prospect of prosecution and imprisonment. For the Voëlfontein Coetzees the whole business was a catastrophe. Dishonesty of any kind went against their grain, and had hitherto been alien to the family. Two bank officials turned up to compile an inventory of the contents of the house. Before the furniture could be sold, however, the matter was resolved. Jack's sister Girlie from Williston advanced money, on condition that he would never again practise as an attorney, and that he would sign an undertaking to repay all his debts. According to the report of the investigating officer, there was one redeeming feature—much of the information had been furnished by Jack Coetzee himself: 'He appeared to be quite open about his misdemeanours and assured us that he was not withholding any relevant information.' Nevertheless the Law Society found that Coetzee had been guilty of unprofessional and unbecoming conduct. He was 'not a fit and proper person to be or remain an Attorney of this Honourable Court'. Quite apart from Girlie's precondition, the Law Society would never have re-admitted him to the legal profession.[51]

The dismal affair played itself out in front of John and David. David was still in Standard Seven and John—'witnessing the shame',[52] the 'disgrace'—was completing his matric and preparing to go to university. There was some pressure from the extended family that, given the family's financial straits, John should rather go out to work. His mother was still teaching, the sole breadwinner. John knew she would make any sacrifice to ensure a tertiary education for him.

He felt he could no longer stay at home as a full-time student dependent on his mother. He decided to find accommodation elsewhere and declare his independence by earning his keep.

CHAPTER 4

STUDENT DAYS AT THE UNIVERSITY OF CAPE TOWN, 1957–1961

I

For John Coetzee the self-evident choice of a tertiary institution was the University of Cape Town, close to his home at 81 Camp Ground Road in Rondebosch. He enrolled there as a student at the beginning of 1957.

The University of Cape Town evolved from the South African College School (SACS), founded in 1829. Tertiary education was introduced here in 1874. It was the first such institution in South Africa, but the South African College received full accreditation as a university only in 1918. At first classes were taught in the city centre in Queen Victoria Street near St George's Cathedral, but these were moved relatively early to Orange Street, closer to the mountain. This campus later became known as the Hiddingh Campus, where part-time students could follow courses in the late afternoon and the evening, and where the Michaelis School of Art and the Department of Theatre and Performance, with the Little Theatre, are still situated today. The Groote Schuur campus was built on the slopes of Devil's Peak between 1928 and 1930. The original complex, with its fine view of Rosebank, was one of the most attractive campuses in South Africa, with creepers covering the walls of the buildings.

Coetzee's classes were mainly offered in the Arts Block, where the departments of English, other languages and philosophy were located, with the Jagger Library conveniently situated on the other side of University Avenue. The Mathematics building, where he would also attend classes, was a stone's throw away. Quick snacks or a cup of tea were available at the Students' Union, on the far side of the Jameson Hall steps. On campus were the two original university residences, Smuts Hall for men and Fuller Hall for women. On the middle campus, closer to Rosebank, was the administration block, where Coetzee enrolled as a student. The South African College of Music was also on this campus, but the well-appointed Baxter Theatre was only erected in the 1970s, at the time when Coetzee was appointed as a lecturer in the Department of English.[1]

As soon as he could afford it, Coetzee moved into a flat at 4 Jefflyn Court, Princess Street, Mowbray, an established middle-class neighbourhood.[2] From Mowbray station there was a bus connection to campus, and a suburban train service into the city. He used the bus only in winter when the black south-easter or the pelting rain made walking well-nigh impossible. Because he had attained the highest marks in English in the exams of the Joint Matriculation Board in 1956, Coetzee received, before the start of classes, a bursary of £88.16.3 from the bequest of I.M. Sacks. He applied successfully to the university for a bursary of £30. This was renewable annually and was increased to £50 in 1958. At the end of his first year he was also awarded a Jardine Scholarship of £30, a grant intended for children of indigent parents. When he enrolled for the honours course in mathematics in 1961, he was awarded a state scholarship of R100,[3] and in the same year was awarded a Shell scholarship of R400 a year for two years. Some of this money he would later use to enrol for an M.A. in English.

Coetzee paid a Cape Town estate agent[4] a monthly rental of eleven guineas[5] for the flat in Mowbray. He had to supplement his income with odd jobs. From his first year as a student he was employed by a cram college for scholars struggling with mathematics.[6] One of his students was John Kensch, a young Briton who had settled in Cape Town in 1958 and needed help to pass matric at university admission level. John Kensch writes:

> I signed up for extra coaching in maths with a cram college in Rondebosch. John Coetzee was my tutor there. We lasted I think about three weeks before he proposed that we move the whole operation to his flat in Mowbray, to save him having to pay a fairly large percentage of his fee to the college. [...] Once a week I trundled around to his flat for tutorials in pure maths. [...] As a maths tutor, he was first-rate, the teaching being very much mixed up with his own mathematical projects, one of which amused us both at the time. He liked to set himself problems, the tougher the better. One such ended up as a manuscript about an inch thick,

the conclusion of which, basically, was that the proposition didn't work. Any kind of complex abstract problem aroused his interest, though, as far as I can remember, nothing literary crept into any of our conversations. [...] He was very amusing, with a wry, self-deprecating manner, but also clearly very much went his own way, as the future was to reveal. The maths tutoring went on for a year, after which I went off to Michaelis Art School, and lost touch with John.[7]

Coetzee had various other jobs. During vacations he compiled statistical data from household surveys for the Division of Public Housing of the Municipality,[8] a project initiated by the Faculty of Sociology[9] of the University of Cape Town. He did night duty at the Jagger Library from 1958, at times when the permanent employees, especially the women, preferred not to be on the isolated mountainside campus and go home in the dark. For this work he was paid £10 a month.[10] In 1960, while studying for the honours in English, he taught at the Cape Tutorial College for a salary of £20 a month.[11] He also conducted group classes in the Department of Mathematics, for which he was paid £30 a week, and on Friday afternoons helped diploma students in drama to study selected Shakespeare comedies. With all this extra income, Coetzee could comfortably pay for his studies and the flat. He provided for his daily meals by cooking a large pot of soup every Sunday with marrow bones, beans and celery, enough to last him the week. These meals he supplemented with seasonal fruit that he bought on Fridays at the Salt River market.[12] As for clothes, he had a jacket and trousers for class, and made sure his clothes lasted. He even saved up enough money to buy a little second-hand Fiat 500 in 1958.[13] He also decided on a few dance lessons to make it easier to socialise with women at gatherings,[14] though he was by no means a party animal, and drank no alcohol on such occasions. His style of living reasssured him that he could row his own boat, 'that each man is an island; that you don't need parents'.[15]

In spite of this declaration, and the statement in *Youth* that 'he uses his independence to exclude his parents from his life',[16] there was no clean break with his parents, especially not with his mother. When his great-aunt and godmother, Aunt Annie, died in Cape Town in 1958, he attended the funeral with his mother and brother and recollected Aunt Annie's words:

'You know so much,' Aunt Annie once said to him. It was not praise: though her lips were pursed in a smile, she was shaking her head at the same time. 'So young and yet you know so much. How are you ever going to keep it all in your head?' And she leaned over and tapped his skull with a bony finger.

The boy is special, Aunt Annie told his mother, and his mother in turn told him. But what kind of special? No one ever says.[17]

Aunt Annie was buried in the Woltemade cemetery. After the burial, the undertaker gave them a lift back to town and remarked to Vera that the deceased had been a teacher. Yes, said his mother, she taught for more than forty years. 'Then she left some good behind,' he commented. What, Coetzee asks, happened to Aunt Annie's books, to all the copies of *Deur 'n gevaarlike krankheid na ewige genesing*?

His mother does not know or will not say. From the flat where she broke her hip to the hospital to the old age home in Stikland to Woltemade no. 3 no one has given a thought to the books except perhaps Aunt Annie herself, the books that no one will ever read; and now Aunt Annie is lying in the rain waiting for someone to find the time to bury her. He alone is left to do the thinking. How will he keep them all in his head, all the books, all the people, all the stories? And if he does not remember them, who will?[18]

What Coetzee was now experiencing with all his odd jobs was a purgatory from which, as he puts it in *Youth*, he would at long last step into the light of art, for whose sake he had to suffer his present hardship:

For he will be an artist, that has long been settled. If for the time being he must be obscure and ridiculous, that is because it is the lot of the artist to suffer obscurity and ridicule until the day when he is revealed in his true powers and the scoffers and mockers fall silent.[19]

Reading *Youth*, one is impressed by the ruthless honesty with which Coetzee confronts himself, an illustration of the principle of 'unflinchingness', possibly to be followed by 'forgivingness'.[20] In these years he had his first sexual experiences: with a statuesque Sandy, a highly strung athletic Adrienne, a subtle transatlantic Joanne, and an enigmatic Mary.[21] He writes about these relationships with callous candour and conceals nothing, not even the pregnancy and abortion of one woman.[22] If *Youth* is a reliable guide, he seems to have experienced only the physical aspect of love, with hardly any sense of a meaningful connection with another person. He reminded himself constantly that he had to suffer this purgatory for a new person to emerge: the human being and writer he was aspiring to be, free from the contamination of family and the past. He was painfully aware of his failure as a lover, which he ascribed to his girlfriends' lack of understanding of a writer's need for withdrawal and solitude. The main question he asked himself was how to transmute his sexual experience into literature: 'how will those emotions ever be transfigured and turned into poetry?'[23]

This question reveals something of the predatory artist in Coetzee, someone who, as an artist, has no use for experience other than as raw material to be distilled into poetry.[24] It is clear that he had taken to heart T.S. Eliot's dictum: 'Poetry is not a turning loose of emotion, but an escape from emotion; it is not the expression of personality, but an escape from personality.'[25] He realised that the true work of art is faithful only to its own immanent precepts and that the task of the poet entails a constant 'wrestl[ing] with words and rhymes'.[26] This formulation suggests that Coetzee knew Eliot's *Four Quartets*. Eliot finds the poet's activity an 'intolerable wrestle/ With words and meanings', demanding that the poet 'get the better of words'. Poetry is

a raid on the inarticulate
With shabby equipment always deteriorating
In the general mess of imprecision of feeling,
Undisciplined squads of emotion.[27]

Coetzee's identification with Eliot's eschewal of direct emotion and his insistence on the hard labour to which the poet has to subject himself, would lead one to expect, even without the evidence of the long schoolboy poem, 'In the Beginning', that Coetzee in his student years would not write any directly confessional poetry, that he would prefer the disguise of images, finding an 'objective correlative'[28] for the inner feeling, and concealing the personal perplexity behind that. It is worth noting that Coetzee at this stage considered himself a poet. Indeed, his years as a UCT student represent his early flowering and also, with a few exceptions, his final efforts as a poet.

II

When Coetzee enrolled at the University of Cape Town in 1957, the National Party had been in power for almost nine years, and had deployed, in the course of the 1950s, a battery of discriminatory laws.

At this time the Extension of University Education Act was under consideration, and with its enactment in 1959 the Universities of Cape Town and the Witwatersrand would be prohibited from continuing to admit coloured and black students, except to courses not offered by the separate colleges envisaged for the different coloured and black population groups. The two universities maintained that the act was an infringement of the academic autonomy recognised worldwide as the right of a university, namely the right to determine what would be taught, who would teach and who would be taught. In a publication entitled *The Open Universities in South Africa*, arising from a conference held in Cape Town in 1957, it was argued that of a university's many functions, the primary one was the pursuit of truth:

> In a university knowledge is its own end, not merely a means to an end. A university ceases to be true to its own nature if it becomes the tool of Church or State or any sectional interest. A university is characterized by the spirit of free inquiry, its ideal being the ideal of Socrates—'to follow the argument where it leads'. This implies the right to examine, question, modify or reject traditional ideas and beliefs. Dogma and hypothesis are incompatible, and the concept of an immutable doctrine is repugnant to the spirit of a university. The concern of its scholars is not merely to add and revise facts in relation to an accepted framework, but to be ever examining and modifying the framework itself.[29]

It was in deference to this supreme principle of the search for truth that the open universities opposed the proposed act:

> The open universities deny the validity of the argument that they should close their doors to non-white students on the ground that in being 'open' they are ignoring an established South African tradition. Apartheid is not the only relevant established tradition

in South Africa. The tradition followed by the open universities has deep roots in the history of the Cape Colony and is no less South African for the fact that it accords with the universality of Christendom.

The open universities would also deny the validity of any argument for compulsory university apartheid which is based upon the adage that he who pays the piper calls the tune. No government would be justified in using its control over the national purse as a lever for such a purpose. All sections of the population contribute to the national income and also to university endowments. State interference with the way in which universities select their students is bad in principle and dangerous in tendency.[30]

Coetzee's reaction to this point of view is not known, but it is to be assumed that he was aware of it, and agreed with it. With the passing of the act in 1959, the University of Cape Town initiated an annual series of 'Academic Freedom Lectures' which was to continue until the repeal of the act. Invited speakers would focus on specific aspects of the task facing the university when its autonomy is jeopardised by the state.

There were, however, other political developments and disturbances that did not pass Coetzee by. In 1959 the prime minister, Dr H.F. Verwoerd, outlined the law on self-governing 'Bantustans', the Transkei being elected as South Africa's showcase of 'separate development'. Blacks would continue to work in South Africa, but would live in their own 'country' and be represented by their own 'government'. On paper this pipe dream seemed to solve the problems posed by the policy of apartheid, but in practice the forced removals of families and the concomitant corruption doomed the whole idea to failure. This was exacerbated by Verwoerd's opposition to the investment of white capital, which might have rendered the Transkei economically more viable.[31]

The resentment of the pass laws felt by black people was fomented rather than defused by such measures. On Monday, 21 March 1960, protest led to violence at Sharpeville in the Transvaal, when the police opened fire on a crowd of peaceful demonstrators, killing 69 and wounding at least three times as many.[32] In the otherwise tranquil Cape six people were shot and killed in the black township of Nyanga, among others a toddler about whom the poet Ingrid Jonker would write the poem 'Die Kind.'[33] The carnage was strongly condemned in the

US, Britain, Norway, Canada and the Netherlands. In *Youth* Coetzee comments on this violence:

> In the Transvaal the police fire shots into a crowd, then, in their mad way, go on firing into the backs of fleeing men, women and children. From beginning to end the business sickens him: the laws themselves; the bully-boy police; the government, stridently defending the murderers and denouncing the dead; and the press, too frightened to come out and say what anyone with eyes in his head can see.
>
> After the carnage of Sharpeville nothing is as it was before. Even in the pacific Cape there are strikes and marches. Wherever a march takes place there are policemen with guns hovering around the edges, waiting for an excuse to shoot.[34]

Coetzee experienced one of the protests indirectly. In the early hours of Wednesday, 30 March, the police conducted a brutal raid in Langa, breaking down doors, dragging people from their beds, assaulting them and chasing them into the streets. This provoked a march of 20 000 people who later that morning proceeded by De Waal Drive, along the slopes of Devil's Peak, towards the city centre. They gathered in front of the police headquarters at Caledon Square and demanded to negotiate with the minister of justice, F.C. Erasmus, about the release of leaders detained the previous day. After Colonel I.P.S. Terblanche had calmed them down by undertaking to arrange such a meeting, the crowd dispersed peacefully towards Langa under police surveillance. There were no incidents, but Erasmus never granted an interview.[35] The march was a culmination of events in the black townships during the previous weeks, 'the result', as Jonty Driver, the poet, novelist and friend of Coetzee's puts it in his biography of Patrick Duncan, 'of the growing groundswell of political elation among Africans, not simply a reaction to the cruelty of the police that morning.'[36]

Coetzee experienced the aftermath of the march while conducting a tutorial in the Department of Mathematics. In *Youth* he describes it as follows:

> It all comes to a head one afternoon while he is on tutorial duty. The tutorial room is quiet; he is patrolling from desk to desk, checking how students are getting on with the assigned exercises, trying to

help those in difficulty. Suddenly the door swings open. One of the senior lecturers strides in and raps on the table. 'May I have your attention!' he calls out. There is a nervous crack in his voice; his face is flushed. 'Please put down your pens and give me your attention! There is at this moment a workers' march taking place along De Waal Drive. For reasons of safety, I am asked to announce that no one is being allowed to leave the campus, until further notice. I repeat: no one is being allowed to leave. This is an order issued by the police. Are there any questions?'[37]

Coetzee was moved to ask himself what the country had come to, when an ordinary mathematics tutorial could be interrupted by such an announcement. He did not believe for a moment that the police, in sealing off the campus, 'this notorious hotbed of leftism',[38] were motivated by concern for the safety of the students: they were more intent on preventing student sympathisers from joining the march. And he wondered whether it wouldn't all end in real violence, with the aid of guns from China.[39]

That the campus was indeed regarded by the police as a hotbed of leftism is evident from an engrossing article by Jonty Driver about UCT students who in the late 1950s and early '6os resisted the government's actions. For many of these their resistance to apartheid was an offshoot of their involvement in student politics. Driver himself was in solitary confinement for a while before he could leave the country, after which, as a prohibited immigrant, he was for twenty years unable to visit South Africa. In his student days in Cape Town, Driver was active as an actor and debater, editor of the student newspaper *Varsity*, at times the editor of the student literary magazine *Groote Schuur*, and the co-founder of the literary journal *The Lion and the Impala*, in both of which publications his own and Coetzee's work was published with that of other young poets like Geoffrey Haresnape, Daniel Hutchinson and Breyten Breytenbach.

One of Driver's friends, Alan Brooks, was vehemently opposed to apartheid, and, like Driver, was involved with the National Union of South African Students (NUSAS) and the Liberal Party, led by Alan Paton and Patrick Duncan. Brooks was later, after being betrayed by Adrian Leftwich, the chairman of the student representative council and of Nusas,[40] sentenced to two years in prison for his part in subversive acts, and afterwards left the country for good. Among the other well-known student activists were Stephanie Kemp, who was also in solitary confinement, later to marry Albie Sachs, and yet later to become the lover of Joe Slovo. Also among the students was Richard (Rick) Turner, who, after studying at the Sorbonne, lectured in political science at the University of Natal in Durban, and was shot point blank, reputedly by a police assassin, one evening in early 1978 when he opened his front door. He wrote, among other works, *The Eye of the Needle*, in which he investigated ethical and political alternatives to the South African situation.

Most of the students Driver writes about went into voluntary exile to escape persecution and never returned to South Africa, even after the democratic elections in 1994. For a country such as South Africa with its shortage of skilled professionals, the loss of such exemplary people, with their strong moral principles and intellectual abilities, is incalculable. 'A common reason,' Driver writes,

> was that they did not want their sons to have to serve in the South African armed forces. Sometimes émigrés found they didn't settle where they had landed and they went back again, or tried another place. More often, they settled perfectly well: in Australia, in Canada, in the USA, in England—and went back only for family weddings and, in due course, funerals until, eventually, they (and their children more especially) became part of the new culture, except for the oddly ineradicable accent.[41]

Apart from Driver, it is not known how many of these people Coetzee knew personally, though he would probably have come across some of them in his student days. The virulence of the state's actions against them would reach a peak with the legislation of the early 1960s, which, under B.J. Vorster as minister of justice, made possible detention without charge or trial, and enabled the police to continue their interrogation and torture of detainees. By then Coetzee had left South Africa.

In spite of his friendship with some of the students, in particular the activist Jonty Driver, Coetzee did not take part in demonstrations or other forms of resistance. While studying, he went his own way, avoiding both the right-wing politics of the National Party (which was virtually non-existent on campus) and the left-wing politics of some of his fellow-students with their violent political rhetoric. The conclusion of *Doubling the Point*, written in the objectified third person that affords him, as in *Boyhood* and *Youth*, a distanced perspective on himself, makes it clear that his withdrawal from active involvement extended also to student politics:

> As a child in Worcester he has seen enough of the Afrikaner right, enough of its rant, its self-righteousness, its cruelty, to last him a lifetime. In fact, even before Worcester he has perhaps seen more of cruelty and violence than should have been allowed to a child. So as a student he moves on the fringes of the left without being part of the left. Sympathetic to the human concerns of the left, he is alienated, when the crunch comes, by its language — by all political language, in fact. As far back as he can see he has been ill at ease with language that lays down the law, that is not provisional, that does not as one of its habitual motions glance back skeptically at its premises. Masses of people wake in him something close to panic. He cannot or will not, cannot and will not, join, shout, sing: his throat tenses up, he revolts.[42]

Coetzee is ever the outsider, contemplating and judging as an observer, without taking an active part.

III

As early as 1957, it had been Coetzee's firm intention to leave South Africa after completing his studies, and to settle overseas. He had had enough of the crushing disgrace his father had brought upon the family with his money laundering and his alcohol abuse; he was tired of the poverty to which they were reduced, and he was appalled at everything the government was doing to the country and its people in the name of apartheid.

It was his intention to devote his time to creative writing, but to earn his bread and butter through a 'respectable' profession. He knew that, initially at least, he would not be able to make a living by writing. 'While perfecting his poetic skills abroad,' he writes in *Youth*,

> he will earn a living doing something obscure and respectable. Since great artists are fated to go unrecognized for a while, he imagines he will serve out his probationary years as a clerk humbly adding up columns of figures in a back room. He will certainly not be a Bohemian, that is to say, a drunk and a sponger and a layabout.[43]

For this reason Coetzee decided to register for pure mathematics, besides courses in English, classical culture and Latin. He eventually majored in English and mathematics, in his second year following a course in logic and metaphysics, and in his third, as backup to pure mathematics, also a first-year course in applied mathematics. With his knowledge of mathematics, which, with English, had been a strong subject at school, he would be able to forge a career abroad. Paul Raiment's statement in *Slow Man* (2005), that he enrolled for a science course at university, could be read as a coded reference to Coetzee's decision to major in mathematics:

> So when I went to university I signed up for science. Science seemed a good bet in those days. It seemed to promise safety, and that was what my mother wanted above all for my sister and me: that we find some safe niche for ourselves.[44]

For someone like Coetzee who, by his own account, is not very visually attuned,[45] and is not particularly interested in his physical environment, the field of mathematics offered an attractive autonomous existence. The abstract, geometrical cogitation of mathematics, as Henri Poincaré puts it, can penetrate to the quintessence of human consciousness.[46] In the Department of Mathematics Coetzee studied under the remarkable Professor Douglas Sears, who patiently taught his students not only mathematics but also how to be mathematicians.[47] In mathematical logic his lecturer was Stanley Skewes, an outstanding mathematician who had worked with the famous A.M. Turing. Skewes was a helpful and lovable person, and highly regarded on account of his important 'Skewes number' article of 1933. He was without affectation, but did not suffer fools gladly.[48] Coetzee's systematic approach to things, as evidenced also by his diligence and dedication at school, provides early evidence of a mathematical intellect and a desire for perfection. One wonders, though, how congenial the abstract ratiocination of mathematics can be for the verbal artist who draws upon the concrete world for his raw material and means of representation, and who has to think with his senses.

For Coetzee this apparent conflict posed no problem; indeed, he once delivered a lecture to the Philosophical Society on 'Poetry and the language of mathematics'. In an interview he has said that he never regretted electing to follow a degree in mathematics. It taught him to read slowly and it afforded him pleasure and amusement. If, he continued, he had known something about chess at an early age, he might have taken that up.[49] That he would keep a life-long interest in mathematics is clear from section 18 ('On Zeno'), that forms part of 'Strong Opinions', the first part of his novel *Diary of a Bad Year*, published as late as 2007,[50] and also from a review he wrote in 2009 of Sarah Glaz and JoAnne Growney's anthology *Strange Attractors: Poems of Love and Mathematics* (2008). In the opening paragraph he draws a connection between poetry and a pronouncement by Aristotle, a connection that was to prove crucial, firstly to his approach to literature and in due course to his practice as a novelist:

> The highest type of intelligence, says Aristotle, manifests itself in an ability to see connections where no one has seen them before, that is, to think analogically. The spark of true poetry—according to one influential school of poets—flashes when ideas are juxtaposed that no one has yet thought of bringing together. Scientific discoveries often start with a hunch that there is some connection between apparently unrelated phenomena.[51]

Although Coetzee appreciated the logic of Latin syntax, he had problems, as at school with the factual content of history and geography, with 'Virgil and Horace, with their haphazard word order and rebarbative word-stock'.[52] In Latin I the love poems of Catullus were studied, as well as translations of Tacitus' 'dry recitals of the excesses and outrages of the emperors,'[53] which Coetzee found compelling, though the Latin was too difficult to follow in the original. He appreciated the work of Anton Paap and Maurice Pope, the two professors of classical culture. His essays for this course were always neatly handwritten and meticulously edited down to the footnotes, and he was usually given an A or a B. These essays dealt with the philosophers Heraclitus and Parmenides, the function of the chorus in classical drama, education in Sparta, and Homer's *Iliad*.

During Coetzee's studies, the English course at UCT comprised two equal compulsory components, in literature and language respectively. In the first year students in the language division were instructed in advanced English stylistics, the history of the English language and selected texts from Chaucer, followed in the second year by courses in Old English and English phonetics in relation to English philology. In the third year students could specialise in either language or literature, but all students had to follow Chaucer and Langland courses in the language division. In the literature division students were given an introduction to literature in English (British, American and Commonwealth) through the study of selected texts in the various genres, and in the second year a further selection from poetry, drama and fiction was taught. In the third year all students had to follow courses in tragedy and modern poetry, with the literature specialists also attending courses in diary literature and the modern novel. Besides a choice from Shakespeare and Milton, the set texts for 1957, Coetzee's first year, included Shaw's *Major Barbara*, Eliot's *Murder in the Cathedral*, Austen's *Sense and Sensibility*, Dickens's *Nicholas Nickleby*, Brontë's *Jane Eyre* and Macnab and Gulston's *South African Poetry: A New Anthology*. In the second year, set texts included, apart from selections from Milton and Pope, Fielding's *Joseph Andrews*, Sterne's *Tristram Shandy*, Conrad's *Heart of Darkness*, James's *The Turn of the Screw*, Forster's *A Passage to India* and Lawrence's *Sons and Lovers*. In the third-year course for 1959 the list included Wordsworth (*The Prelude*), Pound (*Selected Poems*), Hopkins (*Selected Poems and Prose*), Yeats (*Selected Poems*), Eliot (*Four Quartets*) and Thomas (*Collected Poems*). In 1960, honours students specialising in literature had to follow courses in Shakespeare and other classical and contemporary literature, as well as in the principles and practice of literary criticism. A separate component was dedicated to the aims and methods of the study of old manuscripts and the editing of old texts.[54] It is worth noting that as important a novel as James Joyce's *Ulysses* was not on the list of undergraduate set texts, though it was discussed with the English III students of 1959. Coetzee sheds some light on this in a letter to Derek Attridge dated 21 August, 2000: 'You may be interested to know that *Ulysses* was prescribed for Eng III at UCT when I was a student (1957–59). With a note from a parent or guardian you could be exempted from reading it or attending lectures on it.' This may have been Coetzee's first acquaintance with a form of censorship that would soon be applied officially in South Africa, very much to the detriment of literature.

Before Coetzee started studying at UCT, W.S. Mackie was the Professor of English Language and Oswald Doughty the Professor of English Literature. There was a long tradition of friction in the English Department, because the two professors were at loggerheads about methods of instruction and almost everything else. Doughty was a typical traditional British scholar who concentrated on editions of texts and on biographies, and devoted his lectures to the life and works of the great writers.[55] Any 'close reading', such as that practised by the senior lecturer, Philip Segal, following the lead of I.A. Richards and F.R. Leavis, was anathema to him. 'I am very sceptical of immature critics,' he pronounced, 'and think that the best way to make a good critic is to bring the students to enjoy the best things of the past without, as Hardy said, "looking so closely at the text as to lose the poetry."'[56] Mackie, on the other hand, found Doughty's style of lecturing a 'solemn and dreary procession of names and dates and periods and influences and tendencies',[57] totally out of date for students who wanted to get to know more about the texts themselves. Such students were more strongly drawn to Philip Segal. He was celebrated for his 'exuberant and eloquent exploration of the whole spectrum of English literature,'[58] which captivated his audience. 'We could listen to him for hours, fascinated by his flow of immaculate language, crisp wit and irresistible humour.'[59]

When Coetzee commenced his studies in 1957, Lewis Casson was the De Beers Professor in English Language, and the Arderne Chair in English Literature was occupied by Guy Howarth, an Australian by birth. The bad blood in the English Department seems to have been contagious, because Casson and Howarth were not on speaking terms, and when absolutely necessary, communicated with each other by letter, or otherwise through Dorothy Cavers, the attractive Senior Lecturer in Language. 'Casson,' Coetzee has written,

> was a stooped, white-haired man with a reputation as a martinet. I went to his lectures on Chaucer quaking in my boots. He paid no attention to me or anyone else, spoke as if to an empty room, never invited questions. An air of irascible disdain breathed from him. For my part, I was enthralled by the succinct mastery with which he laid out the phonology of the Middle English dialects.[60]

Coetzee's only contact with Casson was thus through lectures delivered from Olympian heights. Casson was indeed a formidable and even a frightening figure, but in an interview long after his student days,[61] Coetzee expressed great admiration for him as a professional and a teacher. The notes he took of Casson's lectures to English II, which he found a remarkable exposition of the history of English phonology, were still in Coetzee's possession in 2009.

With Howarth, Coetzee had a long association, starting in 1957, his first year in English. Coetzee took both English and mathematics, an unusual combination, with both courses being offered at 10.35 in the morning. The only way of doing both English and mathematics was to attend the Mathematics I lecture at 10.35 and then in the afternoon to take the 'Jammie Shuttle' from the Rosebank Campus to Orange Street, or otherwise to travel by train from Mowbray to Cape Town and walk through the Avenue in the Company Gardens, to attend the English I evening class at 6.05pm on the Hiddingh Campus, basically offered for commerce students. The lecturers here were the most junior in the department, because the professors and other senior staff had no taste for driving to town to lecture to exhausted people who had spent a long day in an office.[62] To earn a year mark for English I, all students had to hand in three projects. One of Coetzee's literature lecturers was Dr B. Jones, then still a junior lecturer. The first assignment set by Jones was a critical analysis of a poem by Andrew Marvell. In spite of taking some trouble over this, Coetzee was given only a C.[63] He decided that there was no future for him in writing critical essays for Jones. There was, however, a second option. Students wanting to be under Howarth's dispensation could submit creative work to him to replace the critical essays. For the next two assignments in English I Coetzee thus handed in poems to be graded by Howarth, for both of which he was awarded an A. The high marks disposed him favourably to Howarth. He continued handing in creative work and Howarth took him under his wing. When, in 1959, he arrived in English III, Howarth offered him an assistantship, which was extended in his honours year. In this way he became better acquainted with Howarth.

Howarth, an amateur poet of sorts, also offered a Friday-afternoon non-credit-bearing class in imaginative writing, open to interested students prepared to make creative contributions. Coetzee started attending these classes from his first year. He writes:

> I had my first contact with Guy Howarth as a first-year arts student. Hearing of something called the Imaginative Writing Class that met once a week, I submitted a poem (that was the regulation: you could not attend unless you wrote) and went along. There were a dozen other students in the room, none of whom I recognised. At three o'clock a plump little man in a dark suit and academic gown bustled in. He had a long, rather grave face and a soft manner of speech from which all but the barest trace of his Australian origins had been effaced.

The submissions for the day were handed back to their authors. While Howarth sat in a corner, we stepped forward one after another, read out our pieces aloud, and heard what our fellows had to say about them. Now and then Howarth would chip in, asking questions rather than expressing opinions. At four o'clock the meeting was over.

During my four undergraduate years, Howarth saw many of my poems, sometimes accepting them in lieu of assigned critical essays. In all this time he never told me what he thought of them or of me as a poet. The poems in lieu of essays came back with a neatly pencilled alpha [...] I felt a kindly encouragement emanating from him, but had no reason to doubt that every other young poet was getting the same encouragement.[64]

Before his honours year Coetzee had, apart from the creative writing classes, only in English III taken a course taught by Howarth. It dealt with various sixteenth- and seventeenth-century writers, and most other students found it boring. Howarth would come to class with notes that he simply read out. This was in sharp contrast to Philip Segal, the students' darling, who jotted down only a few principal points on a scrap of paper, and improvised on the subject of a poem or a novel. Coetzee, though, found Segal's style of lecturing a bit showy, and preferred Howarth's professional craftsmanship. During his honours year Coetzee was the only student enrolled for Howarth's Early English Prose course:

They meet once a week in Howarth's office. Howarth reads his lecture aloud while he takes notes. After a few meetings Howarth simply lends him the text of the lecture to take home and read. [...]

The lectures, which are typed in faint ribbon on crisp, yellowing paper, come out of a cabinet in which there seems to be a file on every English-language author from Austen to Yeats. Is that what one has to do to become a professor of English: read the established authors and write a lecture on each? How many years of one's life does that eat up?[65]

Although Howarth was regarded by most students as an uninspiring lecturer, there were a few like Coetzee and Jonty Driver who appreciated him, especially for his encouragement of their creative work. Coetzee was well disposed towards the clumsy and awkward underdog, and felt empathy for this gentle, kindly man who seemed so ill at ease in front of students, reluctant listeners from law and commerce, to whom he was trying to convey some sense of poetry:

> As he stood before this bored and uncouth gathering of young white South Africans, reciting in his sensitive, lyric manner, rising incongruously to his toes as the poem reached its climax, pausing to invite us to consider the force of an enjambment here, a chiasmus there, my heart bled for him, but I kept my distance, wishing he had a little more savvy.[66]

In his subject Howarth was active in two divergent areas. In his youth at the University of Sydney he had concentrated on Australian literature. He founded the periodical *Southerly*, which exists to this day, and did much to promote the poetry of his own generation in his native land, such as compiling *The Penguin Book of Australian Verse* (1958). He was an authority on the Australian poet Kenneth Slessor. Apart from this, his field of enquiry was a continuation of his studies at Oxford: compiling texts from fragmented sources, the area of textual bibliography indicated in the prospectus by the neologism 'bibliology'. This course, probably the least popular in the Department of English, was intended to equip his honours students for careers as literary craftsmen of his kind. His own research in this area concentrated on the seventeenth-century English dramatist John Webster, the author of, among other plays, *The White Devil* and *The Duchess of Malfi*. He was immersed in writing a biography of Webster, though it had been rejected by Cambridge University Press. When Coetzee was living in London a few years later, he undertook some research for Howarth in the British Museum into Webster's sources. Howarth's professional focus was thus on an increasingly dated area, that had yet seemed important at some stage. He had backed the wrong horse, academically speaking. In addition, because of his poor lecturing style and chronic disagreement with Casson, he was not respected in the faculty.[67]

Nevertheless, some students did appreciate Howarth, especially because his courses included South African authors, such as Sarah Gertrude Millin, Roy Campbell, Pauline Smith, William Plomer, Laurens van der Post, Alan Paton and Nadine Gordimer. Besides initiating the course in creative writing, he started, with Jonty Driver, the journal *A Literary Miscellany*, and arranged for an annual visit from an American academic to lecture on American literature. In Coetzee's time this visitor was Professor Joseph Jones of Texas, who was later to be an important contact when applying for a bursary for study in the US. Howarth expressed a caution regarding South African literature that may well later have inclined Coetzee, albeit unconsciously, not to restrict himself too closely to a specific reality in his own creative work:

> The question of the present and future relations between the white and the black races in Africa is of such vital interest and concern that books like Paton's embodying it, may well be temporarily overvalued or given a place of factitious importance, especially among Americans who feel some similarity to the particular problem affecting the United States.[68]

On another occasion, on 12 April 1960, he commented on the South African national ethos and policy in terms that also have a bearing on Coetzee's work:

> This is a country that needs to try to free its mind from colonial struggles and internecine rivalry; that is, if the mind has yet emerged. A refixing of the early Native frontier still seems to be more important than obscurantism and enlightenment.[69]

When Howarth resigned as professor in 1971 and returned to Australia, Geoffrey Haresnape, one of the poets in his creative writing class and a senior lecturer in the UCT English Department, offered this tribute:

> On his arrival [in South Africa] Professor Howarth founded and for some years ran an Imaginative Writing class, which he continued as a vital force in the department until the present day. It is not always possible to gauge the influence of such a class in cold statistics, but it is very pleasing to note that some of its earlier members have since done very well in this field. The novelist C.J. Driver and the poet Stephen Gray (a recipient of a State Award for Verse this year) are just two examples. Who can guess what the class's more recent members may produce in the future?[70]

And Coetzee paid tribute to his contribution to the development of young creative writers and to his dedication to the cause of literature:

Numbers of young South African writers passed through the Imaginative Writing Class and through Howarth's kindly hands. Some of them went on to make names for themselves. To me he is an example of how a teacher who may not have much of inherent significance to convey can still exert a shaping influence on his students. He was the first person I had come across who was transparently devoted to the life of literature.[71]

IV

While at school, Coetzee tried, with the aid of a grammar, a set of records and a series of exercises, to teach himself French. Although he says in *Youth*[72] that the attempt was not successful, he must later have acquired enough knowledge to read the language with reasonable fluency. Spanish, too, he later mastered without much difficulty, but the foreign language he took to most readily was German: 'With the ghost of Afrikaans still in his ears, he is at home in the syntax.'[73]

Coetzee did not want to arrive in Europe as a dim, illiterate country cousin from the colonies. So he read the classics of various literatures, among others Flaubert's *Madame Bovary*, as well as the novels of James, Conrad and Ford Madox Ford.[74] A poet whose work appealed to him increasingly was Ezra Pound. He now preferred Pound to Eliot, who in his dedication to *The Waste Land* had generously called Pound '*il miglior fabbro*', the better craftsman. He read Hugh Kenner's book on Pound as a guide to the series of 'Cantos'. Pound's letters, too, spoke to him, especially a passage from a letter to Harriet Monroe dating from January 1915. This made such a strong impression on Coetzee that he copied large parts of it into a notebook. The passage offers an important key to the later stripped prose style of Coetzee:

> Poetry must be *as well written as prose*. Its language must be a fine language, departing in no way from speech save by a heightened intensity (i.e., simplicity). There must be no book words, no periphrases, no inversions. It must be as simple as De Maupassant's best prose, and as hard as Stendhal's.
>
> There must be no interjections. No words flying off to nothing. Granted one can't get perfection every shot, this must be one's INTENTION.

Rhythm MUST have meaning. It can't be merely a careless dash off, with no grip and no real hold to the words and sense, a tumty tum tumty tum ta.

There must be no clichés, set phrases, stereotyped journalese. The only escape from such is by precision, a result of concentrated attention to what one is writing. The test of a writer is his ability for such concentration AND for his power to stay concentrated till he gets to the end of his poem, whether it is two lines or two hundred.

Objectivity and again objectivity, and expression: no hindside-beforeness, no straddled adjectives (as "addled mosses dank"), no Tennysonian-ness of speech; nothing that you couldn't, in some circumstances, in the stress of some emotion, actually say. Every literaryism, every book word, fritters away a scrap of the reader's patience, a scrap of his sense of your sincerity. When one really feels and thinks, one stammers with simple speech; it is only in the flurry, the shallow frothy excitement of writing, or the inebriety of a metre, that one falls into the easy—oh, how easy!—speech of books and poems that one has read.

Language is made out of concrete things. General expressions in non-concrete terms are a laziness; they are talk, not art, not creation. They are the reaction of things on the writer, not a creative act by the writer. 'Epithets' are usually abstractions—I mean what they call 'epithets' in the books about poetry. The only adjective worth using is the one essential to the sense of the passage, not the decorative frill adjective.[75]

Another important key to Coetzee's later development as a writer is Eliot's essay on John Dryden. Coetzee also copied extracts from the essay into his notebook. Eliot was struck by the element of surprise in Dryden's verse and his masterful control of words. Unlike the showy Swinburne, whose words are 'all suggestion and no denomination', Dryden's use of words is characterised by the cruel precision of the phrasing and the ability to concretise things, not merely suggest them:

A clever versifier might have written Cowley's lines; only a poet could have written Dryden's. They have not the element of *surprise* so essential to poetry. [...] Dryden is distinguished principally by his *poetic* ability. [...] Much of Dryden's unique method consists in his ability to make the small into the great, the prosaic into the poetic, the trivial into the magnificent. [...] Dryden with all his intellect, had a commonplace mind. His powers were, we believe, wider, but no greater, than Milton's. [...] Swinburne was also a master of words, but Swinburne's words are all suggestion and no denomination; if they suggest nothing, it is because they suggest too much. Dryden's words, on the other hand, are precise; they state immensely, but their suggestiveness is almost nothing ...[76]

At UCT, Coetzee was part of a small band of poets that included Jonty Driver, Geoffrey Haresnape, Daniel Hutchinson and Harald Jawureck. Some of their poems were first read out in Howarth's Imaginative Writing classes. Geoffrey Haresnape recalled later that Coetzee approached human relationships with great circumspection, even though his conduct was sometimes unsettling:

He used to read from his short poems, which were usually in the manner of T.S. Eliot or Ezra Pound, and then maintain an absolute silence in the discussions which followed. Silence can be unnerving, especially when it is used by a person who gives every evidence of being confident in it.[77]

The first work of all these poets, as well as that of the Afrikaans poet Breyten Breytenbach, appeared in *Groote Schuur* and other student publications. Although Coetzee was known as a loner whose privacy had to be respected by those who would befriend him, he was, even as a student, very friendly and helpful in his dealings with other people, especially with young writers. The rest of the band looked up to Coetzee as the outstanding intellect, a central figure, and a mentor to the others. Driver writes: 'John was perceived as very clever and talented, though at that stage we didn't see him as a potential novelist. I doubt if he saw himself that way, either.'[78] That in his quiet way he nevertheless assumed a leading role, is clear from the foreword he wrote to the 1959 edition of *A Literary Miscellany*. He comments on the meetings of the Imaginative Writing classes under Howarth's tutelage:

The intention was as much to display to students of literature the basic problems facing a writer as to encourage in young writers a self-critical sense. Members of the class have accordingly fallen into two sets—those who find an opportunity to reach a critical audience for their work, and those to whom an opportunity to hear and criticise new work forms an approach to the vitality of literature. The profit to both writers and critics has undoubtedly been great; in particular, the writers who form the nucleus of the group have gained the encouragement always needed by beginners unsure of themselves.

This firm assumption of authority is evident also in Coetzee's critical commentary on the poetry of his fellow students Haresnape, Coque and Driver in the 1962–1963 edition of *Groote Schuur*. He does not hesistate to express strong criticism of Haresnape and Coque, while commending Driver's greater maturity. The commentary is characterised by Coetzee's insight and erudition, even as a student, and by the considered and balanced way in which he delivers a trenchant judgement:

> Driver has broken from a preliminary discipleship to Dylan Thomas to become as poet far less 'conceited' and 'metaphysical' than before. His best work is now characterized by a powerful, sustained period which grows out of passionate concentration on a single point. One does not look to him yet for variety of tone or subtlety of thought: the poetry is that of a young man, its themes love and death, its manner grand; yet it is revealing to observe how little the ranging of the imagery interferes with the poem's long, low song.

Contrary to the public image later painted by journalists who were not always well disposed to him, Coetzee was often a witty and humorous companion and a charming friend. Driver and his girlfriend at the time, Jann Parry, who would later for many years in Britain write on ballet for *The Observer*, often visited him in his flat in Mowbray. He was known as a good cook, at a time when South African men could at most scorch meat in the open air. Coetzee's soufflé omelette was so exceptional that Driver could recall it fifty years later. Parry was, as a first-year student in the English Department, in one of Coetzee's tutorial groups, but was too inexperienced to get to know him well or engage him in conversation. 'All I remember,' she writes in a letter of 8 March 2010, 'is that he was soft-spoken, serious and rather sweet, with big brown eyes.'[79]

In 1957, his first year at UCT, no poems by Coetzee appeared in any of the student publications, but from 1958 to 1962 five mainly long poems were published, and a series of short poems that he called 'Trivial

Verses.' The 'Trivial Verses', dedicated to 'A Lady' and written in a style dripping with courtly chivalry, generally employ a mythological field of reference and tend to the epigrammatic, expressed by someone with misgivings about an addressee, a woman who seems not to reciprocate his feelings or satisfy his desires. This self-conscious poet-speaker declaims: 'You hardly deserve to be woven into the delicate/pattern of my verses.' In *A Literary Miscellany* of 1958 Coetzee published the long 'The Love Song', written alternately in archaic and modern English, and containing, besides some free-verse stanzas, sections employing an ironic type of rhyme. Coetzee here also engages with Shakespeare in lines such as 'Signifying nothing' and 'Thy eyes are nothing like the sun', while the title and certain poetic turns ('And should I then presume?/And how should I begin?') recall the Eliot of 'The Love Song of J. Alfred Prufrock'. This is no romantic lover addressing his beloved, knowing as he does that she is 'a bundle of mortality' who will grow old and waste away. Tentative and self-obsessed, he should really have been a Hamlet, 'Saying curiously shapéd things/ To vacant spaces'. As opposed to the shorter 'Procula to Pilate', the same edition contains Coetzee's long poem 'Attic', with allusions to the writing group to which he belongs—'a district haunted by the ghosts of major poets', the ghosts putting in an appearance immediately after in his rewriting of 'Prufrock' and 'Preludes':

> The fog has never rubbed its muzzle on our window-pane,
> It has only smothered our view of the chimney-pots.
> The music of the spheres has never led
> Our ancient women in vacant lots.

The equally long 'Truth Lies Sunken' was published in *Groote Schuur* of 1959. This poem, containing some allusion to the myth of Echo and Narcissus, was praised by Louis MacNeice during his visit to South Africa in 1959. It starts with a particularly successful first stanza, creating the image of a well in which Truth lies locked up and from which sound waves emanate that disturb the surface of the water. These waves may then convey a message to humans who are waiting attentively for it. In an article in which he quotes this stanza, Rodney Edgecombe[80] says that Coetzee by this representation attributes to Truth the status of a Greek oracle replying only by means of an echo, a mocking, almost taunting reaction that, in the way of oracles, does not supply direct unambiguous

replies, but prefers to resort to riddles and frustrating vagueness or
obscurity:

> Truth lies sunken in a well,
> Giving forth two echoes when we call,
> Call, now, call.
> Watch the shivering of your image on the water;
> Stand;
> Stand, and, if you do not breathe,
> Watch, it will follow you,
> Though at the bottom of a well,
> Copying the frieze of your repose.
> So these symbols shine to you,
> Reflecting your greater light;
> So, as our faces lie upon the water, I call,
> And wait to hear the echoes of my call
> Collect among our wanderings.

In *A Literary Miscellany* of 1959 Coetzee published the triptych 'Three
Poems from a Cold Climate', in which he comes as close as he ever does
to an unambiguous love poem, although the direct expression of love is
still veiled in images:

> If you will love me now
> we shall not fear
> leopards,
> for over us will stand
> one with an arched bow,
> which is a symbol of love.

> If you will love me now
> we shall not fear
> sand,
> for before us will walk
> a boy with a pitcher
> chased in chrysolite,
> which is a symbol of love.

If you will love me now
we shall not fear
stone,
for over us will stand
a lady, hooded,
and in her hands a heart
carved in jasper
and riven,
which is a symbol of love;

for wondrous figures visit
those who love.

In the 1959 edition of *Groote Schuur* Coetzee published two scenes from *The Last Spring*, a verse drama about the figure of Cervantes's Don Quixote, which he started writing in his last years at UCT, but never completed. In *Youth* he writes that 'the mind of the old Spaniard was too remote, he could not think his way into it.'[81]

At this time John met somebody whom he does not refer to in *Youth* nor, later, in *Summertime*. Philippa Jubber, born on 13 December, 1939, was slightly less than two months older than he. She attended the Wynberg Girls' High School, and matriculated in the same year as Coetzee. But she had lost a year after school because of pneumonia contracted as a result of a horse-riding accident, so in Coetzee's third year, as an assistant in the English Department, Philippa was a member of one of his English II tutorial groups. She was a sister of Cecil Jubber, eleven years her senior, a producer of radio dramas with the SABC in Johannesburg. He was one of the more creative people in the corporation, and in the 1950s had won the coveted Prix Italia for his radio dramas, but after a while he found the working conditions exceedingly frustrating and produced less and less creative work of quality.[82] Philippa followed in her brother's footsteps, studying for a degree in drama and theatre, and appearing in a Shakespeare play at Maynardville, after which she obtained a teacher's diploma. She introduced Coetzee to the works of Anouilh and Ionesco, at the time much studied and performed at drama schools. It was probably thanks to Philippa's influence and encouragement that Coetzee put his hand to a verse drama. This was his only venture ever in this direction. He soon recognised that he was not really interested in writing for the theatre. The meeting between Coetzee and Philippa—a beautiful brunette, slender, with delicate features, and much more socially inclined than the reserved Coetzee—soon led to a firm friendship and a relationship.

Towards the end of 1960 Howarth invited Coetzee for drinks one evening with him and his wife at their house, Myrtle Lodge, in Gardens. It transpired that the Howarths wanted to go overseas for six months and they needed someone to look after their house and other affairs. As this meant rent-free accommodation with few responsibilities, Coetzee accepted promptly, very pleased with the idea. If he could give up his flat in Mowbray, he reasoned, he could save more money and all the sooner be able to afford a passage to England.

The time in the Howarth house revealed the humorous side of the quiet Coetzee to Daniel Hutchinson, who became a good friend at this point, and who later, when Coetzee left for overseas, would take over his house-sitting task. He saw this humorous side, Hutchinson writes, 'not as jests, quips or pratfalls, but ironic discomfiture experienced from a situational impasse, a psychological contretemps or social wrong-footing, that would confront you, or preferably others, with the eternal one-up/ one-down contest. He had a well developed sense of the ridiculous and acute insight into power dynamics between people, their motives and prevarications, which he adroitly concealed.'[83] In Howarth's house they shared much fun:

It was the scene of some pranks, such as visitors' tyres mysteriously deflated or rotor arms removed. Once J and a current date (a memorable Lysistrata) threw a candlelit party for some engineers, who were lured, one by one, into dark rooms and wardrobes, doors slamming and locking behind them. Emerging flushed and mad for revenge they removed, unnoticed, all the carpet pins from the staircase. The carpet gave way when Howarth returned, who fell heavily, broke his ankle and needed a crutch from then on. [...] We would dine weekly together in restaurants around town, chosen by each in turn. (Later he was diagnosed lactase deficient and became vegetarian). Or we drove in his battered brown baby Fiat to friends, mostly of his, often with a bizarre project: to check if three-week-old smuts behind the ear of one had been washed off, to verify if another was still living in picturesque pajamas.[84]

The visits to restaurants and the pranks with fellow-students did not, in Coetzee's case, involve alcohol abuse. In the first month he had to share the house with visitors of the Howarths from New Zealand, a woman and her three-year-old daughter. The New Zealand woman proved, once the Howarths had left and Coetzee had moved in, to be a drinker. One night she came to his room and made sexual overtures, which he repulsed, after which they avoided each other for the rest of her stay, 'averting their gaze when their paths happen to cross'. In *Youth*, where Coetzee recounts this episode, he firmly states his dislike of drink and drunkards:

> He has never been drunk in his life. He abhors drunkenness. He leaves parties early to escape the stumbling, inane talk of people who have drunk too much. In his opinion, drunken drivers ought to have their sentences doubled instead of halved. But in South Africa every excess committed under the influence of liquor is looked on indulgently.[85]

It seems likely that the example of his father and the disruptive influence of drink on family life made Coetzee a life-long abstainer from alcohol. Jonty Driver writes, in a letter of 1 May 2009: 'I suspect there is in the Coetzee family some predisposition to alcoholism — one of the reasons for admiring John is his steadfast self-discipline, not just as a writer.'[86]

V

In 1960 Coetzee was granted special permission by the Senate of the University of Cape Town to register for both English honours and mathematical statistics, since he intended to register for mathematics honours after completing his English honours.[87] At the end of the year he was awarded the English honours degree with distinction and mathematical statistics in the first class. In January 1960 Professor S. Skewes of the Department of Mathematics wrote a testimonial praising Coetzee's abilities and hard work. He had passed in the first class in five of the ten courses for which he had enrolled. Skewes knew that Coetzee, who had in his second year easily achieved a first-class pass in pure mathematics, had in 1959 been handicapped by having had to follow another first-year course in addition to English III and Pure Mathematics III.

[T]he amount of work involved made it impossible for him to do justice to both, so I was aware early in the year that his priority was English III, with the Maths getting what he could spare from reading English. He duly got his first in English, and still contrived to get a good second in Maths III. Had he elected to spend the major part of his time in Maths he would undoubtedly have had a first class in that—he does not lack the mathematical ability. […] Mr Coetzee is a peaceful, industrious citizen, so unobtrusive as to be practically invisible. Nevertheless, for calm competence he is very hard to beat, and he has been a most patient and helpful demonstrator to the most fatheaded of first-years. I can recommend him to anyone requiring a mathematical assistant with every confidence.

After Coetzee had completed the B.A. Honours in English, Howarth, too, wrote him a glowing testimonial. Howarth mentions that of the six students in the course, Coetzee had been the only one who, from the available choice of authors, works and topics in the period 1500 to the present, had studied the whole curriculum and had answered a wide variety of questions in the exam. 'He is, indeed, the best-read candidate in this course since the establishment of the B.A. Honours degree here in 1955.' He continues:

Mr Coetzee combines wide and deep knowledge with accurate scholarship, expressing himself, too, in a style at once faultless and individual. Critically he shows great independence of mind. All in all he has amply fulfilled the promise of his B.A. work in English (Class I at graduation) and manifests a capacity for much further intellectual development.

Mr Coetzee is entirely worthy of a major scholarship and I most strongly recommend him as a candidate for such, particularly one enabling him to proceed to a university abroad for advanced study and research.

Alternatively he could fill with distinction a literary, editorial or academic post. As an imaginative writer in both prose and verse he has shown an exceptional talent; he has successfully co-edited *Groote Schuur*, the students' annual magazine, and has assisted me in the preparation and production of *A Literary Miscellany by Staff and Students of the University of Cape Town*, 1959; he has also had some teaching experience as a 'Demonstrator' in English Literature and is now responsible for most of this tutorial work. I have recommended him for a Graduate Assistantship in the Department, should such a post be established this year.

Personally Mr Coetzee is entirely estimable and can be relied upon in every way.

I believe that he will have a distinguished career in whatever profession he chooses to follow.

In December 1961 Coetzee was awarded the B.A. Honours in mathematics, but he received the degree in absentia, since on graduation day, 15 December 1961, he was on board ship from Cape Town to Southampton.

One reason for his departure was the possibility that in the light of the worsening political situation in South Africa he could be called up for military service. When he left school, the Defence Force called up only one in three white boys for military service, and he had been fortunate enough to be exempted. Things might change; he could at any time receive a letter directing him to report to the Castle at nine o' clock one morning for military service at Voortrekkerhoogte near Pretoria. 'There is only one course open: to flee.'[88]

But apart from his reluctance to serve in the army, Coetzee was convinced that his academic training in South Africa had been lacking in every respect. In an article written in 1984 he puts it as follows:

> In the colonies, where I came from ultimately, I had received a conventional undergraduate training in English studies. That is, I had learned to speak Chaucerian verse with good vowel definition and to read Elizabethan handwriting; I was acquainted with the Pearl Poet and Thomas More and John Evelyn and many other worthies; I could 'do' literary criticism, although I had no clear idea of how it differed from book reviewing or polite talk about books. All in all, this patchy imitation of Oxford English studies had proved a dull mistress.[89]

He ultimately wanted to improve his academic grounding in literature, but for the time being his training in mathematics would enable him to make a living. He was painfully aware of the limitations of his situation in a (former) colony, and he yearned for a metropolis where he would be rid of all restrictions. 'South Africa,' he writes in *Youth*, 'was a bad start, a handicap. An undistinguished, rural family, bad schooling, the Afrikaans language.'[90] The Afrikaners running the country, he writes in *Summertime*, 'isolated within a language spoken nowhere else in the world, [...] had no appreciation of the scale of forces that had since 1945 been sweeping away the old colonial world.'[91]

For Coetzee there were only two or three places on earth where life could be experienced in its full intensity: Paris, the city of love and art; Vienna, the city of logical positivism, Schönberg's twelve-tone music and Freud's psychoanalyis; and London. But, he realises with laconic irony, his French was not good enough for Paris, and Vienna belonged to Jews returning to claim their birthright. That left London, where South Africans needed no visas and where English was spoken.[92] Besides, this was the city where the 'colonials' Eliot and Pound had settled.

A South African passport was issued to him on 20 November 1961, and in December he left by boat from Cape Town to Southampton, and from there by boat train to London, with no clear idea of what to expect. He, fond as he was of the barren plot of ground that was Voëlfontein, could not have foreseen how the London winter would affect him. Neither could he foresee that the 'colonial', especially an intellectual, was often a lonely outsider in the British capital.

II

BRITISH INTERLUDE
(1962–1965)

CHAPTER 5

LONDON AND BRACKNELL, 1962–1965

I

When John Coetzee arrived in London early in 1962, he was, even compared with other young people from the former British territories seeking their fortunes there, intellectually advanced. But he was aware of a colonial disadvantage in his academic training and saw himself as a 'socially disadvantaged, socially marginal young intellectual of the British empire'.[1] He was inexperienced in many areas, especially emotionally. He was only twenty-one, and such life experience as he had, had been gleaned largely from books. But he was enterprising and wanted to '[shake] the dust of the provinces off his feet'.[2] Much later, in *The Master of Petersburg* (1994), he would project something of this feeling onto the figure of Dostoevsky, the protagonist:

> When you are young you are impatient with everything around you.
> You are impatient with your motherland because your motherland
> seems old and stale to you. You want new sights, new ideas. You
> think that in France or Germany or England you will find the future
> that your own country is too dull to provide you with.[3]

Before the First World War Vienna had been the home of the Strauss family, their waltzes perceived as symbolic of the grace and charm of the Habsburg regime. In the 1920s, with the advent of Hemingway, Picasso, Fitzgerald and Joyce, Paris had been a powerhouse of culture and in the late 1940s became the intellectual mecca for post-war artists and intelligentsia, to explore new philosophical movements like existentialism, and to practise divergent art forms, from surrealism to the theatre of the absurd. It was only in the late 1950s and early 1960s that London caught up. Though it was not until 1966 that a prominent article in *Time* hailed London as 'The Swinging City', the formerly chilly, dignified British capital had by 1962 changed quite radically. Five million people under the age of twenty-one, some of them fired up by the Beat Poets and the Angry Young Men of the theatre, were overturning the conventions of British society.

After the sex scandal that brought down John Profumo, a minister in the Conservative cabinet, the Tory era was over for the time being. Harold Wilson of the Labour Party won a narrow victory in 1964; at fifty, he was the youngest Briton ever to be elected prime minister. On Sunday, 24 January 1965, Sir Winston Churchill died, leaving Britain in mourning. His body lay in state in Westminster Hall for three days, and 320 000 people waited for hours to pay their tribute. He was buried on Saturday, 30 January 1965 near Blenheim after a state funeral at St Paul's Cathedral, 'one of the great national events of the decade,' as Dominic Sandbrook put it,⁴ but also a historical watershed. Patrick O'Donovan wrote in *The Observer* the day after Churchill's funeral:

> [T]his was the last time such a thing could happen. [...] This was the last time that London would be the capital of the world. This was an act of mourning for the Imperial past. This marked the final act in Britain's greatness.⁵

Time wrote about the changes confronting the British capital in the 1960s:

> The London that has emerged is swinging, but in a far more profound sense than the colorful and ebullient pop culture by itself would suggest. London has shed much of its smugness, much of the arrogance that often went with the stamp of privilege, much of its false pride—the kind that long kept it shabby and shopworn in physical fact and spirit. It is a refreshing change, and making the scene is the Londoner's way of celebrating it.⁶

Coetzee, stamped at school as resistant to rock and roll, observed with interest, to judge by the evidence of *Youth*, the young people in the streets and on the Underground: the men with long hair, dressed in 'narrow black trousers, pointed shoes, tight, boxlike jackets with many buttons'; the girls 'from all over the world: as au pairs, as language students, simply as tourists [...] their hair in wings over their cheekbones; [...] their eyes dark-shadowed; [with] an air of suave mystery.'⁷ As he had been at school since his sixteenth year, as described in *Boyhood*, he was fascinated by women and their aura of mysterious beauty. He noted, with puzzled disapproval, the way in which the Britons tried to imitate American music and the latest fads from the US:

> The popular newspapers carry pictures of girls screaming their heads off at concerts. Men with hair down to their shoulders shout and whine in fake American accents and then smash their guitars to pieces. It is all beyond him.[8]

Coetzee dealt with the city's hubbub by withdrawing rather than getting involved. He avoided brothels and pubs and ate cheap but filling meals at the Lyons Corner Houses. There could be some autobiographical resonance in the experience of Elizabeth Costello, Coetzee's alter ego, when, in the 2003 novel named after her, she recollects how she 'forty years ago, hid day after day in her bedsitter in Hampstead, crying to herself, crawling out in the evenings into the foggy streets to buy the fish and chips on which she lived, falling asleep in her clothes'.[9]

The society that Coetzee encountered in Britain prized individual and national liberty, unlike the South Africa he had left. Britain was the first of the Western European countries to open its borders to citizens of its colonies in the West Indies, so much so that the demographic profile of a city such as London was gradually altered, at times to the discomfiture of the British. Coetzee read in the newspapers about race riots in Nottingham and Notting Hill, but he was at most an observer, never a participant.

Internationally the 1960s were also a turbulent decade. In 1961 the Berlin Wall was erected by the Communists to stem the flow of refugees to the West. The Belgian Congo gained independence from its European master in 1960, and other African countries followed suit. The post-independence unrest in the Congo was the prelude to other forms of violence in the 1960s. In 1962 the French president, Charles de Gaulle, was obliged to agree to a cease-fire with his colony Algeria and to start negotiations with the outlawed government. In the US the liberal John F. Kennedy was elected the 35th president in 1961, only to be assassinated two years later.

These events are not reflected in *Youth*. Coetzee does, however, react to the march in central London organised by the Campaign for Nuclear Disarmament against the British atomic weapons station at Aldermaston.

He expresses puzzlement at the fact that the British invariably side with the Americans against Russia, a country that in all the wars since 1854 that he knows of has been on the British side:

> It is not as though the British actually like the Americans. Newspaper cartoonists are always taking digs at American tourists, with their cigars and pot-bellies and flowered Hawaiian shirts and the fistfuls of dollars they brandish. In his opinion, the British ought to take their lead from the French and get out of NATO, leaving the Americans and their new chums the West Germans to pursue their grudge against the Russians.
>
> The newspapers are full of CND, the Campaign for Nuclear Disarmament. The pictures they print of weedy men and plain girls with ratty hair waving placards and shouting slogans do not predispose him to like CND. On the other hand, Khrushchev has just carried out a tactical masterstroke: he has built Russian missile-pods in Cuba to counteract the American missiles that ring Russia. Now Kennedy is threatening to bombard Russia unless the Russian missiles are removed from Cuba. This is what CND is agitating against: a nuclear strike in which American bases in Britain would participate. He cannot but approve of its stand.
>
> American spy-planes take pictures of Russian freighters crossing the Atlantic on their way to Cuba. The freighters are carrying more missiles, say the Americans. In the pictures the missiles—vague shapes under tarpaulins—are circled in white. In his view, the shapes could just as well be lifeboats. He is surprised that the papers don't question the American story.
>
> *Wake up!* clamours CND: *we are on the brink of nuclear annihilation.* Might it be true, he wonders? Is everyone going to perish, himself included?
>
> He goes to a big CND rally in Trafalgar Square, taking care to stay on the fringes as a way of signalling that he is only an onlooker. It is the first mass meeting he has ever been to: fist-shaking and slogan-chanting, the whipping up of passion in general, repel him. Only love and art are, in his opinion, worthy of giving oneself to without reserve.
>
> The rally is the culmination of a fifty-mile march by CND stalwarts that started a week ago outside Aldermaston, the British atomic weapons station. For days *The Guardian* has been carrying

pictures of sodden marchers on the road. Now, on Trafalgar Square, the mood is dark. As he listens to the speeches it becomes clear that these people, or some of them, do indeed believe what they say. They believe that London is going to be bombed; they believe they are all going to die.

Are they right? If they are, it seems vastly unfair: unfair to the Russians, unfair to the people of London, but unfair most of all to him, having to be incinerated as a consequence of American bellicosity. [...]

From the frying-pan into the fire! What an irony! Having escaped the Afrikaners who want to press-gang him into their army and the blacks who want to drive him into the sea, to find himself on an island that is shortly to be turned into cinders! What kind of world is this in which he lives? Where can one turn to be free of the fury of politics? [...]

The rally ends. He goes back to his room. [...]

Then a few days later the crisis is suddenly over. In the face of Kennedy's threats, Khrushchev capitulates. The freighters are ordered to turn back. The missiles already in Cuba are disarmed. The Russians produce a form of words to explain their action, but they have clearly been humiliated. From this episode in history only the Cubans emerge with credit. Undaunted, the Cubans vow that, missiles or not, they will defend their revolution to the last drop of blood. He approves of the Cubans and of Fidel Castro. At least Fidel is not a coward.[10]

Although Coetzee repeatedly declared that he wanted to rise above the colonial mentality and be a citizen of the world, or at least of the British metropolis, he remained aware of events in South Africa. He realised that nobody could escape caste — in his case the Afrikaner caste to which he, at least partly, belonged.[11] Under the rule of the National Party, South Africa in the 1960s became more and more isolated from the outside world. This isolation was made clear as early as February 1960 when the British prime minister, Harold Macmillan, in his 'Wind of Change' speech before parliament in Cape Town, expressed misgivings about the direction in which the policy of 'separate development' was driving South Africa, and announced that Britain accepted as a reality the national liberation movements and the struggle for independence of the African countries. She would promote the political emancipation of the British colonies, and withdraw from the continent. When, in a referendum, white South Africa opted for a republican form of government, prime minister H.F. Verwoerd took South Africa out of the Commonwealth because of the strong opposition to its internal race policies. In the chambers of the United Nations and in the ranks of the World Council of Churches vehement criticism of South Africa's policies of racial segregation was repeatedly expressed, and the country was denied participation in most international organisations and sporting bodies. Within South Africa itself there were fierce indictments—initially from English-speaking clerics, but eventually also from the Dutch Reformed Church and from lawyers and philosophers. Unrest among the black populace was countered by the government with the proclamation of states of emergency, the mobilisation of the police and citizen force, the banning of individuals and detentions without trial.

About South Africa's expulsion from the Commonwealth and Britain's reaction to the South African regime, Coetzee writes:

> It is not a good time to be a South African in England. With great show of self-righteousness, South Africa has declared itself a republic and promptly been expelled from the British Commonwealth. The message contained in that expulsion has been unmistakable. The British have had enough of the Boers and of Boer-led South Africa, a colony that has always been more trouble than it has been worth.[12]

In letters to his mother, as reported in *Youth*, Coetzee reacted strongly to the unrest in South Africa, police violence against blacks and the alleged suicide of political detainees:

> [I]nstead of making speech after speech at the United Nations, the Russians ought to invade South Africa without delay. They should land paratroops in Pretoria, take Verwoerd and his cronies captive, line them up against a wall, and shoot them. [...] South Africa is like an albatross around his neck. He wants it removed, he does not care how, so that he can begin to breathe.[13]

While Coetzee was in England, Nelson Mandela, in his forty-sixth year, was sentenced to life imprisonment with seven ANC colleagues, after being charged with recruiting and training personnel to wage a revolutionary war and with conspiracy to invade the republic with the aid of foreign forces. In his four-hour statement before the court Mandela distanced himself from an exclusive black nationalism and from international socialism, and demanded a new constitution for South Africa that could lead to a new state, free from racial boundaries and class differences, based on a unitary economy with scope for private enterprise.

In reaction to the arrest of Mandela and others, the dramatist Athol Fugard wrote to his friend Mary Benson in London: 'Has this poor, blighted country ever been uglier? Is it possible for the stain of injustice on this earth to be deeper? I don't think so ... Yes South Africa is ugly—so ugly that even those who really loved her are now beginning to hate—and this is tragic! Never before had the need for love been greater.'[14]

In *Youth* Coetzee does not comment on the Rivonia trial and the sentences meted out to the ANC members, nor on the night march from Brighton to London by ANC sympathisers on 13 June 1964, when the accused had been found guilty and there was a real possibility that they would be sentenced to death.[15] Much later, however, he would react to these events in *The New York Review of Books*, in response to a book on Mandela. If the South African regime had come to an understanding with the ANC in the 1950s, Coetzee says, it would have had a predominantly pacifist movement under a petit-bourgeois social-democratic leadership to deal with. Instead, it branded the movement as subversive and its leaders as instruments of international communism. This was a move for which South Africa and specifically the Afrikaners would ultimately pay a heavy price.[16]

And yet Coetzee could not escape South Africa. If, for instance, he were to apply to the Home Office for British citizenship, on what would he base his application? He was no refugee and could lay no claim to refugee status. They would not accept that he was being oppressed, or that he did not want to return to South Africa out of boredom or because of the collapse of all moral values. And would they accept that shame, shame at the history of his father and at the years under apartheid, made him cringe for his country?

But then his ambivalence towards South Africa returned. Although 'South Africa is a wound within him',[17] he could not turn his back on the intransigence and fearlessness of his ancestors, sweating and straining in the heat and dust of the Karoo. It was not given to these people to be cheerful and to make merry, and nor was it to him. When, in the reading room of the British Museum, he read travel journals of the early explorers at the Cape, of journeys lasting many days without the sight of another human being, he felt an affinity with the place names of his youth, and realised: 'it is his country, the country of his heart, that he is reading about'. And he asked himself: 'Patriotism: is that what is beginning to afflict him? Is he proving himself unable to live without a country?'[18]

II

On leaving for London it had been Coetzee's plan to find a job on the strength of his mathematical training, to provide a regular income and leave him time to pursue his writing. He realised that at the beginning of his writing career he could not make a living out of creative work. Thus he chose the way of Kafka, Eliot and Wallace Stevens before him, settling for a quiet office existence, using his free time to extend his knowledge of literature and to write.

At first Coetzee lived with his Cape Town friend Paul, who had also settled in London. He had a single room with an annex equipped with a gas stove and a sink, but only cold water. Even though he intended to generate an income through his mathematical skills, he applied for a job as a relief teacher. But the work he was offered did not appeal to him. He succesfully applied for a position at an agricultural station at Rothamsted, where he would be analysing data on a computer. But when he learnt that he would be required to live in Rothamsted, missing out on the possibility of poetry readings, films, meetings with poets and painters and love affairs in London, he turned down the offer.[19]

In the newspapers he came across advertisements for computer programmers, and applied to International Business Machines (IBM), the biggest and evidently the best of these firms. After an interview and an IQ test, he was within days offered a position as a programmer at £700 a year at their offices in Newman Street, off Oxford Street, in the heart of the West End. He was part of the first generation of computer programmers, who still worked on the gigantic Hollerith machines. Although his working hours were from nine to five, he found that the male members of staff tended to stay at the office much later, and that he seldom got home before ten. He shared an office full of grey furniture with nine other people, among them an attractive young woman from New Zealand and a young London man, Bill Briggs, with whom he sometimes talked at lunch about a limited range of topics. With a fixed monthly income, he was able to establish himself in a room in a house near Archway Road in North London, where he prepared his own meals—oatmeal porridge, apples, bread, cheese and sausages—and seldom got a glimpse of the other lodgers.

For recreation, Coetzee visited the Everyman in Hampstead, where he saw films by Antonioni, among others *L'Eclisse*, dealing with a woman, played by Monica Vitti, wandering through the streets of a sun-drenched deserted city, about whose 'perfect legs and sensual lips and abstracted look' he dreamed.[20] He also saw the films of Ingmar Bergman, with their lonely characters, haunted, the newspapers said, by a fear of nuclear annihilation or the uncertainty after the death of God, though *The Observer* opined that these fears were not to be taken too seriously, arising as they did from 'long Nordic winters, nights of excessive drinking, hangovers'.[21] Coetzee also took pleasure in the BBC Third Programme, which took note of new directions in the arts, like the latest American poetry, electronic music and abstract expressionism. He heard music he had never heard before, and listened to talks and discussions worth listening to. He heard, for instance, a series of programmes on the Russian poet Joseph Brodsky, sentenced to five years hard labour in the frozen north of his country on the grounds of being a social parasite. Through the BBC's programmes he also got to know Ingeborg Bachmann and Zbigniew Herbert, the Polish poet, 'telling him again of what poetry can be and therefore of what he can be'.[22] He listened to the music of Schoenberg and Berg and also, for the first time, to Anton von Webern. In the Tate Gallery he saw an exhibition of abstract impressionists, and spent a quarter of an hour in front of a Jackson Pollock painting, which, alas, said nothing to him. In an adjoining room, however, he was transfixed by a painting consisting only of a rectangular black blob against a white background. This was *Elegy for the Spanish Republic* by Robert Motherwell:

> Where does its power come from, this amorphous shape that bears no resemblance to Spain or anything else, yet stirs up a well of dark feeling within him? It is not beautiful, yet it speaks like beauty, imperiously. [...] Is it the same power that makes his heart leap at the sight of one woman and not another? Does *Elegy for the Spanish Republic* correspond to some indwelling shape in his soul? What of the woman who is to be his fate?[23]

On Saturdays Coetzee visited bookstores, galleries or cinemas. On Sundays he read *The Observer* in his room, then walked on the Heath or watched another film. He browsed in the bookshops on Charing Cross Road, which remained open until six o' clock. Foyle's, reputed to stock every book on earth, proved a disappointment, and he preferred Dillons on Gower Street, where he found little poetry magazines like *Ambit, Agenda* and *Pawn*:

> He buys one of each and takes the pile back to his room, where he pores over them, trying to work out who is writing what, where he would fit in if he too were to try to publish.
>
> The British magazines are dominated by dismayingly modest little poems about everyday thoughts and experiences, poems that would not have raised an eyebrow half a century ago. What has happened to the ambitions of poets here in Britain? [...] Have they not learned the lesson of Pound and Eliot, to say nothing of Baudelaire and Rimbaud, the Greek epigrammatists, the Chinese?[24]

Had these young poets never taken note of Eliot's 'objective correlative' and his precept to write away from the self? Coetzee's mathematical background inclined him to approve of statements such as the following in Hugh Kenner's book on Pound:

> Poetry is a sort of inspired mathematics, which gives us equations, not for abstract figures, triangles, spheres, and the like, but equations for the human emotions. If one has a mind which inclines to magic rather than science, one will prefer to speak of these equations as spells or incantations; it sounds more arcane, mysterious, recondite.[25]

After a visit to the bookstores Coetzee could follow the flow of the Saturday-evening revellers and pretend also to be out on the prowl or on his way to meet somebody. Eventually, though, he would have to take the Underground back to Archway and his solitary room, wondering 'What then is he doing in England? Was it a huge mistake to have come here? Is it too late to move?'[26]

If *Youth* is to be trusted, the young Coetzee was morose, trying to make his way in the cold labyrinth of London, dedicated to the lofty ideal of creating great art, inspired thereto by perfect, mysterious women eager to ignite his sacred spark and launch his artistic career. Snared in the monotony of computer programming, he slept with a succession of women, but gained at most physical relief, routine without passion. He had to have art in order, as Friedrich Nietzsche put it, not to die of the truth.[27] He dreamt of being a poet like Ezra Pound, but found himself in a creative and psychological impasse. He wandered through the dismal London streets in the dismal London weather, meeting nobody, making no friends:

> Along Great Russell Street he trudges to Tottenham Court Road, then south toward Charing Cross Road. Of the throng on the sidewalks, most are young people. Strictly speaking he is their contemporary, but he does not feel like that. He feels middle-aged, prematurely middle-aged: one of those bloodless, high-domed, exhausted scholars whose skin flakes at the merest touch. Deeper than that he is still a child, ignorant of his place in the world, frightened, indecisive. What is he doing in this huge, cold city where merely to stay alive means holding tight all the time, trying not to fall?[28]

On the Underground he conspicuously read volumes of poetry, in the hope that some woman would recognise the rare spirit within him, but the hope was never realised.

He received a letter from UCT notifying him that on the strength of his honours results he had been awarded the Croll Bursary of £200 for postgraduate study. The money was not enough to fund study at a British university, so he registered in absentia for an M.A. in English at UCT under the supervision of Guy Howarth. He considered writing on the *Cantos* of Ezra Pound, but eventually decided on the novels of Ford Madox Ford. Pound regarded Ford as the greatest prose stylist of the day and despised the English for ignoring him. Having read five of Ford's novels, Coetzee agreed with Pound's judgement: 'He is dazzled by the complicated, staggered chronology of Ford's plots, by the cunning with which a note, casually struck and artlessly repeated, will stand revealed, chapters later, as a major motif.'[29] He explored Ford's whole oeuvre, spending Saturdays and the two late-opening evenings in the reading room of the British Museum; but Ford's early works proved to be a disappointment, and he searched in vain for a masterpiece among them. Ford's *Mr Humpty Dumpty* was so boring that he could hardly stay awake reading it. His only gift seemed to be for misery:

> There seems to be no limit to the misery he can attract to himself
> and endure. Even as he plods around the cold streets of this alien
> city, heading nowhere, just walking to tire himself out, so that when
> he gets back to his room he will at least be able to sleep, he does
> not sense within himself the slightest disposition to crack under the
> weight of misery. Misery is his element. He is at home in misery like
> a fish in water. If misery were to be abolished, he would not know
> what to do with himself.[30]

There is evidence to suggest that Coetzee's melancholy and misery in
London was not as continuously relentless as *Youth* would suggest. In an
interview with Joanna Scott he has said that in mathematics, the subject
most pertinent to his work as a programmer, he found a certain joy, and
that he enjoyed the element of play in it:

> Mathematics is a kind of play, intellectual play. I've never been much
> interested in its applications, in the ways in which mathematics can
> be set to work. Play is, to me, one of the defining characteristics of
> human beings. I look askance at the word 'work'. When people talk
> of work I ask myself: What is going to be betrayed, sacrificed, in the
> name of work?[31]

Working with computers also taught him to write with even more con-
ciseness and concentration than he had been doing:

> I spent all my time writing system programs, [...] [t]here is a
> premium for condensation. It was quite reasonable to expect that a
> system programmer would produce at the end of the day's labour
> maybe five lines of code. Five lines of instructions which would be
> very ingenious in their ways of saving space and saving time. And
> this was at a very impressionable age in my life, early twenties.
> Writing a few lines every day got me habituated to the notion that
> you could spend endless time revising and cutting down, which is
> the way I work as a writer.[32]

At this time Coetzee also advised his brother David, who after his
schooling at St Joseph's and Rondebosch Boys' High had studied

briefly in Cape Town, to come to London to try his hand at journalism. For financial reasons David had had to interrupt his studies and take up employment with the Wool Board in Paarden Island. At this time he was studying after hours at the Michaelis School of Art and considered a career as an artist, but, much to his mother's relief, abandoned that idea. Like his brother, he was a practical person, deft with his hands: he could strip a car and reassemble it. He had developed into a capable mechanic in a relatively short time. Weekends he spent with young people, some of them of a different skin colour to his own, got drunk with them, and generally led quite a risky life, bordering on the legally proscribed. Later he said that to have led a 'normal' middle-class life with white girlfriends and a 'white' career, would have meant that he had been hijacked by the establishment and apartheid. He returned to UCT and followed a course in African Studies under Professor Jack Simons, who eventually, as a listed communist, had to give up his job and leave the country.[33] In 1965 David also left and, after a detour through Greece, reached London, were he started working as a journalist, and later filled an important position with the North London Newspaper Group.[34] With both her sons in London, Vera visited Britain at this time.

Besides working at IBM, Coetzee expanded his knowledge of literature through reading at the British Museum. Apart from the novels of Ford Madox Ford, he got to know the novels of Samuel Beckett's middle period, from *Watt* to *The Unnamable*. 'I read those books over and over again,' he writes. 'That kind of close, repeated reading tends to influence the cadences of one's prose and perhaps even one's habits of thinking.'[35] He also read more novels by Henry James and D.H. Lawrence, even though the women in Lawrence's books made him feel uneasy, and he had never been a member of his cult. While living in London, he wrote a considerable amount of poetry, but, except for a single story, no prose.[36]

In *Youth* Coetzee refers dismissively to the poems written in London, and none of these were published in magazines or otherwise preserved. He did, however, in *The Lion and the Impala*, II: 1, March–April 1963, a publication of the Dramatic Society of the University of Cape Town, publish an interesting experiment that suggests that his years as a computer programmer did at least yield some engrossing results. The poem, also published in the *Cape Times*,[37] bears the title 'Computer poem' and reads:

Dawn, birds, a stream, a calm morning,
You stand among the trees alone and tense.
You have cried.
You spend the nights away from me,
Terrified, rapt,
Among owls and black men,
Hoping for violence.

Coetzee describes the poem's genesis as follows:

This poem was generated by the 1401 computer at 58, Newman St., London, W.1 and edited by me. I have tried to dilute the 'originality' of the poem as little as possible in editing it—compare the computer output with the edited version with respect to key words—but as the program (written by me) which generated the poem is, comparatively speaking, primitive, without some editing the poem would be, simply, boring.

By using the word 'primitive' I imply that a more sophisticated programme would do most of the work now done by the editor. This consists of planning the structure of the poem, choosing a vocabulary for it, and choosing a final version out of the garbage produced. Obviously, at the low level of sophistication of the programme used, the editor needs elementary critical abilities to create the poem; but it should not be immensely difficult to write a computer programme that could be run by a hack. Anyhow, the procedure I adopted in the present case was as follows:

1. Structure. The poem consists of eight statements based on the elementary paradigm illustrated by:

You lie	Action-present
On the bed	Place
Alone	Action-past
You think	Action-present
In the bedroom	Place
Gloomy	Manner
Hopeless	Manner

Each of these statements is generated in elementary form without the 'you-I- they' qualification; this qualification is added randomly; and then (somewhat cynically) statements of nature-description are inserted randomly.

2. *Vocabulary*: The editor, if lazy and sensible, quickly decides on an area of life, picks a few key words in this area, and using these, out of Roget's *Thesaurus* provides four vocabularies—a vocabulary of actions, one of places, and one of modes (manners), plus a random vocabulary of nature-words. The area of life chosen here was personal estrangement. The vocabularies totalled about 800 words.

3. *Selection*: The computer is provided with the vocabularies, the structure of the poem and its programme, which tells it among other things to go on generating poems until its vocabularies are exhausted, i.e., until all possible poems with the given structure and words have been written. The editor now wades through what has been printed (in this case 2 100 poems at a rate of 75 poems per minute), makes his selection, reduces it to standard form, and sends it to the editor.

In an article published in 1968, in which he looks back in good-humoured satire at the years at UCT when they read out and discussed poems in Guy Howarth's gatherings, Geoffrey Haresnape depicts Coetzee, for whom he chooses the name Perfeddwlad Jones, as somebody who lived on sour milk and eggs and who, with his enigmatic smile, 'liked to be as mysterious as a Houdini'. He also, anachronistically and not without a touch of malice, invokes Coetzee's computer poem:

'You may not know,' he said, 'that a computer possesses a much greater ability to correlate disparate experiences than we do. The machine which produced this example has 350 000 memory banks alone.'

'Do you mean it can really *write?*' blurted out eager Hannah.

This gave Perfeddwlad the opportunity to look as inscrutable as the Delphic Oracle. 'It depends on what you *mean* by write,' he whispered.

He went on to explain that he had fed all the necessary data into his machine and had instructed it to write a poem of passion. If somewhat eccentric, the result could be considered a masterpiece of brevity.

> My red one hic
> In tree blue shade
> We caboobled
> Hic charming flower.

Perfeddwlad hastened to assure us that he had not used a drunken computer. The 'hics' were merely the result of technical hitches. 'Caboobled' ought to be construed as 'considered'.

With this method,' he concluded, 'we can at last press beyond the free associative techniques of James Joyce and the stream of consciousness school. Here are limitless possibilities.'[38]

Apart from the poems he wrote in London, Coetzee completed his M.A. thesis on Ford Madox Ford in a comparatively short time, further evidence that his time in Britain was not as unproductive as he would suggest in *Youth*. The thesis is entitled *The works of Ford Madox Ford with particular reference to the novels*, and was submitted to UCT in November 1963.

Ford collaborated closely with Joseph Conrad at the beginning of the twentieth century, and initially wrote light novels and historical fiction. The greatest achievement of his early career is *The Good Soldier* (1915), which was based on his own experiences and suffering, and which Coetzee describes as 'the finest example of literary pure mathematics in English'.[39] It is an exceptionally subtle account of the lives of four people, narrated by one of them. They lived for more than ten years in apparent harmony and friendship, but the real state of affairs, which is only revealed in the closing pages of the novel, is totally different. From Ford Coetzee learnt the technique of changing perspectives and time shifts—and, above all, to prune his prose. Ford was intent on the correct placing of the correct word, and on making all elements contribute to the whole through stringent selection. He provided Coetzee with a valuable model for his later writing.

The dissertation is notable for its meticulous style, confident use of sources, and the biographical emphasis that would also characterise Coetzee's later essays on literature and his reviews in *The New York Review of Books*. This is the work of a mature literary commentator. An extract from his introduction shows how polished Coetzee's style was at this early stage, and how confidently he could construct an argument:

Until recently, outside the United States, Ford Madox Ford's sole claim to fame seemed to be the footnote in the literary textbooks that read, 'Conrad also collaborated in three slight productions with F.M. Hueffer (Ford).' Twenty-three years after his death Ford was being thought of vaguely as a Pre-Raphaelite friend of Henry James, as an American writer of *belles-lettres* or as one of Ezra Pound's passing crazes. His books were unobtainable.

Such an eclipse seemed a needlessly harsh fate for a man whose career was notable for above all things its brilliance. Born into a famous Pre-Raphaelite family, author at the age of seventeen of a by no means disgraceful novel, friend of James and model for one of his characters, collaborator for years with Joseph Conrad, editor of a famous review which published within months of each other James, Conrad and (for the first time) D.H. Lawrence, editor of a second review which published Joyce, Pound and Hemingway, author of what are often acknowledged to be respectively the finest historical romance of the century, the finest French novel in English and the finest novel about the First World War, an acknowledged influence on Hemingway and Graham Greene, Ford would seem to deserve not only critical but also popular recognition.

Yet his neglect is understandable if unforgivable. His early career was perhaps too brilliant: coming back from the war he found himself, at the age of forty-five, largely forgotten. His early collaboration with Conrad served him badly in that his name was throughout his career overshadowed by Conrad's. The unselfish service he provided to other writers as editor of the *English Review* made him 'Only Uncle of the Gifted Young' and obscured his own achievements. The bulk of his production hid his best novels, and the success of the latter was largely a *succès d'estime*.

But perhaps weightier in sum effect as causes of his neglect were matters only peripherally connected with his writing: his difficult to pronounce surname Hueffer and his confusing change of name in 1919; his German associates; his inability to manage his private affairs discreetly; his appallingly poor taste in titles for his books; the public attacks made on his personal integrity by Conrad's widow and an ex-mistress; his self-exile from England during the last seventeen years of his life; and his turning to an American public which, together with his circular name, labelled him American in the eyes of the average English reader.

Almost forgotten in England, then, Ford has fittingly been restored to his proper place by Americans. His two best novels, *The Good Soldier* and *Parade's End*, have since 1950 been widely read in the United States; since 1948 such critics as Mark Schorer, R.P. Blackmur, Hugh Kenner and Robie Macauley have been subjecting his work to intelligent scrutiny; and in the last two years four books of criticism and scholarship have been published in the United States. Two of these, *Ford Madox Ford* by Richard A. Cassell and *Ford Madox Ford's Novels* by John A. Meixner can be regarded as only introductory; the third, Paul L. Wiley's *Novelist of Three Worlds*, is a penetrating work of criticism which sets Ford in a unique position as historian of his time. Together with the publication in England of *The Bodley Head Ford Madox Ford* under the editorship of Graham Greene, these studies possibly mark the end of Ford's period of limbo.

Yet it is not an exaggeration to say that it is only with David D. Harvey's monumental bibliography of writings by and about Ford that accurate Ford criticism can begin: several of even Wiley's conclusions are invalidated by misdatings and omissions. Harvey's bibliography gives some indication of the vast quantities of unpublished and even unexamined material by Ford in existence: the first work of Ford's scholarship, it opens the fields of criticism but also demands higher standards of accuracy.

Several further studies of Ford are projected. What is most needed, however, is a critical biography to replace Douglas Goldring's valuable but uncritical *The Last Pre-Raphaelite*, for the relation between Ford's life and his work, undeniably close, has been the subject of too much uninformed speculation. Such a study would do much to explain such matters as the notorious inaccuracy of his reminiscences—which his avowed adherence to Impressionism is not enough to explain –, the bases of several themes to which he returns obsessively in his writing, and the reasons behind his vast production of comparatively trivial work.

III

At the beginning of 1963, his second winter in London, Coetzee found that from the £60 he was earning with IBM, he could save barely £10.

He discovered also that a Mr Pomfret, one of IBM's clients, was using data for a new type of bomber that was being developed by the RAF. This meant that Coetzee had '[i]n the most incidental, the most minor way, […] become part of the British defence effort; he has furthered British plans to bomb Moscow. Is this what he came to England for: to participate in evil, an evil in which there is no reward, not even the most imaginary?' In secret he contemplated tampering with Pomfret's data, to 'do his bit to save Russia from being bombed', but, says *Youth*, this caused him another dilemma: 'has he a moral right to enjoy British hospitality while sabotaging their air force?'[40]

Coetzee resigned his post at IBM in the spring of 1963. This was mainly to spend more time on his M.A. dissertation, although his doubts about his function may have played a part. He was not prepared to live with dualisms. He told the IBM management merely that he could not form friendships with his colleagues, an explanation that did not impress them, and left a residue of some resentment against him. Because he now had no income and had to save money on his lodgings, he looked after the house of a woman who was holidaying in Greece. He shared the house with a Malawian woman and her little daughter, and had to protect the house against possible depredation by the owner's estranged husband. At this time he started wearing glasses and grew a beard that would from then on be a permanent feature. In his free time he strolled in the London parks, much as his father in his years of unemployment had wandered through Cape Town whiling away the hours in bars until a respectable time to return home.[41] He soon discovered that his work permit did not allow him to change jobs at will, and that every change had to be authorised by the Home Office. He received an official letter instructing him to renew his work permit within 21 days, failing which he would forfeit his permission to remain in the UK. Somebody at IBM must have betrayed him, and he was at a loss to decide whether to return to South Africa. With a sardonic glance at the writers and artists of Clifton, in particular Uys Krige, who in the 1930s had lived in France and Spain for a long time, and who, with his translations of Villon and Lorca, had brought a Mediterranean freshness to South African literature, Coetzee writes:

> The fact is, if he goes back to South Africa, he will never escape again. He will become like the people who gather on Clifton beach in the evenings to drink wine and tell each other about the old days on Ibiza.[42]

The style of narration of *Youth*, with its distanced third-person perspective, is consistently elusive in the self that it projects. At this point of the book Coetzee goes further, opting to omit certain facts. This is in keeping with what he says in *Doubling the Point* and in his inaugural address at UCT about the nature of autobiography. In one of the interviews in *Doubling the Point* he describes autobiography as 'a kind of self-writing in which you are constrained to respect the facts of your history. But which facts? All the facts? No. All the facts are too many facts. You choose the facts insofar as they fall in with your evolving purpose. [...] You tell the story of your life by selecting from a reservoir of memories, and in the process of selecting you leave things out.'[43] The autobiographer is entitled to present a selection from the available material, because he may decide on personal grounds or for the sake of the structure of his story to omit certain matters. In an interview Coetzee has said: 'The point about selection is an important one. Even if an autobiography is absolutely true to the facts, nonetheless you have a selection of facts, because you can't get everything into a book. So the line between a work of true biography and of fictional biography is not as clear as some people like to think. True autobiography depends on selection of data and omission of data.'[44]

One of the facts that Coetzee omits in *Youth* is that in the spring of 1963, after about a year and three months in London, he returned to South Africa. He flew back via Khartoum and Kampala, and settled in Cape Town at 202 Linden Court, a flat in Gladstone Street, Gardens, where he completed his M.A. dissertation. He renewed his acquaintance with his friend from his student days, Mauna Philippa Jubber, who was teaching at La Rochelle Girls' High School in Paarl. They got married on 11 July 1963 in Johannesburg, where Philippa's parents and brother, Cecil, had settled. Coetzee was still determined to return to England, but they had to wait until the end of the year for Philippa's contract at La Rochelle to expire. After the wedding and their return to the Cape, she stayed in Paarl during the week to work, but joined him in Linden Court over weekends.[45] In his acknowledgements to his M.A. dissertation, Coetzee thanks 'my wife for assistance in the preparation of this typescript'.

The decision to marry was a sudden one, not preceded by a long courtship. Philippa was much more socially adept than the reserved, taciturn Coetzee, and she could at times be merry, though she was not always calm and even-tempered. With her social skills she seemed to complement him perfectly. Did she from the start admire his intellect and talent, and discern in him the writer he was to become? Whatever the case, they were very young when they married: he, just twenty-three; she, a few months older. They could neither of them have foreseen what marriage to the other would entail.

IV

Shortly after the wedding, back in Cape Town, Coetzee started trying to find a job in Britain. In reply to a letter to the British Ministry of Education, he received a letter on 28 August 1963 confirming that his qualifications at the University of Cape Town would permit him to be employed in primary and secondary schools in England and Wales. Evidently he had hoped his application would secure him a letter of appointment that he could show passport and immigration officials on his return to secure permission to remain in England. In a follow-up letter on 19 November he was informed that the principal of the Victorian Secondary School in Watford, Hertfordshire, had a temporary vacancy for a teacher, mainly of English, and had invited him to an interview. This invitation would allow him to stay in Britain for fourteen days. The secretary of the appointments committee writes: 'We are therefore able to send you a letter drafted in terms as approved by the Home Office [...] and this letter should facilitate your entry to the UK. It will constitute evidence that you have prospects of a teaching post when you arrive. To this letter we would advise you to attach the letter you received from the Ministry of Education recognising you as a qualified teacher on taking a post under the Schools Regulation, so that you may show your documents to the passport and immigration officers.' He adds: 'Watford is a pleasant place with a flourishing printing industry, though it has something of the atmosphere of a country town, with a regular market. It is in Hertfordshire, about 18 miles from London, and there is an excellent train service to and from London.' In a letter dated 2 December 1963, Mr T.H. Price, the principal of Victorian Secondary School, asks Coetzee to come and see him on 13 January 1964.

This position would, unlike Coetzee's previous job offer in 1962, have enabled him to remain living in London and enjoy the facilities of the city. But another opportunity arose. In reply to an enquiry he received a letter, dated 16 October 1963, from International Computers and Tabulators Limited (ICT), the British competitors of IBM. The personnel officer wrote that they might be able to help him, but that they would have to meet him first. He enclosed an application form, which he asked Coetzee to complete and forward to him.

Coetzee and Philippa embarked for Southampton from Cape Town on 30 December 1963 on board the Athlone Castle. They disembarked on 10 January 1964. In a letter to Mike Kirkwood dated 25 January 1978, Coetzee describes this voyage as 'long & hot & boring'. On board with them was Rick Turner, an acquaintance from his student days, with whom he had a few conversations. Turner was on his way to Paris, engrossed in Sartre and Norman Mailer. He lent Coetzee Mailer's *Advertisement for Myself*. He was married to the beautiful Barbara Hubbard, with whom he visited the Coetzees a year later in Bagshot, Surrey, with their first child. 'They left behind a half-pint saucepan which I never returned.'

Coetzee probably kept the appointment with the principal of Victoria Secondary on 13 January, but he did not accept this post. The reason for this is not clear. Possibly Coetzee did not want to teach English at such an elementary level. Or possibly the principal preferred another candidate.

On 10 February 1964 Coetzee started working for ICT in Bracknell, Berkshire, at a salary of £1 209 a year, under more pleasant working conditions than at IBM. Bracknell, a small village about 33 miles west of London, set bucolically inside a forest, was founded in 1949 in the aftermath of the Second World War. Coetzee and Philippa did not live in Bracknell, but in Bagshot, an equally small village in Surrey, about half an hour by bus from Bracknell. Coetzee found that smaller towns suited him better than cities. At ICT, based in a manor house, he could play cricket with the other programmers at lunchtime, enjoying it as much as he had done at school. His work brought him in contact with brilliant mathematicians connected with Cambridge University, and he regularly went to Cambridge, where he overnighted at the company's expense.

He soon discovered, however, that the Cambridge Mathematical Laboratory was linked in sinister fashion with the nuclear installation at Aldermaston, and that the laboratory was in effect an ally in the Cold War. By collaborating with Aldermaston, he would be in cahoots with evil, as an accomplice in the conflict between Britain and the US on the one hand and Russia on the other. The involvement with Mr

Pomfret's project in his IBM days seemed trivial compared with this. Could he continue with a project that required him to betray his moral principles? He recalled the well-known words from T.S. Eliot's *Murder in the Cathedral*:

> The last temptation is the greatest treason:
> To do the right deed for the wrong reason.[46]

Taking his cue from these words, Coetzee writes: 'All that matters is doing the right thing, whether for the right reason or the wrong reason or no reason at all.'[47]

In these days Coetzee befriended a fellow-programmer, the Indian Ganapathy, who despised everything about England, much preferring the US, where he had lived and worked for a long time. Coetzee, too, asked himself what he was doing on this miserable island with its atrocious weather. One day, while they were walking in the Surrey countryside, Ganapathy remarked that this environment meant nothing to either of them. At least in America, he said, there were hamburger stalls that stayed open all night. Coetzee did not care much for hamburgers, but the America described by his friend was evidently an improvement on the England he had got to know,[48] even though the newspapers were full of the atrocities marking America's war in Vietnam. Coetzee was so horrified at the appalling behaviour of the Americans that he wrote to the Chinese embassy in London, offering his services as an English teacher as his contribution to the resistance. This letter elicited no response.

In his interview with Shauna Westcott[49] Coetzee says that in Britain he worked for more than two years for two different companies:

> It meant living among people with an uncritical belief in techno-logical progress, in enlightenment, and so forth. Also, being Englishmen, they never doubted that the world they knew was going to last a long time. I felt quite alien & temporary. But there was a lot to admire among them — the habit of hard work, for instance. Also they were very bright, for the most part, particularly the people I met and worked among at Cambridge.

Over-modestly, he claims: 'It was that, finally, that made me decide to quit: I wasn't in the same league, intellectually.' And in an interview with

Fernando de Lima Paulo he says: 'I was not a creative mathematician. As I discovered (rather too late), I had no real talent.'[50]

Nor did his stay in England bring him creative inspiration. For two years he waited for the words that would make a poet of him. But the paper he prepared for writing remained obstinately blank.[51] And yet Coetzee's years in Britain were by no means the failure he described them as in a *Fair Lady* interview of 25 February 1983. Apart from his sustained reading of Pound, he wrote his dissertation on Ford Madox Ford [52] and got to know Beckett's novels, especially *Watt*, which would later occupy him intellectually for the first few years of his academic career. He read in newspapers about the violence in Vietnam, and in the British Museum he explored the accounts of the early travellers in the Cape, both preliminary studies for his first novel. His years as a programmer also prepared him for the connection between mathematics and the study of literature that he would take up again in his research.

Did he find South Africa as repugnant as he would suggest in *Youth*? While living in London, he met the South African poet Sydney Clouts, who had settled in England in 1961. In an interview Coetzee says:

> We used to meet and talk about literature and he showed me some poems of Van Wyk Louw which he had translated. And I wrote back to South Africa and asked my mother to send *Tristia* to me. She sent me *Tristia* and I was immensely impressed by it.[53]

Although he, by his own account, read no other Afrikaans at this time, the publication of Van Wyk Louw's highly praised collection and Clouts' enthusiasm prompted him to take note of it. Certain images from this collection, in particular of his beloved Karoo, the setting of Voëlfontein, perhaps reverberated with him, such as the description of a Karoo town on a summer's evening, with the late afternoon having turned to cream, and the far-flung whistling of trains, and a dapple-white wheatear sitting alert on its clod of earth.[54]

And could he also have shared Van Wyk Louw's yearning that, in his barren, desolate land, olives should grow, and that the small chalk-white buildings should assume a Latinate character, a certain alignment with an older cultural tradition[55]

Coetzee was ambivalent about his own country, yet not happy in the city to which he had escaped. It is doubtful, however, that he was truly as unhappy as he often suggests in *Youth*. He writes, for instance, about a Sunday afternoon when he was stretched out on Hampstead Heath half-asleep and yet conscious of his surroundings:

> It is a state he has not known before: in his very blood he seems to feel the steady wheeling of the earth. The faraway cries of children, the birdsong, the whirr of insects gather force and come together in a paean of joy. His heart swells. *At last!* He thinks. At last it has come, the moment of ecstatic unity with the All![56]

It is worth taking note of the impression Coetzee made on somebody of his own age who knew him in his years in Britain. Lionel Knight, now a retired teacher, got to know Coetzee in the winter of 1962 in the reading room of the British Museum, and often joined him in walks when he and Philippa were living in Bagshot and visited Knight's parents' home in Woking. When Coetzee's mother came to Britain to see her two sons, she stayed with Knight's parents for a week.[57] In an e-mail, Knight writes at some length about the impression Coetzee made on him, presenting an image of his humanity and consideration that has been less evident in later interviews with Coetzee:

> I didn't think of him as a future writer. I have a vague memory of his having shown me something he had written. But I do remember his pride in some published mathematical piece—a competition, I think. And of having lunch with him after he had come from an exit interview at IBM. They wanted to know why he had resigned and he had been, I imagine, quietly and courteously evasive; he felt he'd got the better of the encounter. Did he work for ICL then, or before IBM? He thought it—ICL—wasn't too well organized, I remember, but that he had time for reading en route to Cambridge and whilst waiting there for an assignment. He seemed dissatisfied & was applying for Buffalo,[58] I guess. He quoted approvingly somebody he had heard describe Britain as a 'cooling planet'.
>
> Of course, he lent me his thesis on F M Ford—I think he went back[59] to complete it. Talking of Ford, he praised 'the quality of his sentences'. I recall walking through crowded dirty streets near King's Cross with John enthusing about *Watt* and *Murphy*, books he often referred to. I do remember a vehement comment—unusual to hear him speak aggressively about anyone or thing—once when we were sitting in my parents' garden. Possibly a n'paper article

or someone had asked why some writer wrote so much, why didn't they write less and better, etc. I remember his angry reply to this reported remark: as if any writer worth their salt would not keep writing, as if they could help themselves.

He struck me as leading compartmentalized lives. I didn't meet many of his other friends or acquaintances. Occasional S Africans; once or twice Jonty Driver; his brother David, then an ardent communist, very direct but with some of John's courteous attention to an interlocutor. There was a chap from Madras—John asked after him only a few years ago.[60] Remarkably, I was able to tell him I'd seen him in a public library. But a friendly chat left me none the wiser about him or his life. He may have been a mathematician with literary interests. But he was rather a mystery man; not apparently employed though in his thirties, with quiet direct remarks, at something of an angle to daily life. John liked him. I don't recall his mentioning his father; but his mother, yes. She stayed with my mother once or was it twice? She was a very strong and direct character full of kindness and decency, very proud of her sons, and especially John's achievements (by that time).

I know that people who met him did not forget him. I introduced him to a Cambridge academic friend. His young doctor wife was giving her screaming son a bath in a tub on the carpet that we were sitting around. John's ability to keep talking, fingertips together, with quiet thoughtfulness impressed and amused them a great deal. But John could be very playful. He liked tricks or unusual questions that would put people on the spot, and he watched their reactions closely. I can remember him jumping out from behind trees on walks in Virginia Water, sometimes taking photographs. (We went on long walks—later with my fiancée joining us—and Philippa would, jokingly, I imagine, claim to be tired, so we carried her with one leg on John's shoulder and one on my mine.) I remember that he was *interested* in p'graphs then (and later when he asked us to send family pictures) when I guess I didn't think about them. The same applied to all his aesthetic responses. Calling on me in Highgate, North London, (where he then lived in a house full of African—Nigerian?—tenants) he saw two records, Ravi Shankar and Ustad Vilayat Khan. Neither of us could then have heard much Indian music, but he asked me which I preferred. I chose the superficial—in this case—Ravi Shankar & he told me with the air of someone who knew about these things, that he preferred the singing style of Vilayat Khan. It took me a lot longer to develop a taste.

Although he appeared as someone creating himself to think and speak with unflinching truth and accuracy, I must mention his kindness, with Philippa and with my wife. When we met in Cape Town, he was anything but the detached quizzical observer. He gave us helpful and pressing advice about driving and about travel — my wife is rather conspicuous as a sari wearer. I also remember a grey evening in the Archway Road talking to a wonderfully friendly Philippa whom John had just brought round to me while he had to go somewhere else and discovering she, just married, had arrived in England a few hours earlier.[61]

This letter from Lionel Knight provides a perspective on Coetzee's years in Britain that differs significantly from that in *Youth*. He recalls a playfulness, humour and humanity that have not generally emerged from interviews with Coetzee. When Coetzee says in an interview with Shauna Westcott that he found England cold and grey and adds 'I'm not sure that I learned much except how to use a laundromat',[62] he is exaggerating. The three and a half years in Britain and his work in the British Museum provided him with a basis for his further development.

But the fact remains that Coetzee, in spite of the broadening of outlook that Britain made possible, was not particularly happy there. He looked forward to a change and especially to the opportunity to dedicate himself fully to literature and to his creative work. And that, he thought, he could achieve by following Ganapathy's advice, and exploring the possibility of bursaries to the United States.

III

THE UNITED STATES
OF AMERICA
(1965–1971)

CHAPTER 6

AUSTIN, TEXAS,
1965–1968

I

By mid-1964 Coetzee had started to feel that as a computer programmer with ICL in Bracknell he was in a dead-end. In a later
interview with David Attwell he says: 'In 1964, I was living in England,
working in a computer research laboratory. I was going nowhere; I
needed to change direction.'[1] And, he reasoned, it might be worth his
while to follow his friend Ganapathy's advice to explore the possibility of
a bursary to a university in the US.

His main interest, however, was still poetry, in particular the work
of Ezra Pound, even though, prompted by Pound's high praise, his
M.A. dissertation had dealt with the novels of Ford Madox Ford. He
did by now have a good knowledge of the work of Samuel Beckett from
the years 1947–1951, one of the great creative eruptions in modern
literature: the fiction *Molloy, Malone Dies*, and *The Unnamable* (the
'trilogy'), the drama *Waiting for Godot* (of which he had seen a production
in Cape Town) and the thirteen *Texts for Nothing*.[2] A text that now made
a particular impression on him was the novel *Watt*, which he found
radically different from Beckett's dramas. He asked himself why nobody
had told him that Beckett had also written novels. In Ford there had
always been 'an element of the stuffed shirt' that he had been reluctant
to recognise; Beckett, in *Watt* in particular, pointed in the direction he
wanted his own creative writing to take:

> There is no clash, no conflict, just the flow of a voice telling a story,
> a flow continually checked by doubts and scruples, its pace fitted
> exactly to the pace of his own mind. *Watt* is also funny, so funny that
> he rolls about laughing. When he comes to the end he starts again
> at the beginning.[3]

Because he was now seriously considering further studies in literature, Coetzee wrote to Professor Guy Howarth, his supervisor in Cape Town, asking him to write on his behalf to several institutions enquiring about available bursaries. Coetzee had made a thorough study of all the possibilities: University of California at Berkeley, University of Texas at Austin, New York State at Rochester, Kansas at Lawrence, Washington at St. Louis, Illinois at Urbana, Tulane at New Orleans, Indiana at Bloomington and Colorado at Fort Collins.

Coetzee knew that Professor Jackson Burgess of the University of California at Berkeley had taught in Cape Town in 1962, although he had not met him personally; he had met and attended the lectures of Professor Joseph Jones of the University of Texas at Austin in 1961.

Howarth probably advised him to write in person to these visitors and institutions to enquire about bursaries and assistantships. Coetzee did so. On 22 January 1964 he wrote to Professor Burgess, in terms that he presumably also addressed to other academics and institutions:

> During 1962, when you were Visiting Professor of American Literature at the University of Cape Town, I held a University scholarship which enabled me to spend that year and part of 1963 in London reading for an M.A. thesis on Ford Madox Ford: the degree was awarded, with distinction, last year. My principal interest is, however, twentieth-century poetry, and this year I am working in Britain and reading in the direction of Ezra Pound. Professor Guy Howarth has suggested that I try to get an assistantship in an American university while I continue my studies—I am not eligible for the State Department scholarships for South Africans because I am not resident in the Republic—and has said that you may be able to give me advice. I should be most grateful if you could tell me whether it would be a good idea for me to apply for an assistantship at the University of California (this would be for the academic year 1965–6, as I still have a certain amount to do in Britain). I should need enough to keep two bodies and souls together and allow me enough time for study. My wife is a high-school teacher but I am uncertain of the regulations that would govern her employment in the United States.

Coetzee duly received the application forms for an assistantship at the University of California. If his application succeeded, he would have to register as a student, and would receive a stipend of $2 750. From Texas, Professor Joseph Jones replied on 24 January 1964:

> You wouldn't do badly to consider Texas as a place to study modern American poetry. We have two or three poets on the staff, and a notable library including a great deal of manuscript material. I'm assuming that you'd wish to go ahead for the doctorate. You would find on our staff a man quite sympathetic to your Ford study, in Professor Ambrose Gordon, who has written on Ford himself.
>
> I would suggest that you apply for a Teaching Assistantship and also for a University Fellowship. […] It is quite regular to put in for both and, since fellowships are pretty scarce, to fall back on the Teaching Assistantship. […]
>
> Your wife's work-status will have to be threshed out with the U.S. consulate. They are sticky about such things at times, so it might be just as well to look into it ahead of time.
>
> Austin is not an expensive place to live, comparatively speaking, and I rather think you might like it here. It does not conform to the stereotype image of Texas as flat, sandy and arid; nor is it a cultural desert either.

From most of the universities to which he had applied, Coetzee received offers of assistantships for the academic year 1965–1966, at salaries ranging from $2 200 to $2 800, an indication that, contrary to his repeated asseverations in interviews,[4] he had after all impressed the authorities of these institutions. It was to become a pattern for Coetzee to belittle his own achievements, and later to keep a healthy ironical distance from the many tributes and awards he was to receive. The University of Indiana in Bloomington, for instance, informed him that he had been selected 'from a large group of exceptionally able applicants'.

He decided on the University of Texas at Austin, where he was offered an assistantship at a salary of $2 300,[5] on condition that he enrol as a student. To support his application for a visa, he had to submit to the US consul in Britain the letter of 4 June 1965, confirming that he had been accepted for a Fulbright scholarship in the 'Exchange-Visitor Program of the University of Texas'. The conditions of the Fulbright Scholarship stipulated that successful candidates had to return to their country of origin to contribute their acquired knowledge and values to the culture of that country. In the letter that Coetzee received from Texas, the responsibilities of the university and of the successful candidate are clearly spelt out:

> The University of Texas, in issuing this certificate, assumes certain responsibilities in relation to your stay in the United States. It is, therefore, important that you conform to all pertinent regulations of the Immigration and Naturalization Service while you are in this country. You should contact this office as soon after your arrival as time permits, and keep us informed of any change in your address.

On 30 August 1965 Coetzee and Philippa embarked for New York from Southampton on the *Aurelia*, an Italian ship that had been used as a troop ship in the Second World War, but was now packed with young people from foreign parts wanting to study in the US. Coetzee was twenty-five and ready to enter a new phase of his life. From New York, where they disembarked on 8 September, they travelled to Austin.

Coetzee knew next to nothing about the University of Texas. He did know that the university was reputed to be strong in linguistics, and that, besides holding one and a half million books, the library had a large collection of manuscripts and rare editions in the area of English literature. But he knew nothing about these manuscripts or what they would mean to him in the near future. He did not know that the chancellor, Harry Ransom, had a few years earlier aggressively started accumulating, for large sums, a treasure for the university library. Years later Coetzee said in an interview:

> I went to Texas because they had a strong program in linguistics and literature. Also because they offered me money. […] It is a very large and uneven university, but the department of linguistics is excellent, among the best two or three in the United States.[6]

The stipend of $2 300 was more than enough for him and Philippa, because he was used to living frugally with few luxuries. They moved into an apartment at 708, Groom Street, close to the campus. Later they would move to 2815, Rio Grande Avenue.

II

At the time of their stay, the population of Austin, the capital of Texas, numbered about 186 500. The city was then not yet a fashionable new-technology hub; it was the centre of a variety of industries and agricultural activity ranging from wheat to stock breeding, especially cattle. The main campus of the University of Texas, established in 1881, in Coetzee's time had 23 000 students. In the centre of the campus is the administration building with 32 storeys and a campanile, offering visitors an excellent view of the city.[7]

Coetzee, who disliked cars, explored the city by bicycle. He did not, however, take into account the extreme heat that Texas is prone to in summer, and was once stranded on a farm road near Bastrop, about thirty miles east of Austin. The water he had with him had reached body temperature and provided no relief from the heat. Though he had experienced the Great Karoo during summer holidays on Voëlfontein, the heat of Texas was something else:

> Summer in central Texas. Days dawn warm and steamy. Clouds build up and sit over the land like a lid on a pot. By ten o'clock the weight of the sun lies heavy on your limbs. It is a sun that burns white skins shades of wooden brown, from light oak to deep walnut, not unattractive but without any hint of the luminous honey-gold one sees under a temperate sun.
>
> Nor is it like the sun of the African uplands, which whips the body dry as a bone.[8] Here one moves in a pocket of humid warmth, sweat streaming from one's pores.[9]

Upon his arrival in Austin, Coetzee felt that he lacked an adequate background in languages. At school he had studied, besides English and Afrikaans, only Latin. He had continued studying it in his first year at UCT, but Latin had not given him much pleasure. He had acquired a reading knowledge of French and German in Cape Town and Britain, and could even follow Spanish with the help of a translation, but no more than that. His problem was the same as he had experienced with history and geography at school: to memorise the basics, in this case the vocabulary. In one of his interviews with David Attwell he says:

I would like to be polyglot but am not. My relationship with languages is an intimate but frustrated one. I have a poor ear and a distaste for memorizing. I pick up the principles of a new language quickly enough, perhaps even get a feel for it, then start looking for shortcuts, then get bored. So the pattern has been that I work on a language intensively for a period, usually for an immediate reason, then put it aside and do something else, and as a result never retain anything like a command.[10]

In Austin Coetzee followed courses in German and French, and, inspired by his admiration of Dostoevsky and Tolstoy, even made an attempt to master Russian. In German he made a study of syntax and stylistics, the problem of the German lyric, and European literature in its relation to the Latin Middle Ages. Because he could read, write and speak Afrikaans well, he felt that he should now use this aptitude as the basis for a more extensive knowledge of Dutch and Dutch literature. In London he had got to know the work of Simon Vinkenoog, who had in Holland acted as spokesman and apologist for a new generation of poets, the *Vijftigers* or the atonal poets. Vinkenoog's own creative work, however, was soon overshadowed by that of his contemporaries Lucebert and Gerrit Kouwenaar. In London the John character in *Youth* had found Vinkenoog's writings 'raucous, crass, lacking any dimension of mystery'.[11] And he had concluded, 'If Vinkenoog is all Holland can offer, then his worst suspicion is confirmed: that of all nations the Dutch are the dullest, the most antipoetic. So much for his Netherlandic heritage. He might just as well be monolingual.'[12] In Austin, however, Coetzee had a totally different attitude to Dutch. He followed courses in Dutch language and literature with Professor Francis Bulhof, known in particular as a translator of Dutch and Flemish poetry into English, and of E. du Perron's novel *Land van herkomst*, translated as *Country of Origin*. Coetzee read as much Dutch literature as time permitted, and took exams in nineteenth- and twentieth-century Dutch literature. To refine his sense of the language, he even started making his own translations from Dutch into English.

Coetzee also extended his knowledge of English literature through a study of Old and Middle English; the Augustan satirists; Byron; Henry James; and American fiction since James. He completed a course in Gothic elements in American literature. Whereas earlier in Cape Town he had immersed himself primarily in poetry, he now, especially as regards modern literature, concentrated on prose, suggesting that his creative focus was shifting. His interest in Byron would later provide a frame of reference for his novel *Disgrace*. He completed further studies in stylistics, morphology and syntax, teaching English as a second language and a course in US government that was compulsory for foreign students.

Coetzee studied under some of the greatest practitioners in the field of literature and linguistics, who in the 1960s bestowed prestige on the University of Texas. William B. Todd, the professor responsible for bibliography, taught him to compare two manuscripts with the aid of the Hinman Collator, and to calculate stylistic differences statistically, an interest that connected usefully with his computer experience in Britain. For Winifred P. Lehmann[13] of Early English he wrote a paper on the rhetorical techniques in the sermons of the medieval bishop Wulfstan. His stylistic approach did not please her, for she awarded him an A–; the minus was, in her words, because work like his gave philology a bad name.[14] It was a criticism that he took to heart and that would lead to a change of direction in his scientific approach.

In the 1960s the centre of gravity of American linguistics was shifting gradually from Leonard Bloomfield's structuralism to the transformational-generative grammar of Noam Chomsky. The structuralism of Europe, in particular the ideas of Roland Barthes and Claude Lévi-Strauss, was also starting to gain prominence. The anthropological structuralism of Roman Jakobson in the area of folk poetry led Coetzee to the insight that the distinction between 'high' European culture and a so-called 'primitive' culture was false.[15] He wrote, for the formidable Archibald Hill, grand master of linguistics at the University of Texas, a comparative essay on the morphology of Nama, Malay and Dutch, languages not related to one another, but brought into interaction upon the arrival at the Cape of the Dutch colonists and the slaves from the East. This paper led him deeper into the syntax of exotic languages, to the discovery that the term 'primitive' was meaningless also as relating to languages; that, for instance, each of the 700 languages of Borneo was as coherent and complex as English. In his 1984 article 'Remembering Texas', recalling his years in Austin, he says:

> I read Noam Chomsky and Jerrold Katz and the new universal
> grammarians and reached the point of asking myself: If a latter-day
> ark were ever commissioned to take the best that mankind has to

offer and make a fresh start on the farthest planets, if it ever came to that, might we not leave Shakespeare's plays and Beethoven's quartets behind to make room for the last speaker of Dyirbal, even though that last speaker might be a fat old woman who scratched herself and smelled badly?[16]

And he arrived at the point of seeing English, the language of his studies and in which he hoped one day to produce significant creative work, in its relation to other languages, those known to him as well as those totally alien:

> It seemed an odd position for a student of English, the greatest imperial language of them all, to be falling into. It was a doubly odd position for someone with literary ambitions, albeit of the vaguest—ambitions to speak one day, somehow, in his own voice—to discover himself suspecting that languages spoke people or at the very least spoke through them.[17]

In the same article he recollects how he had passed the office of James Sledd, his professor in Chaucer and English phonology, one Saturday afternoon at five, and heard the sound of a typewriter inside. Recalling years later, in an interview with *Fair Lady*, his time as a student in the US, he says: 'I learned a lot in the United States, particularly from the energy and industry of Americans.'[18] How different, he must have thought wryly, was the lifestyle of his colonial teachers—mere dilettantes consorting idly with their subject. And how different, too, to the vigour and dedication he witnessed in America, was the lazy, empty existence on the farms in the colony from which he came. This was a theme to which Coetzee was to return, and to which he would devote, in his 1988 collection *White Writing*, an insightful introductory chapter called 'Idleness in South Africa'.[19]

One marvels at the results Coetzee achieved in the many courses he completed in preparation for his doctoral dissertation. In all the courses in which he wrote an exam, he was invariably given an A. And yet, besides the dedicated attention to his studies and his fervent reading in the wonderfully equipped library, he still found time for cycling and for Sunday afternoon cricket on a baseball pitch. On page 321 of the 1968 *Cactus* yearbook there is a photo of the University of Texas at Austin's cricket team. Among other players—mainly of Indian and Pakistani origin, all 'nostalgic castoff children from the colonies'[20]—Coetzee stands third from left, a bespectacled young man, almost the tallest, with dark wavy hair and a neatly trimmed beard. He wears the pads characteristic of the game and in his right hand he holds a pair of gloves. For Texas it is an unusual sight.

In 'Remembering Texas' Coetzee writes that the doctoral students among whom he moved, were housed in rented apartments strewn with baby toys. All were completing courses, preparing for oral exams or writing dissertations. Their sole aim was to make a financial success of their lives, 'of getting out, getting a job in Huntsville or Texarkana, getting their hands on real money'.[21] With a less tangible ambition for the immediate future, Coetzee was content to labour on at his Old English texts and his German grammar. Many of his contemporaries at Austin could not remember him at all when he was awarded the Nobel Prize in 2003. This is understandable, given a student body of 23 000, large enough for him to disappear into, but it does bring to mind the pronouncement of Professor Skewes, his mathematics professor at UCT, that Coetzee was 'a peaceful, industrious citizen, so unobtrusive as to be practically invisible'. One contemporary who does remember Coetzee is Thomas Cable, later Professor of English at the University of Texas, who recalls how they attended the classes of the dreaded Professor Hill and discussed the provocative theories of Noam Chomsky. Cable, for one, discerned a touch of brilliance in his quiet colleague.[22]

By his own account, the students whom Coetzee had to teach remained strangers to him. Their whole way of life—their culture, their choice of recreation and their expectations—was inaccessible and incomprehensible to him.[23] He perhaps identified with his admired Beckett, who for a while as a young man had to persuade the sons and daughters of the Irish–Protestant middle classes that Ronsard and Stendhal were worth taking note of.[24] This is, however, another instance of Coetzee's cynical-ironical undercutting of his own success as a lecturer. Because he was so well prepared and could convey his knowledge authoritatively, he made an impression on those students who were interested in the subject. That the Department of English was very satisfied with Coetzee's work as a lecturer is evident from the fact that in his first academic year he was appointed to supervise three students during the summer recess, and that his bursary and assistantship were renewed for the academic year 1966-1967. On 30 March 1967 he was informed by the office of the Dean that a 'Graduate

Fellowship' had been awarded to him, commencing in September 1967. This released him from all tuition fees and other financial obligations to the university, and freed him to devote himself full-time to his academic work. For the academic year 1967–1968 he was promoted to 'University Fellow', another honour entailing a further salary increase.

III

With his preliminary studies behind him, Coetzee could concentrate on his doctoral dissertation. He sensed that there was something in the air, the possibility of somehow combining linguistics, mathematics and textual analysis, while also bringing into play his experience in the world of computers.[25]

While in London, Coetzee had started devouring the prose of Samuel Beckett, developing great admiration for his frugal, even stingy use of words, and deriving near-sensual pleasure from this prose. In an essay in his 2007 collection *Inner Workings: Essays 2000–2005*, he characterises the curious world of Beckett's oeuvre:

> It is a world of confined spaces or else bleak wastes, inhabited by asocial and indeed misanthropic monologuers helpless to terminate their monologue, tramps with failing bodies and never-sleeping minds condemned to a purgatorial treadmill on which they rehearse again and again the great themes of Western philosophy; a world that comes to us in the distinctive prose that Beckett, using French models in the main, though with Jonathan Swift whispering ghostly in his ear, was in the process of perfecting for himself, lyrical and mordant in equal measures.[26]

One is inclined to recognise something of especially the late Coetzee in his reference to Beckett's 'vision of life without consolation or dignity or promise of grace, in the face of which our only duty—inexplicable and futile of attainment, but a duty nonetheless—is not to lie to ourselves'– a validation of his pronouncement in *Doubling the Point* that all writing, fiction as well as literary criticism, is autobiographical:

> Starting out as an uneasy Joycean and an even more uneasy Proustian, Beckett eventually settled on philosophical comedy as the medium

for his uniquely anguished, arrogant, self-doubting, scrupulous temperament. In the popular mind his name is associated with the mysterious Godot who may or may not come but for whom we wait anyhow, passing the time as best we can. In this he seemed to define the mood of an age. But his range is wider than that, and his achievement far greater. Beckett was an artist possessed by a vision of life … It was a vision to which he gave expression in language of a virile strength and intellectual subtlety that marks him as one of the great prose stylists of the twentieth century.[27]

In London Coetzee had developed a particular interest in *Watt*, the novel that Beckett wrote in the 1940s on a farm in Roussillon in the south of France, while eluding the Germans. In the Austin library he now discovered, through a fortuitous confluence of circumstances, Beckett's manuscripts, of which he had been unaware before coming to Texas. Among these manuscripts were a number of exercise books in which Beckett wrote his *Watt*. For weeks Coetzee studied the sketches and numbers and scribblings in the margin, deeply impressed with the sheer effort it takes to produce a masterpiece. 'It is heartening,' he said later, 'to see from what unpromising beginnings a book could grow: to see the false starts, the scratched-out banalities, the evidences of less than furious possession by the Muse.'[28] When Deirdre Bair in her biography of Beckett dismissed *Watt* as a confused book without any system, Coetzee could not contain his impatience and even fury at such a pronouncement. It is rare in his criticism for him to react quite as vehemently as this:

> This is execrable literary criticism. It is foolish to say that Beckett was 'confused' when he wrote *Watt*. It is nonsense to say that he 'steps in to undercut and belie any meaning or appreciation': *Watt* is an important book, and there are a dozen studies which might have helped Bair to understand and/or appreciate it if she had consulted them (I find no evidence that she has). As for 'settling into a warm, cozy read', is this really what she wants from Beckett?[29]

The *Watt* documents at the University of Texas comprise three stages in the composition of the novel: a first design in holograph that was composed from February 1941 in Paris to October 1943 in Roussillon; an incomplete typescript with corrections in holograph; and a collation of a part of the typescript with a new holograph completed in February 1945. Studying the manuscript and its textual history, Coetzee felt, enabled the reader to understand why Beckett himself was unhappy with the completed product and why it took eight years for it to be published.[30] The author of *Waiting for Godot* described his work on *Watt* to Lawrence Harvey as 'only a game, a means of staying sane', and dismissed it to Ruby Cohn as a mere exercise, written to shore himself up against the long hours of boredom and waiting for nothing to happen.[31] In the introduction to the Faber and Faber edition of *Watt*, C.J. Ackerley writes:

> [F]or the first six decades of its existence (as manuscript and book) the text of *Watt* has been a mess. The problem of error is crucial, for as *Watt* interrogates the foundations of rational inquiry, the distinctions between intended errors, authorial errors, mistakes introduced by publishers, changes of intention and other obnubilations loom all the larger. If no distinction can be drawn between deliberate and inadvertent error then all interpretation is fraught. To an extent, this will always be so with *Watt*, because its textual history is so complex; but a first scholarly step must be the determination of the best text possible (if not the best possible text).[32]

The title of Coetzee's dissertation, for which he was awarded a doctorate in 1969, was *The English Fiction of Samuel Beckett: An Essay in Stylistic Analysis*. For permission to quote from Beckett's *More Pricks than Kicks* (1934), he wrote a letter on 19 March 1968 to the publishers Chatto & Windus. Beckett, however, exercised strict control over his creative work, and they were not prepared to approach him before Coetzee had stated which parts he wanted to use. After receiving Coetzee's information, Chatto and Windus granted permission for him to include sections in an appendix to his dissertation — provided, however, that he consult them again if he should consider commercial publication. Beckett's jealous guardianship of his interests is apparent also from a further letter in which the publishers quote from a letter from the author: 'You may give permission for ten extracts (maximum), no extract to exceed ten lines (of Chatto & Windus edition).' This was probably Coetzee's first experience of a prominent writer's strict stewardship of his rights, and may have guided him in his later control of his own creative work.

In his dissertation Coetzee employs among other methods a numerical approach, known as stylo-statistics, and supplements his text with numerous diagrams, lists and charts, comprehensible (only) to somebody who understands computers. Hill was warmly appreciative of the study, but it was eventually completed under the supervision of Thomas Whitbread, one of the professors of English. Coetzee was later to say that his stylistic analysis and the numerological basis of his study led nowhere and had been a 'wrong turning' in his career, 'a false trail both in my career and in the history of stylistics'.[33] Nevertheless, it did make him aware of the possibilities of form in the novel, and of language as a self-enclosed game, an insight that was to prove decisive in the creative prose he would start writing a few years later.

At the end of the dissertation Coetzee comes close to rejecting stylo-statistics as a critical method. He writes:

> The dilemma is that if we give an arbitrary statistical definition for a quality of style such as nominalism we will eventually be faced with a text for which our literary response to its degree of nominalism does not square with the response indicated by the statistical measure; while if we define the quality in such a way as to square invariably with our literary response then we are measuring rather deviously an aspect of our response rather than an aspect of the text. One solution to the dilemma is to interpret statistical measure as correlations, i.e. to say, with a certain degree of probability, a high noun-to-verb ratio occurs together with other stylistic features like Latinism. A more extreme solution, the one I prefer, is to limit statistics to comparative statements. By choosing the latter solution I in effect reject stylostatistics as a creative tool of exploration in single texts. I take this side in the dispute over stylostatistics not because I oppose quantification as such but because I believe that by their nature the statistical techniques currently applied to literary texts oversimplify their material and therefore falsify it.[34]

Apart from the objection that stylo-statistics oversimplifies the material, the method, according to Coetzee, yields no new insights. Whitbread recalls that when they came to discuss that section, Coetzee smiled mischievously, which told Whitbread something about his candidate's sense of humour and his insight into the relative value of his work.[35]

After his student years Coetzee was to return to Austin four times. In 1979 he was a visiting professor, acquainting himself with the latest developments in linguistics, and using the opportunity to complete his third novel, *Waiting for the Barbarians*. Later, in the autumn of 1995, Coetzee presented a course in creative writing. The director of the Michener Center for Writers in Austin, James Magnuson, according to Rae Nadler-Olinick, found him '"immensely conscientious and generous with his time" toward the students, [...] toss[ing] out "very incisive, analytical, thought-provoking" discussion questions for his fiction workshoppers to ponder'.[36] On his return visits Coetzee was fascinated by the extensive Central Market of Austin, which had been established since his student days. A strict vegetarian since 1974, he was struck by the contrast between the different market halls. In the 1995 essay, 'Meat Country', one of his most spirited and assured essays, he wrote:

> Stores like Central Market, as large as two or even three football fields, are familiar to Americans, or at least to affluent, middle-class Americans. They are based on economics of scale and on a single promise addressed to the customer: Everything you can conceivably want, in the way of things to eat and drink, is here, and more. You need go nowhere else.
>
> The 'and more' is important. The cornucopia, the mythological horn of plenty, disgorges a *copia*, a torrent of goods, that is more than anyone can consume. Fundamental to Central Market and stores like it is the cornucopian promise that what is on offer is inexhaustible not only in sheer mass but in variety too: variety of flavour and colour and size, variety of origin, variety of method of cultivation. If the effect is dizzying, that is part of the plan.
>
> Wandering around the first hall of Central Market, the atrium of fruit and vegetables, is indeed like being in the mythic Land of Plenty. Why, then, is the experience of the next chamber, the Hall of Meats (meat, fish and poultry), so different? Partly, perhaps, because the smell has changed. No longer does the air hold the scent of melons and peaches. Instead there is a smell of blood and death, and all the exertions of the smiling assistants behind the counters to scrub and sterilize will not chase it away.
>
> The infernal atmosphere in which they have to operate is not their only handicap. However willing they are to advise, to chop and slice and weigh and pack, they cannot compete, as a show, with Fruits and Vegetables. The very current of modern marketing is against them. The modernist food hall consisting of nothing but

rows and rows of gleaming refrigerated beds holding antiseptic packages, neatly labeled and priced, is becoming an anachronism. The new fashion is rough, homely, mock-rustic: fruit and vegetables cascading out of bushel baskets, with folksy handwritten signs planted in them where they come from, what they taste like, how to cook them. A spectacle, in other words, of origins.[37]

He wonders if the 'Hall of Meats' will adapt to changing times:

Ineluctably the meat halls of Texas and the rest of the United States are being tugged towards the model of the Cantonese market, where you can pick out a goose and have its head chopped off before your eyes; or of the Riviera restaurant, where in their aerated tank lobsters await the distinction of being selected for the cauldron; or even of those Hong Kong establishments where a live vervet monkey is brought to your table and trepanned so that you can spoon out its warm brains (good for potency or longevity or sagacity, I forget which). Towards theatre, in other words.

Yet there is something in the Anglo-American way of life that baulks at such a prospect. For centuries its table culture has been moving in the opposite direction, towards greater discretion, greater delicacy regarding the unpleasant off-stage business of the slaughterhouse and kitchen. The climax of the feast in Petronius's *Satyricon*—the arrival of a giant goose built out of pork, with quail in its belly—would call forth no admiring applause today. On the contrary, the dish would be regarded as vulgar and even offensive. The pig—tail and trotters and eyeballs and all, with an apple in his mouth—has been removed from his showplace at the centre of the table, and replaced with euphemistically or metaphorically named *cuts* (butterfly chop, veal scaloppini, tenderloin) whose relation to the bodies they come from is a mystery to most of the family. The art of carving, which used to be part of a gentleman's repertoire, proving that he was a huntsman and knew how to deal with a dead animal, has become a quaint and faintly comical accomplishment rolled out for Christmas or Thanksgiving; the diner's personal knife has evolved into the table knife, a dull, blunt-pointed tool for pushing food around. The United States in its present mood would simply not stomach the metamorphosis of the meat hall into a theatre of execution, disembowelment, flaying, quartering.

> Respect for life, one might call it [...] It is not death that is
> offensive, but killing, and killing only of a certain kind. Killing
> accompanied by 'unnecessary pain'. Somehow the imagination
> knows what the other's pain is like. [...] What the imagination
> cannot encompass is Death.[38]

In 2001 Coetzee received an honorary doctorate from Texas and the
Graduate School's Outstanding Alumnus Award. At the same time, the
John M. Coetzee Fellowship was instituted to support doctoral studies.
On this occasion Coetzee said:

> Both the state of Texas and the University of Texas were welcoming
> and generous to me from the moment I arrived there in 1965. I
> learned a great deal during my time as a student, as well as during
> my two subsequent academic visits. It is a source of much satisfaction
> to me to have kept up the contact with UT to the present day.[39]

What he missed in Texas, however, was the sight of emptiness, an
empty earth and empty sky, as he had experienced in the Karoo. In
the library he read Burchell's account of his travels in South Africa,
and found in the description of the desert plains and the desolate
Karoo a kind of beauty not provided for by the European picturesque
tradition.[40] The green hills of Texas were to him as inimical and alien
as the Surrey landscape. What he also missed was a language of which
he could grasp the variations of shade and tone. It seemed to him
that Texas speech lacked nuance, or if indeed there were nuances, he
could not pick them up.[41] These strictures on American speech return
in *Diary of a Bad Year*:

> Much of the ugliness of the speech one hears in the streets of
> America comes from hostility to song, from repression of the
> impulse to sing, circumscription of the soul. In the education of
> the young in America, instead, the inculcation of mechanical,
> military patterns of speech. Inculcate, from *calx/calcis*, the heel. To
> inculcate: to tread in.
>   One can of course hear stunted and mechanical speech all
> over the world. But pride in the mechanical mode seems to be
> uniquely American. For in America the model of the self as a ghost
> inhabiting a machine goes almost unquestioned at a popular level.

The body as conceived in America, the American body, is a complex machine comprising a vocal module, a sexual module, and several more, even a psychological module. Inside the body-machine the ghostly self checks read-outs and taps keys, giving commands which the body obeys.[42]

In spite of his aversion to the American landscape and speech, Coetzee retained warm feelings for Texas. In 2010, at the age of seventy, he once again visited Austin, and in a speech he was invited to deliver, expressed his appreciation for what he had gained at the University of Texas in knowledge and general development. The library had given him access to books and manuscripts that he could not have found anywhere else, and his lecturers had given him the freedom to go his own way.

IV

When not having to attend or give classes, Coetzee spent his days in Austin's spacious library. Some years later, in the first part of *Dusklands*, he describes Eugene Dawn working in the basement of a library, and it is not far from the bookish Coetzee's own experience:

> There, among the books, I sometimes catch myself in a state not far from happiness, the highest happiness, intellectual happiness. [...] I sit in libraries and see things. I am in an honorable line of bookish men who have sat in libraries and had visions of great clarity.[43]

And Eugene Dawn's assertion that he cannot do creative work in the library and has to reserve the early morning hours at home for it, chimes with the working hours that Coetzee would reserve for his own creative work:

> My creative spasm comes only in the early hours of the morning when the enemy in my body is too sleepy to throw up walls against the forays of my brain. [...] I rise before dawn and tiptoe to my desk. The birds are not yet yammering outside. [...] I say a grace, holding the finished chapters to my exulting breast, then lay them back in their little casket and without looking at yesterday's words begin to write. New words flow. The frozen sea inside me thaws and

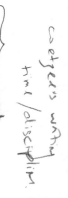

Coetzee's writing/discipline

cracks. I am the warm, industrious genius of the household weaving my protective fabrications.[44]

To his surprise Coetzee discovered in the library the journals of early travellers to the Cape, many of them published by the Van Riebeeck Society, a historical society founded in 1918 to print or reprint rare books and manuscripts dealing with the history of South Africa. Some of these accounts he had read in the British Museum, but he now extended his explorations and came across the travel journals of Lichtenstein, Dapper, Kolbe, Sparrman, Barrow and Burchell. He immersed himself in books on the history of the indigenous peoples of South Africa and South-West Africa, like H. Vedder's chapter on the Herero and C.H. L. Hahn's *The Native Tribes of South West Africa*.[45] He made a study of the ancient languages of South Africa, of which the grammar had been compiled by the missionaries and which, like Khoi, had died out.

In John Barrow's journal he came across an account of farmers in the interior who had succumbed to a life of idleness: the women without any hankering after refinement or culture, the men inert and lacking ambition: 'Very few have those open ingenuous countenances that among the peasantry of many parts of Europe speak their simplicity and innocence.'[46] Many of these farmers, according to Barrow, were exceedingly cruel in their dealings with the indigenous people, especially when pursuing some of the Bushmen who had stolen an ox or a sheep to feed their hunger and their destitute families. On the other hand, he read in Lichtenstein's *Travels in South Africa* how this German, after travelling through the Roggeveld, had been told, on the farm of a Mr Dirk van Wyk of Matjiesfontein, of the extreme cruelty of the indigenous people. What particularly interested Coetzee was a reference to a person who must have been a distant ancestor of his. Lichtenstein's interlocutor had been the witness to a farm murder, an incident which, in retrospect, forms a prelude to one of the incidents in Coetzee's novel *Disgrace*:

> Among the children of this man, who was already advanced in years and singularly corpulent, we were particularly interested by the eldest daughter, from the terrible scenes she had gone through two years before. She had married a person of the name of Coetzé, with whom she was living at the house of his father not far from hence. Their domestic happiness was already increased by the prospect

of her becoming a mother, and the time of her confinement was approaching, when suddenly, in a dark night, the slaves and Hottentots belonging to the establishment (there being, among the latter, many of the Bosjesmans) rose upon the family, and after inhumanly murdering her husband, her father and mother-in-law, and a sister of her husband's, before her face, plundered the estate of everything worth carrying away. She herself was, wonderful to relate, spared. It could only be supposed that even these barbarians were moved with something like compassion on seeing her situation. She was, however, dragged away, gagged, till after several days travelling, they arrived at a place of concealment, whither also they carried all their plunder in cattle, in goods, or in money.[47]

The 1799 edition of *The Journal of Hendrik Jacob Wikar*[48] includes the short account of a journey undertaken by Jacobus Coetzé in 1760 along the West Coast and through Namaqualand to the Orange River and beyond, an account that would form the basis of the second part of *Dusklands*, Coetzee's first novel, which he was shortly to commence.

But Coetzee was not exclusively immersed in South African history and the annals of the early travellers. While he was working away in the library, the US was involved in a military offensive in Vietnam, with constant air strikes on the capital, Hanoi, which he and Philippa witnessed every night on television. In an interview with Peter Temple published in *The Star* in 1974, shortly after the publication of *Dusklands*, Coetzee says:

I think particularly of the effect that televised air strikes had on the small screen. The violence erupted at you, the massiveness of thousands of tons of high explosives dropped. The war was an avenue through which a lot of pent-up aggression, sadism, let itself out, not only on battlefields but in people's living-rooms.[49]

In his collection *Oorblyfsels* [*Remains*], his compatriot Breyten Breytenbach, who had married a Vietnamese woman, was to write the poem 'Bid vir Hanoi' ['Pray for Hanoi'], which, along with other allegedly political poems, could initially not be published in South Africa:

pray for them choking in bitter smoke
for them hiding in dark holes

from the singing shiny angels
  of death
(angels bellyful with bitterness and fire bombs)
(70 000 tons in the spring of March 1967)
confess the children that like bloody beefsteaks blemish the mud
[...]
you who have no gods
but also
like the rest of us
must puking with terror bend the knee
before the Great Rot
the murder machines
  of the New World Democracy
pray for Hanoi
that it may just end soon.[50]

In the first part of *Dusklands* Coetzee, too, would draw on this war, because his own involvement as a computer programmer—an involvement of which he had initially been unaware—with the nuclear weapons developed at Aldermaston had made him see the US military offensive in an intensely ethical light. The two stories in *Dusklands*, the one set against the background of the Vietnam war and the other in the Africa of his ancestor Jacobus Coetsé, were to form for him a parallel with moral degeneration in colonial situations through the ages.

[In *The Daily Texan* Coetzee wrote a satirical comment on the Vietnam war in the form of a letter to the newspaper, a piece so subtle that his anti-war position was misunderstood by some readers. His contemporary Thomas Cable found the letter so outstanding that later, when he was a professor at Texas, he gave it to his first-year students for comparison with Jonathan Swift's eighteenth-century masterpiece, *A Modest Proposal*, professing to advance a solution to the problem of beggars in Ireland. Later he joked that he had been the first person to introduce Coetzee material into his courses.[51] Coetzee's article, under the heading 'Misconception', reads as follows:

This letter is intended as something of a reply to John Morby, who calls the war in Vietnam a 'blunder' and a 'crime' (*Daily Texan*, Oct. 20). Conclusions like these seem to me ingenuous, like the result of a misconception of the war. I hope to show that, both in terms of world strategy and in the more limited terms of strategy within Vietnam, US policy has been the work of intelligent men.

First, in terms of world strategy, it is already observable that the firm line taken in Vietnam has shown national liberation movements all over the world that the Soviet Union lacks the will and China the power to apply significant counterpressure outside the spheres of influence accorded them. With the defeat of the NLF[52] in Vietnam, the US can thus confidently expect the consolidation of friendly governments in Asia, Latin America and Africa, the quiet elimination of national liberation movements there (as has already happened in Indonesia), and the eclipse of China as a would-be world power. This is what Walt Rostow means when he speaks of Vietnam as a scene of the last important war.

In US strategy within Vietnam, we again see the signs of clear and systematic thinking. The NLFSV entered 1965 with a number of advantages: 1) it had the élan of a revolutionary movement believing itself to be moving with the tide of history; 2) it had developed a strategy which had already succeeded against a colonial army; 3) it possessed the only political organization, at all levels, in the South; 4) it has the sympathy of the people; 5) it could bank on the Occidental conviction that lives of white men are too precious to trade, one for one, for the lives of yellow men.

The US started, in the simplest terms, with the advantage of a technology, and US strategy has been to demonstrate: 1) that 'the tide of history' can always be rolled back if one has power enough; 2) that an army with unlimited air support can never be beaten by an army with none; 3) that, no matter how deeply rooted a political organization is, it can be destroyed through systematic interrogation, by trained men using modern and traditional methods, of those suspected of political interests; 4) that popular support can always be broken down if subjected to stern enough reprisals; 5) that the white man can always arrange matters so that he sells his life for the lives of 10 yellow men.

It is in this context that those weapons to whose use Mr Morby so vehemently objects—napalm, fragmentation bombs, tumbling bullets—should be seen. Against an enemy whose resources are human and not material, surely these are precisely the weapons to use. No Vietnamese whose village has been subject to a reprisal raid and who has seen people die of napalm burns can have any doubt that the NLF is helpless to give him the protection it promises. The Vietnamese who has seen a modern technology in action must become aware of the true direction of 'the tide of history'. And it is Vietnamese such as this one who are more likely to defect to the Saigon government, which offers them above all peace and a chance to return to the kind of life their fathers have lived for the last 1000 years.

Why this carefully calculated strategy should be thought a 'blunder' eludes me. History may well show the presidency of Lyndon B. Johnson as marking the beginning of the consolidation and perhaps even expansion of US world interests following the setbacks of the years following World War II. As for 'crimes' in Vietnam, doesn't an arrow in the stomach kill just as dead as a face full of napalm?[53]

While Coetzee was doing research in the library during the day, Philippa, who had not been able to find a teaching job, had a half-day job as a secretary in the Department of Classical Languages, one of the best departments at Austin, offering a variety of courses. One of these was Modern Greek, for which Philippa enrolled, hoping to find a niche of her own. She did manage to translate Ilias Venezis's thirteen tales, which appeared under the title *Aigaio*, but only one tale, 'The Seagulls', was published after her return to South Africa in *Contrast*.[54] It would seem that she admired her husband's application and catholic receptivity to influences, but ultimately she was never really part of the life he was creating for himself, and she felt at a loose end. His stinginess at various levels, he admits openly in *Doubling the Point*, could have played a part in the difficult relationship: *'It's an unattractive part of my makeup that has exasperated people who have to share their lives with me.'*[55] The result was that Philippa could not give Coetzee emotional security in the marriage, nor he to her.

In April 1968 Philippa flew back to South Africa with their son, Nicolas, who was born on 9 June 1966, to show him to her parents in Johannesburg and Coetzee's in Cape Town. There was some talk of a divorce, but Philippa decided to carry on with the marriage. Philippa and Nicolas returned on 10 August and joined Coetzee, who had moved to Buffalo. When Nicolas was a bit older and became obsessed with comic books, Coetzee shared his enthusiasm, and as an adjunct to his reading of nineteenth-century American novels, made a study of the

Captain America stories, which were then all the rage among children.[56]

During his years in the US Coetzee kept abreast of events in his native land. With all the emergency regulations that the government was instituting, South Africa was entering its darkest period. Internal resistance to apartheid had been forced underground by the banning of black political organisations. In Cape Town a Greek parliamentary messenger murdered the prime minister, Hendrik Frensch Verwoerd, on 6 September 1966, while the House of Assembly was preparing for the afternoon session. The afternoon paper *The Austin Statesman* reported it on the front page on the same day:

> Prime Minister Hendrik F. Verwoerd died today at the hands of a white assassin.
>
> The assailant, in the uniform of a parliamentary messenger, stabbed Verwoerd as he sat in Parliament. He plunged a knife into the symbol of South Africa's white supremacy rule, then stabbed him twice more as he slumped on his desk with blood gushing from the wounds. A pool of blood formed on the green carpet. [...] The South African Press association said it understood the assassin was a white man of Greek descent. The South African radio gave his name as Dmitri Tsafendas.

Coetzee experienced an act of violence in Austin itself. On 31 July 1966 Charles Joseph Whitman, 25, an architecture student at the University of Texas, bought binoculars and a knife from Davis Hardware and murdered his wife and mother at their respective houses. The next day, 1 August 1966, he hired a trolley and returned to Davis Hardware, where he bought an M1 carbine for 'boar hunting'. At another store he bought a shotgun. Apart from these two weapons, he took three pistols and other equipment with him on the trolley and entered the central administration building shortly after 11.30am. He took the lift to the 27th floor, one floor below the clock face. When the receptionist asked him for his student card, he knocked her out with a rifle butt, so violently that she later died of her wounds in hospital. Whitman then went to the upper deck of the campanile, a prime position for a sniper, from where he killed ten people and wounded 31 others in a frenzy of shooting, not only at people on campus, but also at people passing by in the streets and at staff through the windows of campus buildings. Apart from the receptionist, two other people died in the tower block, visitors who had come to admire the view. The total number of dead and injured was 45.

Whitman was brought down at 1.22pm by two policemen. At the autopsy it was found that he had a malignant brain tumour, which might have caused his irrational behaviour.[57] He would probably not have lived long.

The events in Austin made headlines nationally and internationally. Coetzee, who was an assistant, was in the office in Parlin Hall that he shared with two other members of staff. It was summer, the university was in recess, and there was not much activity on campus. He heard the sounds of shooting, but did not know what was happening. The sounds persisted, and he put his head out of the window, but could not see anything, and carried on with his work. Suddenly a security guard appeared at the door, saying, 'Get under your desks, there's someone shooting through the windows.' After a while everybody in that part of the building was led to the basement, where there were no windows, and where they had to remain until everything was over. Coetzee was to discover later that somebody had been shot who had, like him, leant out of a window.

For Coetzee it was a shocking experience. Nowadays somebody who has lived through something like that would receive counselling, but at the time counselling was unknown.[58] On 2 August 1966 Coetzee wrote to the South African writer Jack Cope, who had visited Austin in May that year on a Carnegie scholarship, saying that nobody Cope had met in Austin had been killed in the carnage,

> though like a fool I spent five minutes gawping through my office window, not knowing where the shots were coming from.
> The town seems to be in a state of terrified shock. It is 11 a.m., but no one is walking on the South Mall, where most of the dead lay yesterday. Perhaps they are learning to fear their neighbour.[59]

Coetzee left Texas in 1968. In 'Remembering Texas' he says that it was never clear to him why the University of Texas and the American taxpayer had spent so much for him to indulge his idle whims. He was there, however, as a part of the Fulbright exchange scheme, a programme that, in retrospect, was far-sighted and did not expect immediate reactions or economically significant returns from the scholarship students. He enjoyed the academic freedom that Austin gave him:

No one had tried to teach me, for which I was grateful. What I had learned in the course of three years was not negligible, though picked up, for the most part, by accident. I had had the run of a great library, where I had stumbled on books whose existence I might otherwise never have guessed.[60]

CHAPTER 7

BUFFALO, NEW YORK STATE, 1968–1971

I

While working on his doctoral dissertation in the second half of 1967 and the first months of 1968, Coetzee remained attentive to world events. In two bloody months in early 1968, both Robert Kennedy, brother of President John F. Kennedy and potential presidential candidate, and the black activist Martin Luther King were assassinated. In Eastern Europe during the 'Prague Spring' of 1968, Alexander Dubček tried in vain to reform the parliamentary democracy and shake off Russian domination through détente with the West. In the US, attempts at social reform in the late 1960s led to race riots in New York and Detroit, and frustration at the slow pace of change gave vent in the actions of the radical Black Power movement. In 1969, the year the Americans succeeded in a manned moon landing, the Nobel Prize for Literature, often awarded to candidates oppressed by communist or other dictatorial regimes, was awarded to Samuel Beckett, the writer much admired by Coetzee.

The issue that rankled most with Coetzee, through daily subjection to images on the TV screen, was the US involvement in Vietnam. He had already in London become aware of the horrors of the war. 'In a photograph on the front page of *The Guardian*,' he writes in *Youth*,

> a Vietnamese soldier in American-style uniform stares helplessly into a sea of flames. 'SUICIDE BOMBERS WREAK HAVOC IN S. VIETNAM,' reads the headline. A band of Viet-Cong sappers have cut their way through the barbed wire around the American base at Pleiku, blown up twenty-four aircraft, and set fire to the fuel storage tanks. They have given up their lives in the action.[1]

In 1966 the vast majority of American citizens still believed that their country's military struggle against the communist northern part of

Vietnam was justified, and that resistance to it was misguided and unpatriotic.[2] Early in 1967, however, opinion polls showed that 57 per cent of Americans were opposed to President Lyndon B. Johnson's policies. Johnson was steadily caught between opposing demands: those who wanted the war to be escalated and pursued to total victory, and those insisting on the immediate cessation of all US involvement.[3] Resistance on various campuses was fierce, giving rise to student protests and demonstrations, but Johnson was determined to pursue the war. In 1965 there had been only about 25 000 troops in Vietnam, but that number soared to 486 000 in 1967. Johnson dropped his secretary of defence, Robert McNamara, who disagreed with him on the continuation of the war. McNamara needed only twenty-five well-chosen words to clarify his point of view: 'The United States must be careful not to interpret events occurring in a different land in terms of its own history, politics, culture, and morals.'[4] On 30 January 1968 the Northern forces invaded Da Nang, the second largest city in South Vietnam, and seven other bigger cities, an offensive turning the tide in favour of the communists. The American public, up to that point confident that the US was winning the war, was flabbergasted at the images on television. 'What the hell is going on? I thought we were winning the war,'[5] was the standard reaction of many people. Resistance to the war escalated, and protest actions by students increased.

Coetzee was disgusted by the sophistical justification for the continuation of the war formulated by Herman Kahn, a physicist who had earlier been involved in planning nuclear war and, as a founding member of the Hudson Institute, had done research into government policy and served as an advisor to the Department of Defence. In the book *Can We Win in Vietnam?*, which he published with a few colleagues, Kahn articulated and defended inhumane solutions to the war. As a motto to the first part of *Dusklands* Coetzee would a few years later choose an extract from *Can We Win in Vietnam?*:

> Obviously it is difficult not to sympathize with those European and American audiences who, when shown films of fighter-bomber pilots visibly exhilarated by successful napalm bombing runs on Viet-Cong targets, react with horror and disgust. Yet, it is unreasonable to expect the US Government to obtain pilots who are so appalled by the damage they may be doing that they cannot carry out their missions or become excessively depressed or guilt-ridden.[6]

The rest of the paragraph from which this extract is taken brings out the full force of Kahn's words and mindset:

> We all live at various levels of consciousness and repression, and it seems *reasonable and moral* for a pilot to concentrate on his mission, undertaken within traditional or widely recognized laws and customs of war, *and not dwell morbidly on the resulting human suffering.*[7]

In the two paragraphs preceding this quotation, Kahn expatiates on the so-called high standards of conduct that the US upholds, for both political and moral reasons, in its military intervention, though he concedes that his colleagues differ from him on this:

> In many cases, of course, political and moral requirements tend to overlap, though they may require and receive different emphasis; but in some cases, particularly on the question of acceptable weapons and legitimate targets, these issues are not so clear-cut. But except for nuclear, lethal biological, and lethal chemical weapons, all of us feel that questions of morality are more bound up with restricting targets than with using particular weapons. The situation is more complex when it comes to the use of incapacitating chemical or biological agents, for example. Here, we are all interested in drawing lines to prevent the introduction of weapons that are likely to get out of control. *Still, there seems to be little reason to prevent the military from using chemicals that civilian police use for riot control, when such means are so effective in dealing with otherwise extremely awkward problems.* [...] We might be quite concerned about the introduction of tranquilizers, LSD, or similar chemicals to incapacitate the enemy, and we are ambivalent toward such current techniques as large-scale chemical defoliation of forests or bacteriological or chemical warfare against food crops. *There are, of course, powerful arguments for such tactics.*[8]

It is against this background of internal conflict in the US that Coetzee, now far advanced with his dissertation, decided late in 1967 to apply for a better-paying position at an American university. There were no vacancies at the University of Texas, but he was probably advised by one of his lecturers of an opening in Buffalo, a harbour town in New York State, situated on Lake Erie, about 24 miles south of the Niagara Falls and 400 miles northwest of New York City. With about 533 000 inhabitants, it was a bigger city than Austin, and had been the shipping centre of the Great Lakes, even though the harbour was frozen solid for four months of the year. Since the 1920s, however, there had been severe economic decline in this once flourishing harbour town, with considerable urban decay. In 1968 Buffalo was still in a derelict condition with widespread unemployment, which was particularly hard on the strong Polish Roman Catholic contingent in the city.[9]

The administration of New York State was sympathetic to Buffalo's plight, and wanted to restore the city to its former glory as one of the leading commercial and industrial centres of the US. One measure calculated to revive the city economically was the establishment of a large new college campus. The University of Buffalo (UB) had been established in 1846 as a private medical school, to which a faculty of law was adjoined in 1891. In 1915 this was expanded to further faculties, including a faculty of arts. UB had from its inception a significant tradition of academic freedom. The city had always had a strong Roman Catholic presence, about 50 per cent of the population, and the university had the same proportion of Catholic students. The university's emphasis on academic freedom clashed so strongly with the religious beliefs of some of its students that priests and nuns advised the parents of high school children rather to enrol their children in one of the smaller Catholic institutions in the area.[10] This did not, however, affect the conduct of the University of Buffalo.

With the intervention of the state in 1962, the University of Buffalo, on the brink of bankruptcy, was taken over and developed as the flagship of the college system of 59 campuses known as the State University of New York (SUNY). In its edition of 12 January 1968, *Time Magazine* described SUNY as 'the fastest growing, best-financed and most ambitious system of public higher education in the land'. As far as the development of Buffalo was concerned, it was the aim of the president, Martin Meyerson, 'to shake up the traditional academic structure' and to create 'a public model for higher education'. 'To that end,' according to *Time*, Meyerson had 'divided the university into eight major interdisciplinary faculties.' The university soon attracted bright young minds—in 1968 more than 85 per cent of the freshmen had been top of their class in their high schools. The number of students that year was 21 735.[11]

With the incorporation of UB into the SUNY system, the student-body demographic changed significantly, partly because a growing number of Jewish students from New York city came to Buffalo, which brought something of the excitement and creative dynamic of Jewish culture. Unfortunately, their presence in Buffalo sparked off a strong anti-Semitic reaction in the established community, particularly among the Polish Catholic working class, whose children had hitherto had easy access to UB, but now had to compete for places with the Jewish students. Their sons and daughters could also no longer count on finding posts at UB or in the city of Buffalo.

This was the situation in Buffalo when Coetzee became interested in a position there. Apart from the countrywide division on the question of whether the US should quit Vietnam, there were now cities — of which Buffalo was only one — where this split manifested itself in different ways. Whereas the Jews in Buffalo, for instance, were identified with anti-war protests, many Polish Catholics had sons serving in the army and were in favour of the war. The beginning of 1968 saw the start of the worst phase of the war because, apart from the violence in Vietnam, there was a 'war' going on in the US itself, a low-grade civil conflict. The escalation of anti-Semitism was but one manifestation of the polarisation of those years. Relations between the white majority and the black minority in Buffalo were bad, as Coetzee had also experienced in Austin, a city known as a hotbed of liberalism in an exceptionally conservative state, supportive of Lyndon Johnson and his conduct of the war. In an interview, Coetzee elaborated on the situation in which he found himself in the US in 1968:

> There was a certain paranoia in the air, particularly if you felt yourself easily to be identified as an intellectual, a Left-winger, a cosmopolitan, and all these things which were anathema to ordinary people of Texas and to ordinary people in the city of Buffalo.[12]

In applying to Buffalo, Coetzee knew he was venturing into a hornets' nest, but his advance research also reassured him that, if his application were successful, he would find himself in a highly rated English department, working alongside extremely stimulating colleagues. He also knew that Buffalo's cherishing of academic freedom meant he would suffer no interference with his lecturing or his relations with students. From his experience at UCT he knew how an authoritarian government could affect a university, and how hard it could be to struggle for academic freedom under such circumstances. As long ago as 1922, Samuel Paul Capen, chancellor of the then still private University of Buffalo, had issued a declaration on academic freedom with which Coetzee was fully in accord:

> Acceptance by an institution of the principle of academic freedom implies that teachers in that institution are free to investigate any subject no matter how much it may be hedged about by taboos; that they are free to make known the results of their investigation, and their reflection by word of mouth or in writing, before their classes or elsewhere; that they are free to differ with their colleagues and to present the ground of their difference in their classes or elsewhere; that they are free as citizens to take part in any public controversy outside the institution; that no repressive measure, direct or indirect, will be applied to them no matter how unpopular they may become through opposing powerful interests or jostling established prejudices, and no matter how mistaken they may appear to be in the eyes of members and friends of the institution; that their continuance in office will be in all instances governed by the prevailing rules of tenure and that their academic advancement will be dependent on their scientific competence and will be in no ways be affected by the popularity or unpopularity of their opinions or utterances.[13]

Coetzee had to mention in his application that the Fulbright scholarship enabling him to study in Austin expressly stipulated that after completion of his studies he had to return to his country of origin, there to plough back what he had learnt in the US. Moreover, at the time of his application he had not yet completed his dissertation, though he could confidently predict its satisfactory conclusion. He received a letter, dated 12 January 1968, from Professor Norman N. Holland, Chair of the Department of English, informing him that, with the concurrence of the provost, he could make him an offer 'of a one-year appointment as a Visiting Assistant Professor at a salary of $9 800. We understand the complexities of your citizenship situation which necessitate the visiting appointment.' One gathers that Holland and his colleagues, presumably on the strength of Coetzee's study record and his dissertation-in-the-making at Austin, were prepared to appoint him to a temporary post in the hope that the question of his permanent residence would be readily solved. Holland continues:

It is our understanding that this appointment would be contingent upon your completing the requirements for the Ph.D. by September 1. Should they be uncompleted, the appointment would shift to a one-year lectureship, but the salary and teaching responsibilities would be unchanged.

Normally, Holland writes, such an appointment would be made for three years, but in the light of Coetzee's complicated citizenship circumstances, it was being made for one year only, with the possibility of an extension. He would be expected to teach nine hours a week in three courses, of which one was an advanced course of his own design. Holland concludes:

I think you would find Buffalo, as I have, a pleasant place to live, with many opportunities for professional flexibility and growth. Our department includes a variety of different kinds of outstanding people, ranging from creative writers like Robert Creeley and Jack Barth to scholars and critics like C.L. Barber and Joe Riddel, with some AC/DC types[14] like Leslie Fiedler and Albert Cook. There is room here for all sorts of people to develop themselves to the fullest. I hope you will decide to join us.

Coetzee was pleased to have secured this appointment. On 12 January he accepted the appointment telephonically and confirmed it by letter to Holland on the same day: 'I shall be most happy to accept the appointment you outlined in your letter of January 2.'

Coetzee completed his dissertation before leaving Austin, but was awarded the degree only at the graduation ceremony on 12 January 1969. Although he had not made the deadline of September 1968, UB was amenable, and appointed him as an assistant professor nevertheless. Coetzee informed Vic Doyno, one of his new colleagues whom he addressed, in a letter of 27 May 1968, by his first name, that Professor Connolly had arranged accommodation for him in a dormitory for the first days or weeks after his arrival:

I should like to find an apartment as soon as possible, certainly before my wife and child join me about August 10. I have no idea how difficult it is to find housing in Buffalo, but ideally I should like an unfurnished two-bedroom apartment (or, if very cheap, house) within a mile of the campus. I have *no* idea of prices. I assume they are considerably higher than Austin which would be $65—$90. [...] I will pay anything reasonable. Our primary drawback as tenants is that we have a rather wild two-year-old. He is the reason why I should prefer an unfurnished place which I can fill with junk and allow him to demolish.

Coetzee officially accepted the appointment in Buffalo on 15 July 1968. He and Philippa settled with Nicolas in a house at 24 Parker Avenue, and later moved to 127 West Oakwood Plaza. On 10 November their second child was born, a daughter named Gisela Gabrièle. Both children were thus US citizens by birth. In 1971, when Philippa returned to South Africa with the children, Coetzee lived on his own at 334 Dewey Avenue, apartment #5.

Coetzee got to know his new colleagues very soon after his arrival in Buffalo. Norman N. Holland was later succeeded as chairman by Marcus Klein. Among the lecturers were creative writers such as John Barth and Howard Wolf, with whom Coetzee would maintain a long friendship and extensive correspondence. It is evident from more than one of his later interviews that he was very happy in Buffalo and in the Department of English. He tells Shauna Westcott in 1981:[15]

> I had three very interesting years lecturing at the State University of New York at Buffalo. I was teaching in the Department of English, which at the time (the late 60s) had the reputation of being one of the most interesting (and way-out) departments in the country. I came in contact with some remarkable people, both teachers and students who taught me a great deal, opened new vistas for me, particularly in contemporary philosophy and criticism. I think everyone who had been connected with that department at that time afterwards recognized how extraordinarily lucky he/she had been.

II

Shortly after accepting the position at Buffalo, Coetzee was asked to indicate which courses he would like to teach. On 19 January 1968, while still in Austin, he informed Vic Doyno, one of his future colleagues, of his preferences. For the second-year (sophomore) courses, he says he would like to teach, in order of preference, critical approaches; a survey of British literature; a survey of American literature; and Great Books. As for the advanced courses, he has toyed with the idea of presenting courses on the approach to the content and structure of poems and prose pieces that have been the subject of eminent past studies. Those studies that he would want to include in his discussions would then also serve as models of literary criticism. He has in mind examples from twentieth-century literature, and the course would have a linguistic slant. Apart from that, he is considering courses in approaches to style and structure in prose fiction; experimental British and American fiction with excursions into other literatures with the aid of translations; Commonwealth literature in English, concentrating on Australia and Africa, which could be an interesting addition to the Buffalo repertory; and a course on prominent figures, in particular Pound and Beckett.

It is clear from the rest of this letter that he already wanted to clear time for his own research:

A schedule which leaves a couple of days empty would be pleasant, but I shan't complain if it can't be arranged. I'm not sure whether you hold classes on Saturdays, and, if you don't, whether this means that classes on Tuesdays and Thursdays are ninety minutes long. One of the things I don't particularly like doing is trying to interest exhausted students for ninety minutes in the late afternoon. Two of the things I don't mind doing are teaching on Saturdays and teaching in the evenings (the students don't have to run off immediately after class). If it positively comes to a choice between one-hour classes MFW and ninety-minute classes TT,[16] I choose the former.

It would be helpful to me to know whether your library has some kind of reserve desk such that an instructor can place books and articles on reserve for short (one-hour, two-hour, three-hour) loan. And I'd be very grateful if you could, at your convenience, send me reading lists for the current Sophomore sequences, so that I can get an idea of the material they cover.

On 22 March 1968 Vic Doyno informed him that his assignment for the coming year would be two sections of the course on important British authors. The first semester was usually devoted to anything from *Beowulf* and Chaucer to Pope and Johnson, to introduce students to a variety of critical approaches. The other course was a section from what was called 'Problems in Literature, Rhetoric and the Intellectual Tradition.' This was a course designed to accommodate everybody's hobby-horse.

In the almost three years that Coetzee taught at UB, he offered courses on a wide variety of literary directions and figures. He taught the nineteenth-century American novel, as well as courses in stylistics, translation and linguistics, with reference to Empson, Jespersen and Wimsatt & Beardsley. For a study of metaphor, he referred his students to works by Cassirer, Chomsky, Jakobson and Riffaterre. For a translation workshop, students had to submit one or more translations, preferably in verse, from Latin, French, German, Dutch, Russian or Spanish. In an introduction to this course he writes: 'I do not recommend the course for students who have done no original writing. Note, too, that my Russian and Spanish are weak.' In a course on Great Writers he included, among others, works like *Pilgrim's Progress*, *Gulliver's Travels* and *Robinson Crusoe*. His thoughts on some of these books were to feature later in his critical essays, while *Robinson Crusoe* would serve as an intertext for his 1986 novel, *Foe*. That Coetzee was already prepared to deviate from the well-trodden ways is evident from the originality of the assignment set for students in their study of *Robinson Crusoe*:

Write a five-page fragment of an imaginary longer work entitled *Robinson Crusoe in Houyhnhnm Land*, a work which opens with Crusoe swimming ashore from yet another wreck and finding himself in the land which Swift describes in Part IV of *Gulliver's Travels* (a book which Crusoe, born in the 1620s, has of course not read).

It would do you no end of good to make a conscious attempt to imitate the manner of either Defoe or Swift, depending on your point of view, in the fragment.

Without trying to force you into a stylistic straitjacket, let me remind you that it is not for nothing that the word 'realism' is so often associated with Defoe and the word 'irony' so often with Swift.

The fragment can describe any part of Crusoe's experience in Houyhnhnm Land. You may, if you wish, add notes to describe what happens to him before and/or after the incidents you describe.

Coetzee was the only member of the UB English Department from Africa. For that reason he was invited to present a course on African literature.

He found this somewhat ironic. He had left South Africa to become part of a wider world and to divest himself of his colonial past, only now to discover, as he put it in an interview with David Attwell, that his novelty value, such as it was, lay exactly in his African origins.[17] He had by then read the well-known English South African authors, but regarded none of them as of world class. He now reread these authors and immersed himself in the rest of African literature available in the US. He found the drama, especially that from West Africa, more engaging than the poetry and fiction, but nothing really enthralled him. But if he were to remain in the US, he argued, he would willy-nilly have to become an Africanist, a specialist in a peripheral area that he could not bring himself to be enthusiastic about.[18]

He taught, among others, the novels of Alex La Guma, an author who had been charged with treason early in his career, had spent years in custody and under house arrest, and had left South Africa for good in 1966. The lectures on La Guma provided the material for one of Coetzee's first published essays.[19] Coetzee felt a tension between conveying to his students what was unique about South African literature and at the same time measuring that literature by European standards.[20] After all, he had early in his life decided, albeit unconsciously, on hearing Bach's *Wohltemperierte Klavier* in his backyard in Rondebosch, that, if he were ever capable of creative work, he would join the classical European tradition, not remain confined to a small colonial enclave. He thus had to justify the profession of Africanist to his own allegiance to an older literacy tradition. He probably wrote specifically about Alex La Guma because La Guma's world—unlike that of most black South African writers—was the Cape.[21] Coetzee's roots, after all, lay in that strip of land stretching from Voëlfontein in the arid Karoo to Cape Town by the sea. The rest of South Africa was for him largely unknown territory. In *Summertime*, his partly fictional autobiographical novel of 2009, Sophie, the lecturer in French at UCT, gives the fictional biographer, who has come to interview her on the deceased writer J.M. Coetzee, some information that is suprisingly congruent with the real Coetzee's statements in *Doubling the Point*, allowing for the subtle relation of fiction to reality in this book:

> Like many whites, he regarded the Cape, the western Cape and perhaps the northern Cape along with it, as standing apart from the rest of South Africa. The Cape was a country of its own, with its

own geography, its own history, its own languages and culture. In this mythical Cape the Coloured people were rooted, and to a lesser extent the Afrikaners too, but Africans were aliens, latecomers, as were the English.[22]

Coetzee's class notes[23] from his years in Buffalo show that he prefaced his lectures on African literature—preferably, to judge by the list, works in English—with a synopsis of the themes to be discussed and an exposition of the differences between African and American social systems. He expected his students to read extensively on the history of South Africa, and made available to them a list of historical studies. Each student had to hand in a dissertation on a specialised topic stemming from the semester's reading. Among the South African writers he recommended—apart from Alex La Guma—were Alan Paton, Lewis Nkosi, Doris Lessing and Nadine Gordimer. On the setwork list, however, are also the names of Guy Butler, Jack Cope, Dan Jacobson, Sol Plaatje, William Plomer, Richard Rive, Olive Schreiner, Pauline Smith and Laurens van der Post. He also recommended some of Uys Krige's works in English. As far as Afrikaans literature is concerned, he included the translations by A.P. Grové and C.J.D. Harvey in *Afrikaans Poems with English Translations*, and those novels of André Brink, Etienne Leroux and F.A. Venter that had been translated into English.

Some of the subjects discussed or set as assignments indicate the direction in which Coetzee was moving in his teaching: 'The social function of traditional Zulu poetry; Some speculations on the popularity of biography among South African writers; Escapism and/or engagement in post-war Afrikaans poetry; Intellectuals and mass movements in West African literature; The treatment of the theme of revolution in Portuguese-African poetry; The treatment of the theme of the missionary in African writers in English/French; The social background to Olive Schreiner's *Story of an African Farm*; The social structure of Pauline Smith's world; Paternal attitudes in Laurens van der Post (Bushmen, Russians); Attitudes towards social reality in Etienne Leroux; South African society in the fiction of Jack Cope; Literary censorship in South Africa.' Many of these themes were to surface later as subjects in Coetzee's own essays. In an explanatory introduction to a consideration of the absence of revolutionary literature in South Africa, which he handed out to participants in a series of seminars, he writes:

Why, even when we take into account the massive intellectual repression of the government (tribalization of education, censorship, etc., etc.), has no revolutionary literature (i.e., revolutionary art in the medium of language) appeared in South Africa? Why has South African writing become so repetitive that Lewis Nkosi has called for a moratorium on writing until something is done about the political situation? [...]

Two of the more obvious answers are that reading books is a middle-class occupation and that the suppression of the printing and/or circulation of a work is decisive. Further answers, more interesting because they require more explanation, are the lack of political curiosity among the established writers (*as writers* at least) and the predominance of the inherently anti-revolutionary mode of tragedy.

This leaves untouched the vast questions of how, when, and to what ends a *revolutionary* literature.

As for the nature of the literature that may arise after the death of the present system, I would guess that it might look for its roots in the loose forms of the autobiography and the realistic sketch.

After completing a course on Samuel Beckett in Spring 1970, he asked the sixteen participants to comment on the lectures. The course was offered at a time when disruption at the university, and protests and marches against the war in Vietnam, were rife — to such an extent that the meetings could not always take place on campus, and Coetzee had to have some of the meetings at his home. From the feedback he received, it is evident that the students were not only happy with the course, but found him an excellent teacher. One of the students writes:

> I believe that the Beckett course was one of the most interesting courses I have taken in our dept. at SUNAB. I think that literature should be studied as an art form, as we did, instead of studying it as a didactic, moralistic, or metaphysical discipline. In this seminar, I think that I learned more than I have from any other source about the relationship which exists between the artist, the art, and the audience, plus the fact that I gained a new perspective on literature which I feel carried over into my other readings. I attribute the qualities of this course not only to the professor, but to general class discussion, [...] and largely to Beckett himself.

Apart from teaching, Coetzee was from an early stage involved in informal interdisciplinary conferences and symposia organised by the Department of English. In October 1969, for instance, he contributed to a session called 'Aesthetic problems in language theory and the theory of signs', and in April 1970 he delivered two papers, 'The vacuum in revolutionary literature in South Africa' and 'Language study in literature'. He also, by invitation from the department chair, acted as the director of the English component of the 'Training of Teacher Trainers' (TTT) programme. He actively promoted, with some of his Buffalo colleagues, the appointment of the Nigerian writer Wole Soyinka, who was to receive the Nobel Prize for Literature in 1986. In a letter to Martin Meyerson, the president of SUNY at Buffalo, Coetzee writes:

> [I]t is my considered opinion that [Soyinka] is one of the two most distinguished African writers in English. His particular achievement has been to enrich world drama by introducing into it some of the conventions of the complex and vital Yoruba drama. I believe that Soyinka would be a considerable asset to the University, and in particular to the Departments of English and Drama, and the Program in African Studies.

At this time, too, Coetzee published his first critical essays. Apart from the essay on La Guma, he published articles on Samuel Beckett based on his doctoral dissertation. His continuing interest in Dutch literature appears from his translation of *Ballade van de Gasfitter*, a cycle of fourteen sonnets by Gerrit Achterberg, which was published in the Fall 1970 issue of the journal *Anonym*. Much later he would include it, drastically revised, in his collection of translations from Dutch poetry, *Landscape with Rowers*,[24] and in *Doubling the Point* he included an essay on this cycle dating from 1977, which originally appeared in volume 92 of *PMLA* (Publications of the Modern Language Association), the first essay since 1941 on Dutch literature in this eminent journal. In the introduction to *Landscape with Rowers* he cites a characteristic of Achterberg's poetry:

> His oeuvre is dominated by a single, highly personal myth: the search for the beloved who has departed and left him behind, a search that takes him on forays into the land of the dead. In typically high-modernist fashion, Achterberg makes stern demands on his

readers: the Orphic myth works itself into 'Ballad of the Gasfitter'
in ways that may seem cryptic.[25]

In his study of 'Ballad of the Gasfitter', Coetzee does not refer at all to
this central theme that in the past has tempted critics to biographical
interpolation, but relates the sonnet cycle and the quest of the *I* for a
defunct *Thou* to the existential incompleteness that, as Martin Buber
shows in his *I and Thou*, occurs when the *I* loses its fundamental
relation to the *Thou*.[26] Coetzee then sees in this 'poetics of failure'
a similarity to the metamorphosis of the nineteenth-century realist
novel into the 'metafictional commentary on the fictionality of self'
in Nabokov and Barth, which reaches its full potential in Beckett's *The
Unnamable*.[27]

Regarding translation, Coetzee makes the provocative comment
that reading a text is in essence a translation, just as all translation is in
the last instance literary criticism.[28] It is, however, in the nature of the
literary work to confront the translator with problems 'for which the
perfect solution is impossible and for which partial solutions constitute
critical acts'.[29] Coetzee finds an example of this in his translation of the
fourth sonnet in the cycle. The first quatrain reads:

> Eindelijk is het kleine lek gedicht.
> Ik zoek de spullen langzaam bij elkaar.
> Mijn benen zijn als buizen lood zo zwaar.
> Zweetdruppels lopen over mijn gezicht.[30]

Coetzee translates this as follows:

> At last the minor leak is traced and sealed.
> Slowly I collect and pack my tools.
> My legs have grown as heavy as lead tubes.
> Sweat is trickling down my face in beads.[31]

Coetzee writes about the problem of translating the word *gedicht* in the
first line:

> English lacks a homonym to parallel Dutch *dichten*: (1) to seal
> (a hole), (2) to compose poetry (though, on the other hand, it
> possesses the notorious homophonic sequence *whole-hole-holy*).

Around the familiar *dichten* pun the whole poem revolves: the gasfitter sealing off leaks is also the poet at work.[32]

It is clear from this translation and discussion of a complex text, with such sensitivity to the precise meaning of words, that Coetzee had an extensive knowledge of Dutch language and literature. He found it impossible, as any translator would, to play the same homonymic game with the word *dichten* as in Dutch, but he introduced the word 'hole' into the poem immediately before the fourth sonnet, thus anticipating the healing process of both the hole and the poem: 'Should I punch the gaspipes full of holes?'[33] That the problem of translating the word *dichten* into English and the wordplay on 'hole' and 'whole' would stay with Coetzee appears later from a passage in his second novel, *In the Heart of the Country*, when Magda reflects on her own life:

> I move through the world not as a knifeblade cutting the wind, or as a tower with eyes, like my father, but as a hole, a hole with a body draped around it, the two spindly legs hanging loose at the bottom and the two bony arms flapping at the sides and the big head lolling on top. I am a hole crying to be whole.[34]

Coetzee commenced work in 1968 on a much more extensive project: translating Marcellus Emants's 1894 masterpiece, *Een nagelaten bekentenis*. The translation, under the title *A Posthumous Confession*, was to appear only in 1975 as Volume 7 of the Series *The Library of Netherlandic Literature* published by Twayne in Boston. A second edition, this time with an introduction by Coetzee (which is included in his volume *Stranger Shores* (2001)), appeared in 1986 from Quartet in London, followed by a third in 2010 from *The New York Review of Books* in New York.

The novel tells the story of Willem Termeer, biologically and psychologically the product of many preceding generations with whom he is fatally and inescapably interconnected. As the son from a loveless marriage between a vindictive mother and a degenerate father, he is fated, as Coetzee says in his essay on the novel, to become a voluptuary and a sado-masochist. 'Termeer thus presents himself as a victim, a victim of heredity,' Coetzee writes; 'his confession is an agonised plea for pity.'[35] 'It is as if the intensity of Termeer's self-pollution overwhelms one,' Etienne Britz writes in the introduction to his edition of *Een nagelaten bekentenis*, 'as if the energy and the spectacle of the masochistic self-destruction carries one along in pleasurable identification.'[36] Coetzee relates this confession to Jean-Jacques Rousseau's *Confessions*, which, after St Augustine, inaugurated the tradition of the 'modern' secular confession, of which both Dostoevsky's anonymous narrator in *Notes from the Underground* and Emants's *Een nagelaten bekentenis* are pure examples. 'In Willem Termeer,' Coetzee writes,

> we find [...] a helpless drifting in a sea of passions, fears and envies; and an agonised twisting and turning to escape confrontation with the true self his life-history reveals to him: impotent, cowardly, ridiculous.[37]

And then Coetzee states that Marcellus Emants is not to be separated from Willem Termeer:

> the author is implicated in his creature's devious project to transmute the base metal of his self into gold.[38]

Asked why he had translated Emants's novel, Coetzee replied in a letter of 20 October 2009:

> I began work on the Emants translation in Buffalo. There were several reasons why I embarked on it. (1) I had an interest in the naturalist school (Zola, Gissing, Dreiser, to an extent Hardy) to which Emants belonged. (2) Emants hadn't been translated into English (he had into French and German). (3) I wanted to keep up and improve my Dutch in an environment (Buffalo) where there was no interest in Dutch studies.[39]

The informed reader, however, considering Coetzee's translation and his essay on the novel, may discern vague outlines of Coetzee's own life and his interest (via Sarah Gertrude Millin and Albert du Biel) in the motif of degeneration and the crimes of the fathers, 'finding whose fault I am.'[40] In Termeer's recollections of his childhood, as translated by Coetzee, the reader acquainted with *Boyhood* may feel that something resonates of John's tendency to secrecy towards his mother and schoolmates:

> I considered all my activities as coolly as possible, and the arguments in favor of doing something had to be really powerful to triumph over my innate sluggishness, which steered me toward inaction.

This cautious pondering, this detachment from my energetic schoolmates, this skeptical reluctance to give in to an impulse of the moment, naturally gave me the reputation of being secretive, underhand, shifty. I found out about this only in later life; but even as a boy I had the feeling that no one could bear me.[41]

In *Een nagelaten bekentenis* the wanderings of the lonely outsider Willem Termeer in Brussels and Paris remind the reader of the alienated John wandering forlornly through the streets of London, unable to achieve anything meaningful either in literature or in his personal relations with women. Termeer, too, has the passionate urge to write something substantial, but his manuscript is returned by publishers and scorned as trivial. Did Coetzee feel something like what he calls Termeer's 'deepest crisis'?[42] He was now almost thirty and, in spite of brilliant results as a student in Austin and the completion of his doctoral dissertation, he had not yet achieved anything of what he saw as his real purpose in life: to create something that would exist outside his self, that he could show to the world as a work of art he had created, and that would lend substance and meaning to his life.

It could have been Coetzee's personal attraction to the figure of Termeer that drove him to translate the novel, as much as Emants's connection with the French naturalists and the fact that the novel had not yet been translated into English. In Emants's narrator Coetzee had discovered something of his deepest being—in the intensity of the writing, and perhaps also in certain resemblances in character between himself and Termeer, and in the fact that both he and Termeer were trapped in an unhappy marriage. When, in 1969, he contacted Senator Jacob K. Javits about the possibility of permanent residence in the US, he replied to the letter from the senator's assistant only several months after receipt. On 16 October 1969 he wrote to the assistant, Mary Ellen McFerran, in Washington: 'Since I received your long and extremely helpful letter in February, I have been through some domestic trouble which at least for a time seemed to render pointless any attempt to argue for a change in my visa status on the grounds of the US citizenship of my children. There seemed, for a time, a strong chance that my wife and I would be separating. The trouble has now blown over.'

Een nagelaten bekentenis starts with the death of the wife and with Termeer at home on his own after the funeral. In Coetzee's translation it reads as follows:

My wife is dead and buried.

I am alone at home, alone with the two maids.

So I am free again. Yet what good is it to me, this freedom? I am within reach of what I have wanted for the last twenty years (I am thirty-five), but I have not the courage to grasp it, and would anyhow no longer enjoy it very much.

I am too frightened of anything that excites me, too frightened of a glass of wine, too frightened of music, too frightened of women; for only in my matter-of-fact morning mood am I in control of myself, sure that I will keep silent about my deed.

Yet it is precisely this morning mood that is intolerable.

To feel no interest—no interest in any person, any work, even any book—to roam without aim or will through an empty house in which only the indifferent guarded whispering of two maids drifts about like the far-off talk of warders around the cell of a sequestered madman, to be able to think, with the last snatch of desire in an extinct nervous life, about only one thing, and to tremble before that one thing like a squirrel in the hypnotic gaze of a snake—how can I persevere to the end, day in, day out, in such an abominable existence?

Whenever I look in the mirror—still a habit of mine—I am astounded that such a pale, delicate, insignificant little man with dull gaze and weak, slack mouth (a nasty piece of work, some people would say) should have been capable of murdering his wife, a wife whom, after all, in his own way, he had loved.[43]

III

While Coetzee was teaching in Buffalo, his conditions of residence in the US remained a nagging problem. On 11 November 1968 he wrote about this to Professor Marcus Klein, the new chair of the Department of English:

When I applied for the job I now hold I stated that restrictions on the length of my stay would probably make it impossible for me to remain longer than a single year. Three months ago I wrote to the Department of Justice to ask whether there was any chance that I would be given permission to stay in the United States for a second year (1969–1970), or, failing such permission, whether there was any chance that the eighteen-month period allowed me could be broken into two nine-month periods, covering the academic years 1968–69 and 1969–1970.

I have now received a reply which states that the maximum period allowed me will be eighteen months, beginning September 1, 1968, and that this period cannot be broken up. This means that I shall have to leave the United States by February 28, 1970.

I have therefore decided to apply for a position at a Canadian university starting in September, 1969. I take this step with reluctance, since I find myself extremely happy in this Department. I do not, however, see that there is anything else to do.

Coetzee decided to approach more than one Canadian university about possible vacancies. He wrote to the University of Victoria and the University of British Columbia, but also sent an enquiry to the University of Hong Kong, which had a vacancy. In all these letters he mentioned that his residence visa in the US would expire in August 1969. He added: 'Conditions in the Republic of South Africa, of which I am a citizen, make me most reluctant to return there.' He included a curriculum vitae.

Before he received a reply from these universities, however, the University of Buffalo had set the ball rolling to apply on his behalf for permanent residence in the US. The Department of English wanted to keep him, and the extension of his educational visa was advocated by the Washington representative of the president of SUNY at Buffalo. One condition of the educational visa he possessed was that he had to leave the US after expiry of the period and to stay away for two years before applying for readmission. The only way around this was to find somebody in Congress who was prepared to introduce a private member's bill exempting the applicant from the condition. This was a not-unusual procedure, but the applicant had to have somebody with political clout to introduce the private bill and lobby for it. The authorities at UB found Senator Jacob Javits, a senior senator of New York State, willing to introduce a private bill that would permit Coetzee to remain indefinitely in the US.[44]

To help state his case, Coetzee wrote on 11 December 1968 to Robert O'Neil, the executive assistant of the president of UB, giving information about his background and that of his wife and children.

He wrote that he was planning an academic career as a lecturer and researcher in the field of English language and literature. He had learnt much in both areas at the University of Texas and at Buffalo, and added that he had begun extensive research that would be interrupted if he had to leave the US.

Before O'Neill could reply, Coetzee received, on 13 December 1968, a letter from Professor G.H. Durrant of the Department of English at the University of British Columbia at Vancouver, Canada, formerly of the University of Natal in Pietermaritzburg. Durrant offered him an assistant professorship at an annual salary of $10 500. Durrant says that he would like Coetzee to offer part of the course in Modern British literature, but that he would want to hear from him what other courses he wanted to be considered for. Coetzee found this offer very attractive, but would have preferred to remain in Buffalo with its academically stimulating environment and pleasant working conditions. His colleagues were anxious to retain his services for their department. In a letter dated 23 December 1968 Coetzee wrote to Durrant that he had to make a choice between accepting the Vancouver offer or staying in Buffalo until 1970. He said:

> I was not prepared to make a decision on your offer when it arrived because I had received no indication from Washington of what the fate of my application might be. I have now had some news, which is of a rather imprecise nature, but at least allows me to weigh the alternatives. I am informed that, because it is for an extension of stay for only three months, my application has a fair chance of being successful, but that no official decision can be made before July or August, 1969. On the strength of this information, Professor Klein is offering to renew my contract for a year, despite the fact that I may have to leave in the middle of that year.
>
> After considerable inner debate I have decided to remain at Buffalo. The primary reason for this decision is that I find that I have a great deal to learn from my colleagues here.

In reply to Coetzee's enquiry to the University of Victoria in Canada, he received a letter, dated 3 April 1969, asking whether he was still available. He replied that he had already committed himself for the academic year 1969–1970. On 27 February 1969 he received a telegram from the University of Hong Kong offering him a lectureship. On

13 March he gave the registrar of this university an explanation that in the main accorded with his letter to British Columbia.

He did find the Hong Kong offer very attractive, and asked whether it would be possible to repeat the offer later the same year. On 10 April 1969 the registrar informed him that they were prepared to keep the post open for him, on condition that he could accept it on 1 March 1970.

In the meantime O'Neill had been in touch with Mary Ellen McFerran, the expert on immigration in the office of Senator Javits, who believed Coetzee's best strategy would be to apply for the two-year residence requirement to be waived on the grounds of the 'hardship provision of the Immigration Statutes'. An alternative would be to offer a strong argument why it would be in the national interest of the US to retain Coetzee, though McFerran cautioned that the board scrutinised such cases very strictly and did not lightly grant such permission. She therefore preferred the former strategy. In his letter to Coetzee, O'Neill quoted the relevant part of McFerran's letter:

> The argument should be made that it would be a hardship on the Coetzees' American born children to return to the Republic of South Africa. Every conceivable but justifiable reason should be given, i.e., exposure at such an impressionable age to an environment of racial discrimination at its worst and of lack of equal opportunity effect on the pre-school education of the children; hardship to their mother; any economic factors on comparative standards of living; and employment conditions and professional development that might operate adversely on the Coetzees' return should be used.

O'Neil proposed that Coetzee send a draft of his letter to McFerran before submitting his application. If the case were to be made on the grounds of 'hardship', Coetzee would have to supply supporting evidence.

On 6 February 1969 Coetzee sent the draft of his letter, as requested by O'Neil, to McFerran, with a copy to Rowan Wakefield, the representative of UB in Washington. In it, Coetzee gives a synopsis of his sojourn in Texas, his student career and his employment in Buffalo. He applies for the waiving of the requirements for residence for aliens, and bases his application mainly on the fact that his two children are US citizens:

I am most reluctant to expose them, and particularly the elder child, to the racial climate of the Republic of South Africa, as it evinces itself in the educational system and the structure of society in general. [...] The law in South Africa requires that all schooling be racially segregated in a complex way, with 'pure' white children, children of mixed blood, and 'pure' black children taught in separate schools. Furthermore, it requires that within each racial group each child be instructed in his 'home' language. [...] The official rationale for this legislation is that it puts the child among 'his own', but it is clear that the real reasons are (a) to maintain total racial segregation, and (b) to maintain Afrikaner predominance among the whites by cutting off the natural drift in each new generation from Afrikaans-language toward English-language culture. The bulk of legislation to promote racial and linguistic separatism was passed in the late 1950's. I myself therefore largely escaped its effects (I was born in 1940). My son will not. Racially he is a white and will therefore be placed in a segregated white school. The language he now speaks at home is English; nevertheless, there is a fair chance that he will be required to attend an Afrikaans-language school, since, despite the fact that by profession I am a teacher of English, all forbears on both sides of my family have been Afrikaners, the same being true of one side of my wife's family.

The result of this two-way segregation will thus be that at an early and most impressionable age the child will certainly receive an all-white education and possibly an education in a strange language. I need not stress the disturbing effect this latter possibility would certainly have. But I should like to emphasize the effects of a racially segregated education, and indeed the effects of simply living in a society in which segregation is accepted as a way of life. Racial separatism is the official ideology of the South African government. Behind it is the unofficial ideology of white superiority. Both positions are almost universally shared among whites, exceptions being restricted almost entirely to the academic community. There is no way of isolating a child from the daily expression of the racialist position, nor from its more obvious manifestations (residential segregation, segregation in employment and education, segregation in buses and trains, everyday instances of white harshnesses toward non-whites, total lack of social contact among the races, the curfew, etc.), to say nothing of expressions of black resentment. When he goes to school he will hear no criticism of the ideology of *apartheid*, which state employees may naturally not voice in their official capacities; he is far more likely to hear his teachers accept and reinforce the ideology.

I cannot see how the final effect of exposure to this environment for any length of time can fail to have an unfortunate effect on the mind of a child. And everything I have said about the older child holds to a lesser degree for the younger child.

After this exposition of the hardships his children would suffer were they to return to South Africa, Coetzee outlined his own situation:

Despite the fact that this application is made on behalf of my two children, I should like to add that it is by no means certain that I would be permitted to hold an academic post in South Africa for long. There are four English-language universities in the country. Like all the other universities, they are under state control, and one of the regulations governing academic employment is that no 'communist' be allowed to teach. Since a 'communist' is in the vocabulary of South African bureaucracy one who 'advocates the aims of communism', and since the avowed aims of the Communist Party of South Africa include the achievement of universal adult suffrage, I am by definition a communist. (It should be noted that this regulation has been applied with increasing strictness in the last two years, one of the results being a noticeable drop in university standards.)

Finally, let me observe that one of my two fields of professional specialization is African Literature, in which I am currently teaching a course at the State University of New York. No such course could be taught at a South African university, simply because the works of most of the African writers with whom I would deal are banned in South Africa.

Coetzee concludes:

To summarize, then, I am applying for a waiver of the overseas residence requirement on two grounds: (a) that the effect on my American-born children of prolonged residence in South Africa and of education there would be psychologically confusing and morally

deleterious, and (b) that the children may be caused hardship in
view of the fact that it is possible that I may be debarred from the
employment for which I have qualified myself in the United States.

In his letter Coetzee makes a strong case for why he would prefer his
children to continue with their lives in the US, though one feels he
exaggerates the matter. It is, for instance, unthinkable that the South
African government, even in the rigid apartheid era, would have risked
diplomatic repercussions by forcing children with English as their
home language and with US passports to attend Afrikaans-medium
schools purely on account of their Afrikaans ancestry. But Coetzee was
now dealing with politicians, whose perspective differed from that of
academics.

On 13 February 1968 McFerran replied to his letter. She pointed
out that he had not stipulated whether or not he would on his return to
South Africa be able to find academic employment, and, if so, what his
salary would be. He would have to show evidence that he had written
letters in this regard and produce the replies. He would also have to
furnish evidence in the form of newspaper cuttings or letters from
friends that he would probably not be able to find employment:

> The burden of the proof is on you ... not only by letter but by
> documentation. You must have documentation to show the
> Government's discrimination against you, your wife but most of
> all ... please remember our law states *exceptional hardship* against a
> citizen of the United States. You must show by documentation how
> detrimental such discrimination in education would be to children
> who must go back to South Africa even though American citizens.

He would also have to provide evidence that the four English-
language universities of South Africa would classify him, due to state
control, as a communist and on those grounds refuse him employment.
She thus recommended that he apply to the four English-language
universities and include their responses with his application. Further, he
should show, with due documentation, how disadvantageous education
in South African schools would be to American-born children: 'Children
at an early age are most impressionable. They are Americans as you wish
to be and as Americans should not be subject to such an environment.
Do not be so formal in writing your book ... Wave the American flag

high and good luck!' He should also apply for a change to his visa status.

In response, Coetzee enquired from the four English-language universities in South Africa (Witwatersrand, Rhodes, Cape Town and Natal) about their salary scales for a lecturer. On 16 October 1969 he submitted an amended application. Coetzee this time omitted the relatively weak argument that his English-speaking children might be obliged, on the grounds of their Afrikaans ancestry, to attend Afrikaans-medium schools. He quoted from the findings of Kenneth B. Clark, who, in his book *Prejudice and Your Child* (second edition, 1963), had made a study of the effects of racial prejudice on children in the US. Clark alleged, among other things, that white children experiencing the prejudices in American society were taught to develop a feeling of superiority:

> The culture permits and at times encourages them to direct their feelings of hostility and aggression against whole groups of people the members of which are perceived as weaker than themselves. They often develop patterns of guilt feelings, rationalizations and other mechanisms which they must use in an attempt to protect themselves from recognizing the essential injustice of their unrealistic fears and hatreds of minority groups.

If these findings are true of a segregated community in the US, Coetzee argued in his letter,

> it is self-evident that they will be a hundredfold truer for South Africa, where the white population for the most part feels itself to be a beleaguered and threatened minority and therefore experiences paranoia as an everyday state of mind.
>
> I would argue, then, that, on the basis of this evidence, it would be a disservice and a hardship to my children to expose them to the racial climate of South Africa. Both children, I repeat, are citizens of the United States, and I hope that, God willing, both will grow up in the United States. In my view, exposure to present-day South Africa will constitute psychic violence to them, a systematic miseducation for life.

His second argument was that it remained uncertain that he would find an academic position in South Africa equal to that in Buffalo. There were vacancies only at the universities of the Witwatersrand and

Natal, and the salaries offered amounted to about 54 per cent of his present income. Furthermore, since leaving South Africa in 1963 he had expressed opinions and publicly defended positions that would brand him as a criminal by South African law. It was, in terms of the General Law Amendment Act of 1962 and 1963, a misdemeanour for an inhabitant of the Republic while overseas 'to have advocated the bringing about of changes in South Africa by the intervention of or with the assistance of any foreign government, body or institution. [...] The minimum sentence is five years' imprisonment.' Coetzee alleged that he had defended the view that the oppression practised by the South African, Rhodesian and Portuguese regimes in Southern Africa constituted a threat to world peace, that internal change in Southern Africa would be in the interests of the international community, and that such changes could be effected with least violence by intervention on the part of the United Nations—for instance, by a total blockade of South African ports. He had aired these views publicly, in the recent past in a speech at Clarence High School on 14 April 1969. Prosecution was not the only penalty that might face him on his return to South Africa: the minister of the interior had been granted the power to ban anybody whose political views he found subversive. He included a copy of an article from the Johannesburg *Star* dealing with the fate of three banned lecturers. His concluding summary differs in some respect from his original application:

> To summarize, then, I am applying for a waiver of the foreign residence requirement on three principal grounds. The first and most important is that my children, both United States citizens, will be handicapped for the life that their country of birth offers them by being exposed to the obnoxious racial atmosphere of South Africa. The second is that, as their breadwinner, my capacity to provide for them will be, at the very least, significantly diminished if I return to South Africa. The third is that my publicly expressed political views render me liable to prosecution or banning if I should return to South Africa.

Coetzee was to find that it took time to get a reply from the authorities. Towards the end of 1969 his application for permanent residence or citizenship had not got anywhere, and the expiry date of his visa was fast approaching. It is a measure of how unpromising the situation seemed that on 29 October he applied for permanent residence for himself and his family in Canada. On 13 October 1969 he wrote to Professor R.M. Jordan, head of the Department of English at the University of British Columbia, enquiring whether the assistant professorship offered to him the previous year in December was still available. But the vacancy no longer existed. Apparently he was not inclined to accept a post in Hong Kong, but he applied for a position as a linguist at the Rijks Psychologische Dienst in The Hague in the Netherlands. It is not known whether he received a reply. If so, it is not among the extant documents.

On 13 February 1970 Coetzee received the ruling of the US Department of Justice. His application was turned down on the grounds that the arguments he had advanced would apply to every visitor from South Africa, and that he could not lay claim to the '*exceptional* hardship' stipulated by the relevant law. On 25 February 1970 Coetzee appealed against this decision and its main argument. He based his appeal on three grounds:

(1) The 'required adjustments' of which he speaks are required of the exchange visitor. They can surely not be required of children who had not been born at the time when the exchange contract was entered upon, and who are not citizens of the visitor's country but on the contrary citizens of the United States. I detect some inhumanity in a decision that children who are US citizens should suffer hardship simply in order that their foreign national parents fulfill requirements which the Department of Justice has in its power to waive.

(2) To call the transition from the freedom of American life to the racial tyranny of South African life an 'adjustment to differences' is euphemistic, particularly when the 'adjustment' is required not of adults but of children. It implies that the differences between the two societies can be 'adjusted' to without hardship, an implication which I find insulting to the United States.

(3) The distinction made between hardship and exceptional hardship implies that those psychological effects of life in a racial tyranny which I have described do not constitute exceptional hardship. Yet I understand that waivers have been granted to black South Africans on the grounds of exceptional hardship to the US-born children. I can only conclude that the line between hardship and exceptional hardship corresponds in the District Director's

decision to the line between black and white. The evidence which I have cited, however, indicates that the psychological effects of discrimination on white and on black children differ in *kind* rather than in *degree*.

In the third argument of my original application I described the penalties I myself am subject to in South Africa if prosecuted under the General Law Amendment Acts of 1962 and 1963, and produced testimony to show that one of the 'crimes' defined by these Acts has been committed by me.

The District Director's decision makes no specific reference to this argument. I can therefore only assume that the final sentence of the decision, quoted above, is intended as a response to it. If this is the case, I must question whether a five-year prison sentence should be referred to as a 'required adjustment', whether it should not indeed constitute 'exceptional hardship' to both parents and children.

To this appeal Coetzee received an extensive reply from the Department of Justice, dated 2 April 1970:

The first reason in support of his contention is that the children would suffer exposure to the racial climate which exists in South Africa. In spite of the lengthy discussion of psychological factors affecting children in a racially separated society, it cannot be conceded that his children would suffer unduly if they lived in South Africa. To adopt such a finding, it would be necessary to assume that all white children in South Africa are in serious danger.

The second argument is financial in that he could expect a 40 per cent drop in income if he returned to South Africa. This has been found to be one of the *usual* hardships which may be encountered by an exchange visitor leaving the United States and is not recognized as *extreme hardship* which was contemplated by the Congress which enacted the statute.

The third argument advanced by this applicant relates to possible punishment in South Africa if he were to return there because of the remarks he has made in the United States about racial policies of the South African Government. He has attempted to show that his thoughts about South African policies render him subject to prosecution there. However, his concern is pure speculation inasmuch as he has not been accused of any anti-South African activity and there is no reason for anyone in that country to be aware of his feelings.

The conclusion reached by the Department of Justice is thus:

> The hardships indicated in this application would primarily affect the applicant. Residence in South Africa would appear to be distasteful to him, but it would be difficult to find that his two very young children would be adversely affected by residence in that country. Therefore the appeal must be dismissed.

One is led to wonder why Coetzee had turned down the offers from Canada and Hong Kong, since he could have foreseen that the delay in approving his application was a bad omen. Perhaps it was from loyalty to Buffalo, where he was very happy with his colleagues—liberals with whom he could form friendships, even if they ultimately could do nothing to end the Vietnam war, just as liberals in his own country were powerless to prevent the forced delimitation and segregation of people. Whatever the reason, his visa was still valid, and he had no choice but to await the events of the following months.

IV

The situation arising from US involvement in Vietnam had deteriorated markedly all over the country. The majority of Americans now opposed the war; only 26 per cent supported Johnson's policy, and on the campuses there was constant protest and unrest. Johnson was intransigent. The war in Vietnam escalated, with the deployment of the most modern weapons, devastating large parts of the country without dampening the resolve of the communists. Apart from aerial bombardment, the Americans also waged chemical warfare, despite strong criticism from other countries and from inside the US itself. Under Johnson's successor, Richard M. Nixon, the offensive was sustained. The American public was subjected to revelations prompting uncomfortable moral questions about the war. Every evening the American people could follow the violence and the viciousness in Vietnam with their own eyes. 'American television audiences,' writes Stanley Karnow, 'could see the aftermath [of an attack] on their screens: grinning and giggling South Vietnamese soldiers scavenged the Vietcong corpses for money and other valuables, looted the radio station itself, and stole any equipment still intact.'[45]

Years after the war, Ho Thanh Dam, an inhabitant of the area north of the seventeenth parallel where North Vietnamese troops gathered to move southward, could recall the day when US bombers struck his town, Vinh Quang:

> The bombing started at about eight o'clock in the morning and lasted for hours. At the first sound of explosions, we rushed into the tunnels, but not everyone made it. During a pause in the attack, some of us climbed out to see what we could do, and the scene was terrifying. Bodies had been torn to pieces—limbs hanging from trees or scattered around the ground. Then the bombing began again, this time with napalm, and the village went up in flames. The napalm hit me, and I must have gone crazy. I felt as if I were burning all over, like charcoal, and I lost consciousness. Comrades took me to the hospital, and my wounds didn't begin to heal until six months later. More than two hundred people died in the raid, including my mother, my sister-in-law and three nephews. They were buried alive when their tunnel collapsed.[46]

With the escalation of the war, there was serious disruption on the Buffalo campus almost every day, with protests not only against the war, but against the UB authorities. On 8 September 1969 the president, Martin Meyerson, announced that he would be on sabbatical for the 1969–1970 term. He was later castigated for abandoning the university at a crucial juncture: 'He gave his job away,' Bruce Jackson, an assistant professor at UB, writes, 'then hid when the turds started flying. He never came out to play, he never supported or helped any of us who spent so much helping him in the last few years.'[47] In Meyerson's place, the vice-president, Peter F. Regan, an inexperienced administrator, was appointed as acting president. As early as November 1969 a circular issued by Regan showed him to be not the right man for the job. He wrote about the 'ugly and disturbing trend' of uncontained violence, harassment and intimidation on campus, and expressed fears that freedom of speech was being jeopardised by physical violence. In order to maintain order on campus, he warned ominously, he would not hesitate 'to call upon such external or internal security forces as may be necessary to prevent [...] intrusion', a formulation that does not preclude the deployment of the police.

The unrest on campus peaked on Wednesday, 25 February 1970, when 27 people were seriously injured, some of them having to be admitted to nearby hospitals. Five of these people were policemen. So extreme was the tension on campus that the staff in Hayes Hall, the administrative block, were instructed for their own safety to take temporary refuge in a new rented building across the way from the campus, and there await instructions from the president. Regan, however, did not turn up, nor in the weeks to come was he available for directions or consultation. When a group of students took up position in front of the building, and started chanting 'We want Regan' in front of his locked door, they found about 30 members of campus control blocking one of the entrances to the university. The students dispersed the campus-control officers with stones and other weapons, and the Buffalo police arrived to quell the insurrection. On 25 February, at Regan's request, four hundred policemen armed with helmets, truncheons and walkie-talkies occupied the campus to prevent any further disruptive demonstrations.[48] Twenty students were suspended and prohibited from entering the terrain.

The University of Buffalo was under siege. On 5 March the council of the Arts Faculty assembled. Several resolutions were debated and passed with an overwhelming majority, among others:

(1) Recognizing the clear violation of the academic and political rights of those suspended by Acting President Regan on March 5th, we demand that these suspensions be lifted immediately and that no punitive action be taken against any member of the University community until he or she is convicted of violations by due process of law.

(2) Because of the Administration's precipitous calling of police to this campus last Wednesday night, February 25th, because of the Administration's refusal or inability since then to deal directly or honestly with the members of this University community, [...] we hereby express our lack of confidence in the Administration of Acting President Regan.

Regan took no notice of the second of these resolutions, but the suspension of the students was repealed by court order. On Monday, 9 March 1970, the Department of History demanded Regan's resignation for calling in the police, suspending the students without following the prescribed process, for not being available to the university and for his lack of forthrightness. The presence of the police on campus, the department declared, was academically intolerable, making it impossible for lecturers to continue teaching.[49] In spite of this criticism and the request that the siege be lifted, the police stayed on campus.

At about a quarter to one on a cold, bright Sunday, 15 March 1970, after two days of relative calm on campus, 45 lecturers turned up at Hayes Hall for a peaceful protest against the continued presence of the police. They staged a sit-in in the president's office and asked to talk to him about the handling of the internal policy of the university in the larger context of a small-scale civil war. Coetzee was one of the 45. Professor William Bunn, one of his colleagues in the English Department, recalled later that Coetzee was not talkative in political discussions, but that for him, as for the other 44, who all believed in freedom of speech, there were important principles at issue.[50] The 45 handed a declaration to Edward Doty, the vice-president of UB, who was present:

> Peter Regan and his administration have defied the will of the Faculty Senate expressed Wednesday, March 11, for the *immediate* removal of police from campus, thereby making themselves responsible for Thursday's events. Hence, we members of the Faculty will occupy these premises until 1) the police are removed from campus and 2) the injunction is lifted.

Doty phoned the acting president at home for instructions. He then informed the waiting group that they had no appointment with the president. He added: 'If you do not leave in five minutes, you will be subject to arrest for trespass.'[51] The group remained sitting, and informed Doty that they would remain there until the acting president acceded to their requests. They were then arrested by the police. Although they were not handcuffed, all 45 were photographed, their fingerprints taken, their pockets emptied, and all personal effects, including belts and ties, confiscated. They weer free to keep their shoelaces, but all spectacles were removed, which was very inconvenient for short-sighted members of the group.[52] On Monday, 16 March 1970, the 45, after spending a night in the cells, were all charged with criminal contempt of the law and unlawful entry, punishable with imprisonment of one year or a fine of $1 000. A further criminal charge of contempt was laid with the State

Supreme Court of New York, which could carry a sentence of three months in prison or a fine of $250. Judge Hamilton Ward found them all guilty and sentenced them to thirty days in jail, with leave to appeal. In his verdict the judge was exceptionally vehement:

> I hope to impress you that there is justice here and I hope to impress you that when a court of this kind makes an order, those above all that ought to comply with it are those who are charged with the responsibility of teaching our young people.[53]

The whole affair was a politically charged show of strength of the right-wing administration under Regan, who promised stronger action by the police if order was not restored on campus. After their arrest, the 45 were harassed with threatening letters and phone calls. In the local *Courier-Express* there were indignant letters about the arrests. Most of them, however, were critical of the lecturers: 'If people are wondering why students think and act the way they do today they only have to look to the 45 faculty members who were arrested. [...] They are the ones who should be charged with instigating all of the current trouble on the campus. [...] Other universities are also infected with the eggheads or "intellectual snobs". [...] They should be fired.'[54] 'The 45 must be counted as deliberately malicious, or as stupid as the man who lights a match in a dynamite factory. In either case, the 45 must bear some moral responsibility—and they should be removed from our educational system.'[55]

John Huddleston defended his colleagues: 'I am proud of my 45 colleagues who were willing to sacrifice themselves in order to focus attention on the true cause of the trouble on this campus—the Administration's insensitivity to the needs of the people in our University community (students, faculty and staff). By exploiting the instincts for brutality of the local politicians and police officials, the Administration has escalated the repression to the point where the University is in danger of becoming like a police state.'[56] In an official letter in which the Department of History made an appeal for financial support in the imminent trials, it was stated that this was the first time in history that lecturers at an American university had been arrested and locked up after a peaceful protest, while the acting president by his silence failed to pronounce on the matter. Leslie Fiedler, an influential critic and novelist, and a lecturer in the Buffalo English Department, described the action against the 45 as 'completely unprecedented as far as we know'.[57] In a letter to Regan, dated 19 March 1970, thirteen eminent professors at the university expressed their sympathy with the 45:

> It is our belief, based on knowledge of their abilities and respect for them as human beings, that these men and women were primarily moved by sympathy for their students and by a desire to bear witness in their own persons to deeply held convictions. The clear distinction between an act of violence and an act of conscience must be maintained if the University is to survive, and it is our further belief that the presence of these [men] on that day was an act of conscience.

On 5 May 1970 the council of the Faculty of Arts reached the following conclusion:

> This campus is presently under a system of law which has an extended injunction ordered by State Supreme Court Justice Hamilton Ward as its instrument of enforcement as well as its final means of arbitration and adjudication of disputes. This means that this campus has, in effect, no self-government, no administration able to make critical executive decisions and more importantly no executive branch willing AND able to actively mediate and arbitrate disputes. The posture of this administration has been and continues to be: 'If there's trouble we cannot handle it, call the cops, arrest the agitators and provocateurs, then let the Judge summarily sentence them to thirty days or more in the Erie County Penitentiary.'

The Faculty Council found an injunction to be, at best, a clumsy and inappropriate way to enforce laws and maintain public order on a university campus:

> Injunctions tend to intimidate and suppress vocal dissent; to use the standard legal language, they have a 'chilling effect' on civil rights guaranteed by the [...] Constitution of the United States.

For that reason the Faculty Council asked that there be an exploration of the means of undoing the obvious damage which this system of law by injunction has already brought down on the heads of 45 faculty members. [...] Specifically, this Faculty should press charges of administrative irresponsibility, dereliction of duty, and bureaucratic cowardice against [several] administrative officers of this University. [...][58] Further, it is the recommendation of this Faculty that if these administrative officers are found guilty as charged, they be asked to resign immediately their positions as administrative officers of this University.

A year later, all 45 lecturers were found not guilty by the court. (Regan had in April 1970 been obliged to announce his resignation as acting president, to take effect at the end of August.) The New York State Supreme Court rejected the charges on the grounds that the university's total ban and interference with the gathering was unlawful. On 8 June 1971, Thomas E. Connolly, the acting provost, congratulated Coetzee on the fact that all charges against the 'Buffalo 45' had been dropped:

You and your colleagues showed great courage, in the face of severe penalties and financial burdens, to take a moral stand on a serious issue. The point that peaceful demonstration against oppression is proper and right was almost lost, and the opposite lesson was very nearly proved by the action instituted against you. It is a relief to all of us who believe in the right to assemble peacefully that this right has been upheld.

The arrest was, as it would later be called in *Summertime*, 'a turning-point'[59] in Coetzee's career, and killed his chances of remaining in the US. Nobody in Congress could afford politically to be associated with a private bill for someone who had been accused of resistance to the war and of public violence. Immediately after the events, Senator Javits informed the university authorities that he would not persist in pleading Coetzee's cause. The extension of his sojourn was a lost cause, even after all charges against him had been dropped.[60] Coetzee wrote to Richard A. Siggelkow in 1989:

After the sit-in I remained on the UB faculty until May of 1971, and passed through the same legal procedures as the rest of the 45. However, my status vis à vis the Immigration and Naturalization authorities was immensely complicated by the fact that I had been (until the appeal succeeded) convicted of an offense against the law. *Inter-alia*, the re-entry visa that until that time allowed me to leave and re-enter the United States was withdrawn, making travel impossible. This played a large part in my decision to resign and leave the US in 1971.[61]

He said to Joanna Scott in an interview in 1997:

I was indeed arrested in Buffalo at the height of the anti-war demonstrations in 1970, but not in an anti-war demonstration as such. Along with some thirty [Coetzee means 44] colleagues from the faculty, I took part in a protest against the way in which our university—SUNY-Buffalo—was being led, that is to say, by a President who quartered hundreds of police on campus and retreated from his office to a secret bunker. This was not, in our view, a responsible way in which to run a university: it created a highly charged atmosphere in which teaching and learning were impossible. My colleagues and I went to the President's office one Sunday morning and refused to leave until he agreed to come and meet with us. He didn't come. Instead, he sent the police. We were arrested, charged with trespassing, and convicted. A year later, on appeal, the conviction was overturned. That's the history. [...] If I had stayed in the United States I would by now have been a different person. I would have a different history. I wouldn't be here answering your questions.[62]

While Coetzee waited for the verdict in his case in the local court and in the State Supreme Court of New York, Philippa was unsure of what to do. Coetzee's future, and therefore hers and that of their children, had been veiled in uncertainty for a few years. At first there had been the idea that they might remain in Buffalo for a year and then go somewhere else—to Canada, for instance. Next there had been the possibility of continuing in Buffalo, with Senator Javits advocating Coetzee's permanent residence. Then their whole existence had been disrupted by Coetzee's arrest and the imminent danger that, after being found guilty, he would be deported. When Javits withdrew, neither of them knew what would happen next. Coetzee no longer had a valid visa to remain in the US. But if he were to leave the country now, it might be interpreted as fleeing the law. They were thus in a conundrum. Philippa decided to return to South Africa with the children and stay with her parents in Johannesburg until the whole mess had been sorted out. As the mother of her children, she was allowed legally to leave the US. She and the children left in December 1970.

Coetzee had applied for leave of absence from Buffalo, on the undertaking that he would resume his duties if his application for residence was approved and he was granted a visa. Because his situation was still uncertain, he gave the US authorities an undertaking to return to serve his sentence if his appeal should fail. On that basis he was permitted to leave the US in May 1971. As late as November 1971 he was still unsure whether he would be readmitted to the US, because on that date he asked Professor J.I. Fradlin, the new chair of the English Department at Buffalo, for a further extension of his unpaid leave:

> I have recently completed a book-length manuscript, in the area of African Studies, and am commencing a second, a critique of linguistic stylistics. For the present I would like to devote myself full-time to this work.

V

Amid the unrest on campus and the uncertainty as to whether he would be granted permanent residence in the US, Coetzee started working on his first novel. In an interview with Jennifer Crwys-Williams, which appeared on 4 December 1983 in the *Sunday Times*, he said:[63] 'I began to write novels on January 1, 1970, in the city of Buffalo in New York State. My 1970 New Year's resolution was to write a book. I said to myself, "If you don't sit down to it today, when will you ever sit down to it?"'

In this interview, shortly after the release of his fourth novel, *Life & Times of Michael K*, and its winning of the British Booker Prize, he also said: 'The first book, *Dusklands*, was the most taxing to write because I didn't know what I was doing. Things have become easier since then but not much. That's not a bad sign. If a book is easy to write, there must be something wrong.'

Coetzee, then, started writing *Dusklands* in Buffalo. He had, in the reading room of the British Museum, engrossed himself in the South Africa of centuries past, an interest that he had continued in Austin's university library with its extensive collection of books from earlier days. He read from diaries published two centuries before in the Netherlands or Germany or England. It felt odd to sit in London or Austin reading about streets in Cape Town—Wale Street, Buitengracht and Buitensingel—that he had walked. But more interesting than the tales of old Cape Town were the tales of journeys into the interior, in particular the explorations by ox wagon in the semi-desert of the Great Karoo, where the traveller could travel for days without seeing a single living being.[64] And by a lucky coincidence, in one of the early editions, he came across a synoptic account of a namesake of his: Jacobus Coetzee, who, in the second half of the eighteenth century, had undertaken a journey along the West Coast north of the Cape into Namaqualand and across the Orange River. If he were to use this material as a building block for a piece of fiction, that much he could see even before he started, he would have to remain true to that world and teach himself to write from it, even though he would have at the same time to insert material that the chronicler, for whatever reason, was silent about. But even then he would not be able to exceed the horizon of knowledge of that era. He would have to embody the 'common knowledge of a bygone world'.[65] He would have to know how to forget certain things, but he would also have to know *what* to forget.

But at the same time he wanted to compose something derived from the immediate brute reality that, now on a daily basis, he had to deal with in Buffalo, and that chimed in a strange way with the actions and experiences of the explorers who two centuries earlier had sallied forth into the African interior. The war in Vietnam, present to him in all its horror on television, provided him with the connection he was seeking.

In Buffalo he started writing this first novel that, eventually, with many delicately linked parallels, cross-references and related scenes, would comprise two parts. When, in May 1971, he boarded a plane for the fatherland he had wanted to escape at all costs, he was on his way to an uncertain future, but with a half-completed manuscript.

Coetzee's research gave him 'a synoptic account of ... Jacobus Coetzee', whose journey would form the basis of 'Dusklands'. Coetzee was able to include 'linked parallels, cross-references and related scenes' that would illustrate the problems he faced in Buffalo, whilst not exceeding 'the horizon of knowledge' that his namesake would have experienced in SA 155 (+) yrs earlier

IV

SOUTH AFRICA
(1971–2001)

CHAPTER 8

LECTURER IN CAPE TOWN, AND *DUSKLANDS*

I

When J.M. Coetzee returned to South Africa in May 1971, he left the United States in a critical phase of that country's modern history. The US was embroiled in a highly unpopular war in Vietnam, making use of constant air raids and chemical warfare. The American public was kept well informed by television, especially about the devastating effect of tons of explosives on a defenceless populace. Under Richard M. Nixon — president since 1968, and of a different party to his predecessor, Lyndon B. Johnson — the attacks were sustained, albeit with a gradual withdrawal of troops. The offensive was halted only in 1975 after Nixon had been forced to resign in August 1974 as a result of the Republican Party's illegal interference with the Democrats' election campaign.

At an important juncture of his life, Coetzee's major political preoccupation was not with the South African situation, but with the war in Vietnam. He had, in the US, been able to read in the daily press and see on television how the war was 'sold' to a gullible public, with Herman Kahn, whom he would quote in the epigraph to 'The Vietnam project' in *Dusklands,* as the diabolical advocate of the megadeath concept. The television coverage, says Daniel C. Hallin, 'dehumanized the enemy, drained him of all recognizable emotions and motives and thus banished him not only from the political sphere, but from human society itself. The North Vietnamese and Vietcong were "fanatical", "suicidal", "savage", "half-crazed."'[1] In an interview with Peter Temple in 1971 Coetzee commented on this aspect of the war: 'The war was an avenue through which a lot of pent-up aggression, sadism, let itself out, not only on battlefields but in people's living rooms.'[2]

This schizophrenic experience was Coetzee's daily reality. Even though his time in the US had considerably broadened his horizons and he had established remarkably good relations with his colleagues and students in Buffalo, he had always remained something of an outsider. In a letter to Dick Penner he refers to 'ugly, grimy Buffalo'.[3] Buffalo with its icy winters and its snow had not agreed with him, and he had never felt at home in big cities. On 6 May 1966 he wrote to Jack Cope, in the US on a Carnegie scholarship, 'I spent sixteen hours in New York last September, and I never want to see the place again.' As he had felt ill at ease in Britain in the grey, exhausted landscape of Surrey, he missed, cycling through the green hills around Austin, the empty desolation of the Karoo. He writes to Sheila Roberts on 13 August 1985: 'In the six years I spent continuously in the US I never ceased to feel like a stranger. I connected it with (a) having utterly different childhood memories from theirs, and so lacking a certain cultural thickness that one gets from growing up in a culture, and (b) having no feel whatsoever for the American landscape'. In an interview with Folke Rhedin he said: 'I do believe that people can only be in love with one landscape in their lifetime. One can appreciate and enjoy many geographies, but there is only one that one feels in one's bones.'[4]

But what did Coetzee return to in 1971, upon leaving the US? Before his departure he had experienced in the 1950s the full implementation of the apartheid policy intended to safeguard white civilisation at the southern tip of Africa, but representing an affront to the most cherished principles of the Western European civilisation it sought to emulate. The accursed system from which he had tried to flee in 1962 was on his return, as he commenced his writing career, still an accomplished fact with which he would have to co-exist. The African National Congress (ANC) and the Pan Africanist Congress (PAC) were in exile, with some of their most prominent leaders in prison, and the National Party was firmly and fiercely in control of the country. As he had every evening in the US endured the horrors of Vietnam on television, he now had, with the introduction of television in South Africa in 1975, on a daily basis to suffer the parade of politicians, the bullies he had endured during his schooldays in Worcester. Something of this would be reflected in Mrs Curren's anguish in his novel *Age of Iron*: 'I have only to see the heavy, blank faces so familiar since childhood to feel gloom and nausea. The bullies in the last row of school-desks, raw-boned, lumpish boys, grown up now and promoted to rule the land. They with their fathers and mothers, their aunts and uncles, their brothers and sisters: a locust horde, a plague of black locusts infesting the country, munching without cease, devouring lives. Why, in a spirit of horror and loathing, do I watch them? Why do I let them into the house? Because the reign of the locust family is the truth of South Africa, and the truth is what makes me sick? Legitimacy they no longer trouble to claim. Reason they have shrugged off. What absorbs them is power and the stupor of power.'[5]

Shortly after Coetzee's return the geo-political landscape of Southern Africa changed dramatically. In 1974 a small group of officers seized power from Marcelo Caetano, the successor to Antonio Salazar in Portugal, a political change inaugurating the independence of Portugal's African colonies, Angola and Mozambique. With the international arms embargo against South Africa, the guerrilla activity on the northern borders and the unrest in South West Africa (Namibia) and Rhodesia (Zimbabwe), South Africa in the 1970s was in a precarious position, militarily speaking, aggravated by Russian influence and interference, and the presence of Cuban troops in parts of Angola. When the struggle between the Angolan government and the guerrillas threatened to get out of hand, South Africa clandestinely—but with the knowledge and concurrence of two African states and the Ford administration in Washington—sent troops to oppose the communist forces. The result was a drawn-out bush war, which was recorded in the 'border stories' of a young generation of Afrikaans writers. The cost to South Africa was great, both in the loss of young lives and in the humiliation of the withdrawal of its troops in 1976.

In these years the international community intensified its criticism of South Africa. Intellectuals among the Nationalists increasingly came to regard the situation as immoral. Though many black leaders were in prison or in exile, a militant and independent movement started up especially among black workers, leading in 1973 to widespread strikes in Natal. From the Anglican Church Archbishop Tutu drew attention to the anger and desperation among black people, and the young Eastern Cape black leader, Steve Biko, from within the structures of the Black Consciousness Movement, launched a national appeal to black people to free themselves from their shackles. A sentiment of resistance was growing among students in particular. In the mid-1960s Beyers Naudé launched the Christian Institute, closely allied with Spro-Cas, 'Study Project on Christianity in Apartheid Society'. The aim was to investigate South African society in the light of Christian principles, formulate long-term aims for an acceptable societal dispensation, and consider ways of achieving such a new dispensation. The project had the support of liberals from various backgrounds, but also of people like Richard Turner, who had studied with Coetzee at UCT, and black intellectuals and political leaders like Biko, Ben Khoapa, Njabulo Ndebele and Mangosuthu Gatsha Buthelezi.[6] Eventually the Christian Institute was banned and Beyers Naudé was placed under house arrest.

On 16 June 1976, 2 000 pupils from the Johannesburg black township of Soweto marched in protest against a decision by the Department of 'Bantu Education' that Afrikaans, increasingly being reviled in the black community as the language of oppression and apartheid, should be used as the medium of instruction in half the classes in black schools. Police vehicles were deployed to control the crowds, and tear gas was used. The thirteen-year-old black pupil Hector Pieterson was hit in the back by a bullet and several other children were killed. In response to this, schools, clinics, libraries and administrative buildings were burnt down, and the unrest spread to other townships and provinces. The government responded to these riots with police action, the promulgation of states of emergency, mobilisation of citizen force units, increased periods of military service and the extension of police powers (interrogation and detention without charge, solitary confinement, banning and house arrest). Sabotage and other subversive activities were more stringently dealt with under already existing provisions of the Terrorism Act. One of the most sensational court cases in terms of this act was that of the poet Breyten Breytenbach, who in 1975 was sentenced to nine years' imprisonment on the grounds of alleged terrorist activities, of which he would serve seven years.

On his return to South Africa, Coetzee would for the next thirty years expend his vital energies in an effort to understand, through his creative work, what South Africa was doing to itself.[7] His novel *Summertime*, set in the 1970s, opens with a reference to a report that, according to the dating, appeared on the front page of the *Sunday Times* on 21 August 1972.[8] In Francistown, the capital of Botswana, a motor car, a white American model, in the middle of the night stopped at a house in a residential area. Men masking their faces with balaclavas jumped out, kicked in the front door, started shooting, set the house on fire, and drove off. The murderers seemed black, but one of the neighbours heard them speak Afrikaans to each other and was convinced they were whites in blackface. The victims were South Africans, refugees who had moved into the house a few weeks earlier. The South African minister of foreign affairs commented, through a spokesman, that the incident could not be confirmed. The SA Defence Force denied any involvement in the incident, and blamed it on tensions within the ANC. Week by week,

Coetzee writes, these stories from neighbouring states are followed by blatant denials. Reading such reports, the protagonist 'feels soiled', and wonders, 'Yet where in the world can one hide where one will not feel soiled? Would he feel any cleaner in the snows of Sweden, reading at a distance about his people and their latest pranks?'[9]

Coetzee personally had a taste of the dirty tricks that the police and their henchmen, especially the thuggish elements in the security branch, got up to. One evening in 1979, when Frederik van Zyl Slabbert was prominent in South African politics, Coetzee and Philippa, with Slabbert and his wife, Mana, were invited to dinner with Catherine and Ian Glenn at their home in Lower Claremont. Ian Glenn was a colleague of Coetzee's at the University of Cape Town. Coetzee had parked his Volkswagen outside the Glenns' house. When they went out at about half past eleven, they found that a bullet had travelled through the front and the back window. Coetzee concluded that the shooter had thought that the Volkswagen belonged to Slabbert.[10] Later, in the 1980s, Slabbert's study was destroyed in an evident case of arson.[11]

When Coetzee was asked, much later, in 2002, by Wim Kayzer in the television series *Van de schoonheid en de troost*, about specific atrocities in the apartheid years in South Africa, he replied:

> The peculiar cruelty and horror of apartheid was the very un-African aspect of it, a very rigid and ordered and in a sense European derived system imposed on a country and society to which it was really petrifying. And its horror was all the more because it seemed an absurd rerun in Africa of what the Nazis had done in Europe. It seemed a farcical repetition of a history of what then ought to have been obsolete. So you look here at a continent which is prolific of life and where life is cheap and always was cheap, but not in that way, not in a manner of systemized cruelty and extinction. So that has been the peculiar hideousness of the past half-century. In a country and on a continent which is not perhaps beautiful on the human scale, but [...] beautiful in a wild and grand and impressive manner. It is the contrast between the particular ugly, banal, systematic, cruel horror in an environment which is so huge and so lavishly beautiful.[12]

In the interview he elaborates on the unique beauty of Dias beach near Cape Point, an unspoilt bit of Africa, that, despite the activities of a small tourist industry about fifteen minutes' walk away, still looks almost as Africa must have appeared to the first European colonists:

> The beauty of this coastline is not a quiet beauty, it's rough and dangerous, it does not really fit in with the more domestic perception of beauty that perhaps came with the first settlers. In their diaries they continually use the word wild for the coastline. Of course it was dangerous for them as navigators, littered with shipwrecks. You can retreat here from the present reality; it exists almost out of time, pulled out of history.

This Africa arouses both fascination with its wild, unspoilt beauty, and a strange fear on account of its cruel indifference and hostility. This is reflected in the work of many South African poets, English as well as Afrikaans, as Coetzee pointed out later in his collection *White Writing*. When poets strive to contain the topography in words, Coetzee writes in the introduction to *White Writing*, they see:

> South Africa as a vast, empty, silent space, older than man, older than the dinosaurs whose bones lie bedded in its rocks, and destined to be vast, empty, and unchanged long after man has passed from its face.[13]

If writers then imagine this empty landscape as a mother, 'it is more often than not as a harsh, dry mother without curves or hollows, infertile, unwilling to welcome her children back, even when they ask to be buried in her'.[14]

What Coetzee expounds at some length in *White Writing* through reference to specific poets, is adumbrated in one of his early essays, 'The burden of consciousness in Africa' (1977), which was collected in *Doubling the Point*. In this essay he writes about the film *The Guest*, directed by Ross Devenish, with Athol Fugard in the leading role. The film was based on an incident in the life of the poet and naturalist Eugène N. Marais. 'In Eugène Marais,' Coetzee writes,

> South Africa came its closest yet to producing a Genius. Think of Marais's qualifications. He had deep-set piercing eyes. He loved many women. He lived in wild and dangerous places. He was addicted to an exotic drug. He wrote poems about death and thought morbid thoughts. He was mainly unhappy and finally slew

himself. He was plainly in a quite different class from mere bright boys like Jan Hofmeyr and Jan Christiaan Smuts.[15]

After this laconic allusion to the film's projection of Romantic stereotypes, Coetzee shows how the concept of the tragedy of white consciousness in Africa is dramatised in the final scene of the film as Marais's friend, the doctor and poet A.G. Visser, takes him away by car from the farm on which he has stayed for a while. Marais asks Visser to stop for a moment, because he wants to pray in the veld. With Visser looking on, Marais stumbles up a ridge, disappears from sight, and then slowly fades away on the other side. While Africa is, so to speak, swallowing him, the listener hears Marais reciting words from his poem '*Die lied van Suid-Afrika*' ['The song of South Africa.'] and the viewer sees the empty veld, the South Africa speaking from the poem:

> She says: 'I claim as sacred right
> The fruits of endless pain;
> I hurl them over mountains high,
> and smother them in desert sand.'[16]

Who, Coetzee asks, is this South Africa to whom Marais feels capable of praying? He continues:

> A murderous mother-goddess, the poem tells us, who devours her young and in return for love gives only 'endless pain.' Marais's poem is powerful stuff, but I doubt that it would awake much response in most South Africans, to whom (and let us not forget this) Africa is a mother who has nourished them and their forbears for millions of years. South Africa, mother of pain, can have meaning only to people who can find it meaningful to ascribe their 'pain' ('alienation' is here a better word) to the failure of Africa to love them enough. What the closing scene of the film depicts is Marais, bearer of a pain-racked higher consciousness, Genius and Saint become Hero, abandoning civilization and going off to sacrifice himself at the feet of adored but implacable Africa.[17]

After his more than eight years in foreign countries, first in Britain and then in the US, Coetzee, with a developed metropolitan sensibility, informed by European modernism and modern linguistics, returned to the South Africa of his youth that he had wanted to leave for ever. He had not felt at ease in Britain or the US. Deep within him, however much he was racked with disgust, with the 'disgrace' of what was happening in South Africa, there was an attachment to the ground of his being and the caste that he was powerless to flee. He had not wanted to return, but neither had he accepted the opportunities offered to him in Canada and Hong Kong.

This ambivalence was perhaps grounded in an intuitive sense that his real task as a writer and as a human being was not to be found in foreign cities, but in the South Africa he had wanted to flee. When, in the capacious university library of Austin, he had had the opportunity to read so many other books, he had chosen to immerse himself, among other volumes, in the old travel journals of sporadic visitors to the Cape. He had seen in these reports the possibility that a later writer, like himself, might engage in conversation with these early chroniclers and in some way connect with their work, as he was to do in his first novel. From these early journals there gradually developed another kind of chronicle, more aware of and sensitive to the historical crisis of the place, yet also enamoured with the lure of its unique physical reality, landscape, and human and national relations, which make possible an own imagery and idiom.

Later his character Magda in *In the Heart of the Country* would say: 'I am corrupted to the bone with the beauty of this forsaken world'.[18] And in *Age of Iron* Elizabeth Curren says, while gazing, not far from Dias beach, at the view of the mountains across False Bay, 'These seas, these mountains: I want to burn them upon my sight so deeply that, no matter where I go, they will always be before me. I am hungry with love of this world.'[19] In much of his work, leading up to *Disgrace*, Coetzee would exploit his position as a writer with European intellectual allegiances, writing from a place of cruel indifference, where European cultural and intellectual expansion largely failed.

It is to the beauty of this desolate world with which Coetzee was corrupted that he now returned, armed with a formidable knowledge of literature and the latest developments in literary theory. He was to say repeatedly later, possibly as a way of allaying his deep ambivalence, that he did not regard himself as in the first place a South African writer, or as having any particular task in relation to the country: 'my allegiances,' he commented in an interview, 'lie with the discourse of the novels and not with the discourse of politics'.[20] Yet he was in his later books to write some of the most meaningful and profound commentaries on South Africa, the land in which he was about to settle once again. He would become part of the European tradition, the metropole, not by negating his colonial background, but by conscious, nuanced reflection on its cultural crisis.

II

Upon his arrival in South Africa, Coetzee rejoined Philippa and their two children, Nicolas and Gisela, who had returned earlier, in December 1970. Coetzee had been unemployed for a considerable time, and had very little money left. He had to make a concerted effort to provide for his family.

After a short stay in Johannesburg with Philippa's parents, they visited Cape Town, where he saw his own parents. Nicolas accompanied his mother to the Museum in the Gardens, and was fascinated by the display of dinosaurs, of which he already at that early age knew a lot.[21] After this they visited Voëlfontein, the plot of ground on earth that Coetzee loved most, the lonely Karoo farm about which he was later, in *Boyhood* and *Summertime*, to write with such warmth and affection. Whether the family actually knew or thought, as one of the fictional informants tells the biographer in *Summertime*, that Coetzee had left the US 'under some cloud or other, some disgrace', and, worse horror even than the few Coetzees who drank too much or had been declared bankrupt, had spent a night in jail,[22] is open to conjecture, but seems likely to be part of the ludic element of this novel.

Because the family really was out of pocket, Gerald Coetzee, the son of Coetzee's Uncle Son and Aunt Sylvia, arranged for them to live for free in a vacant house on a neighbouring farm. This house was on the farm Maraisdal, about three kilometres from Leeu Gamka (formerly Fraserburg Road), where Grandfather Gert Coetzee had owned the hotel, butchery and general store. In 1971 the farm belonged to one Derek Scheun, but he no longer lived there.[23] Conditions were primitive. There was no electricity and water had to be fetched in buckets. Because they could afford hardly any furniture, the children had to sleep on newspapers on the floor. Nicolas and Gisela found it a delicious adventure. Gisela later recalled how taken she was with all the animals they could keep there and how they had named each animal, but also how scared she had been of the harvester crickets that sometimes came into the house and frightened her with their racket. While staying at Maraisdal, they visited Voëlfontein often, and she later remembered the smell of mealie meal, and how the men went out in the mornings to hunt buck, or how the sheep were driven into pens to be dipped, to be shorn, and even once to be slaughtered.[24]

In spite of the inconvenience, this was a happy time for the family, as is evident from an article by Philippa published in *Fair Lady* on 12 January 1972 under the title 'Karoo Odyssey':

> I want to make a plea for holidaying in the Karoo, something more than a week-end. My family and I have just spent three months on a Karoo farm. The house was previously uninhabited so it was not as though we stepped into a smoothly run establishment. We had to do everything ourselves: chop wood, heat water on an open fire, empty the sanitation bucket daily, cook on gas and primus, read by lamplight at night. We brought in animals for our children and altogether had an interesting and rewarding time. Our chickens laid, Myrtle sat on a batch of eight eggs in a hidden self-chosen corner and we prayed the muishond would not get her; the puppies lazed in the sun, the Karoo cat climbed on the thorn trees and proudly displayed stripy Karoo mice. The farmhouse was near the banks of a river (which came down in flood and we were cut off for eight exciting hours) where hundreds of wild birds have their home—including geese, ducks and hawks. We made the acquaintance of a koringkriek; for those who don't know, this is a spitting beetle the size of a mouse. The reason we found the farmhouse empty is interesting. Wool farming is not as lucrative as it used to be, so many farmers are leaving. I saw three other farms abandoned in the district. In spring and autumn, life on a Karoo farm is ideal. The weather is neither too hot nor too cold; the flowers are out in spring, while in autumn fullness is just going out. This world is positively beautiful and anything but boring. At the nearest town (Beaufort West) I searched for a postcard of a Karoo scene. Perhaps a koppie landscape with some sheep in the foreground or a Karoo homestead with its characteristic windmills, but all in vain. Hosts of zebras and lions from the Kruger Park or the traditionals from the Cape Peninsula were all that were to be had. The Karoo is neglected in many ways, but I certainly recommend it for a holiday.

For those who would like to try it, drive along the dusty farm tracks of the Karoo and find an empty house. Somewhere it will have an owner who might, like ours, let you have it rent-free.[25]

Some of the couple's Cape Town friends sometimes came to visit, like Chris Perold and his wife Sandra. Chris Perold, an English teacher, had been at university with John and Philippa. He had not really known John at the time, but had been friendly with Philippa. When she and Nicolas visited South Africa in 1968, the Perolds had seen her again, and Nicolas had got on well with their daughter Lisa. On the Coetzees' return, the Perolds got to know John as well. They spent several days at Maraisdal, and enjoyed the fresh air of the Karoo, in spite of the primitive conditions. Coetzee, who was still unemployed but could at least afford a little Fiat, asked Perold what it was like to be a teacher in a country town, and if he could expect frequent visitations from the dominee. Perold reassured him that when he'd taught in King William's Town he had not been unduly inconvenienced by the dominee. On the Sunday of their visit the Perolds were invited with John and Philippa and the children to lunch with Uncle Son and Aunt Sylvia at Voëlfontein. As wool was no longer fetching the high prices of former years, Sylvia had to work in the hotel in Leeu Gamka during the week for an extra income. In spite of this, they spared no expense and prepared a sumptuous meal for the visitors.

At the time of the Perolds' visit to Maraisdal Coetzee was writing his first novel, in a rondavel he had constructed at a distance from the house. Coetzee was anxious for Chris Perold to read a part of the manuscript and give him an opinion. Probably, Perold admitted later in an interview, Coetzee had overestimated his friend's literary competence: he was flummoxed by the end notes, the interplay of fiction and reality, and the strange otherness of the novel. He thought submitting it to him was an error of judgement on Coetzee's part. He was not the reader to pronounce on such a radically innovative novel.[26]

The opening of the manuscript on which Coetzee began work anew at Maraisdal, 'The Narrative of Jacobus Coetzee', dated back to his Buffalo years. On 1 January 1970, he had decided, as a New Year's resolution, to start a project he had been cherishing for a long time. This date is confirmed by the manuscript of *Dusklands*, which has found a permanent home in the Harry Ransom Humanities Research Center of the University of Texas at Austin. Formerly it was held, with all Coetzee's manuscripts up to and including *Boyhood*, in the Houghton

Library at Harvard. He started writing *Dusklands* with a black ballpoint pen on lined paper, dating each daily segment as he went. That was to be Coetzee's habit throughout his writing career, to date his work at each section of a manuscript, a modus operandi that makes it possible for researchers to trace the day-by-day genesis of a novel with great precision, even where the author returned to a specific section with a red pen and noted the date of the revision. In the years before the start of the writing, he had discovered, in the university library of the University of Texas at Austin, among the old Cape travel journals, the short *Relaas* (Narrative) of a Coetzee from the third generation of that family in South Africa. The manuscript of this narrative, which is kept in the *Rijksargief* in The Hague, was originally published in 1916 by E.C. Godée Molsbergen in *Reizen in Zuid-Afrika in de Hollandsche tijd* [*Travels in South Africa in the Time of the Dutch*].[27] A second edition, together with an account of the expedition of one Hendrik Hop, was included in 1935 in the Van Riebeeck Society's edition of *The Journal of Hendrik Jacob Wikar* (1779), with an English translation by A.W. van der Horst, and *The Journals of Jacobus Coetsé Janz (1760) and Willem van Reenen (1791)*, with an English translation by E.E. Mossop.[28]

The *Relaas*, as transcribed by a secretary at the Castle of Good Hope, tells how Jacobus Coetsé (as he spelt his name) set out from his farm near the present-day Piketberg with twelve of his Griqua and Nama labourers. Next to the Olifantsrivier, the Groenrivier and the Buffelrivier (Elephant, Green and Buffalo Rivers), he felled two elephants and took the ivory with him. He found the Kamiesberg area a beautiful oasis in a barren environment. From there he travelled past the Koperberge (Copper Mountains), where Simon van der Stel had stopped in 1685, and crossed the dry and desolate Koa Valley. After a journey of twelve days he reached the Eyn or Gariep, which he would name the Grootrivier (Great River), but which was renamed the Oranje in 1799 by Robert Jacob Gordon in honour of the Dutch royal house. Next to the Great River they found pasturage for the cattle, and could take a rest. The territory beyond the Great River, which he crossed at Guados—the 'sheep crossing' that the English transmogrified to Goodhouse—was inhospitable. He followed the course of the Houm River, which he renamed the Leeuwrivier (Lion River), and where the company constantly had to be on their guard against attacks by Bushmen or wild animals. After five days they reached the territory of the Great Namaquas, who found their arrival an unwelcome intrusion. Because Coetsé was proficient in the language of the Little Namaquas, which was also understood by the Great Namaquas, he was able to make them understand that his journey had been officially approved by the governor at the Cape and that he had come with the sole purpose of shooting elephants. He put his case so persuasively and impressed them so strongly with his intrepid and forceful personality, that they let him travel on unhindered. A day later he reached the hot springs of Warmbad (Warmbaths) and the next day the Swartberg (Black Mountain), where he outspanned next to a natural spring. There, however, Coetsé decided to turn back, since he was now 680 kilometres away from his farm. On the return journey he followed a different route, travelling in an easterly direction, where he came across another tribe, the Eyniqua, and encountered many lions and rhinoceroses.

On his return to the Cape, Coetsé reported that the Namaquas had told him about the 'Damroqua' tribe with a yellow skin colour, long hair and linen clothes. This prompted the governor, Rijk Tulbagh, to order another expedition, this time led by Hendrik Hop, to verify the existence of this tribe and to determine whether it would be possible to establish trade relations with them. This company was considerably larger than that of the previous year, and comprised 17 whites, 68 Namas and 15 wagons with 150 draught oxen. Among the whites were experts to draw maps, study plants and test the quality of the copper ore. Coetsé preceded the expedition as scout and guide to report back on soil conditions and the availability of water. After arriving at the hot water springs, the expedition moved on to east of the Great Karasberg and the Xambo River, about as far as the present Keetmanshoop. Coetsé and two others reached part of the canyon formed by the Fish River. They found no trace of the Damroqua tribe. Whereas initially Coetsé had gone on ahead of the company, on the return he made up the rear to explore the territory, especially near the Great River, and to get to know the inhabitants.

This is the background material that 'The Narrative of Jacobus Coetzee' purports to reproduce. It soon becomes apparent, however, that the refashioned history of the eighteenth-century elephant hunter is the work of someone who is familiar not only with the history of the novel, but also with modern literary theory and all the narrative strategies at a writer's disposal. 'The Narrative of Jacobus Coetzee' is presented as a new 'integral translation' of the original Dutch, to which the author adds, as a postscript, his late father's introduction to the original edition by the Van Plettenburg Society, followed by an appendix containing the deposition of Jacobus Coetzee. J.M. Coetzee thus partly aligns himself with the typical eighteenth-century travel journals that in the twentieth century were romanticised as adventurous imaginary voyages of discovery. But he also subverts the tradition with a playful fusion of reality and fiction, decisively distinguishing his text from the kind of colonial literature of the last quarter of the nineteenth century and the first thirty years or so of the twentieth with its emphasis on the typically African, especially the indigenous animals and peoples.

From the title page ('edited, with an Afterword, by S.J. Coetzee, translated by J.M. Coetzee') onward, the whole of the Preface, narrative, postscript and appendix is problematised. The complete 'narrative' is the creation of J.M. Coetzee, but in the Preface he introduces himself as translator, and his father, S.J. Coetzee, as historian and writer of the afterword. All of this, however, is fiction, because J.M. Coetzee's father was not a historian, and no edition of the '*Relaas*' of Jacobus Coetzee was published in 1951 by the (non-existent) Van Plettenburg Society.[29]

J.M. Coetzee represents his new translation of the eighteenth-century narrative as a corrective to the stereotype in which the 'true' stature of the old traveller is effaced by a 'Castle hack who heard out Coetzee's story with the impatience of a bureaucrat and jotted down a hasty précis for the Governor's desk.' The hack writer thus 'records only such information as might be thought to have value for the Company',[30] omitting the colourful adventures, but also the true cruelty of Jacobus's experiences and actions when he, in Derek Attridge's words, 'makes a return visit to punish [the servants] with the utmost savagery'.[31] The hack writer concentrates on things like mineral ore deposits and 'the potential of the tribes of the interior as sources of supply'. The story of the strange northern tribe on which Jacobus had reported, is added purely as a commercial consideration. By contrast, S.J. Coetzee in his Afterword wanted to elevate Jacobus Coetzee to one of the heroic 'founders of our people'. The 'corrective' that J.M. Coetzee effects through his 'translation', however, ironically tells another story. Jacobus is depicted as a sadistic murderer who takes delight in his own atrocities. Because he sees the Hottentots and Bushmen exclusively from a European perspective, they have for him only curiosity value, as appears from his unabashed fascination with their sexual organs.[32] With the additions provided by the 'corrective', the new 'translation' becomes an attempt to bring to light the suppressed facts behind the bare account. In his essay on Achterberg J.M. Coetzee declared that the reading of a text is in essence translation, just as all translations are in the last instance literary criticism.[33] Taking one's cue from this formulation, one could then say that the reading and 'translating' of the eighteenth-century founding text becomes a rediscovery and rewriting of a hidden fragment of history.

Susan van Zanten Gallagher has commented on the manifold textual manipulations of which Coetzee avails himself and on the many filters to which the original text is subjected.[34] The afterword by S.J. Coetzee emphasises the authenticity of the 'new' edition, claiming that it is more complete than earlier editions and for that reason furnishes a more accurate view of Coetzee's experiences.[35] All of it, however, as Gallagher goes on to show, is a parody on the editions of the Van Riebeeck Society, with S.J. Coetzee as the typical conservative, authoritarian and uncritical Christian-nationalist historian proffering his research as a labour of piety towards an ancestor and a pioneer of 'our' people, a man of fortitude. Gallagher writes:

> Although his account has a façade of learning with its many footnotes and foreign words, his use of sources is sloppy at best and deliberately misleading at worst. Many of his footnotes contain slight inaccuracies: the wrong page is cited, several words omitted from quotes, two accounts conflated and presented as one. [...] S.J. claims that Jacobus's own son was murdered by his slaves and cites Lichtenstein's *Travels in Southern Africa* as his source. Lichtenstein does tell of the death of a Coetzee, but it is not the son of Jacobus Coetse (Lichtenstein 124–126). A little bit of historical research easily establishes that S.J. Coetzee is not the best of scholars, even by traditional methods of judgment.[36]

The entire work concludes with a purportedly authentic document, the original '*Relaas*' translated by J.M. Coetzee. Ever since Peter Knox-Shaw's article on Coetzee's sources it has been generally accepted that the deposition of Jacobus Coetzee is the one authentic document in *Dusklands*.[37] This mistaken assumption, however, indicates only that Knox-Shaw and other commentators following him did not take the trouble to check the *Dusklands* text against the original Dutch document. A comparison with Mossop's English translation of 1935 reveals clearly that Coetzee deliberately mistranslated. Some incidents have been omitted and others added, dates have been changed, certain phrases

have been amended and the footnotes are sometimes wrong. David
Attwell has pointed out that the friendly attitude of the Namaquas, their
permission for Jacobus to traverse their territory and the exchange of
gifts have been omitted in J.M. Coetzee's version. On the other hand,
two instances of desertion are added that do not form part of the
original '*relaas*'. The most important alteration is that the voyage of
Hendrik Hop, which was essentially a fact-finding mission to investigate
the economic prospects of possible barter with the unknown northern
tribe, has been expanded into a punitive expedition through which
Jacobus Coetzee could avenge himself on his absconded labourers. The
official document differs from the new version in that the bureaucratic
'hack' of the Castle concentrates only on bare factual considerations
and ignores matters not intended for the eyes of the governor or those
of the *Here XVII* in Holland.[38]

It is clear from the manuscript of 'The Narrative of Jacobus Coetzee'
that the first words that J.M. Coetzee wrote, according to his own dating
on 1 January 1970, were neither that Preface nor the beginning of the
narrative. This first segment, that he marks as the 'Introduction', and
that eventually was to be published as the 'Afterword', is the appendix in
which the historian S.J. Coetzee has his say. A comparison between the
initial 'Introduction' and the final text reveals how meticulously Coetzee
hones a manuscript until the words convey his exact meaning. The first
version starts, with many deletions and alterations that are indicated in
the footnotes, as follows:

> Among those heroes who first ventured into the interior of Southern
> Africa and brought us back the news of what we had inherited,
> Jacobus Janszoon Coetzee has hitherto occupied an honorable
> but minor place. He is known to scholars of our early history as
> the discoverer of the Orange River and the giraffe; but he is also
> pictured[39] as an illiterate boer[40] who brought back to Governor Rijk
> Tulbagh those fables of long-haired[41] men living[42] in the far north
> which[43] led to the loss of so many good men on the[44] expedition of
> Hendrik Hop in (1761).[45]

Coetzee refined this first version to read, as published:

> Among the heroes who first ventured into the interior of Southern
> Africa and brought back news of what we had inherited, Jacobus

Coetzee has hitherto occupied an honourable if minor place. He is acknowledged by students of our early history as the discoverer of the Orange River and the giraffe; yet from our ivory towers we have smiled indulgently too at the credulous hunter who reported to Governor Rijk Tulbagh that fable of long-haired men far in the north which led to the dispatch of Hendrik Hop's fruitless expedition of 1761–62.

According to the dating on the manuscript, the first words that Coetzee wrote on 1 January 1970 were to become the opening of what was to be published as the 'Afterword' in 1974. There must, however, have been an interruption after the initial work in Buffalo, probably owing to his problems with extending his visa, the court cases he was involved in, the departure of his family and his own return to South Africa. When the family settled at Maraisdal he was able to return to his labours. The written manuscript, still with the 'Afterword' at the beginning, was begun on 19 August 1971 and completed on 30 November 1971. While working on this holograph, he also started on the typescript on 1 October 1971, to which he made many alterations by hand.

The fact that the manuscript opens on this 'Introduction', which was later to be published as the 'Afterword', may tempt one to ask whether it might not have been Coetzee's original intention to write a historical account of Jacobus Coetzee, this distant ancestor from the eighteenth century, rather than a novel. This speculation is prompted by a letter Coetzee wrote from Maraisdal on 12 November 1971 to Professor J.I. Fradlin of the Department of English at Buffalo. In it he mentions that he has recently completed a book in 'African Studies', that he intends continuing in this area, and that he also wants to start on a critical analysis of linguistic stylistics. Perhaps Coetzee wanted to convey to Fradlin that he was still working in the literary field, and did not want to reveal that he was also involved in creative writing.

But the way in which the original Preface was to constitute the eventual Afterword of 'The Narrative of Jacobus Coetzee', makes it very clear that he had from the start intended to recast the facts as a novel. 'Recasting' is the appropriate term here, because the presentation of the whole work as a new 'translation', which is at the same time a new interpretation as well as a supplementing and critique of the original deposition, involves a complex interplay of reality and fiction that is far removed from a mere historical account. What was glossed over or simply omitted in bureaucratic slovenliness, becomes the very core of the 'Narrative'. In an interview with Christopher Hope on BBC Radio 3, in February 1993, Coetzee said that 'the old stories of discovery and exploration were in some sense written over much darker stories which have thus been obliterated, so that going back to the past becomes a matter of recovering what was covered up'.[46]

The tale of Jacobus Coetzee thus requires, in the words the fictional S.J. Coetzee uses in another context, 'a positive act of the imagination',[47] the imagination of the novelist who can interpret historical data and revive the essence of concealed material. For that reason J.M Coetzee can use the economic tyranny of the VOC, relentlessly taxing its burghers, as reason for Jacobus's turning away from the Cape and for his northward expansion, even though this motive would achieve full momentum only sixty years later with the large-scale migration of the Great Trek. Also, the depiction of Jacobus's delirium and fever dream is clearly the work of a much better writer than an obtuse hack scribe. And for that reason Jacobus becomes capable of the insight that the Hottentots, who had helped and nursed him during his illness, were not really savages:

> What was true savagery [...]? Savagery was a way of life based on disdain for the value of human life and sensual delight in the pain of others.[48]

What Jacobus verbalises here is in reality a fierce indictment of himself, even though J.M. Coetzee sees to it that his character remains believably immersed in history, enclosed in the eighteenth century, with no trace of the European Enlightenment that apparently never reached the Cape.

The projected study of linguistic stylistics that Coetzee mentioned in his letter to Fradin came to nothing for the time being. He completed the final revision of 'The Narrative of Jacobus Coetzee' on 2 January 1972, according to the information on the manuscript. But by then Coetzee and his family were no longer living at Maraisdal, because something had happened that was to direct his life once again towards an academic career.

III

Coetzee had written to Guy Howarth from Buffalo, enquiring about the possibilities of an appointment in the Department of English at UCT.

Howarth had replied that he would be retiring as professor at the end of 1971, and that he would not be in a position to take any decisions on future appointments.[49]

On 25 August 1971 an advertisement appeared in the *Cape Argus* for a senior lectureship and two lectureships in English at UCT, candidates being asked to indicate whether they wanted to be considered only for a senior lectureship or for a lectureship as well. On 30 September 1971 Coetzee applied for the senior lectureship, but specifying that he also wanted to be considered for one of the two lectureships. He attached details of his academic qualifications, previous positions and publications. As references he cited Professor S. Newman of Buffalo, Professor Arthur Norman of Austin, and Geoffrey Haresnape, the latter formerly one of his fellow-students who had been appointed in the UCT department. Coetzee outlined the subject areas in which he was interested:

> With respect to my application for the Senior Lectureship, I should note that my qualifications and interests are in modern linguistics in the American tradition rather than in historical linguistics in the German tradition. Thus in the field of English language studies I should be interested in teaching general linguistics, modern grammatical theory, the structure of English, and Middle English language and literature.

Middle English had been taught by Professor Lewis Casson until his retirement, but in the other areas mentioned by Coetzee there was on his return little or no interest among English lecturers in South Africa. As far as twentieth-century literature was concerned, English departments in general favoured the principles of I.A. Richards and the 'great tradition' as formulated by F.R. Leavis, with particular attention to the novels of D.H. Lawrence. On his return, then, Coetzee, with some years of study and experience in the US behind him, was excellently placed to effect a renewal in this state of affairs. For all practical considerations he was an excellent candidate.

On 5 November Coetzee received a telegram from the registrar inviting him, at the university's expense, for an interview on 10 November. A fellow-candidate for one of the vacancies was Jonathan Crewe, who was to become a good friend, but who left in 1974 to study in the US, and never returned to South Africa. In *Summertime* the fictional biographer of the 'late' author conducts an interview with one Martin who had turned up with Coetzee at the interview, and who is broadly recognisable as Crewe. In *Summertime* Crewe, rather than Coetzee, was the successful candidate. In fact, both of them were appointed. Whether the other details about the interview accord with the facts, as purportedly derived by the biographer from a notebook of Coetzee's, is thus uncertain, but they at least give some indication of how the interview might have run. Asked which authors he would like to teach, 'Coetzee' replies: 'I can teach pretty much across the board. I am not a specialist. I think of myself as a generalist.' And to himself, long since accustomed to count his words and to keep his replies short and to the point, he thought:

> These people don't want brief answers. They want something more leisurely, more expansive, something that will allow them to work out what kind of fellow they have before them, what kind of junior colleague he would make, whether he would fit in a provincial university that is doing its best to maintain standards in difficult times, to keep the flame of civilization burning.[50]

Apparently there was not time enough to consult with Coetzee's overseas references, and Haresnape was on leave overseas. For that reason Guy Howarth asked Daniel Hutchinson, the only member of staff present, who was also on the point of departure, to write a report on Coetzee. Howarth himself, as outgoing professor, could not serve on the appointments committee. The chairman was Donald Inskip, former Professor of French, who had played an important part in the activities of the Little Theatre and the Drama Department. He had been vice-principal of UCT for years. In his report Hutchinson described Coetzee as 'deceptively modest and unassuming to a fault ... succinct in speech and of exceptional intelligence, [someone who] ... will greatly enhance teaching, scholarship and research'.[51] Without being in a position to know how prophetic these words were to prove, this was the sentence that Inskip selected as a summary of Coetzee's qualities as a candidate.

On 21 December 1971 Coetzee, by now living in Silver Gulls, Kemps Road, in Glencairn, near Simon's Town, received a letter from the registrar of UCT offering him a temporary lecturer's post for 1972. That it was initially only a temporary position may have been attributable to the fact that the new incumbent of the Arderne Chair and successor to Howarth would only be assuming his post on 1 January 1972, and would be given the opportunity to vet the new appointment. The new professor, David Gillham, who had been at the University of Stellenbosch and the University of Natal (Pietermaritzburg) previously, had written a doctorate on William Blake at the University of Bristol. He was an ardent proponent of a simplistic, dated British method of 'practical criticism', which he expected all members of staff to adhere to. He wanted courses in the department to be exclusively devoted to classic British literature, although provision was made to include some American authors. South African literature, and literature from other Commonwealth countries, he regarded as not worth teaching.

The new broom thus was diametrically opposed to Howarth's inclusion of previously excluded material. Gillham had no interest in modern developments in literary theory, nor in modern linguistics, and had no appreciation for his predecessor's work in the field of 'bibliology'. Before Gillham's arrival Howarth had neatly arranged all the assignments of his students and the question papers from his years in office for his successor. Coetzee writes:

> The first thing his [Howarth's] successor in the Arderne Chair did was to have the janitors clear out and burn the tons of essays and poems by students with which Howarth, a great accumulator of paper, had stuffed all the cupboards in the building. The Honours course he had constructed, with its long reading lists and heavy emphasis on bibliography and textual scholarship, was thrown out of the window and replaced with a sparse Leavisite curriculum.[52]

While the janitors were carting away all Howarth's students' work, Daniel Hutchinson noticed in passing a complete set of Coetzee's exam scripts, neatly bound with string and written in his neat hand, with the answer on *Tristram Shandy* crammed into half a page. Hutchinson thought this too valuable to destroy. He writes:

> A trove! When I told him [Coetzee] of my find, he blanched. To literature's loss I gave them to him, no doubt to be passed straight into the flames.[53]

It was inevitable that such opposing approaches to the teaching of literature should lead to friction and eventually to confrontation—not only between Gillham and Coetzee, but also between Gillham and other members of staff. Even so, it was not in Gillham's power to stop Coetzee's permanent appointment in 1972. In 1974 Coetzee would apply for an ad hoc promotion to senior lecturer on the grounds of his lecturing and publications, but he was not recommended for it. When, however, he submitted his curriculum vitae again in 1976, he was successful, and was promoted to senior lecturer. In a letter dated 11 November 1976, the vice-principal, Professor M.F. Kaplan, writes to him: 'I feel sure that you will derive great satisfaction and encouragement from this recognition of your academic achievements and service to the University.'

On his appointment to UCT, Coetzee moved into a small, bare and unattractive office in the Arts Block, looking out onto University Avenue and the Jagger Library. He was tall and lean, dressed simply and without adornment in long pants and a dark jacket, as inconspicuous as possible in his beard, unlike grandiloquent lecturers like Philip Birkinshaw, who, with his instinct for the stage, delivered his lectures in declamatory style. Coetzee had an intellectual approach to posing questions about events, human behaviour and texts. He would often open a proposition with the words 'The question I ask myself is ...' Then he would reveal the problematic aspect of the apparently cut-and-dried, when viewed from an unfamiliar angle. His absolute honesty in his dealings with literature struck everybody who had anything to do with him. As far as his lecturing was concerned, Daniel Hutchinson says: 'He was softly spoken with characteristically ironic emphases in speech, and ending sentences with a rise in intonation or, sometimes, a shrug with upturned open palms. Though his voice was slight, as a lecturer he took no pains to project it and yet his thoughtful material ensured rapt audiences.'[54]

Despite Gillhams's watchful eye, Coetzee immediately started implementing in his courses the knowledge he had gained in the US. He included De Saussure and other theoreticians, demonstrating the benefits of a strict, professional post-graduate education in the US, unlike that of most of his colleagues, with their fixation on further study at British universities.[55] Ian Glenn, one of his colleagues, writes in an article that Coetzee returned from the US with:

> knowledge drawn from the most recent developments in Western thinking. Coetzee's intellectual trajectory is, in other words, that of the dominant mode in contemporary literary studies: American, with strong French influences. Within the literary-intellectual field in South Africa, he has confronted the British-oriented traditions

of literary criticism with recent structuralist and poststructuralist theories. His distance from British models and values, his American postgraduate education in the rising field of linguistics, and his residency in the United States during the 1960s gave him a particular set of interests and views on South Africa and literary studies within it, views which have in general—and in no small measure through his impact—become the dominant ones. [...] As with his theoretical models, many of his literary influences (Kafka, Beckett, Joyce, Nabokov, Borges) belong to no single national tradition but to a major, modern, deracinated, and difficult to classify international tradition.[56]

In an interview with Peter Temple in the *Cape Argus* of 19 June 1974, Coetzee says, modestly: 'I have no particular talent for teaching and I devote much time to a kind of niggling preparation than I ought to be doing ... basically I'm afraid of the lecturing situation.' His class notes, however, held at the National English Literary Museum in Grahamstown, suggest that Coetzee prepared his courses extremely carefully and was a dedicated lecturer with a lively interest in his subject. His first-year students received meticulously typed worksheets on poems, with Socratic questioning and commentary,[57] which pointed them to a thorough investigation and to which the dedicated students reacted with enthusiasm. Lesley Marx, later a senior member of the English Department, remembers Coetzee as a brilliant and inspiring lecturer who in her undergraduate years lectured on Henry James's *Washington Square*, T.S. Eliot's poems and Patrick White's *Voss*. She writes: 'I also took the third-year seminar on Nineteenth-Century American Fiction taught by him and other colleagues in my third year and the Honours-level course on Realism in the Novel, also co-taught by him and other colleagues. Both courses were superlative. [...] John was a kind friend and very supportive colleague, notably when I became head of department.'[58] For his students, as many of them testify, he was prepared to sacrifice anything, and he would go out of his way to promote their interests and to help them in their future careers.

It is clear, however, from his instructions for attendance at his poetry tutorial groups that he did not tolerate idle students turning up unprepared at class: 'Please do not come to your tutorial if you have not done the assigned work. All written work will be marked.' One of the courses he offered at honours level in 1974 was devoted to 'Art and

the End of Art: Pound, Faulkner, Stevens, Beckett.' He outlines his aims
clearly for prospective students, an indication of the generous ambit of
his course:

> In this section we will trace certain changes toward the social
> function of the artist, the nature of the imagination, and the nature
> of language. We will first read three writers who in their different
> ways find a bedrock of certitude in the creative imagination:
> Ezra Pound, transmitter of the wisdom of the ancients, doctor of
> language; William Faulkner, master of the art of memory as ecstatic
> recapture of and liberation from history; and Wallace Stevens, the
> artist who re-names the world into existence. Side by side with these
> writers we will read some poems by Rilke. Then, after looking again
> at Nabokov's *Pale Fire* and at the stories of Jorge Luis Borges for
> the growing ambivalence they show about the powers of art, we
> will take up the experience of the rupture between language and
> things in Sartre's *Nausea*. We will then read one of Samuel Beckett's
> later novels, in which the art-work is seen stripped of metaphysical
> sanction. From Beckett we will look ahead to the practice of Alain
> Robbe-Grillet and John Barth.

Coetzee's notes on T.S. Eliot, the basis of a course he offered in 1974,
demonstrate not only a thorough knowledge of the literature on the
poet, but also the depth of the insights he could convey to his students,
immersing himself with the full force of his personality in the study of
the poetry. One may even speculate that these notes on Eliot were partly
aimed at the Leavisites in his immediate vicinity with their veneration of
Lawrence. Coetzee writes:

> Now it is a matter of history that it was Eliot and not Lawrence
> who came effectively to create the image of the 1920's for itself
> as a 'waste land' of debilitation, impotence, boredom, and vague
> menace. And when a poet is welcomed with the flood of second-
> hand imitation and crazed vituperation that greeted Eliot, it must be
> that deep-lying nerves are being touched. This never happened with
> Lawrence. Why? In his later poetry Eliot used the metaphor of the
> wounded surgeon for the artist. The wounded surgeon, the tainted
> diagnostician—perhaps that is the reason for Eliot's profound
> insight into, and profound effect on, his age: being afflicted with

the late-industrial, late-imperial, post-Christian malaise, perhaps he was in the best position to see what was wrong with his civilization.

Coetzee's later work as a writer, invoking as it does an extensive literary frame of reference, suggests that the notes on Eliot contain an element of self-characterisation. From Eliot's essay on the metaphysical poets he quotes an important pronouncement on Donne: 'When a poet's mind is perfectly equipped for its work, it is constantly amalgamating disparate experience.'[59] Coetzee's commentary on this brings to the informed reader's mind, in some of the pronouncements, a veiled self-image. His comments on Eliot's poetry hold true for his own creative work:

> That is the miraculous thing about Eliot: that a man so profoundly split within himself, with a mind continually so near disintegration, should in a different way have been able to confront experience in so integrated a way. For what he writes [in his essay on Donne—JCK] is absolutely true about himself. His poetry is learned, full of the past, but the learning is never something superadded. Intellectual experience, emotional experience, sense experience are somehow all on the same plane in Eliot.

Upon settling in Cape Town, Coetzee started taking part in the general literary life and published some of his first critical essays. In 1978 he acted, with Mark Swift, as a judge for the Ingrid Jonker Prize, which they awarded to Colin Style. Coetzee provided this sober and concise commendation: 'The best of Colin Style's poetry is accomplished, lucid, compassionate. He knows what it is to live in Africa. He gives us the sights and smells of this life, but also its sudden mysteries.' His discussion of Wilhelm Fucks's *Nach allen Regeln der Kunst* in *Style*, V: 1, 1971, a kind of guide to the stylostatistics that Coetzee practised in his doctoral dissertation at the University of Texas, is a settling of scores with the type of statistical approach to literature that confines itself to measurable units (word lengths, sentence lengths, grammatical function, etc.). In 1973, in *UCT Studies in English*, he discussed *The Pound Era* by Hugh Kenner, a critic whose work had impressed him even in his early student days, and whom he now called 'the most accomplished *reader* of his generation, superior even to Roland Barthes'. In 1974 he published in the same journal a short study of Nabokov's *Pale Fire*, which had fascinated him in Buffalo by its various levels of reality and its questioning of its own 'fictional premises'. In a second article in this journal, he discussed George Steiner's *On Difficulty and Other Essays*, expressing admiration of Steiner's formidable command, both of technical literature in the fields of linguistics and the philosophy of language, and of the major European literatures. In 1974 he published his essay on Alex La Guma, lamenting the fate of so many of his South African writer colleagues: 'So much of the intelligentsia is in prison or in exile, so much serious work has been banned by the censors, that the work of black South African writers has become a kind of émigré literature written by outcasts for foreigners. There can thus be no argument, as in independent Africa, that a vital if crude national school of writing will eventually both educate and be educated by its audience, for the work of the South African exile is deprived of its social function and indeed of the locus of its existence in a community of writers and readers.'[60]

Coetzee wrote two reviews in Afrikaans at this time. In his review of Stephen Gray's novel *Local Colour* he pointed out its relation to Melville's *Moby Dick* and noted some criticisms of Gray's novel. His review of Adam Small's drama *The Orange Earth* (the only time in his career that he wrote about drama) traces the development of an emotionally damaged boy to the point when, found guilty of terrorism, he awaits execution. Both reviews show insight, but one does get the impression that Coetzee is not at ease writing in Afrikaans and sometimes uses a word that does not altogether fit its context.[61]

In a review of Michael Wade's study of Nadine Gordimer[62] Coetzee points out that Gordimer in the first phase of her writing career had explored the ethos of the dominant white South African elite, showing the loss of the moral foundations brought from nineteenth-century liberal Britain by their ancestors. In her novels *The Late Bourgeois World* (1966), *A Guest of Honour* (1971) and *The Conservationist* (1974) she identifies the European past as the wrong past to discover, and implies that the way to the future must be based on an African past. What Gordimer thus achieves, according to Wade, is 'a new sense of history', a judgement Coetzee endorses, though he poses some questions about the discrepancy between the moral principles people believe themselves to value, and the reality—the love of comfort, the exploitation and the discrimination—of their social behaviour. Apropos of this, Coetzee writes:

What I would have liked further, [...] would have been a more searching investigation of the grounds for her accedence to the liberal myth. [...] The past that white South Africa must accept is a past based on colonialism and neo-colonialism, exploitation, and repression.

With his appointment as lecturer at UCT, Coetzee became part of a happy academic milieu, even though he would in the years to come have to deal with a head of department who sought to impose his own critical approach on his colleagues. It was admittedly a shock to discover how limited South African library resources were, compared with Austin and Buffalo. More than before his departure in December 1961, he now found that all the songs on the radio came from America, while the newspapers diligently reported the fads and foibles of American film stars, and slavishly aped American obsessions like the hula hoop. There was thus now an infiltration of popular culture and less of the conservative element than before.

As opposed to these superficial influences, Coetzee and Philippa had brought with them an element of American counterculture, which made for a refreshing change to the British orientation of most other members of the English Department. At first they lived in Glencairn in a partly built house, but then moved to 24 Prospect Hill, Wynberg. Yet later they settled in Tokai Road, Tokai.[63] Because Coetzee, apart from his lack of money, was averse to assuming a position of authority over coloured people, the family employed no domestic help or gardener. If the details in *Summertime* are to be trusted, the house in Tokai had formerly been a farmhouse. Over the years the house had fallen into disrepair and Coetzee, partly as recreation, spent some time working on it, among other jobs by covering the bricks with cement. Whether everything happened in just this way is less important than the spirit that this activity conveys to the reader of *Summertime*:

> Week after week, using a shovel and a wheelbarrow, he mixes sand, stone, cement and water; block after block he pours liquid concrete and levels it. His back hurts, his arms and wrists are so stiff that he can barely hold a pen. Above all the labour bores him. Yet he is not unhappy. What he finds himself doing is what people like him should have been doing ever since 1652, namely, his own dirty work. In fact, once he forgets about the time he is giving up, the work begins to take on its own pleasure. There is such a thing as a well-laid slab whose well-laidness is plain for all to see. The slabs he is laying

will outlast his tenancy of the house, may even outlast his spell on earth; in which case he will in a certain sense have cheated death. One might spend the rest of one's life laying slabs, and fall each night into the profoundest sleep, tired with the ache of honest toil.[64]

With her interest in Greek culture and literature, Philippa named the house Ithaka, the place, according to the poem by Constantine Cavafy, to which one has been voyaging all one's life, until on 'a summer morning ... you come into harbours seen for the first time'.[65]

IV

Early in 1972, before the start of classes at UCT, Coetzee sent his translation of Marcellus Emants's novel, *Een nagelaten bekentenis,* entitled *A Posthumous Confession,* which he had completed in the US, to William Heinemann in London. Shortly afterwards, W.R. Smith of Heinemann's informed Coetzee that they had carefully considered the manuscript:

> This is certainly an interesting work, but in our opinion it would have only minority appeal in this country and in the circumstances we do not feel able to make an offer.

It was only in 1973 that the translation was accepted for publication by the *Stichting ter Bevordering van de Vertaling van Nederlands Letterkundig Werk* [Foundation for the Advancement of Translation of Dutch Literary Work]. In a letter from D.J.J.D. de Wit of this Foundation, the readers are quoted as saying that Coetzee had retained the 'atmosphere and style' of Emants, while yet remaining 'lively and interesting'. The editor of *The Library of Netherlandic Literature,* of which it would form part, also felt that this book deserved a place in the series. It appeared in 1975 from Twayne in Boston.

But Coetzee was now mainly interested in having his latest work, an attempt at a short novel, published. At about the same time as he was submitting *A Posthumous Confession,* he sent the manuscript of 'The Narrative of Jacobus Coetzee' to James Brown Associates, a New York-based literary agency. He had clearly envisaged international marketing of his work from the start, not wanting to be branded as a writer from the colonies. Hermann Wittenberg, who has made an extensive and meticulous study of the 'archeology' of *Dusklands*, notes that from the start of his writing career Coetzee 'repeatedly expressed reluctance to be included in a narrow, nationally defined category of South African writing or a geographically constrained provincialism'.[66] It is noteworthy that he offered only the tale of Jacobus Coetzee for publication, not the complete *Dusklands* as it would later be published. Indeed, the first part, 'The Vietnam Project', had not been written.

Coetzee's intention to market his works internationally was in keeping with the realities of the book trade in Africa at the time. London and Paris, and sometimes also New York, were regarded as the metropoles. African writers generally submitted their manuscripts to publishers in the relevant metropole, from where they were once again exported to the province, and marketed elsewhere.[67] In reply to his submission, David Stewart Hull of the James Brown agency wrote to Coetzee on 12 January 1972 that he found the work to be a 'tour de force' and that he would like to handle it. He adds, however: 'I must be quite honest and say that it will be difficult to place the manuscript, as it is so unusual, and the length—on the short side—might be an additional problem, but I'd like to give it a try.'

Probably on account of the South African themes and the strange experiment in the relation of reality and fiction, Hull did not succeed in placing Coetzee's manuscript with an American publisher. In an interview with UCT's *Monday Paper* Coetzee says, without mentioning names, that 'The Narrative of Jacobus Coetzee' had been rejected by four publishers. Andrew van der Vlies, too—who derived his information from Mike Kirkwood, later of Ravan Press—says in an article that the 'manuscript of *Dusklands* was rejected by a number of foreign publishers',[68] again without any indication as to their identity. According to Wittenberg, Coetzee's manuscript was then rejected by all the 'normal' South African publishers.[69] He mentions the case of Ad Donker, who read it in bed and found it not to his taste.[70] Apart from Donker, it is not clear from Wittenberg's account which publishers he has in mind here. One he could have mentioned is Human & Rousseau, a Cape Town firm, known since its inception in 1959 as the publisher of the new generation of often avant-garde Afrikaans writers in rebellion agains the taboos of a conservative society. Coetzee knew some of these writers, and would have identified with their ambitions. He submitted the manuscript of 'The Narrative of Jacobus Coetzee' on 28 December 1972 to Human & Rousseau. Again, however, it was rejected.

Given all the rejections, one must agree with Wittenberg that '*Dusklands*'s initial rejection reflects badly on the state of publishing in South Africa in the 1970s [...], but it also put Coetzee in the illustrious and long list of famous writers who struggled to have their first book published.'[71]

Even before submitting 'The Narrative of Jacobus Coetzee' to Human & Rousseau, Coetzee, at this late stage of his dwindling poetic ambition, sent the poem 'heroic poetry' to the editors of *boundary 2*, a magazine published by the English Department of the State University of New York at Binghampton. He made this submission on 14 April 1972. When by 28 August he had still not heard from the journal, he enquired again and added:

> Magazines seem to have a habit of folding as soon as I submit things to them. So if you can't yet let me have a decision about the poem, you might at least reassure me that *boundary 2* still exists.

To his humorous reproach, the editors replied that they were still 'alive and kicking', but had decided against publication of the poem:

> It is not easy to say why, but it probably has something to do with a certain laboured quality in the verbal accumulations.

Coetzee's submission, on 24 October 1972, of a long experimental poem titled 'beowulf' to the magazine *Extensions* in New York was once again unsuccessful. Coetzee may well have realised by now that his poetic endeavours were not bearing fruit. It is worth noting, however, that once again he opted to submit his work to foreign journals, rather than, for instance, to *Contrast* or *Standpunte*, which were both published in Cape Town. He did, with Daniel Hutchinson, contribute short articles on Sydney Clouts and Alex La Guma to their colleague Alan Lennox-Short's *English and South Africa*,[72] but as far as poetry was concerned, he admitted to Hutchinson, 'I just haven't got it.'

Apparently David Stewart Hull's comment on the modest size of the tale of Jacobus Coetzee and the rejection by Ad Donker had set Coetzee thinking, because on 11 June 1972, with the first semester of his first year as a lecturer behind him, he started work on a second tale, which occupied him until 12 September. In a 1994 lecture to the English Department at the University of Tulsa, Oklahoma, Coetzee said that he wrote the 'Narrative' first, but thought that it couldn't stand on its own, and so had started on a 'companion piece', the tale of Eugene Dawn.[73] Whether this really was the reason for the second tale, or whether it had been prompted by the repeated rejections of the Jacobus narrative, is impossible to establish.

The second tale progressed relatively slowly. After the initial work on it, there was an interruption, probably due to Coetzee's lecturing load in the second semester. In the period December 1972 to April 1973 he reworked the text, followed by a final revision and the typescript, which he completed on 24 May 1973. The final typed copy comprises fifty pages.[74]

'The Vietnam Project', which was later combined with 'The Narrative of Jacobus Coetzee' to constitute *Dusklands*, focuses on a totally different setting and period. The narrator is a man named Eugene Dawn, who in or around 1970, in service of the US Department of Defence, has to write a report on how to undermine the enemy in Vietnam psychologically by propaganda. Dawn has to submit his report to a man called Coetzee, somebody, according to Dawn, without imagination, 'who does not believe in magic',[75] whereas he himself is of artistic temperament, and couches his report in the avant-garde tradition that Coetzee finds too new-fangled and experimental. Although Coetzee pretends to be satisfied with the report and to be pleased at being associated with somebody who can write so well, Dawn is nevertheless obliged to revise his report to 'convince of the justness of your recommendations' the 'slow-thinking, suspicious and conservative'[76] military types. In the new report, the core of the tale, Dawn recommends that they should take account of the collective psyche of the Vietnamese rather than think of them as individuals. The charges of cruelty against the Americans, he argues, are meaningless if they can't be proved—a reaction reminiscent of the justifications of the South African government in the 1970s, which Coetzee, fresh from the US, would have heard in news bulletins on the radio. 'Atrocity charges are empty,' says Dawn, 'when they cannot be proved. 95 per cent of the villages we wiped off the map were never on it.'[77] When Dawn studies photos of the mutilated and poisoned bodies of the Vietnamese who died in the US offensive, he is not filled with revulsion, but, ironically, with regret that the Americans were not accepted as liberators by their enemies. Coetzee's prose here derives some of its force from the reader's realisation that the shocking reality can also stand as metaphor for conditions in South Africa:

Why could they not accept us? We could have loved them: our hatred for them grew only out of broken hopes. [...] We landed on the shores of Vietnam clutching our arms and pleading for someone to stand up without flinching to these probes of reality: if you will prove yourself, we shouted, you will prove us too, and we will love you endlessly and shower you with gifts.

But like everything else they withered before us. We bathed them in seas of fire, praying for the miracle. In the heart of the flame their bodies glowed with heavenly light; in our ears their voices rang; but when the fire died they were only ash. We lined them up in ditches. If they had walked toward us singing through the bullets we would have knelt and worshipped; but the bullets knocked them over and they died as we had feared. We cut their flesh open, we reached into their dying bodies, tearing out their livers, hoping to be washed in their blood; but they screamed and gushed like our most negligible phantoms. We forced ourselves deeper than we had ever gone before into their women; but when we came back we were still alone, and the women like stones.[78]

Both narratives in *Dusklands* thus, in spite of the distance of nearly two hundred years separating them, deal with people who are complicit in a particular kind of development that enlists them in subjugating and exploiting those whom they regard as inferior. Whereas the story of Jacobus Coetzee is set during the conquest of Southern Africa around 1760, Eugene Dawn's narrative concerns the exploitation and subjugation of Vietnam, as orchestrated by a state department of the US. Both tales deal with aggression and the ways in which a dominant group is prepared to impose its authority on other cultures, even though it may entail premeditated mass murder. So preoccupied is Dawn with his project that he cannot sustain a satisfactory relationship with his wife, 'the swimwear model I married',[79] even though he finds her physically entrancing. It is no coincidence that her name recalls Marilyn Monroe, one of the great sex goddesses of the twentieth century.[80]

The strange genesis of *Dusklands* leads one to question whether the two narratives in fact cohere as a single unit, and thus if it can be called a novel. In an interview with Joanna Scott, Coetzee says:

'The Vietnam Report' [Project—JCK] grew out of my feelings' about what was going on in Vietnam. Because I lived in the United

States while it was a country at war, those feelings could not be other than intense. [...] The two narratives have a relation at the level of ideas, but otherwise the relation is loose. Is it so loose that the two parts might as well be separate publications? I don't know. I don't want to dodge your question, but a novel is ultimately nothing but a prose fiction of a certain length. It has no formal requirements to satisfy; to that extent, the question of whether X or Y is 'really' a novel can't be very interesting. By itself, 'The Narrative of Jacobus Coetzee' is no more and no less of a novel than, say, *A Journal of the Plague Year*, where Defoe also invested some energy in faking an authentic record.[81]

In spite of the huge distance in time and space between the two tales there is a dialectic between them in terms of subject matter, moral questions and motifs, as well as cross-references linking the two.[82] In both tales the fictionality of the narrative is signalled through the use of the name Coetzee, and the twentieth-century history of US involvement in Vietnam is paralleled by colonial atrocities in eighteenth-century Southern Africa, as if the two stories were echoing each other. A clear link is established between Dawn and Jacobus in Dawn's claim that he could have been a pioneer and explorer: 'Had I lived two hundred years ago I would have had a continent to explore, to map, to open to colonization.'[83] Pascal Carré, also quoting this sentence, adds: 'Jacobus Coetzee is the embodiment of Dawn's dreams: he is that explorer, that colonizer who made his way through unexplored, unmapped countries, two hundred years before Dawn's time.'[84] Both narrators have something of Defoe's *Robinson Crusoe* about them, the first English novel to reflect an element of European expansion and the conquest of new territories for financial gain, often disguised as a Christian crusade. Both Jacobus and Dawn have, in Pierre Macherey's term, the giant figure of Crusoe as 'thematic ancestor'.[85] Even so, the methods of the two differ from each other through the distance in time and by the fact that the Crusoe figure in Coetzee's debut novel is not yet as prominent a presence as in the later *Foe. Dusklands* introduces the motif of the master-servant relation in Coetzee's work, through which he connects directly with the philosophy of Friedrich Hegel.[86] In both tales there are signs of a feeling of guilt: in Dawn's story, on account of the American atrocities in Vietnam; in the tale of Jacobus, the guilt of the ancestors at the history of oppression.[87]

But there is something else present in *Dusklands*. Derek Attridge writes:

> Both works make a claim to be documentaries of sorts, the first an autobiographical account by an expert in psychological warfare that includes verbatim the report he has written for the American military, in numbered sections, and the second a scholarly publication translated from Afrikaans and Dutch by one J.M. Coetzee.[88]

In the Jacobus tale J.M. Coetzee plays a complex game with reality and fiction in the rewriting of the voyage of an eighteenth-century Coetzee, whereas Eugene Dawn must submit his report to one Coetzee who is never identified more closely. Both parts of the text contain, however vague and camouflaged, a fragment of autobiographical data that, especially in the Dawn character, can be related to recognisable aspects of the author. In his youth Dawn was accustomed to the 'adulation'[89] of his mother, and was a clever child who was seen but not heard.[90] Like Coetzee in Austin, Dawn spent his days in the Truman Library, a 'bookish man' with iron discipline, at his best, like Coetzee, early in the morning: 'My creative spasm comes only in the early hours of the morning when the enemy in my body is too sleepy to throw up walls against the forays of my brain.'[91] Again like Coetzee, Dawn in his youth exposed himself by composing poetry, 'derivative but not shamefully bad',[92] even though he believes that his best work, like that of the mathematician Coetzee as a programmer in England, is his 'New Life' project, which is also a form of poetry. This is why he eventually, now badly ill and institutionalised, can say that he is a mere cipher, a mathematician. It is a glimpse into himself that can lead to knowledge, because 'We cannot know until we can measure.'[93]

V

With both sections of *Dusklands* completed, Coetzee once again seriously considered publication. 'The Narrative of Jacobus Coetzee' had, however, not been followed up by his American agent, and had been rejected by South African publishers. He wrote to the journal *Contrast* on 26 May 1973, in the hope that Jack Cope, the editor, could find a home for it. He now for the first time used the unifying title *Dusklands*, a title recalling Spengler's *Der Untergang des Abendlandes* (The Decline of the West), Nietzsche's *Götten-Dämmerung* (Twilight of the Gods) and W.E.B. du Bois's *Dusk of Dawn*.[94] In Coetzee's letter to Cope, he tells him about his vain attempts to have his work published:

> I am sending you today, by separate registered post, a 126-page manuscript called DUSKLANDS. It consists of two novellas, 'The Vietnam Project' (about 19 000 words) and 'The narrative of Jacobus Coetzee' (about 29 000 words).
>
> Can you use either for *Contrast*? If you can't—and I realize that length is a big deterrent factor—I should really be most grateful for any comment you might care to make about the works themselves, and for any advice you might have on how to get either or both published.
>
> The earlier work, 'The Narrative of Jacobus Coetzee,' has been in the hands of a New York agent, James Brown Associates, and in the hands of his London affiliate, Lawrence Pollinger, since early 1972. Neither has reported a nibble; in fact, neither sounds particularly enthusiastic about it. It has been seen by one South African publisher, Human & Rousseau, who turned it down without comment.[95] Quite aside from internal demerits, 29 000 words is an inconvenient length, and the subject—nominally the expedition of Jacobus Coetzee to the Orange River in 1760—not one to lure an audience, much less an overseas audience. It would seem more natural to try to publish it in South Africa. Should I translate it into Afrikaans and become a Sewentiger? The idea is absurd.
>
> 'The Vietnam Project,' which is about America, has occupied me over the past year. I will be sending copies off to New York and London within the next few days.
>
> I feel uneasy about foisting a manuscript of this length off on to you. But here I sit with a block of paper whose value I have no clear idea of: I would really appreciate an estimate I can trust.

Coetzee's letter exudes a despondency at having to dispose of a work that he had now, at least as far as the second tale was concerned, tried to market a number of times. His efforts had been so fruitless that he was starting to doubt the quality of his work. His diffidence is evident from the fact that he could even consider submitting tales of this length to a literary journal, knowing that publication of the manuscript would far exceed the available space of a single issue of *Contrast*. Cope's reply has not survived, but it is clear that he was not altogether taken with the two tales. On 25 July 1973 Coetzee thanks him for reading *Dusklands* and for 'your kind if discouraging comments'. In a desperate effort he sent the manuscript on 25 July 1973 to the South African branch of Macmillan in Johannesburg, only to receive it back on 15 October with a brusque rejection: 'After careful consideration and lengthy discussions we have, much to our regret, come to a negative decision regarding the publication of your manuscript, which we hereby return.'

Coetzee was now at his wits' end. At this stage Jonathan Crewe who, like Coetzee, had at the beginning of 1972 started as a lecturer at UCT, had become aware that his colleague was also writing, besides essays on literature, creative work. Crewe read some of the essays and commented on them, but Coetzee never showed him the manuscript of *Dusklands*, probably because he was now uncertain about its quality and was in any case diffident about his creative work. Many years later Crewe recalled how it had come about that he got to read the manuscript:

> With some trepidation I asked to read it, since more often than not it is embarrassing to have to respond to one's academic colleagues' fictional and poetic efforts. After reading just a few pages of *Dusklands*, I felt stunned and excited; it immediately seemed to me like an extraordinary breakthrough in S.A. writing in English at that time, the field being defined by people like Paton, the earlier Gordimer, Jack Cope, and Dan Jacobson. I couldn't have defined it in these terms at the time, but in retrospect *Dusklands* marked the arrival of the postmodern novel in SA. (I believe Coetzee's *Youth* gives a good account of the impasse high modernism had created for an aspiring writer of his generation.)
>
> *Dusklands* clearly seemed like a strange beast to many readers at the time of its publication. (I'm now amused at how practically any literary conversation among South Africans, including writers, turns within moments to Coetzee.)[96]

Because he was convinced that a work of such high quality should be published, Crewe got in touch with Peter Randall who had recently, along with Danie van Zyl and Beyers Naudé, started the small firm Ravan Press, as an adjunct to the Christian Institute's Spro-Cas project.[97] Randall had worked for Oxford University Press in South Africa since

1953, but had left when they expected him to concentrate exclusively on school handbooks. With the establishment of Ravan in 1972, Randall decided to concentrate on oppositional writings in social studies and history, but he was also interested in publishing poetry and fiction. Like two other small publishers, David Philip in Cape Town and Ad Donker in Johannesburg, Randall dared to publish books that were risky in the light of publications control legislation. Like Philip and Donker, Randall was under the scrutiny of the security police, and the victim of all sorts of intimidation and harassment.

In the year of its founding, Ravan published a collection of protest poetry by James Matthews and Gladys Thomas under the title *Cry Rage*, followed the next year by Wopko Jensma's *Sing for our Execution*. Fairly soon after publication, *Cry Rage* was banned, a fate that was soon to befall several other of Ravan's books. In a 1997 article on the early years of Ravan, Randall writes:

> From the beginning the policy was to publish only material relating to contemporary southern African issues and to foster the work of new black writers. Merit was to be a major criterion in the selection of both literary and socio-political manuscripts. [...] The company constantly walked a financial tightrope and further bannings could have been disastrous. Some bookshops were afraid to stock our titles and some were visited by the special branch to dissuade them from doing so.[98]

Coetzee was very grateful for the word Crewe had put in for him with Ravan, and was prepared to submit his manuscript to this new publisher. Later he was to say to Peter McDonald: 'I knew nothing about Ravan except that it had been in trouble with the government, which was a good sign, and that it had some kind of Christian background, which was not necessarily a good sign. I was surprised that they took the book: *Dusklands* was quite a "literary" book, and Ravan was not a "literary" publisher.'[99]

On 22 October 1973 Coetzee sent *Dusklands* to Ravan, accompanied by a covering letter. 'The courteous, formal, slightly distant tone of the covering letter, as well as its brevity,' Hermann Wittenberg writes, 'effaces any sense of affect a first author might be expected to have when submitting his first book, and the laconic closing sentence signals his willingness to accept a negative outcome.'[100] Coetzee writes:

I enclose for your consideration a manuscript entitled DUSKLANDS. It consists of two short fictions, THE VIETNAM REPORT[101] (19000 words) and THE NARRATIVE OF JACOBUS COETZEE (29000 words).
    I also enclose return postage.[102]

In his reply of 2 November 1973 Peter Randall writes that, as far as the manuscript is concerned, he is 'in no doubt as to its quality and significance' and that he is eager to publish it. Since fiction, however, is 'new territory' for their firm, he would like to know from Coetzee whether the book will also be published by a British or American publisher; whether, in view of the fact that they have hitherto been a non-profitmaking concern with little capital, he would be expecting a royalty; whether he would settle for paperback publication; and whether he insisted on American spelling as in the submitted text or would be prepared to change it. As far as royalties are concerned, he points out that Ravan had offered Wopko Jensma payment after the costs incurred in the publication of his poetry collection *Sing for Our Execution* had been covered. Randall concludes: 'Let me emphasise my keenness to publish your book. I merely want to explain our position in fairness to you, and to have your reaction to the above points.'

In his reply of 5 November 1973 Coetzee expresses his satisfaction that Ravan wants to publish *Dusklands*, but it is clear that he wishes to deal very precisely and carefully with his creation. He writes:

Let me try to answer your questions as clearly as I can.

1. I am of course interested in publication overseas as well as in South Africa. But as long as I retain the overseas rights, previous publication in South Africa is no disadvantage, at least to US publishers. Ravan Press is the only publisher in South Africa presently considering the manuscript. There is another copy in the hands of my agent in New York. He would have to vet the contract, but I don't anticipate any difficulty.
2. Royalties. I am under no illusions about the amount of money to be made from first novels on the South African market. You mention that your arrangement with Wopko Jensma is that after your expenses have been recouped you will pay a royalty. I would find a similar arrangement satisfactory. As for soft covers, I have no objection: the Jensma volume seems to me an excellent piece of book production.

3. I don't mind the spellings being anglicized in *The Narrative of Jacobus Coetzee*, but I would prefer the American spellings to stand in *The Vietnam Project.*

Coetzee expresses his disappointment that because of a full programme Ravan will not be able to start production before the beginning of 1974. He would appreciate a firm commitment to publication in April 1974.

On 5 November 1973 Randall sent Coetzee a draft contract for *Dusklands* in which he cedes the international rights to Coetzee, and undertakes to print 4 500 copies and to pay 15 per cent of the income from sales as soon as the publisher's costs in production and promotion have been recouped. He asks an undertaking from the author to give Ravan a first option on any similar manuscript that he might seek to publish in South Africa in the following two years.

As far as the 15 per cent royalty is concerned, Wittenberg comments that it testifies to 'Ravan's commercial inexperience',[103] since such an amount, based on retail price, is unusually generous. Furthermore, a print run of 4 500 copies was extremely ambitious for a writer as yet unknown. On 19 December 1973 Coetzee sent the signed copy of the contract to Randall, mentioning in a covering letter that he had abandoned the somewhat absurd idea of keeping the American spelling in 'The Vietnam Project'. Although it was not in his province to concern himself with the physical appearance of the book, he recommended that the cover designer cast an eye on plate XII in L. Schultze's *Aus Namaland und Kalahari* (1904) in which two 'Hottentotten Mädchen' are depicted in front and side view. He hoped that the blurb would not give a distorted version of the book, an indication that Coetzee did after all, very politely, want to signal to his publisher that he would like to be consulted also on these matters.

In another letter Coetzee provided, apparently at Randall's request, a blurb of two hundred words, to which Randall was free, in Coetzee's words, to add 'the X's and Y's' in the closing paragraph. Randall also asks for a photograph of Coetzee for publicity purposes and a few biographical details:

Could you also supply a few more personal details for possible use — we are often criticised for not telling readers about our authors. While I do not want to over-do this, some more information about your school education, for example, or your family background, may be useful. I leave this to you.

To this, Coetzee replied on 17 January 1974:

> I am in two minds about supplying the particular personal in- formation you suggest, not because I am at all against idle curiosity, and not either because I think the facts of a writer's background irrelevant to his work (they are and they aren't), but because the information you suggest suggests that I settle for a particular identity I should feel most uneasy in. A few words about my schooling, for example, make me a player in the English-South African game of social typing and can even be read as a compliment to those monsters of sadism who ruled over my life for eleven years. As for my family background, I am one of the 10 000 Coetzees, and what is there to be said about them except that Jacobus Coetzee begat them all?

His interests, he concludes, are 'crowd sports; other people's ailments; apes and humanoid machines; images, particularly photographs, and their power over the human heart; and the politics of assent'.

One gathers that Coetzee was not only averse to providing personal details, but also from the start shied away from being introduced as a writer from one of the colonies, someone with a 'particular identity'. In a following letter he reminded Randall that the epigraph from Herman Kahn was protected by copyright and that permission for its use would have to be obtained. On 6 March he requested that a number of copies be dispatched, mainly to friends in the US. He also drew Randall's attention to some international journals that should receive review copies. As far as his writing name was concerned, he writes: 'I should like to be styled J.M. Coetzee on the title page.' On 29 March he returned the corrected proofs, with commentary showing the meticulousness of his control. He made some changes to the blurb sent to him. 'I think the "Dr Coetzee" angle should be avoided,' he added. He was clearly even at this stage a very conscious writer who wanted to keep control of his creation, and, though he had not yet made it internationally, knew very well which road he wanted to take.

Jonathan Crewe had, on the strength of the manuscript, written an article about *Dusklands*, which Coetzee described in a letter of

13 February 1974 to Randall as 'an intelligent and favourable review essay'. Crewe was hoping to place this article in *Contrast* or elsewhere. For this reason Coetzee enquired whether the scheduled publication in April would still take place. Randall confirmed early April as the publication date and asked for a copy of Crewe's essay. He also mentioned that they had scrutinised the catalogue of pictures in the Africana Museum and had made a small selection for consideration for the cover, since it had proved difficult to adapt Coetzee's suggested picture to a cover design.

On 18 April 1974 the first printing of *Dusklands* appeared in hardback, with a press release by Randall praising the novel as 'as one of the most important works of literature to have been written in South Africa'. The retail price was R4.80.[104] The blurb contains a quotation from Jonathan Crewe's essay which was soon to appear in *Contrast*:

> *Dusklands* is a very remarkable first book, written with a fastidiousness and power that are rare on the South African literary scene, or any literary scene.

The larger part of the blurb, however, was, at Randall's request, written by Coetzee himself, the only time he has consented to pronounce in this manner on his own work. He may have agreed in order to help a publisher who was relatively inexperienced in publishing and marketing fiction. Coetzee writes:

> A specialist in psychological warfare is driven to breakdown and a murderous assault by the stress of his work on a cold-blooded RAND-type project to destroy Vietnam.
>
> A megalomaniac frontiersman wreaks vengeance on his Hottentot captors for daring to see him as a man, fallible and absurd, rather than as a white god.
>
> In *The Vietnam Project* and *The Narrative of Jacobus Coetzee* we visit the dead souls of the explorers, conquistadors, and administrators whose work it is, in 1970 as in 1760, to absorb the wilds into the Western dusklands. Is it contempt for their victims, or is it fear of the damage that love may do to the screens of abstraction through which they see the world, that makes them monsters of callousness? Are they simply the barbarians of 'progress,' or are they creatures of the apocalypse determined to involve mankind in their personal

damnation? 'I have taken it upon myself to be the one to pull the
trigger,' says Jacobus Coetzee, philosopher of the gun, 'committing
upon the dark folk the murders we have all wished.'

The dust cover on which Ravan decided was a watercolour of Namaqualand attributed to Thomas Baines, an early colonial representation of
the interior of Southern Africa with its koppies and sandy landscape,
with a wagon and a horse and a little group of Hottentots with the white
owner of the wagon. Probably because this cover evoked a colonial
illusion and an idyllic reality, Coetzee later regarded it as inappropriate,
also from a marketing point of view. As part of the text on the back
cover Randall included the details about the author's interests, as well
as, without Coetzee's permission, information about his place in the
family tree as one of the descendants of Jacobus Coetzee, exactly the
kind of information that the author did not want to provide for public
consumption. Much later, in 1978, after Randall had been banned
by the government and could no longer openly perform his function
at Ravan, his place having been taken by Mike Kirkwood, Coetzee
objected that the biographical information had been lifted from a
letter without permission. Hermann Wittenberg writes about this in
his article:

> It is clear then that Coetzee's eccentric self-stylization on the jacket
> cover of *Dusklands* was not an aberration of a writer who went to
> unusual lengths to keep his personal life and opinions separated
> from his books, but a publishing error, perhaps attributable to
> Randall's well-meaning inexperience as a fiction editor. In all
> subsequent editions of *Dusklands*, as well as in the following novels,
> biographical information was kept to a prosaic minimum that
> concerned itself rather with the books than with the person who
> wrote them.[105]

When the first copies of *Dusklands* were being produced, Coetzee wrote
to Ravan asking why the CNA store in Rondebosch, where most of the
UCT students bought their books, had not yet received any copies or
any information about the book or publisher. In a letter of 10 October
1974 he enquired about sales, and whether there was any competition
for which *Dusklands* was eligible. On 16 October Randall reported that
the book had been submitted for the annual CNA Literary Award, that

they had already sold 1 300 copies and that *Dusklands* had, according to reports, been set for 1975 at both the University of Natal at Durban and the Rand Afrikaans University in Johannesburg. Randall would be able to recoup his costs after the sale of 2 500 copies, so that Coetzee could expect to start receiving royalties at the end of the first year after publication. On 20 February 1975 Randall wrote to Coetzee that of the 4 800 copies of the first edition 160 had been free copies for publicity and reviewing and that the remaining stock on 31 December had been 3 046. Thus in the period from April to December 1 594 copies had been sold, yielding an income of R5 101, as against printing costs of R8 400. A balance of R3 299 would thus have to be recouped before payments to the author could start.

The correspondence between Coetzee and Randall about the publication of *Dusklands* shows clearly that Coetzee had from the start involved himself in every aspect of the production of the book and in his public persona as author, as is evident from his minute enquiries about every detail and the precision with which he checked the proofs. It is also clear that from early on he realised or suspected that his manuscripts would be of value to researchers later on; he preserved all phases of the genesis of the novel and repeatedly asked Randall to return the proofs to him after the publishers had done with them. Wittenberg points out in his article that the correspondence with other Ravan authors, like Nadine Gordimer and Njabulo Ndebele, was much smaller in extent than with Coetzee. Wittenberg writes:

> [T]he sheer volume of letters in Coetzee's case indicates that this was an author who exercised an unusually thorough oversight over his book. Randall commented that Dusklands had been the 'cleanest ms [he] had ever received'.[106]

VI

Jonathan Crewe submitted his essay on *Dusklands* to Jack Cope on 14 February 1974 for publication. The book, he wrote, was supposed to appear in April, and his essay was based on the manuscript. He requested that the essay be held over until publication of the novel. When the book reached proof stage, he asked, in another letter a week later, that a few changes be made.

Cope, who had from the first not been very much taken with *Dusklands,* found the length of seven pages a problem, and he asked Crewe to shorten the essay. He also objected to the comparison of *Dusklands* with Conrad's *Heart of Darkness.* Cope wrote to Crewe on 25 March 1974:

> Also a note of caution, I think you might look again at the point in which you compare the book with Conrad's 'Heart of Darkness'. Personally I don't feel that comparisons carry one far in criticism and to stand any book up against Conrad will be to invite attack and so really sidetrack a serious approach to John Coetzee's book.

Even though Crewe was obliged to shorten his article by almost three pages, and even though it only appeared in *Contrast,* IX: 2, August 1974, later than some reviews, it constitutes the first serious discussion of Coetzee's work. Crewe had unerring insight into Coetzee's work, immediately divining the importance of the novel, and wrote penetratingly about it. In an interview much later Coetzee said he was 'basically very grateful to Crewe for his enthusiasm about the book, helping me to find a publisher for the novel and the propaganda work he did for it'.[107] Crewe placed *Dusklands* not within the context of South African English literature, but as a contribution to contemporary fiction. He writes:

> *Dusklands* can be judged by no standards but those created by the best modern fiction, and however it fares under that judgement it makes no appeal to any qualified standard whatever; which is to say that one can forget the considerations which normally apply to South African writing. In *Dusklands* the modern novel in English arrives in South Africa for the first time. [...] The fields of external reference in *Dusklands* are America and South Africa: the Americans in relation to Vietnam and the white man in relation to South Africa. Neither of these can be called a strangely neglected topic. Need one say more about Coetzee's achievement than that on both he is continuously and often brilliantly illuminating?

In spite of Cope's warning, Crewe maintained his comparison with Conrad:

> Though quite unlike Conrad's work, 'The Narrative ...' is a South African *Heart of Darkness*—and it is not absurd to mention both works in the same sentence.[108]

He concludes:

> The two solitary selves, Jacobus Coetzee and the worker on the Vietnam Project, are historical and psychological paradigms of the utmost interest. The former is historically antecedent to the latter, but the stories are published in reverse-chronological sequence, reminding us that we are looking at *recto* and *verso* of the same coin—the Western consciousness in its exploded and imploded condition. It is a spectacle that prompts some serious reflection, and it is a pleasure to salute the book that makes this possible.

Other reviewers praised the book. In *The Star* of 24 April 1974 Peter Wilhelm writes: 'Technically and morally this book begins where most South African fiction leaves off. It carries no banners saying, "I protest, therefore I am"; and there are no easy paths into its recesses. [...] Some might find *Dusklands* stark and obsessional. But starkness and obsession can illuminate, and the novel is a metaphor on ourselves which has unquestioned power and even grandeur.' In the *Cape Argus* of 1 May Peter Temple called the author 'a major talent'. He said it was difficult to believe that this elegant and 'profoundly disturbing work' was a debut novel. He writes: 'The author's vision is not pleasant. But it has the compelling power of a genuine insight and it is set out in a splendidly supple style and in diamond-hard language.' In his review in *Rapport* of 19 May 1974 André Brink, who knew nothing about Coetzee or his background, assumed that he was Afrikaans-speaking, and felt that he could have become a central figure in the new Afrikaans literature if his work had been in Afrikaans. Brink found *Dusklands* to be an impressive debut and hailed Coetzee as one of the finest contemporary stylists in English in South Africa. He was less appreciative of the story of Eugene Dawn; according to him, it did not quite escape the charge of melodrama, deliberateness and superficiality, even though it remained 'a disturbing case study of human disintegration under pressure of violence'. His preference was for the tale of Jacobus Coetzee: not in the first place for the multiple perspective, but for the deceptive simplicity of the journal section. He found *Dusklands* to provide 'a disturbing look at a kind of Twilight of the Gods, a Decline of the West', important as 'an inescapable statement about South Africa and the world today'.[109]

When Coetzee received the Nobel Prize in 2003, Brink wrote

an article in the *Sunday Times*[110] praising him for his stark use of language, but also for his dry sense of humour. As for *Dusklands*, he once again pointed out the connection with Spengler. Apparently he had overcome his objections to 'The Vietnam Project', because he now expressed admiration for the book as a whole. *Dusklands* is 'a revision of the colonial world through postcolonial eyes, a fascination with "how myths operate in human society, how signs are exchanged", an exploration of power and of what it does to societies and to the individual, [...] and an abiding involvement with South Africa in its historical, ethical and psychosocial dimensions'.

In the *Cape Times* of 5 June 1974 Francis Bowers called *Dusklands* 'stimulating, disturbing and beautifully written, showing a fresh, original talent'. In *Reality* VI: 3, July 1974, Pauline Fletcher wrote: '*Dusklands* is an extremely powerful and disturbing book; but what makes it particularly interesting is that its power to disturb springs not merely from "strong" writing and the exploitation of highly emotive issues, but from the penetrating intelligence of its author.' In *Management* of July 1974 Philip Birkinshaw advanced several contentious and debatable interpretations, but did express admiration of *Dusklands*: 'The vision is bleak, tragic and sardonically funny, and reminds one of the masters of this mood, Swift, Voltaire and Kafka. The writing is as incisive as the material is unexpected, and the impression is of originality in a great idiom. Obviously J.M. Coetzee has written an important book.' In *Snarl*, I: 1, August 1974, Lionel Abrahams was also very positive: 'It is hard to say in which respect *Dusklands* makes its most important contribution. It boldly diversifies our fiction and relates it to modernistic modes. It reveals, as persuasively as anything in our fiction, the foundations of bad conscience in South Africa. It invigorates and substantiates the criticism of Western civilization that both White and Black thinkers among us are conducting.' Tony Morphet in *Bolt*, December 1974, writes even more favourably: 'Reading *Dusklands* is a bitter, often troubling but finally exhilarating experience. It is certainly the best novel from a South African in English since (say) Dan Jacobson's early works. It is also without qualification the most avowedly literary and intellectual work in South African fiction. Its ancestors are not South African at all. Eugene Dawn has *Herzog* and *Voss* on his motel bedside table and one can speculate that the pile on J.M. Coetzee's desk includes beside these two, the novels of Barth, Pynchon, Nabokov, and Borges.'

A particular section of 'The Narrative of Jacobus Coetzee' was problematic to the publisher and some readers alike, leading to a pronouncement in one of the reviews and a correspondence once again illustrating Coetzee's basic authorial position. On page 100 of the published text, Jacobus tells how Klawer, while they are crossing the Great River, feels out the bottom with a stick, inexplicably misses a hippopotamus hole, loses his balance, is swept into the deep water by the violence of the current and drowns. On page 101, however, it appears that Klawer is still alive, but gets so ill on his and Jacobus's joint voyage southward that Jacobus is obliged to abandon him in the mountains to die.

To Randall's query in his first letter asking whether this was 'a deliberate technique' that he was too dim to grasp, Coetzee replied tersely: 'No, there is no oversight on my part.' Because this reply did not resolve Randall's quandary, he returned to the matter in his letter of 18 February 1974:

> Incidentally, both our readers were puzzled by the point I raised earlier, regarding Klawer's deaths. I was unable to explain what you intended, and wonder whether you could give me an explanation. I am sure reviewers are going to stick on this, with irrelevant comments and questions. It would help me if I were able to answer any queries.

But even at this early stage of his career it was a matter of policy on Coetzee's part not to assume a position of authority as the writer by providing an interpretation of his work, but to leave it to his readers and literary scholars to make sense of the novel. For this reason he includes in his letter of 24 February a copy of Crewe's essay on *Dusklands*. As far as Randall's request is concerned, he reacts as follows:

> Regarding the alternative deaths of Klawer: I don't believe in the principle of authorial explication, so what I have done is to ask Crewe—who gave the work a reading which was in my eyes amazingly responsive—what he made of the pages in question. He referred me to the passage on p. 2 of his review[111] where he discusses 'the disclosure of the stage-machinery,' and suggested (a) that Jacobus Coetzee is telling stories to cover up the 'facts' of Klawer's death, and (b) that someone (who?) is writing a document

called 'The Narrative of Jacobus Coetzee' and has been caught with the edges of his revision showing. I don't know how you feel about this interpretation. I find it quite plausible.

Randall had no choice but to make do with this explanation, but the alternative deaths of Klawer were to generate another postscript. In her discussion of *Dusklands* in the *Cape Times* of 5 June 1974, Francis Bowers wrote that there was 'evidence' of 'careless editing' that was not the author's fault, without explaining what she meant.[112] Since this comment reflected poorly on his editing, Randall wrote to Bowers asking her to explain what she was referring to. In her reply of 12 July 1974 she identified the two deaths of Klawer as the problem. She adds:

> It seems to me (and to others to whom I have shown these pages) that the author changed his mind about Klawer's fate, but omitted to delete the first version. If I am right, this is certainly in the first place the author's fault, but I suppose ultimately the publisher would be responsible for letting it through. Having read the passage several times, I can come to no other conclusion. Or am I being stupid? I considered some brief mention ought to be made in a review of what seemed to me as a careless oversight, although I would like to say that it is quite evident that in all other respects you did take 'inordinate pains' as you point out, because it is most beautifully printed.

In his reply Randall told Bowers he had suspected that she had had the Klawer incident in mind. He assured her, however, that it had been the author's considered and deliberate intention to render the incident as printed. He had mentioned the matter by letter to the author after his first reading of the manuscript and again later, since he had suspected an error. He adds: 'and even now [I] do not fully understand what he meant by it. The author's wish must, however, prevail.'[113] In an article written in 1982, Peter Knox-Shaw suggests that with the competing versions of Klawer's death, Jacobus Coetzee as the narrator of his tale not only wants to demonstrate to the reader that he is in control of the fictititious aspect of his narrative, but that he also wants 'to alert us to the ease with which a sole witness may falsify facts prejudicial to his self-presentation'.[114] To this Gallagher adds: 'As the all-powerful chronicler of history, Jacobus can construct his story as he pleases, and we are helpless before his narrative power. The contradictory accounts of Klawer's death and the entirely different story told in the deposition remind us that we have no way of knowing what actually took place on Jacobus's journey; we can only know the story he chooses to tell us.'[115]

VII

In the years after its first publication many articles were devoted to various aspects of *Dusklands*. But what impression did Coetzee's debut make at first on readers from different generations?

In a programme called *Passages* made by SATV in 1999, which Kai Easton in an exemplary discussion calls a 'dazzlingly minimalist montage',[116] Lionel Abrahams, who had written a review of *Dusklands*, said that on a first meeting he had not formed such a favourable impression of Coetzee:

> I first encountered Coetzee at the conference on South African poetry in Cape Town in 1974 at which he delivered a short paper on the academic uses of poetry, and I found his approach unsympathetic, daunting, chilling. My prejudices—but this meant that by the time I read his first book, *Dusklands*, a year or two later, I was not predisposed in its favour. Nevertheless, its originality and power and brilliance impressed me and I became open to him.[117]

Lesley Marx, considerably younger than Coetzee, who had studied under him at UCT, said in the same programme:

> The first of John Coetzee's novels that I tried to read, was *Dusklands* which came out in 1974. And I think that many of us, who tried to read the novel, were naïve freshers who had not before come into contact with literature of that sophistication at all. The most modern the English Department was at that time was D.H. Lawrence's *Sons and Lovers*; so a novel that was playing, experimenting with voice, with narrative point of view, with narrative strategies, was really something that we were not trained to deal with. In later years we came back to it with immense pleasure to see that that book was a seedbed for so much of the working with South African history, with colonialism, the Afrikaner past that is very important to a number of Coetzee's novels.'[118]

Stephen Watson, a younger colleague of Coetzee's, later wrote an incisive essay on Coetzee's work, in which he concisely discusses the impact of *Dusklands*:

> Never before has a South African novel broken so obviously, even self-consciously, with the conventions of realism and so candidly announced its own artificiality. In the pseudo-scholarship in which the second half of the novel was embedded, the example of Jorge Luis Borges and Vladimir Nabokov was palpable. The very conjunction of the two narratives seemed to suggest that their relation to reality (and I mean *historical* reality) was problematical, hardly a simple matter of representation or mimesis.[119]

Years later, in April 2004, after Coetzee had received the Nobel Prize, *World Literature Today* published an issue dedicated largely to him. Under the title 'Reading Coetzee in South Africa', Tony Morphet, who had been a lecturer in English at the University of Natal in Durban at the time of Coetzee's debut, wrote about his response to the novel:

> When *Dusklands* was published in 1974, I was given a copy soon after publication by Alan Paton, who had received it from the publishers who were promoting the young and unknown writer. I had been working as a reader for Paton, and in handing me the book, he gruffly explained that he couldn't make out what it meant. He asked me to read and report on it at our next meeting.
>
> I read the book in one sitting, exhilarated but confounded. The narratives were intense and compelling, yet, as I progressed, I felt the pattern of meaning eluding me. I knew it was there, somewhere, but exactly where and in what form remained beyond reach. When I described my experience to Paton, he gave a characteristic dismissive chuckle. It wasn't for him.
>
> The reading, however, convinced me that *Dusklands* was a herald. A new form of narration, a new way of imagining—a new prose had entered South African literature. It had a strong claim to academic attention. Out of an academic English department of twenty-three, only two of us had read the book, but our enthusiasm managed to persuade a majority to accept the text for a contemporary course curriculum. Staff agreed to read the work in order to decide teaching responsibilities.

The results of the departmental reading were startling. Objections erupted over the politics, the history, the obscure psychology, the disturbing point of view and the vocabulary—especially regarding the body and race. All readily agreed that the prose was distinguished, but the sense of a violation of the canons of a liberal and humanist study of literature was deep and intense. The author was not to be trusted: in a universe of horrors, his 'position' was elusive and unclear. The book would be a danger to students. Nevertheless we went ahead and taught it.

These were early reactions, and on a very small scale, but they signalled Coetzee's impact on South African literature: the same kind of impact had continued to carry the aura of scandal in spite of the massive reputation his work has subsequently achieved throughout the world.

But reactions to Coetzee's debut were not unanimously appreciative. Even in later years *Dusklands* was seen as a reaction to the realistic, and therefore politically engaged, work of other South African writers, notably Nadine Gordimer. There were complaints that it was too modernist, cerebral and cold. Michael Vaughan's criticism, from a Marxist perspective, was that Coetzee, also in his later work, did not attend closely enough to the material aspects of the struggle and oppression in South Africa in the apartheid years.[120] According to him, the tone of ambivalence and ambiguity dissipates the necessary political urgency and does not relate to the historical 'facts'. In similar vein Peter Knox-Shaw in his article on *Dusklands* criticises Coetzee for the 'existentialism of the armchair': 'It is regrettable that a writer of such considerable and varied talents should play down the political and economic aspects of history in favour of a psychopathology of Western life.'[121] The objection is thus, as Sue Kossew puts it, 'that the post-modernist angst of his protagonists involves the narratives in self-defeating discourse that fails to confront the particularity of the political conditions of oppression in South Africa.'[122] Many writers and activists, so the argument ran, had been banned or had emigrated. The intellectuals remaining were duty-bound to express themselves against apartheid. Instead of asking why Coetzee does what he does, they analyse, according to Alastair Bruce, his fiction in terms of what he should, according to them, be doing.[123] By contrast, Dick Penner, in his critical study *Countries of the Mind: The Fiction of J.M. Coetzee*, says that:

the demand from J.M. Coetzee's works is related to the world's interest in the politics and society of South Africa. However, Coetzee's fictions maintain their significance apart from a South African context because of their artistry and because they transform urgent societal concerns into more enduring questions regarding colonialism and the relationships of mastery and servitude between cultures and individuals.[124]

Dusklands was a contender for the annual CNA Prize, but it went to Nadine Gordimer, an established writer, for *The Conservationist.* That the choice between the two books was not self-evidently in Gordimer's favour, is clear from the correspondence between Arnold Benjamin, one of the judges, and Jack Cope.[125] Benjamin writes: 'Some time or other—if necc. over much red wine—I'd like to debate with you the respective merits of *Dusklands* (which I placed first) against *The Conservationist* which I was told the other two judges voted for. It's history now, but I thought Coetzee's book was fantastic and that Nadine's—well, as an American critic put it—"Her normal style is oblique—this one is oblique to the point of being opaque"'. Jack Cope replied to this:

> I was very interested in what you said about the CNA Award in which we differed over the winner. I don't know whether I could put up much of a speech about the relative merits of *Dusklands* and *The Conservationist.* I guess my method of judgement, if you can call it that, is perhaps subjective. As D.H. Lawrence is supposed to have said 'You've got to feel it here'—grabbing to his solar plexis. I know Nadine's style is rather like embroidery. But then Jane Austen once wrote that her writing was on the scale of a small slip of ivory and history has shown she was anything but a miniaturist. My thing about *Dusklands* is that it fell between just about every stool you can think of. It's not a novel nor a memoir and the two bits don't hold together; the style is neither real nor surreal and to my way of feeling it just doesn't grip. I think Coetzee might yet write something very individual though he is an extremely slow worker and still much too self-conscious about style etc. Against this Nadine is every inch an accomplished writer and even if her characters tend to be negative, her total presentation in *The Conservationist* is a tour de force, much as I would criticize the book in detail. She is just not my kind of

writer but that doesn't mean to say I don't recognize and admire her tremendous achievement.

Upon publication of *Dusklands*, Coetzee sent a copy to James Brown Associates, the literary agency in America to whom he had originally submitted the manuscript. David Stewart Hull thanked him for sending the book and expressed his regret that, mainly on account of the brevity of the text, he had not been able to place it with a publisher. Coetzee also received a friendly letter from Celia Catchpole of Murray Pollinger thanking him for the copy he had sent her. She had tried the previous year to sell the novel to Macmillan and to Chatto & Windus, but it had proved impossible to get the two tales, with their difficult length, accepted, in spite of their literary merits. She would, however, be very interested in future to receive a full-length manuscript from him.

In 1975, after most of the favourable reviews of *Dusklands* had appeared, Randall also made an attempt, supported by an enthusiastic recommendation from Nadine Gordimer,[126] to sell the book to Gollancz in Britain or Viking in the US. Alan D. Williams of Viking commented favourably, but foresaw problems in marketing the book in America. He wrote to Randall on 9 December 1975:

> A number of us have read J.M. Coetzee's *Dusklands* with admiration for its originality and for the author's highly individual and muscular style. Mr Coetzee conveys disturbance and anger with a voice that demands to be heard. Nevertheless, we feel that the whole of this book is somehow less than the sum of its rather too disparate parts. We think it would be especially difficult for an American reader to make the transition from the first to the second section who would instead find them both offputtingly exotic despite the American setting of the first. We feel that strong texture alone is not enough to sell a book where the organic and overall purposes remain hidden.

At this stage, then, *Dusklands* was not yet acceptable to publishers in the US and Britain. This state of affairs was soon to change.

CHAPTER 9

IN THE HEART OF THE COUNTRY AND THE CLIMATE OF CENSORSHIP

I

As early as the 1950s, when Coetzee was a pupil at St Joseph's Marist College in Rondebosch, the apartheid government appointed a commission to investigate 'the evil of indecent, offensive or harmful reading matter'. It was chaired by Professor Geoff Cronjé, one of the theoreticians of apartheid, the policy that brought the National Party to power in 1948.[1] In its 1957 report the commission recommended draconian measures, such as censorship before publication, the scrapping of appeal to the courts, and the licensing of all printers, publishers and booksellers — all of it purportedly to ensure the 'spiritual welfare of the nation'.

The extreme recommendations of the Cronjé Commission were rejected by the government. South Africa would nevertheless from the early 1960s to about 1980 establish what Coetzee later called 'one of the most comprehensive censorship systems in the world' — though the censors preferred to refer more euphemistically to 'publication control'. Compared with existing forms of censorship by the police, the legislation of 1963, which finally institutionalised censorship under an authority of a Publications Control Board, was, on paper, less extreme. But the oppressive climate of censorship by then permeated the atmosphere.[2] Some publishing houses were already practising pre-censorship, for fear of a book being banned.

Compared with the earlier recommendation there were certain concessions in the 1963 law, such as the possibility of appeal to the courts and the stipulation that a majority of Publications Control Board members were expected to have expert knowledge of art, literature, language or law. This relenting prompted N.P. van Wyk Louw, a highly regarded poet and a prominent figure in Afrikaans literature, to intercede with the minister concerned to ward off bids to obtain the chairmanship of the board from ambitious lesser figures such as Abel Coetzee and Abraham H. Jonker, who would have been disastrous choices. On Van Wyk Louw's recommendation, Gerrit Dekker, a literary historian and recently retired professor at Potchefstroom University, was appointed chairman of the board. Dekker saw to the part-time appointment of three of his ex-students, A.P. Grové, T.T. Cloete and Merwe Scholtz, who kept their respective university posts. C.J.D. Harvey of Stellenbosch was elected as the English expert on the Publications Control Board. Whether it was wise of Van Wyk Louw to enter into this compromise with the government is a moot point, but it ensured that Afrikaans books that would certainly have been banned under Abel Coetzee or Jonker were tolerated. No Afrikaans book was banned until after Dekker's retirement, when André Brink's *Kennis van die Aand* [*Looking on Darkness*] was banned in 1975. The most peculiar aspect of the system was that the Nationalist government placed extraordinary, even unlimited, power in the hands of the censors. The participation of Afrikaans literary figures and writers lent an appearance of legitimacy to the system, bizarrely elevating the 'literary police', as Peter McDonald calls them in his extensive and thorough study of publication control in the apartheid years, from enemy to ally.[3]

From the outset the most vehement criticism of the law was directed at the criteria for a banning, in particular the fact that a work could be found to be offensive or harmful to public morals on the grounds of a single word or paragraph, without consideration of the context in which it appeared. Literary scholars and writers rightly feared that works of literary quality could be banned if the Publications Control Board were to be usurped by people of questionable literary judgement. This danger was for the time being seemingly averted by Van Wyk Louw's action, but it was soon clear that the 'literary police' did not hesitate to exercise their powers. The law on censorship proceeded from the mistaken assumption that—employing known principles of functionality, structure and self-sufficiency—there was consensus as to the nature of literature and its evaluation. The censors were not plagued by doubts on these matters. Their reports frequently testify to an overweening confidence in the face of questions that literary commentators over the ages have approached with the greatest circumspection.[4]

Foreign publishers suffered under the unpredictability of the literary 'stewardship' of the censors. The stringent legislation and the fear of financial losses led some British publishers to put pressure on writers to expurgate their work themselves and to cut potentially offensive scenes. South African publishers too were sometimes obliged, as Peter Randall of Ravan Press put it, to practise self-censorship merely to survive. Light escapist literature that according to the censors did not resort under the rubric 'literature'—books by writers such as Wilbur Smith and Stuart Cloete—were banned on moral grounds. The assumption that great literature should transcend contemporary politics led to the banning of Brink's *Kennis van die Aand* [*Looking on Darkness*], Jack Cope's *The Dawn Comes Twice*, two novels by C.J. Driver (*Elegy for a Revolutionary* and *Send War in Our Time, O Lord*) and some of Nadine Gordimer's first works. Gordimer's relatively innocuous novel about multiracial socialising, *A World of Strangers*, was tolerated in hardcover in 1958, before the passing of the law on censorship, but the cheaper Penguin edition was later banned. With Gordimer's growing international stature in the 1980s, the censors became more circumspect and tolerated her novels. But the censorship system came down particularly harshly on black poets writing protest poetry about the sabotage trials and their experiences of apartheid in the officially white cities. Work by black prose writers such as Peter Abrahams, Alfred Hutchinson, Alex La Guma, Es'kia Mphahlele and Todd Matshikiza was repeatedly banned. A whole generation of black writers were victimised by the censors and most of them were gagged and silenced.

The first stirrings of censorship and the institution of the Publications Control Board coincided with the publication of the first works of a number of Afrikaans writers—among whom Jan Rabie, Etienne Leroux, Bartho Smit, André Brink and later also Breyten Breytenbach—who deviated from the well-worn characterisation and traditional inoffensive motifs of Afrikaans literature. In 1962, the year before the appointment of the board, André Brink's *Lobola vir die Lewe* [*Lobola for Life*] and Etienne Leroux's *Sewe Dae by die Silbersteins* [*Seven Days at the Silbersteins*] were published, two novels that, with Brink's *Die Ambassadeur* [*The Ambassador*] (1963) attracted immediate attention, also internationally through translations into English and other languages. Some of these authors were to experiment in various directions, and write more openly than in the past about sex and politics.

Apart from the new generation of writers, many other young Afrikaners rebelled in the late 1950s and the '60s against the mores, values and political practices of established Afrikanerdom. This coincided with changing attitudes, especially among young people, all over the Western world. Serious students from Afrikaans homes, albeit a minority of them, were influenced by new philosophical, artistic and political currents of thought reaching South African universities especially from the US and Europe. The message of informality, spontaneity and freedom, disregard for traditional inhibitions and taboos, rejection of traditional prejudice against difference, and tolerance of individualistic and unconventional behaviour influenced the younger Afrikaans generation, especially in urban areas and at universities.

Many of the new Afrikaans writers emerging in this era of change protested in and outside of their creative work against what they experienced as the injustices of South African society. The renewal of Sixty (as the Afrikaans literary movement of the 1960s was denoted) brought about, as Brink was to put it later, 'a daring, an honesty, a realisation of form, an adventurous readiness to experiment'.[5] They were, as Leroux put it, 'blood brothers in oppression, joined against the older generation'[6], at a time when the Church, the National Party and professors in Afrikaans departments could issue unquestionable ex cathedra decrees. They were unified in their resistance to the imminent danger of censorship, the new law that, in the words of Brink, got off the starting blocks alongside the *Sestigers*.[7] Brink was the main spokesman, in repeated statements to the press spelling out his resistance to the system of censorship, and paying a high price for his political stand. In an interview with the magazine *Insig*, in the issue of November 2004, J.M. Coetzee said: 'There was a time when he was in almost daily conflict with the powers of censorship. He was hounded; often petty-mindedly, sometimes intimidatingly. Even though I did not yet know him personally at the time, I suspected that it cost great courage and integrity and that he was an example of how an intellectual should behave when confronted with authority.'[8]

After his term as chairman of the Publications Control Board, Dekker was succeeded by Jannie Kruger, who, on the grounds of his publications and lack of standing as a literary scholar, did not command the same respect. In the 1960s the board several times banned issues of the magazine *Scope*, only to have these bannings overruled by the Supreme Court. Apart from the unfavourable public attention this attracted, the system and members of the controlling body became the targets of fierce criticism and satire. In 1972, after Coetzee's appointment as a lecturer at UCT, a commission investigated the application of the law, but before an amendment could be proposed, the Cape Supreme Court confirmed the banning of Brink's *Kennis van die Aand*, the first Afrikaans literary work declared undesirable by law.

The Publications Act of 1974, which superseded the 1963 legislation, brought about radical changes in the system of control. The Publications Control Board was abolished, and replaced with a Directorate, consisting of a director, a deputy and a number of vice-directors, which had to enforce the law as a purely administrative body. The directorate appointed a number of committees from a list furnished by the minister of the interior, whose function it was to declare works undesirable or not undesirable. Appeal to the courts was abolished and an appeal board was instituted. The chairman of the appeal board was appointed by the state president, and he in turn appointed two members. As was the case under the previous act, any member of the public could obtain a ruling on a publication from a committee. In case of dissatisfaction with the decision of a committee, a publisher or writer and the directorate could appeal to the board. The minister was empowered to request the appeal board to reconsider a decision. As far as the definition of undesirability was concerned, the new act corresponded verbatim with that of 1963, except that the 'probable reader' was no longer taken into account.

The legislation was objected to on various grounds: a committee could now also prohibit possession of a publication; the minister could authorise anybody to enter premises and confiscate books; the right of appeal to the courts had been abolished; and the minister had acquired too many arbitrary powers. Apart from the clumsy administration, vagueness as to objections, and misgivings as to the abilities of committee members, the prime defect of the system from a literary perspective remained the fact that a work was not judged as a whole and that aesthetic considerations were irrelevant in the eyes of the law. Judge Lammie Snyman was appointed as chairman of the appeal board. His mindset and arrogance are evident from the dim-witted declarations he from time to time made in the press: 'Every Afrikaner cannot go and buy and read every book that is published to decide whether he likes it or not. Now there is a body that does it on his behalf. We'll tell him whether or not he's going to like the book.'[9]

After the banning of *Kennis van die Aand*, the work of younger Afrikaans writers such as André le Roux, Welma Odendaal and John Miles also came under fire. The most sensational banning in the 1970s, which led to two court cases, was that of Etienne Leroux's *Magersfontein, o Magersfontein!* Lammie Snyman's decision speaks of an unimaginative and rigid application of the law. The general opinion of the literary experts, Snyman says, 'is that the purpose of the book is to satirise the folly, the extravagance, the ostentation and moral decline of our own time against the background of a heroic past', but he asks whether society 'is prepared to tolerate the means whereby this purpose is achieved'. Filthy language is often used and the name of the Almighty taken in vain. Language, according to him, can be 'regarded as coarse if it is not in common use in the mixed company of educated men and women'. Human & Rousseau lost the initial case with costs of around R20 000.

The banning of Leroux's *Magersfontein, o Magersfontein!* was a watershed. Coetzee writes about this banning in a 1990 essay on Brink which was later collected in *Giving Offense.*

> In the *Magersfontein* case, the board had adopted a highly confrontational posture toward those Afrikaans intellectuals who had come forward to testify on behalf of Leroux's novel. The banning of the book, with the clear proof it gave that the censors were determined to continue to apply the most conservative standards, threatened to alienate even middle-of-the-road Afrikaans academics and intellectuals.[10]

A new turn in the application of the law came in 1980 when the appeal board suspended the banning at the request of the publishers. The appeal board was now under the relatively enlightened chairmanship of J.C.W. van Rooyen, Professor of Criminal Law at the University of Pretoria. It is virtually certain, says Coetzee in his essay on Brink, that the prospect of the defection of its intellectual and academic constituency had influenced the government in its appointment of Van Rooyen.[11] In its decision the appeal board says that the probable reader rather than the average person should be taken into account, while the fact that the concepts 'literature, language and art' were mentioned for the first time in the Publication Amendment Act of 1978 meant that the appeal board in its judgement could take these factors into account. In this regard the appeal board would be led by the advice of a committee of experts, which was made possible by the new legislation, and would not lightly deviate from this advice. Under Van Rooyen's chairmanship the law was applied in a much more nuanced way after the regime of Lammie Snyman, and the banning of most Afrikaans literary works after *Magersfontein, o Magersfontein!* was rescinded. Even so, South African writers had to wait for a new democratic dispensation in 1994 before the legislation as a whole was struck off the statute book.

The drastic change in the censorship dispensation under Van Rooyen, after the dark days of Lammie Snyman, was welcome also to Coetzee, who, like many of his fellow-writers, was fiercely opposed to the system. In an interview with Hugh Roberton of the *Pretoria News* on 18 August 1983, he says that the censors, under the guidelines of the new dispensation, were displaying a far more tolerant and civilised approach to what could realistically destroy public mores or subvert the state. He feels that the only writers still seriously hampered, would be those who did not distinguish between writing and a more or less direct political act. This does not mean that the laws have been abolished or that the censorship apparatus has vanished, only that a greater tolerance has been established. 'One upshot is that what stands between the reading public and innovatory, unsettling new writing is not so much the grim-lipped censor as the economics of the book trade, which dictate that the South African bookseller should only import safe books, books for which a market already exists, as opposed to books that, in the course of time, make their own market.' Economic realities of the book trade are, according to him, also largely to blame for the tendency of South African authors to seek overseas publication.

In 1972, however, the outlook for a young writer was completely different. Unlike Nadine Gordimer and André Brink, Coetzee never had a book banned, and unlike Athol Fugard, he was never subjected to the concerted scrutiny of the authorities or placed under house arrest. In a 1992 interview with David Attwell he says: 'I regard it as a badge of honor to have had a book banned in South Africa, and even more of an honor to have been acted against punitively, as Fugard and others were officially, and Brink and others unofficially. This honor I have never achieved nor, to be frank, merited. Besides coming too late in the era, my books have been too indirect in their approach, too rarefied, to be considered a threat to the order.'[12] As a writer whose first publications were, nevertheless, submitted to the censors before publication, he reacts with a measure of vehemence:

> Being subjected to the gaze of the censor is a humiliating and perhaps even enraging experience. It is not unlike being stripped and searched. But at the same time it is a sign that one's writing is being taken seriously [...] Writing under threat of official censure

concentrates the mind wonderfully. I have no doubt that the intensity, the pointedness, the *seriousness* of Russian writing from the time of Nicolas I is in part a reflection of the fact that every word published represented a risk taken. *Mutatis mutandis*, I would say the same about much postwar writing from Eastern Europe. [...] [T]he ease with which books [in English] can be published abroad renders the actual powers of the South African censor rather vacuous. Nevertheless, no one can deny the pointedness and seriousness of the best of South African writing since 1948. [...] But writing under threat also has uglier, deforming side effects that it is hard to escape. The very fact that certain topics are forbidden creates an unnatural concentration upon them. To give one example: when it was forbidden to represent sex between blacks and whites, sex between blacks and whites was widely written into novels.[13]

Apart from this, he says, he has pragmatic reasons for his distrust of censorship, because the cure in his experience is worse than the disease:

> The institution of censorship puts power into the hands of persons with a judgmental, bureaucratic cast of mind that is bad for the cultural and even the spiritual life of the community.[14]

Furthermore, Coetzee continues, he has never been impressed with the intellectual qualities of those censors he has had contact with: 'Censorship is not an occupation that attracts intelligent, subtle minds.' He goes on to say:

> The censor acts, or believes he acts, in the interest of a community. [...] I cannot find it in myself to align myself with the censor, not only because of a sceptical attitude, in part temperamental, in part professional, toward the passions that issue in taking offense, but because of the historical reality I have lived through and the experience of what censorship becomes once it is instituted and institutionalized.[15]

But the whole question of censorship and its application in South Africa had been a worrying reality for Coetzee since shortly after assuming his lectureship in 1972, long before he was to devote a book to the subject. On 19 October 1972 all heads of department at UCT received a circular from the registrar, asking them to comment, for forwarding to the secretary of the Committee of University Principals:

> to inform him to what extent this University is affected academically as a result of censorship and the banning of certain books regarded as essential for the proper study of a subject or subjects.

Heads of department were requested not later than 30 November 1972 (i) to comment on the extent to which teaching and research were affected by censorship; (ii) to provide a list of banned books, publications or any other material that they regarded as essential to a thorough study of their subject.

David Gillham, the head of the Department of English, sent the circular to Coetzee for reply. He replied on 27 October in a detailed three-page response, testifying not only to his capacity for intensive labour, but also to his concern about censorship. The information he supplies is shocking. In his letter to Gillham Coetzee says:

> I have recently subjected myself to the dreary and dejecting task of reading through the list of some 16 000 publications banned in South Africa by the Publications Control Board. I did this partly because I did not want to become an inadvertent criminal, but mainly because I wanted to get a clear idea of the bounds within which I have to confine myself in my reading and teaching. You may be interested to look over the following condensation of how our censors have impoverished our lives: we are, after all, people whose professional and private lives are bound up with books.

Coetzee then supplies a list of writers and books that have been banned. He divides them into American literature, British literature, South African literature in English and 'World Literature'.

Especially American writers had attracted the displeasure of the censors. Among works that Coetzee would have expected his students in twentieth-century American literature to have read, the following were banned: William Faulkner's *Sanctuary*, Nathanael West's *Miss Lonelyhearts* and *The Day of the Locust*, James Farrell's Studs Lonigan trilogy, Richard Wright's *Native Son* and Vladimir Nabokov's *Lolita* and *Ada*. Among the contemporary American writing that he wanted to introduce his students to, were works by Gary Snyder (*Earth House Hold*), Norman Mailer (*An*

American Dream, Why are we in Vietnam?), James Baldwin (*Another Country*), Bernard Malamud (*The Assistant*), Joseph Heller (*Catch-22*) and John Barth (*The End of the Road*). Books by writers that he would recommend as necessary background vacation reading were frequently banned: Norman Mailer (4 bannings), Bernard Malamud (4), Terry Southern (1), Joseph Heller (1), William Burroughs (5), LeRoi Jones (2), John Barth (1), James Purdy (1), Philip Roth (2), Nelson Algren (1), William Styron (1), Edmund Wilson (1), Henry Miller (5), Robert Coover (1), Jerzy Kosinski (1), James Baldwin (5), Robert Penn Warren (1), Mary McCarthy (3), John Updike (4), Jack Kerouac (3), Robert Gover (2), John O'Hara (5), Truman Capote (1), R.V. Cassill (5), Evan Hunter (2), Paul Bowles (1), James Jones (1), Gore Vidal (2), John Rechy (1) and Mordecai Richler (Canadian) (1).

As for British literature, two prominent works—John Cleland's *Memoirs of a Woman of Pleasure* and D.H. Lawrence's *Lady Chatterley's Lover*—were still banned, even though Lawrence's novel had been unbanned more than ten years earlier in a sensational court case in Britain. Among important British writers on the list were Christopher Isherwood, David Caute, Simon Raven, Frederic Raphael, Colin Wilson, Doris Lessing, Brigid Brophy, Brendan Behan, Paul Ableman, Kingsley Amis, Andrew Sinclair and Alan Sillitoe.

Black South African writers were particularly hard hit. 'The bannings,' Coetzee writes, 'leave the field of Black South African writing in English almost empty.' Among the authors were Ezekiel Mphahlele (*The African Image, The Wanderers*), Richard Rive (*African Songs, Emergency*), Alex La Guma (*A Walk in the Night, And a Threefold Cord, The Stone Country*), Bloke Modisane (*Blame Me on History*), Lewis Nkosi (*Home and Exile, The Rhythm of Violence*), Peter Abrahams (*A Night of their Own, Tell Freedom, A Wreath for Udomo*) and Alfred Hutchinson (*Road to Ghana*). Among the white South African authors who had fallen foul of the censors were C.J. Driver (*Elegy for a Revolutionary*), David Lytton (*The Goddam White Man, The Freedom of the Cage*) and Nadine Gordimer (*The Late Bourgeois World*). All paperback editions of Gordimer's *A World of Strangers* were banned, although the hardcover edition was available.

As far as 'World Literature' was concerned, at least one work of each of the following authors was banned: Pietro Aretino, Nikolai Gogol, Marquis de Sade, Maxim Gorky, Arthur Schnitzler, Guillaume Apollinaire, Jean Cocteau, Henry de Montherlant, Nikos Kazantzakis, Alfred Jarry, Vladimir Mayakovsky, Pablo Neruda and Jean Genet. Next to these classical or neo-classical authors appeared also the works of a number of contemporary writers: Fernando Arrabal, Philippe Sollers, Pauline Réage, Alain Robbe-Grillet, Italo Calvino, Juan Goytisolo, Pier Paolo Pasolini, Roger Vailland, Carlos Fuentes, Alberto Moravis, Junichiro Tanizaki, José Yglesias, Violette Leduc, Jerzy Peterkiewicz and Mikhail Sholokhov.

Coetzee concludes his stock-taking and his letter to Gillham as follows:

> On the evidence of these lists, I would be prepared to accuse the Publications Control Board of three specific evasions of duty.
>
> 1. It is guilty of working by the rule, 'If I do not understand a book, ban it.' Two examples:
>
>> (i) The Russian text of Gogol's play *The Inspector-General* is banned though the English translation is not.
>>
>> (ii) The French translation of Pablo Neruda's *Canto General* is banned, though neither the Spanish original nor the English translation is (Neruda is, incidentally, one of the four Nobel Prize winners with works on the list).
>
> 2. It is guilty of working by the easy rule, 'If I banned a work by this writer in the past, I can ban every new publication of his without reading it.' The worst victim of this malpractice is James T. Farrell, some fifteen of whose novels are banned, none, in my estimate, with any justification whatsoever. (The authoritative *Penguin Companion to Literature* calls his work 'an immense *roman fleuve* which offers an effective, at times moving and indignant, history of 20th-century America.') Other notable victims of the practice of mass banning are Richard Wright, Bernard Malamud, Mary McCarthy, and R.V. Cassill.
>
> 3. It is guilty of following the easy practice of making decisions based on the publisher's advertising material, ignoring the fact that today as a matter of course publishers make exaggerated promises of sex and violence in blurbs whose purpose is to sell the book rather than accurately summarize its contents. Thus, for example, the cover of Gary Snyder's *Earth House Hold* states that Snyder writes revolutionary poems. The censors have banned the book, apparently unaware of the fact that Snyder's revolution is the Neolithic revolution.

The extent of the bannings as you know, affects several of the courses we offer in the English Department. After going through the Board's lists in full, I am convinced that, in particular, the number of works by serious American writers of our day proscribed quite emasculates any course we might offer in the twentieth-century American novel.

Besides spelling out in this letter the malign influence of censorship on the reading and teaching of literature in South Africa, Coetzee was involved in an incident that would have been hilarious had it not been so dismal. With the passing of the new legislation in 1974, Dr Connie Mulder, the minister of the interior, responsible for publications control, called for nominations of people to serve on the directorate's committees. He issued declarations describing the new dispensation as an easing of control. According to the application form, which was available from the secretary of the interior, prospective candidates had to indicate not only their academic qualifications, command of language and professional experience, but also their race, religion and cultural connections. 'That careful vetting was involved was obvious to most observers,' Peter D. McDonald writes about this form. He continues:

As J.M. Coetzee remarked, most people he knew were, like him, 'convinced that "suitably qualified" was code for sharing the government's view of the world'. Nonetheless, in early 1976,[16] when the government was on a drive to recruit more English speakers, he decided to test its bona fides by taking the radical step of applying himself. As a young bilingual academic at the University of Cape Town, who could also read three European languages, he was eminently well qualified.[17]

In reply to his application Coetzee received a letter from the secretary of the interior on 17 March 1975:

With reference to your recent application I regret to inform you that your name has not been included in the list of names which in terms of section 5 of the [Publications Act, 1974] has been compiled by the Honourable Minister of the Interior for the period 1 April 1975 to 31 March 1976.

> I wish to add that many more persons applied than were needed and that in consequence it was not possible to include the names of all applicants in the abovementioned list.

Coetzee was later to elaborate on this in an interview:

> I never expected to be accepted. I did it because they were claiming that they were opening up the censorship system to become more accessible to writers and intellectuals. I didn't believe a word of it and made an application. I thought on paper my qualifications were excellent, but they turned it down. It was exactly what I expected. I have written a whole book on censorship and it is a question that comes up again and again: what position should one take in as a writer and as an intellectual towards censorship? Should one take a hard line from the beginning and have nothing to do with people working within the system? When one works within the system, at least one can prevent it from becoming too harsh. It happened in Russia in the 19th century. If we had known in 1960 what was going to happen, we would perhaps have behaved differently.[18]

Regarding his unsuccessful application, Coetzee writes, laconically and concisely, a single sentence to Peter Randall dated 26 March 1976:[19] 'I have applied to become a one-day-a-week censor and have been rejected.'

Years later, in 1982, Professor A. Coetzee, director of publications, asked Coetzee to read *Cities of the Red Night* by William Burroughs and to write a report on it, evidently with a view to releasing the book for distribution. From his report, dated 29 November 1982, it is clear that Coetzee was not, as was customary among members of the committees of the Publications Control Board, going to gloss over matters so that the book could be permitted on the grounds of certain putative literary and moral qualities. He even alleges blatantly that there are many passages intended to be obscene and indeed are so, though they are neither erotic nor pornographic. He indicates passages that are blasphemous and in which homosexual intercourse is described in detail. Furthermore, he does not find the book to be of high literary value. He would almost seem to be daring the state machinery to ban the book. The unequivocal way in which Coetzee formulates his opinion of Burroughs's novel constitutes an indirect mockery and a demonstration of the contempt he feels for the South African system of censorship:

> I find that I am unable to summarize the contents of the book because it is structured in a deliberately modernistic or avant-garde way and does not follow a narrative line. However, for convenience it may be thought of as a set of interweaving fantasies revolving around biochemical poisoning and coloured by paranoid fears of global psychological/political control.
>
> There are numerous passages which are obscene and are intended as such, for example passages describing homosexual intercourse on pages 23, 121, 175.
>
> I do not regard the book as undesirable. It is consistently obscene but neither erotic nor pornographic. The spirit behind it is, if anything, one of despair and disgust, though there is an element of satiric humour. The key phrase is given on page 13: 'Everything is permitted.' This is adapted from Dostoevsky: 'If God does not exist, everything is permitted.' All Burroughs' works reflect a universe without God, without any transcendent principle, in which human beings are free to prey upon each other like insects for their own (usually sadistic) gratification. It is a relentlessly materialistic universe. People do not have souls but are animated by bio-electrical transfers in the brain; hence the emphasis on drugs and drug addiction in Burroughs.
>
> I cannot conceive of any reader who could receive illicit sexual pleasure from reading Burroughs.
>
> Though Burroughs is generally regarded as a significant writer, perhaps the major prose writer of the generation of the 1950s in the United States, I do not myself regard him as a major writer, if only because he has been repeating himself for the past twenty-five years.
>
> I appreciate this opportunity to present my opinion of Burroughs to the Publications Control Board, and apologize for having taken so long to submit it. I have not completed the reverse side of form 1G because I do not wish to be paid. Like many—perhaps most—other writers and literary academics in this country, I am not convinced that the system of publications control we have is a desirable one, and do not wish to become part of it.

II

With the publication of *Dusklands* and its generally favourable critical reception, Coetzee established himself as a powerful new voice in South African literature. Even though he could not yet achieve international marketing, his South African publisher, Ravan Press, was satisfied with the good sales. From publication in April 1974 up to February 1976, 2 300 copies were sold, a total which gradually increased over the years. In reply to Peter Randall's question whether he could produce a full-length manuscript to follow up on the success of *Dusklands*, Coetzee replied cautiously on 8 March 1975: 'I wish I had something to offer; but I am, to put it crudely, stuck.'

In truth he had, according to the dating of the manuscript, started his second novel on 1 December 1974, and had made rapid progress over UCT's summer break. This was a rudimentary first draft, due to be written out later in longhand. He started on the final holograph on 26 February 1975 and completed it on 25 January 1976. The final typescript of both versions of the text was completed in April 1976. He wrote the manuscript, as in the case of 'The Vietnam Project' on UCT exam books, revising and cutting considerably, also while on a short visit to the US in 1975.[20]

Whereas in *Dusklands* Coetzee had reached back to a piece of eighteenth-century colonial history in which one of his ancestors had played a part, *In the Heart of the Country*, as the second book would be called, harks back to the empty world of the Karoo that he had come to know intimately as a child on visits to Voëlfontein. Some parts even recall the young John Coetzee's memories of the annual family gatherings. In the farmer inspecting his farm dressed like a real gentleman in a jacket and tie, the informed reader recognises Gert Maxwell Coetzee, the author's grandfather. With the children of the farm labourers the narrator looks for khamma roots in the veld, feeds the motherless lambs with cow's milk, and hangs over the gate while the sheep are dipped and the Christmas pig is shot. With the coloured children the narrator sits at the feet of their grandfather, while he tells how man and beast in days gone by trekked to lower-lying farms in winter to secure grazing for the sheep: 'At the feet of an old man I have drunk in a myth of a past when beast and man and master lived a common life as innocent as the stars in the sky' (16).²¹ What is being evoked here is the Eden which Coetzee pictures in *White Writing*, a life of pastoral simplicity and honest labour: 'Blindness to the colour black is built into South African pastoral. As its central issue the genre prefers to identify the preservation of a (Dutch) peasant rural order, or at least the preservation of the values of that order.'²² As *In the Heart of the Country* runs its course, however, this idyll will yield to a whole web of failed relations.

As in Coetzee's first novel, this one too features a first-person narrator, but with a notable difference.²³ In 'The Narrative' Coetzee would for the first and last time employ a speaker inflicting pain with violence and from a lust to power. In the novels to follow, as David Attwell points out,²⁴ such characters would be the antagonists of the narrator. As against Jacobus Coetzee, the narrating Magda in *In the Heart of the Country* is the victim of the pain, with her overbearing patriarchal father as the antagonist.

Magda is an unmarried woman on a lonely farm in the Karoo at the end of the nineteenth and beginning of the twentieth century. The period of the novel is clear from the absence of electricity and running water in the house and the transport by means of donkeys and horses, in spite of Magda's characteristic uncertainty about the information she provides. Thus she asks whether there were bicycles (5) or photos (38) at that time. That the events take place after 1925 (the year in which Afrikaans was accepted as an official language), is evident from the letter in two languages that she receives in section 238, and from the machines flying in the air (239).²⁵

A conspicuous feature of the novel's external structure is its division into 266 numbered units, not ordered chronologically but relating freely to time and often containing contradictory versions of events, causing them to shift kaleidoscopically past one another. The numbers do not occur in the first draft; they were added at the second stage, during the revision and pruning of the manuscript. In an interview with Joanna Scott, Coetzee says the numbers permitted him to do away with the pretense of continuity, enabling him to create abrupt transitions or facilitate transitions. They also made sharp juxtapositions possible, and telling the same story twice, but in different versions.²⁶ In one of his interviews with David Attwell in *Doubling the Point* Coetzee says that there are similarities between *In the Heart of the Country* and the French *roman nouveau*, especially that of Alain Robbe-Grillet, but that his novel also shows the influence of film and photography. In the heyday of modernism, he continues, first poets and then novelists tried to execute narration as quickly as possible and looked for inspiration to films employing montage to link short consecutive sequences in long narratives through jumps and an episodic narrative. This made the novel a rather different affair to the nineteenth-century novel that builds up its narrative in a leisurely unfolding of material. About the resemblance of the novel to the technique of films such as those by Chris Marker and Andrzej Munk, Coetzee says:

> What impressed me most about films like these was, paradoxically, what they could achieve through stills with voice-over commentary: a remarkable intensity of vision (because the eye *searches* the still image in a way it cannot search the moving image) together with a great economy of narration. More than economy: a rapidity, even a forward-plunging quality.[27]

Although Magda refers to herself as 'a spinster with a locked diary', fighting against 'becoming one of the forgotten ones of history' (10), the numbered units should not be read as diary entries. At the end she laments the fact that she had not had the idea to keep 'a journal like a good castaway' (237), a formulation revealing Coetzee's fascination with the character of the castaway, which was to emerge in the novel *Foe* and its adaptation of the tale of *Robinson Crusoe*. Nevertheless, it is clear from the start that Magda makes use of written words in her effort to survive on the pitiless, merciless piece of land and in her struggle against the great forgetting of death, disappearing without a history. In the isolation of the desert world in which she lives, where normal family ties and the happiness of marriage are out of her reach, she wants to create a life for herself. 'Is it possible,' she asks in section 27, 'that I am a prisoner not of the lonely farmhouse and the stone desert but of my stony monologue?' In this sense the numbered sections are segments of her alternating narratives, thoughts or meditations, except in those sections where she abandons her monologue to enter into dialogue with other characters. It is noticeable, too, that Magda narrates in the present as the events gradually unfold, seldom reproducing earlier incidents in the past tense. This technique, of writing in synch with history, is one that Coetzee will also employ in later works to lend immediacy to events. And in the figure of Magda is reflected his own ambivalence to the Afrikaner part of his cultural heritage—both a fascination with the landscape, the people, their folklore and their linguistic habits, and an antagonism towards the patriarchal value system and the master-servant relation that he experienced there.[28]

The opening of the novel places the reader *in medias res*, and the differences from the traditional farm novel, both in English (Olive Schreiner and Pauline Smith) and in Afrikaans (Jochem van Bruggen, D.F. Malherbe and C.M. van den Heever) are immediately evident:

> Today my father brought home his new bride. They came clip-clop across the flats in a dog-cart drawn by a horse with an ostrich-plume waving on its forehead, dusty after the long haul. Or perhaps they were drawn by two plumed donkeys, that is also possible. My father wore his black swallowtail coat and stovepipe hat, his bride a wide-brimmed sunhat and a white dress tight at waist and throat. More detail I cannot give unless I begin to embroider, for I was not watching. I was in my room, in the emerald semi-dark of the shuttered late afternoon, reading a book or, more likely, supine with a damp towel over my eyes fighting a migraine. I am the one who stays in her room reading or writing or fighting migraines. The colonies are full of girls like that, but none, I think, so extreme as I. My father is the one who paces the floorboards back and forth, back and forth in his slow black boots, And then, for a third, there is the new wife, who lies late abed. Those are the antagonists.

The opening signals clearly that *In the Heart of the Country* deviates from the realistic farm novel. As against the custom-sanctioned brave and self-sacrificing woman with a noble spirit, Magda suffers from migraine and hides in her room with a book, instead of labouring over the pots and pans in the kitchen like a dutiful farm woman. It is soon clear that Coetzee is deviating also from the traditional realistic setting of the farm novel, as Magda's version of events cannot decide between a horse cart or a donkey cart for the newly married couple, because she has not witnessed the arrival personally and bases her account on mere speculation and fantasy, as the word *embroider* suggests. Then there is a temporal leap when she refers to the woman 'who lies late abed', an observation she could only have made after the new arrival had become part of the routines of the household. At the end of the first lemma she identifies her father and his new wife as the antagonists, a moment in her narrative when the novel takes stock of its structure, as it were, underlining the fictive nature of the events.

That the events, including the arrival and presence of a new wife in the household, exist only in Magda's imagination, is apparent from lemma 38, in which the opening, with verbal echoes, is repeated. Now, however, it is the coloured labourer Hendrik bringing his new wife, later known as Klein-Anna,[29] to the farm:

> Six months ago Hendrik brought home his new bride. They came clip-clop across the flats in the donkey-cart, dusty after the long haul from Armoede. Hendrik wore the black suit passed on to him by my father with an old wide-brimmed felt hat and a shirt buttoned to the throat. His bride sat by his side clutching her shawl, exposed and apprehensive. Hendrik had bought her from her father for six goats and a five-pound note, with a promise of five pounds more, or perhaps of five goats more, one does not always hear these things well.

As before, there is the 'clip-clop' sound of the donkey's hooves, though the alternative possibility of a horse cart is eliminated. Instead of the swanky swallow-tail coat of the father, Hendrik, in keeping with his lowly status, is dressed in a suit inherited from the owner of the farm. The addition of an old felt hat contrasts with the smart, albeit second-hand, clothes he is sporting and the top hat the father wears on his arrival. This time Magda feels no uncertainty about her perceptions, but wavers on the precise amount of lobola Hendrik had to pay. When, later in the same lemma, she has to describe Armoede, Klein-Anna's home town, she once again fabricates, because by her own account she has never been there, though she can vividly picture the shabby houses, the chickens and the snot-nosed children. Reality and invention constantly intertwine in the novel, effacing boundaries. It is impossible to establish whether any of the events really took place or whether they are figments of Magda's disturbed and over-active imagination. Replying during a lecture in Lexington to a question about the unreliability of the narrator in this novel, Coetzee said:

> When you opt for a single point of view from inside a single character, you can be opting for psychological realism, a depiction of one person's inner consciousness. And the word I stress there is realism, psychological realism. And I suppose that what is going on in *In the Heart of the Country* is that kind of realism is being subverted

because, you know, she kills her father, and her father comes back, and she kills him again, then the book goes on for a bit, and then he's there again. So that's a different kind of game, an anti-realistic kind of game.[30]

After the arrival of her father and his bride at the beginning of the story, Magda's jealousy increases to the point where she spies on them in their intimacies like a voyeur, and murders them with an axe. That this is another figment, is apparent from her father's actions after the arrival of Hendrik and his bride. His growing interest in Klein-Anna leads him eventually to rape the young woman, and whereas Magda had earlier yearned for his body near-incestuously, she now fatally wounds him with a gunshot through the bedroom window. With her father now (apparently) dead, Magda seeks to appease Hendrik and Klein-Anna. She wants to escape from the hierarchy into which she was born and reverse the traditional roles of master and servant or master and slave. She invites them to live with her in the house, and seeks to befriend both Klein-Anna and Hendrik. She admires Klein-Anna's body, which radiates a contented womanliness, and wants to enter it completely ('I would like to climb down her throat while she sleeps and spread myself gently inside her', 211). Klein-Anna, however, does not respond to her blandishments, and Hendrik insults her physically and rapes her. This rape is described five times, each time from a different perspective (205–209),[31] and poses the question whether this may not be a creation of Magda's wishes and her lust. She says, for instance: 'I am a hole crying to be whole. [...] there is a hole between my legs that has never been filled' (87). In 217–219 Hendrik visits her in the night (in reality or in her imagination?) on an irregular basis, but the meetings remain brief and loveless. Through the (second) death of her father and her relationship with Hendrik, Magda realises, as Susan van Zanten Gallagher puts it,[32] that the burden of the patriarchal system cannot be shed that easily. This is a development that Coetzee also refers to in his interview with Folke Rhedin: 'At a certain point she tries to drop the master/slave relationship in favour of a relationship of equality which I think is entirely sincerely intended on her part. But it fails, and it fails because a mere effort of the will is not enough to overcome centuries of cultural and spiritual deformation.'[33]

   Hendrik, too, perpetuates the patriarchal system: he demands payment for his work, whereas Magda wants them to co-exist in an Eden without mercantile values and demands. When the neighbours start asking questions about her father, Hendrik and Anna flee, abandoning Magda on a derelict farm—though the reader never knows which part of this report is fictitious and which not. Fantasy and reality are constantly interwoven, as Derek Attridge points out in his commentary on the novel:

> The consistency of style, the lack of any overtly signaled transitions between what might be fantasy and what might be reality, the improbabilities that remain in the latter (culminating in the impossible final pages, in which Magda's father is once more alive—unless he has been alive the whole time): all these make clear distinctions highly problematic. As a result, Hendrik and Anna remain enigmatic presences, never wholly grasped by the machinery of the text, never securely 'in their place'.[34]

Although Magda lives on a farm, she differs in very specific respects from the characteristic Afrikaner woman of the past, venerated by poets for her courage, faith and purity. Something of the authoritarian patriarch of the traditional Afrikaans farm novel does remain in the behaviour of the father, whose feet are washed in silence by his daughter in the evenings when he returns from the fields. But the way in which he, in full sight of Magda, carries on with his new wife and later embarks on a relationship with the wife of a coloured labourer, is a far cry from the substance of the Afrikaans farm novel, in which conservative moral values and a clear distance between employer and employee are maintained. And, as Gallagher points out:

> Magda's character and narrative [...] rewrite the nationalistic myth in their subversion of Afrikaner patriarchal discourse. By centering his novel in Magda, Coetzee reinscribes the figure of the woman that is commonly employed to validate the Afrikaner myth. [Magda's] feminine history attempts to break out of the patriarchal hierarchies on which traditional Afrikaner identity is based. Her narrative presents an alternative version of South African national consciousness as she struggles to find her identity in relationship to the land, her father, and the Africans of color with whom they share the land.[35]

The Afrikaans farm novel characteristically introduces the reader to a predominantly male world, with the woman a peripheral figure, playing no significant part in the action. Every farm is, as Coetzee points out in *White Writing*, 'a separate kingdom ruled over by a benign patriarch with, beneath him, a pyramid of contented and industrious children, grandchildren, and serfs'.[36] In this microcosm the coloured or black labourers are conspicuously absent. Coetzee says that the novels of Olive Schreiner and Pauline Smith make no space worth mentioning for the labourers. This is true also of the Afrikaans farm novels. Where they do occur, it is, as in Jochem van Bruggen, D.F. Malherbe and C.M. van den Heever, confined to a single chapter for comic relief, in scenes where lucerne is harvested or the vineyards are dug over and the workers start an impromptu race. The silence about the place of the labourer in these novels represents, according to Coetzee, 'a failure of imagination before the problem of how to integrate the dispossessed black into the idyll (or in Schreiner's case the anti-idyll) of African pastoralism'.[37] Attridge comments:

> There are no communicative breakthroughs in Coetzee's fiction; just moments at which a character talks himself or herself into a new mental position, a new constellation of thought and feeling, with no guarantee that the addressee will take the slightest notice—with the likelihood, in fact, that the alterity of the addressee will be underscored all the more.[38]

In her final meditations (230–266) Magda is living on the farm, caring for her father—now mute, probably after a stroke—and believing that the messages she receives from the machines in the air are of divine provenance. In her reactions, as Dominic Head has shown, paraphrases and quotations from a whole spectrum of Western literature and philosophy are interwoven, intensifying the unreal element in her character:

> The construction of Magda is ultimately a textual problem, in the sense that she is shown to be the product of different textual influences. Her narrative is peppered with quotations from, or allusions to, many important figures in modern Western literature and philosophy, including Blake, Hegel, Kierkegaard, Freud, Kafka, Sartre and Beckett. The fact that she is versed in contemporary

literary theory makes her seem, in the words of Ian Glenn, 'a kind of Emily Dickinson with therapy and a thesis in critical theory'.[39] Clearly, the extraordinarily rich and diverse composition of Magda's intellectual identity underscores her position as a metafictional device to facilitate the exploration of character construction, and the nature of the 'I-figure' in fiction.[40]

Her communication with the 'sky-gods', to whom she represents herself with letters on stones as Cinderella, creates in her a certain expectation drawing on Beckett's *Waiting for Godot*. The traditional poems about the desolate plains—by poets such as Thomas Pringle, Jan F.E. Celliers, Toon van den Heever and Guy Butler, about whom Coetzee writes extensively in Chapter 2 of *White Writing*—are too facile for Magda and probably rhetorically and emotionally too shallow. She does confess to her great love of this landscape. To her it is an Eden, to such an extent that she never considers flying away with the 'sky-gods':

> There are poems, I am sure, about the heart that aches for Verlore Vlakte, about the melancholy of the sunset over the koppies, the sheep beginning to huddle against the first evening chill, the faraway boom of the windmill, the first chirrup of the first cricket, the last twitterings of the birds in the thorn-trees, the stones of the farmhouse wall still holding the sun's warmth, the kitchen lamp glowing steady. They are poems I could write myself. [...] I am corrupted to the bone with the beauty of this forsaken world. If the truth be told, I never wanted to fly away with the sky-gods. My hope was always that they would descend and live with me here in paradise, making up with their ambrosial breath for all that I lost when the ghostly brown figures of the last people I knew crept away from me in the night. I have never felt myself to be another man's creature (here they come, how sweet the closing plangencies), I have uttered my life in my own voice throughout (what a consolation that is), I have chosen at every moment my own destiny, which is to die here in the petrified garden, behind locked gates, near my father's bones, in a space echoing with hymns I could have written but did not because (I thought) it was too easy.

In the Heart of the Country is not notable in the first place for its critical survey of colonialism or of an earlier master-servant dispensation, but for the lyrical quality of the prose that with the interweaving of the realistic and the fantastic at times acquires a near-magical element. Derek Attridge comments on the import of both *Dusklands* and *In the Heart of the Country* in the context of Coetzee's oeuvre:

> The importance of *Dusklands* and *In the Heart of the Country* does not lie in their critique of colonialism and its various avatars; there needs be no Coetzee to tell us that the white world's subjection of other races has been brutal and dehumanizing, for both its victims and for itself. These novels—unlike some that are classified under the rubric 'postcolonial'—provide no new and illuminating details of the painful history of Western domination. All this brutality and exploitation is certainly there in the novels to be felt and condemned, but it is not what makes them singular, and singularly powerful. It is what they do, how they happen, that matters: how otherness is engaged, staged, distanced, embraced, how it is manifested in the rupturing of narrative discourse, in the lasting uncertainties of reference, in the simultaneous exhibiting and doubting of the novelist's authority. Whether we call this modernism or postmodernism is, finally, inconsequential; what is important is the registering of the event of meaning that constitutes the work of literature—the event that used to be called 'form' and that was given new potential by modernist writers. In Coetzee's hands the literary event is the working out of a complex and freighted responsibility to and for the other, a responsibility denied for so long in South Africa's history. The reader does not simply observe this responsibility at work in the fiction, but, thanks to its inventive re-creation of the forms and conventions of the literary, experiences, in a manner at once pleasurable and disturbing, its inescapable demands.[41]

III

On 27 June 1975, when he had made considerable progress with *In the Heart of the Country*, Coetzee wrote to Peter Randall, at a time when Judge Lammie Snyman with his rigid notion of censorship was heading the government's Directorate of Publications:

I am working on a book-length fiction which, if published in South Africa, might conceivably be banned on one or both of the grounds that (1) it impairs good race relations, (2) it is obscene etc.

(a) Assuming that Ravan Press were interested in publishing the book, and assuming that I had no objections, would you be prepared to submit the MS to the Publications Control Board for scrutiny? And if they asked for cuts, what would you do?

(b) If you were not prepared, on principle, to submit any MS to the PCB, would you be prepared to publish a book which, although in your opinion of literary merit, stood a good chance of having official action taken against it? To what extent would considerations like these influence your decisions on form of publication, size of printing, etc.? To what extent would the (presumably beneficial) repercussions of banning on overseas publication and sales enter into consideration? In other words, to what extent would such a risky act of publishing have to be insured by prior agreements with publishers overseas?

At this stage Coetzee's enquiries were only an exploration of the likely economic realities for Ravan Press if they were to accept a book featuring a relationship across the colour line and of which parts could be regarded as morally corrupting or even pornographic in terms of the legislation. Coetzee was concerned that, in the light of a possible ban, the manuscript might be too great a financial risk for Ravan.

Although Wopko Jensma's second collection, *Where White is the Colour, Where Black is the Number*, a Ravan publication, had been banned in June 1975, the publishers were dead set against making any submissions to the Publications Control Board. In his letter of 21 July 1975 to Coetzee, Peter Randall writes: 'We have taken a policy decision that we shall not under any circumstances submit a ms to the PCB.' As for the answers to the questions under (b) in Coetzee's letter, Randall writes that that would depend entirely on their assessment of the merits of the manuscript:

If I believe that it has great merit, we shall publish it irrespective of possible banning by the PCB. The only legal criteria we would consider would be the specific laws relating to obscenity, libel, state security and the Suppression of Communism Act (i.e. quoting banned people etc).

Inevitably, if I believed that a book stood a good chance of being banned, this would influence my decision regarding the amount of capital to be risked. For example, we might well decide on a soft cover edition in a limited printing whereas normally we would go for a hard cover.

All this applies irrespective of the prior sales of rights overseas, although clearly this would be of importance to us.

Ravan's finances are still very tight, but I believe that we have little justification for our existence if we cannot take considered risks. I am hopeful with the new titles we are bringing out we shall have sufficient income to act as a cushion against further bannings.

A few months later Coetzee informed Randall that the book was progressing well and that he hoped to be able to work on it while the students were writing exams and during the university's long summer break. On 30 September 1975 he writes: 'I watch myself carefully to see whether I notice this notorious sense of the-censor-at-my-elbow that people write about, but I haven't found it yet.' Although humorously meant, the statement indicates to what extent censorship and the danger of a banning could influence a writer in the 1970s. In his 1996 collection, *Giving Offense*, Coetzee was to write:

The tyrant and his watchdog are not the only ones touched by paranoia. There is a pathological edge to the watchfulness of the writer in the paranoid state. For evidence one need only go to the testimony of writers themselves. Time and again they record the feeling of being touched and contaminated by the sickness of the state. In a move typical of 'authentic' paranoids, they claim that their minds have been invaded; it is against this invasion that they express their outrage.[42]

A few pages later Coetzee writes, clearly with his work on *In the Heart of the Country* in mind:

Working under censorship is like being intimate with someone who does not love you, with whom you want no intimacy, but who presses himself upon you. The censor is an intrusive reader, a reader who forces his way into the intimacy of the writing transaction, forces out the figure of the loved or courted reader, reads your words in a disapproving and *censorious* fashion.[43]

On 26 March 1976 Coetzee writes to Peter Randall to say that he is completing the manuscript with parts of the dialogue in Afrikaans. On the assumption that they may want to publish it, he wants to know if the rumours are true that Ravan is on the point of bankruptcy. He also wants to know whether it would be a drawback from their point of view as publishers if parts of the dialogue were in Afrikaans. As for Ravan's position on publications control, Randall had clarified that in an earlier letter. 'May I then ask whether,' Coetzee continues, 'if you thought publication worthwhile but risky, you would contemplate any special manoeuvres, like the subscription manoeuvre adopted by André Brink,[44] or a small trial printing? Is Ravan Press in a position to survive the financial effects of a banning [...]?' He also wants to know whether Ravan has printers who would be prepared to undertake a project that could be seen as dangerous from a legal point of view. He writes:

> In the case of a book that may be banned, one enters the whole ethical minefield of the effects of banning on publication and/or sales overseas. Such effects are obviously a concern of mine. Would they also be a concern of yours, or does Ravan Press drop out of the picture for good in the event of a banning?

In his reply of 29 March 1976, Randall reacts in the first place to the rumours about Ravan's financial position: 'Please disregard the rumour. Ravan is less likely to fold now than at any time in the past two years.' As for the use of Afrikaans in sections of the dialogue, it would make no literary difference, though it could have a negative effect on sales. He can decide on possible manoeuvres in order to market the book in the face of an imminent banning only once he has read the manuscript. There should be no problem in getting a printer. 'Printers are not affected by PCB bannings, but are afraid of prosecutions under libel, sedition or obscenity laws.' On the question of overseas marketing and Ravan's probable share in it, Randall writes:

> We are able to negotiate sales abroad (i.e. of reprint/translation etc rights) after a banning. Obviously we would be keen to keep in the picture, if only to try to recover some of our outlay. Bannings here *may* stimulate interest abroad.

He points out that the Afrikaans dialogue could pose a problem in such a case. But since he had in the meantime completed the exclusively English version of *In the Heart of the Country*, Coetzee sent it to Randall on 21 May 1976, with a request for an opinion on the manuscript. Randall wrote to him on 29 June 1976 saying that he had read the novel and had no doubts that they would want to publish it.

Because he was afraid that publication in South Africa might come up against a banning, which would entail a large financial loss for a local publisher, Coetzee got in touch in March 1976 with David Stewart Hull of the literary agency James Brown Associates in New York, to whom he had earlier unsuccessfully submitted *Dusklands*, and with Celia Catchpole of the Murray Pollinger agency in London. He sent them each a copy of the completely English version of *In the Heart of the Country*. He does think, he writes, that in spite of the censorship problem, he might be able to find a local publisher if his novel is not accepted in the US and Britain. 'If I do have to publish locally,' he adds, 'it will be a somewhat different version of the book that will appear, with the dialogue in the *patois*.'

On 5 May he received a reply from Celia Catchpole. Two members of her agency had read *In the Heart of the Country* and there was no doubt in their minds that it was 'a brilliant and curiously compelling piece of writing', especially remarkable because the situation in the novel was so bleak and 'the characters so lacking in attractive human qualities that I am still wondering what exactly it was that made me to read the script so avidly!' Although she thought it would be difficult to sell the manuscript to a British publisher, she hoped that there would be an editor compelled by the 'intricate virtuosity' of the work. On 10 May Coetzee also received a letter from David Stewart Hull, saying that he had been very impressed with the manuscript: 'It is a beautiful piece of writing of the kind one all too rarely sees, and I am most enthusiastic about it.' He has, Hull writes, received a letter from an American publisher visiting London, who had heard news of Coetzee's work there, with a request to see the manuscript.

On 25 May Celia Catchpole told Coetzee enthusiastically that she had been quite wrong about marketing the manuscript in Britain, since Tom Rosenthal of the highly regarded firm Secker & Warburg had immediately been prepared to accept it by virtue of its quality, even though he was convinced it would not be passed by the South African censors. Later Rosenthal would write to Coetzee, describing his book as a 'small masterpiece'. In a letter of 31 May Coetzee expresses his joy to

Catchpole at her successful marketing, and accepts Secker & Warburg's offer with thanks. The possible ban in South Africa raised questions regarding strategy. His comments on the Afrikaans dialogue in the original version are revealing of Coetzee's own vision of its function:

> Besides the version of the novel I sent to you, I have a second version [...] in which all the dialogue, constituting perhaps 10 per cent of the text, is given in Afrikaans, in a patois which stands in roughly the same relation to literary Afrikaans as the speech of Faulkner's crackers and poor Negroes to literary American English. In preparing the English text I was unable to find a stylistic variety which was non-regional and yet had a rural, traditional flavour; I therefore translated it into a rather colourless colloquial English. For this reason, and for other reasons, I prefer the mixed or bilingual version to the English version, though it is obviously unsuitable for publication anywhere but in this country. Although no one has yet seen the bilingual version, I have discussed it with Peter Randall of Ravan Press (publisher of Dusklands). Randall says that, if he believed strongly enough in the new book, he would be prepared to publish it in the bilingual version whether or not he thought it would be banned, though of course the size of the edition would depend on the riskiness of the venture.

In the light of this Coetzee asks whether Secker & Warburg would be prepared to forfeit their South African rights if Ravan, regardless of the danger of a banning, wanted to proceed with publication of the bilingual edition. In the event of the British edition being banned in South Africa, he wants to know if Secker & Warburg would agree to a bilingual edition being produced for the South African market by Ravan. He is making these proposals against the background of a growing mood of confrontation between authors and certain publishers on the one hand and the censorship board on the other. He feels that the strongest possible attempt must be launched as a matter of principle to make the book available in South Africa, also because he feels the bilingual text to be the most authentic version.

Catchpole replies that Secker & Warburg have decided not to cede their South African rights, but that they consent to a bilingual edition by Ravan, on condition that it appears nine months after the British version. In a letter of 9 June Coetzee asks Catchpole to see to it for bibliographical reasons that the British version has the words 'English version prepared by the author' added to the colophon.[45] He points out that with the new legislation in South Africa it is now possible for authors or publishers to submit manuscripts to the Control Board for a decision as to its desirability. Writers and publishers, to his knowledge, have thus far refused to do so, mainly on the grounds, which Coetzee agrees with, that this facilitates the task of the censor. It is, however, up to Secker & Warburg to decide what to do, since they would be investing money in the edition.

Shortly after dispatch of this letter, on 16 June 1976, the political situation in South Africa deteriorated drastically when black school-children rioted in Soweto against the compulsory use of Afrikaans in the teaching of some subjects. Soon the unrest spread countrywide. Hermann Wittenberg, in his incisive study of the publication history of *In the Heart of the Country*,[46] points out that, apart from the constant threat of a banning on account of the relationship across the colour bar in the book, the prospects of publishing *In the Heart of the Country* worsened dramatically with this unrest, and that international publication was Coetzee's only option.

Coetzee thought it advisable to inform Peter Randall that Secker & Warburg were interested in accepting the exclusively English edition for publication, with South African rights. The choice facing him, he writes in a letter of 9 July 1976, is for Ravan to publish the bilingual version and for him to forego overseas publication, or for him to give the rights for an English-language version to an overseas publisher. He continues:

I might even have been prepared to turn down Secker's offer were it not for the prospect of the same dilemma recurring with the next novel I might write. At some moment or other I have to break out of the local market, and it appears that if one writes minority-taste novels one has to offer up the local market as the price for overseas publication.

The one concession Secker is prepared to offer is to allow a separate South African edition on condition that it appears no earlier than nine months after original publication and at a price which does not undercut Secker's prices. Obviously I can't offer this to you as a proposition, since from a publisher's point of view it is not a proposition. However, it seems to me that there are two possible events which might justify a later local edition. The first is

that the UK edition is not marketed here because of the banning
or fear of banning; in such a case some kind of edition, even with
occasional blank pages, might be worthwhile. The second is that the
book sells well and steadily past the nine-month mark.

Coetzee asks whether Randall would still like to see the bilingual manuscript.

Coetzee's letter came as a shock to Randall, who had already accepted
In the Heart of the Country for publication. Although Coetzee's contract
with Ravan for *Dusklands* had contained the customary clause that his
next work should be submitted to them, Randall decided not to stand
between an author and the posssibility of international recognition and
worldwide sales. In a letter of 21 July he writes: 'I am very glad for your
sake that Secker & Warburg have accepted *In the Heart of the Country*.
I am disappointed, however, that you did not let me know you were
negotiating with them.' He expresses the hope that somewhere in the
Secker & Warburg edition there might be a mention that Coetzee's
first novel had been published by Ravan. When this edition appeared,
however, there was no mention of Ravan. Later, looking back on the
early years of Ravan, Randall wrote: 'It was painful to know that as a
small publisher we could not compete with international houses to
retain authors for whom we had taken the initial risks.'[47]

For Coetzee the acceptance of his manuscript in Britain and his
accession to the Secker & Warburg list was an important development
in his growth as an author. He had always wanted to market his work
internationally, but with *Dusklands* he had not been able to find an
American or British publisher prepared to take this risk for a totally
unknown author with an unconventional manuscript. With his entry
into the international market Secker & Warburg allowed him to present
himself as a novelist 'pure and simple', unlike Ravan Press, who had
featured him as a 'South African novelist' — a literary role that he on
more than one occasion declined to play.[48]

In the meantime Coetzee heard from his American agent, David
Stewart Hull, that the publisher Alfred A. Knopf had turned down *In
the Heart of the Country* on the grounds of an overly cerebral approach.
Shortly afterwards, Hull cabled him the news that Harper and Row
had accepted it and wanted to make an offer. There was a problem, as
outlined by Corona Machemer in a letter of 21 October 1976. It seemed
that Harper and Row had some years earlier published a book by

William Gass called *In the Heart of the Heart of the Country*, a book that was still available in paperback and appeared on university setwork lists. She was not so much concerned about possible confusion among reviewers as about computer mix-ups of orders. She wanted to know whether the title could be changed to *Here in the Heart of the Country*. She concluded: 'It is a superb novel; I wish I could read Afrikaans so that I could read the version you prefer.' In reply, Coetzee wrote on 29 October that the problem of the title is 'an unfortunate business':

> It's galling to have to make a change that really means something for the sake, not of a machine (I know computers), but of a hypo-thetical day-dreaming punch-machine operator. 'In the Heart of the Country' was not simply a phrase I picked on after I had written the book, it is a motif that recurs with a certain rhythm throughout the text. I can't accept 'Here in the Heart of the Country' because it is too long and (I think you will agree) rather unmemorable. The best compromise I can suggest is: 'From the Heart of the Country'. Beginning with an *F*, this will *surely* not be confused with a title beginning with an *I*. [...]
>
> Your jacket copy is, I think, more informative than Secker & Warburg's. I would quibble only with 'awesome land' (4th paragraph)—the topography of this country is not particularly awesome and I don't think the book suggests it. Perhaps you might like to think along the lines of barren, vast ...

In London Tom Rosenthal of Secker & Warburg was still concerned about a possible ban on *In the Heart of the Country* in South Africa. For this reason Coetzee got in touch with Andrew Stewart of Heinemann's in Johannesburg, who managed distribution and sales for Secker & Warburg. 'My own feeling,' he writes to Stewart on 30 July 1976, 'is that, though the book may offend some people, the people it may offend are not likely to read it. Therefore if the PCB has any sense it will take no action. Unfortunately, the PCB does not always behave in the most sensible way.'

In spite of this uncertainty, preparation of the manuscript for setting went ahead in London. In May 1977, however, Coetzee received a letter from Alison Samuel of Secker & Warburg with the bad news that their sales director believed there was no chance that it would be possible to distribute *In the Heart of the Country* in South Africa:

Even if the censors weren't being particularly strict at the moment—which apparently they are—a book which explicitly mentions miscegenation in the blurb is, I'm told, a hopeless proposition. [...] Even if it didn't, though, and even if we did manage to persuade a few bookshops to take it, I'm told that they would be bound to return them almost immediately: it's happened before and the whole process is a waste of energy, I gather, and simply destroys any goodwill the bookshops and distributors may have accumulated towards Seckers and the Heinemann Group.

Coetzee replied on 26 May 1977. His opinion was, and he asked her to bring it to the attention of those in her organisation concerned with this decision, that Secker & Warburg was making a double error. In the first place, it was a tactical error, in the light of the South African censorship system, for a publishing firm to censor itself:

The authorities here have created a situation in which the publishers feel that it might be so financially ruinous to put out books that might offend dominant white mores that they prefer to try nothing risky. Thereby they play into the authorities' hand. For the authorities do not like banning works by South African writers. There is invariably an unpleasant hullabaloo in the press, the size of the hullabaloo depending on the newsworthiness of the writer. The press, English and Afrikaans, is pretty much united on the issue of censorship of serious literature. Therefore there is every reason to press the authorities to make a decision.

I need not point out, further, that self-censorship places both Seckers and myself in an untenable moral position.

In the second place, he thought, Secker & Warburg might find that they had misjudged the likely sales in South Africa. Their adviser at the South African branch of Heinemann's was attuned to the sale of school textbooks on the local market. He himself thought it highly improbable that *In the Heart of the Country* would be banned. They should also bear in mind, he said, that Ravan Press did not have any distribution and marketing system of note. *Dusklands*, for instance, had not been bought by the CNA, and still sold 2 700 copies through no more than seven or eight 'serious' urban bookstores. Secker & Warburg's foreboding of bookstores sending back copies with a degree of rancour was very unlikely. He therefore proposed that they submit the book to the censors—proof of how the censorship system could drive even a writer of Coetzee's integrity to despairing actions that he would normally have abhorred. 'This step costs almost nothing. If you are not prepared to take it, I will have to take it myself.' If the book was not banned, he recommended that they revisit the matter of distribution.

Coetzee's letter elicited a reply from Tom Rosenthal himself on 1 June 1977. He expresses sympathy with Coetzee, because he is as frustrated with the system of censorship as Coetzee himself. He reassures him, however, that it is not a matter of self-censorship, but of whether they should spend a substantial sum on shipping books to South Africa, only to have to reimburse bookstores afterwards for sending them back. They are prepared to submit the book to the board, 'but unless the censorship board has radically changed over the years, it seems to me that since the book deals with miscegenation, and that is the ultimate moral crime in the Republic, they have no choice but to ban it'. For that reason, unless Coetzee insisted on it, he thinks it would be unwise to submit the book to the board. He concludes:

> So let me assure you that we are not acting as self-censors nor are we being cowardly. We simply have to cope with the pragmatism that we know. If you can advise us that our views are erroneous, no one will be happier than me and we will do whatever you want. We want to sell these books as much as you do and since I am passionately committed politically in those directions that you might expect, I will do whatever you say within the limits of financial prudence.

Coetzee replied to Rosenthal's letter on 8 June. He realises, he writes, that the South African censorship system will expose Secker & Warburg to substantial financial risks, and he is the last person to ask them to undertake unnecessary risks. He agrees that submitting the book to the censors, only to have it banned, would place everybody in a weaker position than at present. Anybody exporting the book to South Africa after such a banning would be guilty of a criminal offence. He thinks, though, that Alison Samuel, in her letter of May 1977, was taking too sombre a view of the possible censorship by bookstores. The CNA, he thinks, is in a position to return books, but this certainly does not apply to the good urban bookstores in the country. Rosenthal may well be right that the book may be banned on the grounds of the scenes in which inter-racial sex takes place. He does, however, want to point out that André Brink's novel *'n Oomblik in die Wind* (1976), which was published in an English version as *An Instant in the Wind* by W.H. Allen, is freely available in South Africa, and deals with a love affair between a white woman and a black man. 'My information,' Coetzee adds, 'is that today's censors are harsher towards "portraying the police in an unfavourable light" than towards miscegenation.' He continues:

> Finally, I must say that I will find myself in an unacceptable position if a situation arises in which the book is neither banned nor available in this country, while no moves are occurring in any direction, i.e., a position of stalemate. If the book is not going to be available in the only country in which it really attains its full significance, I must at least have the comfort of knowing that I am not responsible.

For that reason he suggests that he should, through the few contacts he has, obtain an informed prediction of the censors' likely actions with regard to *In the Heart of the Country*. Once he has this information, he'll write to Rosenthal again. In the meantime he'd like to suggest that Rosenthal send review copies to the main South African newspapers. The reason for this is that after a banning it is illegal to discuss a book's merits in public. Thus if there were no reviews before such a banning, nobody would even know the book existed. By informing the public, reviews at least make it more difficult for the censors to suppress the book indefinitely.

Since Rosenthal balked at the expense of returning copies in case of a banning, Coetzee was prompted once again to get in touch with Peter Randall. On 14 June 1977 he informed him that the British edition had appeared the previous day. Secker & Warburg, however, 'at the last moment got cold feet about trying to market the book in South Africa. As matters stand, they don't even want to try.' On the same day he wrote to Rosenthal that he had been in touch with the writer Elsa Joubert, married to Klaas Steytler—also a writer, journalist, a member of the dissident Afrikaanse Skrywersgilde (Afrikaans Writers' Guild) and attached to Tafelberg Publishers—who had served on one of the panels of the Directorate of Publications. According to Steytler, *In the Heart of the Country* would be passed for distribution in South Africa, because it was mainly police torture that was 'the current no-no' subject for the censors. Steytler recommended that a copy of the book be submitted as soon as possible to the directorate, so that it would not later feel pressurised. Coetzee said he was leaving it to Rosenthal to decide whether he wanted to do that. Randall, who had in the meantime also been in touch with Rosenthal, informed Coetzee that Ravan was prepared to print a thousand paperback copies of the bilingual edition, on the understanding that Secker & Warburg would not import any copies of their edition. He warned Coetzee not to proceed with the plan to submit the book to the censors, as a matter of principle, but also, if there were no banning, to protect their own publication against the British edition for distribution in South Africa.

On 28 June 1977 Coetzee received a letter from Rosenthal, informing him that they had decided against submission to the censors, and that they intended, after a survey by Andrew Stewart, to deliver a small number of copies of their edition to some bookstores in South Africa. They would also send review copies to newspapers about three weeks before shipping, so that the books would be available when the newspapers announced the publication. The bookstores could then choose to order more copies. Rosenthal sent a copy of this letter to Randall, and in a letter of 28 June consented to the Ravan edition on condition that the text differed markedly from theirs, with the insertion of the Afrikaans dialogue, and that the whole was reset. Ravan had to draw up a proper contract with the author regarding royalties. The only concession Rosenthal made was that, probably in the light of the financial riskiness of the enterprise, he would not demand any compensation from Ravan. In a subsequent letter to Randall he says that he regrets not being able to delay the import of copies to South Africa, since review copies have already been sent out.

The delivery of the Secker & Warburg copies for distribution in South Africa made a local edition more risky for Ravan, especially since nothing prevented the British publisher from supplying additional copies in large numbers to bookshops if the book were not banned. In spite of this, Randall was prepared to proceed with the Ravan edition. He asked Coetzee to let him have the manuscript as soon as possible. In reply Coetzee wrote to Randall on 8 July that he was convinced the book would not be banned. In case of problems, Randall could consider a toned-down blurb (not mentioning a relationship across the colour bar), and an edition with four or five paragraphs blanked out. Randall requested copy from Coetzee for a diluted blurb and asked him to indicate which paragraphs should be omitted. Coetzee replied:

I think you misunderstand me on the subject of omitted paragraphs. I'm not suggesting that we omit paragraphs at this stage. But if the situation does arise where your edition is set up and the Secker edition is banned, I would suggest putting out (if necessary, submitting it to the censors first, though I know you are opposed to compromises like this) a version with the four or five most 'offensive' paragraphs blanked out.

As for the blurb, S & W say that their advice is that the blurb is not suitable for selling the book in this country; they regret passing it in the first place. If you think they are essentially correct, I'd be happy to draft a less 'offensive' blurb. Certainly, reading the first British reviews, it has struck me forcefully how vitally important it is to have a blurb which reviewers can paraphrase in the form of a review when they haven't actually got time to read the book itself.

In the meantime articles had appeared, as in the *Sunday Tribune* of 12 July 1977, in which the British edition of *In the Heart of the Country* was sensationally announced as a publication in which the South African censors were sure to interest themselves. Secker & Warburg's strategy was clearly to arouse public interest in the book by concentrating on matters like black–white sex. In the blurb this is focused on, in particular in relation to Magda's father and his desperate 'bid for private salvation in the arms of a black concubine'. Hermann Wittenberg comments on this marketing strategy: 'Far from quietly slipping in a few copies, Secker & Warburg was in effect broadcasting the fact that it was bringing a politically controversial novel on to the South African market, manufacturing a controversy that the censors would now certainly be unable to ignore. It is difficult to judge the motives here of Secker & Warburg, but possibly a high-profile confrontation with the state [...] would enable them to occupy the moral high ground—and generate publicity for international sales.'[49]

Randall wrote to Coetzee that they probably now had no other option but to submit the manuscript of the South African edition to the censors, probably with Coetzee's proposed omissions. It might then just be possible for the Ravan edition to be allowed if the British edition was banned.

But the ever-alert censorship system had already been set in motion. On 11 July 1977 Customs at Cape Town harbour confiscated the shipment of *In the Heart of the Country* intended for distribution in South Africa. On 19 July Rosenthal writes to Coetzee:

> I am afraid that the censorship boys have already struck on *In the Heart of the Country* and the book has been embargoed, so no one quite knows what will happen from now on.
>
> There is no way that one can legally get copies in once a book has been embargoed or banned, as you well know.
>
> So I am afraid that we must just wait and see in the light of this by no means unexpected development.

Randall heard the news at the same time as Rosenthal. On 20 July he writes to Rosenthal: 'I sometimes think only lunatics try to publish anything other than travel guides and gardening books in this country!' In Cape Town, in the July edition of *UCT News,* Coetzee expressed doubt that the book would ever be available in South Africa, a statement that he recanted later in the same month in a press interview, saying that it had been a private speculation which had been taken as gospel.

On 19 July Coetzee replied to Randall's letter of 13 July in which he had asked which paragraphs should be omitted. Coetzee suggested three possible courses of action: Randall could have the text set in its present form, have it proof-read, and keep options open to the last minute. If, when all the production work had been completed, there was still no action against the British edition, he could assume that all was in order. If the book was acted against, he could leave sections 206, 209 and 221 blank or submit them to the censors, explaining that the submitted sections differed from the British edition. A second possibility was to do nothing and await the fate of the Secker & Warburg edition; or he could submit the South African edition, with or without the omitted sections, immediately. Coetzee's only stipulation was that the omitted sections should indeed look like deletions, in other words that section 206 should be followed by 43 blank lines, number 209 by 32 and number 221 by 4 blank lines.

The three passages selected by Coetzee for deletion all have to do with the rape and sexual humiliation of Magda, which in terms of the law could be seen as obscene or harmful to public morals. Section 206 describes the moment when Hendrik, the coloured farm foreman, evidently rapes Magda; in 209 she is unwilling to be orally stimulated by him; and in 221 she is humiliated by him:

> He turns me on my face and does it to me from behind like an animal. Everything dies in me when I have to raise my ugly rear to him. I am humiliated; sometimes I think it is my humiliation he wants.

Wittenberg points out that, even with the proposed cuts, the reader would still know from other parts of the novel what was happening to Magda here, since sections 205 and 206 recount the same incident in a different way.[50]

In September 1977 the embargo on *In the Heart of the Country* was lifted. This still did not mean that the book was freely available in bookshops. In a letter of 6 December 1977 Coetzee complains to Sheila Roberts:

> [The] distributors are so reluctant to sink money into bringing copies into the country (they think the censors' decision will be reversed as soon as the book becomes public) that the book is not available in the bookshops. The situation has become quite ridiculous, in fact, since two newspapers have published reviews (the reviewers got copies of the book through unorthodox channels—one read it in MS, the other read the censors' copy).

The members of the panel appointed to decide the fate of *In the Heart of the Country* were not the type of 'dark-suited, bald-headed censor, with his pursed lips and his red pen'[51] that Coetzee had mockingly imagined in *Giving Offense*, but academics and writers. The chairman of the committee was Merwe Scholtz, Professor of Afrikaans and Dutch at UCT, and thus a colleague of Coetzee's, with F.C. Fensham, Professor Emeritus in Semitic Languages at the University of Stellenbosch, and the writer Anna M. Louw also submitting reports. All three expressed great appreciation for the exceptional literary quality of the novel and recommended that it be passed, even though they referred in their detailed reports to certain passages in which sex was described. Scholtz pointed out that the scenes depicting sex across the colour line belonged historically to an earlier period and thus were not a contravention of the country's laws; he also emphasised the novel's inaccessibility to the ordinary reader, making a case that only a highly developed reading public would be interested in the novel. Scholtz writes:

In many respects a dark, densely woven and therefore exceptionally difficult novel to access. And according to three (experienced) readers exceptional and even outstanding; indeed, according to one of them, 'one of the few works of stature in the South African English book sphere'. Sex across the colour line does take place, but the characters are historically-geographically so situated as to render it entirely acceptable. Besides, the sexual act is never described in such a way as to be stimulating, provocative or lust-inducing. For that matter, the reader does not always know where the boundary lies between reality and the rich, tormented fantasy world of the spinster-narrator. In any case, as mentioned above, a difficult, obscure, multi-levelled work that will be read only by intellectuals, that will even to them not easily deliver all its 'layers'. The Committee confidently recommends to allow. [Translation M.H.]

Fensham found certain passages describing sexual acts problematic, and pointed out that section 259 might offend some readers on the ground of blasphemy, but thought the novel so 'excellent' and 'strongly intellectual' that only intellectuals would read and enjoy it.

The most extensive report is that by Anna M. Louw, who was so impressed with the novel that she based two reviews on it and chose it as her book of the year 1977. Peter D. McDonald, who in *The Literature Police* offers a comprehensive account of the restrictions Coetzee's first three novels came up against, says that the peculiar blend of cultural assumptions, of an aesthetic, nationalistic and unselfconsciously humanistic nature, was particularly evident in the reports on *In the Heart of the Country*, especially in the way in which they justified the scenes depicting sex across the racial divide:

All the readers agreed that the complex narrative mode, which, as Merwe Scholtz put it in his chair's report, left the reader unsure about 'the boundary between reality and the rich, afflicted imaginary world of the spinster-narrator', meant it would not give offence or threaten the established order. In her own report, however, Louw took indeed the aestheticist argument one step further, linking it directly to the shibboleth of universality. 'Owing to the striking technique employed by the writer,' she claimed, 'the reader is made to see the events taking place as if through a bell-jar so that details and incidents that might, in a different context, be questioned as being undesirable function, by means of the distancing achieved, solely as parts of the mystery of human being.' On this reading, the first-person mode of narration presumably had a neutralizing effect because it was simultaneously aestheticizing and universalizing, or, indeed, because these two conventionally prized powers of the literary were in some sense causally related. The narrative's universal scope was reinforced, she thought, by the title, which suggested that *Country* was 'essentially' about what happens 'in the secret human heart—that seat of emotion and consciousness—and not only to people of a specific time and place'. In an absurd twist, Fensham claimed that the scenes of miscegenation could be justified on more narrowly realist grounds as well. 'The circumstance of the spinster who is cut off from all life's comforts, who sits alone on a farm, can develop into a situation when things across the colour-bar can occur,' he claimed. 'The same goes for Magda's lonely father.'[52]

With the Secker & Warburg edition now officially released, Randall's plan was to proceed immediately with the Afrikaans dialogue edition, even though the South African representatives of the British firm were energetically marketing their edition. At Randall's request Coetzee sent a proposal for a blurb that was in essence a long extract from Maev Kennedy's review in *The Irish Times*. The review, Coetzee writes, 'seems to summarize the book intelligently and give a useful characterization of it'. Unlike the blurb of the British edition, which concentrates on the theme of sex across the colour bar, Kennedy draws attention to the central character's delusions and fantasies, her emotions, her loneliness and her sense of a wasted life:

> The form of the book is deliberately artificial. The text is divided up into sections hung on the page like pictures in an exhibition. It only takes two or three pages to realize that no objective truth is going to emerge. The woman's own life shimmers and shifts in her mind like a mirage in the heat. [...] The link in all the delirious versions of her life is the woman's isolation from whatever events she conjures up, her constantly rebuffed efforts to partake. The truth that emerges is the searing loneliness of this life, the echo of her feeling of waste and futility, painfully and vividly conveyed. It is a very restrained, spare book, depicting intense emotion in matter of fact words, very few events, four characters. It is

also haunting, putting its finger on several common terrors of mankind and blowing them up to fill the whole canvas, so that they leave a disturbing after-image even when you turn your eyes away.

Before Randall could make much progress with the South African edition, he was served with a banning order of five years in terms of the Internal Security Act. He was removed from public life and could no longer function as a publisher. On 28 October Coetzee wrote to Randall at his home address:

> I don't know whether to congratulate you or sympathize with you. Both, perhaps. You are certainly in most honourable company, if one looks down the roll through the years. But it can be no joke living under these circumstances.

In Randall's place, Gill Berchowitz initially handled the Ravan edition of *In the Heart of the Country*. When Coetzee received the proofs, he discovered to his dismay that the numbers of the sections had been left out. He wrote to Berchowitz on 1 December 1977, in a letter demonstrating once again Coetzee's jealous guardianship of all aspects of his work, including the graphic design, and his craftsman's decisiveness in dealing with deviations from his high standards:

> The omission of the section numbers is a serious mistake and must be corrected. I don't know who took it upon himself to order their omission, but I was not consulted and would certainly not have authorised it. The manuscript, by numbering and spacing, indicates a clear distinction between sections and paragraphs. Now that the text is no longer even in galley form I don't know what you are going to do to introduce spacing. But the numbers have to be restored—there can be no argument about this—even if (a suggestion) they go into the margins in bold face.
>
> I have written the numbers into the proofs. It will require a careful second check to see that the restored numbers are correctly aligned. Otherwise there are no serious problems. Since your copy editor began the job of changing American spellings to British, I completed it.

On 1 December 1977 Coetzee also wrote to Mike Kirkwood, a former lecturer in English at the University of Natal, who had taken Randall's place as publisher with Ravan Press, to convey his dismay over the omission of the numbers:

> Someone made a major fuckup and authorized the deletion of all the section numbers. I have written to Gill Berchowitz about this. She should have the letter and the proofs tomorrow morning. The numbers will simply have to be restored. I don't know what this is going to do to their schedule. As for the cover, I hope your friend Andrew Verster (about whom I heard good things) can have some effect on Ravan. The cover of *Dusklands* was a mistake from every point of view, I think, including the commercial.

After further revision Coetzee returned the proofs to Kirkwood on 9 January 1978, and the Ravan edition of *In the Heart of the Country*, with Afrikaans dialogue, appeared at the end of February. In the light of the competing British edition, the print run was reduced to 700.[53] In a letter of 19 January to Coetzee Kirkwood added his plaudits to those the novel had already received:

> After *Dusklands* it is like moving from Descartes to Pascal. I see it as something of a minor miracle that novels like yours should be coming out of South Africa at this late hour.

Although with the publication of *In the Heart of the Country* by Secker & Warburg Coetzee now had a British publisher that could promote his interests also in other languages, he did not terminate his association with Ravan Press. Wittenberg suggests that this may have been partly due to the easing under Van Rooyen of the rigid censorship of earlier, after the lifting of the ban on Leroux's *Magersfontein, o Magersfontein!* Coetzee may also have thought that he owed some loyalty to Ravan and would also have enjoyed working with the new editor, Mike Kirkwood. Kirkwood, like Coetzee, had been a lecturer in English literature, with some shared assumptions, such as their rejection of the Leavisite principles that still dominated the study of literature at many South African universities. Thus three of Coetzee's novels would in the 1980s be co-published by Secker & Warburg and Ravan Press, even though this meant little more than local distribution and a new dust cover.[54] When

Kirkwood started the magazine *Staffrider* in 1978, mainly as a platform for black South African writers, Coetzee contributed a poem titled 'Hero and bad mother in epic', using elements of the villanelle form. This was to be his last published poem. It is also the only of his writings to fall foul of the censors, not because of anything 'offensive' or 'improper' in the text, but because the whole first issue of the magazine was banned by the censors. The parts singled out as undesirable in a letter from the Director of Publications 'are those in which the authority and image of the police, as the persons entrusted by the State with maintaining law, internal peace and order, are undermined'.[55]

Coetzee was interested in the renewal brought about by young writers and small publishers, and he wanted to be part of it. With his return to South Africa in 1971 his interest extended also to the writers who had started publishing in Afrikaans since the 1960s. In 1973 the University of Cape Town organised, as part of its annual summer school, a series of lectures on the 'Sestigers' in which most of the writers of this generation participated. These lectures were prominently reported in the press. Especially the lecture by the poet Breyten Breytenbach, who was for the first time since his marriage to the Vietnamese Yolande allowed to enter South Africa, elicited great interest, and was attended by Coetzee. Later Coetzee would write that the audience gave this 'prodigal son' of Afrikaans literature 'a rapturous welcome.'[56] In his novel *Summertime* (2009) he also lingers over the Breytenbach visit to South Africa:

Breytenbach left the country years ago to live in Paris, and soon thereafter queered his pitch by marrying a Vietnamese woman, that is to say, a non-white, an Asiatic. He not only married her, but, if one is to believe the poems in which she figures, is passionately in love with her. Despite which, says the *Sunday Times*, the Minister in his compassion will permit the couple a thirty-day visit during which the so-called Mrs Breytenbach will be treated as a white person, a temporary white, an honorary white.

From the moment they arrive in South Africa Breyten and Yolande, he swarthily handsome, she delicately beautiful, are dogged by the press. Zoom lenses capture every intimate moment as they picnic with friends or paddle in a mountain stream.

The Breytenbachs make a public appearance at a literary conference in Cape Town. The hall is packed to the rafters with people come to gape. In his speech Breyten calls Afrikaners a bastard people. It is because they are bastards and ashamed of their bastardy, he says, that they have concocted their cloud-cuckoo scheme of forced separation of the races.[57]

In the 1970s Coetzee would write several reviews and articles on the latest Afrikaans literature. With the bilingual *In the Heart of the Country*, Wittenberg writes, Coetzee explored 'a form of authorship that differentiated itself sharply from the liberal South African English novelistic tradition (exemplified by Paton, Butler and Gordimer) — and foregrounded his affinities with an avant-garde Afrikaans literary culture. [...] As several critics have pointed out, *In the Heart of the Country* was a rewriting of the "plaasroman", a genre that Coetzee saw exemplified in the farm novels of the Afrikaans writer C.M. van den Heever.'[58] An extract from Coetzee's novel appeared in *Standpunte*, 29: 4, August 1976, the literary journal founded in 1945 by N.P. van Wyk Louw and W.E.G. Louw, which predominantly featured Afrikaans literature, although contributions in English and Dutch were accepted from its inception.[59]

IV

The first reviews of *In the Heart of the Country* appeared soon after its publication. In the *Rapport* of 9 October 1977 André Brink was the first to point out that in Magda's relationship with Hendrik and Klein-Anna a gradual reversal of roles takes place, Magda becoming the slave of her erstwhile slaves, making herself available to Hendrik, 'randily, humiliatingly and fervently sexually'. The novel becomes 'a quest after a *truth* which is sought through manifold fictions', and the events are a 'mirage' of Magda's 'feverish jealousy': a mindset as intense and distorted as that in Robbe-Grillet's *Jalousie*. He concludes:

> I know, to get to the point, of no other South African, Gordimer included, who can manipulate language like Coetzee. It varies from a flamboyant volcanic spectacle such as that of Henry Miller or Roy Campbell, to the stiletto-like precision of a Beckett.

When he had, in *Die Burger* of 2 December, to elect his book of the year, Brink placed *In the Heart of the Country* first, calling it a novel with something to say 'about loneliness, about the craving for love, about the relation between master and servant and between black and white, and the human being's worldly anxieties and his yearning for salvation'.[60] In contrast to this glowing review, Reg Rumney wrote an exceedingly negative review in *Oggendblad* of 24 November. He finds that the way in which Coetzee 'is seen to be manipulating the interminable philosophical cum theological gropings of his character', renders the book very unsatisfactory. He continues:

> It is a literary book, and while I applaud the learning and the effort, and the skill, which has gone into its making the applause mirrors the essence of the work: Just the sound of two hands clapping.

Like Rumney, Barry Ronge in *Die Transvaler* of 22 April 1978 thought the tale a mere 'romantic cliché', Magda a caricature and the 'highly artificial style' more of 'a technical exercise than anything else'. Probably the most negative assessment came from Cherry Wilhelm in *Standpunte*, 32: 3, June 1979, deploring the 'intellectual élitism' and the 'irritating show-off' manner representing for her Coetzee at his worst. For Stephen Watson, who wrote a particularly searching essay on the first four novels, it was precisely the intellectual quality of Coetzee — 'the most bookish of all authors in South Africa' — that lent a work like *In the Heart of the Country* its distinction. He mentions the authors that Coetzee draws on, and describes the book as 'a tissue of borrowings' stretching from Hegel (with his master-slave relation) and Kafka to Conrad, Beckett and Sartre — '"all of Europe" (and North America) has gone into the making of Coetzee — or at least into the making of his books. He has produced by far the most intellectual and indeed intellectualising fiction of any South African or African writer.'[61] Jos Baker in the *Cape Times* of 18 January 1978 described it as 'a brilliant book'. The reader 'is swept along on sensuous waves of imagery'; the author 'uses words as music [;] sentences and phrases flow into each other, building up rhythm and tempo as the central character plots her revenge'. Scott Hague in the *Cape Argus* of 15 February 1978 writes: 'Mr Coetzee's prose artistry and sense of drama make one a captive reader right to the last page.' In his review in *SA Outlook* of March 1978, Philip Cohen pointed out that in the figure of Magda Coetzee had aligned himself with a Western epic tradition, from Homer to Saul Bellow and Patrick White, but that he also, partly through the use of Afrikaans dialogue, in an original sense belonged to the heart of this particular country and utilised its attributes. It was in connecting a literary tradition and the common traits of a divided country that *In the Heart of the Country* was 'a gripping book'. In an illuminating review in *Oggendblad* of 28 April, Jean Marquard concludes:

> There can be no question [...] about the brilliance of [Coetzee's] linguistic resources and the skill of his experimentation. In using the novel as a critical tool, aimed not only at the South African way-of-life, but at the literature which has traditionally reflected it, he creates for the tradition a new direction.

In *The Friend* of 3 May 1978, a reviewer with the initials MHF wrote that in J.M. Coetzee South Africa possessed a world-class English-language author, comparable with Athol Fugard, somebody with the potential to be compared with the greatest writers like Graham Greene and John Updike. Tony Morphet, who had judged *Dusklands* very favourably, felt that in this instance, the prose, though 'startling in its precision, solidity and power', lacked the capacity of masters of the genre to register 'layers and relativities of the consciousness'. He does, however, add:

> But in what other writing can one discover such a power of pene-tration — such a capacity to create the shape and feel of things — such a sense of the inward workings of emotion and thought and above all such an experience of entering the deep dark recesses of hidden states of mind, especially when the mind is our own inheritance.

For her review in *Beeld* of 23 January 1978, Anna M. Louw reread the book after writing her report for the censors. Whereas, according to her, indigenous English literature was struggling to liberate itself from the European view of 'mysterious black Africa', or tended to oversimplify the racial dynamic in political terms, in Coetzee's novel one recognised 'immediately the wide, bright, stone-faced land in which the Protestant outlook on life had so often fought in a spiritual corner.' She says that one could speculate about the levels of meaning of the work:

> Is it basically a case study of a lonely unattractive spinster with a Freudian father-fixation coupled with a fervent imagination and an extraordinary ability to verbalise her affliction? Is it a fable about 'consciousness adrift' as the blurb has it? For me, as a reader,

there are indications that it is much more. Questions thus arise: Could Magda's unfolding emotional life, because there is never stasis, perhaps be seen as a metaphysical account of the—mainly Protestant—search for God? Quite early in the novel and shortly after the arrival of the (imagined?) stepmother Magda gives utterance to the recognition of the 'Godshaped hole' in her that is virtually a basic premise, for instance for Calvin in his *Institutes*: 'I'm a being with a hole inside me,' Magda says on page 9, 'I signify something. I do not know what.' [...] I would not want to make the mistake of over-interpretation, but could Magda's apparent insanity, when she remains behind alone on the crumbling farm, be seen as the condition of 'God's harlequin'? In this case a Protestant harlequin who to the bitter end clearly and in solitude discovers, analyses and tries to process mentally the facts of life? Who questions through prayer, not out of mystical conviction but on rational grounds. 'Am I going to yield to the spectre of reason and explain myself to myself in the only confession we Protestants know?' Magda asks on the penultimate page of the novel.

Anna M. Louw decides: 'To my mind Coetzee has in this work succeeded in composing a finely honed and monumental metaphor such as you rarely find in the modern literature of anywhere you care to name.'[62]

In his review of 15 May 1978 in the *Rand Daily Mail*, Lionel Abrahams refers to the 'silvery brilliance' of Coetzee's style, 'an art strong enough to ballast the intellectual and philosophical thrust by which this author is bringing a new dimension to South African English fiction'. Later Lesley Marx was to say, in the video *Passages*: 'The fascinating tension in Coetzee's work for me is the tension between the potentially very bleak vision and the exquisiteness of the prose. Even with something as grim as *In the Heart of the Country* those sentences are so perfectly formed that there is a kind of aesthetic delight I gain from that. And I think in some ways it could be argued there is a moral vision attached to that aesthetic perfection, that you can only put a sentence together perfectly if you engage in the discipline of writing a combination of your soul and your imagination, your artist's skill.'[63]

Reactions to the first publication of *In the Heart of the Country* in the UK were by and large confined to short notices that gratefully availed themselves of the blurb. The work did not attract much attention from the reviewers who helped shape literary taste in Britain. That attention

308   J.M. COETZEE: A LIFE IN WRITING

would come only after the publication of Coetzee's third novel, *Waiting for the Barbarians*, when its success prompted Penguin to bring it out in paperback. In the US, too, reaction to *In the Heart of the Country* was lukewarm, though the South African poet Barend J. Toerien recommended the book strongly in *World Literature Today* of Summer 1978: 'I can hardly recall a work more steeped in the authentic and historical South African situation. Over it hangs a brooding intensity, intermixed with a crazy humor.' It was only in a 1978 article by Josephine Dodd, pointing out the theme of colonial exploitation, that the novel received more serious attention.[64]

The international interest in *Waiting for the Barbarians* prompted the publisher Nadeau to publish a French translation of *In the Heart of the Country* in 1981. The important weekly French magazine *Express* described the book as a masterpiece, and the literary journal *La Quinzaine Litteraire* devoted two whole pages to it. In a letter of 2 October 1979 Coetzee explained to the translator, Sophie Mayoux, the meaning of words like *muishond* [skunk], *karos* [kaross], *sening* [sinew], *koppie* [hillock] and *Verlore Vlakte* [*Desolate Plain*]. The book appeared in Holland in 1985, translated by Peter Bergsma. Coetzee's Dutch, which he had studied in Austin, was still so good that he was able to check the translation and answer the translator's queries. In a letter dated 15 November 1984, Bergsma says that he is 'very much obliged' to Coetzee for his cooperation.

V

As early as June 1975 Randall had alerted Coetzee to the fact that manuscripts were being invited for consideration for the Mofolo-Plomer Prize. On 26 April 1976 Coetzee wrote that he would like to enter two copies of *In the Heart of the Country* for this prize, but that two problems had arisen. In the first place he had heard that Chinua Achebe, who would find the Afrikaans sections unintelligible, would be one of the judges. In the second place, the prize was intended for writers under 35, and he had turned 36 in February. He writes:

> If I submit *In the Heart of the Country* as it presently stands, I sus-
> pect that Achebe might have either to recuse himself or pass a
> conditional verdict or decline to consider the work. If it is necessary,

I am prepared to translate the Afrikaans, but that entails a lot of work, since literally every second page is affected. Is it therefore not possible to get guidelines, from whomever runs the competition—I have no idea of how things are run—on the question of the language and the question of whether a point will be stretched on the age limit? I would hate to go to all the trouble of preparing a revised manuscript solely for the competition only to find that it is ineligible.

Randall replied that the Mofolo-Plomer Prize had been initiated by Nadine Gordimer, and that she would have to decide the matter. She was overseas, and would only return by the end of May. He advised Coetzee to submit the manuscript with the Afrikaans dialogue, with a covering letter stating that, if necessary, he would provide a translation of the Afrikaans sections.

In the Heart of the Country was not, however, submitted for consideration in 1976. On 9 June 1977 Peter Randall asked Coetzee if they could consider the manuscript for submission for that year's Mofolo-Plomer Prize, as the age limit had been scrapped. On 20 September Randall reported to Coetzee that the prize of R500 had been awarded to him, and that André Brink and Peter Strauss had been the judges. Coetzee wrote to Rosenthal of Secker & Warburg on 6 October 1977 with the news that *In the Heart of the Country* had been released by the censors and that it had won the Mofolo-Plomer Prize. 'This prize counts as the second most prestigious award for English-language fiction in South Africa, after the CNA Prize, which is awarded in December. The CNA Prize is, to some extent, an "establishment" prize; the Mofolo-Plomer Prize is not.'

In March 1978 Coetzee received a letter informing him that the CNA Prize for 1977 had been awarded to *In the Heart of the Country*. The prize of R2 500 would be handed over at the Country Club in Johannesburg. In his speech on the occasion Coetzee reacted to the regime of censorship under which South African writers were obliged to labour. It was humiliating to expend one's best energy on work that would be scrutinised by people who had no particular interest in it, people who could see no reason why doors closed by their great-grandparents should not remain tightly shut until Doomsday, people for whom propriety, decorum and decency were the cardinal virtues. When, in future, people wanted to know what life was like in the twilight of the republic, they would not approach the Department of Information, but read the books of authors like Alex La Guma and Nadine Gordimer. 'Not because writers hold any monopoly of truth, but, firstly, because what they write is written to be memorable and, secondly, because history finally gets written by that shadowy class, the intelligentsia, which has its own loyalties.'[65] During the Cape Town Book Fair of 1979, Marilyn Honikman, at the time married to Mike Kirkwood, saw to it that two shelves in the Ravan stall displayed nothing but copies of *Dusklands* and *In the Heart of the Country*. 'Through this kind of marketing we wanted to make a statement: this is South Africa's great new author.'[66]

Apart from his work as an academic and novelist Coetzee was active in other related fields in the 1970s, especially where literature or individual freedom was at stake. When the writer Sipho Sepamla was refused a South African passport for a second time in 1976, Coetzee signed a petition in November, drawn up by Richard Rive and Nadine Gordimer, stating that the refusals were 'deplorable infringements' of Sepamla's liberty, especially since no satisfactory explanation had been given. Other writers who signed the petition were Jack Cope, Douglas Livingstone, Tania van Zyl (on behalf of the South African PEN Centre, Cape), Jan Rabie, Adam Small, F.A. Venter, J.J. Degenaar, Elsa Joubert, Lionel Abrahams, Peter Randall, Guy Butler, André Brink, Alan Paton and Richard Rive. At the end of 1980 Coetzee joined the ranks of the Afrikaanse Skrywersgilde (Afrikaans Writers' Guild) as a member, though he was never really active in this organisation. He wrote reviews and essays in these years, but it is clear that he also wanted to undertake more analysis of popular culture, such as reviewing Ross Devenish's film *The Guest*. When Mike Kirkwood asked him for contributions to *Staffrider*, Coetzee replied on 1 December 1977:

> I am at present interested in doing reasonably exhaustive analyses of the kind of text that doesn't usually get critical attention. [...] In other words, I am interested in finding a way of talking intelligently about popular contemporary texts and less interested in 'high' literature. I'd be happy to write about films or popular writing for the magazine.

Staffrider, however, was not the place for contributions on contemporary popular texts; Coetzee's articles with an academic but slightly 'lighter' slant did not for the time being materialise.

Apart from cricket, which he played regularly at UCT with colleagues such as John van der Westhuizen and Geoffrey Haresnape, Coetzee kept a lively interest in rugby. He wrote 'Four notes on rugby' for the July and August 1978 edition of the periodical *Speak*, an article that he later reprinted in *Doubling the Point*. It was clearly intended for a broader audience, but Coetzee maintained a strong logical structure and even mathematical precision in his argument, with the same stylistic polish as in his more 'serious' work. He points out that sports like cricket and rugby established a foothold in the great British public schools and were exported from there to the colonies. In South Africa rugby was a way in which the economically disadvantaged Afrikaners could prevail over the English. For enthusiasts more fervent about rugby than religion, who during the week were rigidly ruled by a work schedule, the Saturday afternoon match at a stadium was a greater escape than the Sunday morning service.

As in his high school article on cricket, Coetzee starts with a historical survey and a general characterisation of the game:

> Rugby is one of a family of games of great antiquity and wide distribution: two teams of unarmed men struggle for possession of an object which they try to carry home with them. The game is inherently violent, and has at various times been outlawed ('Nothing but beastly fury and extreme violence' — Sir Thomas Elyot, 1531). The present-day football codes attempt to isolate a non-violent variant. The rugby code in particular forbids any attack ('tackle') on a player not carrying the ball. The question of how the ball-carrier is to be dispossessed, and how another player is to possess himself of the ball, is approached via a complex, even labyrinthine set of laws. Despite repeated chopping and changing, these laws remain unsatisfactory, and for a number of reasons. (a) They are inexact inasmuch as they allow a variety of interpretations. (b) They yield a phase of play without aesthetic interest. (c) They fail to prevent injuries and allow some covert violence. (d) By and large they fail to keep the ball 'live' as they are intended to do. (e) They contribute heavily to making rugby a game whose outcome is decided by prowess at goal-kicking.

Something of the pre-television South African custom of attending the weekly rugby match on Saturday afternoons is reflected in Coetzee's *Summertime*, in the description of the character John's father putting on his coat and setting off without a word, like a lonely child, to Newlands: 'On Saturdays the stands at Nuweland,' he writes,

> are full of them, solitary men in grey gabardine raincoats in the twilight of their lives, keeping to themselves as if their loneliness were a shameful disease.[67]

VI

In June 1979, while Coetzee was teaching and researching linguistics at the University of California in Berkeley, he received a letter from James Polley, attached to the UCT Department of Extramural Studies, and director of the Cape Town Film Festival. Polley expressed his admiration of *In the Heart of the Country* and inquired about the possibility of acquiring the film rights. He would appreciate Coetzee's answer, as there was a degree of urgency. He intended to produce the best possible South African film with the collaboration of the best technicians and actors in the country.

Coetzee wrote to Polley on 19 June 1979, saying that Francis Gerard, a director with the BBC and maker of a series on the Afrikaners called *The White Tribe of Africa*, which had been turned down for screening by the SABC, had corresponded with him on the subject and had negotiated with various people for funding, but without success. Coetzee regarded himself as informally committed to Gerard, but that could change if Gerard could generate no funding. The question was whether Polley would be interested in using Gerard as a director. The agreement with Gerard was that Coetzee would provide a first draft of a screenplay as a basis for the film. He would like to know whether Polley, in the light of possible censorship, had in mind an exclusively foreign market, and how he proposed to deal with the use of two languages in the book.

It transpired that Polley had not had somebody like Gerard in mind, but wanted to use South Africans in making the film. Later letters between Coetzee and Polley mention Manie van Rensburg as a possibility. Coetzee was not much taken with this suggestion. In a letter of 6 December 1979 he writes to Polley that he gets the impression that Van Rensburg is not very enthusiastic about the project, that he wants a screenplay acceptable to West German television, and wants to make a version for local consumption that would not offend the man in the street. He once again appealed to Polley to consider Francis Gerard, as he was enthusiastic about the book and wanted to approach the project in a serious spirit. If Polley found it impossible to go this route, it was pointless to negotiate any further.

Coetzee had received another film offer from Johannesburg. After lengthy negotiations he signed a contract with Clive Levinson in April 1980, on condition that Levinson raised the necessary funding for the filming within two years. It was not long, however, before major differences arose between the two on the realisation of the film, for instance whether or not a voice-over should be used. When Levinson suggested that the film could benefit from being based, after the model of *Days of Heaven*, on 'folk wisdom or the colloquialisms of the Karoo', Coetzee reacted quite strongly. In a long letter, which sheds light once again on his concern for the proper realisation of his work, in this instance the screenplay, and on his vision of the novel, he writes:

> There are three observations that need to be made here. The first is that many many people were struck by the kid sister's commentary in *Days of Heaven*, and we can be sure that in years to come we are going to see many clones of her appear; so it may be a good idea to get off that bandwagon right now. The second is that she had available to her the accent and the argot of working-class Chicago, whereas we in South Africa have nothing *unless* we descend to the pseudo-translation of folksy Afrikaans which has been the bane of South African film & drama for a long time. The third is that I have lived in the Karoo for extended periods and can report with some assurance that it has no particular folk-wisdom or colloquialism: the minor dialectical variations are invisible except in Afrikaans.

With a pointer to his investigation into the incorporation of respectively Afrikaans and Zulu into the work of Pauline Smith and Alan Paton, which he was to deal with in Chapter 5 of *White Writing*, Coetzee writes:

> In *In the Heart of the Country* I very deliberately steered clear of all the wrecks of previous efforts to produce Afrikaans effects in English, from Pauline Smith onwards. Aside from the dialogue, which was written in Afrikaans and translated for the UK edition, the language is an English about as international, or non-national, as we can get. I chose that standard consideredly: first, because pseudo-Afrikaans

English is kitsch; and second, because I don't anywhere in the book claim the kind of truthfulness that you claim when you locate an action in a specific time, place, society, milieu, etc.

As regards the 'importance' of themes and individual characters, he preferred not to commit himself on that, as he did not think in such terms while writing. Nor did he want to comment on the relation between reality and imagination:

My 'central concern' is not to 'discuss reality and imagination'. I wrote a book, which effectively unrolls from p. 1 to p. 134. Certain pages in the book revise certain other pages. The book doesn't claim to be reality, and by revising itself it doesn't even claim to imitate reality. Now we are engaged in making a film, which also unrolls from left to right. Again certain sequences revise certain other sequences. You object, 'The audience will not understand what is going on.' Very well, I suggest that certain signals occur which are not present in the book, and which mark off a scene from the revision of the scene, even to the extent of indicating which is the more trustworthy, though in fact it turns out at the end that nothing, or very little, has been trustworthy.

So, rather than discussing themes, we might better occupy our time in discussing whether this treatment is at all workable. If it is, how should it be done? If not, is there an alternative?

My argument, in the 'if not' case, is that there is no alternative to hand. Because the basis of the film is the book; and the book is a very thin affair indeed, full of gaps and self-contradictions, if one tries to lay it out as a naturalistic narrative.

Now on to the craziness of Magda. There are, of course, no crazy people at all, only ways of regarding people as crazy. The difference between the two 'time-blocks' lies in two different ways of looking at Magda: in the first as ridden by violent and erotic imaginings, in the second as being around the bend.

From Coetzee's conclusion to this letter one can deduce that the differences between him and Levinson were great, even insurmountable:

Perhaps I misread your letter seriously, but it appears to me that we are several miles apart in our thinking. Perhaps it would be better if you let me have your response to the comments I make in this letter before we set up a meeting. If you think a compromise is possible, a date in June would suit me best.

In his reply Levinson attended at length to the use of a voice-over and to parts of the screenplay that he did not find satisfactory. In addition the text was long enough only for an hour-long television production, not for a feature film. For that reason he proposed an amendment to the contract: that Coetzee would get 10 per cent of the net profits of the worldwide television productions, with the remaining 90 per cent going to investors from whom he had received contributions that he estimated at R100 000. From his reply it appears that Coetzee was not prepared to make such a concession. He felt that the film, which dealt mainly with bored people and was set in a slow and spatially extended world, could precisely not be hastened along. He proposed that they continue on the basis of the original agreement, until such time as it should prove that a feature film was not viable. In such a case the contract would have to be amended so that he would receive a substantial non-refundable advance on the 10 per cent.

Further negotiations persuaded Coetzee that what Levinson had in mind differed radically from what he expected from the filming. If he had known he was signing a contract that left an option open between a production for the screen and for television, he wrote to Levinson, he would probably not have signed it, and the new financial arrangement would in all probability be to his disadvantage. For that reason he wanted to insist that the original contract be honoured, and he could not accept the amendments proposed by Levinson. In a letter of 25 June 1980 to Francis Gerard, with whom he was now again in contact regarding the possible filming, Coetzee provided more details regarding the differences between him and Levinson:

(1) Levinson seems to be nonplussed about what I have called the non-naturalistic stretches and has several times asked me to 'explain' them. I have preferred not to do this (I just don't work that way), suggesting that he simply play them as written; but this is obviously not satisfactory. I would have more sympathy for his position if he had positive suggestions, but he has none, except perhaps to leave these sequences out. In that case, I have pointed out, there isn't enough substance left for a film. Impasse.

(2) Levinson wants more humour, more earthy touches, folk characters, etc. I, on the other hand, am most resistant to turning anyone into a comfortable & familiar stereotype (bluff Boer frontiersmen, etc.). The book isn't about Afrikaners or the Afrikaner character, it is in fact deliberately vague about social identity.

(3) Levinson wants to make Magda a more clearly sympathetic character, e.g. by casting a 'handsome' rather than a 'plain' woman in the part and by cutting out scenes [...] that show her in an unfavourable light.

In September 1980 the agreement between Coetzee and Levinson was terminated,[68] and Coetzee once again started negotiations with Gerard. In a comprehensive letter of 11 January 1981, Gerard commented on the text of the screenplay that Coetzee had sent him, and came up with constructive suggestions that could enrich the film and also provide enough length to make it acceptable to distributors, such as details about farm life and the characters, to follow upon the opening scenes. Most of these suggestions Coetzee found acceptable, except scenes featuring the slaughtering of sheep and the fixing of a windmill, which could hamper the flow and be experienced by the viewer as 'padding'. To Gerard's comment that there is no mention of religion or faith and his question whether a scene in this regard would get in the way of the story, Coetzee reacted very firmly: 'I don't think there should be any references [to religion], otherwise one is opening a whole can of worms.' Gerard thought that the film would cost about £350 000 to produce.

While these negotiations were under way, Coetzee received a letter from Chester Dent of Moonyeenn Lee Associates, who were also interested in filming the novel. Negotiations broke down at an early stage because of insurmountable differences: the filmmakers did not want to spend time on a project before they had at least an option on the book, and Coetzee was not prepared to sign a contract giving him no control of any kind. Even though Gerard had gone some way in planning the film and had secured the prominent South African actress Janet Suzman for the role of Magda, he could not find the financial backing. In a letter of 4 January 1983 Gerard told Coetzee he was shattered by the fact that he had to admit defeat—'it's been running in my head like an old friend for so long'.

Another possibility had opened up. The Belgian Marion Hänsel, director of the successful feature film *The Bed* (*Le Lit*), based on the

French novel by Dominique Rolin, approached Coetzee's agent, Murray Pollinger, for permission to film *In the Heart of the Country*. She was very enthusiastic about the novel and could identify with the voice of Magda,[69] a woman desperate in her loneliness, unhappy and wounded. In a letter of 26 September to Marion Hänsel, Coetzee gave his views on the filming, making some comments that are of interest in understanding *In the Heart of the Country*. For him, the linguistic relationship between Magda, Hendrik and Anna forms the heart of the book:

> It is unacceptable to me that Hendrik & Anna should be represented speaking a language which informed viewers know not to be their first language. The language spoken by Hendrik & Anna must be *the only language they have*. The question of whether the language of the film is English only or English and Afrikaans is a secondary (though very important) question. The crucial point is that Hendrik and Anna should not have another language (Xhosa, say) and speak English /Afrikaans to their masters only, because to give them their own language gives them a world of their own *which they do not have*. That is the reason why I see questions of casting as central to the film. One cannot cast indigenous Africans as Hendrik & Anna because to such people English and Afrikaans are second or third languages, and an intelligent audience knows it.

He wants to clear up any misunderstanding Hänsel may have regarding the setting of the novel:

> Not knowing South Africa, you speak of 'the veld' as though it were all the same. In fact, the book is set in a huge arid region of this country called the Karoo. That is where I would like to see the book filmed. But I know that for practical reasons people like to shoot in 'tame' countryside in close reach of cities where the crew can relax, etc.

Coetzee sent Hänsel the screenplay, to which she responded on 28 December 1982. She thought it of prime importance that the characters be represented at the beginning of the film in every detail of their physical appearance, and that the accent should fall on Magda, as the main character. The arrival of the father with his new bride and of Hendrik with Klein-Anna would also cinematically be represented as repetitions and parallels. She expressed misgivings about the voice-over technique:

As far as the voice-over is concerned I am very careful with the use of it, because it nearly always is a failure. Too many films use it when they don't know how to *show*, and I often resent it as a weakness of the construction of a story.[70]

Hänsel visited Cape Town in April 1983 to introduce her film *The Bed* at the Cape Town Film Festival, to visit the Karoo, and to have discussions with Coetzee. In March 1984 she told Coetzee she would start filming in September. As she had not been able to raise any money in South Africa, and the intimate relations between people of different skin colour could cause problems with the authorities, not to mention the Belgian cultural boycott which prohibited her filming in South Africa, she had decided on a farm in southern Spain as the setting. For Magda she had considered Glenda Jackson, who to her regret was not available at the scheduled time. Jane Birkin was available, and Trevor Howard could play the father. For Hendrik she had obtained the services of John Matshikiza, a South African, with Nadine Uwampa and Lourdes Christina Sayo as Anna and Klein-Anna respectively. From Coetzee's letters it is clear that he was not particularly happy with Spain as a setting, and that he found Jane Birkin a very attractive woman, unlike the Magda of the book. In the absence of the authentic South African landscape and of the archaic and old-fashioned society reflected in the novel, as well as the intellectual substructure of Magda's monologue, he wrote to Hänsel on 29 April 1984, one is ultimately left with melodrama and little else. Coetzee did not realise that to secure financial backing for the film, Hänsel had had no choice but to cast an internationally known actress in the lead.

Although he had reservations, *Dust*, as the film was eventually called, was a reasonable success. Hänsel had not distorted the novel to make a political statement. 'I want to make a human film,' she said in an interview.[71] With the launching of *Dust* at a film festival in Venice in August 1985, the two stars, Jane Birkin and John Matshikiza, received a standing ovation, and the film was described as 'a harrowing study of loneliness and sexual desperation'. The South African premiere was on 23 September 1985 in Pinelands, Cape Town. In a review of the film Janet Maslin praised the 'remote, barren setting for the story', even though it was shot in Spain rather than in the Karoo. She was particularly impressed with the acting of Jane Birkin and Trevor Howard:

Miss Birkin, who progresses from impassivity to pure hysteria during the course of the story, presents her haggard, beautiful features to the camera in a wholly unselfconscious way. Trevor Howard, who plays her father, must perform in an even more passive style, since his character has been given almost nothing to say. In the film's opening passages Miss Hänsel simply records the quiet monotony of their life together, observing their daily rituals and the tattered gentility that seems so out of place in this deserted setting. These wordless scenes are slow and uncomplicated, but they do create a strong sense of deprivation.[72]

VII

While John Coetzee was establishing himself as an academic and writing his way into a place in South African literature with his first two novels, his brother David returned briefly to South Africa and accepted an appointment with the *Cape Argus*. One day he was summarily dismissed and escorted off the premises. Although no grounds were given for his dismissal, he was convinced that news had reached the directors of his involvement in the anti-apartheid movement in London, and that they had deemed it not in the interests of the paper to employ him. Since he was by now a British citizen, he returned to London, where, also in an editorial capacity, he collaborated with newspapers and magazines with an African focus. In 1980 he was a co-founder of *Africa Now*, a Nigerian-owned magazine based in London, in which some of his seminal articles on African governments and political events appeared. From his relationship with Irene Fick, a son, Samuel, was born in 1979. When this relationship foundered, he started living with Akwe Amosu in 1982. They were married in 1994, their son, Corin, being born in the same year. In 2000 he was awarded a master's degree in Oriental and African Studies with distinction by the University of London. In the same year he and his family moved to Washington, but they also spent two years (2004–2005) in Ethiopia.[73]

In Cape Town, Vera, John and David's mother, continued teaching, since she and Jack had to live frugally on small salaries. After being struck off the attorneys' roll, Jack was unemployed for a while, but then accepted a position at a meagre salary with a firm selling motor spares. People who knew him then described him as a slight man and an introvert, quite a contrast to his earlier sometimes flamboyant lifestyle with his friends. He must have overcome his drinking problem to a large extent, because Agnes Heinrich, a cousin of the Coetzee sons, never saw him out of control.[74] Nellis du Biel, one of the grandsons of the writer Albert du Biel, did later recall his 'crooked yellow teeth and his whiskey breath' when he visited Jack and Vera Coetzee in their flat in Rondebosch and he and his brother played carpet bowls with Jack.[75] To John and Philippa's friends Jack was a nonentity, Vera being the dominant figure in a marriage that had never known much happiness. She was a large, warm person, very proud of both her sons, especially of John's achievements, and a wonderful grandmother to Nicolas and Gisela.

Although John Coetzee was known as an intensely private person, he still attended the family gatherings at Voëlfontein. His cousin Carol Goosen was impressed with his affectionate nature, gentle manner of speech and his non-verbal communication.[76] On his Voëlfontein visits, so his cousin Gerald Coetzee recounts, John would often start walking at five in the morning to the far end of the farm with its jackalproof fencing and only return to the farmhouse at about eleven.[77] As in his youth, the family would then be congregated on the stoep of the beautiful home, with the bougainvillea to the right and the orange orchard in front of the house. Above the farmhouse was the dam, but there was nothing left of Outa Jaap's house. Of Bloemhof, where the first farmhouse had been, only the foundations and the palm tree remained.

In the late 1970s Coetzee and his family, after living in Wynberg and then Tokai, moved to 11 Toll Road, Rondebosch, a corner house with an avocado tree in front. His daily working routine was to get up at five in the morning and devote about two hours to his creative work before delivering the children to school on weekdays at half past seven and leaving for the university for his classes. Then he would return to mark essays and prepare lectures for the following day. It was difficult to keep to such a strict programme, as he had to shoulder a full burden of lectures, no allowance being made for creative work.[78]

Philippa was a more outgoing person, very generous, at ease in mixing with people and a good conversationalist. In some respects she was also a difficult and eccentric person, as was apparent from time to time from her choice of clothes, odd hairstyles and 'mad' ideas. She had a very close relationship with her homosexual brother, Cecil Jubber, who dominated her. Cecil was attached to the SABC in Johannesburg and was a very successful producer of radio plays, for which he had received a Prix Italia in the 1950s. He was a hyperactive person and later a complete alcoholic, repeatedly arrested for drunken driving, before being stripped of his licence.[79] Through his father's abuse of alcohol, John was aware of its dangers. Apart from an occasional glass of wine with friends, he avoided liquor, and later became a total abstainer. He decided in 1974 to cut meat and fish from his diet and become a vegetarian, probably motivated by his moral convictions regarding the rights of animals. His self-discipline in the midst of family members with a history of excessive consumption earned him the admiration of his fellow-student Jonty Driver, with whom he kept up a friendship, even though Driver had been living in Britain for years.[80]

To her children Philippa was a caring mother. She took an interest in their schooling and education, but cherished the odd 'American' idea that they had to make their own way and not get too much help. At UCT she worked as a secretary in the Department of Chemical Engineering. She still had a passion for all things Greek, and exerted herself to study modern Greek, without ever really mastering the language. This may have been one reason why she felt inferior to her brilliant husband. John was a compulsive worker and secretive about his creative work. It was a world of which she could never really be part and to which she was not really granted entry. She may have sometimes found him melancholy, 'the self-consumer of [his] woes',[81] as he would later in *Slow Man* quote from John Clare, somebody 'who took books too seriously'.[82] Unlike her husband, Philippa had religious leanings, and was later admitted to the Roman Catholic Church. Both were strongly opposed to the apartheid policy and to the measures adopted by the government in the 1970s to deprive people of their freedom, but in this Philippa was the more demonstrative, through her membership in the Black Sash movement.[83]

Although preoccupied with his work, John Coetzee gave his children ample attention. There was a strong bond between him and the introvert Gisela, who as a child physically resembled him. When friends visited, she liked sitting on his lap in company. As a child she developed a resistance to eating and tended towards anorexia. A friend of John's gave Gisela a French anorak, which she wore constantly, winter and summer, almost as if warding off onslaughts from outside.[84] Nicolas, who resembled Philippa, was an extrovert, self-assured, fairly courageous and inclined to perform risky feats. Relations between the two children were not good. Gisela, her father's favourite, had to endure Nicolas's jealousy, bad temper and non-physical violence, and at times was scared of him.[85] At their house in Wynberg and again later in Tokai, John Coetzee built them and their playmates a playhouse in the backyard by digging a trench of about one and a half square metres, with vertical props in the corners and a roof of galvanised iron. The rabbits that they kept in cages and that burrowed in the soil were a great curiosity and attraction for the children of Chris and Sandra Perold, at the time very close to the Coetzees. Chris in time decided that the underground passages could collapse and forbade his daughter Lisa and her sister from entering them.[86] Lisa Perold, a real tomboy as a child and attracted to Nicolas, recalled later how he and she played cricket and drove go-karts. She found Nicolas's knowledge of the history of cricket incredible. He could remember matches of years earlier to the last detail, who batted in what order and on what day and what the individual scores were.[87] Their childhood days were wild, and they rebelled against all forms of authority, especially that exerted by teachers.

As a father John Coetzee shied away from assuming a position of authority. Daniel Hutchinson was later to recall how once, when he and his wife were visiting the Coetzees in Tokai, the young Nicolas had arrived home late and in a tempestuous and fractious mood. An upset and exhausted Philippa begged John in vain to discipline the child. Daniel overheard John's melancholy reply: 'You know I can't.'[88] In 1976, shortly after her arrival from her native France, Catherine Lauga du Plessis was visiting the Coetzees at their house in Tokai with her first husband, Ian Glenn, a colleague of John's at UCT. The Coetzees were very hospitable and she found John unpretentious and Philippa very pleasant and an excellent cook to boot, but she did wonder whether John's abhorrence of exerting authority did not disqualify him in advance as a parent. When Philippa told the ten-year-old Nicolas that it was bedtime, he refused to go to bed. John did not lift a finger, and it was Ian Glenn who had to grab hold of the struggling Nicolas and put him to bed.[89] Even so, John could act decisively in an emergency. Daniel Hutchinson remembers that they were visiting the Coetzees and were lying next to the pool, engrossed in conversation. Suddenly Daniel's wife exclaimed 'Where's Kolya?', their two-year-old son. Everybody jumped up in a panic, but John was first in the pool to drag the child out by the hair, just in time to save him from certain drowning.[90]

The lack of communication between John and Philippa Coetzee made for a tense marriage, and close friends expected a breach. Philippa complained to friends like the Perolds that John could sometimes be cruel in his actions. The Perolds remembered that John in their years in Wynberg sometimes shot at cats with a shotgun. In Tokai the Coetzees owned a dog that Philippa was very fond of, but John not. Since the house was situated on the busy and dangerous Tokai Road, the dog was kept in the yard behind a locked gate. According to Philippa's account to the Perolds, John one day deliberately left the gate open. The dog slipped out, landed under a passing motor car, came back and crawled under Philippa's bed to die.

If indeed the incident with the dog was a deliberate act by John and not a misinterpretation on Philippa's part, it might represent a turning point in the life of someone who later in his work would take a very strong stand on animal rights. It could be that his conversion to vegetarianism was also connected with this, as well as his aversion to all forms of violence, even in cases where it could lead to a political solution. In a 1992 interview with David Attwell in *Doubling the Point* he says: 'Violence, as soon as I sense its presence within me, becomes introverted as violence against myself: I cannot project it outward. I am unable to, or refuse to, conceive of a liberating violence.'[91] It is well to recall that this pronouncement comes from the creator of Eugene Dawn, the architect of unflinching violence against the Vietnamese, and the eighteenth-century Jacobus Coetzee with his monstrous lust for revenge and retribution against the Namas.

The Coetzees returned from the US with the idea of an open, broad-minded marriage in which both partners could go their individual way, free to pursue other relationships and to return to each other when it suited them. Philippa was very open about this with friends like the Perolds.[92] They gradually started drifting apart. John was in the US more than once to present courses, while Philippa spent some of her time visiting Greece. At one stage John even said to Daniel Hutchinson, then attached to the Department of English at UCT, that he would not object if he started an intimate relationship with Philippa. John considered a divorce, but was concerned about its possible effect on his mother, and he was not much cheered to hear from Hutchinson how well *his* mother had handled his divorce. On the eve of the publication of *Dusklands* in 1974 John was involved in a triangular relationship with the wife of a colleague. Philippa did not know about this, and both men were terrified to admit to each other what was happening. The whole affair is oddly reminiscent of the strange ambivalence of the quartet in Ford

Madox Ford's novel *The Good Soldier*, the author Coetzee elected as the subject of his M.A. dissertation. After a phase of near-hypnotic paralysis for all the participants, John's colleague and his wife moved to the US. John was left behind to care for his rabbits, and the husband continued his academic career in the US.

At last the marriage landed on the rocks. One evening John arrived at the Perolds' with a typed document and a somewhat odd request. Philippa and he, he said, had agreed to a divorce, and he wanted the Perolds to sign the agreement as witnesses.[93] The divorce happened at a bad stage of Nicolas and Gisela's lives, when they were fourteen and twelve years old respectively. The Coetzees seldom had meals together and had for years not really functioned as a family. John and Philippa did not sit down with Nicolas and Gisela to discuss the process and implications of the divorce. The children thus did not have the support to see them through the situation, and their response was a strong feeling of anger.[94] They were extremely upset by the divorce, and both, particularly Nicolas, believed that John and Philippa would eventually reunite. After the divorce Philippa stayed on in Cape Town for a while, living in a house in Observatory, before leaving for Johannesburg to be with her parents and brother Cecil. While both parents were still in Cape Town, the children, who did not get along with each other, took turns to live with John and Philippa, Gisela mainly with John and Nicolas with Philippa.

For John this was a difficult time. Apart from his UCT obligations and the time he wanted to devote to his creative work, he had to care for two children who required constant attention. In the years after the divorce he and Philippa got on reasonably well. John got the impression that she was basically well disposed towards him and wished him well in his career as a creative writer.[95] Sometimes, in spite of valuing his privacy, he enjoyed it when friends turned up unexpectedly. 'My idea of a nice evening,' he said in 1983 to a journalist from *Fair Lady* in an interview that apparently was never published, 'is that friends drop in unexpectedly in a famished state, whereupon I cook up a quick, simple, nourishing meal. They eat everything on their plates, compliment me on my cooking, and go home early without requiring me to make conversation.'

The children gradually became aware that they were living with a parent who was developing into an important international author. Gisela, who was closest to him, recalls the sound of his typewriter and the intellectual life that, with the visits of the few good friends of the Coetzees, they could witness from the periphery. As an adult, she said in an interview, she could see that he had often been absent as a parent, but she did not blame him for this. It would in any case now be too late for accusations. He was not really cut out to be a parent, but, she said in a moving tribute to John Coetzee, 'he did his best, his very utmost best, without sacrificing himself.'[96]

CHAPTER 10

WAITING FOR THE BARBARIANS AND INTERNATIONAL RECOGNITION

I

In 1962, the year John Coetzee started working in London as a computer programmer, thinking to divest himself of South Africa as 'a bad start, a handicap',[1] the Sabotage Act was passed in the country of his birth. The aim was to limit political activity among black people and restrict the movements of students and academics at English-language campuses, who were suspected of seditious and subversive activities. The act gave the minister of justice far-reaching powers, such as detaining suspects without trial for interrogation and torture. Quite a few of the detainees were people whom Coetzee had known personally as fellow-students at UCT. Many were interrogated, humiliated, tortured and kept in solitary confinement, and some, like Jonty Driver, left South Africa permanently.

Shortly after Coetzee's return to the country he had wanted to disown, the measures employed by the security police were stepped up as the unrest in the black townships intensified, especially after the Soweto Uprising of 1976. Overseas television showed the police brutally acting against fleeing groups of schoolchildren, sometimes with a sadistic pleasure and a ferocity far exceeding the limits of what could be deemed necessary for the maintenance of order.[2] No longer prepared to tolerate the oppression of apartheid, the pupils reacted by boycotting schools, vandalising public buildings, marching in the streets and organising stay-away actions. 'During sixteen months of chaos,' Mary Benson writes, 'recorded deaths numbered some six hundred but were thought to be nearer a thousand—all but two of them black, and most of them school pupils shot by the police. Nearly four thousand were injured; thousands more vanished into detention, some to spend five years in solitary confinement, some never to be seen by their parents again.'[3] The security crackdown also led to the banning of eighteen organisations and three newspapers, while 47 black leaders and seven prominent whites were detained or banned. Since the institution of the security measures at least 64 detainees had died as a result of the physical and psychological abuse inflicted upon them.

Of those dying under suspicious circumstances, it was in particular the death, on 12 September 1977, of Steve Biko, charismatic Eastern Cape leader of the Black Consciousness Movement, that sparked worldwide outrage. His influence and actions were held responsible for the Soweto uprisings of 1976, and the authorities were targeting him. On a night in August 1977 the security police stopped his car at a road block near Port Elizabeth and took him to the cells for questioning. Biko had been arrested before, and could hold his own against his interrogators. A later statement by the security police claimed that Biko had assaulted an officer and in the ensuing struggle hit his head against a wall. What really happened was never established, but he fell into a coma, his brain fatally damaged in the assaults. The interrogators claimed they were under the impression that he was pretending to have been injured. They kept him shackled and naked for three days, lying unconscious in his cell on a mat that was drenched with the urine seeping out of him. The state doctors called by the police to examine him remained silent on what they had seen. He was, still naked and handcuffed, loaded into the back of a Land Rover, and without any accompanying medical reports, taken to a prison hospital in Pretoria, a distance of about 1 000 kilometres. There he died the next day, without having received any medical attention.[4] Later three medical doctors who had examined Biko in detention admitted that they had given false evidence regarding him. The inquest magistrate found that Biko had died of head injuries, probably sustained in a struggle with the security police in their Port Elizabeth offices, and that on the basis of the available evidence the death could not be ascribed to anybody's negligence or criminal action.[5]

In spite of international protest the government tried to cover up the events with fabricated medical reports. Jimmy Kruger, the minister of police, vehemently denied any police complicity. He said Biko had died after a hunger strike and that his death left him cold. He threatened to close down the *Rand Daily Mail*, which had published information on the true course of events. The threats were so intimidating that the editor was obliged by his directors to publish an apology. In the rest of the world, however, the reaction was damning. The London *Times* wrote in a leading article: 'Mr James Kruger's behaviour after the Biko affair was of such a degree of disgrace that in any country upholding civilized norms he would have been put out of office immediately.' From Afrikaans commentators in South Africa the response was also extremely negative. The journalist Rykie van Reenen wrote that she had once had a long conversation with Biko, and that she saw him as a builder rather than a breaker, wanting to uplift black people through community service. What had stayed with her was 'the image of the new black man trying with all his might and fearless dedication to prepare himself and his people for greater responsibility'. She found it disconcerting that 'a voice such as his has disappeared from the critical dialogue in our country'.[6]

What appeared most trenchantly from the events around the death of Biko was an expression of the Hegelian master-slave relation in its most hideous form in the confrontation of interrogator and accused. The former newspaper editor Donald Woods, who testified in the inquiry into the death of Steve Biko, wrote later that cross-examination for the first time dragged the security police into the light of public scrutiny from the dark torture chambers where they interrogated prisoners:

> For the first time, these men, products and inheritors of the Afrikaner Nationalist tradition, were flushed out of their police stations and their little interrogation rooms. For once they were in the position of having to account for themselves. These men displayed symptoms of extreme insularity. They are people whose upbringing has impressed upon them the divine right to retain power, and in that sense they are innocent men — incapable of thinking or acting differently. On top of that they have gravitated to an occupation that has given them all the scope they need to express their rigid personalities. They have been protected for years by the laws of the country. They have been able to carry out all their imaginative torture practices quite undisturbed in cells and rooms all over the country, with tacit official sanction, and they have been given tremendous status by the government as the men who 'protect the State from subversion'.[7]

Coetzee did not respond publicly to Biko's death, but in a letter of 20 September 1977 to Sheila Roberts he expressed his dismay and his suspicion that the government would contrive to cover up the atrocity:

> Biko's death has cast a pall over everyone. It would seem that the pathologist is going to report that he was murdered; my guess is

that the government is then going to brazen it out—refuse to hold an inquiry or else hold some kind of low-level cover-up, such as an 'internal' police inquiry—and to hell what people think.

The depth of his feelings about the death of Biko and other people in detention, such as that of Ahmed Timol in 1971 and Neil Aggett in 1982, is evident from two of Coetzee's important essays in the 1980s and early '90s: 'Into the dark chamber' (1986)[8] in *Doubling the Point* and 'Breyten Breytenbach and the reader in the mirror' (1991)[9] in *Giving Offense*. In the latter of these essays Coetzee refers to the lies told by John Vorster's security police in cases of death in detention, such as that the prisoner slipped on 'a piece of soap', an explanation that in reality, in the linguistic practice of totalitarianism, acts as a coded message for 'death under torture'. It is the kind of lie that testifies to a shameless contempt for the truth. In the essay in *Doubling the Point* Coetzee quotes the poem 'In detention' by Christopher van Wyk to illustrate how people mangle the truth:

> He fell from the ninth floor
> He hanged himself
> He slipped on a piece of soap while washing
> He hanged himself
> He slipped on a piece of soap while washing
> He fell from the ninth floor
> He hanged himself while washing
> He slipped from the ninth floor
> He hung from the ninth floor
> He slipped on the ninth floor while washing
> He fell from a piece of soap while slipping
> He hung from the ninth floor
> He washed from the ninth floor while slipping
> He hung from a piece of soap while washing[10]

When the court then obliges the torturers to leave their dark chamber and account for their deeds, as in the Nuremberg trials and that of Adolf Eichmann in Jerusalem, it is the disproportion between the dwarfishness of the accused and the enormity of their crimes that strikes Coetzee. He discerned the same kind of paradox in the investigations into the deaths of Steve Biko and Neil Aggett, during which 'members of the security police have briefly emerged from their native darkness into the public gaze'.[11]

330 J.M. COETZEE: A LIFE IN WRITING

Inside the torture chamber in John Vorster Square the tortured is, however, thanks to a set of corrupt laws, at the mercy of the torturer. In his essay in *Doubling the Point* Coetzee refers to works by Sipho Sepamla, Mongane Wally Serote and Alex La Guma, in which the writers have to use their imagination to depict the torture, since the events in the torture chamber are accessible only to the participants. 'The dark, forbidden chamber,' Coetzee writes, 'is the origin of novelistic fantasy per se; in creating an obscenity, in enveloping it in mystery, the state unwittingly creates the preconditions for the novel to set about its work of representation.' [12] After his discharge from prison Breyten Breytenbach would comment in *The True Confessions of an Albino Terrorist* (1984) on those stages of the interrogation when torturer and tortured experience their closest, most intimate and most destructive meeting: [13]

> The interrogator will be someone who looks and behaves as if *normal*. He will lead an unremarkable family-life. [...] These people are not monsters: they know that they are tolerated and accepted by the powerful. They may even fondly believe that they are implicitly supported by the so-called silent majority. They will at most consider theirs to be 'a necessary if dirty job'. [...] The prisoner will inevitably end up confessing [...] He will have the leftover knowledge that he has been used as a tool, that he was coldly and expertly manipulated, that he was confronted with his own weakness. Worse, far worse — that he ended up looking upon his tormentor as a confessor, as a friend even. [...] The two of you, violator and victim (collaborator! violin!), are linked, forever perhaps, by the obscenity of what has been revealed to you, by the sad knowledge of what people are capable of. We are all guilty. [14]

In his essay in *Giving Offense* Coetzee gives extended attention to the poem 'Brief uit die vreemde aan slagter' ['Letter from abroad to butcher'], which he rightly calls one of Breyten Breytenbach's 'major poems'. The poem, which Breytenbach 'dedicates' to 'Balthazar', John Vorster's second name, is a reflection from a prison cell on the behaviour of both the prisoner and the 'butcher'. It appeared in the collection *Skryt* that was published in the Netherlands and banned for distribution in South Africa. In the poem the prisoner speaks in a dramatic sequence, ranging from 'The prisoner says' through 'alleges' to 'confesses', about his own suffering when he notices the first signs of decline and corruption ('a first fly'), prepares for the journey to death when 'his dreams at last are crushed' and he is prepared 'shivering underground/ to feed the insects.' Death comes as a deliverance when he—with an allusion to the case of the political prisoner Timol—'*tumbles* from the tenth storey of heaven/ to salvation on a street full of people.' Then comes the direct address as the prisoner asks whether the 'butcher' also shows emotion when torturing:

> *And you, butcher*
> you who are charged with the security of the state
> what do you think of when the night starts to show her skeleton
> and the first babbling scream is pressed from
> the prisoner
> as with a birth
> the fluids of childbearing?
> Are you then humbled before this bloody thing
> with its all-too-human shudder-shocks
> with the broken breath of dying
> between your hands?
> does your heart in your throat erect itself too
> when you touch the spent limbs
> with the same hands that will caress your wife's secrets?[15]

Coetzee comments on 'your wife's secrets' that

> Breytenbach might as well have written *secret parts*. The exposure to public gaze is not just of the forbidden secrets of the torture chamber, not just of the (putative) private revulsions of B.J. Vorster himself (the irony is complex here: Breytenbach asserts that Vorster has a conscience and dares him to deny it), but of the mysteries (forbidden to the public gaze by decency itself) of the Vorster marriage bed. The poem is a low blow, a dig at the private parts, not of the man, but of his defenceless wife; an insult to male honor, more rather than less offensive when one considers the age of its targets (Balthazar and Tini were in their mid-fifties in 1972). The excess of the poem is an excess of intimacy.[16]

It is notable that Coetzee in his essay on Breytenbach in *Giving Offense* gives so much attention to 'Letter from abroad to butcher', just as in

'Into the dark chamber' in *Doubling the Point* he quotes Christopher van Wyk's 'In detention' in full; his interest is of a piece with his fascination, in *The True Confessions of an Albino Terrorist*, with the representation of the spiritual atmosphere in which the security police live, people who find it possible in the morning to leave the breakfast table, kiss their children goodbye and drive to the office to commit obscenities.[17] In 'Into the dark chamber' Coetzee refers to his novel *Waiting for the Barbarians*, which he published in 1980 and which deals with the impact of the torture chamber on the life of a man with a conscience. Although both essays appeared after publication of the novel, they are useful keys to understanding *Waiting for the Barbarians* and the influences shaping it, as often with Coetzee, whose creative work and literary criticism frequently stand in osmotic relation to each other. That Coetzee, for instance, despite the vague setting in space and time, has in mind a South African set of possibilities, becomes clear quite early in the novel when Colonel Joll, in his report to the magistrate on the death of a prisoner, uses data from the torturing of Biko and the lies told by the security police about his death. The report is written in the typical style and register of the security police, with among other tics the repetition of the word *prisoner*. The lies in the report are similar to those Christopher van Wyk alludes to in his poem:

> During the course of the interrogation contradictions became apparent in the prisoner's testimony. Confronted with these contradictions, the prisoner became enraged and attacked the investigating officer. A scuffle ensued during which the prisoner fell heavily against the wall. Efforts to revive him were unsuccessful.[18]

When the magistrate later examines the corpse, he discovers swollen lips, broken teeth and one empty bloody eye socket, injuries reminiscent of Biko's.

But it is more particularly the questions of the prisoner to the torturer in 'Letter from abroad to butcher' that resurface in the magistrate's troubled question to Joll: how does he deal with a prisoner who is telling the truth but finds that he is not believed, and what (moral) responsibility weighs on the interrogator in such a case? Joll says there is a certain 'tone' from which he can deduce whether the man is telling the truth. He must also attempt to plumb the truth by applying pressure. With the callousness of the trained security man Joll says:

'[...] First I get lies, you see—this is what happens—first lies, then pressure, then more lies, then more pressure, then the break, then more pressure, then the truth. That is how you get the truth.'[19]

When he ponders the tactics and technique of Joll, the magistrate asks himself whether the torturer experiences any emotion when he penetrates the secrets of the tortured, a question in which the words of the prisoner to the 'butcher' in Breytenbach's poem also resonate:

Looking at him I wonder how he felt the very first time: did he, invited as an apprentice to twist the pincers or turn the screw or whatever it is they do, shudder even a little to know that at that instant he was trespassing into the forbidden? I find myself wondering too whether he has a private ritual of purification, carried out behind closed doors, to enable him to return and break bread with other men. Does he wash his hands very carefully, perhaps, or change all his clothes; or has the Bureau created new men who can pass without disquiet between the unclean and the clean?[20]

And close to the end of the novel, when the magistrate is a free man again after his own torture, he asks Mandel, Joll's assistant, how he finds it possible to eat and consort with his family and friends after completing his gruesome task:

Forgive me if the question seems impudent, but I would like to ask: How do you find it possible to eat afterwards, after you have been ... working with people? That is a question I have always asked myself about executioners and other such people. Wait! Listen to me a moment longer, I am sincere, it has cost me a great deal to come out with this, since I am terrified of you, I need not tell you that, I am sure you are aware of it. Do you find it easy to take food afterwards? I have imagined that one would want to wash one's hands. But no ordinary washing would be enough, one would require priestly intervention, a ceremonial of cleansing, don't you think? Some kind of purging of one's soul too—that is how I have imagined it. Otherwise how would it be possible to return to everyday life—to sit down at table, for instance, and break bread with one's family or one's comrades?[21]

II

In August 1977 Coetzee visited Canada to attend the third international conference on computerisation in the humanities at the University of Waterloo in Ontario, a subject in which he had kept an interest from his years as a programmer in Britain. On his way back he spent a few days in Buffalo, where he saw some of his former colleagues again. Whereas *In the Heart of the Country* was at this time being approved for distribution by the censors, Etienne Leroux's novel *Magersfontein, o Magersfontein!* was being targeted. Connie Mulder, the minister concerned, had personally requested the appeals board of the Directorate of Publications to have another look at it. In a letter to Sheila Roberts of 6 December 1977 Coetzee says that the banning was a victory for a Pretoria pressure group called *Aksie Morele Standaarde* (Action Moral Standards), who had 2 000 correspondents on their address book, an all-too-willing administrative machine, and a commitment to purifying all Afrikaans books written in the previous fifteen years.

On 20 September 1977, shortly after his return from Canada, Coetzee started writing *Waiting for the Barbarians*. In the earliest version of this novel he placed the events in South Africa, specifically in Cape Town, but he abandoned this fairly soon in favour of a more indeterminate time and space. The earliest versions were once again written in UCT exam books, and were dated from 20 September 1977 to 28 March 1978. A month later, on 28 April 1978, he started a further version that he completed on 28 October 1978. Yet another version occupied him from 1 November 1978 to 8 April 1979. This version was started in Cape Town and continued in the US while Coetzee was lecturing first at the University of Texas and then at the University of California at Berkeley.

Coetzee comments on this visit in one of his interviews with David Attwell:

> I spent 1979 on leave from the University of Cape Town, working on *Waiting for the Barbarians* and getting back to grips with linguistics. Though I had intermittently taught courses in grammar and in stylistics in Cape Town, I had lost touch with new developments. I spent a semester in Texas, in the Department of Linguistics, sitting in on Lauri Karttunen's seminar on syntax, doing a lot of reading,

and generally trying to reposition myself in a discipline that was expanding so rapidly in so many directions that no one could expect to command more than one or two branches. After Texas I went to Berkeley for another three months. [...] It was a lonely period but a productive one.[22]

During his time in Austin Coetzee completed three essays on questions of syntax, more particularly on the rhetoric of the passive voice in English, and the agentless sentence as a rhetorical device. These essays were collected in *Doubling the Point*. He also continued working on *Waiting for the Barbarians*. In April and May 1979 he edited the manuscript with a red pen. He completed the typescript on 1 June 1979, adding further amendments in black ink. The proofs of the Secker & Warburg edition, which are kept with the various versions of the novel in the Harry Ransom Center at Texas, contain only a few corrections in black.

As against the numbered units of *In the Heart of the Country*, the novel *Waiting for the Barbarians* is divided into six chapters following chronologically upon one another, but in the Ravan edition separated into shorter sections with asterisks (in later editions, for typographical reasons, replaced with more white space by the publishers).

The time span extends over more than a year, the turning of the seasons marking its course. This gives the novel a less 'experimental' aspect than both *Dusklands* with its play of different Coetzee identities, and *In the Heart of the Country* with its repetitions of similar scenes and its juggling of time. In *Waiting for the Barbarians*, though, the setting, unlike that of the first two novels, does not represent a recognisable world, and it is impossible to determine the period in which the events take place. The setting has a hybrid quality, with salt pans and deserts on the one hand, and the lake and snow-covered mountains on the other. The castle and the use of horses and swords correspond in part with the Roman Empire, but the vastness of the landscape has elements of both the Steppe of Central Asia and the South African Karoo. The themes of torture and violence vaguely recall Germany under the Nazis, or Russia under the czars and the Soviet Union under the communists, but it is impossible to miss the parallels with South Africa of the 1960s and '70s, especially in the references to 'emergency powers', so characteristic of South Africa in the 1980s and earlier. In the *Newsweek* of 31 August 1982 Coetzee is quoted as saying to Peter Younghusband: 'I wanted to create characters and a setting that belong to no recognizable contemporary situations. But people who know South Africa will probably pick up allusions.' In an interview with Joanna Scott Coetzee said that the challenge in writing *Waiting for the Barbarians* had not been to describe an unfamiliar landscape, but to construct a landscape he had never seen, that probably did not exist,[23] and to which he had to remain faithful throughout the novel. In an interview with David Attwell Coetzee says: 'the landscape of *Barbarians* represented a challenge to my power of *envisioning'.*[24] Thus in this novel those fictional events apparently rooted in actuality cannot *directly* be traced to any specific country, including South Africa. In this indeterminany resides what many commentators have called the allegorical aspect of the novel, through which the events assume relevance to other countries and events. At the risk of using the word rather loosely, one could say that *Waiting for the Barbarians* is an allegorical version of the abuses in South Africa in the apartheid years.[25]

The tale is told by a nameless narrator identified only through his function as the magistrate, a man serving out his years in a remote corner of the Empire. As a functionary of the Empire he maintains law and order, but he is an elderly man who wants to live in peace on the border, perform his duties, albeit somewhat reluctantly, wait for retirement and his pension, and pass his time in tranquillity, reading the classics and deciphering the strange script on a number of poplar slips he has come upon in the course of his archeological excavations. For relaxation he visits one of the prostitutes on the second storey of the inn.

The novel opens with the arrival at the border post of the sinister Colonel Joll—an unfeeling bureaucrat of the Third Bureau in the capital, a security corps that invites comparison with the Gestapo or the KGB.[26] He is notable for his irritatingly affected manner and the ominous dark glasses concealing his eyes and masking his evil nature. Joll is a prototype of the warped humanity produced by a depraved political system; but the fact that the magistrate sees only his own reflection in the opaque glasses is an indication that he too has been affected by the rotten system. Joll alleges that the barbarians are preparing to revolt. He launches a raid on them and returns with a group of nomads in chains, to interrogate and torture them. The magistrate, who cannot act decisively, does not want to get involved in these investigations and distances himself from the visitors and their methods, even though he later is compelled by honesty to admit that he, as a servant of the Empire, is just as guilty as they are. Towards the end of the novel he says:

For I was not, as I liked to think, the indulgent pleasure-loving opposite of the cold rigid Colonel. I was the lie that Empire tells itself when times are easy, he the truth that Empire tells when harsh winds blow. Two sides of imperial rule, no more, no less.[27]

Coetzee's novel is intertextually related to both Joseph Conrad and Franz Kafka. Like the young Kurtz in *Heart of Darkness*, the magistrate believes in enlightened, liberal government and takes a dark lover, but is later suspected of being out of his mind. The Kafka echoes are even clearer, specifically the tale 'In the penal colony', with its implication of sadism as embodied in Kafka's officer.[28] The title of Coetzee's novel recalls Samuel Beckett's *Waiting for Godot*, but is in the first place derived from Constantine Cavafy's poem, 'Waiting for the Barbarians', of which the closing line in particular has bearing on the novel:

> Because night has fallen and the barbarians have not come.
> And some people have arrived from the frontiers,
> and said that there are no barbarians anymore.
>
> And now, what will become of us without barbarians?
> Those people were some sort of a solution.[29]

At the end of the novel the army pursues the barbarians beyond the borders of the Empire, but the soldiers return in tatters, reporting that the enemy had lured them into the desert and then simply vanished. Joll and his men's waiting for the barbarians comes to nothing. The anticipated barbarians do not materialise because they are in truth an ideological convenience, like the 'black peril' that for years was the subject of dread in white South Africa. These people can bring no 'solution', because they never appear. The roles are reversed and the true barbarians are the soldiers of the Empire under Joll's command.

Increasingly, as the tale unfolds, the magistrate develops sympathy with the victims, especially a girl who in the course of torture is left half blind and with broken feet. When the colonel leaves the outpost, the magistrate takes the girl into his house and his bed and cares for her, every evening anointing her body with almond oil and washing her feet—a ritual and a penance, through which he wants to cleanse himself of his assumed guilt and complicity. The relationship between the magistrate and the girl is consummated just once, and by not talking she remains a mystery, even a hallucination. The magistrate's relationship with her forms a contrast with his meetings with the girl at the inn, which are rife with the lies that accompany bought sex. Later, accompanied by two soldiers and a guide, he undertakes an arduous journey through the desert to restore the girl to her people, a part of the novel recalling the chronicles of the early travellers in South Africa, but in which Coetzee remains remarkably close to the fictive setting of his world.

Back at the border post, the 'black flower of civilization',[30] the magistrate discovers that in his absence the army has turned up to fight the barbarians. He is taken prisoner, and, on the grounds of his alleged negotiations with the enemy, accused of high treason, incarcerated, tortured and humiliated. He is summoned before a 'stiff little colonel presiding and his henchman reading the charges and two junior officers as assessors to lend the proceedings an air of legality'.[31] His situation is acutely ironical: a person who is part of the colonial order is now labelled an enemy within the empire. He who was earlier in a position of authority is now one of the tortured. The master-slave dialectic, which featured in Coetzee's two earliest novels, thus becomes, through the reversal of roles, a particularly complex affair, in the relation between the magistrate and Joll (and his officer Mandel) as well as between the magistrate and the girl. The magistrate's situation uses, in Derek Attridge's words, 'the solitary individual in a hostile human and physical environment to raise crucial questions about the foundations of civilization and humanity'.[32] During his imprisonment the magistrate, although weakly , at last reflects: 'Let it at the very least be said, if it ever comes to be said, if there is ever anyone in some remote future interested to know the way we lived, that in this farthest outpost of the Empire of light there existed one man who in his heart was not a barbarian.'[33] He later tells Joll: '*You* are the enemy, *you* have made the war, and *you* have given them all the martyrs they need—starting not now but a year ago when you committed your first filthy barbarities here! History will bear me out!'[34] For Joll, however, history is a trivial matter, because the Empire of which he forms part runs counter to the normal order of things and conspires against history. One idea rules supreme in this Empire, and here the application to South Africa of the 1970s and '80s is striking: 'how not to end, how not to die, how to prolong its era'.[35]

Waiting for the Barbarians contains some of Coetzee's most brilliant and cleanest prose. It also demonstrates a stylistic flexibility that enables him to switch from the elevated style of some sections to a dialogue that matches the speech of his characters. When a roof-strut under the reed and clay snaps and one of the men on the roof falls through the opening, his foul-mouthed reaction reflects the rough speech of the soldier:

'Shit!' he says. 'Shit, shit, shit, shit, shit!' His friends howl with laughter. 'It's not funny!' he shouts. 'I've hurt my fucking thumb!' He squeezes his hand between his knees. 'It's fucking sore!' He swings a kick at the wall of the hut and again I hear plaster fall inside. 'Fucking savages!' he says. 'We should have lined them up against a wall and shot them long ago—with their friends!'[36]

When the magistrate is summonsed for interrogation in the course of his detention, Colonel Joll demands to know the meaning of the writing on the poplar slips found in his possession, implying that they could contain messages in an unknown language. In an important passage,[37] the magistrate, who was himself unable to decipher the writing, uses the opportunity to present his interrogator with a number of provocative possibilities, with subtle reference to Joll's recent torturings and atrocities. Just as Coetzee's novel does not contain a direct, simplistic or single political 'message', the magistrate in his putative 'translation' offers different interpretations of what the writing on the slips could mean: a domestic diary, plans for a future attack or a history of the last years of the Empire. Behind these multifarious choices the informed reader will spot the 'seven types of ambiguity' with which Coetzee, the literary scholar, expert in literary theory and the interpretation of texts, is acquainted. The explanations the magistrate offers play with ambiguity and the various potential levels of a text, without settling for a clear exposition of a single specific meaning:

'Now let us see what the next one says. See, there is only a single character. It is the barbarian character *war*, but it has other senses too. It can stand for *vengeance*, and, if you turn it upside down like this, it can be made to read *justice*. There is no knowing which sense is intended. That is part of barbarian cunning.

'It is the same with the rest of these slips.' I plunge my good hand into the chest and stir. 'They form an allegory. They can be read in many orders. Further, each single slip can be read in many ways. [...] There is no agreement among scholars about how to interpret these relics of the ancient barbarians.'[38]

In a chain of related scenes a group of children appears repeatedly, in reality or in the magistrate's dreams, building a fort for defence, or a castle and a whole city, suggesting a social dispensation. The children reappear at the end of the novel, but the return is preceded by an important passage in which the magistrate, now restored to his legitimate position, starts writing. But he makes no progress. The last years in the annals of this outpost are not what he wants to record, because he has achieved an existence outside history. He wants to wait until winter, when the actual barbarians may be at the gates of the city, to bid farewell to the rhetoric of the public servant and to start telling the truth. But then he once again observes a group of children in the square. Unlike earlier, they are not building a fort or a castle, but a snowman. When he sees this he feels 'inexplicably joyful',[39] even though he notes that the figure is clumsily made. He does not upset them by pointing out the shortcomings:

> They are not alarmed. They are too busy to cast me a glance. They have completed the great round body, now they are rolling a ball for the head.
> 'Someone fetch things for the mouth and nose and eyes,' says the child who is their leader.
> It strikes me that the snowman will need arms too, but I do not want to interfere.
> They settle the head on the shoulders and fill it out with pebbles for eyes, ears, nose and mouth. One of them crowns it with his cap.
> It is not a bad snowman.
> This is not the scene I dreamed of. Like much else nowadays I leave it feeling stupid, like a man who lost his way long ago but presses on along a road that may lead to nowhere.[40]

Although the figure lacks arms, the magistrate does not interfere, because arms have, as Gallagher has shown,[41] the negative connotation of weapons. Instead he feels inexplicably happy at the sight of the children's creation, suggesting to him something of the hope that is in store for a next generation, even though that hope, according to the final sentence, will no longer dawn for him. And this tentative image of hope for a new generation is confirmed by the dedication of the novel to Nicolas and Gisela, Coetzee's two children.

As with *In the Heart of the Country*, there were various people anxious to film *Waiting for the Barbarians*, among others James Polley, who wanted to bring in Manie van Rensburg, and Moonyeenn Lee, who wanted to collaborate with the director Chester Dent. Francis Gerard, too, was interested, but Coetzee instructed his new agent in the US, Peter Lampack, to proceed with one of the three people who had approached him for film rights. Lampack decided on Wieland Schulz-Keil, who was considering Jack Nicholson for the part of the magistrate. Coetzee wrote to Schulz-Keil on 26 October 1984 that Nicholson was a very talented actor: 'It is difficult,' he continues, in a section revealing his own vision of the character of the magistrate,

> to divorce Nicholson from the roles one has seen him play. I would only say that to play the Magistrate, Nicholson would have to divest himself from certain qualities of what I can only call slyness and subversive humor, which have been part of his hallmark in other roles. [...] Generally speaking, I would say that a European would find it easier to feel his way into the part than an American. What is required in the part is, on the one hand, intelligence and a capacity for self-doubt, and, on the other, a genuine commitment to duty, without the first subverting the second; i.e., an integration of the two sides, rather than a switching from the mood of the one to the mood of the other. Not easy.

In the end, the film came to nothing, probably because Schulz-Keil could not raise the necessary funds. Only in 2005 did *Waiting for the Barbarians* achieve its transmutation into another genre: an operatic adaptation by the German company Theater Erfurt, with music by Philip Glass and a libretto by Christopher Hampton, staged in Amsterdam and in Austin. For Austin, where Coetzee had been a student, the production, in January 2007, was adapted to align the veiled allegory with the situation at the time in Iraq—a provocative strategy in the city where President George Bush had served as Governor of Texas.

III

On 24 July 1979 Coetzee posted the manuscript of *Waiting for the Barbarians* from Berkeley to David Stuart Hull, his agent with James Brown Associates in New York. Coetzee alerted Hull to the fact that he had received a letter from Corona Machemer of Harper & Row, who had published *In the Heart of the Country* in the US, asking him if he had anything ready for publication. He deduced that they might be interested in the new manuscript. He sent a second copy to Murray Pollinger, his agent in London, who had handled the sale of the French rights of his second novel.

Apparently Pollinger succeeded almost immediately in selling the manuscript to Secker & Warburg, because by 8 October 1979, on his return to Cape Town, Coetzee received a letter from Tom Rosenthal of Secker, describing *Waiting for the Barbarians* as 'a novel of quite devastating power'. He also refers to the 'remorseless clarity' of Coetzee's prose:

> It is a nightmare world which you have described and the character
> of the magistrate is so real with not a single short cut or soft option
> taken in the writing that one practically lives with the poor man.

For the South African market Rosenthal arranged for Mike Kirkwood to take over 1 000 hardcover copies and 2 000 in paperback in the name of Ravan Press. The British edition appeared on 16 October 1980, and the South African edition a few months later, in 1981. In a letter of 2 November 1980 Coetzee wrote to Kirkwood that on the cover of the Secker & Warburg edition a man called Martin Seymour-Smith is quoted as calling Coetzee 'the best Afrikaans novelist to emerge in the last decade'. Coetzee writes:

> I wasn't asked to check the jacket copy, so I could do nothing about
> this. But if you use the same jacket for your edition, we will all look
> pretty silly.

On 29 November Coetzee informed Murray Pollinger that he was unhappy with the publisher Maurice Nadeau, who, two years after buying the French rights of *In the Heart of the Country*, had not yet managed to publish the novel. He told him he was working on a fourth novel that he hoped to complete in the first half of 1982.

Most British reviewers welcomed Coetzee's new novel, though Peter Lewis in the *Times Literary Supplement* of 7 November 1980 felt that, in spite of 'its gripping narrative and moral insight', it did not, after Dan Jacobson's *The Confessions of Josef Baisz*, contribute anything substantial to the tradition of political allegory, and that the characters were close to stereotypes. Bernard Levin in the London *Sunday Times* insisted on the importance of *Waiting for the Barbarians*, his glowing review finally placing Coetzee as a writer in the international arena. Levin calls Coetzee 'an artist of a weight and depth that puts him in a category beyond ordinary comparisons'. He continues:

> On the surface, the story, though a metaphor, directly indicts [Coetzee's] country as one ruled by 'people who assert that there are higher considerations than decency'. But beneath the surface it is timeless, spaceless, nameless and universal. Coetzee sees the heart of darkness in all societies, and gradually it becomes clear that he is not dealing in politics at all, but inquiring into the nature of the beast that lurks within each of us, and needs no collective stimulus to turn and rend us. [...] Each of us, it seems, is waiting for the barbarians, and if Coetzee is right, none of us will have long to wait.

Levin points out that Coetzee evokes the deceptive and elusive anxiety of Kafka, but that the paring down of the magistrate's humanity goes further than the fate of Joseph K. When the magistrate compares himself with Colonel Joll, he says (as quoted above):

> I was the lie that Empire tells itself when times are easy, he the truth that Empire tells when harsh winds blow.[42]

Levin decides:

> I have never known an author so willing to bare his own back to his own rod, to declare himself at once part of suffering humanity and of that which makes it suffer.
>
> And I have known few authors who can evoke such a wilderness in the heart of man to compare with the wilderness of the barren plain across which the barbarians are relentlessly advancing. This book is the work of an Old Testament prophet who sees no escape from the rain of fire even for those who warn of its coming, and who knows that it is both important and futile 'that in the farthest outpost of this Empire of light there existed one man who in his heart was not a barbarian'. In the turning of Coetzee's pages there sounds the bitter storm of desolation, which is the more bitter for the fact that he sees no hope that man will ever succeed in closing the Pandora's box from which the storm escaped.

When Coetzee was asked later, in an interview with the *Cape Argus* of 21 April 1982, what he thought of Levin's review, he said he was vaguely bemused by the glowing praise and the assertion that he had with his novel transcended the tragic dilemma of South Africa. Levin's description of the novel as 'timeless, spaceless, nameless and universal' prompted Coetzee to say local critics should take local products more seriously and should not wait for them to be discovered overseas. As for Levin's praise, he said that words like 'universal' and 'transcend' were too big for him. All he did was write. To the question whether the 'tragic dilemma' of apartheid had impelled him to write, he replied that nobody started writing from a motive carefully established in advance. What one writes is an investigation and discovery of his own motives for writing.

When the Secker & Warburg edition of *Waiting for the Barbarians* reached the Cape Town docks, the customs officials embargoed it, as they had done with *In the Heart of the Country*, and the book was submitted to a selected group of censors. In 1981, one Major G.J. Petzer, a zealous police officer, also submitted a copy of the Ravan edition to the Directorate, but it was returned to him with the comment that the novel had already been brought to the attention of a committee. Reginald Lighton, a member of the Cape Town censorship committee to which the book had been sent, commented in his report that the scene in which Warrant Officer Mandel reads out the charges against the magistrate, ranging from incompetence to high treason, could be interpreted as a reference to political unrest, especially when the magistrate says that they will use the law against him as it suits them and then resort to other methods. Lighton also finds the character of Mandel problematic, in that he could just as readily make a living from a life of crime as in the service of the Empire. Even the fact that the book does not have a contemporary South African setting does not suffice to dispose of certain questions to Lighton's satisfaction. Nevertheless he concludes that the locality of the novel is obscure, an oasis in a dry region situated north of the equator and not near South Africa. He thus stresses that in terms of locality there are no self-evident parallels with South Africa, although certain symbolic correspondences might be found. In his general summary he comments on the possibility that figures like Mandel and Joll could be read as representatives of 'the arrogant tyranny of State senior ideologists—their blinkered ideological outlook & ruthlessness'.[43] Even though the method of torture, given the circumstances of Biko's death, has clear relevance to South Africa, Lighton in his report takes pains to suggest the converse by pointing out the universal theme of the novel. He adds: 'Though the book has considerable literary merit, it quite lacks popular appeal. The likely readership will be limited largely to the intelligentsia, the discriminatory minority. There are less than a dozen "offensive" words, and all are commonplace & functional in context. To submit these is no convincing reason for declaring the book undesirable.' The book was accordingly passed for distribution in South Africa.[44]

In South Africa Bernard Levin's review, to Coetzee's dismay, was taken over by the *Daily News* on 12 December 1980 and by the *Argus* on 26 March 1981. Coetzee would have preferred original reviews. The Ravan edition of the novel appeared in January 1981, announced before publication by *The Natal Witness* as a book with which 'Mr Coetzee has risen to the front rank of South African literary talent.' The *Natal Mercury*'s reviewer declared on 5 February 1981: 'I doubt whether I have read another book as powerful as this one.' In his review in the *Financial Mail* of 6 February 1981 Peter Wilhelm wrote that many people would read the book as an allegorical commentary on South Africa:

> But the deliberate, and masterly, universalisation of character and place, rendered in language of extraordinary beauty and precision, leads the reader into a meditation on the meaning of civilisation itself, its corrupting quest for perpetuation and stability, and its fragility in the face of encroaching barbarism, internal as much as any perceived external menace.

Wilhelm concludes his review with a panegyric on the effects of the novel on the reader:

> The strange landscapes, part-African, part a country of the mind; the sense of action and thought scarcely disturbing the flux of time; the crystalline lucidity of the language — these will haunt the reader long after the novel has been laid aside.

Compared with this, Cherry Clayton in the *Rand Daily Mail* of 8 March 1981 is relatively restrained in her praise, Coetzee remaining for her an intellectual and even cerebral writer, even though she sees the novel as a welcome corrective in a literary arena where daring protest and simple documentation are sometimes over-praised. As against this, Jean Marquard expresses admiration for his 'deceptively bare prose style' and his 'evocations of brutality and suffering in a timeless setting'.[45]

From his agent in the US, David Stuart Hull,[46] Coetzee heard that the manuscript of *Waiting for the Barbarians* had been submitted to Harper & Row, Houghton Mifflin, Viking and Doubleday, but that it had also gone to Penguin, who was considering both the new novel and a reissue of *In the Heart of the Country*.

In his letter Hull does not explain why the manuscript was submitted to so many publishers. In an article in *Publisher's Weekly* of 20 November 1981, however, Joann Davis tells how Hull was lunching one day with Kathryn Court of Penguin to discuss a number of properties and the purchase of American houses. During the conversation he told Court about the British publication of *Waiting for the Barbarians*. He said:

> Here's an example of something good that a number of American publishers have turned down. The author has received three distinguished prizes abroad, but nobody here is interested in him.

Her interest piqued by the disparate reactions of the British and American publishers, Court agreed to take a copy of the British edition of *Waiting for the Barbarians* along on her impending holiday. 'It really wasn't the kind of book one chooses to read at the beach,' she said later to *Publisher's Weekly*. 'But I took it along any way in order to find out for myself.' Court, who had never before heard of Coetzee, was, as she says in her interview, totally bowled over by the South African's work:

> It's easy to come up with clichés, but I think what impressed me the most was the way the book allows the reader to look at the darkness in men's souls and to grasp, in an emotional way, the moral dilemmas that political situations can create. I don't know of many writers who can invent a character examining his own beliefs and ethics at the deepest level, and not get mired in rhetoric.

While still on holiday, Court informed Hull that she would very much like to publish *Waiting for the Barbarians*, and that he should spare no effort to acquire the rights for her. A few days after his previous letter, Hull on 6 May 1981 brought Coetzee the good news that Penguin had decided to accept both *Waiting for the Barbarians* and *In the Heart in the*

Country for publication in paperback, and to offer an advance of $7 500 for the package, which he advised Coetzee to accept. Although Harper & Row owned the reprint rights for *From the Heart of the Country*, he would ask for a reversion of rights, since the hardcover they had published was out of print.

On receipt of the signed contracts from David Hull, Court wrote to Coetzee on 6 November 1981, saying that Penguin would publish *Waiting for the Barbarians* in April 1982, and that she and many of her colleagues were very excited about it. She continued:

> It is an extraordinary novel, not only because of the quality and spareness of your writing, and the intensity of your imagery, but especially because it allowed me to make a sort of 'emotional leap' — to understand in a non-intellectual way the awesome nature of choice.
>
> As you know the novel will be published as an original trade paperback. This should allow us to reach a much larger audience. It will be the first time Penguin here has published a novel in this way, and this will of course draw additional attention to the book. [...]
>
> I also wanted to let you know that we have printed advance reading copies to help in publicity and promotion, and which I sent to a number of people for quotes. Nadine Gordimer, Graham Greene and Michael Arlen gave us the following responses (respectively):
>
> 'J.M. Coetzee's vision goes to the nerve-centre of being. What he finds there is more than most people will ever know of themselves, and he conveys it with a brilliant writer's mastery of tension and elegance.'
>
> 'A very remarkable and original book and under the circumstances a very courageous one.'
>
> 'It's a stunning book. I expect it's going to stay in my head for a long time.'

Court concluded: 'I am of course certain that this is just the beginning and I will let you know how everything progresses.'

The American edition of *Waiting for the Barbarians* appeared in April 1982 in a first printing of 30 000 copies. Since Penguin had made extensive publicity for the book before publication, and sent advance copies to journals, several editors now also took an interest in Coetzee. On 6 November 1981 David Hull let him know that he had received calls from quite a few editors enquiring whether there were short stories of Coetzee's available for publication in their magazines. One of the calls was from *The New Yorker*, 'which is the toughest market to crack in this country'. Melissa Baumann of the magazine *Harper's* wrote to Coetzee on 2 December 1981, saying that *Waiting for the Barbarians* was 'a wonderful book' and that it should have been published in the US long ago. She asked whether an extract from the novel could be made available for publication in her magazine. If not, she would like to know whether he could submit a shorter piece of fiction, a 'letter from South Africa' or, with reference to the growing right-wing movement of 'Marais and Blanche, is it?'[47] he could write an essay on contemporary South African literature. In his reply on 20 December 1981 Coetzee writes that he would be happy for her to publish an excerpt from the book. He continues:

> As for the alternatives you suggest, I'm afraid I just don't have a short piece at the moment that would be suitable. A 'letter from South Africa' on Marais, Terre'blanche, and their followers would be interesting, but I know nothing more about them than what I read in the newspapers, and I think one needs more first-hand information than that. As for the literary scene, it's actually rather dull at the moment—at least, that's my impression. Let me give the matter some more thought and get in touch with you again in a couple of weeks.

In the event Coetzee did not follow up immediately on the 'letter from South Africa', but it is possible that the idea planted a seed for an article that he was to work on later.

In *New York* of 26 April 1982 Anthony Burgess pronounced *Waiting for the Barbarians* a 'grave and admirably written story', a 'powerful fictional indictment not only of the stupidity of the separatist ideology that sustains Coetzee's own country but of that stupidity in all of us that finds its most typical expression in destruction.' George Steiner, a prominent literary scholar and philosopher who was known for works like *The Death of Tragedy* (1961) and *Language and Silence* (1966), provided, in *The New York Review* of 2 December 1982, an important exposition of the Hegelian concept of the master-slave relation as a preamble to his review. What particularly engrossed him was the depiction of the love affair between the magistrate and the girl:

> The Hegelian equivocations on mastery and subjection, on how the possessed come to possess their possessors, are beautifully rendered. The Magistrate is erotically and morally obsessed by the pain that has been inflicted on the dark creature. He washes, he kneads her torn feet, looking for the buried roots of sadistic hurt. Mr Coetzee conveys to us how a man who does not yet know torture at first hand will seek out in others the seeds of endurance, of recuperation. [...] It is in his subtle inference of this love, and of the waste that may come of liberation, that Mr Coetzee is at his best.

In the US *The New York Times Book Review* gave great prominence to *Waiting for the Barbarians*, in a review by Irving Howe on the cover page of their edition of 19 April 1982. In the preamble Howe refers to the problematic position of the writer in South Africa, who could find the daily furore of the racial conflict so deafening that his anger could overpower his psyche and paralyse his creative work. In *Waiting for the Barbarians*, according to Howe, Coetzee had found a narrative strategy to contain the tension between circumstance and writer by placing the tale in an imaginary Empire in an unspecified time, but simultaneously recognisable as a 'universalised' version of South Africa. This procedure enabled him to keep an aesthetic distance from his material, without getting swamped by the chaos and hideousness of the present era. Like Steiner, Howe finds the relationship between the magistrate and the barbarian girl the most brilliant part of the novel. He provides an insightful summary of the story. At the end of the review he posits a possible loss attendant on the strategy of an imaginary Empire, even though *Waiting for the Barbarians* remains for him 'a distinguished piece of fiction'. He takes issue with a pronouncement of Levin's:

> One possible loss is the bite and pain, the urgency that a specified historical place and time may provide. To create a 'universalized' Empire is to court the risk—especially among sophisticated readers for whom the credos of modernism have become dull axioms—that a narrative with strong political and social references will be 'elevated' into sterile ruminations about the human condition. As if

to make clear what I'm getting at, Mr Coetzee's American publishers quote from a London review of the novel by Bernard Levin: 'Mr Coetzee sees the heart of darkness in all societies, and gradually it becomes clear that he is not dealing in politics at all, but inquiring into the nature of the beast that lurks within each of us ...'

This is a profundity very much in the spirit of our time, but perhaps I'll be forgiven if I say that it's a shallow profundity. Why should we suppose that it's a virtue in a novel such as *Waiting for the Barbarians* that it does not deal 'in politics at all'? Of course it deals in politics: what is Colonel Joll but the representative of one kind of politics and the magistrate another? Nor is politics, as Mr Levin seems to imply, some sort of surface triviality, a mere scum on the waters of life; politics is a fundamental human activity, the way we structure our shared existence. To scant the politics of Mr Coetzee's novel, is to pull its teeth.

That 'a heart of darkness' is present in all societies and a beast 'lurks within each of us' may well be true. But such invocations of universal evil can deflect attention from the particular and at least partly remediable social wrongs Mr Coetzee portrays. Not only deflect attention, but encourage readers, as they search for their inner beasts, to a mood of conservative acquiescence and social passivity.

I cannot believe this was Mr Coetzee's intention or, perhaps more important, that it is warranted by his novel itself. True, the Empire is abstract, timeless, placeless; but through the scrim of Empire, *Waiting for the Barbarians* renders a moment in our politics, a style of our injustice. Precisely this power of historical immediacy gives the novel its thrust, its larger and, if you wish, 'universal' value.

Waiting for the Barbarians brought Coetzee much praise. Some of his close friends congratulated him by telegram, letter and telephone. He received a letter from Dennis Worrall, a South African politician and in the 1980s an ambassador to Australia, expressing his admiration of the novel: 'I have just read with enormous interest and pleasure your *Waiting for the Barbarians* and, for what it is worth, wish to compliment you.' Worrall asked if Coetzee could recommend a review of the novel, upon which Coetzee sent him Irving Howe's review in *The New York Times Book Review*, which, according to him, 'at least addresses some of the central issues of the novel'. John Barth, of the Johns Hopkins University in Baltimore, whom he had got to know during his Buffalo years, also sent a congratulatory letter: 'Congratulations indeed on the enthusiastic critical reception that *Waiting for the Barbarians* got in this country. Congratulations again on having written a book that actually deserved that reception. We're teaching it already in our 20th Century Fiction course here at Hopkins.' Barth enquires whether Coetzee will be back in Buffalo in the spring of 1984 and wants to know whether he will be able to come to Baltimore to speak to their creative writing students and to deliver a public lecture on his work. Coetzee replied that he would indeed be in Buffalo for the spring semester, during which he would be offering a course on Realism (whatever that might be), and that he hoped to visit Jonathan Crewe in Baltimore. He would thus be pleased to speak to Barth's creative writing students on this occasion.

Penguin in Britain decided to follow the example of their American sister company and to publish the book also in paperback. Translation rights were sold to publishers in France, Sweden, Denmark, Germany and Holland, and in due course in many other countries and linguistic regions. In the Netherlands, in particular, Coetzee was to garner an extremely large readership. Initially he was published by Uitgeverij Ambo, later by Uitgeverij Cossee, who also took over the earlier novels and republished them in attractive editions. Reactions to the Dutch translation of *Waiting for the Barbarians* were extremely favourable. In *De Volkskrant* of 24 June 1983 Ena Jansen wrote that *Wachten op de Barbaren* was an engrossing blend of exact description and introspection:

> The descriptions of landscapes and people are very specific, but the evocation is oddly enough that of a primitive landscape in which the underlying melancholy of a doomed way of life and the resistance of one solitary man can be emphasised. The theme is universal: about people of all times who cannot accept that they are complicit in a repressive regime.

In the 'Cultural Supplement' of the *NRC Handelsblad*, also of 24 June 1983, Frans Kellendonk finds that Coetzee writes 'in an unusually earthy and unruly way' and that *Wachten op de Barbaren* contains nothing 'disguised or allegorical':

> It would be wrong to relate Coetzee's work too narrowly to the tragedy of his fatherland. The apartheid he is writing about is not

political, but existential. Race is a fetish, and racism and anti-racism alike are false statements. It is rather a matter of recognising and respecting the real differences, which are cultural. People are equal only in so far as they are all different.

And in *Vrij Nederland* of 28 January 1984 Aad Nuis discusses the original English editions of Coetzee's first four novels, pronouncing *Waiting for the Barbarians* the high point—a novel in which the form of the narrative is conventional, even though reality is deviated from, in a different way to *In the Heart of the Country*. Colonel Joll, with whose visit from the capital the novel opens, is revealed as the new barbarian, a much greater threat to civilisation and humanity than the old barbarians ever could be. More than in other novels, Nuis writes, there is a correspondence between the position of the liberal magistrate and that of the author himself, something which contributes to 'the enrichment of the characters':

> not only as symbols of time-bound attitudes, but also of a convincing particularity with particular needs. As a critique of the South African situation the book is circumspect, but authentic. Its power lies exactly in the fact that the well-meaning section of the ruling group, to which the author himself belongs, is placed in the merciless spotlight of the imagination. That South Africa is not mentioned by name, is on the one hand a matter of self-preservation, but it also has a positive aspect: the novel's reach is extended all the more by it.[48]

With the publication of *Waiting for the Barbarians* Coetzee achieved his international breakthrough. Apart from the intrinsic quality of the novel, the timing was right, because with the publication of so many books on the South African situation, international outrage at the apartheid policy was mounting. *Waiting for the Barbarians* was selected by the *New York Times* as one of the best books of 1982. The novel, according to them, 'contributed a powerful and moving voice to the international discourse on torture in the eighties'.[49]

With all the attention Coetzee was receiving, Penguin, in the year of the publication of *Waiting for the Barbarians*, also reissued *In the Heart of the Country*, which had been published by Harper & Row in the US in 1977, with limited success, under the title *From the Heart of the Country*. In 1982 Coetzee's success also prompted his

LEFT: Balthazar du Biel and Anna Louisa Brecher, maternal great-grandparents of J.M. Coetzee. Du Biel was a Rhenish missionary and the author, among other works, of *Deur 'n gevaarlike krankheid tot ewige genesing*, which was translated from the German into Afrikaans by his daughter Annie. In *Boyhood* Coetzee writes: 'In the photograph in Aunt Annie's bedroom Balthazar du Biel has grim, staring eyes and a tight, harsh mouth. Besides him his wife looks tired and cross.' *(Stefan Wehmeyer)*

RIGHT: Gerrit Maxwell Coetzee with his daughter Irene circa 1902. He was the paternal grandfather of the author, and the owner of the farm Voëlfontein, which played an important part in John Coetzee's life, and features in books such as *Boyhood* and *Summertime*. *(Maxwell Coetzee)*

BELOW LEFT: After the death of his first wife, Gerrit Maxwell Coetzee married Magdalena Catherina (Lenie) de Beer (1884–1978) in 1905. In her youth she studied the piano, organ and violin at Stellenbosch and at an advanced age she was still an excellent pianist. *(Sylvia Coetzee)*

BELOW RIGHT: Johann Albert Ernst du Biel, son of the missionary and his wife, Anna Louisa. Under the name Albert du Biel he achieved a modest place in the annals of Afrikaans literature in the 1920s and 30s with novels such as *Die misdade van die vaders* (1919); *Kain* (1922) and *Die verraaier* (1931). *(Dion du Biel)*

ABOVE: The Cape-Dutch homestead at Voëlfontein, the Karoo farm belonging to John Coetzee's grandfather. In *Boyhood* Coetzee writes: '... there is no place on earth he loves more or can imagine loving more'. *(Lynette Märki)*

BELOW: The house on the farm Maraisdal, approximately three kilometres from Leeu-Gamka, where the Coetzees lived after their return from the United States in 1971, and where John Coetzee completed 'The narrative of Jacobus Coetzee' in *Dusklands*, his debut novel of 1974. *(Wium van Zyl)*

TOP LEFT: Vera Hildred Wehmeyer, mother of the author. *(Stefan Wehmeyer)*

TOP RIGHT: Jack Coetzee, father of the author, with his 'dapper little moustache and his cocky look', as described by John Coetzee in *Boyhood*. *(Lynette Märki)*

RIGHT: Son and Sylvia Coetzee, with their children Gerald and Valmé. This photo was taken circa 1954 by John Coetzee, already a competent photographer, in front of Jack and Vera Coetzee's home in Plumstead, Cape Town. *(Gerald Coetzee)*

LEFT: John Coetzee with his father dressed in his uniform as a member of the South African forces in the Second World War. This photo was taken in 1943 in Johannesburg. *(Family album)*

BELOW: John Coetzee's father, Zacharias (Jack), *(seated front left)* with his five brothers. *Back row left to right*: Alfred Kenneth (Bubbles), Stanley Maxwell Buller (son from Gerrit Maxwell Coetzee's first marriage) and Gerald Zacharias (Son or Sonny), the last of these the author's favourite uncle and later owner of Voëlfontein. Seated next to Jack in front are Alan Hubert and James Mills. *(Sylvia Coetzee)*

RIGHT: Vera with her two sons, John *(left)* and David. *(Stefan Wehmeyer)*

BELOW LEFT: John Coetzee at age ten in Worcester in 1950. *(Family album)*

BELOW RIGHT: John Coetzee in 1949 in Worcester in his Scout uniform. *(Family album)*

ABOVE: The matric class of 1956 at St Joseph's Marist College. John Coetzee is in the third row, third from the left. (*St Joseph's College Magazine*, 1956)

BELOW: The First Eleven cricket team of St Joseph's Marist College in 1956. John is in the second row far right. (*St Joseph's College Magazine*, 1956)

ABOVE: The Arts Block on the main campus of the University of Cape Town, site of most of John Coetzee's classes when he started studying in 1957. When he returned to South Africa in 1971, he was appointed as a lecturer in the Department of English, and had an office overlooking the Jagger Library on the other side of University Avenue. *(Anton Naudé)*

RIGHT: Guy Howarth, Arderne Chair in English Literature at the University of Cape Town. Coetzee had a long association with him and attended his course in creative writing, among others. Coetzee wrote: 'He was the first person I had come across who was transparently devoted to the life of literature.' *(A.L. McLeod)*

LEFT: Coetzee in Cape Town in 1963. *(Family album)*

ABOVE: Philippa Jubber, married to Coetzee in 1963. This photograph was taken in 1976. *(Family album)*

BELOW: With Philippa in Cambridge, England, in 1964. *(Family album)*

The main campus of the University of Cape Town, where John Coetzee studied from 1957 to 1961, and lectured from 1972 to 2001. *(Alex Pratt)*

LEFT: David Coetzee, brother of John. *(Family album)*

BELOW: John Coetzee *(left)* with his mother and his brother, David, during their mother's visit to London. *(Family album)*

Philippa in Surrey, England, in 1964. *(Family album)*

In Surrey in 1964. *(Family album)*

ABOVE: A peaceful student demonstration in Buffalo.
(Richard A. Siggelkow, *Dissent and Disruption: A University under Siege*, Buffalo, NY, Prometheus Books, 1991)

BELOW: When 45 lecturers at Buffalo arrived at the administration building on Sunday, 15 March 1970 in peaceful protest against the continued police presence on campus, demanding a conversation with the president, they were arrested and had to spend a night in the cells. Among the 'Buffalo 45', as they were later called, was John Coetzee. Here are some of these lecturers behind bars. (Richard A. Siggelkow, *Dissent and Disruption: A University under Siege*, Buffalo, NY, Prometheus Books, 1991)

ABOVE: Philippa with her two children, Gisela *(left)* and Nicolas. *(Lisa Perold)*

LEFT: Gisela and Nicolas, 1970. *(Lisa Perold)*

The first page of 'The narrative of Jacobus Coetzee', which, according to the annotation at the top, was written on 1 January 1970, thus constituting the start of Coetzee's career as a novelist. (*Harry Ransom Humanities Research Center, University of Texas*)

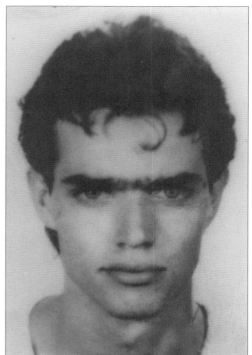

Top left: John Coetzee with Gisela in Muizenberg in the early 1980s. *(Family album)*

Top right: Nicolas Coetzee. *(Family album)*

Above: Dorothy Driver. *(NELM)*

ABOVE: Dorothy Driver and John
Coetzee during their visit to the
Johns Hopkins University in
Baltimore in 1986. *(Family album)*

LEFT: In the 1980s Coetzee took
up cycling as a form of sport and
recreation. He took part
in the annual Argus Cycle Tour
in Cape Town fifteen times. In
1991 he clocked his best time,
completing the race in three hours
and fourteen minutes, a feat he
repeated in 1994. *(Family album)*

ABOVE: John Coetzee during a visit to Switzerland with his boyhood friend Nic Stathakis in 1987. *(Family album)*

BELOW: In June–July 1994 John Coetzee undertook a cycle trip from Paris to Avignon in the south and then to Toulouse in the west, with seven companions, among whom was his daughter, Gisela. Eventually only two members of the group, Coetzee and Gisela, reached Toulouse on 13 July, having covered about 1 250 kilometres. Here is Gisela on her bicycle, with acre upon acre of sunflowers to her right. *(Family album)*

With an allusion to T.S. Eliot's essay of 1944 by the same title, Coetzee delivered the lecture 'What is a classic?' in Graz, Austria, in 1991. *(Family album)*

LEFT: John Coetzee looking on, while the archaeologist Jane Klose sorts sediments near Churchhaven. (Carmel Schrire, *Digging through Darkness: Chronicles of an Archaeologist,* Johannesburg, Witwatersrand University Press, 1995)

BELOW: With a group of writers and friends at Silvermine Nature Reserve in Cape Town in the early 1990s. *From left to right:* Dorothy Driver, John Coetzee, Julian Judd, Gisela Coetzee, Tony Morphet, Breyten Breytenbach, Zoë Wicomb and Ingrid Fiske. *(Family album)*

In 2000 in Amsterdam with the group of writers, artists and scientists who participated in Wim Kayzer's television series *Van de schoonheid en de troost*. In the second row from the back, third from the left, is George Steiner, with Wole Soyinka in the third row from the back, second from the left. Second from the right in the same row is John Coetzee, with the Dutch painter Karel Appel standing next to him. Between Soyinka and Coetzee is Dubravka Ugrešic, the Croatian writer now living in Amsterdam. Diagonally in front of Soyinka is the Dutch poet Rutger Kopland. On the far right is the Hungarian author György Konrád. *(Family album)*

ABOVE: In June 2000 Coetzee was awarded the Commonwealth Writers' Prize for that year. He received it in person from Queen Elizabeth II in London at Buckingham Palace. *(Family album)*

BELOW: On 27 September 2005 Coetzee was awarded the National Order of Mapungubwe (Gold), which he received in person from President Thabo Mbeki in Pretoria. *(Family album)*

ABOVE: In 2002 the University of
Oxford awarded John Coetzee
an honorary doctorate.
(Family album)

LEFT: On 10 December 2003
John Coetzee received his Nobel
Prize from King Carl XVI Gustaf
of Sweden. *(Family album)*

British and American publishers to publish his first novel, *Dusklands*, which had previously been published only in South Africa. As early as April 1978, Lemuel A. Johnson had reviewed the Ravan edition of *Dusklands* in *The African Book Publishing Record*, calling the tale of Jacobus Coetzee's trek over the Great River 'at once a baroque, comico-nightmarish safari as well as a profound exploration of those dilemmas which racial differences, cultural imbalances, and beliefs in "manifest destinies" can provoke'.

In the London *Sunday Times* of 23 January 1983, Victoria Glendinning pronounced very favourably on *Dusklands*:

[Coetzee's] writing gives off whiffs of Conrad, Nabokov, of Golding, of the Paul Theroux of *The Mosquito Coast*. But he is none of these, he is a harsh, compelling new voice. Like his characters, Coetzee has 'an exploring temperament', and drags his reader with him into uncomfortable patches of perception. I wish everyone would read his books.

IV

With the publication of *Waiting for the Barbarians* and its breakthrough into other countries, Coetzee now received international awards. From Scotland he was awarded one of the oldest and most influential prizes in Britain, the James Tait Black Memorial Prize. It was instituted in 1919 in memory of James Tait Black, a partner in the publishing firm A&C Black, and is administered by Edinburgh University. In his commendation Professor A.D.S. Fowler of this university described Coetzee as the best South African novelist of the previous decade. From England Coetzee received the Geoffrey Faber Memorial Prize, instituted in 1963 in honour of the founder and first chairman of the publishing house Faber and Faber, a prize awarded in alternate years to a poetry collection or to a work of fiction by a Commonwealth writer under the age of forty.

Like *In the Heart of the Country* in 1978, *Waiting for the Barbarians* was awarded the CNA Prize for 1979. The members of the adjudicating panel were Professor D.R. Beeton of the Department of English at the University of South Africa, Charles Barry of the Argus Printing and Publishing Company, and Dr Thelma Gutsche, a prominent Johannesburg writer.

The award ceremony took place at the Johannesburg Country Club in Auckland Park on 23 April 1980.

On this occasion Coetzee delivered one of his most important public speeches,[50] in which he posed the question of what exactly one understood by the concept of 'national literature', and whether it was possible to talk of a national literature in English in South Africa. Coetzee had from the start of his writing career been at best ambivalent about his own South African origins. On the publication of *Dusklands* he had objected to Ravan Press's labelling of him as a South African writer. *Dusklands* contained two stories respectively situated in the US and South Africa, but the cover had been based on a watercolour by Thomas Baines, the nineteenth-century Africana painter, depicting a South African landscape from the colonial era, with ox wagons and distant hills. The blurb hailed the book as 'probably the first truly major South African novel'. If one bears in mind further that after completion of his studies at UCT, Coetzee had planned to leave South Africa permanently, to escape the colonies and settle in the metropolis, his pronouncements on what he sees as a national literature assume cardinal importance for an understanding of his interpretation of his own task as a writer.

If one were to place Coetzee's understanding of a national literature in the context of the greater South African literature, one could note that N.P. van Wyk Louw had already in March 1936 concerned himself with this question in a lecture in Stellenbosch, from the perspective of the Afrikaans writer. In this lecture Van Wyk Louw resists the 'easy-going local realism' that before him had dominated Afrikaans literature, especially its prose variant. It amounts, according to him, to a colonial and thus 'fragmentary' literature that cannot contain 'complete humanity'.[51]

In accepting the CNA Prize, Coetzee said that the annual CNA awards marked an important event on the South African cultural calendar, since they charted something of the growth of South African literature in English and Afrikaans. Whether or not the committees consciously played this role or not, what they produced was at least:

> a record of changing tastes and changing concerns among South African writers and critics, and perhaps even, however human and fallible their choices may be, an incrementing list of more important South African books of the past few decades.

The decisions of the awards committees, Coetzee continues, may be seen as part of a larger communal project: to define a South African national literature—in reality two South African literatures, one in English and one in Afrikaans. What he has to say about Afrikaans in his address, will be peripheral. What he wants to talk about, is South African literature in English (including black anglophone writing), to ask whether it is a good and true idea to think of it as a national literature, or as an emerging national literature. It is in this respect that the established approaches to English and Afrikaans literature respectively are particularly striking:

> The running battle between Afrikaans writers and the Afrikaans establishment during the 1970s can fairly be seen as a battle about what it meant to write within an Afrikaans national tradition; whereas a comparable conflict between English-language writers and that much more nebulous entity, the English establishment in South Africa, is hard to imagine. [...]
>
> But if the question of whether English South African writing constitutes a national literature seems purely academic today, it is not likely to remain so in the South Africa of the future, in which English will very likely be overwhelmingly the major literary language. For there exists a more radical view of what it means to be part of a national literature, a view that prevailed among Afrikaners: that a national literature gives expression to national aspirations and, in some general sense, becomes part of the national struggle for survival, independence, unity, hegemony, or whatever. There is every indication that pressures on South African literature in English to take on this kind of role will mount in the future.
>
> The question I should like to ask tonight is a simple but, I think, radical one: whether there is adequate reason for calling any of the bodies of writing in English coming out of Africa and carried on within national boundaries national literatures; or, to put the question more precisely, whether there can be a good motive for thinking of them as national literatures other than the political motive of wishing to span in the energies of writers for national ends.

Coetzee goes on to say that he does not want to get entangled in the larger question of the task of the writer, or in the question whether the nation and the state are identical. He wants to restrict himself to the smaller question of whether, from the perspective of literary history, it is a misnomer to call South African literature in English a national literature. The practising writer, to his mind, deals on a daily basis with the problem of connecting content with form. Content is easy, if the writer possesses the requisite passion and imagination and a few other qualities. But content does not exist independently of form. What you can say and think and feel, is limited to and determined by the forms in which it can be expressed. And these forms, literary and linguistic, are not easy to change, while new forms are not often invented. Coetzee finds it striking that the important formal changes that have been made to express new things have not usually taken place at the peripheries of civilisation. They usually occur in the cultural centre of a civilisation, which Coetzee designates as the 'metropolis'—even though the more refined communication networks of the late twentieth century would make it possible for a metropolis not to be restricted to a single defined location. As far as the South African position is concerned, Coetzee says:

> I want to assert that our relation in South Africa to the West European and North American centres of the dominant world civilization remains that of province to metropolis, to be a provincial literature.

It was precisely this province from which Coetzee had wanted to escape, first through his departure for Britain, but since 1974 also in his creative work, which he did not want to be labelled specifically South African. But his thinking on what a provincial literature really is, is also more ambiguous, and complex:

> If I am right to say that what we are doing is not building a new national literature, but instead building on to an established provincial literature, then it seems to me that the most constructive way to behave—certainly a more constructive way than pitying ourselves for our provincial lot, or plotting an escape to the metropolis—is to set about rehabilitating the notion of the provincial so that being a provincial writer becomes a fate one can embrace without ignominy. Provincialism usually carries connotations of the backward, the smug, the philistine. It also carries a stigma of inferiority. I do not see that any of this is necessary. A provincial literature is not necessarily minor. Russian literature of the age of Dostoevsky and Tolstoy is

provincial and major. There are quite other values associated with provincialism that one can cultivate, for example, a sense of cultural and historical continuity at the level of the lives ordinary people lead; a respect for localities; craftsmanship; sobriety.

Coetzee feels that it is not always easy to be a provincial artist, in particular at times when his orientation towards and connection with the metropolitan heritage brings him into conflict with the provincial mores, as the writer in South Africa experiences on a daily basis through censorship. It is also not easy to accept that what he regards as the invention of a new form is really only a repetition of what has already been done in the metropolis. He has to learn to live with this, as with the clarion call of metropolitan critics to produce through his art something 'authentically' South African that does not ape European or American models. 'Demands of this kind,' he says, 'come out of a naïve, idle, and typically metropolitan yearning for the exotic, a yearning we should recognize as of no importance.' Coetzee concludes with a thought he will elaborate on a few years later in another prominent address:

> I remember a British colleague saying: 'What paradise to be a writer in South Africa! Everything else may be wrong, but at least you have a great subject staring you in the face!' Perhaps. South Africa may offer a great subject, but great subjects do not make great novels. Oppression and exploitation on a massive scale, the struggle against oppression and exploitation — these are certainly not a new subject. [...] What I am suggesting this evening is that the South African writer may have to learn to be modest, to accept that his historical destiny, and the destiny of his society, are in no way special, that despite the flags and anthems and other national paraphernalia, his relationship to the metropolis, like that of other African writers in English, is not all that different from what it was seventy years ago.

After the award of the CNA Prize, a review of *Waiting for the Barbarians* appeared in the magazine of the South African Students' Press Union (SASPU) by Menán du Plessis, at the time a student and later a well-known novelist. She not only comments unfavourably on the novel and its (to her) lack of political relevance in the burning reality of South Africa, but also launches a fierce attack on the integrity of the author: 'As the CNA award shows, this is a book which will be enthusiastically assimilated into the very system it (vaguely) condemns. In the end it is not a disturbing book, and ultimately it challenges nothing. Coetzee is a fine writer. It's a pity he isn't a bolder one.' In a later article[52] she expresses a completely different opinion, and sketches the circumstances that had compelled her to this judgement. When the censors could find nothing offensive in the book, and it was on top of that awarded the prestige prize of the establishment, students with Marxist expectations of the book were disappointed. Now, however, she sees the book and Coetzee differently: 'Ultimately [...] there is no distinction to be made between [Coetzee's] fineness and his boldness. If readers do not sense the searing directness of the challenges he makes, the failure, I am afraid, is not Coetzee's.'

V

In the 1980s Coetzee remained active as a translator, critic and occasional speaker. In October 1981 he was invited to Durban to appear before a meeting of the South African Teachers' Union. When, however, he was asked, besides reading from his work, to talk on 'authorial concerns in relation to themes and techniques', and received a list of questions and topics, he demurred. He wrote to M.F. Cassim, the union's vice-president, that three of the questions implied he would have to talk about his own work, something he wanted to avoid. He continues:

> I find newspaper interviews painful, and try not to give them; I think that talking about my own work to a large audience would be, if anything, more painful. (One of the compensations of not having to earn a living by one's writing is that one doesn't have to involve oneself in 'promoting' it.) Couldn't we therefore talk, at that point, a little more generally about the state of writing in South Africa?

In December 1981 Koos Human of the publishing house Human & Rousseau approached Coetzee to undertake the English translation of *Die Kremetartekspedisie* by Wilma Stockenström, an Afrikaans novel that, differences apart, shows a certain similarity to Coetzee's work. The sustained monologue of a former slave woman in a language with particular sound combinations and unusual syntax invites comparison with that of Magda in *In the Heart of the Country*, and the indeterminacy of the milieu is reminiscent of that in *Waiting for the Barbarians*, even though Coetzee's is mainly a desert region while Stockenström's is tropical. Most importantly, in both Stockenström's novel and Coetzee's there is a waiting for something to happen.

Stockenström's novel had made a strong impression on Coetzee, and he was immediately prepared to undertake the translation. He enquired in writing from Stockenström regarding the names of plants and trees occurring in the novel.[53] Apart from the South African edition of the translation, it was published in Britain by Faber and Faber and afterwards in several other countries. In Italy it was judged the best non-Italian book to appear in Italy that year.

In reply to an enquiry about his working methods and principles from Ria Vanderauwera, doing doctoral research on English and American translations of Dutch fiction at the Universitaire Instelling Antwerpen, Coetzee wrote on 3 June 1981 that in theory he preferred fidelity to the source text to fluency in the target language, but that he had seldom found he could achieve both aims in the translation of prose:

> I would not try to translate a 19th-century novel into a variety of English that is recognizably of the late 20th century. On the other hand I would not imitate features of diction and syntax uniquely characteristic of late 19th-century English. My general aim has been to make my English as invisible as I can to the reader.
>
> When, as result of cultural differences, there are no exact equivalents in the target language, the translator is faced with a problem:
>
> I would cite here: terms referring to items of clothing and culinary items, as well as specialized vocabularies (e.g. of banking and finance). Only in a highly academic translation has one the luxury of the footnote. I have done as most translators do: translated the problem term into what I regard as an equivalent in the structure of the target culture. In the case of culturally similar societies, the degree of mistranslation caused by this principle is trivial. In the case of culturally remote societies, of course, this principle (which lies behind all so-called 'creative' translation) can raise major philosophical difficulties.

Through the translation of *Die Kremetartekspedisie* Coetzee renewed contact with Koos Human, who was tackling a new project with Faber and Faber, with which André Brink, at that time Professor in Afrikaans and Dutch at Rhodes University in Grahamstown, was also involved. At the invitation of Robert McCrum of Faber and Faber, Coetzee and Brink undertook an anthology of South African literature since 1976. Coetzee made a selection from the available material in English, and Brink was responsible for the Afrikaans section (with translations into English by the authors or by available translators). The compilers selected tales and poems reflecting contemporary South Africa, and ignored all restrictions imposed by censorship. Because one of the contributors, Mazisi Kunene, living in the US, was not to be quoted in South Africa in terms of the law on the suppression of communism, Human & Rousseau rescinded their intention to market a local edition. On 4 August 1986 Coetzee wrote to Mike Kirkwood: 'You may have heard that Human & Rousseau pulled out of the arrangement they had with Faber to publish a South African edition, largely out of nervousness that they might be prosecuted under the emergency regulations (there are some poems in the book by Mazisi Kunene.)' *A Land Apart*, as the anthology was eventually called, appeared in 1986 from Faber and Faber, and was published in Holland as *Ons geduld heeft zijn grenzen* (1987) [*Our Patience has its Limits*], with an introduction by Coetzee and Brink. In general the reaction to the book was very favourable. David Caute wrote in the *New Statesman* of 29 August 1986 about the 'remarkable vitality of contemporary South African writing, the inspiration it draws from the grotesque contours of daily life'.

In the reviews that Coetzee published in the 1980s, he attended to both English South African and Afrikaans literature. What is striking about his reviews of Richard Rive's *Writing Black* (1981) and Athol Fugard's *Notebooks 1960–77* (1984) is how these two books enable him to position himself in relation to South Africa. In his review of *Writing Black*[54] he comments on how Rive's life story, though somewhat one-sided and selective, casts light on a black South African who would have preferred not to spend his life in this or any other racially categorised society, and who looks forward to the day when there will no longer be any 'black writing'. One of Coetzee's comments on autobiography is of particular interest in the light of his own later autobiographical works: 'To write an autobiography is inevitably to embark on a program of self-justification.' Of primary importance in his discussion is the theme of the possible effect of a long-term banning on a writer. For the writer to be removed from his real readers and to have his citizenship revoked, can be dispiriting and paralysing, draining him of inspiration. On a visit to Canada, Rive found coloureds from South Africa living in Toronto in a kind of lower middle-class psychological limbo, with a flickering South African existence, entailing bobotie evenings and attempts to speak Afrikaans. Exile thus entails, among other impoverishments, a loss of roots and a dwindling of creativity. In spite of this interest, Coetzee found Rive's book to be superficial, concentrating too much on his overseas visits, with too little on his life as a writer in South Africa.

Athol Fugard's *Notebooks 1960–77* (1984)[55] was for Coetzee 'a record of the inner experience of a self-aware and articulate creative consciousness [...] [The *Notebooks*] are also the autobiography of a man of intelligence and conscience who chose to remain in South Africa at a time when many fellow-writers were opting for (or being forced into) exile.' Confronted with a government characterised by a remarkably loveless approach to its subjects (or some of them), Fugard revealed the meagre portions of love in the hearts of people inhabiting this lovely country. For Fugard the great problem was the way in which the dignity of life, and in particular the life of the black man, was affected. Fugard, Coetzee writes,

> is close enough to the Afrikaner to know that the humiliation of the weak by the strong has been a characteristic practice of the Afrikaner within his own culture, a practice underpinned by a perhaps perverted reading of Scripture which gives inordinate emphasis to authority and its converse, abasement. The humbling of children by parents, of students by teachers, and generally of the younger by the older (the uninitiated by the initiated) — humbling that does not cease until face has been lost — is part of the life experience of most Afrikaners, and is kept alive, against liberalizing counterforces, by such institutions as the armed forces, which reach into most white households. There are many authoritarian societies on earth, but Afrikanerdom strikes one as a society in which castration is allotted a particularly blatant role.

For him, this mindset is what gave birth to the idea of white supremacy.

An Afrikaans novel published in the 1980s that Coetzee valued very highly was Karel Schoeman's *'n Ander land* [*Another Country*].[56] This is the tale of the Dutchman Versluis, who, suffering from tuberculosis, travels to Bloemfontein, hoping to find a cure in the dry climate, only to discover that no cure is possible any more. The sojourn in the alien, initially hostile, country leads to the discovery that the South African landscape ultimately exerts a hold on you, and that under the civilised exterior of people there is a deeper spiritual self. Coetzee finds it a novel virtually without any dramatic events, concentrating only on daily life and social occasions, all seen through the eyes of Versluis. The novel is 'a symphonically constructed work in which the *weight* of all the slow, stately preparation is architecturally necessary to give the ending its correct proportions'. For Coetzee the climax of the novel occurs when Versluis is virtually forced one evening to watch by the bedside of the clumsy, young, rude Dutchman Gelmers—who, like Versluis, is suffering from his lungs—only to have the young man die in his arms. A question that occupies Versluis in his conversations with the two Germans, Scheffler and his sister Adèle, is what place European culture has in Africa, a vital issue for Coetzee, considering, for instance, his acceptance speech for the CNA Prize for *Waiting for the Barbarians*.

For Coetzee there is a lack of congruence between the European consciousness and the reality of Africa, the meaning of Africa and how it can be known. 'The thesis of the novel,' he writes, 'is clearly that it becomes possible to live in Africa once you have accepted that you will die in Africa. But this thesis is not what will remain with the reader from his reading. What will remain rather is the feeling of having been carried forward in the symphonic movement of the novel from a stage of doubt and alienation to a stage of reconciliation and acceptance.' Coetzee goes on to speak of Schoeman's 'superlative art, whose virtue is to be an art that conceals art. [...] I cannot think of any Afrikaans prose that matches the sober magnificence of the last pages.' When he was asked in December 1985 by the *Weekly Mail* to name his book of the year, Coetzee chose *'n Ander land*: 'It's one of the most beautiful pieces of writing I've read for a long while.'[57]

In these years Coetzee's most comprehensive work in literary criticism and what he calls the 'culture of letters in South Africa' was a series of articles of which the earliest was published in 1980 in *English in Africa*, and which was eventually collected in 1989 as *White Writing*, a joint publication by Yale University Press and (for the South African market) Radix, an imprint of Century Hutchinson. As against Richard Rive's *Writing Black*, Coetzee characterises the *White Writing* of his title as writings 'generated by the concerns of people no longer European, not yet African'.[58] The volume comprises seven essays dealing with themes like 'Idleness in South Africa', 'The Picturesque, the Sublime and the South African Landscape', the way in which South Africa is represented in poetry, the use of language in Pauline Smith and Alan Paton, racial degeneration as depicted in the novels of Sarah Gertrude Millin, and the '*plaasroman*' [farm novel], an Afrikaans word that he internationalised through his study of the work of C.M. van den Heever and others, and that was later taken up by other critics pursuing the same train of enquiry. For his essay on the *plaasroman* and C.M. van den Heever, the English Academy of Southern Africa awarded him his second Thomas Pringle Prize.

One of the ideas that Coetzee investigates in *White Writing* is that after the European settlement on the southern tip of Africa, the myth of a garden, a return to the innocent Eden, never found expression in literature here. Unlike America, which aroused a kind of geographical excitement in the explorers, and which introduced them to people 'in a state of original innocence',[59] Africa was part of a known Old World, 'peopled by natives whose way of life occasioned curiosity or disgust but never admiration'.[60] When British travellers explored the interior of South Africa in the nineteenth century, they found both the natives and the Afrikaans Boers in a brute state, lazy and stupid. In the pastoral novels the farm is a bastion of familiar feudal values, ruled over by a kind-hearted patriarch, a white world, with the black or coloured labourers at most on the periphery or present for comic effect. The farm is thus, as in Olive Schreiner, a microcosm of colonial South Africa, a small community set against the enormity of nature, 'pettiness in the midst of vastness',[61] in which, as in Pauline Smith, something of the rural order of England is transplanted to South Africa. In C.M. van den Heever rural values are extolled as against the 'evil' city, a legacy that the descendants of the pioneers have to safeguard, even when creditors, people without visible traditions or ancestors, want to claim it.

On the other hand the land is experienced as empty, still and old, a land of stone and sun, hostile, barren. This is depicted, for instance, as Coetzee says, in J.H. Pierneef's 'scenes of empty plains, blank mountains, and towering skies'.[62] The question Coetzee poses is whether there is a language in which people of European descent can talk about Africa—a central problematic for him, and one that he discerns also in those poets, English as well as Afrikaans, from whose work he quotes.

Coetzee would later strike a similar chord in his essay on the nineteenth-century English South African poet Thomas Pringle: 'Pringle rather uninventively assimilates his data under the categories provided for him by the dominant models of his time and place.'[63] In his essay 'Reading the South African landscape' Coetzee goes further. 'The questions that trouble white South African poets above all,' he writes, 'are whether the land speaks a universal language, whether the European can be at home in Africa',[64] or 'whether native African languages may not be in harmony with the landscape as European languages are not.'[65] Is there a language in which people of European identity or of problematic colonial descent can speak to Africa? Coetzee creates an image of the lonely, solitary poet trying to initiate a dialogue with Africa in an English that with its 'downs and fells, oaks and daffodils, robins and badgers'[66] is redolent of a very different kind of natural world. The true South African landscape, Coetzee writes, 'is of rock, not foliage'[67]—and here he is thinking of the Karoo and the farm Voëlfontein of his Coetzee grandfather, not of the Cape Peninsula with its winter rains in which one can sink into 'leafgreen dreams'[68] and picture in one's mind's eye the damp Surrey landscape. Coetzee talks, in relation to Schreiner's *The Story of an African Farm*, of 'the stony truth of Africa',[69] of Africa as a demanding rather than a bountiful mother, with the danger of an underlying prehistoric force threatening to erupt out of history, as in Roy Campbell's 'Rounding the Cape':

> The low sun whitens on the flying squalls,
> Against the cliffs the long grey surge is rolled
> Where Adamastor from his marble halls
> Threatens the sons of Lusus as of old.
>
> Faint on the glare uptowers the dauntless form,
> Into whose shade abysmal as we draw,
> Down on our decks, from far above the storm,
> Grin the stark ridges of his broken jaw.[70]

Coetzee concludes his book with a paragraph on the idea of an uncommunicative Africa:

> In all the poetry commemorating meetings with the silence and emptiness of Africa—it must finally be said—it is hard not to read a certain historical will to see as silent and empty a land that has

been, if not full of human figures, not empty of them either; that is arid and infertile, perhaps, but not inhospitable to human life, and certainly not uninhabited. From William Burchell to Laurens van der Post, imperial writing has seen the truest native of South Africa the Bushman, whose romance has lain precisely in his belonging to a vanishing race. Official historiography long told a tale of how until the nineteenth century of the Christian era the interior of what we now call South Africa was unpeopled. The poetry of empty space may one day be accused of furthering the same fiction.[71]

Three literary scholars reviewing *White Writing* pointed out that Coetzee at times bases his argument on selective quotation, especially when he tries to support his notion of Africa seen as an empty land from arbitrarily selected examples.[72] This does not detract from the fact that South African poetry does often address the barrenness and inhospitability of Africa. Several commentators found *White Writing* one of the best collections of essays yet published on South Africa literature. Shaun Irlam wrote in *Modern Language Notes*, 103: 5, 1988:

> The strength of Coetzee's collection is to interrogate succinctly and acidly the presuppositions inhabiting the language with which 'white writers' have addressed and presumed to ventriloquize Africa. With an alert and responsive eye he discloses the mystifications and blindness inherent in European schemata for thinking Africa.[73]

Another group of essays that Coetzee wrote after his return from the US is grouped under the rubric 'popular culture' by David Attwell in *Doubling the Point*: essays such as that on rugby and on Captain America, which Coetzee himself denigrates as 'barely deserv[ing] the name of work'. Another series of essays written at this time and dealing with the Afrikaners, 'deserve,' according to him, 'a quiet death'. It is likely that these essays were elicited by the invitation from Melissa Baumann of *Harper's* magazine to write something on this subject.[74] In an article that *Fair Lady* reprinted in their edition of 28 May 1985, Coetzee conducts interviews with a number of Afrikaners in the Stellenbosch area—not, according to him, a location known in earlier days for being a liberal sort of place. He is surprised to discover how open and receptive these people are to the imminent changes in South Africa, and how prepared they are to change their attitudes and way of life. In another article, 'The white tribe', in *Vogue* of March 1986, he expresses stronger criticism of Afrikaners who believe that the changes will entail a loss of their 'tribal culture' and will result in a merging of identities or a diaspora. Coetzee himself, however, does not make any claims for these essays. He said to David Attwell: 'I am afraid that at a certain stage of my career—the mid-1980s—I slipped a little too easily into the role of commentator on South African affairs. I have no talent for that kind of political/ sociological journalism. To be more specific, I am too suspicious of the genre, of the vision it locks its practitioners into, to give myself wholly to it, yet I lack enough zeal to try to turn it upside down or inside out. Anyhow, I am far too bookish, far too ignorant about real people, to set myself up as an interpreter, much less a judge, of the lives they live.'[75]

VI

When Coetzee began his lectureship in English at UCT, a new regime was instituted by David Gillham, a regime that sought to impose a dated form of 'practical criticism', modelled on the teachings of F.R. Leavis, on all members of the department. As an academic Leavis had reacted fiercely to the philological studies which were in vogue at Cambridge, and of which Guy Howarth, Gillham's predecessor, had also been an exponent. Leavis, and Gillham after him, found this kind of factual 'scholarship' futile. Leavis also believed that no theoretical discussion of literature should be sustained for too long without recourse to critical practice. Gillham went even further. He found it unnecessary for any attention to be devoted in his department to the theory of literature. Like Leavis, he wanted lecture courses to be devoted to the 'great tradition', the great writers of British literature, with no space for writing originating in the colonies.

It was to be expected that Coetzee, with his extensive knowledge of the latest trends in literary theory, would not be happy with this. He was appalled at the fact that all South African literature and the writings of prominent writers in other former colonies were excluded, other than perhaps a few works prescribed in the first year. Gillham had not published prolifically: his single major publication, *Blake's Contrary States: The 'Songs of Innocence and Experience' as Dramatic Poems*,[76] was a reworking of his doctoral thesis. Coetzee, on the other hand, was producing, apart from his creative work, important critical studies. It would not be surprising if Gillham soon began to see Coetzee as a threat to his status as head of department, and he may even have resented his prominence. Gillham apparently did not realise that Coetzee was not in the least interested in burdening himself with a power base such as the headship, with all the red tape that it entailed. All he wanted was to reach a position in which he could teach his subject in peace and with his own insights, and carry on with his own creative work and research.

Colleagues complained that Gillham was autocratic in his dealings with them. He would, for instance, check their library orders, and scrap some of the titles, without informing the lecturer concerned. He would at times interfere when a lecturer had, according to him, awarded too high a mark to a student; and would moderate the mark. When one lecturer objected to this procedure, Gillham suggested that they take the matter to the dean or even higher in the university hierarchy, leaving the colleague intimidated.[77]

In spite of the friction between him and Gillham,[78] Coetzee was promoted to senior lecturer and fellow, and at the beginning of 1981 was promoted ad hominem to associate professor. Perhaps Coetzee weathered the tension in the department thanks to his long spells as visiting lecturer at various US universities. In the first semester of 1984 he studied and lectured at the State University of New York at Buffalo, and in 1985 and again in 1989 spent a semester in each year at the Johns Hopkins University in Baltimore.

Nevertheless, Gillham's methods of imposing his own views on the teaching of literature violated Coetzee's every principle of academic freedom. In Buffalo, before his return to South Africa in 1971, Coetzee had experienced a department in which all members of the academic staff, down to the most junior lecturer, could contribute to decisions. Gillham was set on being the sole authority. He had been known to contend that the democratic model was not desirable for an academic department at a university: the ecclesiastical model, with its clear hierarchy, was more appropriate.[79] In appointing new lecturers, he saw to it that his sycophants got the jobs, people who would not question his authority.

The discord between Coetzee and Gillham thus had an ideological basis, but it also often caused personal friction between them. Coetzee was carrying a full lecturing load, which he had to combine with his research and creative work. With the dissolution of his and Philippa's marriage he also had to look after two small children who needed

368 J.M. COETZEE: A LIFE IN WRITING

a lot of care and had to be carted to school every day and collected again. Gillham, however, was intransigent, and would allow no relief in Coetzee's lecturing load, not even when after publication of *Waiting for the Barbarians* he was accorded international recognition.

The university authorities, however, were not blind to the importance of Coetzee's work and the prestige his publications brought the University of Cape Town. In a letter of 4 August 1983 he was informed by the registrar that he had been promoted ad hominem to the rank of full professor. Gillham had no choice but to tolerate this promotion, though it is very doubtful that he had initiated it.

In order to continue with both his creative and his critical work, Coetzee was starting to consider reducing his commitments to a part-time basis, but this, too, Gillham would not countenance. This prompted Coetzee in July 1984, upon returning from six months' leave in the US, to bypass Gillham and appeal directly to Professor A.D. Carr, the vice-principal charged with academic matters. In a lettter of 24 July 1984 he writes that while he was in the US he had been approached by several universities to join their faculty, both in a full-time and a visiting capacity. He had promised a response by September. He continues:

My personal inclination is to refuse, and to maintain the connection with Cape Town and with UCT. However, the fact is that I have never enjoyed working in the English Department; and I doubt that things will improve under a new Head, given the people who have been appointed to tenured posts in the Department during the past twelve years. Furthermore, it no longer makes financial sense for me to spend most of my energies on undergraduate teaching which could be done as well or better by any competent younger lecturer.

I would therefore like to work out a *modus vivendi* that would allow me:

(1) to retain my position at UCT;

(2) to take leave, including leave of absence, fairly regularly;

(3) to reduce my connection with the administration and day-to-day operation of the English Department to a minimum; and

(4) to reduce my teaching load.

I don't know whether there are precedents for such an arrangement, but it does not strike me as impossible to work out, particularly if I take a cut in pay.

There was now, Carr realised, an imminent danger that UCT could lose the services of Coetzee. He knew it would be an irreparable loss and unmitigated disaster. Carr brought the matter to the attention of Dr Stuart Saunders, the principal of UCT, who called an urgent meeting with Carr and Coetzee on 23 August 1984. The day after the meeting Coetzee put to paper his revised role, as he envisaged it for himself, in the Department of English:

1. I will teach the following courses, and conduct the following supervisions, in the Department of English:

(a) Supervise up to two PhD theses concurrently.

(b) Supervise up to four M.A. theses concurrently.

(c) Teach two one-semester Honours courses per year. (These courses will involve one 90-minute class per week, plus consultation times.)

(d) Supervise up to four Honours dissertations per year. (Each dissertation counts as one-fifth of the Honours candidate's programme.)

(In all, this quota equals slightly over half of the present load carried by full-time members of the department.)

1. I will be relieved of routine administration duties in the department, though I will remain eligible for Faculty and Senate duties.

2. I will retain the rank of Professor, and my rights as a full-time tenured member of the academic staff will be unaffected.

3. Like any other academic officer, I will be expected to carry on academic research.

4. I will remain eligible for Department, Faculty and University research awards.

5. It will be understood that, from time to time, I may apply for periods of Special Leave, unpaid, with rights, to pursue research and creative work.

6. My salary will be that of a Senior Lecturer at the top notch of the Senior Lecturers' scale.

Coetzee concludes his letter:

> I should like to express my appreciation to you and Professor
> Carr for giving me a chance to redefine my relationship with the
> Department of English. At the same time I believe that, when it is
> taken into account that the reduction in my teaching commitment
> would be balanced by a drop in salary, the arrangement I propose is
> not unfair to the University.

On the same day as writing his letter to Saunders, Coetzee wrote to
Gillham, saying that since his return from the US it had become clear
to him that he could not continue to shoulder a full lecturing load as
at present, while also continuing with his research and creative work.
For that reason he had appealed to Vice-Principal Carr for a review
of his contractual commitment to the university. Since this, after a
conversation between him, Carr and the principal, would probably lead
to a reduction in his work load from the beginning of 1985, he thought
it appropriate that Gillham be informed of these developments.

Gillham refrained, perhaps prudently, from replying in writing, but
it is clear he was not happy with Coetzee's proposed reduction of duties.
From Coetzee's reaction, in a letter of 3 September 1984, it is possible
to deduce Gillham's objections:

> I have given some thought to both the general and specific reser-
> vations you have expressed regarding the proposal I have made for
> a reduced teaching and administrative role in the department.
>
> I cannot agree with your view that, if I do not teach under-
> graduate courses, few students will know who I am and therefore few
> students will enrol for whatever Honours courses I teach. Honours
> students have to submit their choice of courses for approval, and it
> has always been department policy that their choice should be an
> academically balanced one. I therefore see no reason why students
> should not be steered into my courses, when these are appropriate
> to their interests.
>
> You also say that the change I propose is likely to cause bad feeling
> among senior members of the department. Whether it will in fact
> do so I cannot say. The changed proportions in my responsibilities
> to the University in the areas of teaching, administration and
> research will be accompanied by a cut in salary. I would expect that

the University administration would see to it that the salary arrived at was a just one. So if there is bad feeling, I cannot concede that it would be justified, particularly in view of the fact that the University employs Research Professors who are paid a full professorial salary in return for a research commitment and only minor teaching duties — duties certainly slighter than those I have offered to take on.

I understand your wish that members of the department should teach across the full range of courses from English I to Honours, and take a fair share of the department's administrative chores. I do not think that anyone would claim that since 1972 I have not done precisely this. However, I am at a point in my career at which it has begun to seem pointless to me to spread my energies so widely, and perhaps so thinly. The entire thrust of my proposal is that the time I put into teaching would henceforth be concentrated at the Honours and post-graduate levels, where it would have a direct relation to my research interests.

It seems to me that at this point my career interests and your interests, as Head of Department, diverge. I understand your point of view, and even sympathize with it. Nevertheless, I wish to continue to urge the proposal I have made, in its original form.

Today it is common practice for universities to allow creative artists to perform creative labour, with a much reduced academic commitment, even on full salary. It is strange that Gillham could or would not see that the prestige of his department and university was much enhanced by Coetzee's presence. Even during and after Coetzee's negotiations with Carr and Saunders he persisted in his unyielding attitude. In the meantime Coetzee wrote to Carr that in the light of the encouraging conversation with him and the principal, he had decided to decline the offer of a job at SUNY at Buffalo. He was doing it in full confidence that a modus vivendi could be arrived at for him in the department and that a new lecturer would be appointed to take over his undergraduate work in 1985.

That Gillham found it difficult to agree to Coetzee's altered commitments appears from a confidential note that Carr wrote to Coetzee on 25 September 1984:

We [Gillham and Carr] have come to a somewhat uneasy truce on this matter but the essential thing is that we can proceed into next year with you remaining in the Department of English under the conditions which you find acceptable. Should this not work out for various reasons, then we will look at other options which would be acceptable to you.

I received your note stating that you have decided not to take up an appointment at Buffalo and am very pleased indeed. We can use people of your calibre on this campus and look forward to your being here under conditions which will enable you to continue your writing.

On the same date Carr wrote to Gillham, a letter which, if read between the lines, more or less compelled him to accept the amended conditions of service Coetzee had negotiated. Carr refers to Saunders's sense of the importance of Coetzee's continued involvement in research and teaching for the university. He realises that Gillham does not agree that Coetzee should be granted a special and sheltered position in relation to other members of the English Department; but, although the arrangement arrived at does not accord with Gillham's preferences, Carr requests him to resign himself to the decisions taken in this regard by Saunders and himself. For the sake of completeness he details Coetzee's work load, as agreed upon, on the understanding that the arrangements are temporary, until they have managed to create alternatives acceptable to both Coetzee and the university.

By the time Gillham retired in 1986, the Department of English, which had a long history of discord and friction among colleagues, had, through many reforms gradually introduced, become a happier place to work in. Over the years it developed into one of the most prominent English departments in South Africa, with members of staff such as Geoffrey Haresnape, Ian Glenn, Kelwyn Sole, Stephen Watson, Lesley Marx, Rodney Edgecombe and Dorothy Driver. The department also initiated undergraduate courses in creative writing, led by Stephen Watson, giving the kind of guidance to aspirant writers that Guy Howarth had initiated in the 1950s, though then not as part of the academic programme. From 1993 Coetzee instituted an honours course in creative writing that gradually expanded to an M.A. and beyond, reinforced by the appointment to the English Department of André Brink, who had been Professor in Afrikaans and Dutch at Rhodes University. Coetzee and Brink's collaboration dates from this time. In an interview Coetzee later elaborated on their relations as colleagues:

I've known André since the middle of the seventies, I worked together with him on an anthology. Although we worked at a distance,
I really enjoyed working with him. He is efficient, practical and an
intelligent person; not at all the type of person which you get to
know from all the talking around him. Later he joined the UCT's
English Department and again we worked together, particularly with
postgraduate students, working with M.A. Literary Studies (an M.A.
by coursework), and M.A. Creative Writing. I attended classes he gave
and he attended some of my classes, and I was always impressed with
the response he received from students. He seemed to me a better
academic than most of my colleagues. He read more, he thought
more, he was an excellent teacher and it was a pleasure to work with
him. We also met socially, there was a certain 'circle' around the
French Embassy, diplomatic people concentrating only on cultural
life ... We got along very well. I like him, get on with him and admire
him.[80]

VII

In the 1970s, while John and Philippa's marriage was disintegrating,
Dorothy Jane Driver, the younger sister of Jonty Driver, was studying
English Literature at Rhodes University in Grahamstown. She was born
on 22 July 1946 in Grahamstown and is slightly more than six years
younger than Coetzee.[81]

In 1974 Dorothy completed her M.A. under the supervision of Nick
Visser, an American lecturer at Rhodes, whom she married. He later
moved to the Department of English at UCT, where he died at an early
age of pancreatic cancer.

In the years 1973–1976 Dorothy was a junior lecturer in the English
Department at Rhodes, and also assistant editor of *English in Africa*. After
that she worked for what was later to be known as the National English
Literary Museum (NELM). One of her tasks was to obtain manuscripts
from authors for the museum, but because of her rather timid manner
she was not very successful at this. As Dorothy was the sister of Jonty,
with whom Coetzee had been firm friends since their student days, Nick
Visser wrote to him in 1979 asking him if they could visit him in Cape
Town. The visit was a success and Dorothy, who had by then read *In
the Heart of the Country*, was impressed with Coetzee's intellect, charm,

friendly manner and good looks. He was obliging enough to give her a copy of the proofs of *Dusklands* for NELM's collection.

As an employee of NELM, she had to attend a conference on censorship at UCT in 1980, where Coetzee would also be. Coetzee's marriage had ceased to exist in all but name, and Dorothy's marriage to Nick Visser was also on the rocks. On this visit John and Dorothy saw much of each other, and fell in love. In December Coetzee turned up in Grahamstown with a pickup truck, packed up all of Dorothy's possessions, and on Christmas Day they travelled back to Cape Town together. Dorothy was sure Coetzee was the right man for her. In Cape Town each had a separate home, though they were often together.

In Cape Town Dorothy worked for the publishers Maskew Miller for a year, mainly dealing with books prescribed for schools. Although she was pleased to be in Cape Town, this was an extremely unhappy year for her, because the whole setwork system, she discovered, was corrupt. In 1982 she was appointed as assistant lecturer in English at UCT, later to be promoted to lecturer and senior lecturer, in 1993 to associate professor and in 1997 to full professor. Her doctoral dissertation, which she completed at Rhodes in 1986, was on the author Pauline Smith. Over the years she often delivered papers at conferences, and she has been a visiting professor in the US and Australia. Her publications deal mainly with South African English literature and women's and gender studies.

In Dorothy Driver John Coetzee found a partner who complemented him well. She is always his first reader, and she can tell him where her attention flags, where he could tighten up things slightly and where he could improve his choice of words. He listens to her, though at times he follows his own head. They often tease each other about matters pertaining to their subject. But apart from their professional bond, they are emotionally well matched and share interests not restricted to literature. Dorothy was moved when Philippa, after meeting her, told her she wished John only the best and wanted to see him happy.

CHAPTER 11

A FIRST BOOKER PRIZE AND A
ROBINSONADE

I

In the 1980s the protest actions by black South Africans escalated, fanned by the crisis in black education, the hostility to the tricameral parliament making no provision for black people, and the increased rents levied by the discredited and corrupt controlling bodies in the local black management councils. Within the ranks of the ANC and its military wing, Umkhonto we Sizwe (the Spear of the Nation), individuals branded as agents of the government or sell-outs were savagely dealt with. Black members of the police were primary targets. In 1985 the ANC changed to a strategy of 'people's war', aimed at making the country ungovernable. The guerrilla activities of earlier were linked with mass mobilisation.[1] Strikes, processions, boycotts and attacks proliferated, the houses of black policemen were firebombed and police informants were killed by having a petrol-filled car tyre 'necklace' put around their neck and set alight.

When Nadine Gordimer spoke before the New York Institute of the Humanities in 1982, the title of her address was 'Living in the Interregnum'. She started by sketching the stormy atmosphere in Johannesburg in those days: 'I live at 6 000 feet in a society whirling, stamping, swaying with the force of revolutionary change. [...] It is not for nothing that I chose as an epigraph for my novel *July's People* a quotation from Gramsci: "The old is dying, and the new cannot be born; in this interregnum there arises a great diversity of morbid symptoms."'[2]

In an attempt to contain the riots, the burning of schools, the gang violence of a 'lost generation', the necklace murders and other militant situations, P.W. Botha in 1985 declared a state of emergency in certain districts, granting the government well-nigh unlimited powers. The state of emergency was imposed on the whole country in 1986, in terms of which the United Democratic Front (UDF) and other

affiliated organisations were banned in 1988 and the Congress of South
African Trade Unions (COSATU) was prohibited from involving itself
in political activities.[3] The extent of the intervention can be deduced
from a statement by the minister of law and order that in 1985 close to
19000 people (of whom 72 per cent were under the age of 20) were
arrrested on unrest-related charges, including public violence, arson
and murder. In spite of its sweeping powers to detain suspected activists,
the government could not contain the resistance. This led to the
escalating liquidation of people seen as enemies of the state. According
to David Welsh:

> Many of the killers who formed the death squads were psychopaths
> with criminal records who appeared to derive considerable job
> satisfaction from their activities. The most notorious of the death
> squad camps was Vlakplaas, a farm near Pretoria that had been
> acquired by the police in the late 1970s for the purpose of 'turning'
> so-called 'askaris' — that is, inducing captured black guerrillas — to
> work for the security forces, invariably by none-too-gentle methods.
> Two of Vlakplaas's commanders, Dirk Coetzee and Eugene de Kock,
> became legendary killers. De Kock [...] was involved in killing some
> 70 people between 1983 and 1993.[4]

Conditions in South Africa prompted Desmond Tutu, winner of
the Nobel Peace Prize in 1984 and Anglican Archbishop of Cape Town
since 1986, to advocate international sanctions to force the government
to negotiations. From the mid-1980s international resistance to the
government's apartheid policies increased in severity. There was a worldwide campaign to release Nelson Mandela and other detained leaders.
Economic pressure on the country became more stringent when the US
Chase Manhattan Bank announced it would not be extending its short-
term loans to South Africa, a move followed by similar cancellations by
other organisations. Pik Botha, minister of foreign affairs, advocated
a crucial change of direction in the government's policies, which
P.W. Botha was widely expected to announce in a speech at the Natal
congress of the National Party. The international expectation was that
Botha, who had assumed the mantle of executive state president, would
announce sweeping changes and the release of Mandela. But Botha's
'Rubicon' speech turned out to be a huge let-down. He was, as he put
it, not prepared to deliver white South Africans to the communists and

to lead them down the road of surrender and suicide. Mandela and his sympathisers would be released only when they forswore violence. Within days of this speech the South African currency unit plummeted to an all-time low. The US Congress prohibited all new investment in South Africa, a decision emulated by the Commonwealth, which banned all imports from South Africa.

Apart from the internal unrest, the government in the late 1980s had to contend with the activities of Swapo (South West Africa People's Organisation) on its northern border. In 1986 Van Zyl Slabbert resigned as a member of parliament and leader of the opposition, saying that the white-dominated parliament had become irrelevant to the solution of South Africa's problems. On the initiative of Slabbert and Breyten Breytenbach, a first meeting took place in 1987 in Dakar between leading members of the Afrikaans community and exiled members of the ANC, a meeting followed by a gathering of Afrikaans writers and intellectuals at the Victoria Falls in Zimbabwe for discussions with the ANC.[5]

J.M. Coetzee did not respond directly to the political developments in the 1980s, although he had opposed all forms of apartheid ever since he became conscious of the political situation. The National Party, with the help of the Afrikaner Party, had assumed power when he was eight years old, and started reversing the course of history. 'Apartheid,' he wrote in 1991 in an essay on the mindset of Geoff Cronjé, the theoretician of apartheid in the 1940s, 'is a dream of purity, but an impure dream. It is many things, a mixture of things; one of the things it is, is a set of barriers that will make it impossible for the desire to mix to find fulfillment.'[6] 'Its programs,' he said in 1992 in one of his interviews with David Attwell,

> involved a radically discontinuous intervention into time, in that it
> tried to stop dead or turn around a range of developments normal
> (in the sense of being the norm) in colonial societies. It also aimed at
> instituting a sluggish no-time in which an already anachronistic order
> of patriarchal clans and tribal despotisms would be frozen in place.
> This is the political order in which I grew up.[7]

In addition, the culture in which he was educated was permeated with a 'home' mentality nostalgically harking back to a little corner of England that had no relevance to the realities of South Africa.

Reviewing Mary Benson's *Nelson Mandela: The Man and the Movement* in 1986,[8] Coetzee wrote that if the South African government had reached some kind of accord with the ANC in the 1950s, they would have had a predominantly peaceful movement under a petit-bourgeois social-democratic leadership to deal with. Instead they had branded the movement as subversive and its leaders as instruments of international communism. In the 1980s the regime found itself in the ironical position that it could not, without a humiliating loss of face, release those same leaders it had arraigned in 1964. Whether the apartheid government had won any time by banning the ANC was open to question, because in 1986 they were up against a mass movement of far greater rebellious and seditious power than that of a quarter of a century earlier, and one that had international opinion squarely behind it. Coetzee posed the question whether the old guard of the ANC, if they were to be released, would be capable of containing the power that embitterment and fury had built up in the black community, and of leading the way to the utopia of liberty, fraternity and equality and to the prosperity of which the Freedom Charter spoke. His answer to this was prophetic: it would depend largely on the personality of Mandela and how he acted after his release. Mandela's incarceration had by no means removed him from the public eye in South Africa.

By 1980 the concept of 'Mandela on Robben Island' had, according to Mary Benson, achieved near-mythic proportions. His face, on T-shirts and posters, was to be seen all over, and the slogan 'Free Mandela' was daubed on the walls of prisons and public buildings alike. Nevertheless the Reagan and Thatcher administrations in the US and Britain respectively still cherished the view that the stronger the South African economy, the greater Botha's capacity to bring about a new dispensation. The contrary view was that the Afrikaners would be prepared to negotiate only when South Africa was isolated and under military and economic pressure. Those who saw Botha as a reformer advanced the argument that he was able to make his reforms acceptable to a terrified white electorate only by misleading them—by wearing a mask of intransigence while negotiating behind the scenes for power sharing. Those who saw him simply as the last in a line of defiantly bellicose Afrikaner nationalists pointed to the gap between his promises and his insignificant achievements. Both interpretations, Coetzee wrote, made him out to be a public liar, having to mislead either the South African public or international opinion.

In his review of *White Boy Running* by Christopher Hope,[9] a South African by birth who had lived in England since 1975, Coetzee also pronounced on the South African politics of the day. In 1987 P.W. Botha called an election for the white electorate to approve his gradual reform of apartheid, a process that according to Coetzee was proceeding at a snail's pace. The election was fought without any particular battles or issues, and was won by the National Party. The only surprise was that the far-right Conservative party emerged as the second-strongest party, leaving behind the Progressive Federal Party with its ethnic base among the English-speaking whites. Christopher Hope's point of view in his book is that there is no such thing as a South African nation, only a conglomerate consisting of antagonistic groups. Coetzee writes, and one feels that he is here to an extent identifying with Hope:

> Part of the trauma of his [Hope's] coming of age in South Africa, he records, was realizing that there was no place in this Afrikaner-Calvinist homeland for an English-speaking Catholic of mildly anti-social tendencies who hated, above all, the 'stultifying, lethally boring business of having to belong to a group in the first place. [...] The sense of exile we felt within our own country is something which has never left me. We were a generation that went into exile before we left home.'

Nevertheless, just as Coetzee returned in 1971, Hope never severed his ties with South Africa. He writes: 'this place is a fever, an infection, a lingering childhood disease I simply cannot get over'. These words are reminiscent of Coetzee's own declaration of love for the meagre landscape of the Karoo and the rude beauty of the Cape Peninsula, as expressed in the words of Elizabeth Curren in *Age of Iron*: 'These seas, these mountains: I want to burn them upon my sight so deeply that, no matter where I go, they will always be before me. I am hungry with love of this world.'[10]

Coetzee did not react in articles or declarations to the riots, the violence and the actions of Umkhonto we Sizwe in the 1980s. His next novel, however, which was eventually to be called *The Life & Times of Michael K*, resonates with a sense of the 1980s, even though it is nominally placed in a near future, with the country on the verge of a race war. According to the dating of the first version of the manuscript, Coetzee started work on this novel on 31 May 1980. At first he employed various story lines, a multitude of characters and frequently revised configurations, among others with the protagonist as a first-person narrator, which he later rejected. Six handwritten versions produced a completed manuscript on 12 July 1982, more than two years after the start. A first typescript was completed on 29 September 1982, followed by a more final version, with corrections in pencil, which was completed on 28 February 1983.

The fact that Coetzee started writing this novel more than four months before the publication of *Waiting for the Barbarians* suggests that creative labour had become a daily necessity for him. Asked in an interview by Stephen Watson whether writing exerted a certain compulsion on him, he replied: 'It's far from a compulsion. It's bad if I do write and worse if I don't.' He has to observe certain artificial rules to make sure that everything does not fall apart, 'such as not skipping a day or else the temptation to skip another day becomes too great'.[11] He told Edwin Hart that he worked very slowly, taking about two years over a novel, at first writing with a pen and making many alterations.[12] As with his first novels, he continued, it was his habit to pen his designs early in the morning, when he was fresh, then to rewrite again and again, restarting frequently, until it was in a satisfactory shape. It was only then that he started typing the manuscript, refining it further in pencil as he went. At this stage of his life Coetzee found it difficult to manage his creative work along with looking after the household and attending to his children as well as his duties as a lecturer, from which he had not yet been granted grudging relief by David Gillham. He usually started working at five in the morning and continued until half-past seven. Then he took the children to school, after which he saw to his lectures and administration at the university, returning home to grade papers and prepare his lectures for the next day.[13]

When asked where particular novels originated and why he decided on a particular theme, Coetzee found it well-nigh impossible to reply. In an interview with Joanna Scott he said: 'I simply don't remember how books I have written started off. Part of the reason is that the beginnings generally get abandoned during the course of revision. If there's an archaeology of the book, then the beginnings are deep under the surface, under the soil.'[14] His view was that the book should speak for itself; otherwise the writer has failed in his duty. Asked whether there is a moment when he knows that something is a viable project, he replied: 'Yes, there is: when I've invested so much time in it that I can't afford to stop, can't afford to face the fact that I've wasted six months of my life, or whatever. So I soldier on, and the book gets written.'[15]

II

Unlike *Waiting for the Barbarians*, which is not set in a recognisable place or particular time, *Life & Times of Michael K* opens in a city identifiable as Cape Town from the naming of suburbs, specific places and streets. As against the first-person narration of his first three novels, Coetzee here in the larger part of the novel employs an omniscient third-person narrator focused on Michael K as protagonist.[16]

The action is situated in a relatively near future in which the country is on the brink of civil war as a result of constant violence and the consequent collapse of virtually all public services, though it is never clear which political parties or issues are in conflict. In an interview with Tony Morphet, Coetzee said that the geography in the novel was not quite as accurate as it seemed at first, because it was not a priority with him to create a precise version of the 'real' world. The alternative was to create an imagined world, as he had done in *Waiting for the Barbarians*, but that aspect of the earlier novel had been 'an immense labour', and would in any case not have made much sense in the case of *Michael K*.[17]

Although not explicitly stated, the immediate background of the novel, as Dominic Head has shown, is the social disintegration after the Soweto Uprising of 1976, the concerns and fears of the apartheid regime, and the attacks on the oil and coal industries in 1980 in an effort to make the country ungovernable.[18] In the novel various measures are in force, such as the introduction of a curfew and permits curtailing freedom of movement, in an attempt to contain the escalating chaos and lawlessness. Unlike in *Waiting for the Barbarians*, where evil is embodied in specific individuals, here it is the system in itself that is the primary vehicle of evil. Because the people oppressing Michael represent the institutional violence of South Africa, most of them are nameless. Their identity is less important than their role in the power structure; thus they are indicated only by their professions: the railway clerk, the policewoman at the desk, the nurse, the soldier, the shop assistant. By contrast with these anonymous bureaucrats, the institutions to which they are attached all have proper names.

Michael K—and, given Coetzee's admiration of Kafka, the reader can't miss the allusion to Joseph K's *The Castle* and *The Trial*[19]—has been fatherless since childhood, was born with a harelip and no great intellect. He grew up in the sombre and stifling atmosphere of an orphanage. Later he worked as a gardener in the city council's department of Parks and Gardens, a position he left to work as a night watchman at the public toilets on Greenmarket Square, before returning to Parks and Gardens to rake leaves in De Waal Park. Unlike in Coetzee's other novels, the central character is someone from a disadvantaged background, probably a coloured man, though his skin colour is never explicitly mentioned.

When Michael's elderly mother, a domestic servant with the Buhrmann family in a flat building in Sea Point,[20] starts suffering from dropsy and swollen legs, and her salary is cut by her employers, she tells Michael that she wants to return to the world of her youth on a farm in the Prince Albert district. Because the permits they need do not turn up and because they could be stopped by the police if they took a bus or a train, Michael decides to transport his ailing mother in a rebuilt wheelbarrow, a totally impractical vehicle for such a long journey—a detail demonstrating that Coetzee's novel does not aim to continue the realistic tradition of its predecessors in the travel tale. They get as far as Stellenbosch before his mother dies in hospital there. With her ashes, which he wants to scatter on the farm of her birth, he continues his voyage through the Karoo, where he sees signs of devastation everywhere. He is detained for a while to remove fallen rocks from the railway track through the Hex River Pass with a gang of hard-labour prisoners. Then he travels on, to be captivated by the silence of the Karoo, where he intends to realise the ideal of a peaceful, pastoral refuge by settling on a plot of land—a motif typical of the farm novels that Coetzee was at this time studying in the work of Olive Schreiner, Pauline Smith and C.M van den Heever, given a personal dimension through his love of this region, as later to be expressed in *Boyhood* and elsewhere.

It is in this landscape that Michael feels at home. 'I could live here forever, he thought, or till I die.'[21] When he reaches the farm that he assumes to be his mother's birthplace, his commitment to recover his true calling as a gardener returns as he plants the pumpkin seeds. The myth of a garden and the return to an innocent Eden, that according to Coetzee in *White Writing* never took hold with the arrival of the Dutch colonists at the Cape, now manifests itself in Michael's impulse to cultivate the land, with which he senses a connection. The dam speaks to him: 'He felt at home at the dam as he had never felt in the house. He lay down and rested with the black coat rolled under his head, watching the sky wheel above. I want to live here, he thought: I want to live here forever, where my mother and my grandmother lived.'[22]

His wish to own a plot of ground is denied by the arrival of a young man, the grandson of the absent farm owners. This grandson, a deserter from the army, recalls for Michael the gatherings of the extended Visagie family every Christmas, the house bursting at the seams with all the visitors: 'I've never seen such eating as we used to do. Day after day my grandmother would pile the table with food, good country food, and we would eat every last scrap. Karoo lamb like you never taste any more.'[23] Coetzee is here reworking the persistent memory of the gatherings he experienced as a child on the family farm Voëlfontein, about which he was later to write in *Boyhood* and *Summertime*.

When the young Visagie tries to make a servant of him and send him to Prince Albert to do shopping, Michael foresees the imminent loss of the freedom he has started to taste in the Karoo, and the danger of being reduced to a vassal in service of a master. This reprises the theme of master and servant from Coetzee's first three novels. Michael takes refuge in the Swartberg, where he can maintain his freedom and live on roots and insects. He becomes so emaciated that he is eventually forced to return, but he is captured by soldiers near Prince Albert and taken to Jakkalsdrif, a labour camp, where he becomes aware of the condition of the other prisoners. The captain's diatribe, accusing the prisoners of not appreciating all that the rulers are doing for them, sounds not only like Eugene Dawn's reproach to the 'ungrateful' Vietnamese, but also echoes the complaint frequently heard in the apartheid years that the blacks did not appreciate the houses, schools and hospitals the government built for them:

> 'Yes, you, you ungrateful bastards, you, I'm talking about you!' he shouted. 'You appreciate nothing! Who builds houses for you when you have nowhere to live? Who gives you tents and blankets when you are shivering with cold? Who nurses you, who takes care of you, who comes here day after day with food? And how do you repay us? Well, from now on you can starve!'[24]

Michael manages to escape, returns to the farm, discovers that his plants have died, but hides in a hole in the ground and plants vegetables again. Once again close to starvation, he is discovered by soldiers who assume that he is providing food to the rebelling guerrillas.

Part II of the novel is narrated by a military doctor working at the hospital in Kenilworth where Michael is convalescing. The doctor, fascinated by Michael's refusal to eat, develops a strong interest in him and tries to get him to ingest something, not realising that it is exactly the 'detention' in hospital that is depriving him of any will to eat, except now and again a bit of pumpkin. When Noël says to the doctor that Michael will die of hunger if he doesn't eat, the doctor replies: 'It's not a question of dying. It's not that he wants to die. He just doesn't like the food here. Profoundly does not like it. He won't even take baby-food. Maybe he only eats *the bread of freedom.*'[25] Obsessed with his patient, the doctor even imagines that Michael is the product of a clumsy God: 'someone had scuffled together a handful of dust, spat on it, and patted it into the shape of a rudimentary man, making one or two mistakes [...], but coming up nevertheless in the end with a genuine little man of earth'.[26] David Ward comments that the allusion to *The Waste Land*[27] is not incidental, because, like T.S. Eliot, Coetzee sends his character on a quest through a desert. In spite of his physical deformity and his sexlessness, he can make the desert bloom in his Karoo garden. 'Once again, like Eliot,' Ward writes, 'he [Coetzee] sets his Man on his journey against the background of a sinister history, the collapse of human institutions in anarchy and barbarism. And last of all, like Eliot, the quest is in the end towards a desperate, minimal, preservation of self amidst the ruins.'[28]

According to Allister Sparks, on the authority of the author, Coetzee got the idea of the virtually fasting Michael from a newspaper report on a large panda that had been conditioned to eat only bamboo shoots, refusing all other food in captivity, and choosing rather to die.[29] Michael rejects all approaches from the doctor and escapes, to find his freedom again, in Part III of the novel, in the familiar domain of his mother's former room in Sea Point. 'I have escaped the camps,' he thinks to himself, 'perhaps, if I lie low, I will escape the charity too.'[30] Charity he sees as merely another form of oppression, through which he is reduced to a slave, forced to accept a relation in which the doctor exerts authority over him. Now once again referred to in the third person, Michael is back in Cape Town, where amid the war-ravished ruins he meets a few prostitutes who, like the doctor, treat him as an object of charity. Alone, wanting to go to sleep in his mother's deserted room, he considers the possibility that somebody looking for a travelling companion may want to join him:

It did not seem impossible that whoever it was who disregarded the curfew and came when it suited him to sleep in this smelly corner (K imagined him as a little old man with a stoop and a bottle in his side pocket who muttered all the time into his beard, the kind of old man the police ignored) might be tired of life at the seaside and want to take a holiday in the country if he could find a guide who knew the roads. They could share a bed tonight, it had been done before; in the morning, at first light, they could go out searching the back streets for an abandoned barrow; and if they were lucky the two of them could be spinning along the high road by ten o'clock, remembering to stop on the way to buy seeds and one or two other things, avoiding Stellenbosch perhaps, which seemed to be a place of ill luck.

And if the old man climbed out of the cart and stretched himself (things were gathering pace now) and looked at where the pump had been that the soldiers had blown up so that nothing should be left standing, and complained, saying 'What are we going to do about water?', he, Michael K, would produce a teaspoon from his pocket, a teaspoon and a long roll of string. He would clear the rubble from the mouth of the shaft, he would bend the handle of the teaspoon in a loop and tie the string to it, he would lower it down the shaft deep into the earth, and when he brought it up there would be water in the bowl of the spoon; and in that way, he would say, one can live.[31]

With this moving, imagined scene the novel ends. In an interview with Stephen Watson, Coetzee deprecated any placing of *Life & Times of Michael K* in a national or regional context:

I don't see any as forbears but I don't make that statement in any spirit of pride. This is not a great literature and there are no really gigantic figures in it. Those who are classed as gigantic, say Schreiner and Campbell, I don't happen to have much interest in. As for people writing nowadays … in practice one can read only so much, and I read mostly the stuff that, crudely speaking, I can cannibalize. There aren't many South African writers I feel like cannibalizing. If I want a good meal I go elsewhere. I read Nadine Gordimer because I think she's extraordinarily accomplished.[32]

If, however, one reads *Life & Times of Michael K* against the background of Coetzee's inquiry into the farm novel and the effect of landscape on South African literature, as in *White Writing*, it is clear that he took note of the work of his predecessors in this field, even if only to write against the tradition.[33]

Where there are similarities, as in *Life & Times of Michael K*'s kinship with the farm novel and the travel tale, he nevertheless, notably in the protagonist's yearning for an earthly paradise, deviates so much from his predecessors that the tradition at most serves as a cautionary counter-example. Coetzee has said in an interview with Hugh Roberton that he believes there are too many fictional situations in South African literature that have become stereotyped and exhausted by repetition, such as the white woman and the black man falling in love and being persecuted by the police, or the heroic black patriot resisting his sadistic interrogators.[34] This stricture would presumably apply even more strongly to the depiction of the 'evil' city and the return to the safe haven of the farm.

The mere fact that Coetzee immersed himself so thoroughly in the South African literary landscape preceding him, implies that he has in his creative work taken account of it *and* deviated from it. *Life & Times of Michael K* was, as Teresa Dovey puts it, generated in the first place by a specific reading of Kafka's texts,[35] as can be seen from a comparison of the novel with the allegorical *The Trial* and the short story 'The Burrow'. Susan van Zanten Gallagher writes: 'Coetzee is fully aware that his fictional mode is quite unusual for a South African writer, and he claims that he doesn't see any South African writers as his forbears. Instead, he lists Beckett, Nabokov, Pound, Rilke, Herbert, Neruda, and Barthes[36] as influences. However, influences can be both positive and negative, and Coetzee's awareness of the traditions of South African writing and his concern with how discourse informs thought suggest that South African writing might actually influence his work more than he admits.'[37]

III

On 19 May 1982 Coetzee wrote to Mike Kirkwood of Ravan Press: 'I am struggling with a novel I have been working on for a couple of years, and am hoping to have it finished by the end of the year.' Although he completed a more final typed version only in February 1983, Coetzee was by October so satisfied with the first typescript that he decided to submit it to his publishers. On 28 October 1982 he wrote to Kirkwood:

> I mailed today the typescript of a 65 000-word novel entitled *Life & Times of Michael K.* I hope you like it. Copies have gone off to my agents in New York[38] and London.[39] In the UK Tom Rosenthal has first option on it. But if both you and he like it enough, perhaps you could again come to some kind of arrangement.

The reaction of his publishers to this submission was exceedingly favourable. On 26 November 1982 Mike Kirkwood wrote: '*Life & Times* is superb, everything pared away until the understatement magically encounters a layer of unobvious, self-evident truth. What gentleness those familiar, unblinking sentences are now revealing ... and I think it deliciously appropriate that this work, which moves closest to registering the "real" ambience, should turn out to be the most metaphysical of any you've given us. It must have been a particularly difficult book to end, and I'd like to say that the cadence of the last section seems to me exactly, wonderfully right.'

Tom Rosenthal of Secker & Warburg sent an even more favourable response on 2 December 1982. Recently returned from the US, Rosenthal had cabled Coetzee immediately after reading the manuscript: 'Feeling totally disintegrated by this superb novel. Have offered terms to Murray.' He has never, he continues, believed in ranking books within the oeuvre of an author; thus it makes no sense to say whether *Life & Times of Michael K* is Coetzee's best book or not. 'What I do know,' he writes,

> is that it is an immensely disturbing one and I really cannot remember when the reading of a work of fiction has upset me so much.
>
> I always feel terribly nervous about writing to you and expressing my true feelings when what you write, while obviously universal, is also so close to the bone in local political terms so I will have to spare you that until we next meet.
>
> However, I have never come across so much cruelty, brutality, wanton wickedness and so on, expressed with such hopeless delicacy.
>
> If one thinks back over the narrative, barely a blow is struck and yet the horror is quite as bad as that of Mr Kurtz[40] and I do not invoke him lightly.

It is a book, he concludes, that 'we passionately [want] to publish. [...] We will definitely enter the book for the Booker Prize and would like to publish it therefore in the early autumn, that is something like the first week of September.'

In the same month, on 20 December 1982, Kathryn Court of Viking Penguin in New York wrote to say how impressed and moved she had been by the new novel: 'It is quite extraordinary how you are able to draw the reader into the mind of a character who on the surface seems very unappealing. I particularly loved the sections when he is on the veldt, aware of the minute changes all around him. I was amazed too by the ending of the novel which seemed to me to be a real celebration of the human spirit. I very much hope that Viking Penguin will publish it.'[41]

As far as the book's sombre impression on Rosenthal was concerned, Coetzee reassured him on 8 December: 'Perhaps you will feel less gloomy if I let you in on a little secret: "Michael K doesn't die."'[42]

In a letter of 11 February 1983 Rosenthal wrote that since his previous letter the manuscript had been edited by Alison Samuel, and that she had several questions for Coetzee. As the British publisher of Kafka's work, and he apologises if he sounds pompous, it is his duty as Coetzee's publisher 'to point out that the world is not full exclusively of lovely people and there might well be reviewers who object to the inevitable resonance of Kafka.' In a letter of 10 February 1983 Alison Samuel asks: 'Why "K"? Having read the book twice I'm almost persuaded that the name is Michael's property but not quite; Kafka still has the edge. It seems a hostage to fortune which the critics will latch onto. Have I missed something? If so, could you explain? If not, it seems to me that the name casts too long a shadow.'

No further letters have survived on the problem in relation to the letter K,[43] so it seems safe to assume the matter was discussed in a telephone conversation anticipated by Rosenthal in his letter. In any case, Coetzee did not change the name of his character.

Before production of the first edition, extracts from the novel appeared in Britain in the *Times Literary Supplement,* in the US in *Harper's* magazine, and in South Africa in *Contrast* and *Standpunte.* When the consignment arrived at the Cape Town docks, the customs, as in the case of *In the Heart of the Country* and *Waiting for the Barbarians,* embargoed it, and submitted copies to the censors. In her report, as chair of the committee of experts to which the book was sent, Rita Scholtz writes that the novel deals with specific sensitive political matters in South Africa. It 'contains derogatory references to and comments on the attitudes of the state, also to the police and the methods they employ in the carrying out of their duties'.[44] She is of the opinion, however, that the 'likely readers of this publication will be sophisticated & discriminating with an interest in literature'. They will experience the novel 'as a work of art & will realise that although the tragic life of Michael K is situated in South Africa, his problem today is a universal one, not limited to S. Africa'. She is convinced that the readers will find that 'this rich novel could be read on many levels — as a fable, as a comment on the human condition in South Africa or as a protest novel: in the sense that it protests against the way in which people are caught up in processes beyond their control'. She finds Michael K to be alienated from the world and therefore a 'puppet [...] thrown from one situation into another'. A scene that could easily run counter to the moral principles of some readers occurs fairly close to the end of the novel when a Sea Point prostitute sits down next to Michael after he has drunk brandy on an empty stomach and is feeling dizzy:

> There was whispering; then someone unbuttoned the last button of the overalls and slipped a cool hand in. K opened his eyes. It was the woman: she was kneeling beside him fondling his penis. [...] She bent down and took his penis in her mouth. He wanted to push her off but his fingers recoiled from the stiff dead hair of the wig. So he relaxed, allowing himself to be lost in the spinning inside his head and the faraway wet warmth. [...] [S]he lay down next to him on the driftsand, still holding his sex in her hand. [...] She smiled. Leaning on an elbow she kissed him full on the mouth, her tongue cleaving his lips. Vigorously she pulled on his penis.[45]

Scholtz finds this description of fellatio to be not morally repugnant or disgusting: 'when Michael K submits to this act it is the ultimate stage that he has reached as an object of pity. The probable reader will only feel compassion & sympathy when reading these two pages.' The other readers on the committee agreed with Scholtz, and the book was released for distribution in South Africa in November 1983.

The danger of a banning did not deter Ravan Press from publishing and marketing the book in South Africa. As in the case of *Waiting for the Barbarians*, Tom Rosenthal and Mike Kirkwood agreed that 5 000 copies of *Life & Times of Michael K* would be made available for distribution in South Africa under the Ravan Press imprint, but printed and bound in London.

IV

As early as August 1983 it was announced that *Life & Times of Michael K* had been submitted for consideration for the Booker Prize. Nadine Gordimer, until then the only South African winner, shared the prize in 1973 with J.G. Farrell. In 1983 the competition was stiff because as well as novels by John Fuller, Graham Swift, Anita Mason and Malcolm Bradbury, Salman Rushdie (who had won the Booker in 1981 with *Midnight's Children*) was also in the running with *Shame*. The panel comprised the novelist and feminist Fay Weldon as chair, and, as members, the fable writer and essayist Angela Carter; the Australian poet and critic Peter Porter; the literary editor of *The Observer* and Proust translator Terrence Kilmartin; and Libby Purves, the broadcaster and previous editor of *The Tatler*.

Meanwhile British reviewers, like those of *The Standard*, *The Guardian* and *The Times*, were full of praise for *Life & Times of Michael K*. In *The Guardian* of 27 September 1983 W.L. Webb writes:

> J.M. Coetzee's *Life & Times of Michael K* is a spare and bleakly beautiful book, a tour de force not least in presenting the world through the eyes and mind and senses of a poor and very simple man—a hare-lipped labouring gardener from the bottom of Cape Town's festering social heap. It is the world of an imminent South Africa, dissolving in the civil war so long expected, and in the course of his journey away from the storm centre all the casual brutality of that morbid society is revealed with irrefutable clarity. Coetzee shows us the human creature worn down to the bone and irreducible spirit, and does it in prose of bone-fine purity and simplicity.

The betting company Ladbrokes offered bets on the finalists for the Booker Prize. At one stage Graham Swift's *Waterland* was the favourite, but he dropped from 7–4 to 2–1, while Coetzee's novel rose from an outsider position of 4–1 to the favourite at 7–4, with Salman Rushdie's *Shame* on its heels at 5–2.[46]

Given Coetzee's valuing of his privacy and his tendency to shun literary social occasions, it was to be expected that such an affair would not be to his taste. Tom Rosenthal insisted by telephone that Coetzee should come to England, grant interviews and attend the dinner in Stationer's Hall on 26 October 1983, where the winner was to be announced. Coetzee, however, was not to be persuaded, even when Rosenthal mentioned the example of Anthony Burgess as warning that writers who don't attend, don't win. Coetzee wrote to Mike Kirkwood on 30 September 1983: 'After some thought I declined: I can't imagine anything better calculated to reduce me to misery than the Booker circus.' Rosenthal suggested that Coetzee should plead pressure of work at UCT rather than aversion to the ceremony as reason for not attending, and that, if Rosenthal could persuade them, declare himself willing to cooperate with a BBC team intending to make a programme composed of interviews with the finalists. This Coetzee consented to do.

On 26 October, in his absence, Coetzee was announced the winner of the Booker Prize. Fay Weldon pronounced very favourably on the novel: 'It is a novel of remarkable power and simplicity; a work of great inventiveness and imagination superbly controlled.' There were all kinds of sinister rumours to account for Coetzee's absence. A London radio station announced in a news bulletin that there had been speculations that the author would lose his job at UCT if he were to attend. According to *The Guardian*, the South African authorities (whoever they might be) had objected to his being absent from his work on campus during the academic year.[47] Those present at the occasion, though, saw a film in which an interview was conducted with Coetzee before announcement of the award. In it Coetzee said he was astounded when he was shortlisted, because he had considered the whole tenor of the book to be so South African that it could hardly arouse the interest of foreign readers. As reason for his absence he mentioned, apart from bashfulness, the exam period at UCT—a reason few writer-academics would have advanced. He said to the *Weekend Post*: 'I regret I was not able to be present. But it is a very busy time of the year at the university and I couldn't go off for days on end, leaving my colleagues to do all the work.'[48]

The Booker Prize brought Coetzee enormous sales and immediate canonical status, ensuring that his novel would be set at universities and schools. It transpired later that there had been vigorous differences of opinion among the members of the Booker panel, with half of them strongly favouring Salman Rushdie's *Shame*. Fay Weldon broke an

392 J.M. Coetzee: A Life in Writing

apparent deadlock by casting her deciding vote as chair in favour of Coetzee's novel just twenty minutes before the start of the evening's proceedings.[49]

On 27 October, the day after the announcement, many journalists were eager to get Coetzee's commentary. When he heard the news of the award, Coetzee disconnected his home phone, locked the front door of his house in Rondebosch, and left for UCT. All calls were directed to two helpful secretaries, who saw to it that not a single call was put through to Coetzee. One resourceful journalist even turned up on the doorstep of his empty house.[50] Years later, Lesley Marx, an ex-student of Coetzee's and later also a member of the English Department at UCT, recalled the day when the award was announced:

> Everyone was terribly excited. [...] People were phoning from all over, the bookshops were phoning, journalists wanted interviews. And one of these calls happened to come through to my office. I told this woman that she couldn't see or speak to him because he was invigilating an undergraduate exam. She was absolutely outraged: 'The Booker Prize winner invigilating an undergraduate exam! It is completely ridiculous! He should be treated like royalty, he should not do these humdrum prosaic kind of things!' But, you see, Coetzee's professionalism is so strong. That comes through in every aspect of my experience of working with him, apiece with his writing.[51]

To the journalist Jennifer Crwys-Williams, Coetzee expressed his dislike of unprepared journalists who wanted to interview him, and of bothersome people who wasted his time: 'They don't bother to prepare themselves, even to the extent of reading up what is on the flyleaf of one of my books. They don't even know my initials. Why should I give anything to them?'

V

At the time of the award of the Booker Prize, *Life & Times of Michael K* was still under embargo and under consideration by the censors. On 15 November 1983, a week after the arrival of the consignment in Cape Town and almost a month after announcement of the prize, the embargo was lifted and the book became available for distribution in South Africa.

Although the official version was that the embargo had been a mere 'formality' and that all consignments of books were examined before release, the opinion of academics was that a novel written by a South African that had achieved international prestige should not be subjected to the red tape of customs and censors. Professor Alan Lennox-Short, a colleague of Coetzee's in the English Department at UCT, said such actions could only harm South Africa abroad. Mike Kirkwood said in a declaration that the relaxing of censorship under Kobus van Rooyen was merely a relative and selective process, since the Act itself with all its restrictions was still in force. In a strongly worded letter, published on 9 November in *Beeld*, the journalist Wilhelm Grütter wrote that the whole handling of the embargo and the release of *Life & Times of Michael K* focused the attention on 'a few interesting principles':

> One of these is that the confiscation was described as a 'mere formality'. For this mere stupidity would have been a more accurate description. What was at issue was a work of such high literary value that it had then just been awarded one of the most sought-after international prizes of its kind.
>
> That, under these circumstances, cultural goods can be confiscated as a formality, is bad enough. That it can happen in the author's native land, is a blot on the international reputation of that country. [...]⁵²

Apart from the Booker Prize, *Life & Times of Michael K* received many accolades. In December 1984 the novel was included, along with Milan Kundera's *The Unbearable Lightness of Being*, Mario Vargas Llosa's *The War of the End of the World* and Saul Bellow's *Him with his Foot in his Mouth*, in *The New York Times Book Review*'s list of the fifteen best books that had appeared that year in the US, and in 1985 it received the Prix Femina Étranger—a new prize for foreign authors publishing in France—for the French translation. On 26 April 1984 the annual CNA Prize was awarded during a dinner at the Johannesburg Country Club, but of the winners only Henriette Grové was present, sharing the Afrikaans prize with Breyten Breytenbach, whose prize was collected on his behalf by Ampie Coetzee of Taurus publishers.

At the time of the awards ceremony, Coetzee was in the US, lecturing at the State University of New York at Buffalo, and promoting his novel in New York by means of a reading. He sent a copy of the speech he was supposed to deliver to Madeleine Jennings, who was in charge of the administration of the prize. In a letter from New York of 15 April 1984 he informed Mike Kirkwood that he had received Jennings's letter of 4 April only the previous day:

> What people outside this country don't realize, what I didn't know before arriving here a few months ago, is that the Reagan administration is quite deliberately winding down the US Post Office, encouraging private carriers to take over its functions. No one here uses the Post Office if they want to get an item somewhere in a hurry. For a city of about a million, there are five post offices. For the rest, you can buy stamps at a few drugstores, and that's it. […] I'm immensely relieved not to be attending the banquet. It has almost been worth coming to America to miss it. Will you please, as you so kindly offer, take over the speech-making function?

The speech, however, did not arrive in time. In his thank-you speech on Coetzee's behalf, Kirkwood quoted Coetzee's strictures on Reagan and the US postal system, but diplomatically suppressed Coetzee's relief at not having to attend the ceremony. The speech is based on an article[53] that Coetzee submitted to Hugh Murray, the editor of *Leadership SA*, and later, in adapted and expanded form, included in *White Writing*. It starts with the yearning for the Great National Novel, in English as well as Afrikaans, that frequently crops up in conversations and debates about South African literature. In the case of Afrikaans literature it is related to a somewhat limited ethnic concept of what 'national' exactly comprises, whereas in local English literature it is part of a striving to rise above anachronistic provincialism. The question is whether it is possible to find someone with a profound enough knowledge of South African society:

> to present it in the depth and fullness we would demand of a Great National Novel. […] Has South African society that degree of organic unity that it can actually be known and represented from the inside out? […] In what sense is South Africa a single society, to what extent merely an agglomeration of people within a more or less unitary economic organization? […] Is it possible to write

a Great Novel which will characterize more or less the whole of a
society at a certain time in history, when the society is marked by
disunity, fragmentation, internal antagonisms, anomie, and above
all by a multiplicity of languages?

According to Coetzee, the English language has an uncomfortable relationship with the South African landscape and has never succeeded in
naming certain parts of it. Afrikaans, which is in all structural respects
a European language, has, with minimal borrowing from older, more
indigenous languages, adapted to the landscape of southern Africa, to
such an extent that English had to adopt words like 'koppie', 'krans'
and 'kloof' from it. After almost two hundred years English has still not
developed a South African linguistic awareness of the landscape in the
spoken language. Coetzee believes that there is a better chance that the
authentic South African novel will be written in Afrikaans, but only if
the author can make a complete break with the traditional Afrikaans
novel and idea of the farm. For the sake of the national self-image
the educational authorities would like to promote the Great Writers.
For South African writers, however, this could be dangerous.'To be
acknowledged, and used by the system, as the author of a Great National
Novel during one's lifetime', Coetzee concludes,

> seems to me at best a kiss of death, at worst a proof that one is
> a fraud. [...] If the Great South African Novel ever comes to be
> written in our midst, let us pray that it is not recognized too widely
> and too soon, particularly by the national-cultural authorities.[54]

Having won the Booker Prize and three CNA prizes, Coetzee was now
a celebrated author. Friends and colleagues, magazine editors and
publishers congratulated him on his achievements. Dr Stuart Saunders,
principal and vice-chancellor of UCT, issued a statement expressing his
joy at the news:

> The university recently recognised John Coetzee's excellence
> by promoting him to full professorship and the conferral of a
> fellowship. I personally am delighted, and I am sure the whole
> university is delighted, that he has been given this award, which
> acknowledges his outstanding ability.

For students at UCT it was a privilege to be taught by someone known both as a prominent author and a respected academic — a rare combination.

VI

Reviewers did not pronounce on *Life & Times of Michael K* with unanimous praise, though many of them wrote with great insight about the novel. Berryl Roberts wrote in the *Sunday Times* of 13 November 1983: 'Michael K is a survivor who has learnt that living life on one's own terms, however minimally, is the only future man can have. It's a stark depressing message, but beautifully delivered in polished prose.'

The Dutch literary scholar W. Bronzwaer wrote in *De Volkskrant* of 16 December 1983:

> This is a novel of rare power, both in its refined design and its humane sensibility. To understand it in the last detail is not possible — or perhaps not yet possible. Behind it one discerns the contours of the great twentieth-century literary tradition, which the book becomes part of, and in which it can hold its own. It is, however, also a work of ennobling humanity. It describes a course of life that is also a via dolorosa. The book answers to our deepest hope of life on earth, here or in South Africa.[55]

Alberto Manguel, in *Commonweal* of 13 July 1984, says that in the tale of Michael K Coetzee has 'recreated the myth of the wanderer — the Wandering Jew, the Flying Dutchman — the man who tries to find, and is denied, a place on this earth'.

It was, however, Michael K's quietness, even quietism, his ethical challenge and his resistance to the attempt to make him function within post-colonial literary criticism and within a politically charged South Africa that met with most resistance. In *The New York Review of Books* of 27 February 1984[56] Nadine Gordimer published an assessment of *Life & Times of Michael K* under the title 'The Idea of Gardening' that led to lively debate. Gordimer starts by saying that Coetzee has chosen allegory as the form of his first novels. She questions his choice of this form, in particular the problem of making the individualistic Michael K a representative of the oppressed black people of South Africa. She appreciates the fact that the novel addresses some difficult questions in the political climate of the 1980s, but laments the 'revulsion against all political and revolutionary solutions'. Coetzee 'does not recognize what the victims, seeing themselves as victims no longer, have done, are doing, and believe they must do for themselves'. She accuses Coetzee, as Patrick Hayes puts it, 'of making a false portrayal of black heroic identity: in choosing as the hero of the novel a man who opts out of a revolutionary role in troubled times and elects instead to concern himself with the cultivation of the land'.[57] For Gordimer, who in *The Conservationist* presented a certain kind of protagonist that critics interpreted as a representative white South African, the main problem is exactly Coetzee's choice of a main character. She does not find Michael K representative of the black people of South Africa. Although she finds the idea of gardening an attractive feature of the novel, Michael K's misfortunes, according to her, are multiplied to the extent that the reader loses patience: 'Does the man have to be harelipped, etc. on top of everything else?'

Gordimer's misgivings were shared by neo-Marxist critics who were disappointed at Coetzee's avoidance of the kind of realism that they found in Gordimer's work. One attempt to castigate Coetzee from this point of view came from Michael Vaughan, who maintained that with *Life & Times of Michael K* Coetzee's work had ended up in a cul-de-sac. Coetzee, however, presents the South African situation as simply one manifestation of the more comprehensive problem of colonialism, and he does not want to restrict himself to that which is uniquely South African.

Coetzee's implied attitude was not new. In South African literature, and specifically Afrikaans literature, there were in the 1950s and later repeated calls for writers to take note of the political situation in their country and to write about it, calls that writers such as D.J. Opperman and Etienne Leroux resisted, arguing that it is dangerous for literature to be recruited as propaganda for a cause. Unlike writers such as André Brink and Nadine Gordimer, Coetzee was not interested in representing the South African political dilemma realistically in his novel. He did not reply to Gordimer's criticism in so many words; but in 'The Novel Today', a lecture he delivered in 1987 during the *Weekly Mail*'s Book Week at the Baxter Theatre in Cape Town, he referred to the pressure on South African writers to act as 'cultural workers' and the demand that their work be of historical significance. This, according to him, reduces the novel to a supplement of the historical text. But 'the novel that places itself outside history, generates its own myths and conclusions, outside the terms of class conflict, race conflict, or any other of the oppositions out of which history and the historical disciplines erect themselves.' Novelistic truth and historical truth are thus for Coetzee two competing truths, and he resists history's claim that it reflects 'reality' authentically. Later, in 1994, he was to quote Doris Lessing approvingly: 'There is no doubt that fiction makes a better job of the truth.'[58] Coetzee wishes to resist what he regards as the 'colonisation of the novel by the discourse of history'. He emphasises instead 'storytelling' as 'another kind, an other mode of thinking', a view that implies reservations about the kind of social realism and committed literature practised by writers like Gordimer and Brink.

Concerning the reaction to his work in the 1980s, and specifically to *Life & Times of Michael K*, Coetzee said in an interview:

> I seem to have two sorts of critical publics, one of which is in the United States. [...] The other is in South Africa. And the terms in which these two publics operate [...] are rather different. [...] On the one hand, the body of people in the United States read these books in the general terms in which books are read by intelligent, mainly academic type of critics in the U.S. Back in South Africa, there is another type of framework in which they are read, which is heavily influenced by Marxism, by general Third World thinking. ... The primary question ... is 'Where does this book fit into the political struggle?' It is a dominant question there. These are actually the people I live among. I don't want to disparage them at all. ... They are serious, intelligent people, but they are reading the books in a particular way.[59]

Coetzee provided a fuller version of these reflections in reply to a question from David Attwell as to whether one could see Michael's resistance to belonging to any camp as a valuable symbolic gesture on the part of the novel:

> If one takes Michael K seriously as a hero, a paragon, a model, it can only be as a hero of resistance against—or rather, withdrawal from or evasion of—accepted ideas of the heroic. But insofar as this resistance claims a social meaning and value, I see no great distance between it and the resistance of the book *Michael K* itself, with its

own evasions of authority, including its (I would hope successful) evasion of attempts by its author to put a stranglehold on it.

There is a moment in *Michael K* at which Michael hides away while a group of guerrillas camp beside 'his' dam. He is tempted to come out into the open and ask to join them, but in the end he doesn't.

This is, I suppose, the most politically naked moment in the novel. If one reads the novel simply, K offers himself as a model either of modest prudence or of cowardice masquerading as commitment to a humbler function (one of his reasons or rationalizations for not joining, as I remember it, is that someone has to stay behind and grow pumpkins for the men in the front line: the context tempts one to read humble as noble, growing pumpkins as more important than shooting people).

Why doesn't K go off with the guerrillas? Why doesn't he abandon his dam and his pumpkin patch, head off into the night with the donkey train and its sacks of mortar shells, hide in the Swartberg, blow up trains, ambush army convoys, and eventually get killed in action?

In a more sophisticated form, this became the question Nadine Gordimer asked in her review of the novel. What kind of model behavior in the face of oppression was I presenting? Why hadn't I written a different book with (I put words in her mouth now) a less spineless hero?

To a reader taking this line, much of the text of *Michael K* is just one fancy evasion after another of an overriding political question: how shall the tyranny of apartheid be ended? In this perspective, the moment when the text turns in upon itself and begins to reflect upon its own textuality is thus simply a moment of evasion. The question of why K does not go off with the guerrillas and the question of why textuality is given a symbolic value become the same question.

How do I respond to such readers?

One writes the book one wants to write. One doesn't write the books one doesn't want to write. The emphasis falls not on one but on the word *want* in all its own resistance to being known. The book about going off with guerrillas, the book in the heroic tradition, is not a book I *wanted-to-write*, wanted enough to be able to bring off, however much I might have wanted to have written it — that is to say, wanted to be the person who had successfully brought off the writing of it.

What, then, do I *want-to-write*? A question to prospect, to open up, perhaps, in the present dialogue, but not to mine, to exploit: too much of the fictional enterprise depends on it. Just as it is not productive to discover the answer to the question of why one desires: the answer threatens the end of desire, the end of the production of desire.[60]

VII

On 25 October 1985 Coetzee wrote to Mike Kirkwood: 'I'm in the last stages of preparing a novel MS (as yet untitled). Would you, in principle, be interested in the possibility of a local edition, and would you be interested in seeing the MS?' He added: 'I must caution you that it is a rather abstruse book. I began work on it in 1982, when the temper of the times was rather different from what it is now.'

It may well be that Coetzee had already in 1982 started the research and preparation for this new novel, but according to the dating of the manuscript, the first five holographs were written between 1 June and 14 October 1983. He started working on an extensively amended text on 28 July 1984, but revised this even further with numerous alterations made in red pen. The final text was commenced on 2 May 1985.

The 'temper of the times' to which Coetzee refers in his letter to Kirkwood probably had to do with the United Democratic Front's response to the tri-cameral parliament and the increased tension that, with the protests, boycotts and daily violence, was starting to dominate the South African political scene in the second half of the 1980s. In July 1985 P.W. Botha proclaimed a state of emergency in parts of South Africa, including the Eastern Cape and the central Pretoria-Witwatersrand-Vaal area. A few months later it was extended to the Western Cape and in June 1989 a state of emergency was declared countrywide that would remain in force up to the election of Botha's successor. Extraordinary powers were given to the security forces; organisations, meetings and even funerals could be banned; thousands were detained without trial; and it became an offence for the media to photograph or report on security force actions without written permission from the government. For Coetzee, having been accused by Gordimer and other commentators of a lack of political commitment in *Life & Times of Michael K*, now to produce an abstruse and even more elusive novel, which on the face of it had no explicit bearing on South African problems, could be seen as grist to the mill of his critics. Hence, presumably, his warning to Kirkwood.

As framework or matrix for the events in *Foe*, as the novel would eventually be called, Coetzee used *The Life and Strange Surprising Adventures of Robinson Crusoe, of York, Mariner*. This novel by Daniel Defoe (born Foe, in 1695, with the prefix 'De' added), published in 1719, is the tale of a castaway who lives on an island for more than 28 years before being rescued by a passing ship. He survives in orderly fashion on the island by building shelters, making clothes and establishing plantations. He rescues the black man Friday, whom he employs as his servant, from certain death at the hands of cannibals. Robinson Crusoe's tale, with its series of thrilling adventures, was extremely popular from the start and with succeeding generations of readers, but with the renewed interest in the colonial era the protagonist gained a new relevance as the prototype of the Western European colonist, with his disapproving take on the 'uncivilised' behaviour of other races. Lewis Nkosi, for instance, a well-known South African novelist and critic, sees *Robinson Crusoe* as a central cultural text for the myth of the superiority of Western European civilisation.[61]

In the introduction to his edition of *Robinson Crusoe* in the World's Classics series of Oxford University Press, Coetzee relates this tale to Homer's *Odyssey* and Cervantes' *Don Quixote*: 'Like Odysseus embarked for Ithaca, like Quixote mounted on Rocinante, Robinson Crusoe with his parrot and umbrella has become a figure in the collective consciousness of the West, transcending the book which [...] celebrates his adventures.'[62] Since its first publication there have been many editions and translations of *Robinson Crusoe*, and the tale has spawned many imitations and adaptations. Even at school, according to *Boyhood*, Coetzee was enthralled by Johann David Wyss's *The Swiss Family Robinson*, a tale following in the tracks of Defoe's, and dealing with a shipwrecked family living for a while on one of the East Indian Islands.[63] Over the years the desert island myth produced many Robinsonades throughout European literature on the model of Defoe's novel, from adventure novels for boys, like Robert Louis Stevenson's *Treasure Island* (1883), to Jean Giraudoux's *Suzanne et le Pacifique* (1921) and Michel Tournier's *Vendredi ou les limbes du Pacifique* (1967), followed somewhat later by Patrick White's *A Fringe of Leaves* (1976) and Brink's *'n Oomblik in die wind* [*An Instant in the Wind*]. Elleke Boehmer has pointed out that the development of the sub-genre 'Robinsonade' is indicative of the paradigmatic power of Robinson Crusoe, but also of the energy that Defoe unleashed with the metaphorical derivations and reproductions within the broader tradition of the colonial narrative and the adventure novel. Defoe's novel is the power source driving the many tales of mutiny and shipwreck, ingenious settlement and cultivation of a desert island, discovery of treasure, slave experiences and fear of cannibalism.[64] To such an extent has the tale of the castaway on an island appealed to the imagination of succeeding generations of readers that the book was not regarded as a piece of fiction, but as the true story of the protagonist. Readers tended to refer to Robinson Crusoe as the author, forgetting that the tale was a creation by Daniel Defoe: 'It is a tribute to an author, one supposes, though of a rather backhanded kind, that he should be eclipsed by one of his creations,' Coetzee writes in his introduction.[65]

Coetzee's appropriation of the tale of an old castaway as the matrix of his new novel can be traced back to his childhood reading of the novel and to his fascination with the journals of early travellers at the Cape that he had discovered in his years in London and later in the library of the University of Texas at Austin. In his preface to *Robinson Crusoe* Defoe emphasises the truth of the adventures and reduces himself to a mere editor of the tale he is telling: 'The editor believes the thing to be a just history of fact; neither is there any appearance of fiction in it.'[66] But what fascinates Coetzee about *Robinson Crusoe* is not in the first place what he sees as the obsolete autobiographical pretence. It is rather, as he puts it in his introduction, the view of the human being as an island and every life, seen in an allegorical light, as a life of isolation under the searching regard of God. What engrosses him, then, is how a piece of fiction can give rise to a prominent archetype in European literature: the essential solitude of the human being on an island of the self. Defoe is not, according to him, a realist in the mould of the great European writers of the nineteenth century, whose novels were based on a confidential compact between author and reader on the 'truth' of their narratives. Defoe's novel is a kind of mock-autobiography strongly influenced by the genres of the deathbed confession and the spiritual autobiography.[67]

It is clear from the outset that *Foe* is a retelling of Defoe's tale of a castaway. Coetzee's novel, however, offers a variant on this in that *Foe*'s

Cruso (now spelt differently to Defoe's Crusoe), presents a different perspective, not in the first place that of the castaway. In place of the exclusive position hitherto occupied by Crusoe, Susan Barton now introduces a wholly new dimension to the classic tale. After her ship is wrecked she ends up on the island on which Cruso is living with his tongueless slave Friday. Her deliverance comes when a ship arrives at the island. Cruso, sick with fever, resists the rescue; Friday flees to the rocks above the northern coast but is brought back by sailors and forced aboard. Susan offers to accompany the sailors, but the captain firmly refuses. While she is enjoying, after a year on the island, a 'civilised' meal and a glass of port with the captain in his cabin, talk turns to the strangeness of her shipwreck and the possibility of writing down her experiences:

> 'It is a story you should set down in writing and offer to the booksellers,' he urged — 'There has never before, to my knowledge, been a female castaway of our nation. It will cause a great stir.' I shook my head sadly. 'As I relate it to you, my story passes the time well enough,' I replied; 'but what little I know of book-writing tells me its charm will quite vanish when it is set down baldly in print. A liveliness is lost in the writing down which must be supplied by art, and I have no art.' 'As to art I cannot pronounce, being only a sailor,' said Captain Smith; 'but you may depend on it, the booksellers will hire a man to set your story to rights, and put in a dash of colour too, here and there.' 'I will not have any lies told,' said I. The captain smiled. 'There I cannot vouch for them,' he said: 'their trade is in books, not in truth.'[68]

On the way to Bristol Cruso dies and is buried at sea. In England, Susan, encouraged by the captain's words about the possible publication of her adventures, tries to get in touch with the writer Daniel Foe (as Defoe was in truth called) to have her story told. When, after a protracted exchange of letters, she eventually tracks him down, she discovers that she can tell her story only with the help of the mute Friday. Susan says to Foe:

> The story of Friday's tongue is a story unable to be told, or unable to be told by me. That is to say, many stories can be told of Friday's tongue, but the true story is buried within Friday, who is mute. The

true story will not be heard till by art we have found a means of giving voice to Friday.[69]

It is this concealed subtext in Defoe's report, which Lewis Nkosi refers to, that Coetzee brings to the surface. In Coetzee's version Cruso has no stories and indeed attaches no value to stories, whereas Susan, on the contrary, believes that a written version of her experiences may be of interest to posterity. Because Friday was deprived of his tongue by a slave trader, his silence may be read as the psychological damage inflicted upon the black man by the coloniser with his racism. Friday's silence is comparable to that of the barbarian girl in *Waiting for the Barbarians* whose feet have been mutilated in prison. Apart from the action of writing, which becomes a major motif of the novel through Susan's insistence on a true account of her experiences, Coetzee's retelling of *Robinson Crusoe* reveals the silence and suppression at the heart of the classic story. It is a silence that affects the whole of Friday's humanity, because he cannot write if he cannot speak to express his deepest being. Susan is here alluding to the creative power of the Word with which God created the universe; she then posits an alternative, whereby Friday could develop a wordless writing with his fingers: 'God's writing stands as an instance of a writing without speech. Speech is but a means through which the word may be uttered, it is not the word itself.'[70] To illustrate this creative power, Coetzee employs the image of whirligigs writing the name of God on the water—an image that his study of Dutch poetry enabled him to borrow from a poem by Guido Gezelle, the Flemish priest-poet: 'The waterskater, that is an insect and dumb, traces the name of God on the surfaces of ponds.'[71]

The main difference between Defoe's and Coetzee's treatment of the material lies in their respective interpretations of the roles of Crusoe/Cruso and Friday. The way in which the diligent Crusoe cultivates his island to make it a better place, using Friday for this purpose, places Defoe's tale within the ambit of British imperialism. By contrast, Coetzee's Cruso has very little of the enthusiasm, energy and optimism of Defoe's character. Cruso is much more closely related, as Dick Penner has pointed out, to the kind of character inhabiting Beckett's cheerless landscapes, a character who devotes himself, with Friday, to the totally absurd construction of massive terraces in which, unlike Michael K in Coetzee's previous novel, they cannot plant anything, because they lack seed—an activity as pointless as that of Sisyphus condemned to rolling rocks up a mountain only to watch them roll down again.[72] When the practically inclined Susan asks what is to be planted or sown in the cleared terraces, Cruso replies, 'We have nothing to plant—that is our misfortune. [...] The planting is reserved for those who come after us and have the foresight to bring seed.' [73]

But there are essential differences also between the Fridays of Defoe and Coetzee. Unlike Defoe's Friday, Coetzee's is clearly from the African continent, not a member of one of the indigenous American peoples. Within the imperialistic world of which Defoe's Crusoe is a denizen, the relationship between him and Friday is that of a master and an underling executing his commands. For Coetzee, who had in his first four novels also employed the master-slave relation as a dominant theme, the servility of Friday was a problem. In an early version of *Foe* a note testifies to his concern about the burgeoning novel: 'Defoe's text is full of Friday's Yes; now [74] it is impossible to fantasize that Yes; all the ways in which Friday can say No seem not only stereotyped (i.e. rehearsed over and over again in the texts of our time) but destructive (murder, rape, bloodthirsty tyranny). What is lacking to me is what is lacking to Africa since the death of Négritude: a vision of a future for Africa that is not a debased version of life in the West.' [75] Unlike Defoe's subordinate Friday, Coetzee's does not possess the power of the word. When Friday does not respond to Susan's request to bring 'wood', and Cruso amends it to 'firewood', a word that Friday does understand, Susan asks Cruso:

'How many words of English does Friday know?'
'As many as he needs,' replied Cruso. 'This is not England, we have no need of a great stock of words.' [76]

From the rest of the conversation it transpires that Friday's tongue has been cut out, probably by a slave dealer from Africa. Cruso continues:

Perhaps the slavers, who are Moors, hold the tongue to be a delicacy. Or perhaps they grew weary of listening to Friday's wails of grief, that went on day and night. Perhaps they wanted to prevent him from ever telling his story: who he was, where his home lay, how it came about that he was taken. Perhaps they cut out the tongue of every cannibal they took, as a punishment. How will we ever know the truth? [77]

Friday's inability to tell his tale is an extension of the silence on the position of the black man in the idyllic farm novels that Coetzee comments on in *White Writing*, and of the problem of the white writer in South Africa to give a voice to Africa and the people of Africa. Later, when Susan starts a writing lesson to convey words to Friday, she can represent Africa only by means of a few clichés, like a lion or a row of palm trees. The question is whether people of Western origin have words to interpret Africa.

Apart from the use of Susan Barton as a female castaway, a further difference between *Robinson Crusoe* and *Foe* is in Coetzee's use of details from Defoe's life and his other fiction. From *Roxana*, for instance, he adapts the mother-daughter plot that creates a certain tension between Susan as a new writer and the famous author Foe. The daughter, also called Susan, claims that Susan is her mother, but she rejects the daughter's claim, as Roxana rejects her mother. Coetzee thus rewrites the whole history of Defoe's *Roxana*, and adds details from *Moll Flanders*, Defoe's other novel. Indeed, other writers are audible in the text, even Shakespeare, whose *Tempest* is added to the mix. In this respect *Foe* is a multi-layered postmodern text. Julia Kristeva refers to this kind of effect as a 'mosaic of quotations',[78] and Sheila Roberts has pointed out the multiple voices in the novel: 'We close the covers of *Foe*, with the faces from a transhistorical collage of accomplices staring at us knowingly as we try to retell ourselves the story of John Coetzee's Foe — the story of his enemy and ours, the colonizer who engendered us.'[79]

It is the fourth and final part of *Foe* in particular that readers found problematic.[80] The events take place many years after those in the first three sections. An unnamed narrator now enters the house of 'Daniel Defoe, Author', identified by the blue-and-white plaque which in England indicates a house of historical interest. Inside he sees, side-by-side in the bed, what would seem to be the corpses of Susan and Foe, their skins dry as paper and stretched tight over their skeletons, the lips drawn back, the teeth visible, as if smiling. Apparently three hundred years have elapsed, the period between Susan's arrival in England and Coetzee's publication of *Foe*. Because the time lapse places the events in a contemporary frame and because the novel represents Coetzee's own confrontation with *Robinson Crusoe*, there may well be a connection between the narrator and Coetzee, at least at the point in time when this narration commences.

Section four of the novel offers two separate endings in which the narrator approaches Friday, opens his mouth and tries to make the silence speak. All he can hear the first time, however, are the sounds of the island, nothing that can be identified with Friday. The second version is a repetition of the first, again with Susan and Foe in the bed and with Friday in the adjoining summer house. Now, however, the narrator does not try to reach Friday directly through his mouth, but by means of a text: the first words of Susan's manuscript, which are also the first words of the novel *Foe*: 'At last I could row no further.' What would seem to be a lived-through experience, the vital first sentence of the novel, now acquires a momentum when the narrator takes over the rest of Susan's first words ('With a sigh, making barely a splash, I slipped overboard'), but alters them ('With a sigh, with barely a splash, I duck my head under the water') thus acknowledging their supplementary status.

By presenting this second ending as a piece of writing, the narrator can now descend into the sunken wreck that is compared to Friday's mouth. In this underwater scene we discover with the narrator the actual 'home of Friday', a place that is not yet 'a place of words', but 'a place where bodies are their own signs'. We are entering a prelinguistic Eden. Then follows the final paragraph of *Foe*:

> His mouth opens. From inside him comes a slow stream, without breath, without interruption. It flows up through his body and out upon me; it passes through the cabin, through the wreck; washing the cliffs and shores of the island, it runs northward and southward to the ends of the earth. Soft and cold, dark and unending, it beats against my eyelids, against the skin of my face.[81]

Patrick Hayes says about this conclusion:

> The ending of *Foe* remains one of the biggest interpretative conundrums of all of Coetzee's writing: we seem to leave the carefully documented world familiar to readers of novels, in which Friday is tongue-less, story-less, and silent, and enter a type of storytelling that operates according to altogether different rules, where Friday mysteriously takes on an expressive power—this is some sort of literary genre in which 'bodies are their own signs'.[82]

VIII

Even before Coetzee sent the manuscript of *Foe* to Ravan Press, Mike Kirkwood informed him that they would definitely be interested in a local edition, and that he would prefer to sign a contract directly with him rather than with Secker & Warburg. When he received the manuscript, he wrote on 17 December 1985 to Murray Pollinger, Coetzee's London agent: 'Everyone at Ravan who has seen the book is very excited: we feel that the art of narration, with *Robinson Crusoe*, will never be the same again.' He wrote to Coetzee the following day: 'Reading your book is rather like dreaming a dream in which access to all other dreams becomes possible—and indeed, I've noticed a distinct improvement in my own dreams since Susan Barton turned up with a sigh, making barely a splash.'

Coetzee was preparing to leave for Johns Hopkins University in Baltimore in the US, where he would be lecturing until the end of April. On 24 December 1985 he informed Kirkwood that both Secker & Warburg and André Deutsch were interested in publication. The interest from Viking in the US was more muted, probably because they had been expecting a different sort of book from South Africa. En route to America, Coetzee travelled through London, where he met Murray Pollinger and expressed the wish that Secker & Warburg and Penguin, the latter for the paperback, handle the book in Britain, but with the proviso that he was eager for the South African edition to be published by Ravan. In a letter of 26 February 1986, Peter Grose of Secker & Warburg wrote to Mike Kirkwood that they would respect the author's wishes, although reading between the lines one can deduce that they would have preferred to market their edition also in South Africa. He writes: 'We have to accept that, in the wake of the Booker Prize and the sales that resulted from it, John has moved into a new league in terms of his sales and the prices he can command.' He did, however, accept Kirkwood's proposal regarding the South African edition and the advance offered to the author, and made the necessary financial arrangements between them. Because of various organisational upsets, Secker & Warburg failed to deliver the film of the book to Ravan in time, with the result that the South African edition could not, as agreed, be published simultaneously with the British edition on 8 September 1986.

Foe, eventually published before the end of 1986 by Ravan, was the last of Coetzee's works to be published by a South African publisher. In future he would deliver all new manuscripts to publishers in Britain and the US. The reason for this was the administrative chaos that befell Ravan Press after the departure of Mike Kirkwood and with the quick turnover of successors.

With the publication of *Foe*, one could have anticipated, locally as well as abroad, that not all critics would take kindly to a novel that *seemed* to have nothing to do with South African actualities of the time. The fascinating close to Coetzee's most postmodern novel to date was open to various interpretations, and many commentators glided so lightly over it as to make one suspect that they did not really understand that section of the novel. The question was, however, whether Coetzee in this novel did veer away from the burning issues of 1980s South Africa. Asked by Tony Morphet in an interview for *TriQuarterly* whether *Foe* represented a retreat from explicitly South African themes, Coetzee responded: '*Foe* is a retreat from the South African situation, but only from that situation in a narrow temporal perspective. It is not a retreat from the subject of colonialism or from questions of power. [It …] may also be called the question of who writes? Who takes up the position of power, pen in hand?'

Not all critics would settle for such a declaration. On 30 August 1986 William French wrote a fairly positive review in *Globe and Mail,* but with some reservations:

> Susan's role as a woman is clear-cut, but her role as a symbol is ambiguous, probably deliberately; through close contact, she comes to respect the austere Cruso, even to have sympathy for him. And Coetzee's last chapter is enigmatic and unsatisfying, again probably deliberately, to deflect the viewpoint away from making a connection with South Africa. But these deficiencies don't seriously detract from the virtues of a haunting and courageous novel.

In *The Times* of 11 September Nicholas Shakespeare, too, was rather lukewarm:

> *Foe* is a novel of silences — the silence of a woman who cannot write the truth, and the silence of a man who cannot speak it. As ever, Coetzee's prose is that of a true craftsman, detached and granite grey, and chipping away to reveal a cold polished work. What prevents it from stirring is the sense he is working out some private riddle between himself and the Crusoe myth. Wrenching this familiar tale into an allegory pertinent to Southern Africa has the same effect on the reader as listening to Friday's mute hum.

In the *Times Literary Supplement* of 12 September, P.N. Furbank wrote:

> Coetzee does what we did not want him to do and still manages
> to win our goodwill. It is hard to say in what spirit this inventive
> and provocative allegory of the creative process was composed, but
> one suspects a rather light-hearted one, and the more Pirandellian
> paradoxes, about created fictions and their right to a life of their
> own, occasionally fall a little flat. The myth of those unplanted
> terraces, though, takes hold of the imagination. One may add that,
> after all, his is not too bad a genesis-story for *Robinson Crusoe*—no
> wilder than some of the fantasies about Defoe promulgated by his
> biographers.

As against this moderate praise, Harriet Gilbert in the *New Statesman* of
12 September was downright negative, asking indignantly: 'Postmodern
games while Soweto burns?', an indication of the angle of incidence
of her objections.[83] André Brink, too, who in the past had written with
great insight and appreciation on Coetzee, was, in a *Rapport* review of 26
October, less impressed with *Foe*:

> Technically *Foe* is a masterpiece: the first half is without any reser-
> vation excellent. But after that the pace—and especially the
> density—cannot be kept up. It remains a reading adventure of
> exceptional alloy, but in Coetzee's formidable oeuvre, and taken as
> a whole, yet a less satisfying novel than the previous ones. [84]

In the *Weekly Mail* of 5 December Stephen Clingman, the author of
The Novels of Nadine Gordimer (1986) and later of *Bram Fischer: Afrikaner
Revolutionary* (1998), concludes:

> For all its modernity, its toying with history and narrative (and
> Coetzee shows himself to be a story-teller of ever-increasing power),
> the book is in many ways a conservative one: it is a quest for meaning,
> inserted in that gap between experience and words. This will not
> make Coetzee popular with those who want their politics hard and
> straight. But I don't know if Coetzee will care; he is a marginal kind
> of hero—one who refuses to be what anyone wants him to be, and
> writes phenomenal stories.

Under the title 'Postmodern palimpsest' Douglas Reid Skinner wrote incisively in *Contrast*, XVI: 2, December 1986: 'Never satisfied with worn sensibilities, *Foe* is highly inventive and displays a rare degree of insight into complex and difficult matters. The characteristic assurance and economy of style and form are once again a lesson in technique. This book seems to me to be Coetzee's finest work since *In the Heart of the Country*.'

In March 1996 the Théâtre de Complicité performed an adaptation of *Foe* by Mark Wheatley in the West Yorkshire Playhouse in Leeds and afterwards toured the UK, but the actors found it difficult to bring to life in theatrical terms such a multi-levelled play. More successful was the adaptation that Peter Glazer produced in October 2003 at the University of California at Berkeley.

Coetzee received the Jerusalem Prize for *Foe* in December 1986. It was awarded to him, according to the mayor of Jerusalem, Teddy Kollek, in recognition of the literary quality of the work and of the author's sustained resistance to apartheid, violence and oppression in all its forms. The prize enjoys great prestige in the literary world, as evidenced by previous winners such as Bertrand Russell, Graham Greene, Eugène Ionesco and Milan Kundera.

To receive the prize money, which amounted to $5000, Coetzee travelled to Jerusalem, where on 9 April 1987 he delivered one of the most important addresses of his career, more important even than those for his two CNA prizes. In the address, later collected in *Doubling the Point*,[85] he spoke feelingly, 'in a calm and measured fashion',[86] about the history of colonialism and its relation to apartheid. In the 1950s a law was promulgated declaring sexual relations across the colour line to be a crime. Symbolically the origin of this was in fear and denial: 'denial of an unacknowledgeable desire to embrace Africa, embrace the body of Africa; and fear of being embraced in return by Africa'. At the heart of this denial of Africa lay, according to Coetzee, 'a failure of love':

> To be blunt: their love is not enough today and has not been enough since they arrived on the continent; furthermore, their talk, their excessive talk, about how they love South Africa has consistently been directed toward the land, that is, toward what is least likely to respond to love: mountains and deserts, birds and animals and flowers.

The price to be paid for this was a 'deformed and stunted inner life' that also makes itself felt in the literature:

> South African literature is a literature in bondage, as it reveals in even its highest moments, shot through as they are with feelings of homelessness and yearnings for a nameless liberation. It is a less than fully human literature, unnaturally occupied with power and the torsions of power, unable to move from elementary relations and contestation, domination, and subjugation to the vast and complex human world that lies beyond them. It is exactly the kind of literature you would expect people to write from a prison. [...]
>
> Two years ago Milan Kundera stood on this platform in Jerusalem and gave tribute to the first of all novelists, Miguel Cervantes, on whose giant shoulders we pigmy writers of a later age stand. How I would like to be able to join him in that tribute, I and so many of my fellow novelists from South Africa! How we long to quit a world of pathological attachments and abstract forces, of anger and violence, and take up residence in a world where a living play of feelings and ideas is possible, a world where we truly have an occupation.

The problem faced by the South African writer is thus, as Irving Howe suggested in his review of *Waiting for the Barbarians* in *The New York Times Book Review* of 18 April 1982, that the racial conflict is so central that it infiltrates his whole psyche and leaves no space for other themes. How, Coetzee asks, do we escape the violence-ravaged world that for metropolitan critics constitutes the 'authentic' South Africa? Cervantes's Don Quixote left hot and dusty La Mancha behind him and travelled into a world of the imagination. What prevents the South African writer from following a similar course, to write himself out of a situation in which his art is too slow and old-fashioned and indirect to have even the slightest effect on the community or the course of history? What prevents him is the power of the world in which he lives, that dictates to him and ultimately infiltrates also his imagination. 'The crudity of life in South Africa,' Coetzee writes, 'the naked force of its appeals, not only at the physical level but at the moral level too, its callousness and its brutalities, its hungers and its rages, its greed and its lies, make it as irresistible as it is unloveable.' 'We have art, said Nietzsche, so that we shall not die of the truth,' Coetzee concludes. 'In South Africa there is now too much truth for art to hold, truth by the bucketful, truth that overwhelms and swamps every act of the imagination.'

The trip to Jerusalem gave Coetzee a chance to get to know a city and a country that he had not visited before. Although he had to meet lots of important people and grant interviews to journalists, and felt constrained by the guide assigned to him, he was able to visit a large part of northern Israel and talk to many people. 'I came away,' he wrote on 27 May 1987 to his friend Howard Wolf in Buffalo, 'feeling a great deal of warmth for the writers and artists I met, and more than a little overwhelmed too by Jerusalem. A terrible pity, though, [...] that the ultra-Orthodox have such a stranglehold—or seems to have—over the lives—and ultimately the futures—of ordinary people.'

After Jerusalem Coetzee visited Finland, his first experience of a country where over the years he would gain many readers. He wrote to Howard Wolf on 10 July 1987: 'Finland was a pleasure, a surprising pleasure, since I hadn't expected much and since it rained most of the time I was there. But the rain, and the real pain the Finns felt at not being able to offer their visitors a taste of their summer, seemed to make people more receptive and kinder to one another.'

IX

Besides the local and international awards for his creative work, Coetzee was accorded other distinctions in the 1980s. In 1982 The English Academy of Southern Africa awarded him the Thomas Pringle Prize for 1980–81 for his article on 'Blood, flaw, taint, degeneracy: The case of Sarah Gertrude Millin' that had appeared in *English in Africa* in January 1980. In his report, A.E. Voss says on behalf of the panel of judges that they wanted to recognise the 'sensitivity, scholarship and style of this work'. He continues:

> Professor Coetzee's essay develops a profound argument in comparative literary study involving South African (English and Afrikaans) and European writing. The whole is enlivened by linguistic tact and delicacy and charged with an imagination sensitive to myth. At the same time there is no lack of historical acuity and hence no easy reading of the problematic relation of texts to their social context.

In 1983 Coetzee was awarded a prize of R500 for his creative work by the English Academy, and invited to become a full member of the Academy.

Apart from his creative work, his lecturing duties and his increasingly frequent visits on invitation to present courses at American universities, Coetzee was now frequently involved in a range of literary activities. In 1982 he was one of the judges who recommended Nadine Gordimer's *July's People* for the CNA Prize. In September 1983 he joined the editorial board of *Standpunte*, a literary journal launched in 1945 by N.P. van Wyk Louw, W.E.G. Louw and H.A. Mulder, which from its inception had published pieces in English and Dutch in addition to its main focus on Afrikaans, and was for years to play an important part in the literary and cultural life of South Africa. In 1985 he also joined the editorial board of the newly established *Journal of Literary Studies*. For his original academic work of outstanding quality, meriting special recognition, he was promoted to the rank of Life Fellow by UCT in January 1984. In the citation mention is made of the prizes he has won with his creative work and the translations made of his work, whereas as innovating critic his output extends from studies of Beckett, Nabokov and Dostoevsky to articles on pure and applied linguistics and semiotics, from translations from Dutch and Afrikaans to contemporary articles on Kafka. In 1981 he was invited by the Chinese University of Hong Kong to deliver lectures on linguistics and his own novels. Other commitments prevented him from accepting this invitation, though he did not preclude the possibility of a future visit. In September 1983 Bernth Lindfors of the English Department at Austin asked him if he could put his name forward for an appointment to teach creative writing and linguistics, but at this stage Coetzee was not prepared for such a change. He did accept an invitation to fill the Butler Chair, a visiting professorship, at the State University of New York at Buffalo in spring 1984, where he offered a single post-graduate seminar and a number of public lectures, and had the opportunity to travel and do readings from his work. In 1985 he and Breyten Breytenbach joined a selected group of international authors in New York at a PEN conference initiated by Norman Mailer, aimed at bringing authors together to discuss their common circumstances. The occasion was announced as the most comprehensive meeting yet between American and foreign writers and included the leading literary figures of the time, especially in the field of fiction, such as V.S. Naipaul, Czeslaw Milosz, Italo Calvino, Günter Grass, Gabriel García Márquez, Carlos Fuentes, Iris Murdoch, Alice Munro, Graham Greene, Léopold Senghor, Milan Kundera, Tadeusz Konwicki, George Konrád, Danilo Kis, Anthony Burgess, Harold Pinter and Antonia Fraser.

In the 1980s Coetzee wrote, more frequently than before, many literary essays. In 1984 he started writing reviews and essays in some of the most important intellectual journals in the US, such as *The New Republic* and *The New York Review of Books*. At first these contributions dealt mainly with South African literature. In the three years separating *Life & Times of Michael K* and *Foe* Coetzee accepted a new role as a promoter of South African literature for an international readership.[87] He became, however, increasingly reluctant to comment on his position as a South African novelist, even though he had become, with Gordimer, canonised as a literary spokesman for South Africa. In many international forums he was cast, in spite of his resistance to the role, as a representative South African voice and as an authority on his country and its politics. It is illuminating to read what he said in a review in *The New Republic* of 8–15 January about *Cry, the Beloved Country*: 'Paton was turned, not wholly unwillingly, into a sage and oracle, the guide for editors and interviewers in search of wisdom on South Africa. [...] The effects can be seen not only in the increasingly ex cathedra tone of his pronouncements, and in his tendency to think, speak, and write in brief, easy-to-chew paragraphs, but in his failure to break new ground and to develop as a writer.'

A distinction conferred upon Coetzee in April 1985 was an honorary doctorate in literature from the University of Strathclyde in Glasgow, the first university to honour him with its highest academic accolade. Whereas Coetzee had not been prepared to travel to London in 1983 for the Booker Prize, he was now, on a particularly cold day, present in Glasgow to receive the honorary doctorate. In his citation, Professor Derek Attridge, at the time head of the Department of English at Strathclyde, said:

> For some, the name J.M. Coetzee will trigger the phrase 'South African novelist'. And it is true that all his work bears the marks of the anguish and anger—but also the courage and compassion—that permeate that extraordinary society; it is true also that as a South African writer he belongs to a group of distinguished and powerful artists who in the face of ignorance and brutality are producing something of lasting beauty. But J.M. Coetzee's work—and the physical and spiritual suffering that it portrays—cannot, for us, be comfortably located in a distant country; its domain is humanity. If that sounds like another equally comfortable platitude, let me be more

precise: J.M. Coetzee's work questions, in the most uncompromising way possible, what it is to be human and to acknowledge others as human. All his fiction deals with the experience of individuals who find themselves, like Michael K, at the limits of the human: isolated, exposed, clinging to some last, central, hard grain of identity, in the face of those massive shifts of history that leech out of a society its humanity and its capacity for love.

For scholars working in my field, there is another J.M. Coetzee: the author of a series of important essays demonstrating in exemplary fashion how the insights of linguistic theory can be utilised in literary criticism, to the benefit of both disciplines. While it is true that, as the saying goes, birds don't make particularly good ornithologists, Professor Coetzee's writing is proof that novelists can analyse the processes and procedures of fictional language as acutely as the most uncreative critic, at least if they have the special talents which he has.[88]

The awards continued. In June 1985 he became the first recipient at UCT of the newly instituted annual prize, a certificate and a bursary, for *Waiting for the Barbarians*. Coetzee received this prize as part of the university's half-yearly graduation ceremony. An indication of the importance of the novel, according to the commendatio, was that it had already been translated into fourteen languages, including Hebrew, Polish and Turkish. The commendatio continues:

> This novel [...] was the work that established [Coetzee] firmly as a major figure in contemporary fiction writing. [...] The novel escapes the particular confines of a South African setting or situation but speaks powerfully and intensely to present day South African political and social concerns. It deals with themes that recur throughout our and other literatures, with torture and violence, collaboration and resistance, learning and responsibility, imprisonment and freedom, pity and restitution. It revitalises these themes by insisting on human and social complexity and by an artistic and imaginative power that creates new insights and resolutions.

In an interview with UCT's *Monday Paper* of 24 June–1 July 1985, Coetzee's wry reaction to the award was: 'It is all very gratifying but fortunately I live in the sanity that is Africa.' In the same year he spoke at a conference of the Association of University English Teachers at UCT, and also at the annual meeting of the Afrikaanse Skrywersgilde held at the University of the Witwatersrand. In January 1986 he attended another PEN meeting in New York, this time with Nadine Gordimer, Sipho Sepamla, Dennis Brutus and Breyten Breytenbach, to take part in the movement Writers Against Apartheid. The meeting was initiated by Norman Mailer and Susan Sontag, and attended by Elizabeth Hardwick, Margaret Atwood and Toni Morrison. The South Africans created a sensation when, with a large group of other writers, they boycotted the opening of the proceedings by George Schultz, the US Secretary of State, on the grounds that the Reagan administration supported governments that silenced their subjects for their convictions by detention and torture. Schultz was heckled several times while commending Reagan's stance on freedom of speech.

In 1987 Coetzee accepted an invitation from the University of Reading in the UK to become one of the patrons of the Samuel Beckett Foundation. In 1988 he was elected Fellow of the Royal Society of Literature and in the same year nominated as Chevalier dans l'Ordre des Arts et des Lettres. In 1989 he was made an 'honorary fellow' of the Modern Language Association and in 1989 an 'honorary foreign member' of the American Academy of Arts and Science. In turn Coetzee recommended Peter Klatzow in 1985 as a Fellow at the University of Cape Town, as a musician whose compositions had elevated him 'to a position of unquestioned pre-eminence among living South African composers'.

Along with other writers Coetzee objected when the writer Njabulo Ndebele was refused a visa in 1988. In 1990 he was instrumental in having UCT award an honorary doctorate to Mazisi Kunene, a poet, dramatist and novelist writing in Zulu, who had translated some of his poems into English, and was held in high regard abroad. He arranged for Kunene, former Professor in African Languages at the University of California at Los Angeles and later Professor in English at the University of Wyoming, to visit UCT in 1994 to lecture in the English Department for a few weeks.

X

On 31 October 1988 Coetzee was due to appear in the Baxter Theatre in Cape Town at a week-long literary conference, along with Salman Rushdie, another Booker Prize winner, born in India but living in

Britain.[89] This conference was arranged jointly by the Congress of South African Writers (COSAW) and the *Weekly Mail*. There had already been worldwide protest against Rushdie's novel *The Satanic Verses* by Islamic groups who claimed it calculatedly distorted the history of Islam and the prophet Mohammed. This protest was still at an early stage, and nobody anticipated the eventual extent and vigour of the attack on Rushdie: the fatwa that would be issued in February 1989 by the Ayatollah Khomeini. Even before the start of the conference, one of the committees of the Directorate of Publications banned the book in South Africa, the last important literary work to fall foul of the censors. It is clear that the ban was effected with over-hasty zeal under pressure from the Islamic community in South Africa. Copies of the book were not yet available in South Africa, and it seems this book of more than 500 pages was banned before the members of the relevant committee had had time to read it.

The week-long conference leading up to the evening of 31 October was, as Chris Louw would put it in an article in *Die Suid-Afrikaan* of December 1989, a spectacle of ironies. Mansoor Jaffer, convenor of the 'Save the Press' campaign working for freedom of speech, never turned up at the opening, in deference to death threats from the Islamic community. Wally Serote, a writer and member of the ANC, expressed himself strongly against censorship—but promised that his party, once they were in power, would apply selective censorship to eradicate racism. Hilda Grobler, a lecturer at the University of Natal, objected strongly to all forms of censorship—but then asked that members of the board of appeal on publications be more representative. The *Weekly Mail*, which had organised the conference along with COSAW, was, according to a statement by Marilyn Kirkwood, that morning informed of a banning order that would extend for a month. Professor Fatima Meer, an anti-apartheid activist from Natal, declared that she was no longer prepared to take part in the conference, because the book week had degenerated into a podium for Salman Rushdie. 'In the final analysis,' Meer said, 'it is the Third World that is being attacked by Rushdie, the belief in the Third World itself and its institutions which he besmirches [...] His attacks are especially painful because of the brilliance of his literary skill and because of the assertion that he writes from inside.' These words were too much for Irving Freeman, a book dealer from Cranford's in Long Street, and he repeatedly shouted 'Shame!'– by chance the title of one of Rushdie's novels—declaring that they were having to listen to Islamic fundamentalism plain and simple. Meer concluded her declaration with the confession that she was condemning the book without having read it.

At the last minute COSAW, against the wishes of the *Weekly Mail*, which was defending Rushdie's right to free speech, decided to withdraw the invitation, allegedly because in the light of the threats from the Islamic community they could not guarantee his safety. In the place of Rushdie, Nadine Gordimer, a committee member of COSAW, flew from Johannesburg to appear with Coetzee. Gordimer would say later that two days before her departure from Johannesburg she had, with members of COSAW and representatives of the *Weekly Mail*, debated the situation for six hours with members of the Islamic community. After two hours they retreated into separate rooms to arrive at some kind of a compromise. After the discussions the Islamic delegation was informed that COSAW would not give ground on Rushdie's visit to South Africa. COSAW recognised the Muslims' right to protest, but asked them to refrain from threatening Rushdie with death and endangering the lives of the audience in the Baxter. COSAW would then give members of the Islamic community an opportunity to read a public statement. But the Muslims had not changed their position. One of them said that Rushdie could not set foot on South African soil. If he were to come, they could not guarantee his safety. From the discussions it became obvious that not one of the representatives of Islam had read the book. Gordimer and her fellow-members of COSAW pointed out that the book was banned in South Africa and could do no harm. The Muslims, however, refused to accept this argument. COSAW then decided to withdraw the invitation. To them the man's life was more important than their principles.

All the tickets for that evening in the Baxter had been sold. Muslims arrived to see what would happen, because the possibility had been mooted of a telephonic connection with Rushdie in London (which did not happen). The atmosphere was tense. Before their appearance Coetzee and Gordimer spoke amicably to each other.

What followed was, as Ian Glenn would put it later, one of the most dramatic public differences of opinion ever in South African letters. 'It is difficult,' Glenn wrote, 'not to sympathize with Gordimer and the Congress of South African Writers, but the dangers of censorship and the paths down which Gordimer's association with and commitment to a political movement seemed to be leading were clearly perilous.'[90]

At the heart of Coetzee's action was not in the first place an attack on COSAW and Gordimer, but a statement of principle on the relation between the spirit of fundamentalism and the free spirit of literature. He said that a whole segment of the South African intellectual community, in which he includes himself, comes out of the affair looking pretty stupid. He suspects that behind the scenes some kind of trade-off took place, some kind of compromise in which the Rushdie visit was given up for the sake of unity of the anti-apartheid alliance and in particular for the sake of not making life too difficult for Muslims in the alliance:

> I am here for three reasons. The first is to register publicly my protest against the silencing of Mr Rushdie's voice, in the first place by the Muslim Right and then for their own hypocritical reasons by the South African censors. [...]
>
> The second reason is that I want to say something about Islamic fundamentalism which no one else seems in a hurry to say. Islamic fundamentalism in its activist manifestation is bad news. Religious fundamentalism in general is bad news. We know about religious fundamentalism in South Africa. Calvinist fundamentalism has been an unmitigated force of benightedness in our history. Lebanon, Israel, Ireland, South Africa, wherever there is a bleeding sore on the body of the world, the same hard-eyed, narrow-minded fanatics are busy, indifferent to life, in love with death. And behind them always come the mullahs, the rabbis, the predikante, chanting their blessings. I do not exclude Cambodia from the list, I do not exclude the madness of the secular apocalyptics.
>
> These words are addressed particularly to the Congress of South African Writers. Don't get involved with such people; don't get into alliances with them. There is nothing more inimical to writing than the spirit of fundamentalism. Fundamentalism abhors the play of signs, the endlessness of writing. Fundamentalism means nothing more or less than going back to an origin and staying there. It stands for the one founding Book and after that no more books. [...]
>
> The third and final reason why I am on the platform here is that I am as much part of this defeat as anyone else. [...] That loose and fragile alliance of people, those who believe in freedom of speech and those who believe in freedom of speech for some people—we have suffered a crushing defeat. [...] We are so demoralised, afraid even to pick up a telephone and dial Mr Rushdie's London number for fear that someone will throw a bomb at us, that we have no sense

of whether the Rushdie affair will in a year's time have vanished from people's memories or, on the contrary, will go down in history as a moment after which people simply got tired of pretending that there was any place for the liberal shibboleths, freedom of speech, freedom of association and the rest, in the anti-apartheid struggle.

There was loud applause from the audience when Coetzee took his seat. It was unexpected and may have even surprised Coetzee, as it previously seemed as if the assurances of COSAW were accepted by the majority of the liberal intellectual and literary establishment.[91]

Gordimer was shocked at the way in which Coetzee waded in and exposed fallacies in COSAW's thinking. When her turn came to speak, she was shaky:

> I must begin by saying that I am extremely surprised, and shocked, and distressed to find that I have come here apparently to defend the Congress of South African Writers rather than to state the opposition of myself personally, the Congress of South African Writers, and all of us to the situation that has arisen over Salman Rushdie. I think that it is very surprising, to me, that my friend and colleague, John Coetzee, without really discussing it, with me or with anybody in the Congress of South African Writers, has sprung this public attack upon us. But that is his democratic right and that is what we're here to defend.

Later, when talking about the debate in one of his interviews with David Attwell, Coetzee was to say: 'I became involved in an unforeseen and unsettling public disagreement with Nadine Gordimer over Salman Rushdie's *Satanic Verses*. Rushdie had been invited to lecture in South Africa and had accepted: the disagreement was over whether, in the light of various menaces to his life (I am speaking of the time before sentence of death was passed on him by Khomeini), the invitation should be withdrawn. I argued that it should not. In retrospect I think Gordimer, in her prudence, was right, I was wrong.'[92]

This does not detract from the fact that Coetzee's statement on the night was principled. He was not cowed by the threats from fundamentalists, and exposed COSAW's inconsistent stand on censorship.

CHAPTER 12

JOYS AND LOSSES

I

On the publication of *Foe* in 1986, John Coetzee was a man of 46, attractive but slight, with a prematurely greying beard, horn-rimmed glasses, a low voice, a taciturn demeanour and a certain asceticism of appearance.[1] The reticence and privacy with which he surrounded himself would over the years become his main defence against unwelcome intrusion from outside, also against critical onslaughts to which he would in general reply only very indirectly. Any attempt to penetrate his privacy, as many a journalist experienced, would make him clam shut immediately. Asked why his family moved about so often in his childhood, he replied simply: 'I don't remember.'[2] His private life was as much outside the public domain in South Africa as abroad. It was known that he was divorced and that he lived with his two children, Nicolas and Gisela, in a small suburban house in a narrow street; also that his partner, Dorothy Driver, lived on her own, not permanently with him. Close friends knew that he was a vegetarian and that early in the 1980s he had been diagnosed with a lactase deficiency that forced him to avoid dairy products. The street in which he lived — 11 Toll Road in Rondebosch, about twenty minutes' walk from UCT — did not in those years feature on maps of the city, and his entry in the telephone directory listed a fictitious address. When he made a rare appearance at a social occasion, he preferred to stand in a corner talking to a single person.

This urge to privacy caused many journalists to over-emphasise the uncommunicative side of his personality and the dark, sombre aspect of his fiction, creating a one-sided image of the real J.M. Coetzee. The journalist Rian Malan, who conducted a few interviews with Coetzee in the 1990s, characterised him as 'the prince of darkness' and his early books as 'awesome, [...] lit from within by a cold and terrible light, haunted by unanswerable questions'.[3] Outlined against the crepuscular light of his small office in the Arts Block at UCT, the author seemed to Malan 'a

pale and austere presence in his grey slacks and tweedy sports jacket'.[4]
His first question was met with a blank silence: Coetzee wrote the words
on his notepad, considered them, and in his reply made an analysis of
the assumptions underlying the question. All his questions, according
to Malan, were given this treatment. When Malan risked the comment
that he read in *Foe* the unbearable allegory of a country in which most
white and black people could find no way of reaching out to each other,
and asked Coetzee what he thought of this interpretation, the reply
was: 'I would not wish to deny you your reading.'[5] When Malan, clearly
desperate, asked Coetzee what kind of music he enjoyed, he replied:
'Music I have never heard before.'[6] In one of his interviews Malan calls
Coetzee 'a man of almost monkish self-discipline and dedication. He
does not drink, smoke or eat meat. He cycles vast distances to keep fit
and spends at least an hour at his writing-desk each morning, seven days
a week. A colleague who has worked with him for more than a decade
claims to have seen him laugh just once. An acquaintance has attended
several dinner parties where Coetzee has uttered not a single word.'[7]

Coetzee's reaction to Malan's questions, however, surely demonstrates, as in other interactions with journalists, a measure of mis-
chievousness not without an element of refined humour. It also betrays
impatience with the kind of questions with which journalists all too often
plague him. In one of the interviews David Attwell conducted with him
in *Doubling the Point*, Coetzee elaborates on this impatience. In the first
place journalists all too often exceed the boundaries of the genre and of
decency by trespassing on what he regards as his privacy: 'I don't regard
myself as a public figure, a figure in the public domain.'[8] In the second
place, there is the lack of professionalism of so many of the journalists
who approach him with little knowledge of his novels or real interest in
his work, and whose questions are utterly predictable. In the third place,
there is the question of control over content. A writer, says Coetzee, does
not easily surrender control of his text, whereas journalists, sometimes
shoddily, edit and censor the text, leaving out all that is unique and
peculiar to it. Coetzee continues: 'But my resistance is not only a
matter of protecting a phantasmatic omnipotence. Writing is not free
expression. There is a true sense in which writing is dialogic: a matter
of awakening the countervoices in oneself and embarking upon speech
with them. It is some measure of a writer's seriousness whether he does
evoke/invoke those countervoices in himself. [...] Whereas interviewers
want speech, a flow of speech.'[9]

As against Rian Malan's version of Coetzee as a surly, aloof and un-communicative person, there are many friends and acquaintances who testify to another side of his personality. Jonty Driver, the poet and the brother of Dorothy, Coetzee's partner, has written:

> I have always found the public attitudes to him (especially in the press) strangely difficult to understand; yes, he is a very private man and hates intrusions—but he is also exceptionally kind and helpful (for instance to other writers, especially young ones), often very witty with a delightful sense of humour, and can be a charming companion. My wife—who is admittedly a chatty soul—loves being seated next to John at dinner parties. When I helped arrange a visit last year to the New Worlds Writing Partnership at UEA, I know the organisers were nervous about his reputation as a difficult, even curmudgeonly, guest. I don't think they accepted my reassurances; but after he had left I was told what an easy person he had been to look after. Sometimes I think journalists especially want to think of him as difficult, because it gives them something to write about—other than the books they haven't bothered to read.[10]

In interviews, it is true, journalists have found him cautious and hesitant. Aware as he is of the provisionality of an interview situation, there are often silences, as he searches for the best possible formulation. He is, in interviews as in his creative work, a perfectionist, struggling with words—although he has commented mischievously in an interview that his perfectionism does not extend to 'all walks of life'.[11] He does, admittedly, not encourage intimacy and has no patience with dumb questions. But if somebody wins his confidence by demonstrating his own qualities, Coetzee can open up. In his letters his approachability is even more evident from the manner in which he replies to questions, although even here he uses words sparingly, his letters always to the point and precisely worded. He is also capable of great empathy. Howard Wolf, who got to know Coetzee well in his years in the English Department in Buffalo and on his frequent visits since, once wrote to Coetzee that he felt his twenty years as a lecturer had not been as rich as they might have been. Coetzee replied, on 27 May 1987, that we all experienced a sense of disappointment at times, which we then ascribed to our chosen career, our marriage or the city in which we lived: 'But middle age brings its lugubrious spells for all of us.'

When Coetzee entertains at home, his friends are constantly aware of his cool, observant intellect. His casual clothing at such intimate gatherings, however, shows that he can relax in familiar surroundings. Even on more formal occasions he avoids, if possible, formal wear or even a tie. His friends find him humorous, warm and generous. He is an engaging host, who likes to fill his guests' glasses, even though he does not drink himself. He has said 'I simply don't like the taste of wine',[12] though it seems likely that he may have retained an aversion to alcohol from childhood memories of his father's over-indulgence. He is an excellent cook, and likes preparing food such as gnocchi and richly flavoured Indian food.

Daniel Hutchinson, who got to know him as a student, has spoken of his long and warm friendship with Coetzee, whom he always found to be an honest, frank, engaging and charming person.[13] Howard Wolf[14] found Coetzee 'mordantly witty' in conversation, though the novels were, for him, 'dark, oppressive, painful and torturous'.

Coetzee liked in his free time to go walking on Table Mountain. He also liked, as in his years in London, to go to the cinema. Although he in general avoided large crowds, and never during his years at UCT took part in political demonstrations, he was very fond of attending rugby and especially cricket matches at the crowded Newlands in Cape Town. Although he expressed some reservations about the politicising of rugby in the 1980s, its use to reinforce the authoritarian male personality and as opium for the masses, he enjoyed watching the show of strength on the field.[15] He often played cricket with other members of the university staff on a Sunday. He was a valuable member of the team, both as opening batsman and as an off-break bowler. He was the only team member who turned up regularly for practice.

In these years Coetzee started cycling seriously, as a sport and as recreation. He had been fond of running, but found that one of the advantages of cycling was that he suffered fewer muscle injuries. He bought quite an expensive bicycle, and between 1983 and 2001 took part fifteen times in the annual Argus Cycle Tour, often with the poet Gus Ferguson. He achieved his best time in 1991, when he completed the race—104 kilometres—in three hours and fourteen minutes, a feat he repeated in 1994.[16] This is an excellent time for this gruelling race. Regular cycling kept Coetzee very fit, as evidenced by the fact that he once cycled from Rondebosch, along Voortrekker Road and through the northern suburbs, for tea with his colleague, the historian

Hermann Giliomee, in Stellenbosch—and then cycled all the way back.
He often combines his overseas trips with a cycle tour, in France in
particular. On 23 October 1987 he wrote to Howard Wolf how, during
a visit to the Rhône Valley, he had cycled through acres and acres of
sunflowers—intended for cattle feed and cooking oil. This is probably
the trip during which he followed the route, referred to in *Diary of a Bad
Year*,[17] that Ezra Pound had taken in 1912 from Foix to Lavelanet past
Roquefixade, in the footsteps of the troubadours of the Middle Ages.

In an engrossing article in *Leadership*, XIII: 5, 1994, titled 'Travels
in space and time', he describes a cycle tour undertaken with seven
companions, among whom his daughter, Gisela, from Paris to Avignon
and then westward to Toulouse. Eventually only two of the company,
Coetzee and Gisela, reached Toulouse on 13 July, having covered about
1 250 kilometres. They had been together for a week, concentrating
wholly on the cycling, and in the evenings having excellent meals and
then sleeping in adjoining rooms in a hotel—for Coetzee one of the
most pleasant holidays of his life, and confirmation that parents and
children can, in spite of everything, still co-exist and love each other.
Coetzee writes about how such a cycle tour differs from a journey by
car or train, about what the cyclist comes across along the way, what
impression the French landscape and people make on him, and
especially about how much easier it is to cycle in a country such as
France than in South Africa. In France motorists do not seem to have a
grudge against cyclists, and acknowledge their right to share the road.
In South Africa cyclists are obliged to be defensive, because they have a
good chance of deliberately being run off the road:

> Why this animus against the bicycle? A simple explanation: be-
> cause drivers are aggressive, because the law is not interested. A
> fancy explanation: in the early decades of the century the bicycle
> was slotted into the mythology of rural Afrikaners as the opposite of
> the horse, and has never escaped the stigma. The suitor who comes
> courting on a bicycle is a man without property, a figure of comedy
> but also a harbinger of social levelling; the suitor on horseback is
> the embodiment of traditional values, dashing yet safe. (Horses and
> rifles also go together, as bicycles and rifles most certainly do not.)
>
> Social history. After World War II black men began to acquire
> bicycles, and for a while the bicycle took on a new signification
> in black society: riding a bicycle was modern, it placed one above

those who had to walk. This was very likely the moment when white opinion, linking the bicycle to black aspirations, concluded that whites who rode bicycles were letting the side down.

Today the bicycle as a means of transport is looked down on from all sides. To young blacks a man on a bicycle is marked as old-fashioned, rural. To them it is the car or nothing.

This article, intended only as an occasional piece and unjustly not considered for collection, demonstrates once again Coetzee's fine powers of observation, his precise formulation, and how logically and originally he surveys a subject. He observes the daily life of a French housewife in slippers and an apron with a bunch of keys round her waist—emblematic of rural France, unchanged since the Middle Ages—watching over her tidy beds of spinach, beans, tomatoes and potatoes, and hiding her money under the mattress. Even though nobody in the hotel industry nowadays welcomes a cycling tourist, Coetzee appreciated how freely a cyclist can move about the roads of rural France. He did have misgivings about the Formule Une hotel in Orange to which the guest gains access by slipping his credit card into a slot, which unlocks the door while it debits the card with f135. For this he is given a tiny room with a bed, a washbasin and television and a toilet that flushes automatically when you leave, just in case you forgot—everything in clinical plastic with no sharp edges or corners. The traditional concierge, bellboy and clerk of the old French hotels have been replaced by PIN codes and cameras monitoring the movements of the guests. He found it odd that in this country with its glorious culinary tradition there was so little provision made for vegetarians. In an *auberge* outside Lavaur he ordered the menu of the day for f55, but asked the *patronne* to omit the ham from the salad and to replace the *agneau* with an omelette—in spite of which he received a salad with tinned tuna, because a cook in France, according to the hostess, cannot imagine a life without meat, just as the Chinese pour a thin chicken-leg gruel over vegetables to add a meaty taste. For someone with his apparently eccentric perspective, the French culinary imagination is more limited than French cooks are prepared to accept.

In spite of this he enjoyed the daily cycle journey. Unlike just about all other advances in Western technology, the discovery of the bicycle, he thinks, has no negative aspect. 'It has brought only good with it,' he writes. 'It has extended the horizon, physical and mental, of billions of people, not least among them children. It has multiplied the weight we can carry and the distance we can travel, and has done so without any noticeable harm to our environment. To the extent that speed is joy, it has also brought quantities of happiness into the world.' On 10 July Coetzee and his daughter were cycling in the Languedoc: 'The road winds downhill, mile after mile. We swoop through the curves, cutting the wind. Around us a pungent smell of herbs whose names we do not know. No sound but the hum of tyres on the road. God, I say, let me live forever in this world you have made.'

In several of Coetzee's books, such as *Boyhood* and the later *Slow Man*, the central characters are at their happiest when cycling. In a letter to the Dutch cycling magazine, *De Muur*, Coetzee writes about the democratic nature of cycling. The bicycle, he says, is wrongly called a machine. Unlike machines that generate an own power source, the bicycle is more of an instrument, dependent on the exertion of the cyclist.[18] In the same issue of *De Muur*, Tim Krabbé, a Dutch cyclist and the author of two cycling books, tells how he and a few other enthusiasts took Coetzee for his first cycling trip in Holland, the country of bicycles:

> The manner in which the Australian-naturalised writer took off showed experience. Coetzee was a cyclist with the technique of a practised climber. [...] Entering Monnickendam he revealed his cautiousness. Calmly negotiating without taking risks, he rode over the cobbled roads of the town, sometimes responding in a startled fashion to the sudden looming up of a car. Whoever was so inclined, could recognise scenes from *Slow Man* or other books describing a scared person.[19]

Acquaintances of Coetzee's have often been struck by his original perspective on matters, coupled with a tendency to a contradictory or unexpected point of view. When an interviewer from *Fair Lady* asked him, in the edition of 28 August 1983, about his 'sombre' novels, he answered provocatively: 'Everyone seems to see bleakness and despair in my books. I don't read them that way. I see myself as writing comic books, books about ordinary people trying to live ordinary, dull, happy lives while the world is falling to pieces around them.' When, in the same interview, he was asked what he thought of feminist literature, he answered: 'Do you mean feminist writers, or women writers who are today claimed by feminists to be feminists or both? I don't go out of my way to read women, just as I don't go out of my way to read men. There are smart women around, there are smart men. Also one shouldn't forget that we live in a country in which the best novelists have been women.' When Wim Kayser put to him, in an interview in the series *Van de schoonheid en de troost*, the predictable but boring question: 'When you are down and out, what do you do? Listen to Bach or Beethoven or Webern or start drinking? Writing? What are you doing?', Coetzee took the opportunity, after a moment's thought, to come up with a perverse reply: 'I cook. It's simple, it's good in itself and the results are immediately available and in itself it is very consoling.'[20] And congratulating his friend, the poet Douglas Reid Skinner, in a letter of 28 August 1983, on his proposed second marriage, he calls it, with good-humoured cynicism and alluding to Samuel Johnson, 'the triumph of optimism over experience'. In his tendency to look at things from an often surprising perspective and to hold unexpected views, Coetzee resembles C. Louis Leipoldt, the medical doctor, botanist, gastronome and versatile writer who, early in the twentieth century until about 1930, figured as one of the most prominent Afrikaans poets, and who on his death in 1947 was accorded the epitaph: 'Dr Leipoldt preferred to contradict. He was the apostle of the opposite view.'[21]

But more important than any other occupation is his creative work, the central focus of Coetzee's life from the moment on 1 January 1970 when he wrote the first words of *Dusklands*. This was the founding moment of an oeuvre that would grow more impressive with every new novel. Coetzee is the kind of writer whose art has to a large extent become the substance of his life. In English letters of the last century he may be comparable only with Samuel Beckett in the centrality of writing to his life.[22] Like James Joyce before him—who had the capacity to write every day, irrespective of his personal circumstances—Coetzee is able to make time for writing every day of his life, including Sundays and holidays. He prefers to write in the early morning when he is fresh and clear-headed. He first writes the manuscript by hand and then switches to the computer. 'I don't like writing,' he has said in an interview, 'so I have to push myself. It's bad if I write but worse if I don't.'[23] When Wim Kayser asked him whether the writing action for him contained something beautiful and consoling, he was very decided: 'Writing in itself,' he said, 'is industry, total engagement, hard thought, verifiable activity, verifiable results, productiveness. Beauty and consolation belong not to the activity, but to the results of that activity. It may or may not be consoling. Looking back having written a book, may be or not be consoling to the author.'[24]

The daily commitment to writing means that Coetzee must be focused and organise his day. When, for instance, he has a lecture at half past eight, he will get up at half past five and put in a few hours' writing. If he only needs to be at the university in the afternoon, he will sleep to a more conventional hour. Over the years writing has become easier for him, and a way of life. The full professorship and the more convenient arrangements he could arrive at with the university authorities in 1984, despite David Gillham's resistance, made his life much easier, even though he had to attend to his children and run a household. In one of his interviews with David Attwell he compared the writing of fiction with the writing of criticism. Fiction gives him greater freedom, because it is responsible to something still in the making, whereas in criticism, he is always conscious of a responsibility 'toward a goal that has been set for me not only by the argument, not only by the whole philosophical tradition into which I am implicitly inserting myself, but also by the rather tight course of criticism itself'.[25]

II

In the 1980s Coetzee was still very actively involved in teaching at UCT. The courses he offered are notable for their originality of approach and for the kind of material he chose for discussion. In 1980, for instance, he offered a course on the 'Narrative Act' in which, using Vladimir Propp's *Morphology of the Folktale* as point of departure, he examined the fairy tales of the Brothers Grimm, then the narrative element in a variety of genres (popular fiction, films and comics), concluding with a discussion of two of Chaucer's *Canterbury Tales*. After the death of Sydney Clouts he devoted a course to this poet's work, with particular attention to the sources and the critical commentary on his poetry. At this time the English Department instituted an M.A. in Literary Studies. For this degree Coetzee offered a course in realism, starting with a theoretical-historical survey of the concept and an exposition of different authors' interpretation of the term. The care with which Coetzee structured his courses is evident from the brochure he compiled for part of the module 'Colonial Discourse', a component bearing the title 'The production and consumption of literature'. He writes:

In [this] component of the Colonial Discourse option we will be mapping some of the ground for a sociology of literary culture in Africa, with an emphasis on South Africa and anglophone West Africa. We will be addressing such questions as: What are the special features of the economics of publication and distribution on the continent of Africa? Within what frameworks (aesthetic, intellectual, cultural) and environments (social, economic, mate-rial, ideological) are the activities of writing and reading carried on today? [...]

[This] component is a research component. There will be no instruction (though students will consult with the lecturer about the progress of their researches). Instead, the last weeks of the semester—from roughly the end of September to mid-October—will be occupied with a series of 90-minute seminars. In each of these an assigned student will deliver a 20-minute report to the class on his/her work, and each of the other students will deliver a 5-minute critique of the report, after which there will be general discussion.

It is therefore necessary for each student to be not only an authority on his/her own topic, but to have an informed and critical awareness of the issues involved in the topics chosen by other members of the class.

Students from [the other] component are welcome to attend the seminars for [this] component, but in that case will be required to deliver critiques like everyone else.

The research report delivered at the seminar should be regarded as a draft of the research essay, which should be submitted in final form *no later than 16 November*. The length of the essay will obviously depend on the nature of the research undertaken, but 20 pages (typed, double-spaced, including detailed and accurate notes and bibliography) should be taken as a minimum. The mark for the essay is the mark for the component; the mark for the component is 25 per cent of the mark for the Colonial Discourse option.

I want to stress that the work undertaken for this component is research work. The field in which we will be working has barely been explored before. There are no ready sources, no handy and complete bibliographical aids. The source-list [...] is only a beginning; the project will entail patient, time-consuming work in the library, not all of which will necessarily show rewards. All that can be guaranteed is that you will learn something at first hand about the sometimes frustrating nature of research work.

The work that goes into the [two] components constitutes $\frac{1}{16}$ of the entire M.A. (Literary Studies) course. At a rough computation, you should therefore be spending the equivalent of about *three weeks* of *full-time* work, i.e., some 150 hours, in researching, writing and revising the essay. This makes the time you invest in it *quantitatively* different from the time you invest in essays for options with an instructional component.

The subjects that Coetzee outlined for the assignments testify to the renewal he brought to the training of students, and to the manner in which he gave direction to their literary research:

1. What have been the obstacles to the evolution of a publication and distribution industry (for books) in Africa in general? What is the present state of affairs in the African book industry? To what extent has South Africa constituted a separate case, and why?

2. What similarities and differences are there between the mass British reading public of the first half of the nineteenth century, as described in Altick's *English Common Reader*, and the mass Black reading public in South Africa today? What are the more significant similarities and differences between the rise of mass reading habits in Britain and the growth of mass reading among Black readers in South Africa?

3. Outline the life-histories of some of the following South African literary magazines and—insofar as these can be inferred—analyze their editorial policies. What effect have these policies had on the development of literary culture in South Africa? (See *English in Africa* 7: 2, 1980.) *Bolt, Classic, Staffrider, Izwi, New Classic, Purple Renoster, Contrast, New Coin.*

4. Discuss the activities of the expatriate or multi-national publishing houses—particularly British-based houses—in post-World War II Africa. What has been the case against them, and how have they defended themselves? What role do they currently play in South Africa?

5. In the light of Edward Shils, *The Intellectuals and the Powers*, pp. 335–371, discuss evidences of a tension between a metropolitan orientation and a provincial orientation in South African literary culture, both historically and in the South Africa of the late 1980s.

6. What has been the role of official US and British programmes of

cultural exchange in the formation of elites in (a) West Africa, (b) South Africa? To what degree have these elites come to influence literary-cultural life in each case? To what do you ascribe differences between (a) and (b)?

7. What differences are there between 'World Literature written in English (excluding British and American)' and 'Commonwealth Literature', particularly at an ideological level? (Include discussion of the journals *World Literature Written in English (WLWE)* and *Journal of Commonwealth Literature*.)

8. What are the characteristics of first-generation (roughly pre-1980) introductions to and surveys of African literature published in the UK and USA? Who wrote these books, for whom were they written, and what are their critical-ideological points of departure?

9. Discuss the reception of African literature by Black American readers—particularly critics and scholars—since 1960. To what extent has a Black American readership served to shape African writing (a) before 1960, (b) since 1960?

With such a logical exposition of what was expected of them, it was natural for Coetzee's dedicated students to respect and appreciate him. In his undergraduate classes, some students, aware that he detested verbosity, sometimes counted the number of words he uttered during a lecture, because compared with his engaging but sometimes much too garrulous colleagues, what he had to say was said in a few minutes. He could be unnerving in class, because the students were constantly aware that he weighed every word before pronouncing it.

Students in his M.A. courses could testify to the meticulous attention he accorded their assignments, always annotated in his small, tidy hand. Alex Smith, who attended Coetzee's M.A. classes, later wrote that she had to suppress her own whims and fancies for the sake of survival when dealing with 'the king of the comma, the gaunt genius of spare and stern'.[26] Evert le Roux, who after his honours at Stellenbosch went to UCT to do his masters in comparative literature (English and German) under Coetzee and Peter Horn, had a very good relationship with Coetzee, got excellent marks and was awarded the degree *cum laude*. He could never understand why people said Coetzee was cold and unfeeling, because he experienced him very differently. After Evert's early death, according to his mother, Marina le Roux,[27] Coetzee often phoned her and her husband and asked 'Are you coping?', a token of his empathy

434 J.M. COETZEE: A LIFE IN WRITING

with parents who had lost a gifted son. David Attwell, one of Coetzee's students, later professor of English at the University of the Witwatersrand and currently at the University of York, said: 'He is very attentive to one's project and utterly astute in his guidance. He had a reputation with undergraduates for being formidable, but my experience was that if you took your work seriously, he would take you seriously.'[28] Shaun Irlam, Attwell's fellow student and currently professor in comparative literature at Buffalo, said: 'He doesn't have time for frivolities. But if he recognized that one was seriously engaged in the study of literature, he would be absolutely transformed into the most responsive and engaged mentor.'[29]

On his appointment as full professor, with effect from the beginning of 1984, Coetzee delivered an inaugural lecture devoted to 'Truth in autobiography'. As starting point he used the opening of Jean-Jacques Rousseau's *Confessions*, and stated the position that confession contained ambivalence between *finding* the truth and *telling* the truth:

> Telling the story of your life [...] is not only a matter of representing the past [,] but also a matter of representing the present in which you wrestle to explain to yourself what it was that *really* happened that day, beneath the surface (so to speak), and write down an explanation which may be full of gaps and evasions but at least gives a representation of the motion of your mind as you try to understand yourself. Indeed, the lies and evasions may be more interesting than the visit itself.[30]

In this pronouncement lies the germ of Coetzee's later autobiographical works, in which he was to recall, in the distanced third-person form and from the perspective of the 1990s and later, his life as a child and a young man. Coetzee did not reprint his inaugural lecture in any of his later collections, but he did incorporate it, in 1985, in the larger frame of his essay, 'Confession and double thoughts: Tolstoy, Rousseau, Dostoevsky', one of his most important essays, which he included in 1992 in *Doubling the Point*.

Apart from lecturing at UCT, Coetzee several times in the 1980s, more frequently than in the previous decade, visited the US, Europe and other parts of the world to present courses at universities or to deliver addresses at conferences or symposia. In 1984 and in 1986 he travelled to the US to occupy the Butler Visiting Professorship in English at Buffalo. On his first visit, he travelled via London, with his daughter, Gisela, who would live with him in Buffalo and go to school there.

During his two visits to Buffalo Coetzee for the first time offered courses in creative writing, a course he would offer in the 1990s in Cape Town with André Brink. He found that American students wrote on a wide variety of subjects, while their South African counterparts tended to a political content that sometimes overwhelmed everything else. He wrote to Douglas Reid Skinner from Cape Town on 28 August 1983 that in the course of his visits he would also do readings from his works at other institutions: 'It's not that I want to do readings—I suspect I'll be rather bad at it, and absolutely dread the political turn such events might take—but it's going to be expensive maintaining two establishments (here and in Buffalo), plus paying alimony.' At the time of the state of emergency and widespread unrest in the black townships, Dick Penner, who would in 1989 publish an important study of Coetzee, *Countries of the Mind: The Fiction of J.M. Coetzee*, nominated him for a Chair of Excellence at the University of Tennessee; Coetzee replied that he found the situation in South Africa appalling, and that he was torn between anger and despair:

> I do not need to tell you of the turmoil in this country, turmoil which is reflected in the minds of everyone who lives here. My own feeling is that I want to live here as long as it is possible to do some good, in whatever way I can. As a writer I don't want to go into exile, if only because I have seen what exile does to writers.[31]

After his visits to Buffalo, Coetzee was in 1986 and again in 1989 the Hinkley Visiting Professor of English at Johns Hopkins University in Baltimore. On his first visit he left in December 1985 to spend time in London first, then attend the PEN conference in New York, to arrive in Baltimore in time for the spring semester. During this visit he also delivered lectures at Princeton, Texas and McGill University in Montreal, Canada. In September 1986 he read from his work in New York, an occasion that coincided with the second edition of *A Posthumous Confession* and the US première of *Dust*, the film of *In the Heart of the Country*.[32] He wrote to Douglas Reid Skinner from Baltimore on 5 November 1986: 'All is going along quietly here, which is how I would wish it to be. I was in Montreal for a reading earlier this week, and was very impressed with what I saw of the city. The reading was OK. Winter isn't quite here, but the temperature is down to freezing. It will be my third winter in a row. I'm missing Cape Town, the warmth, the cycling, friends, Dorothy.' One condition of Coetzee's appointment to the Hinkley chair in 1988–'89 was that he would deliver a lecture on literature and the law. He chose as subject 'D.H. Lawrence and censorship', and later reprinted the lecture in the collection *Giving Offense* (1996). His experience had been that there was often heated debate about censorship, but that too little considered, logical thought had been given to the matter. In his lecture he concentrated on *Lady Chatterley's Lover* and on Lawrence as a transgressor—not of any law in particular but of taboo and decorum.

In the 1980s, Coetzee by invitation started writing reviews for the London *Times Literary Supplement* (*TLS*) and *The New York Review of Books*. When approached by the *TLS*, he wrote on 9 December 1983: 'I would indeed like to review for the TLS—in fact would be honoured to do so—as long as I don't, as a rule, get invited to review South African material (I am willing to consider exceptions). I am rather concerned to avoid the more limiting implications of the label "South African novelist J.M. Coetzee". I hope you will understand.'

But it was in *The New York Review of Books* that many of his most important essays would appear in the subsequent years, often on writers from Russian or Polish background not generally known in English. The underlying literary theory, explicitly present at times in his earlier work, is here osmotically incorporated into the whole. When devoting an essay to a particular author, he generally writes from a knowledge of the previous work of the writer and of the literary landscape from which he or she has emerged. As a perceptive literary anthropologist he is able to trace the underlying literary currents of a specific time and place and identify the myths and other binding and meaning-producing mechanisms shaping the literary context of a particular work. Adjectives and summary judgements are rare in his critical essays. The analysis of an oeuvre proceeds mainly from the forces implicitly contained in the work itself. In Coetzee's essays the critic is a companion; as a mouthpiece for judgements he is virtually invisible.

From the many essays submitted to *The New York Review of Books* and reprinted in his collections, it is clear that his initial interest in theoretical matters had waned, in the interests of a broader overview of an author or a single work, often with a biographical or historical orientation. His friendship with Howard Wolf had in part been based on their common interest in literary theory and postmodern literature. When Wolf asked him, in 1998 during a visit to Cape Town, whether his planned early retirement was in any way related to a feeling that literary theory had become too abstruse and sterile, too far removed from direct observation and from the human condition, he answered in the affirmative.[33] When Howard Wolf sounded him out about the newly vacant McNulty Chair in Buffalo, he replied in a letter of 23 September 1986: 'My feeling at the moment [...] is that I'm in the process of at least partly retracting from academic life, rather than going deeper into it; and that what the department needs is someone in the chair with a great deal of energy and commitment.' Although Coetzee would retain his chair in Cape Town for another decade or longer, he clearly was already considering a withdrawal, at least partly, from academic life. This may be one of the reasons why in 1998 he declined an invitation from Johns Hopkins to apply for the chair formerly held by John Barth.

Apart from the lecturing visits to the US, Coetzee took part in several conferences on literature. In 1980 he was part of a panel discussion of censorship at UCT, and in 1985 he took part in a conference on aesthetics at Houwhoek in the Western Cape. Later he would frequently visit Europe and other continents to deliver papers at conferences as far afield as Mexico, Essen in Germany, Djibouti in the Horn of Africa, Dartmouth College in Hanover, New Hampshire, Budapest in Hungary, Canberra in Australia, and Victoria in British Columbia, Canada. In 1997 he visited the French city of Aix-en-Provence, to appear with a group of South African writers.

The symposia he attended gave Coetzee the opportunity to get to know some of the foremost writers and critics in the world, and to visit many countries, often with his partner, Dorothy. Though he has said[34] that he does not like travelling and prefers books, there has since 1980 not been a single year in which he did not undertake at least one long journey to another continent. He said in an interview that Dorothy enjoys travelling and visiting unfamiliar places, and that he is more than happy to accompany her. He prefers France, because he is able to combine his visits with long cycle tours. In spite of what one might be led to believe by his novel *The Master of Petersburg*, he has never been to Russia. When visiting foreign countries, he does not go to museums or churches, because they soon exhaust him. Although he is very interested in music, he does not attend concerts, preferring to listen to recordings at home. He likes accompanying Dorothy to restaurants, but the initiative is usually taken by her. Like him, she is a vegetarian.[35]

In July 1991 Coetzee, with about 240 other academics, attended a conference on narrative in Nice. He used the chance to undertake a cycling trip through Provence along the famous coastal strip—the Esterel Corniche with its spectacular clay-red cliffs descending into a clear, blue ocean—between St Raphael and Nice. On 2 August 1991 he and Dorothy left for Australia, where for three weeks he acted as 'writer in residence'[36] at the University of Queensland in Brisbane and then spent a week in Melbourne. This was his first visit to Australia, and he explored the country. The week in Melbourne was the best. After Brisbane they spent a week in Sydney. He also travelled to Tasmania to visit an old friend, and was reminded of Scotland and Norway by the snow on the ground and the coastline. A few weeks of his sojourn in Australia were spent in an artists' colony in rural New South Wales. There he had a cottage to himself close to five artists with their studios, with the nearest supermarket 25 kilometres away. He felt attracted to Australia—the landscape, the bird life and the general tranquillity—and tried to persuade Dorothy, at first without much success, to move there. He found the people pleasant.

An invitation came in the autumn of 1991 to lecture at Harvard. He was accompanied by Dorothy, who had also been invited as a visiting professor. They arrived in September 1991 and stayed in Eliot House, a university residence close to Harvard's impressive libraries and even closer to the indoor swimming pool, which Dorothy visited twice a day. They undertook a few very pleasant cycling trips to the west and north of Boston to enjoy the autumn leaves.[37]

During his stay at Harvard, Coetzee travelled to Berkeley, which struck him as more run-down and impoverished than during his visit in 1979. He also went to the University of Wisconsin for three weeks and afterwards to Indiana and Northwestern for a week each. On their way home he and Dorothy visited Verona in Italy. Returning to Cape Town in November 1992, he found that his house in Toll Road had been burgled, which contributed to his decision eventually to move to a flat in Rondebosch. This offered a quiet retreat, until some rowdy students moved in downstairs.

With them at Harvard on a Fulbright Scholarship was Manju Jaidka, later professor of English at the Punjab University in Chandigarb, India, well known for her contributions to the study of American literature in India, and the writer of respected critical works. In an article she published later, Jaidka writes that she had not at first known of Coetzee's literary achievements. When she discovered them, she was amazed that somebody with such a low profile could have such an eminent career. She found no pretension or affectation in him. He conformed, for her, to the kind of image that T.S. Eliot projected, with his belief that a writer should wear a mask and live a conventional and conformist life. She writes:

> John Coetzee is [...] like Eliot in the way he deliberately keeps his private life out of the public eye. A researcher seeking information on his biography invariably draws a blank. The writer is hard to contact; it is near impossible to get an interview or even a response from him. [...} His job is to study the world and write about it. Material gains, rewards, international awards, nothing seems to matter much.[38]

III

While John Coetzee was lecturing at UCT in the 1970s and '80s and starting to achieve international recognition with his novels and visits to American universities, his parents were settled in a flat in Rondebosch, where their grandchildren, Nicolas and Gisela, often visited them. Jack Coetzee travelled to central Cape Town every day by train, where he had an apparently soul-destroying job as a bookkeeper with a motor spares firm. Vera was still teaching.

The two of them were getting on in years, and they started to think of exchanging life in Rondebosch for something in a smaller and cheaper place. Vera's cousin owned such a property, in Greyton, about a hundred kilometres from Cape Town, and urged Vera to buy the plot next to his. Because Vera had always believed in property as a safe investment, she did buy the plot. Both plots previously belonged to a coloured owner who had run a small farm there, but the renovated house was on the cousin's section, and Vera had only a borehole and the vegetable plots on her section. John bought her a prefabricated house from the South African Naval base on a slope in Noordhoek and transported it piecemeal to Greyton by lorry. When the house had been assembled, the local council took one look and decided that Greyton did not need prefabricated houses. So John had to disassemble the house and get a retired builder in Greyton to design and build a brick-and-mortar house.[39]

Vera and Jack moved into the new house in Greyton early in the 1980s, but the change was disastrous. They did not like Greyton, they had no friends there, and they had to get by without a car. Vera's eyes started giving in, and she had trouble reading, although she was not quite blind. They returned to Rondebosch, but Vera's health kept deteriorating. Apart from her visual impairment, she developed heart problems. She died after a heart attack on 6 March 1985, in her eighty-first year.

Jack and Vera had had no happy marriage, but her death left Jack at a loss. Men of his generation had been brought up to be more or less helpless at practical housekeeping, with no experience of cooking or coping in the kitchen. He simply faded away. In the last months of his life he developed cancer of the larynx, for which he was operated on. After this he was unable to speak, and spent his last days in the Arcadia old-age home in Observatory, where he died on 30 June 1988 at the age of seventy-six. His brother Mills and his family commemorated him in the *Cape Times* of 1 July 1988 with a death notice: 'Jack passed away peacefully after a long illness bravely fought.'

Even though John had had a fraught relationship with his father, his death, just more than three years after that of his mother, was a palpable loss. In *Summertime* (2009) Coetzee depicts a single John, after his return from the US in the 1970s, living with his father in a house in Tokai. This is part of the fiction that *Summertime* interweaves with fact, because Vera and Jack died in the 1980s, while in the 1970s John was married with children. Jack did not at any stage live with John's family. Nevertheless, *Summertime* clearly dramatises a rapprochement of sorts between John and Jack, as in the descriptions of John accompanying his lonely father to rugby and in summer to cricket at Newlands.[40] Later, John is imagined going to help his father with his bookkeeping in the evenings during annual stocktaking, his presence making the job that much easier.[41] He also recalls, in the diary entry with which the book ends, his father's return from the war in 1945, having acquired a taste for Italian opera in Rome, and his belting out opera passages in the bath, to the irritation of John with his preference for Bach. Once, according to this narrative, he damaged his father's recording of arias by Renata Tebaldi with a razor blade. This deed compels him many years later, upon his return from the US, to give his father a new Tebaldi record, only to find that his father no longer recognises Tebaldi's voice. Whether John Coetzee had really accompanied his father to Newlands, helped him with stocktaking and actually damaged the record, is not important for the reader of the novel to know. What is important is the spirit of conciliation with the father, what it represents after all the years, and the development of compassion in the John figure.

Previously, the death of Vera was a great loss for John Coetzee. In spite of his references in *Boyhood* to her suffocating love, which made him treat her dismissively, she was in his early youth the centre of his existence. 'He cannot imagine her dying,' the young John thinks in *Boyhood*. 'She is the firmest thing in his life. She is the rock on which he stands. Without her he would be nothing.'[42] At her funeral in Cape Town, Stefan Wehmeyer, the author's second cousin, found a sombre John Coetzee and expressed his condolences. 'Thank you,' Coetzee replied, 'but you can do nothing about it.'[43]

There was a further bereavement: the death of Philippa Jubber, Coetzee's ex-wife. After the divorce Philippa had stayed on for a while in Cape Town, but then settled in Johannesburg, where her parents and her brother, Cecil, lived. In Cape Town she had worked as secretary in the Department of Chemical Engineering at UCT, and on moving to Johannesburg, filled the same post in the same department at the University of the Witwatersrand. Later she moved to a secretarial position at the Council for Scientific and Industrial Research, with offices next to the Wits campus. She got to know the much older Louis Levine, a salesman who sold various wares to shops, such as toys and other objects made in Taiwan. They fell in love. Although they did not get married, she had a happy relationship with him. At this stage of her life she converted to Roman Catholicism.

While Coetzee was working on the first rough design of *Age of Iron*, Philippa developed breast cancer. Her daughter, Gisela, who had always had a better relationship with her father, was shocked, on a visit to Johannesburg, at Philippa's appearance, and made up her mind to go and live with her and help her in her illness.[44] Shortly before her death Philippa went to Cape Town to say goodbye to her friends. On 7 June 1990 Coetzee wrote to Howard Wolf:

Philippa was in Cape Town for ten days in May, more or less saying goodbye. She has advanced cancer, as I may have mentioned. She has given up the very strict diet she has been on, since there seemed not much point in continuing with it. Whether it is because her metabolism has been disturbed by the treatment I don't know, but she eats wolfishly. Not at all one's picture of a dying person. She has no strength in her limbs, and can hardly climb stairs. But the combined radiotherapy and chemotherapy seem to have stalled the three brain tumours she has, and she is once again able to do things like reading.

Philippa died in hospital on 13 July 1990, before Gisela, who was studying at UCT, could go to Johannesburg again to look after her mother. On 4 August Coetzee wrote to Howard Wolf:

Philippa died two weeks ago. She had been hospitalized at the end of June, with fluid on the lungs. This problem was patched up; but in the process it became clear that her whole body was riddled with cancer. There was an unexpected lesion of the wall of the bowel; before an operating theatre became available — for an operation which she would probably not have survived anyway — she was gone. There was no time to call anyone to the bedside. My cousin's wife, who was paying a regular visit, was fortunately there, and stayed till the end. Philippa was heavily drugged and not in pain.

Gisela has spent ten days there in June, so she doesn't have to feel bad about not getting a chance to say goodbye. She is holding together well, but I'm not sure that the impact has fully worked through yet.

The funeral was appalling. It was held in the Catholic cathedral — Philippa had converted to Catholicism some years ago — and the arrangements had been made by her brother. Whether he had not stressed sufficiently that she was divorced and living in a deep monogamous relationship with another man, or whether the priest as a matter of dogma simply refused to hear about divorce, I don't know. But throughout the service he referred to Gisela, Philippa's brother, and me as the 'bereaved ones'; Louis' name wasn't so much as mentioned. And this for a Jew who was having to go through all the motions of a Catholic funeral mass! I was enraged; but Louis said, 'It doesn't matter, it's what's here that counts' (touching his heart). Philippa was so lucky to have him. I could not have coped, as he did, with her long illness, during which she was not at all times an angel of patience (who would be?).

She and I were married for seventeen years, not particularly happy years (not her fault by any means). She appointed me executor of her estate, and I have had the dreary duty of going through her papers, which I brought down to Cape Town from Johannesburg — a carful.

Catherine Lauga du Plessis, later Coetzee's regular translator into French and at the time of Philippa's death married to Coetzee's colleague Ian Glenn, was a close friend of Philippa's. Philippa's remains were reburied in the cemetery near the Fountain in Rondebosch. At the time of the commemoration Catherine was in the US attending a translators' conference.

On her return she went to the grave to put flowers on it. On the spur of the moment she went to Coetzee's house nearby, in Toll Road. She found Coetzee in the kitchen, cooking. When she told him she had visited Philippa's grave, he looked at her and started crying uncontrollably.[45]

IV

Coetzee's next novel, which appeared in hardback in 1990 with Secker & Warburg, and after that as a paperback with Penguin in the United Kingdom and the US, was called *Age of Iron*. Apart from *Waiting for the Barbarians* and the collected edition of his three autobiographical works, *Scenes from Provincial Life* (2011), it is the only one of Coetzee's works to carry a dedication. The first of these is to his parents: Vera Hildred Marie Coetzee, born Wehmeyer (1904–1985), and Zacharias Coetzee (1912–1988). They are indicated only by their initials.

Although a dedication in a literary text can be a gesture of respect or affection to (often departed) family, friends or mentors, the ritual of dedication may sometimes also function as an integral part of the text, pointing towards the raw material or motifs to be developed in the text. From large sections of *Age of Iron* in which the longing for the child is expressed, the informed reader may deduce a longing for the dead mother. The novel often recalls the narrating central character's childhood with her mother; and at times even her mother's recollections, which had been recounted to the narrator as a child. One such section occurs as early as the manuscript of *Boyhood*, but Coetzee omitted it from the final text of that book. This section, which now forms part of *Age of Iron*, considerably pruned from the manuscript version, functions as a memory of the mother who in her childhood in the days of ox wagons had travelled with her parents, brothers and sisters from Uniondale to Plettenberg Bay at the mouth of the Piesangs River. One of the stopping-places on the long journey was at the top of a mountain pass. While the parents slept in the wagon itself, the children had to sleep under it, and through the spokes of the wheel she could see the moving stars. She wondered if it was not perhaps the wheels rather than the stars that were moving, and what would happen if the wagon started rolling.[46] We can assume that this material is biographical. It recurs repeatedly in the manuscripts, is reduced to just three paragraphs in the final text of *Age of Iron*, and is alluded to again later in the novel.[47] Even a detail in *Boyhood*—the character John causing his brother David to get his finger caught in a machine—recurs in *Age of Iron*, but now transposed to the narrating mother who takes her daughter to the emergency section of a hospital after the injury.[48] Again and again the childhood and past of the mother return as material for the novel. In its entirety *Age of Iron* is a novel about love that exceeds boundaries, an elegy, a lament on death and dying.

At the end of the novel are the dates '1986–89'. These indicate not only the dates of the genesis of *Age of Iron*, but also the time frame in which the events in the novel take place. Although it lacks the external paraphernalia of the epistolary novel, the form is that of a very long letter from an elderly woman—Mrs Curren, a retired lecturer in classical languages—to her daughter, who left South Africa in the anxious apartheid years to settle permanently in the US. There she has married and had children, vowing never to return until the day when the rulers of the apartheid state are swinging by their necks from the lamp posts.

The events take place in winter in the mid-1980s, and start on the day that Mrs Curren, who narrates the novel,[49] is informed by her doctor that she has terminal cancer and probably won't see the summer she longs for so ardently.[50] The absence of her daughter is for Mrs Curren an abiding grief, rooted in a desperate attempt at contact, expressing a love that cannot be returned, and that she can only exorcise by putting words on paper to reach out to her daughter. 'I am feeling my way towards you,' she writes, 'with each word I feel my way.'[51] Her letter is a testament, a bequest on the threshold of death, a raw cry from her deepest self, lamenting the last phase of her life as well as the last phase of the apartheid state, a land 'in the process of being repossessed'.[52] In truth the cancer[53] afflicting Mrs Curren is a metaphor for the moral mutilation of a country that, with the abuse of power by the apartheid structures, has lost its humanity. It is no coincidence that the words 'disgrace' and 'shame' that will culminate in Coetzee's novel of 1999, recur several times in *Age of Iron*.[54] The letter to her daughter represents also a recourse to language as a last resort, just as it was an escape route for Magda in *In the Heart of the Country*, her 'ancestor' in Coetzee's oeuvre.[55]

Unlike Coetzee's previous novels, which were set in a specific time far in the past ('The Narrative of Jacobus Coetzee'), against a vague fictional geographical background (*Waiting for the Barbarians*) or somewhere in a near future (*Life & Times of Michael K*), the setting of *Age of Iron* is the bloody history of South Africa in the 1980s. The naming of specific residential areas and streets places the action clearly in the Cape Town of the 1980s. The events take place against the backdrop of the violence in the townships, with militant, rebellious children burning their schools, choosing liberation before education, and with their taunting of the police heeding the call of their banned leaders to make the country ungovernable; while the armed forces of the regime meet the insurrection with remorseless onslaughts on the young people, 'legalized tyranny' as the historian Leonard Thompson calls it.[56]

Because the radio, television and newspapers are silent about what exactly is happening in the townships, Mrs Curren at the outset of the novel is ignorant of the real extent of the violence. That shots are being fired in Guguletu and children are in peril, she does not know. 'In the news that reaches me,' she writes, 'there is no mention of trouble, of shooting. The land that is presented to me is a land of smiling neighbours.'[57] Events gather momentum only at the beginning of the second section of the novel, when her domestic help, Florence, returns to work, accompanied by her two little daughters. With them is her school-going son, Bheki, who has been brought along because of the unrest in Guguletu, and whose friend John soon joins him. Mrs Curren becomes drawn into the violence when the police, looking for the two boys, engineer an accident, hurting John so badly that he is taken to hospital by ambulance. When, at the beginning of the third section of the novel, Florence is told by phone late at night that Bheki is in trouble, Mrs Curren drives her and the little girls to Guguletu. This turns into a descent into the underworld reminiscent of Book VI of Virgil's *Aeneid*, a Dantesqe vision of hell: she witnesses the burning of houses and sees five bodies, among them that of Bheki, lying in a devastated hall. Later, at home, she witnesses the murder of John, who has been hiding from the police in the servants' quarters. A central incident of the visit to Guguletu is the dispute between her and Mr Thabane, Florence's brother, a former teacher but now working for the struggle. He supports the idea that children should be part of the struggle, whereas Mrs Curren blames people like Thabane for enticing children to the 'mystique of death'.[58] Unlike the tongueless Friday in *Foe*, the blacks in *Age of Iron* have found their voices and unanimously reject an authority and laws they regard as illegitimate, a rejection articulately voiced by Mr Thabane in his defence of the comrades. The novel thus, according to David Attwell, demonstrates 'the necessity, certainly the desirability, of a reconstructed ethics in which certain traditional liberal values find a new relevance within an all-consuming and humanly damaging political struggle'.[59] But at this stage Mrs Curren abhors the call to sacrifice that leads to young people dying in the mud:

> War is never what it pretends to be. Scratch the surface and you
> find, invariably, old men sending young men to their death in the
> name of some abstraction or other.[60]

What Mrs Curren wants to say, from her classicist's world view, is that political aims efface the ethical implications of the deaths of children. When, early in the novel, she criticises the violence in the townships, saying that in her youth parents considered education a privilege and would deny themselves in order to keep their children at school, Florence replies: 'I cannot tell these children what to do. It is all changed today. There are no more mothers and fathers'[61] As Derek Attridge comments in his illuminating discussion of the novel, Mrs Curren considers this reply a manifestation of the 'age of iron' in which she lives, distorting the future that traditionally belongs to children. In this respect there is a kinship between these children and her own daughter, who has left the country, determined not to return until the dawn of a new dispensation.

But her experiences bring about a change of heart in Mrs Curren. Especially the death of John brings her to accept a new ethos calling for direct action: the insight that the values and ethics she has cherished are no longer valid in the violence-riven South Africa of the 1980s:

> But now I ask myself: What right have I to opinions about com-
> radeship or anything else? What right have I to wish Bheki and
> his friend had kept out of trouble? To have opinions in a vacuum,
> opinions that touch no one, is, it seems to me, nothing. Opinions
> must be heard by others, heard and weighed, not merely listened to
> out of politeness.[62]

She comes to the realisation that the politics of the day need to be corrected by ethical considerations, not vice versa. Derek Attridge puts it thus:

> It is an age of iron, the worst of times, and its particular defor-
> mations of the human spirit call for a response that is neither
> moralizing nor cynical. Mrs Curren has to acknowledge that nothing
> she can say will detract from the heroic self-sacrifice of the township
> children, made vivid to her in the deaths first of Bheki and then
> of John; theirs is a situation in which the only possible ethic is an
> ethic of comradeship, single-mindedness, and blind courage. For
> Mrs Curren, and by implication for J.M. Coetzee and the majority
> of his readers, who are in a markedly different situation, the ethical
> appears in another guise: as the difficult task of responding with full
> justice to the moment, with a trust in the other and the future that
> is ultimately beyond measure. [...] An ethical response on the part
> of privileged South African whites to the violent and dehumanizing
> campaign of the townships would be one which is neither
> condemnation nor approval, neither detachment nor immersion,
> but a living-through (in concrete action as well as in thought and
> emotion) of the torsions it produces in shared value-systems.[63]

Attridge concludes this aspect of his discussion with the thought-
provoking statement: 'What is enacted in this novel is the acute ethico-
political trauma of the post-colonial world, where no general rule
applies, where a conflict of values is endemic, and where every code
of moral conduct has to be tested and justified afresh in terms of the
specific context in which it is being invoked.'[64]

On the day she receives the news of her terminal illness, Mrs Curren
notices a homeless tramp called Vercueil in her garden, a person ex-
traneous to the accepted norms of society.[65] However oddly for her as
a refined person, a peculiar relationship gradually develops between
her and this man, whose name evokes the Afrikaans words *kuil* (a

pool), *verskuil* (conceal) and *verkul* (cheat). He is the person to whom she entrusts her deepest thoughts (in a dialogue that is really a long monologue), and whom she binds to a promise to post her 'letter' after her death to her daughter in America. The mutilation of his hand through an accident (he cannot move his index finger and thumb, and the other three fingers are curled back into the palm) links him to Michael K with his harelip and the mute Friday. Like Michael K, he is a gardener, however reluctantly, for which he receives money from Mrs Curren on which to get drunk. But he is also her chauffeur, confessor, a surrogate for her child, nurse and ultimately her messenger who must post her bequest to her daughter. In the closing scene of the novel he is the angel of death. From the manuscript it appears that Coetzee at first wanted to call the novel *Rule of Iron* and later considered the title *Winter*, and the novel would have ended on the words: 'But spare a thought for this man left behind who cannot swim, does not yet know how to fly.'[66] It was only at the very end that Coetzee added the last five paragraphs. In the final paragraph Vercueil, as angel of death, mercifully helps Mrs Curren to die: 'He took me in his arms and held me with a mighty force, so that the breath went out of me in a rush. From that embrace there was no warmth to be had.'[67]

In an essay touching on *Age of Iron*, James McCorkle suggests that the title of the novel alludes to Olive Schreiner's pseudonym Ralph Iron, and that the plot evokes Olive Schreiner's lonely death in Cape Town.[68] Most readers will probably find these connections far-fetched. But if we bear in mind that in the years that he was working on this novel, Coetzee was also writing the essays that were in 1988 collected in *White Writing*, and in which he repeatedly returns to *The Story of an African Farm*, the suggestion may not be as improbable as it seems at first sight. Other allusions are possible: in Mrs Curren dying of cancer a memory of Coetzee's former wife, Philippa; in the many pages about love a hidden homage to the dead mother, Vera; and even in the dissipated figure of Vercueil an indirect reference to Coetzee's father, who, like Vercueil, took refuge in liquor while tramping through Cape Town in search of work. (Coetzee's Du Biel second cousins, who played carpet bowls with him on their visits to Jack and Vera, would remember his father by his whisky breath and his 'crooked yellow teeth'.)[69] Patrick Hayes, basing his interpretation on the reference to Cervantes in Coetzee's acceptance speech for the Jerusalem Prize, sees in Vercueil Coetzee's own version of Sancho[70]—not in the first place to mock Mrs Curren, but rather 'like a companion in folly, being foolish enough himself to believe, at least in part, though with growing dubiousness, aspects of Quixote's illusion'.[71]

The reception of *Age of Iron* was exceptionally favourable. In *The Listener* of 13 September 1990, Harriet Gilbert calls Coetzee 'perhaps the most gifted and skilled living novelist, his vision magnificent and terrible, his writing as supple as a hairspring'. She continues: '*Age of Iron* appears to have stepped entire from Coetzee's head, deft in its subtle integrity, to explode inside ours and illuminate not just the South African child-killing fields but a whole world of poisoned chalices carelessly pushed against children's lips.' In *The New York Times Book Review* of 23 September 1990, Lawrence Thornton writes: 'In this chronicle of an aged white woman coming to understand, and of the unavoidable claims of her country's black youth, Mr Coetzee has created a superbly realized novel whose truths cut to the bone. His readers will "suffer the shame" of injustice that came to occupy the old Magistrate's [in *Waiting for the Barbarians*] heart, but they will also witness the inevitable flowering of the age of iron.' In *The Spectator* of 29 September 1990, Francis King praises 'the writing, so spare, so strong, so iron-hard, [...] wholly and magnificently original. There is no hope in this book for either Mrs Curren or South Africa; but there is ample hope for the future of the novel when writers like Coetzee are around.' In the *Chicago Sun-Times* of 14 October 1990, James North anatomises the 'hypnotic minimalist prose that is the equivalent of the steady drip of rain on a dank and gray winter day in Cape Town. Coetzee dispels some of the romantic aura that has grown up around the struggle for liberation, especially from afar, and forces us to press our noses up against the glass and look closely at the ugly, unbelievably brutal things that people are capable of doing to other people.' The Nijmegen critic, W. Bronzwaer, writes in *De Volkskrant* of 22 May 1993:

> The theme of the farewell to the daughter is worked out movingly and poignantly. The form of the novel, which is in effect a letter in which the mother recounts the last six months of her life to her daughter in America, is admirably suited to this purpose. Because South Africa too, will have to say farewell to what it holds most dear: the ideals of white, liberal humanism, and yield the stage to the children of the new age, the age of iron, the children with hearts of stone: the violent ones, the rebellious oppressed. To them love and care will have to be extended—there is no other solution.'[72]

The highest praise came from Tony Morphet in the *Weekly Mail Review of Books* of 7–13 December 1990. He describes Coetzee's earlier work as 'masterly' — but '*Age of Iron* has opened a gate and released a current of profound feeling. It is this which gives the book its place at the head of his achievement. A masterpiece.' What strikes him in particular, is the power residing in the movement of the language:

> The sentences seem to write themselves directly out of the thought of the characters. The meanings emerge slowly from within, and they carry a sense of natural inevitability. They follow the rhythms of the thinking mind, unfolding themselves through repetitions, extensions, balanced oppositions, parallel constructions and sudden unexpected openings. All the while, as they go, they elaborate an intricate network of cross reference and illusion.

In a second review, this time in the *South African Literary Review*, I: 2, April 1991, Morphet writes:

> The wonder of the book is its discipline. It is the discipline which yields not only the powerful illusion that the book has written itself 'from within', as it were, taking the experience of people in a particular time where it found it, but also that individual lives have been felt, heard and weighed within a profound current of feeling illuminated by an exceptional intelligence.

In *Vrye Weekblad* of 1 March 1991, Gerrit Olivier, too, expresses great admiration for the novel:

> Age of Iron is a book that brings the reader from the very first page, in language both poetic and knife-sharp, very close to the narrator and her dilemma, and this intensity is sustained almost throughout. [...] What Coetzee achieves here is not only an extraordinary evocation of a personal death, but also a diagnosis of a whole society from the perspective of somebody dying of shame and disgust.

Ernst Lindenberg, in his review in *Die Suid-Afrikaan* of April–May 1991, concentrates particularly on the failure of a liberal mindset in the South Africa of the 1980s:

Perhaps some of the questions raised by the book may be answered if we see the heroine's fate as the death of liberalism in South Africa. Liberal values as such are not denied, but they have proved ineffectual. *Age of Iron* with its convincingly sustained female perspective constates or diagnoses this failure, but sorrowfully. The lasting impression is of an endless grief at the withering, at the insight that also Mrs Curren and her daughter with their stiff-necked pride, in spite of everything, are also affected, are also of iron. The frustrated reaching-out, the realisation of futility and the longing for deliverance vibrate in the words, page by page: it is a compelling reading experience, and assures *Age of Iron* a worthy place with its five predecessors. It compensates in intensity for what it lacks in epic dimension.[73]

In a concise review in *Sesame* 15, 1991, Lionel Abrahams, the Johannesburg writer and literary critic, trenchantly analyses the essence of the novel, and, like Morphet, expresses the highest admiration for it:

Coetzee's novel, though relentless in its contemplation of the condemned woman's special loneliness, as of public savagery, mindlessness and dread, though charged with accusation, warning, grief, anger, shame and perhaps even despair, transcends its material, transcends, amazingly, some of its own judgements and ideas—because the telling is so impassioned, so full of Mrs Curren's love and her sense of human identity, so paced by the beat of life's race against death; also because the narrative art is so aesthetically fulfilled.

These (passions, rhythmic urgency, symbolic potency, and inspired expressiveness) are the qualities that render this as much a titanic poem as a novel that, surely, dwarfs just about everything else in South African fiction so far.

This appreciative assessment prompted Coetzee to the unusual step of writing to thank Abrahams. In a letter of 27 May 1991 he writes: 'We get the readers we deserve, they say. But what did I do to get a reader and a reading like this? Thank you. It makes the whole enterprise of a life suddenly worthwhile.' He concludes: 'Thank you too for your continual steadying presence in South African letters, like a hand on the tiller.'[74]

Age of Iron was considered for the CNA Prize, but it was awarded to Nadine Gordimer for *My Son's Story*. Coetzee did win the Book of the Year 1990 prize of £20 000 awarded by the British *Sunday Express*. The South African actress Janet Suzman accepted it on his behalf at a lunch in the Café Royal in London. The literary editor of the paper, Graham Lord, wrote:

> Anyone who cares about South Africa, that beautiful, tormented land where blacks are now killing blacks in a vicious tribal war, will tremble to read Coetzee's superb, gripping new novel. [... It] depicts vividly the nightmare and shame of white South African anti-apartheid liberals who have suddenly been forced to realise that history has overtaken them.

Coetzee also received, with Kathleen Coleman, the University of Cape Town's annual book award. The actress Yvonne Bryceland read the book on the BBC's Radio 4. This was repeated in 1995 on the English service of Radio South Africa.

V

Among the dedicatees of *Age of Iron* appear also the initials of a third person: 'NGC (1966–1989)'. This is Nicolas Guy (Talbot) Coetzee, the son of Coetzee and Philippa, who was born on 9 June 1966, and died, according to the dedication, in 1989.

How did Nicolas come to die at such an early age, before turning twenty-three? On several websites writers clearly not in possession of the facts maintain that he died in a car accident. Shortly after his death rumours circulated among staff at UCT that he had committed suicide and that the Security Branch had been looking for him. The rumour concerning Nicolas's so-called political involvement was probably re-inforced by details that readers of *The Master of Petersburg*, Coetzee's 1994 novel, wanted to link to biographical circumstances.

The facts are different. Although he was not well disposed to the apartheid regime, Nicolas never displayed any political involvement nor, during his student days at UCT, did he take part in protest marches or demonstrations. Although it may be true that in Johannesburg he on occasion scribbled graffiti on walls for fun,[75] it is highly unlikely that there is any truth in the rumour of political involvement.

But was it suicide?[76] Nicolas started his schooling at one of the Waldorf schools and continued it at the Western Province Preparatory School in Rondebosch.[77] After this he attended Westerford High School. At this stage *Waiting for the Barbarians* was published. Nicolas was very proud of the international recognition the novel received, and was probably very pleased that it was dedicated to him and Gisela. For one of his school assignments he did an oral presentation on the novel.[78] He idolised his father, and, to their mutual amusement, tried to persuade him to write a best-seller.[79] But then John and Philippa got divorced. This came as a great shock for both children, because, in spite of the tension in the home, they were completely unprepared for it. Their parents had not taken them into their confidence, and offered them little support. To sit down with Philippa and talk the children through the process of the divorce would have gone against Coetzee's instinct for secrecy and privacy. To make things more difficult for the children, this happened while they were contending with the onset of puberty. Nicolas in particular was badly shaken, and irrationally placed all the blame for the divorce on his father.

After Philippa's departure for Johannesburg the children saw less of her, though they did from time to time visit her over holidays. They were mainly looked after by Coetzee in the 1980s, which Nicolas found difficult: he looked very much like his mother and was closer to her than to his father, against whom he was in revolt. In his quiet way John Coetzee is a very dominating figure and Nicolas probably, as he got older, had to contend with the syndrome of a famous father and having to find a niche for himself in life.[80]

At school, too, things started going wrong for Nicolas. Often Coetzee could not get him out of bed in the morning, and he would wake up only in the afternoon, having missed school. He thought the kind of instruction to which he and his friends were subjected was rubbish, and he was in revolt against the hierarchy of the school and the discipline maintained by the teachers. Because he did no work whatsoever, he fell behind, despite his exceptional intelligence. Everything started going downhill for him. Along with a few friends he smoked pot, and indulged in other drugs and alcohol. He once drank so much that he had to be hospitalised. This youthful recklessness took a serious turn when, with two or three other boys, he got involved in housebreaking and other criminal activities while they were supposed to be at school. Once Coetzee had to go to the Claremont police station to bail him out after he and his friends had been arrested.

Because he could not abide the discipline at school, and because someone had told him it was easy to matriculate as an independent candidate, Nicolas left school. He enrolled at a correspondence college and registered for the easiest subjects he could find. One of the subjects, notorious for being impossible to fail, was criminology, a bizarre matric subject, actually intended to recruit candidates for the police force. John Coetzee scrutinised some of the exam papers, and found it scandalous that anybody could be given a certificate for an examination with such ludicrously easy questions that could be answered with a minimum of knowledge and common sense. Nicolas did get his matric, but very unconventionally, by not attending school, doing no work, and persisting in his idle existence.

With matric behind him, Nicolas at eighteen decided to avoid compulsory military service. He left for the US, since by his birth in Austin he was an American citizen. He settled in San Francisco on an allowance that Coetzee sent him. Here he led an extremely meagre existence, because even that mecca of hippies and rebellious youth could be very tough on an 18-year-old. He tried registering at an American university, but his matric certificate was unacceptable as an equivalent to a high school diploma in the US. He had a variety of casual jobs, like gardening, but could not cope. After about a year he was back in South Africa. He was accepted at UCT, without his father smoothing his way, but also completed some courses through the University of South Africa. He enrolled for the B.A. degree, majoring in history, passed all his subjects with a minimum of effort, with an average well above 60 per cent, even scoring 70 per cent or higher in history, with a first for the module 'Colonizer and Colonized'.[81] Nicolas was, however, estranged from his father and refused to accept money from him. On 22 December 1987 Coetzee wrote to his friend Howard Wolf: 'Life [is] full of conflict with my son, who (at the age of 21) still can't put me behind him and occupy himself with other things. Perhaps one day he will write a *Forgive the Father* too.[82] Or perhaps not.' On 7 September 1988 he wrote to Wolf:

> Ingratitude isn't what I get from Gisela. In fact, she isn't the 'problem' child in that sense. Nicolas is the one who gives me headaches with a bizarre trick he has of refusing to take anything directly from me, so that I have to create elaborate chains of fictional benefactors — usually including his mother — via whom to

get money to him—money without which he would either starve or drop out of college. So that in the end he can maintain his stance of independence from his father. The day he comes to me to play out the reconciliation scene, I'll really have some truths to tell him.

After completing his studies at the end of 1988, Nicolas decided to settle in Johannesburg, where his mother was living with Louis Levine, and to start a career in the film industry. To establish yourself in this industry, he discovered, takes hard work. He had to start right at the bottom, and could only get a job as a chauffeur for film crews at a film company, supplementing his income at night by manning a telephone for a security company, receiving reports of burglaries, etc. Although he often visited his mother, by now seriously ill with cancer, Nicolas had his own flat at 115 Sunny Ridge, Claim Street, Hillbrow. Because his income was so meagre, Coetzee had to keep supporting him financially.

At the beginning of 1989 Coetzee went to the Johns Hopkins University in Baltimore to lecture for a semester. On Monday morning, 24 April 1989, he received a message to phone Philippa urgently. Her first words were: 'Nicolas is dead.' She and Louis Levine had been in Cape Town for the weekend.[83] When they returned, there was a message from the police to get in touch with them. They told her Nicolas had fallen to his death from the balcony of his flat on the eleventh floor.

Coetzee flew back to South Africa as soon as he could. He wrote to Howard Wolf in Buffalo from Baltimore on 28 April 1989: 'A note in haste—I leave Baltimore in a few hours. My son Nicolas was killed a few days ago. He fell from the eleventh floor of an apartment block in Johannesburg. The funeral is on Tuesday.' He attended the funeral on Tuesday, 2 May in Johannesburg with Dorothy, Philippa and Louis Levine.

The inquest took place on 23 October 1989 in the magistrate's court in Fox Street, but neither Coetzee nor Philippa atttended it. According to the bare facts in the 'Register of deaths' in the Johannesburg state mortuary,[84] the body was found at a minute past midnight on 22 April on the corner of Claim and Jettah Streets, Hillbrow, by one Constable Du Toit, who brought it to the mortuary. It was identified by Louis Levine and the cause of death in the register is indicated as 'multiple injuries'. Although the date of death in the register is 22 April, it should be 21 April, since the body was found a minute after midnight on 22 April. On 24 April an autopsy was performed by a Dr Maar. The autopsy report has not survived, but in the 'Register of deaths' under

'General comments' the word 'Jumped' appears, suggesting a verdict of suicide. In the absence of an inquest report the word 'Jumped' should probably be ascribed to a facile conclusion by a functionary at the police station. It is an understandable conclusion, given a death of this kind. At first, before going to Johannesburg for the funeral, Dorothy and John Coetzee also assumed it must have been suicide.[85] But somebody in the flat building opposite, according to Lisa Perold a medical doctor, told Philippa he had seen Nicolas swinging from the lower part of the balcony, and heard him calling: 'I can't hold on, can you help me?' He had struggled and tried to pull himself up, but the railings were slippery, he lost his grip, and fell. Dorothy found this plausible, because she had not known Nicolas to have suicidal tendencies. And he had not left a suicide note.

The question remains what Nicolas was doing on the balcony that night. According to Gisela Coetzee,[86] her brother had been listening to a cassette that night. She is convinced he lost his balance, slipped and then tried to climb back into the flat. Many of his organs were so badly injured by the fall that death must have been almost instantaneous. Gisela tried to establish whether he was perhaps under the influence of alcohol or drugs, but could not gain access to the report of the inquest.[87]

On their arrival in Johannesburg, John Coetzee and Dorothy went to Nicolas's flat, and saw the fingermarks left by his attempts to get back onto the balcony. These marks, though not conclusive evidence, seem to exclude the possibility of suicide. John found them very distressing. Years before he had rescued Daniel Hutchinson's little son from death by drowning, but his own son he could not save. Apart from John and Dorothy, Lisa Perold also travelled from Cape Town to Johannesburg for the funeral. John and Lisa went to the mortuary to view the body. According to Lisa, he looked very peaceful, but the cosmeticians must have had an enormous job cleaning and preparing the wounded body. John and Dorothy spent the night before the funeral with Jacqueline Cock, and according to Marilyn Honikman,[88] John cried all night. His devastating grief was distressing to behold. When his friend Chris Perold, who at that stage had a very bad relationship with his daughter Lisa, Nicolas's childhood friend, phoned to express his condolences, John's words were: 'Just be reconciled with your daughter. Please take this advice from me.'[89] Although Nicolas, according to Gisela, had been moving towards a reconciliation, he died without reaching that point.

For John Coetzee the death of Nicolas remains a constant, corrosive pain from which there is no deliverance. The loss of his son casts doubt on the hope for a future generation that he tries to imagine at the end of *Waiting for the Barbarians* through the group of children with their snowman. And the dedication of this novel to Nicolas along with Gisela becomes, against the background of his early death, very poignant.

Coetzee returned to the US on 20 May 1989 to receive an honorary doctorate from the State University of New York at Buffalo. When Howard Wolf met him at the airport and hugged him, his words were: 'It's OK, it's behind me.' They spoke no more about it. When Wolf and Coetzee arrived for lunch at the home of the poet Mac Hammond, Coetzee looked up at a plane passing above them, and said: 'My son could be up there, he's a drifter.' Wolf found this an unusually frank remark from Coetzee, who is not inclined to self-revelation. He told Wolf that at the time of his death Nicolas had a postcard from his father in his possession. He was apparently gladdened by the thought that he, in spite of their estrangement, was still able to reach his son in this way. For Wolf, who was also caught in a difficult relationship with his daughter, it was heartbreaking to see Coetzee deriving comfort from this single postcard.[90]

For the rest of Philippa's life she and John remained on a friendly footing, and there was never an actual breach between them. John always felt she was well disposed towards him. She wished him a happy life with Dorothy, and the shared grief of Nicolas's death brought them closer together.

Philippa, by now very ill with the cancer that had metastisised through her whole body, wrote to Sylvia Coetzee, John's favourite aunt and the wife of his uncle Son:

> Life for me has become very sorrowful. Not because of illness but because of Nicolas's death. When I thought I was facing death from cancer, I really felt very sorry for myself, but what I feel now, after Nicolas's death, is far far worse. There can be nothing worse than the death of a child. The pain just seems to go on and on. Cancer has become a mere trifle, an irritation, a common cold. The correct order of things is for a parent to die before a child.

VI

Although *Age of Iron* reflected the political actualities of the 1980s in South Africa, the novel also develops a metaphor of motherhood,[91] against the background of Coetzee's personal loss with the death of Vera Coetzee. In *The Master of Petersburg* (1994), as earlier in *Foe*, Coetzee apparently digresses from the politics of the day by placing the events in the Russia of the second half of the nineteenth century, a country that with its specific social problems of the time was far removed from South Africa. Nevertheless the reader gradually discovers that the events form, however vaguely, a certain parallel with those in the South Africa of the 1980s. But at the centre of the novel stands the dominant theme of the father-son relationship, and behind that looms Coetzee's grief at the death of Nicolas. It was a theme that Coetzee knew from Ivan Turgenev's *Fathers and Sons* and Franz Kafka's *Brief an den Vater* (1919, but only published in 1960); it now formed warp and weft of his own novel.

From the material in the Harry Ransom Center at Texas, comprising ten printouts of the manuscript and the proofs of the Secker & Warburg edition, it appears that Coetzee started work on the novel on 21 February 1991, almost two years after the death of Nicolas. At first he had wanted to call it *Falling*, showing how crucial the theme of the fall is for him in this novel. He abandoned the idea because Susan Schaffer had already used the title in 1974 and David Hughes in 1979.[92]

As in *Waiting for the Barbarians* and the larger part of *Life & Times of Michael K*, Coetzee here employs an omniscient narrator. The central figure on whom this narrator focuses is the Russian writer Dostoevsky, who, according to the novel, returned to St Petersburg clandestinely in October 1869 from Dresden, where, with his second wife and his child, he had tried to escape his many creditors. The purpose of his visit, under an assumed name and with a forged passport, is to investigate the circumstances and mysterious death of Pavel Isaev, his stepson from his first marriage, who had fallen from a high tower building. He also wants to retrieve his son's documents and belongings, which the czarist police have confiscated.

The events in the novel extend over a few weeks. Coetzee chooses a short period from the writer's life, when Dostoevsky was forty-nine and Pavel twenty-three, a difference that correlates exactly with the age difference between Coetzee and Nicolas at the time of Nicolas's death in 1989.

On his arrival in St Petersburg, Dostoevsky goes to the address he knows from Pavel's letters. He rents the room in which Pavel lodged, from his landlady Anna Sergeyevna. A relationship develops between Dostoevsky and Anna, and he is fascinated by her young daughter, who had been very close to Pavel.

The questions to which Dostoevsky has to find answers during his visit are whether Pavel's death had been suicide, whether he had been pursued and murdered by the police, or whether he had been killed by the terrorist group with whom he had been collaborating. The attempt to retrieve the papers leads him to Councillor Maximov, a figure whose bureaucratic behaviour is reminiscent of that of Colonel Joll in *Waiting for the Barbarians*. The possibility that Pavel could have been involved in terrorist activities is confirmed when Dostoevsky meets Nechaev, a character that Coetzee based on an actual figure from Russian history, Sergey Gennadiyevich Nechaev (1847–1882). Nechaev was a revolutionary with fanatically nihilistic views, who had a large following among Moscow students in particular. He is regarded by some as the father of modern terrorism. Along with Mikhail Bakunin he wrote a book entitled *The Revolutionary Catechism*, in which he justifies lies, fraud and even murder as legitimate tools of the struggle.[93] The group of anarchists under his leadership tried by acts of violence to create an atmosphere of confusion and revolt, intended to lead to the destruction of the old society, paving the way to a new socialist state. The radical application of this theory—the murder of one of his followers, the student Ivanov—led to Nechaev's indictment and imprisonment, where he tirelessy preached his views up to his death.[94] In the novel a meeting between Dostoevsky and Nechaev leads him to the exact spot from which Pavel fell:

> He grips the railing, stares down *there* into the plummeting darkness. Between *here* and *there* an eternity of time, so much time that it is impossible for the mind to grasp it. Between *here* and *there* Pavel was alive, more alive than ever before. We live most intensely while we are falling—a truth that wrings the heart![95]

Dostoevsky, however, rejects the nihilism of Nechaev. In his conversation with Councillor Maximov he declares his resistance to it:

> Nechaevism is not an idea. It despises ideas, it is outside ideas. It is a spirit, and Nechaev himself is not its embodiment, but its host; or rather, he is under possession by it.[96]

Later in the novel Nechaev tries to exploit Dostoevsky's literary talent for his political aims by getting him to compose pamphlets for his movement, which Dostoevsky is not prepared to do.

An investigation of the historical record soon reveals that *The Master of Petersburg* is not a factually faithful novel. Coetzee allows himself many distortions and manipulations of the historical data. It is true that Dostoesky lived in Dresden until shortly before the time in which Coetzee's novel is set, and that he there surrendered to his gambling mania. His banishment to Siberia is also factually correct, as are his epileptic fits. However Dostoesky did not go to St Petersburg in 1869; he went in 1871, but accompanied by his second wife, Anna Snitkina, and their child. Pavel did not die in Dostoevsky's lifetime, but survived his stepfather. In actual life he was an irresponsible, flashy coxcomb who caused Dostoevsky much trouble, vexation and embarrassment. Pavel, indeed, thought up many a machination to undermine Dostoevsky's marriage with Anna Snitkina.[97] It is also historically unfounded that Pavel could have committed suicide or been murdered by the police or a terrorist group. What Coetzee did was to telescope the figures of Pavel and the student Ivanov, who left the Nechaev group and was probably executed by them. Dostoevsky and Nechaev also never met in real life. This revolutionary nihilist, however, is the raw material for the character Verkhovensky in *The Possessed* (also known as *The Devils*)—probably the best novel of all times about a revolutionary plot. Shatov's murder in the novel corresponds with that of Ivanov—a police agent who in *The Master of Petersburg* is disguised as a tramp. In the novel Coetzee not only adapts data from the life of Dostoevsky, as recorded by, among others, Joseph Frank in his comprehensive biography.[98] He also engages intertextually with Dostoevsky's work, among others *Poor Folk* and *Crime and Punishment*, but in particular *The Possessed*, so that Coetzee's novel becomes a palimpsest of Dostoevsky's life and work. The final chapter of *The Master of Petersburg* is based on a segment of *The Possessed* in which the character Stavrogin confesses his paedophilic experiments—a segment that was rejected by the editor of the magazine *Kathov*, in which the novel appeared in serial form. Coetzee adapts this material in the relationship between Dostoevsky and his landlady's daughter, Matryona.

As earlier in the case of *Life & Times of Michael K*, critics questioned Coetzee's decision, amid violent upheavals in the black community of South Africa, to write a novel apparently reflecting nothing of this turmoil. Once again they expected an unambiguous political stand from him. But apart from this, the way in which he connects history and fiction in *The Master of Petersburg*, distorting the historical data and providing a misrepresentation of Dostoevsky and other characters in the novel, earned him some of the fiercest criticism ever in his novelistic career. In the *Times Literary Supplement* of March 1994, Zinovy Zinik goes so far as to call the novel 'an act of literary terrorism', and Victoria Glendinning in *The Telegraph*[99] states that Coetzee's fictional Dostoevsky is nowhere as convincing as Dostoevsky's own troubled anti-heroes, merely coming across as neurotic and unpleasant. James Wood accuses Coetzee in the *Weekly Mail & Guardian* of 18–24 March 1994 of 'a tendency to mummify his characters in strips of ratiocination, to make them the arrested victims rather than the dynamic sources of thought'. This is an objection that Richard Eder, in *The Jerusalem Post* of 8 December 1994, shares: 'Any of Dostoevsky's characters, after only a few pages, makes the heart freeze and the eyes weep. Coetzee achieves a measure of freezing; the eyes stay quite dry.' In *The New York Times* of 18 November 1994, Michiko Kakutani pronounces extremely unfavourably on Coetzee's distortion of history: 'Though Mr Coetzee's manipulation of [the] facts and fictions is perfectly nimble, it also feels completely arbitrary. For the reader, at least, there seems to be no larger purpose to his clever sleight of hand: he has simply confused the record of Dostoevsky's life and blurred the outlines of his famous novel without shedding new light on the art of fiction-making or the craft of writing. Indeed, one finishes *The Master of Petersburg* marveling at the waste of Mr Coetzee's copious talents on such an odd and unsatisfying enterprise.' John Skow, in *Time* of 28 November 1994, objects to the 'confounding falsification' that deceives the reader, and to the distortion of history: 'It's true that telling invented stories is what novelists do; but what of novels that are part history, that take their weight from the known stature of real people? Isn't the point to use fictional techniques to get the history right?' The Dostoevsky biographer Joseph Frank also deplores Coetzee's fictionalised version of the Russian writer's life: 'Coetzee is a novelist, of course, and he has the novelist's right to play with history. Still, it is regrettable that he did not include a warning to his readers, many of whom will be unfamiliar with the details of Dostoevsky's biography, not to take his fiction as fact.'[100]

However, Patrick McGrath, in *The New York Times* of 20 November 1994, admires the central figure that emerges from the pages of this novel: 'the master himself, in his tortured unhappiness, his terror of the next epileptic seizure, his restless sexuality and his desperate gambling with God'. Peter Wilhelm, in the *Sunday Times* of 13 March 1994, praises the dialogue in the novel, and admires the 'ambience of doom against which Dostoevsky must wager upon the very existence of God'. He continues:

> *The Master of Petersburg* is not the first satellite book written by Coetzee, a novel that orbits another book. *Life & Times of Michael K* orbits Kafka; *Foe* orbits *Robinson Crusoe*; *Waiting for the Barbarians* has fairly specific reference points in world literature, especially the poet Constantine Cavafy of Alexandria.
>
> Should we be concerned with this issue, which is that of what is left for the modern writer to write about? In and of itself *The Master of Petersburg* has a strange beauty, like that of the *aurora borealis*, a high and distant flickering which is not of necessity comprehensible. Of who and what Dostoevsky was, the reader need know little.

In the *Harvard Review* 8, Spring 1995, Athena Andreadis writes:

> This is a brilliant book, a *tour de force* but difficult and unrewarding to a casual reader. Its relentless melancholy and avoidance of neat endings make it frustrating, though the rich texture more than compensates for the effort. To attempt to write from inside another writer, and so successfully, is an amazing feat. To convey the sometimes distasteful contradictions within a human mind is risky and bold—and here it pays off: the story rings with authenticity.

Although Richard C. Crepwau, in the *Orlando Sentinel* of 22 January 1995, makes the point that Coetzee does not surpass or equal Dostoevsky, he does feel that he achieves 'something [that] most writers would love to achieve every time out. He has created several marvelous characters, placed them within a compact, compelling story and, in the process, has produced some very elegant prose. Who could ask for more?' And in the Canadian periodical *Chimo* of Spring 1995, T. Kai Norris Easton writes: 'This is a brilliant and absorbing book, a stunning measure of creative play and serious meditation, of subtle wit and deep intellect. In this tension between aesthetics and ethics, neither claims supremacy, rather, both attempt to find a space. Whether there is such a place is precisely the question Coetzee reserves.'

Asked in an interview with Joanna Scott[101] why he had chosen this specific historical period for his novel, Coetzee said that Dostoevsky at this time was struggling with the composition of a novel and did not know what it would be about: 'In fact he tried to write at least three different books using the same material—material in an abstract rather than concrete sense. The book that eventually emerged was *The Possessed*. The record of that period is absorbing and very humbling to follow. My novel takes up that period and reimagines it, so to speak.' In reply to critics who, in spite of the 'disrespect' of modern novelists for historical fact, still have problems with *The Master of Petersburg*, Coetzee says:

> Not my concern. In *The Possessed* the names of personages are not historical names and the identities are not historical identities. Yet no one is going to say that *The Possessed* is not about the Russia of 1870. It's not as though Dostoevsky himself does not imagine or reimagine history, imagine or reimagine the scene around him.

Coetzee goes on to say in this interview that the death of Pavel gave him the opportunity for the meeting between Dostoevsky and Nechaev, which had not happened in real life, but which could bring together two very important figures from this period. As for the relation between history and the novel, he sees it as a kind of rivalry, a point of view that replies, albeit not explicitly, to the critics who deplore his distortion of history:

> There can be rivalries of various kinds, but when the crunch comes, the relation between history and fiction is still a rivalrous one. People say the discursive models in the human sciences are giving way to narrative models. I know of a few instances, principally from anthropology and archaeology. But these instances don't persuade me that the grand discourses have yet been abandoned in favor of narrative—narrative with all its implications understood and embraced and appreciated (that's worth underlining).

What critics of this particular blending of fact and fiction have lost sight of, is that as early as 1987,[102] seven years before publication of the novel, Coetzee had expressed his resistance to the claim that a novel should remain true to 'reality'. A novel, according to this claim, must be made subservient to history and thus be reduced to a mere supplement, whereas in fact the novel creates its own reality, conveying its own validity and truth. In the same year in which *The Master of Petersburg* was published, Coetzee approvingly quoted a pronouncement of Doris Lessing in a review of her autobiography: 'There is no doubt that fiction makes a better job of the truth.'[103]

Monica Popescu writes: 'In this context, Coetzee's novel, *The Master of Petersburg*, arises not as a denial or a rejection of the importance of the historical context, but as a claim to engage with it on one's own terms within fiction.'[104] It is a pity that some critics who commented on Coetzee's novel in their reviews were apparently totally unfamiliar with his statements on the relation between history and fiction. Had they been versed in these, they could have responded more knowledgeably and with greater insight into what he was doing in *The Master of Petersburg*. If they still had objections, they could have formulated their criticisms in a more nuanced fashion. Through the (fictitious) encounter of Dostoevsky and Nechaev, Coetzee wants to convey something, however veiled, of the Russian writer's reaction to the revolutionary ideals of a group of activists and to the ways in which young students were drawn into their ideas. By implication Dostoevsky's sentiments may contain something of Coetzee's own thoughts on the South African situation, as also verbalised by Mrs Curren in *Age of Iron*. The nineteenth-century events in Russia covertly allude, in spite of all the ideological differences between the Russian nihilists and the South African Umkhonto we Sizwe,[105] to the political disorder of the 1980s in South Africa. Black children were made activists and martyrs in the name of the struggle, disempowering the parents completely. 'It has become a sickness of this age of ours,' says Dostoevsky, 'young people turning their backs on their parents, their home, their upbringing, because they are no longer to their liking! Nothing will satisfy them, it seems, but to be sons and daughters of Stenka Razin or Bakunin!'[106]

For Dostoevsky, Nechaev represents not the power of life, but the power of death: 'A child can kill as dead as a man can, if the spirit is in him. Perhaps that again is Nechaev's originality: that he speaks what we dare not even imagine about our children; that he gives a voice to something dumb and brutal that is sweeping through young Russia. We close our ears to it; then he comes with his axe and makes us hear.'[107]

The Master of Petersburg is, finally, a novel about a great personal loss and the consequent grief and regret. This is embodied in the writer

Dostoevsky mourning the death of his son Pavel. For the reader with knowledge of Coetzee's own life, alert to the autobiographical play in some of his novels, behind Dostoevsky and Pavel loom the figures of the South African author and his son, Nicolas. From a detail in the manuscript, not included in the final text, it is clear what an impact the telephone conversation with Philippa had on Coetzee: 'The words "Your son is dead" echo in my head to this day, each word with its full and final weight, and the spaces between the words with their due weight too. They do not go away: four bells, four dull bells, pealing in my head.'[108] Nicolas's tardiness in getting out of bed and his frequent absence from school leave their traces early in the novel: 'My son had a scattered education. [...] I had to move him from school to school. The reason was simple: he would not get up in the mornings. Nothing would wake him. I make too much of it, perhaps. But you cannot expect to matriculate if you do not attend school. [...] It was not just sluggishness. Nothing would wake him—shouting, shaking, threats, pleas. It was like trying to wake a bear, a hibernating bear! [...] It was not easy to bring him up alone. I had better things to do than to coax a boy of that age out of bed. If Pavel had finished his schooling like everyone else, none of this would have happened.'[109] And Pavel, too, like Nicolas, had 'rough friends'.[110] In spite of the estrangement between father and son, Coetzee derived some consolation from the fact that after Nicolas's death a postcard from him had been found on the body. This detail recurs when Dostoevsky, during his conversation with Councillor Maximov, is shown a letter. 'It is the last letter he wrote from Dresden, a letter in which he chides Pavel for spending too much money. Mortifying to sit here while a stranger reads it!'[111] The grief at the loss is never-ending: 'Mourning for a dead child has no end.'[112] Particularly terrible is the moment of falling, and the realisation that his son knew nothing could save him:

> What he cannot bear is the thought that, for the last fraction of the last instant of his fall, Pavel knew that nothing could save him, that he was dead. He wants to believe Pavel was protected from that certainty, more terrible than annihilation itself, by the hurry and confusion of the fall, by the mind's way of etherizing itself against whatever is too enormous to be borne. With all his heart he wants to believe this. At the same time he knows that he wants to believe in order to etherize himself against the knowledge that Pavel, falling, knew everything. [...] Upon him bursts the thought of Pavel's last

moment, of the body of a hot-blooded young man in the pride of life striking the earth, of the rush of breath from the lungs, the crack of bones, the surprise, above all the surprise, that the end should be real, that there should be no second chance.[113]

Behind the characters of Dostoevsky and Pavel Coetzee conceals a mythological-poetical allusion, the burning desire to bring the dead Nicolas back to life with a spell or charm. He avails himself of a well-known representation in the poetry of Gerrit Achterberg, the Dutch poet on whom early in his literary career he wrote a searching essay, and whose sonnet cycle *Ballade van de Gasfitter* he translated. A central motif in Achterberg's poetry is the quest for the word that has the magical power to bring the dead woman back to life. In his introduction to his anthology, *Landscape with Rowers: Poetry from the Netherlands,* Coetzee describes it as follows: 'His oeuvre is dominated by a single, highly personal myth: the search for the beloved who has departed and left him behind, a search that takes him on forays into the land of the dead.'[114] Achterberg repeatedly invokes the mythical figure of Orpheus who in a near-swoon has to speak the magic word that will bring the beloved back to earth. One of Achterberg's collections is called *Eurydice* (1944), but the Orpheus motif recurs throughout his oeuvre, among others in poems like 'Woord', 'Diaspora', 'Thebe' and 'Majesteit'. In all these verses the finality of death is denied and rationality and logic rejected in an attempt to revive the dead woman with the magical power of the word. In 'Thebe', in particular, Achterberg uses the Orpheus figure in his design:

> Equipped with life for both,
> I entered tonight the corridors
> leading to you.
> The underground vault was filled with
> a silence, that with reluctance
> bore my footsteps.
>
> The walls were as if saturated
> with rough mould; air and light,
> forever damaged,
> corroded me; only the will
> to be with you on Judgement day
> kept me going.

The labyrinth dwindled in windings
of similar, blinder circles.
For your sake?
I no longer know how far I went.
How did they bring, those who buried you,
such a thing so far?

Until my feet were stayed against you:
from total darkness
I saw your eyes opening;
your hands, which I could not lift,
I felt caress the life,
that beat in me;
your mouth, concealed in death, asked.

A language for which there is no sign
in the universe,
I understood for the last time.

But I had not breath enough
and fled into this poem:
emergency stairs to the morning light
faded and far too soon.[115]

In *The Master of Petersburg* the Orpheus reference also recurs repeatedly. It is prominently present for the first time early in the novel when Dostoevsky is lying on the bed and tries to restore Pavel to life like a magician:

The curtains are open. Moonlight falls on the bed. He is there: he stands by the door, hardly breathing, concentrating his gaze on the chair in the corner, waiting for the darkness to thicken, to turn into another kind of darkness, a darkness of presence. Silently he forms his lips over his son's name, three times, four times.

He is trying to cast a spell. But over whom: over a ghost or over himself? He thinks of Orpheus walking backwards step by step, whispering the dead woman's name, coaxing her out of the entrails of hell; of the wife in graveclothes with the blind, dead eyes following him, holding out limp hands before her like a sleepwalker. No flute, no lyre, *just the word, the one word,*[116] over and over. When death cuts all other links, there remains still the name. Baptism: the union of a soul with a name, the name it will carry into eternity. Barely breathing, he forms the syllables again: *Pavel.*

His head begins to swim. 'I must go now,' he whispers or thinks he whispers; 'I will come back.'[117]

The novel acquires a deeper religious dimension when Nechaev tells the story of the mother of God who at the last judgement will descend into hell and return only when all the suffering souls have been redeemed. Dostoevsky, however, is oppressively aware of an eternal damnation permitting no redemption. A fate that he cannot escape is his life in Russia and *with* Russia. 'It is not a life that will bear much scrutiny. In fact, it is not so much a life as a price or a currency. It is something I pay in order to write. That is what Pavel did not understand: that I pay too.'[118] All he knows is that the death of his son will provide raw material for his writing. In his mercilessness and predatory quest for material, writing becomes an evil profession and a voracious demon. It is his task, and here Dostoevsky has in mind both his own epileptic fits and the death of Pavel, to emerge unscathed from the fall, engage in battle with the 'whistling darkness'[119] and transform the fall into flight. If he were once again to be asked, as Maximov asked him earlier, what kind of books he writes, he knows what his reply will be: 'I write perversions of the truth. I choose the crooked road and take children into dark places. I follow the dance of the pen.'[120]

Ultimately, then, The *Master of Petersburg* is a book about grief and loss, but also about the amoral writer who claims everything for his writing and in the process does not hesitate to commit treason, even against those he loves. In the closing pages Dostoevsky becomes a Faust figure who concludes a pact with the devil for the sake of his art. He becomes so inspired that he talks in a voice that is not his own. As Stephen Watson puts it: 'He becomes the medium of another voice the good or evil of which he cannot determine, let alone foretell, and to the seductive powers of which he cannot help but give himself. Thus in his creative trance — as the novel now tells us — Dostoevsky is in some sense beyond the human, beyond man.'[121] In the end there is, then, for the writer no forgiveness for the deal he has struck:

He has betrayed everyone; nor does he see that his betrayals could go deeper. If he ever wanted to know whether betrayal tasted more like vinegar or like gall, now is the time.

But there is no taste at all in his mouth, just as there is no weight on his heart. His heart, in fact, feels quite empty. He had not known beforehand it would be like this. But how could he have known? Not torment but a dull absence of torment. Like a soldier shot on the battlefield, bleeding, seeing the blood, feeling no pain, wondering: Am I dead already?

It seems to him a great price to pay. *They pay him lots of money for writing books,*[122] said the child, repeating the dead child. What they failed to say was that he had to give up his soul in return.

Now he begins to taste it. It tastes like gall.[123]

VII

In December 1995 Coetzee travelled to Holland, where he delivered a lecture on 'What is realism?' before the Stichting Literaire Activiteiten Amsterdam. In April 1996 *The Master of Petersburg* was awarded the Irish Times International Fiction prize, for which award he travelled to Dublin. The University of Cape Town once again honoured him with their annual book award. He also received the Commonwealth Writers' Prize for the Africa region for his novel. Coetzee travelled to Harare in Zimbabwe for the prize-giving ceremony. In their report the jury wrote:

Incident, character and setting are probed by the narrator with deep psychological and ideological insight. Though stark, subject-matter is lightened by witty and varied dialogue, subtle humour softens up the angst in the self-searching, soul-excoriating interior monologue. Diction is on the whole evocative, lyrical and impressive.[124]

On a more personal level, Coetzee received, after publication of his novel, a short note from his colleague André Brink: 'I am enthralled & deeply moved by *The Master of Petersburg.*'[125] And from his brother-in-law, Cecil Jubber, who knew more than his closest friends about the circumstances of Nicolas's death and Coetzee's reaction to it, he received a letter dated 15 February 1994:

Thank you so much for getting your publishers to send me a copy of *The Master of Petersburg.* I read it straight through at one sitting & then read it again, more slowly.

Knowing something of the circumstances behind the book's writing, I was very moved to find you had the courage to set down what I am sure you felt had to be set down. Apart from the absolute clarity of the writing — always so striking in your work — I have at length come to believe that M of P was an act of contrition & to a certain extent one of exorcism. Congratulations. I hope you have a big success.

CHAPTER 13

AUTOBIOGRAPHICAL EXCURSIONS, *THE LIVES OF ANIMALS*, *DISGRACE* – AND A DISPUTE

I

Shortly after F.W. de Klerk became state president in August 1989, the Berlin Wall fell and the end of world communism seemed imminent. South Africa could no longer try to justify its policy of separate development to the US and Britain on the grounds of a possible communist threat. Because the collapse of the Soviet Union deprived the ANC of an important traditional ally, De Klerk came to the view that in a negotiated settlement the ANC would recognise the democratic right to property and a free-market system, and maintain cordial relations with future foreign investors. Western powers, he felt, could put pressure on the ANC to accept a settlement.

De Klerk felt at liberty, in his address at the opening of parliament on 2 February 1990, to lift the ban on the ANC, the PAC and other liberation movements, and to announce the imminent release of Nelson Mandela and other political prisoners. In a later interview John Coetzee expressed his joy at the somewhat risky step De Klerk had taken. He admired De Klerk, who in all probability had had to do an enormous amount of work behind the scenes to prevent the army from intervening: 'It could so easily have come to the point where the military stepped in and said we'll run the country. I thought it was a triumph of reasonableness that De Klerk was able to get so many people behind him.'[1]

Internationally De Klerk's announcement was greeted with jubilation, and doors that had been closed to South Africa were gradually re-opened. In a referendum on whether the reform process should proceed, 69 per cent of the electorate voted in favour. In a letter to his friend Howard Wolf, Coetzee wrote later: 'An enormous sigh of relief has gone over this whole country after the white electorate's endorsement of reform policies. It almost begins to seem possible that the future may be a peaceful one.' As for his role as a writer in a changing South Africa, however, Coetzee pronounced with some caution, because he was not entirely sure that such a role existed: 'To me a story is a way of thinking—an archaic way of thinking, non-analytic,' he said in an interview with Rian Malan. 'It's the sort of thinking I do best. I certainly don't see any way for a person to think in stories and at the same time act on a political stage. So, to return to your question, the role I see for myself is to write stories.'[2]

From the day of his release Nelson Mandela made a tremendous impression with his unique qualities that, as Hermann Giliomee put it, 'suited the situation superbly. He had a strong presence, combining gravitas and charisma with a sense of humour and humility. [...] He did have an autocratic streak—a combination of the style of a tribal chief and that of a democratic leader—but it was always accompanied by courtesy and good manners. He knew that it was not necessary to be bellicose. In the eyes of the world apartheid had been totally discredited. [...] In his effort to persuade the Afrikaners to surrender power, he knew and respected their history. He condemned apartheid as a serious crime against humanity, but he regarded Afrikaner nationalism as a legitimate indigenous movement that had, like the blacks, fought against British colonialism.'[3]

After the release of Mandela and the return of the exiled ANC leaders, the negotiations around a democratic constitution[4] started in Kempton Park. In the first free democratic elections of 27 April 1994 the ANC obtained by far the majority of votes and on 10 May 1994 Nelson Mandela was sworn in as the first democratically elected president of South Africa. A government of national unity came into being, with the collaboration of De Klerk's National Party (NP) and Buthelezi's Inkatha Freedom Party (IFP), with De Klerk and Thabo Mbeki as deputy presidents. In his five years in office Mandela impressed everybody, even those who differed from him politically, with his wise statesmanship, his emphasis on reconciliation as the central theme of his presidency despite all differences of race and colour, and the smooth transition from the old government to the new. Mandela says in his autobiography: 'From the moment the results were in and it was apparent that the ANC was to form the government, I saw my mission as one of preaching reconciliation, of binding the wounds of the country, of engendering trust and confidence. I knew that many people, particularly the minorities, whites, Coloureds and Indians, would be feeling anxious about the future, and I wanted them to feel secure. I reminded people again and again that the liberation struggle was not a battle against any group or colour, but a fight against a system of repression. At every opportunity, I said all South Africans must now unite and join hands and say we are one country, one nation, one people, marching together into the future.'[5] Part of Mandela's reconciliation effort was the institution of a Truth and Reconciliation Commission (TRC) in 1995, chaired by Archbishop Desmond Tutu. It was the task of this commission to investigate violations of human rights since 1960, with the power to grant amnesty to transgressors who made a full confession.[6] Some aspects of the commission's procedures would figure later in Coetzee's novel *Disgrace*, when the protagonist is forced to appear before a disciplinary committee on charges of sexual harassment of a student.

Some white observers, but also black commentators like Moeletsi Mbeki and Mamphela Ramphele, and even writers like Njabulo Ndebele, expressed reservations about the manner of implementing affirmative action, the policy of granting preference to black people and women in appointments. Although Coetzee never commented directly on this, his character Señor C in *Diary of a Bad Year* does remark on the naive optimism prevalent in South Africa after the abolition of job reservation in 1990. Well-meaning whites had assumed that with the end of apartheid there would be no boundaries or divisions of race or colour between individuals. 'Hence,' Señor C continues, 'their bafflement when the African National Congress brought in legislation that privileged blacks on the job market. To liberals there could be no step more retrogressive, a step back into the old days when the colour of one's skin counted for more than education or aspirations or diligence.'[7]

Mandela was succeeded as president in 1999 by Thabo Mbeki, who in 2004 was elected for a second term with a more than two-thirds majority. He regarded himself as an African who wanted to lead his people, after the long years of colonialism, to a better life through a call to an African renaissance. His charm, elegance and erudition made him an impressive leader and politician. But the chronic unemployment, the high crime rate, the unfulfilled hopes and the increasing inefficiency of the law-enforcement agencies frustrated his ideal of an African renaissance. In the face of all medical evidence, Mbeki at first obstinately denied that AIDS was caused by a virus, with the result that the government dragged its feet in combatting with anti-retrovirals the pandemic that threatened to wipe out large sections of the populace. The high incidence of rape of women and children, the highest in the world, led the journalist Charlene Smith to say that South Africa had developed a culture in which rape was endemic. When Robert Mugabe, the president of Zimbabwe, in spite of repeated interventions by the supreme court, continued his policy of the illegal occupation of white-owned farms, and caused opposition supporters to be intimidated during elections, Mbeki followed a policy of 'quiet diplomacy' that created the impression that solidarity with a former freedom fighter weighed more heavily with him than the crimes that his Zimbabwean counterpart was openly committing.

Coetzee's initial response to De Klerk's initiatives was very favourable, and he admired him for his courage. Even so, quite soon after the speech on 2 February 1990, he was moved to scepticism by the wave of protests and the chronic violence in South Africa. In the black townships and among the black youth there was still unrest, accompanied by the torching of lecture halls, violence among students and a blockading of highways. He wrote to Howard Wolf: 'The post-February euphoria in this country lasted about three weeks. Now, though the media try to keep up the euphoria, the general feeling seems to be just about what it was before. The precipitant has been the plunge into violence in the black townships. No one has anything intelligent to say about it. Even the leadership of the political Left seems to be bewildered. My own feeling is that it is pre-political, far down beneath any level that the political can reach. A lifestyle of violence has grown up which is the lifestyle of a huge sector of black youth, and they aren't going to give it up.'

When *Waiting for the Barbarians* and *Disgrace* were both translated into Czech in 2002, the journalist Alexandra Buchler sent Coetzee some questions in writing. Asked to comment on the changes in South Africa between the publication of the two novels, and whether the 'brutal tyranny' of the first novel had been replaced by the 'brutal anarchy' of the second, he replied in April 2002:

I wouldn't describe the situation of present-day South Africa as 'brutal anarchy.' *Anarchy* is too strong a word, and *brutal* is simply insulting. What we have, rather, is a demographic and economic situation all too common in Africa: millions of young people with a poor education behind them and no prospects in life, plus underfunded and demoralized organs of law enforcement—police, courts, prisons. To which one must add a collapse of public morality, evinced in lack of respect for the law at all levels of society.

> But this does not add up to anarchy. South Africa can in fact be
> an exciting country in which to live, if you have an adventurous
> temperament—adventurous and perhaps fatalistic too.

In Coetzee's response there is still an element of optimism, however
qualified. Other commentators pointed more openly at the danger signs
threatening the future of the country. A year before Mandela stepped
down as president, Patti Waldmeir, the author of *Anatomy of a Miracle*,
wrote in her postscript that the euphoria of the new South Africa had
dissipated since the completion of her book,

> leaving South Africans with a massive post-liberation hangover, and
> a painful case of depressed spirits. They have awakened to a world
> where Nelson Mandela has begun to lose his aura of sainthood;
> a world where corruption and incompetence have emerged to
> taint the new administration; where fear of crime and violence is a
> constant companion; and where the arrogance of power has begun
> to claim its victims.[8]

II

Coetzee, who in 1984 had been promoted ad hominem to full professor
at UCT, was in 1993 elected to the Arderne Chair in English Literature,
the position held by Howarth and Gillham before him. It was not a matter
of his wanting this chair. It was offered to him and he accepted it at the
urging of his colleagues, because no suitable outside candidate could
be found. With the freezing of the De Beers Chair in English Language,
there was a real danger that the Arderne Chair could be abolished.

In the late 1980s and the 1990s Coetzee was still active as a lecturer,
although he devoted most of his time to postgraduate students registered for the honours and M.A., by coursework, dissertation and
creative writing. For the M.A. course in modern literature offered in
1993, for instance, he concentrated on texts by Denis Diderot, Alain
Robbe-Grillet, Samuel Beckett, Vladimir Nabokov, John Barth, Thomas
Pynchon, A.S. Byatt and Alasdair Gray. Apparently, he observes in
his class notes kept at NELM in Grahamstown, there is nothing new
about the postmodern reaction to modernism. 'What is new is that
Postmodernism, as a highly intellectual movement, brings into question

the whole notion of parentage/paternity, as part of its interrogation of historicity and its general textualization, not only of history but of life. […] The enemies are identified as style, taste, asceticism.' In telegraphic style he devises lectures on Beckett, with particular attention to the mode of presentation as a crisis of language, the representation of a world without God, and, with reference to Descartes, the problem of knowing that what one experiences is real and not a dream. The only sciences, according to him, capable of conveying exact knowledge, are arithmetic and geometry. Of particular interest is what he says in his lectures on Nabokov:

> Circumstances forced N to live in America and write in English. It is here that the interesting turn in his career takes place. N's feeling for English words is exact, but deliberately remains that of a connoisseur, an outsider. This yields the extraordinarily tessellated feel to his prose, the air of being a construct of words, as opposite as can be to the transparency of realism.
>
> N chose to love and admire America—a version of America of small, ethnically white, Republican-voting college towns. He became a specialist, a connoisseur of American life and particularly of middleclass culture of the Eisenhower years, which he was careful never to condescend to. In this respect he differed from most of the European exiles who chose to live in big cities and to lament the hold of mass culture over the American people.
>
> It is this fascination with, and embrace of, American popular culture, seen best in *Lolita*, that oddly takes N from fin-de-siècle aestheticism to postmodernism (one of whose poses is also that of the dazzled aesthete).

Coetzee could confront his students with engrossing subjects, often in peripheral areas of literature. One of the assignments that he mentions as a possibility to his M.A. students in 1994 is formulated as follows:

> (a) Besides 'Kubla Khan', what literary works in English are known to have been written under the effect of chemical substances? (b) Are there any studies of artistic production under the influence of drugs? Any medical-scientific studies? (c) What has been written since 1965 about artistic production in drug-influenced or trance states, in societies past and present?

Coetzee was not a lecturer for students with a lukewarm interest in his subject. It would be a fallacy to equate him with his character, Professor David Lurie in *Disgrace*, who month after month grades assignments, achieves nothing with his lectures, and persists in his job merely for subsistence.[9] Coetzee was highly appreciated as a lecturer and as a supervisor. Anne Landsman could recall attending a course on realism in the novel and a seminar on Ezra Pound and T.S. Eliot:

> I can still see the sun streaking into the classroom, dust motes dancing as we listened to Coetzee's precise voice, the elegant turns and curves of his crystalline intellect. He had a way of carving his questions into the air with devastating simplicity. Quite often, the class was stupefied, perhaps by the heat, perhaps by the difficult times we were living in, perhaps by being nineteen and twenty and not knowing very much about anything.
>
> Or perhaps everyone felt the way I did: heart in my throat, stunned into silence by this small, quiet man's brilliance. His gifts as a writer were becoming known but he had not yet been crowned as one of the greatest writers of our time. When I began to read his novels, I heard his voice speaking the words, the same spare prose he used in the classroom, the same economy and honesty. In this way, he continued to be my teacher and moral compass through the darkest days of apartheid. By that time I was living in the United States, and reading about South Africa—in particular, reading *Life & Times of Michael K*—took me on a journey to the earliest part of myself, to my childhood in Worcester, a small Boland town ringed by mountains. The physical descriptions of the land were searingly familiar, and the excruciating solitude of Michael K so vivid.
>
> In the late '80s, Coetzee gave a reading at Endicott's bookstore on the Upper West Side. I spoke to him there, reminding him I was once a student of his and letting him know I now lived in New York City, writing screenplays. He said drily, 'You escaped the UCT English department,' and gave a faint smile. When I began writing my first novel, *The Devil's Chimney*, in 1994, I couldn't help recalling the desiccated landscape of *In the Heart of the Country*, the harsh world of *Waiting for the Barbarians*. But working in his shadow, guided by his influence, was never overwhelming or suffocating.[10]

A few years later André Brink, who in the 1990s was also professor of English at UCT, co-taught the M.A. course in modern literature with Coetzee. 'For me,' writes Brink, who attended some of Coetzee's classes, 'his group discussion of writers like Balzac, Zola, Joyce, Beckett, Nabokov and many others brought a stimulation that I was able to follow up many years later.' For the students, Brink continues, Coetzee's presence was 'a form of shock therapy'. When a student delivered a rather slipshod offering, he would ask with a poker face 'Do you really think you've put enough effort into this?' or simply say 'I'm afraid that was not the best you could do.' At other times he could make a student beam with the reaction: 'Now that wasn't bad at all' or 'I rather liked that.' And Brink decides: 'I don't think a single student who ever studied under Coetzee could have emerged at the other side unchanged or without some deep impression.'[11]

The creative writing workshop that Coetzee offered, often in collaboration with Brink, was a systematic course for which all participants had to prepare thoroughly. This is clear from guidelines that he outlined for the course in 1995:

> The class meets on Wednesdays, 15:30–16:45. (1) Each student offers an original piece of prose fiction to the workshop as assigned. Copies are made available to the rest of the class by 13:30 on the Monday preceding the relevant meeting, at the student's expense. Each of the other students in the class writes a brief, *constructive* critique (1–2 pages). These critiques form the basis of class discussion. At the end of the class the critiques are handed in. (2) Two passages are assigned from the course reader each week. These passages come from the openings of the unidentified short stories. Each student selects one of these passages and continues the story for at least another page (300+ words). The continuations will be discussed in class, and handed in at the end of the class. The reader comprises anonymous texts by a variety of authors.

Just as he never wanted to position himself as a 'herald of the community',[12] Coetzee was also not the prescriptive pedagogue given to monologues. In a letter of 17 May 2001 to Laurel Bernard he writes: 'I'm not the kind of teacher who tells his students things. I just try to get them to read slowly and pay attention to the words.' Patricia Schonstein, the author of *A Time of Angels*, which was a product of the UCT creative writing course, talks, in the *Sunday Times* of 12 October 2003, of the excellent guidance she received from Coetzee. He never prevented her from going in the direction she wanted to go. When he commented, it was always keen-witted and to the point. In a feedback report on his supervision she wrote:

> Professor J.M. Coetzee supervised my thesis. Through his astute commentary and guiding questions, I learnt to write with great care, and to go over and over a piece of work until it is as close to perfect as possible. I will carry his influence with me into my future works. He showed me the need for thoughtful focus; discipline; fine crafting of words; proper observation of characters; careful overview of the whole plot as it develops; and consideration of the reader's integrity. This is not to say I now consider myself an accomplished author. I see myself as an emerging author, one still learning the trade, but one who has been watched over, for one project at least, by a master of literature, and therefore one who knows how valuable is apprenticeship.[13]

Apart from his lecturing and post-graduate supervision at UCT, Coetzee regularly, as in the 1980s, went abroad to attend conferences, to deliver papers or to spend a term or a semester, by invitation, at some American university. Such visits were often combined with appearances at other institutions — at first to deliver papers, but, towards the turn of the century, more frequently to read from his work. He started feeling increasingly that he wanted to divest himself of the academic responsibilities to which he had devoted a good thirty years, and to dedicate himself to what he saw as his prime task: his creative work. He was also unhappy about the direction in which universities were developing — not only in South Africa, but worldwide. He found it a pity that the old model of a training in the classics and a broad literary-historical schooling, such as he had, despite all shortcomings, had as a student at UCT, was being supplanted by subject areas that could be calculated in terms of rands and cents for social upliftment. In reply to a paper by his colleague André du Toit, professor of philosophy, Coetzee said: 'Now, all over the Western world, this old model of the university finds itself under attack as an increasingly economistic interrogation of social institutions is carried out. There is only a tiny market for philosophy and the classics, the argument goes, therefore the study of philosophy and the classics ought to constitute only a tiny part of the enterprise of the university. Similarly for other venerable fields of study: history, philology, etc.'[14] What happened to universities in the 1980s and '90s, he later wrote in *Diary of a Bad Year*, 'was pretty shameful, as under the threat of having their funding cut they allowed themselves to be turned into business enterprises, in which professors who had previously carried on their enquiries in sovereign freedom were transformed into harried employees required to fulfil quotas under the scrutiny of professional managers.'[15] In an interview in April 2004 with Sylvia Colombo of the Brazilian newspaper *Folha de São Paulo*, he said that a crisis in the humanities had arisen at universities: 'The university, which used to be based on the humane studies, and to provide a home for humane studies, has lost interest. Humane studies have been pushed into a neglected corner while the university goes ahead with its new business, namely, servicing the neoliberal economy. Should humane studies adapt to new circumstances? No, not if that means changing their nature.'[16]

Coetzee at this time declined many invitations to lecture—for instance, to deliver the six Clark Lectures at Cambridge, to appear at the Sligo Festival in Ireland, to attend a conference in Amsterdam, to deliver an address at the graduation ceremony of the University of the Witwatersrand, and to talk in Chicago about the national character of South Africa. He wrote to John Gouws, who had invited him to take part in a conference in Grahamstown on the history of the book: 'Thanks for letting me know about the conference you and Peter McDonald are organizing. It sounds as if it might be interesting. However, I am in the process of withdrawing from academic life to concentrate on my own work. I can't envisage preparing a conference paper.' He also declined an invitation in 1998 to assume the Charles Norton Chair for 2000–2001 at Harvard; so, too, in September 2001, the invitation from Dorothy Lane, Associate Professor of English at the University of Regina in Canada: 'There are practical considerations, however, that make me reluctant to accept, principally the travel: I am in my sixties, and I find long flights across time zones harder and harder to bear. [...] If the visit to Regina were part of a more extended stay in western North America the situation would perhaps be different. But for the present I am afraid I must decline.' Lane then invited him to deliver a series of lectures in August 2002 at Regina, but this invitation, too, he declined, writing, on 12 September 2001: 'Thank you for extending your invitation, but I am on the point of retiring from my position at the University of Cape

Town. I am looking forward immensely to being a writer pure and simple. Taking on new teaching engagements is, I am afraid, the last thing I want to do.'

He also refused numerous requests to comment on his own novels. In an e-mail of 28 October 2000 he writes: 'I am afraid I make it a rule not to discuss my own work. I have always believed that books should not be burdened with authorial interpretations.' To another e-mail, on 16 July 2001, he replied: 'I have always followed a policy of allowing my books to make their own way in the world without intervention from my side. In particular, I do not want to saddle them with authorial interpretations.' To a request from Sandra Chait of Washington to visit her class and talk about his books, he replied in an e-mail on 7 September 2001: 'Frankly, I've always been reluctant to get into situations where I have to "explain" my books or lend my authority to some or other reading of them, and it's difficult to explain this to students. So maybe I should pass on that.'

Even though he did in the 1970s on a few occasions comment on social and political issues, he soon realised that this was not the kind of article he enjoyed writing. He declined an invitation from *The Guardian* to spend three to seven days in Israel and write an article on the situation there. He wrote to his agent, Bruce Hunter, on 1 November 2000: 'I'm afraid I can't accept, either now or in the future. It's a kind of assignment that I have no talent for and no interest in.' He also declined all requests from journalists for an interview,[17] except in a few instances, which he granted grudgingly.[18] He became increasingly averse to long flights to launches of new publications. In August 2000 he was invited to Spain for the launch of the Spanish translations of *Boyhood* and *Youth*. The publisher Grijalbo was prepared to bear all expenses, and the South African embassy in Madrid was planning to make a big event of it. But Coetzee was not interested. He wrote to Sandy Blanton, his agent in London: 'There is absolutely nothing in it for me in paying such a visit. Two days are knocked out of my life travelling there and back, and the pound of flesh my hosts will require will be that I sit down with one journalist after another answering questions I have heard scores of times before. Then the Embassy will mount a reception and I will have to shake hands with strangers and answer questions like "How long will you be in Madrid?" I won the Booker Prize without doing a single UK interview. The Viking edition sold thousands of copies in the US without the aid of interviews. Why does Grijalbo need interviews?'

An invitation that Coetzee gladly accepted annually was to a visiting professorship in the Committee on Social Thought at the University of Chicago.[19] This interdisciplinary committee was founded in 1941 by the historian John U. Nef, the economist Frank Knight, the anthropologist Robert Redfield, and Robert M. Hutchins, then President of the University. Their premises were that the serious study of any academic topic, or of any philosophical or literary work, is best prepared for by a wide and deep acquaintance with the fundamental issues presupposed in all such studies, that students should learn about these issues by acquainting themselves with a select number of classic ancient and modern texts in an inter-disciplinary atmosphere, and should only then concentrate on a specific dissertation topic. Over the years, temporary and permanent members of the Committee have included Hannah Arendt, Saul Bellow, Allan Bloom, Mircea Eliade, T.S. Eliot, Friederich Hayek, Paul Ricoeur, and many others. The Committee differs from the normal department in that it has no specific subject matter and is organised neither in terms of a single intellectual discipline nor around any specific interdisciplinary focus. Robert Pippin and Jonathan Lear persuaded Coetzee, who was lecturing regularly at Texas, to come to Chicago as well. Coetzee found that the intellectual environment and spirit agreed with him, so much so that he decided to repeat the visits annually from September to November, also because the English Department, which in the past had counted Wayne C. Booth, R. S. Crane, Norman Maclean and other illustrious figures among its staff, was prepared to make provision for Dorothy. The downside for Coetzee lay in his aversion to big cities, even though the university bordered an enormous lake, and in the flatness of Chicago and the coldness of its winters. Increasingly, however, Chicago became his academic and intellectual home, and in Jonathan Lear he found a friend with whom he could consort on a human and personal level. They had weekly dinners and relaxed conversation at each other's homes, with Dorothy and Lear's wife, Gabriel. Conversation, in fact, formed the Socratic basis of Lear's vision of the ideal university. 'There is a shared understanding,' he said in a welcoming address to freshmen, 'that if, in this brief time we are alive, we are going to figure out anything genuinely worthwhile, it will be through conversation. Each of our individual ideas needs to be tested against the countervailing thoughts of others; but even more important, it is the imagination of others that sparks our own.'[20]

This was a mindset that Coetzee admired, against what he perceived as the trend for university authorities to pursue profit. In his novels something of Coetzee's critique on the modern university emerges, masked by the personae of Elizabeth Costello and the 72-year-old Australian writer known as Señor C in *Diary of a Bad Year*. If Elizabeth Costello were to be asked 'to name the core of the university today, its core discipline, she would say it was moneymaking'.[21]

This spirit of merchants was not to be found at the University of Chicago. Every autumn Coetzee and Lear lectured on a specific book, or, rather, conducted relaxed Socratic conversations on a common topic with the students. The aim was an honest, open dialogue and the careful reading of works such as *War and Peace, The Brothers Karamazov* and *In Search of Lost Time*. An example of such a discussion programme is the information sheet Lear circulated to students about the Proust course:

> As I think you all know, John Coetzee and I are giving a course in the fall on Proust's *In Search of Lost Time*. We are requiring that anyone taking the course read the entire work this summer. (We are using the latest translation of Montcrieff, revised by Kilmartin and D.J. Enright, 6 volumes, available in paperback.) We shall then read 100–150 page segments from throughout the work each week. Because of this requirement, we are also requiring that students seek permission from the instructor before taking the course: obviously, we don't want students to read the whole book then get rejected from the course.
>
> Three more important facts you need to know: (1) We want to keep the class small—a real working seminar. Thus (2) we shall not allow any student auditors. And (3), most importantly, the seminar is getting filled 'as we speak' by students who are now asking us to be in the course.
>
> We want to give preference to CST students if there are any who want to take the course. On the other hand, you should know that the seminar is filling up on a first-come, first-served basis.
>
> So: if you want to take the course, I suggest you email me asap. At the current rate of email requests and the percentage of acceptances / rejections of those requests, I suspect the seminar is going to fill up quickly. I thought you would want to know.

Lear was impressed with Coetzee's knowledge of philosophy, such as his insight into the thought of Kierkegaard. He was also amazed at Coetzee's dedicated attention to the students. He had never met anybody who spent more time on students. Coetzee assumed full responsibility and sat on committees that he had no need to. His professional approach to his teaching extended to making himself available for conversations and remaining in e-mail contact with his students. Lear admired his generosity, honesty, trust and general openness towards the students. He also found that Coetzee, though not a chatterer, loved to laugh. In Chicago he had found an intellectual home that he did not have in Cape Town.

Coetzee kept up his visits to Chicago until 2003, and occupied the Arderne Chair in English Literature at UCT until 1997. On 3 March 1997 he wrote to John Martin, the deputy vice-chancellor:

> I have, as you know, held the Arderne Chair of English since 1994. For ten years before that date I held a personal chair. During both tenancies I have had a reduced teaching and administrative load, and have drawn a correspondingly reduced salary.
>
> I would now like to explore the possibility of resigning the Arderne Chair and executing some kind of sideways move that would allow me to go ahead with the supervision of graduate students, and with my own research and writing, but would relieve me of a role in the Department of English.
>
> I have two broad reasons for wishing to make a move of this kind, the first to do with the Department, the second of a more personal nature.
>
> André Brink and I are at present the only two full professors in the Department of English; there is a third chair, but it is not occupied. André and I are both in our late fifties. Neither of us is particularly interested in the issues of educational policy and the role of English education in a changing South Africa that—quite properly—preoccupy the rest of the department. Both of us are frequently away on leave.
>
> I cannot speak for André, but with regard to myself I feel I am not providing the kind of academic leadership in the department that one would expect from a chairholder. In my defence I can only say that I did not apply for the Arderne Chair. It was offered to me only because no one suitable could be found; I accepted—under

pressure from colleagues—only because discontinuance of the Chair was being threatened.

With the De Beers Chair frozen *sine die*, it seems to me appropriate that the Arderne Chair should be taken over by someone whose interest in the general field of academic development is stronger than mine. This would extract me from a position I find more and more invidious.

At a personal level, I would like to make a move because, as I grow older, I find less and less pleasure in classroom teaching. If I have anything left to contribute as an educator, it is, I feel, as a research supervisor working with graduate students.

With the introduction—as of this year—of the M.A. by thesis in creative writing, and with my continuing participation in the M.A. (Literary Studies) programme, I find that I am anyhow doing half of my teaching and supervision outside the Department of English, under the aegis of the Faculty of Arts. One possible route for me to follow would therefore be to take up a position located in the Faculty but in no department in particular.

I am not sure how strong the precedents are for a move of this kind, but would be grateful for any advice you could offer.

The Council of UCT acceded to this request and nominated Coetzee as Distinguished Professor in the Faculty of Arts. At the nomination ceremony, the Dean of Arts, Professor Wilmot James, said: 'This is the highest academic appointment UCT can make. Such appointments are made rarely, for academics who have either excelled beyond their discipline or are considered to be national intellectual assets. Professor Coetzee is a writer of global distinction. His work has won nearly every major Commonwealth literary award. [...] His work was also nominated for the Nobel Prize in Literature in 1996.[22] [...] We are honoured to have him as a member of our academic staff.'

Underlying this request, which resulted in his resorting for administrative purposes directly under the Dean of Arts, was Coetzee's disgruntlement with the Department of English, to which he had been attached since 1972, and in which he had never been particularly happy. This is evident from a letter he wrote to Professor Wieland Gevers, deputy vice-chancellor, providing reasons for his resignation as professor of English in 1999. Coetzee writes: 'One of my main reasons for resigning in 1999 was to escape what I regarded and continue to regard as a depressed and depressing work environment, namely the Department of English Language and Literature. I took on the new commitment on the understanding that I would not be a member of the English Department but would report directly to the Dean of Humanities. I would like to ensure that under the proposed new dispensation I report directly to the Dean of the Graduate School.' Professor Gevers granted this request and Coetzee was absolved from reporting to the head of the Department of English, although he continued to supervise post-graduate students of the department. This disgruntlement may well also be the reason why he referred to the University of Chicago, where he had established a vital relationship with Jonathan Lear, as his true intellectual home.

In the late 1980s and 1990s Coetzee received numerous other tributes. In 1989, shortly after the death of his son, Nicolas, he flew to Buffalo to receive an honorary doctorate from the State University of New York. In his citation the president, Dr Steven B. Sample, said:

> You have distinguished yourself as a powerful writer whose message serves both to compel and to disturb, and in so doing you have ably demonstrated literature's capacity to heighten the social conscience of its audience.[23]

On this occasion Coetzee was given an exceptionally valuable statuette of an American buffalo by the French glass designer René Lalique, engraved with Coetzee's name. When his friend Howard Wolf took him to the airport and handed him the statuette, Coetzee said: 'Keep it. It is too heavy for me.' Wolf was flabbergasted. He was silent for a moment and then said: 'I'll wait for seven years. If you still do not ask for it, I'll keep it.' Coetzee's reply was a characteristic silence. Seven years later, with still no reply from Coetzee, Wolf added the object to his collection of documents at Amherst College. En route from Buffalo to London, Coetzee's suitcase, containing the certificate he had travelled so far to collect, got lost.[24]

In 1995 UCT awarded Coetzee an honorary doctorate. The orator was his colleague André Brink, who said that it is not often that a university confers an honorary degree on one of its own active members. That UCT has decided to take this step is a measure of the exceptional esteem in which Coetzee is held and of a desire to demonstrate to the world that the old adage about a prophet in his own country does not hold true in all places and at all times. He continued to say that he does have the advantage 'of having come a long way' with John Coetzee:

> 234 years, in fact, ever since in 1761 Carl Frederik Brink set off into the heart of the country in the company of Jacobus Coetsé, in search of a tawny-coloured tribe of long-haired people who reputedly wore linen clothes. It comes as no surprise that they never found the mysterious tribe; but what they did find, jointly and severally, was a fascination with Africa and with human nature which persists to this day.

After recounting the course of Coetzee's life, his academic career and the awards he has received, Brink states:

> As a novelist, with seven novels translated into a dozen languages, John Coetzee has changed not only the South African literary landscape but the shape and horizons of the novel as a genre.

On 18 April 1996 Coetzee received an honorary doctorate also from the University of Natal in Pietermaritzburg. Professor Colin Gardner of the Department of English said that Coetzee was not only a highly respected and intellectually discerning academic, but, more importantly, the most original novelist South Africa had yet produced. In his speech Coetzee congratulated the students in the arts on their achievements and said they were better prepared for the future than students in the practical disciplines. While the latter were trained to solve problems, the arts led to free and creative thought. Leaving the university without marketable skills was not a problem, because such skills could be acquired in a few afternoons, whereas it was more difficult to realise that the human being can be taken over by the machine. 'There are many examples,' he said. 'The roads are full of human beings being driven around by cars.'

On 31 May 1996 the Cape Tercentenary Foundation gave Coetzee its Award of Excellence for 1995 for his life-long services to literature. In the same year he received an honorary doctorate from Skidmore College in New York. It was awarded on 14 October 1996 with Professor Robert Boyers as the orator:

> J.M. Coetzee: Novelist, political thinker, critic, linguist, theorist, anatomist of power; you have created a body of work impressive

for its vividness and restraint, for its immediacy and its enigmatic austerity, for its shapeliness and its intellectual courage. Writing out of a South African experience, with all its peculiar stresses and obsessions, you have resisted the easy moral posturings and false heroics that often disfigure dissident writing, and you have found a way to talk about the play of particular historical forces without limiting your perspective to a single time or country. A close student of oppression, brutality and injustice, you have taught your readers how to think about freedom and about the difficulties entailed in attempting to represent it.

You are someone, as you have said, 'who has intimations of freedom (as every chained prisoner has),' and whose representations are never more than 'shadows … of people slipping their chains and turning their faces to the light.' To read you is to understand that nothing valuable is easy or conclusive, and that the writer himself, however passionate or full of conviction, must at present be painfully alert to the limitations of his own language. To get things right—so you have helped us to understand—to feel adequate about our capacity to name and to judge, as one of your characters says, 'you would need the tongue of a god'. So you make us believe, and so you make us feel the weight of that difficult proposition.

In the early years of your professional writing life you did the kind of linguistic and stylistic analysis that would later inform several of your novels. You developed a sophisticated critique of naïve realism and studied the impact of history upon the post-colonial writer. One thinks of you as the most theoretical of our great novelists, the one most interested in philosophical issues and capable of addressing them in narratives that never seem merely theoretical or arcane. For all that you have done to make your novels reflect an interest in issues of authority, gender, imperialism, indeterminacy, the fiction has always seemed to us remarkably human, sensual, intimate. Though deconstructionists and semioticians have a field day with your work, most of us—common readers—are grateful for the energy of your prose, the rhythms and surprises of your narrative, the disturbing suggestiveness of ideas that never seem superfluous or willed.

Of course it is tempting to speak of you as the master of a certain kind of fiction, but so various are your books, so eager have you been to take on fresh challenges, that one knows not quite how to describe you. Some speak of your academic precision, your analytic scruple. Others describe you as allegorist, psychologist, realist, ironist, post-modernist. Reviewers of *In the Heart of the Country* praised the biblical cadences of the prose, while later reviewers of *Waiting for the Barbarians* rightly praised its stark, spare, introspective intensities. In the novel *Foe* you moved away from the South Africa you explored in novels like *Age of Iron* and *Michael K* to offer a recasting of the Robinson Crusoe story, this one narrated by an eighteenth-century Englishwoman obsessed with the mystery of one person's submission to another. In *The Master of Petersburg*, you dared to offer a fictional portrait of Dostoevsky, a figure so believably Dostoevskyan in its perversity and its combination of compassion and cruelty that at certain moments it seems to have been fashioned by Dostoevsky himself.

Of course you are interested, in your Russian novel, not merely in character or psychology but in exploring the very genesis of fiction. So, in *Michael K*, you are interested not simply in a person and a situation but in what one critic calls 'the rules governing the production of ... discourse'. Though it is impossible to say what precisely a novel by J.M. Coetzee must look like or cover, we can say that each of your works is about many things—literary ideas and persons and politics—and that no one of the works much resembles any other.

In short, we are moved by the range and the venturesomeness of your imagination, by the shapeliness and torsion of your narratives, by the penetration of your political analysis and the cunning of your portraiture. Most of all, we are moved by the vision that informs everything you have written, a vision that goes—as Nadine Gordimer has memorably said—'to the nerve-centre of being' and enables you to find there 'more than most people will ever know about themselves'.

In October 1998 the California-based Lannan Foundation announced that Coetzee had received a grant of $75 000 for his exceptional contribution to English literature. He was one of eleven recipients of this award in the field of fiction, poetry and non-fiction, and the only one from outside the US. On 10 April 1999 Rhodes University awarded Coetzee the degree D. Litt *honoris causa*. Professor Vivian de Klerk, head of the Department of English, said:

He has displeased some of his critics for two reasons: firstly, because, in their view, he has not been politically relevant enough, and has refused to show them the agonised white consciousness they all seek; he has insisted on his freedom to be what he is; he does not see himself as a South African writer *per se*, but as someone writing in the world at large, his allegiance lying with the discourse of novels, rather than the discourse of South African politics.

A second reason for their displeasure has come from the fact that his writing is not always easy to understand: he challenges the orthodox definitions of the role of the writer, and, instead of making things nice and clear for his readers, he often leaves them with evocative pointers and questions, and gives them the freedom to interpret for themselves.

His work has been described as serious, sophisticated and brilliant, uniting intellectual rigour and ethical scrupulousness with the aesthetic. With unflinchingness and forgiveness, Coetzee offers his readers the cold solace of understanding.

In 1994 Coetzee received the Premio Mondello and in 1995 the Premio Feronia, both of them from Italy. In 1995 he won the Irish Times Literary Award. In 1999 he was selected by a *Financial Mail* panel as their South African writer of the century. In the edition of 17 December 1999 this magazine quotes Coetzee's words on the essence of writing from *Doubling the Point*:

> As you write — I am speaking of any kind of writing — you have a feel of whether you are getting closer to 'it' or not. You have a sensing mechanism, a feedback loop of some kind; without that mechanism you could not write. It is naïve to think that writing is a simple two-stage process: first you decide what you want to say, then you say it. On the contrary, as all of us know, you write because you do not know what you want to say [...] That is the sense in which one can say that writing writes us.[25]

In October 2000 Coetzee received an honorary doctorate from the University of Hartford. He was praised for his powerful prose, his novels and other works covering a wide variety of subject, extending from apartheid to animal rights and censorship. 'You have provided a strong voice for South Africans who have suffered from the effect of imperialism, apartheid and post-apartheid violence. [...] [Y]our striking, uncompromising writing has enriched and challenged us, and forced us to confront truths about ourselves and our world.' On 17 June 2002 the University of Oxford awarded Coetzee a doctorate. The addresses, in Latin and in English, were later published in the *Oxford University Gazette*. Part of the English text reads:

> Born in South Africa, [Coetzee] had before his eyes the spectacle of that tyrannical regime which imposed on the native peoples the separation which was known as Apartheid. He took the more liberal side, and he worked for better things, but he did not make the naïve mistake of supposing that in such a situation there was no complexity, no ambiguity, nothing which might cause feelings of doubt or uncertainty even in the minds of decent people. The ancients were long ago aware that tyranny offered intractable moral problems, and that the position of the tyrannicide was far from unambiguously clear. Professor Coetzee brought some of the discussions of the philosophers, which at times seem remote from the world, into contact with real life in a series of novels which depicted people with vividness in the action of engrossing plots. He shows us Michael, with no advantages of appearance or education, without even a surname except the letter K, always somehow ill omened; if I may slightly distort the words of the poet Horace about the wanderings of Ulysses,
>
> > He travelled widely, towns and camps and sand,
> >
> > Saw world and men, and did not understand.
>
> He too was trying a home-coming, but alone—he had no Odyssean companions. The story is a harrowing and moving one. Elsewhere he gives a new and original turn to the story of Robinson Crusoe; and he shows a Professor involved in *Disgrace* (*absit omen!*), driven out to a farm, attempting to give a little dignity to the death of the stray dogs which are daily put down. In his work we see individual people represented in such a way that their experiences illuminate the society in which they live.

In 2001 Coetzee was elected as 'outstanding alumnus' and as 'writer of global distinction' by his American alma mater, the University of Texas. Having earlier won the Commonwealth Writers' Prize for the Africa region, Coetzee in 2002 was awarded the Overall Commonwealth

Writers' Prize for 2000, which he received personally from Queen Elizabeth II at Buckingham Palace. He described this event to Geoff Mulligan of Random House in London: 'The meeting with Her Majesty went off smoothly, after Colin Ball (of the Commonwealth Foundation) and I had been given a quick lesson in etiquette from a Royal Equerry in an anteroom. HM gave the impression of being really interested, which, considering the number of people she must meet from all walks of life, struck me as pretty professional.' And in June 2003 Coetzee received the Italian Grinzane Cavour Prize in the International section, one of the most influential and prestigious fiction prizes in Europe.

III

It was to be expected that a writer like J.M. Coetzee would excite the interest of literary scholars engaging with post-modern fiction and in literary-theoretical matters. What could not have been foreseen, is that since the 1980s a whole critical industry would develop around his work. Some of these studies, such as the work of dedicated experts like David Attwell and Derek Attridge, are not only excellent studies of Coetzee, but also highlights of contemporary English literary criticism. His work has elicited some of the most penetrating commentaries being published on specific literary works, and has been a focal point of literary-theoretical questions.

A seminal publication early in the 1990s, which had a strong influence on the Coetzee industry, was the collection of essays from the years 1970 to 1989 that Coetzee combined with a series of interviews with David Attwell in *Doubling the Point* (1992). Read together, they form an intellectual autobiography of Coetzee. The interviews place the essays within the context of the larger autobiographical whole and serve as a link with Coetzee's novels. The book was published by Harvard University Press and was the runner-up for the Alan Paton Prize, which was awarded to Tim Couzens for *Trader Horn*.

David Attwell has provided engrossing details about the genesis of this important book.[26] According to him, after the publication of *White Writing* Coetzee was asked by Harvard University Press to produce another collection of essays of linguistic studies not tied to South Africa. Coetzee was not inclined to do this, as he felt he had left that kind of work behind him. He came up with a counter-proposal of a selection from his essays, interspersed with a series of conversations on the relation between fiction and non-fiction, thus initiating a kind of intellectual biography.

Attwell, then attached to the University of the Western Cape, and recently returned from a sabbatical at the University of Texas, sent Coetzee a few questions and a thesis proposal on his creative writing that he had developed under the supervision of Bernth Lindfors in Austin. Coetzee's response, rightly, was to question his own appropriateness as collaborator. He intended to distance himself from the kind of ideological criticism that Attwell was engaged in, which regarded literature as secondary to historical discourse. Attwell himself realised that in certain respects he would have to deviate from Marxist literary criticism if he wanted to do justice to the historical subtlety of Coetzee's fiction.

In an exchange of letters Coetzee suggested that Attwell might be interested in collaborating with him on the book that would eventually become *Doubling the Point*. This was probably on Coetzee's part a risky but generous proposal, since he knew that there were theoretical divergences between himself and Attwell. But he did not want a collaborator who agreed with him on all points; he wanted the potential of gradually developing dialogues. From the conversations, as published later, it transpired that Attwell tended to approach the topics through the perspectives of prominent theoreticians like Lacan, Derrida and Foucault, whereas Coetzee preferred to anchor his comments in the practice of other writers—Beckett, Ford Madox Ford, Hardy.

As for the genesis of the book, Attwell says that at the outset Coetzee sent him all his extant non-fiction in unsorted form. Attwell writes: 'I read it, read it again and began reading some of his reading, to begin making sense of it all in my own terms. When I was ready, I would propose a cluster of essays and shorter items on a particular theme. He would respond to the selection by drafting notes, recalling the resonances of the essays and their situatedness in whatever story of their genesis might suggest itself. I took these notes, drafted questions, trying to reprise the notes and open new angles. He would respond with more text, then I would send more questions and so forth, until we felt the conversation had reached a natural conclusion. Then we would start on another theme and cluster. So it went on.'

At first the interchanges between Coetzee and Atttwell took the shape of live conversations in Cape Town, with nothing being recorded. Eventually everything was committed to writing, letters were exchanged, and the whole edited. The various sections, each prefaced by an interview, comprised essays on Beckett, 'The poetics of reciprocity', popular culture, syntax, Kafka, autobiography and confession, obscenity and censorship, and South African writers. Attwell points out that all the central questions in *Doubling the Point* have a bearing on language. If the book in any way tackled the reception of Coetzee's work, it was, according to him, to eradicate the misconception that Coetzee was apathetic in the face of South African politics. Nowadays there is little disagreement among people who read Coetzee attentively—they are united in rejecting the notion of his allegedly irresponsible political stand. The consensus is that Coetzee is in fact deeply involved in South Africa's violent history.

Translations of Coetzee novels appeared as early as the 1980s, but this gained momentum in the '90s, when his books became available in, apart from the familiar Western European and Scandinavian languages, also languages such as Icelandic, Catalan, Brazilian, Polish, Russian, Serbian, Slovenian, Hebrew, Mandarin, Indonesian, Japanese and Korean. Of the some 25 languages into which his books have been translated, Coetzee knows only three moderately well. Of the other translations he knows little, except when a bilingual reader compares the two reports to him. In an article, 'Roads to translations: How a novelist relates to his translators',[27] Coetzee provided fascinating details about the pitfalls of translation.

'Sentence by sentence,' Coetzee writes, 'my prose is generally lucid, in the sense that the syntactic relations among words, and the logical force of constructions, are as clear as I can make them. On the other hand, I sometimes use words with the full freight of their history behind them, and that freight is not easily carried across to another country. [...] I do tend to be allusive, and not always to signal the presence of allusion.'

His novel *Waiting for the Barbarians* created problems for translators, because it is set in a non-specific space and time. It is virtually impossible to place the milieu as Western, but the imperial palace referred to is not necessarily situated in the East either. All the dialogue could be construed as translations by an invisible hand from an unspecified language into English. Such passages are characterised by a simplified syntax and vocabulary. The central character is referred to simply as the 'Magistrate.' He is at the head of a legal system in his specific border area, but in English there is no term for somebody who is both judge and mayor. In modern German the term *der Magistrat* refers to the whole judicial system, not a specific individual. The standard translation of the English 'magistrate' is *Friedensrichter*, but that translates into English as 'Justice of the Peace'. For that reason the German translator revived the old meaning of *der Magistrat*, which is still current in Switzerland.

The Chinese translator enquired whether the summer palace in *Waiting for the Barbarians* referred to the historical building in his country. Coetzee replied that he had not consciously referred to the palace in Beijing, but that he had wanted to suggest some connection with imperial China, just as elsewhere in the book, with 'Third Bureau', he had wanted to establish a resonance of czarist Russia.

Foe, if it can be said to deal with a single subject, is about authorship: not only in its professional sense, but also in the sense that verges, if not quite on the numinous, then on the demiurgic: sole writer, sole creator. In Serbian, however, the problem was that 'Autor' is not a profession, so that the translator had to consider the word 'tvorac' (maker, creator, founder) instead of 'scribe/scrivener'; but ultimately they decided on 'makir'.

The Serbian translation of *Elizabeth Costello*, too, presented a problem: Costello sees her books on the library shelf next to those of Chaucer, Coleridge and Conrad, but notes that her nearest neighbour is Marie Corelli; but in Serbian all these names except Chaucer are spelt with a K, so that Chaucer had to become Keats. Corelli is spelt with a K, but would be meaningless to a Serbian reader, so she had to be replaced with Agatha Kristi.

Coetzee is sometimes asked about unfamiliar English idioms or unusual words. The Korean translator, for instance, wanted to know the meaning of '*dies irae*' and '*stoksielalleen*' (the Afrikaans for 'totally alone'), and the Icelandic translator of the same book enquired about '*muti*', '*snoek*' and '*Kaffraria*'.

Coetzee's last five books have as a rule been published in the Dutch translation a few months before the original English text from the British publisher Harvill Secker. To a large extent this very generous concession is thanks to the good relations Coetzee has established with Eva Cossée, his Dutch publisher. Coetzee's work was first discovered in the Netherlands by the Bussum publisher Evo Gay, who was later connected with the publishing house Ambo. After *Waiting for the Barbarians*, he published Coetzee's first autobiographical works, but his function at Ambo was taken over by Eva Cossée, who published Coetzee's later works, and started her own publishing firm named Uitgeverij Cossee in 2001. This is a publishing house that, with a maximum of about 25 titles a year, concentrates on quality and produces books in a very attractive format.[28] Coetzee's books are accorded particular attention by this publisher, regarding production and artistic finish as well as publicity and marketing. Holland is the country, other than the UK and the US, in which his books sell most copies in relation to the population.

IV

Coetzee's interest in younger writers and in promoting important new work led him, in the 1990s and later, to provide concise assessments of the manuscripts of mainly first-time authors, which could then be used as cover copy. Thus, for instance, he enthuses over Zoë Wicomb's novel *David's Story*: 'For years we have been waiting to see what the literature of post-apartheid South Africa will look like. Now Zoë Wicomb delivers the goods. Witty in tone, sophisticated in technique, eclectic in language, beholden to no one in its politics, *David's Story* is a tremendous achievement and a huge step in the remaking of the South African novel.' Hermann Giliomee's standard work, *The Afrikaners*, is also accorded a warm and illuminating reception: 'A book to welcome—a history of the Afrikaners from the first European settlement to the present day written by a proud and even patriotic Afrikaner which is nevertheless critical in its approach and untainted by Afrikaner nationalism. It includes an account of the origins and demise of apartheid that must rank as the most sober, objective and comprehensive we have.'

Coetzee also accepted invitations to write introductions to editions, such as the one he wrote for the World's Classics edition of *Robinson Crusoe*, and for an anthology of English translations from the Dutch poet Rutger Kopland under the title *Memories of the Unknown*. In 2000 he collaborated with Carolyn Christov-Bakargiev and Dan Cameron on a monograph on the artist William Kentridge.

After his illuminating essays on the 'culture of letters' in *White Writing* (1988), he collected, in *Giving Offense* (1996), a series of studies on censorship, in South Africa as well as in countries like Britain, Russia and Poland. Many of the essays he wrote in the 1990s for *The New York Review of Books* were in 2002 reprinted in *Stranger Shores*.[29] He wrote comprehensive studies of, among others, the Dutch writers

Harry Mulisch and Cees Nooteboom, and of the German poet Rainer Maria Rilke. 'Harry Mulisch,' he remarks, 'has written frequently, even obsessively, about his ancestry, and particularly about his father (among the few books in Max Delius's apartment is Franz Kafka's *Letter to My Father*, the cry of another son struggling to escape from under the suffocating weight of a father).'[30] In the light of his comment in *Doubling the Point* that all writing, even literary criticism, is autobiographical, we may wonder if Coetzee, in making this observation, did not have in mind his own difficult relationship with his father. Apropos of the book (in its English translation) *In the Dutch Mountains*, Nooteboom's novelist-narrator asks, in the course of a debate about truth and fiction, why he should have this ungovernable urge constantly to fictionalise, to tell lies—something that Coetzee was to do in his novels and especially in his autobiographies, eventually taking it to an extreme in *Summertime*. Coetzee also points out in his study of Robert Musil's diaries how Musil fictionalises his own childhood and adolescence, looking back on the accursed time in which he lived, trying to understand what Europe did to itself and why the German nation ended up in revolt against civilisation. The essay on Rilke reveals a parallel between the German poet's attempts as a young man to detach himself from his fatherland in pursuit of a larger whole, and Coetzee's own earlier striving to escape the restrictions of the colony and settle in the metropolis. Coetzee writes: 'As a young man [Rilke] liked to say he was *heimatlos*, homeless, without a country. He even asserted a right to decide his own origin. "We are born, so to speak, provisionally, it doesn't matter where; it is only gradually that we compose, within ourselves, our true place of origin, so that we may be born there retrospectively."'[31]

In the essay on Rilke, Coetzee makes some further extremely important statements on the task of the translator. He is responding to the work of William Gass, Rilke's biographer and translator. To translate a literary text, Gass said, it was not enough to understand the source language. You also had to understand the work. Coetzee wants, in response, to lend nuance to Gass's pronouncement: 'The translator does not first need to understand the text before he translates it. Rather, translating the text becomes part of the process of finding—and making—its meaning; translating turns out to be only a more intense and more demanding form of what we do whenever we read.'[32] This is exactly Coetzee's position also in relation to his translation of Achterberg's *Ballade van de Gasfitter*[33]; it is also what his fictional Elizabeth Costello will say in her lecture on 'The humanities in Africa': 'Textual scholarship meant, first, the recovery of the true text, then the true translation of that text; and true translation turned out to be inseparable from true interpretation, just as true interpretation turned out to be inseparable from true understanding of the cultural and historical matrix from which the text had emerged.'[34] In an article on the various English translations of Kafka, Coetzee voices many objections. Also of note in this essay is his reference to the 'obscene intimacies of power',[35] which can be related to his *Waiting for the Barbarians*.

Coetzee often writes about writers and subjects with whom or which he has a connection or common ground. One can discern a parallel between Coetzee and J.L. Borges, who, like Coetzee, returned to his native land after many years, but then transcended the regional and the local, also writing in a spare, controlled and economical prose style.

On the model of T.S. Eliot's 1944 essay, 'What is a Classic', Coetzee in 1991 delivered a lecture in Graz, Austria, bearing the same title and alluding to his predecessor. This was to prove one of the most important lectures of his career. Like Eliot, Pound and V.S. Naipaul (about whom he was to write later in *Inner Workings*), Coetzee too in the 1960s exchanged the 'colony' for the metropolis. For Eliot the conservation of literary creativity in any community comprises an unconscious balance between tradition and the originality of the current generation. Eliot ascribes a central position in European civilisation to Virgil. 'Virgil,' Eliot writes, 'acquires the centrality of the unique classic; he is at the centre of European civilization, in a position which no other poet can share or usurp. The Roman Empire and the Latin language were not any empire and any language, but an empire and a language with a unique destiny in relation to ourselves; and the poet in whom that Empire and that language came to consciousness and expression is a poet of unique destiny.'[36] Virgil thus provides us with a criterion; without him we are inclined to become provincial.

Coetzee was struck by the fact that Eliot, who had settled in London, nowhere in his lecture referred to his American roots. Did this, he asks, stem from anglophilia, solidarity with the intelligentsia of the English middle classes, or from embarrassment at what he regarded as his barbaric American origins? By 1944 Eliot had become very conscious of where exactly the metropolis of a particular culture was to be found, and where its provinces. Eliot famously had declared impersonality to be a mark of great poetry, but, paradoxically, Coetzee found Eliot's lecture surprisingly personal and autobiographical. Behind the man talking about Virgil and seeing it as his task to purify the dialect of his tribe and rewrite the Latin poetic oeuvre, Coetzee discerned a subtext dealing with the person and life of Eliot, the man from the colonies who was now deliberately constructing a new identity for himself in the metropolis.[37] 'Born in a half-savage country, out of date,' Coetzee quotes Ezra Pound. He continues:

> The feeling of being out of date, of having been born into too late an epoch, or of surviving unnaturally beyond one's term, is all over Eliot's early poetry, from 'Prufrock' to 'Gerontion'. The attempt to understand this feeling or this fate, and indeed to give it meaning, is part of the enterprise of his poetry and criticism. This is a not uncommon sense of the self among colonials—whom Eliot subsumes under what he calls provincials—particularly young colonials to match their inherited culture to their daily experience.[38]

Underlying Coetzee's essay is a tacit autobiographical subtext, the question whether Coetzee, as somebody from South Africa, somebody from the colonies, could ever succeed in writing a classic. Does Eliot's definition of the word 'classic' not render it impossible? Pound's sentiment, Coetzee finds, is not uncommon among young colonials:

> To such young people, the high culture of the metropolis may arrive in the form of powerful experiences which cannot, however, be embedded in their lives in any obvious way, and which seem therefore to have their existence in some transcendent realm. In extreme cases, they are led to blame their environment for not living up to art and to take up residence in an art world. This is a provincial fate—Gustave Flaubert diagnosed it in Emma Bovary, subtitling his case study *Mœurs de province*—but particularly a colonial fate, for those colonials brought up in the culture of what is usually called the mother country but in this context deserves to be called the father country.[39]

Coetzee refers to the incident when he as a young boy of fifteen heard Bach one afternoon in the garden and experienced the impact of a classical work. He argues that it is possible to experience and understand the classic as speaking with its own immanent force and illustrates how it is possible for classical works to endure. Following the poet Zbigniew Herbert he argues that the concept of the classic manifests itself in people's perceptions not as the opposite of the Romantic, but of the barbarian; furthermore, classic versus barbarian is not so much an opposition as a confrontation:

> It is not the possession of some essential quality that, in Herbert's eyes, makes it possible for the classic to withstand the assault of barbarism. Rather, what survives the worst of barbarism, surviving because generations of people cannot afford to let go of it and therefore hold on to it at all costs — that is the classic.
>
> ... the interrogation of the classic, no matter how hostile, is part of the history of the classic, inevitable and even to be welcomed. For as long as the classic needs to be protected from attack, it can never prove itself classic.
>
> ... rather than being the foe of the classic, criticism, and indeed criticism of the most sceptical kind, may be what the classic uses to define itself and ensure its survival. Criticism may in that sense be one of the instruments of the cunning of history.[40]

In another essay in *Stranger Shores*, prompted by the Kenyan Ali Mazrui's television series *The Africans*, Coetzee comments on how writers in the past have seen Africa. 'One year,' he writes, 'the image of Africa is of herds of giraffe sailing across boundless sunlit plains. The next year it is of stick-like starving children with ballooning bellies and great sad dark eyes. Another year it is of soldiers in tattered fatigues lobbing mortar shells into the bush in yet another incomprehensible war. Africa is still peripheral enough to the West for the West to be able to afford to see it in terms of a repertoire of images like these, purveyed by journalists to a public impatient of far-off complexities.'[41]

For centuries, Coetzee writes, it was the fate of Africa to be used by the West as a kind of image bank from which emblems could be drawn. Sometimes of cruelty, brutality and hopelessness, sometimes of innocence, simplicity and good nature. Even for well-disposed outsiders, Africa remains a place to be studied, to which one sends teachers and aid. Africans are not people from whom one can learn anything. The wealth of Africa's resources is acknowledged, but they are natural resources, not human. What Africa can offer, is always raw material: raw ore, raw people, raw experience. What Africa receives in exchange, is complete systems, clinics, computers. Against this, African intellectuals will talk of a continent that is exploited and patronised by strangers, an Africa that still—bitter, resentful—lives in the aftershock of colonialism. In his series Mazrui presents a variety of images of Africa, like neglected roads, deserted factories, empty schools, derelict clinics, but next to these also 'the old Africa of sturdy, self-reliant peasants, respected elders, tight family ties, deeply ingrained myths and observances, out of which, one day, the true Africa of the future will be born'.[42]

Coetzee is of the opinion that Mazrui is romanticising the old Africa and shying away from the economic realities of which proponents of Black Consciousness need to take account. He admits that Mazrui makes an attractive case for a unique African future, faithful to its old traditions, at present negated by its mere aping of the West. 'But,' he continues, 'there are some hard questions it has to face. One is this: unless it imports Western technology on a larger scale, and along with Western technology the problem-solving Western outlook, Western materialism and Western values, can Africa hope for anything but economic stagnation, which coupled with a fast-rising birth rate, will mean that the future promises not a return to Eden but to a hell of disease and starvation?'[43]

In an essay on Gordimer and Turgenev, Coetzee writes about Gordimer's position as a writer, a commentary that is equally germane to his own:

> Writing is a lonely business, writing in opposition to the community one is born into even lonelier. It is understandable that Gordimer, as an oppositional South African writer, should have sought for and annexed historical precedents and antecedents wherever she could find them.
>
> As for why she should have worked herself into a position of on the one hand listening to, accepting, even approving the repudiation of Europe by black fellow-writers (thesis), while on the other hand asserting her own allegiance to a powerful European literary-political tradition (antithesis), and yet (synthesis) claiming an overriding commonality of purpose with her black colleagues, all one can say is that the reasons are complicated. They have a great deal to do, one suspects, with the two halves of the imaginary audience to whom Gordimer, at least at that time, was addressing herself: inside South Africa, to a radical intelligentsia, mainly black;

outside South Africa, to a liberal intelligentsia, mainly white; each
(as she was acutely aware) listening with one ear to what she was
saying to them, with the other ear to what she was saying to the
other half.[44]

As far as other South African writers are concerned, Coetzee does
not pronounce on Athol Fugard (apart from the *Notebooks 1960–
67*), because by his own admission he is not particularly responsive
to the theatre. He admires the role that André Brink played in the
struggle against censorship, even though he finds him at times
unnecessarily vehement in his formulations.[45] If he feels himself
closer to Breytenbach than to Gordimer, it is because Breytenbach
more readily accepts that stories must tell themselves. If he does
have certain reservations about Breytenbach, that is because of a
narcissistic element in his prose which is not present in his poetry.[46]
He was never party to Breytenbach's feud with Afrikanerdom, because
his first language was English, because he was never embedded in
Afrikaner culture and was formed by it only in a perverse way (by his
peripheral contact during the Worcester years).

In *Stranger Shores* Coetzee discusses Breytenbach's autobiographical
triptych: *A Season in Paradise, Return to Paradise* and *The True Confessions
of an Albino Terrorist*, the last of these his prison memoir. Coetzee finds
something wild and uncontrolled in Breytenbach's railing against all
parties: the white liberals, the South African Communist Party, the
bourgeois Left and the ANC. The best pages, he feels, are dedicated to
his rootedness in a landscape, and to a reflection on what it means to
him to have been born in Africa. Although he lived for most of his life
in Europe, Breytenbach does not feel himself to be a European: 'To
be an African is not a choice, it is a condition.'[47] In *Dog Heart* (1999)
Breytenbach restricts himself to the Western Cape, indeed to the town
of Montagu, not far from his birthplace, where he and his wife bought
and restored a house. It is an area with a predominantly white and
coloured population, with Afrikaans as their home language, the kind
of heartland where, according to Breytenbach, the restless nomadic
kind of hybrid Afrikaner without social pretensions was bred—a
claim that probably, Coetzee adds, would not stand the test of close
scientific investigation. It does, however, provide Breytenbach with the
opportunity to develop his revised version of the Afrikaner pioneer:

Whereas in the establishment version these pioneers were white-skinned farmers who, Bible in one hand and gun in the other, trekked into the interior of Africa to found republics where they would govern themselves free of British interference, in Breytenbach's version they become people of inextricably mixed genetic origin who followed their herds and flocks into the interior because they had learned a wandering lifestyle from the Khoi pastoralists. And (Breytenbach's argument goes) the sooner the modern Afrikaner discards the illusion of himself as the bearer of light in the African darkness, and accepts himself as merely one of Africa's nomads—that is to say, as a rootless and unsettled being, with no claim of proprietorship over the earth—the better his chance of survival.[48]

Although Coetzee doubts the scientific verifiability of this theory, he nevertheless finds attractive the notion that the original pioneers were mere visitors to Africa granted a temporary residence. This is a theme that will return in *Boyhood*, the first of his autobiographical works, when he describes the Coetzees of the family farm Voëlfontein in the Karoo: 'the Coetzees, drinking tea and gossiping on the farmhouse stoep, are like swallows, seasonal, here today, gone tomorrow, or even like sparrows, chirping, light-footed, short-lived.'[49]

But Breytenbach connects the two elements of his ethnic philosophy, the hybrid and the nomad, a connection in the light of which one must see the gruesome attacks on whites on farms in the new South Africa. 'These stories,' Coetzee writes, 'make disturbing reading not only because of the psychopathic violence of the attacks themselves, but because they are being repeated at all. For the circulation of horror stories is the very mechanism that drives white paranoia about being chased off the land and ultimately into the sea.'[50] The motif of the farm attack, which appears in Breytenbach's *Dog Heart* in 1999, is of course also a feature of Coetzee's *Disgrace*, published in the same year.

V

Before starting to write *Disgrace*, Coetzee began preparations for a book that would eventually constitute a new departure in his oeuvre. This is a specialised form of autobiography that was to be embodied in the next decade or so in two works: *Boyhood* (1997) and *Youth* (2002).

Coetzee's interest in autobiography as a genre, and in the particular kind of truth it can convey, was evident from 'Truth in autobiography', his inaugural address delivered in October 1984 at UCT. 'Autobiography,' the lecture starts, 'is a kind of writing in which you tell the story of yourself as truthfully as you can, or as truthfully as you can bear to. Autobiography is usually thought of not as a kind of fiction-writing, but as a kind of history-writing.'[51] Such an undertaking, Coetzee continues, with reference to the work of Jean-Jacques Rousseau, derives from a will-to-truth, which aims both to *find* the truth and to *confess* it.[52] The inaugural address is in truth a preliminary study for the comprehensive essay that Coetzee wrote in 1985 and reprinted in *Doubling the Point* under the title 'Confession and double thoughts: Tolstoy, Rousseau, Dostoevsky'. In an interview with David Attwell he says he regards this as a key essay in his development as a writer for two reasons:

> One, that there I see myself confronting in a different genre — the essay — the very question that you have faced me with in these dialogues: how to tell the truth in autobiography. Two, that I find the story I tell about myself has a certain definiteness of outline up to the time of that essay; after that it becomes hazier, lays itself open to harder questioning from the future.[53]

Shortly after his mother's death on 6 March 1987, Coetzee started making notes for a book that he at first wanted to call *Scenes from Provincial Life*, eventually to be published in 1997 as *Boyhood*, though keeping the original title as a subtitle to the British edition. The initial notes deal with a night that his mother spent as a child with her parents, brothers and sisters under an ox wagon on the Swartberg Pass, followed by scraps of memories from his childhood, all told in the first person. The night on the Swartberg Pass does not appear at all in the final text, but does return in *Age of Iron* as a youth memory of the central figure, Mrs Curren. It is clear from the fact that *Boyhood* was published only in 1997, after *Age of Iron*, *The Master of Petersburg*, *White Writing* and *Doubling the Point*, that Coetzee initially worked very slowly at this project. The holograph kept with other manuscript information in the Harry Ransom Center at Texas was completed only in July 1995. This holograph contains more material than the eventual book, and Coetzee evidently pruned the final text considerably. One change is that the teachers who emerge with less than credit from the book have had their names changed, although Coetzee kept the name of Mr Gouws, who, though Afrikaans-speaking, had excellent command of English and was aware of fine nuances of usage that English-speaking students at UCT were to prove largely ignorant of. Quite early on, too, he changed the first-person narration to third-person. His uncertainty as to the direction the text was to take is apparent from a note he made on 8 August 1993: 'Not a memoir but a novel, a slim novel.' And on 16 September 1993 he writes: 'Think about all I did not do in this memoir: bring the atmosphere to life, tell anecdotes.' Derek Attridge nevertheless thinks that there is nothing in *Boyhood* to suggest that it is deliberately unhistorical: 'and part of its singular power undoubtedly comes from the reader's sense that this is not fiction (in the narrow sense of the word).'[54]

The subtitle of *Boyhood* is borrowed from William Cooper's 1950 novel *Scenes from Provincial Life*. David Attwell has pointed out, though, that behind Cooper looms also Flaubert's *Madame Bovary*, whose sub-title is *Moeurs de province* ['Provincial customs/life']. The title *Boyhood* furthermore refers to Tolstoy's *Childhood*, *Boyhood* and *Youth*, a trilogy that is fictional, but rooted in reality and autobiography. 'When still only a boy of nineteen,' Rosemary Edmonds writes in the introduction to the Penguin edition of the trilogy, Tolstoy 'confided to his Diary that he wanted to know himself through and through, and from then until his death at the age of eighty-two he observed and described the morphology of his own soul. [...] It was not intellectual curiosity, nor hunger after the wisdom through knowledge, that drove Tolstoy to spend his life from first to last in observing and recording: it was despair and the fear of death, of nothingness.'[55] One is tempted to ask whether there may not have been something of the same driving force behind the autobiographical project that Coetzee undertook after the death of his mother, followed by that of his father and his son.

Boyhood is one of Coetzee's most accessible books, recounting the story of a boy looking for a place in which he is at home, at first in relation to his own immediate and extended family and then in the larger community. Within this family and this community, however, there are irreconcilable contradictions. He was born into a family of Afrikaans descent, but to parents who preferred English as their home language. Within the strongly Christian conservative community of Worcester they were agnostic and opposed to the policies of the National Party that came to power in 1948 on its slogan of apartheid. In the confusion attendant upon these contradictions, the boy declares himself at school to be a Roman Catholic, and sympathises with the Russians under the 'fatherly' Stalin, rather than with the Americans who are the heroes of his classmates. The book ends with the father's misconduct, barring him from practising as an attorney, and with the death of the John character's great-aunt Annie, who had had faith in his intellectual abilities. *Boyhood* differs markedly from traditional trips down memory lane, with false sentiment about the days of yore. Coetzee is consciously writing against this tradition.[56]

Youth, the autobiographical work following on *Boyhood*, was begun on 11 October 1996,[57] and first published by Secker & Warburg in 2002. Apparently it was Coetzee's plan to start the book with the arrival of the character John in London; the first part, dealing with his student years in Cape Town, was added later. *Youth* continues the tale of *Boyhood*,[58] with John studying at UCT, experiencing at first hand the political violence in South Africa, and deciding to go to London to avoid compulsory military service and to work as a computer programmer. Whereas in *Boyhood* he was trying to find himself within a community to which he felt himself an outsider, he now, amid various loveless experiences with women, tries to carve out a niche for himself as a writer. All he achieves, however, is to indulge in a frenzy of reading. His suffering in solitude in the great city, apparently, does not suffice to ignite the creative spark in him. Nevertheless, *Youth* can be seen as a *Künstlerroman*, in the tradition of Joyce's *Portrait of the Artist as a Young Man*. The John character, in his solitary wanderings through a city he experiences as hostile, is remarkably similar to Willem Termeer, the protagonist of Marcellus Emants's *Een nagelaten bekentenis*, which Coetzee had translated years earlier as *A Posthumous Confession*.[59]

As early a work as *Dusklands*, his debut novel in 1974, contained an autobiographical element, even if only in the various characters with the surname Coetzee. In both *Boyhood* and *Youth* the complicating feature of the structure is the narration from a third-person perspective. It is through this perspective that the boundaries of autobiography are shifted, because the autobiographical burden to offer the 'truth' through a faithful rendering of the 'facts' is undermined and subverted through the created distance between the John figure and the narrator. By contrast with novels like *Robinson Crusoe*, *Jane Eyre* and *David Copperfield*, which invite the reader through all kinds of stratagems to accept the real existence of the protagonist, thus creating an autobiographical illusion,[60] the reader of *Boyhood* and *Youth* becomes aware of a distance, often an ironical distance, between the adult writing the book and the child that he was, creating an image of a childhood in which the mature man's voice at times usurps that of the boy. There is thus a distance created between the I-as-child and the I-as-adult, to a large extent by the ironical use of a third-person narrator, rendering the thought, feelings and observations of the focaliser those of an adult rather than of a child. Especially in *Boyhood* the intellectual distance between the protagonist and the narrator is particularly in evidence in relation to the boy's sexual awakening. 'The time when the protagonist becomes aware of his sexuality,' writes Anna Cichoń, 'is focalized internally by his young self, but the language, notably the question: "What is desire *for*?", cannot but appertain to the narrator as a mature person.'[61] The narrator thus looks back with an ironic regard at his younger self as a somewhat strange creature, a regard that subverts the autobiographical charge even further. As Matthew Cheney writes: 'In *Boyhood* and, especially, *Youth*, the John Coetzee presented to us is an alienated and alienating figure, one who challenges the reader's sympathies not only through point of view but through the actions and perceptions conveyed to us by the narrator.'[62]

Coetzee's agents received the manuscript of *Boyhood* with great enthusiasm. Reviewers, too, reacted very warmly to it. In *The New York Review of Books* of 20 November 1997, John Banville writes: 'It is both a curse and a blessing for an artist to live in the "interesting times" of a totalitarian regime, as Coetzee is well aware. His achievement is that his books are so concentrated, so poised, so intensely *mediated*, that they are wholly autonomous, and do not depend for their power on our knowledge of where and in what circumstances they were written. Surely this is one of the identifying marks of authentic, enduring works of art.' '*Boyhood*,' writes T. Kai Norris Easton in *The Boston Sunday Globe* of 26 October 1997, 'is a masterfully told, spare, and accessible memoir, and an unexpected companion to Coetzee's intellectual autobiography, *Doubling the Point*. [...] The chapter on the farm must be singled out: It is a triumph of storytelling. Coetzee's prose magically evokes the pastoral beauty of the farm, while his unusually perceptive boyhood self ponders his sense of belonging in the landscape.' David Attwell, too, in the *Sunday Independent* of 2 November 1997, praises the lyrical and at times searing look at the Karoo farm and finds the book 'in every detail [...] poised and compelling. Its frank and searching account of one phase of the author's childhood will do much to humanise and illuminate what has often been received as unnecessarily remote intellectualism.' Karen Rutter writes in the *Cape Times* of 21 November 1997 that *Boyhood* 'moves beyond the strictures of biography in terms of its socio-cultural setting. Coetzee's observations on language, class, gender and history, whilst seen through the eyes of a young child, are razor-sharp.' And in the *Times Literary Supplement* of 9 January 1998, Ronald Wright commends the narrative technique and the way in which a 'solitary child's detachment' is conveyed. He concludes: 'In *Foe*, Coetzee wrote that the myth of a human being alone on an island is perhaps the only story there is. With extraordinary candour, eloquence and vividness, *Boyhood* shows us the need for islands and the terrors of rescue for those who have guessed the nature of the world beyond.'

The manuscript of *Youth*, too, was enthusiastically received. Alan Taylor writes in the *Glasgow Herald* of 21 April 2002: 'Coetzee's *Youth* records with almost too-painful honesty the circuitous route a man must take to realise his desire to become a writer. For those who succeed, there are books such as this one to prove it; for those who don't, there is only silence, and another question: what if?' Hilary Mantel, in *The Spectator* of 20 April 2002, writes about Coetzee's 'solemn intensity, the magisterial calm and the clarity of his prose'. In the *Evening Standard* of 22 April 2002, David Sexton calls *Youth* 'a wonderful book, a *Bildungsroman*, or portrait of the artist as a young man, to rank with any in the canon'. Peter Porter, the reviewer of the *Times Literary Supplement*, was perturbed at the book's negative take on the British capital. In his review on 26 April 2002 he finds a correlation here with Coetzee's absence from the Booker ceremony: 'The literary world attributes Coetzee's reluctance to travel to London to receive his Booker prizes to purely private considerations. *Youth* suggests that the remembered horrors of 1960s England have been keeping him away. If so, it has been literature's gain, since his preoccupation with life in his native land has led to some of the finest novels of the past century. There is no requirement that he shows us to ourselves. On the other hand, what can solace an admirer of [his books] in the face of the oddity and lack of sympathy of this pinched and obsessive performance?'

The American reviewers were no less favourable in their responses than the British. Martin Rubin writes in the *San Francisco Chronicle* of 14 July 2002: '*Youth* is a delight to read. It will make you angry, amused, scornful and sympathetic by turns. It also has the virtue of genuinely enlightening you about the mind that produced those spare, stark novels.' The novelist John Updike, in *The New Yorker* of 15 July 2002, concludes his long assessment as follows: 'A delectable tension exists in this writer between a youthful wariness of tired, termite-ridden words and a childish desire to spill ink, out of control, to unload what is in his head. Even the low-energy years described in *Youth* take on, in the clipped telling, a curious electricity; the astringent pages leave us keen to read on.' In the *Chicago Tribune* of 4 August 2002, Dan Cryer writes: 'Fiercely honest, *Youth* provides an indelible portrait of a young man so in thrall to art that he is consumed by fear of failure. Its heights are so lofty and his means of ascent so puny that climbing seems utterly preposterous. Likewise, for any adolescent, that's how perilous the path to adulthood can seem.'

In Australia, where Coetzee was by now receiving increasing attention, the reviewers were full of praise. In the *Australian Book Review* of June/July 2002, Jim Davidson, for instance, found it 'a meticulous analysis of vulnerability, and of negative capabilities', but also 'fearfully honest […] and a compelling read'.

In the Netherlands, where Coetzee was building up a large readership, *Youth* was the first of his books to appear in a Dutch translation several months before the publication of the original English text. Here, too, the critics wrote with great appreciation of his work. Jeroen Vullings expressed himself warmly in *Vrij Nederland* of 16 March 2002 on *Youth*, translated as *Portret van een jongeman*: 'Never before has Coetzee written in so pared-down a style, without frills and lyricism'. And Pieter van Os calls it, in *De Groene Amsterdammer* of 1 June 2002, a brilliantly written work, an 'unmistakable pearl of gloom'.[63]

In the US, *Youth* was, as the subtitle indicates, marketed as a novel, whereas in the UK the title was published without any indication as to genre. In this regard Coetzee exchanged e-mails with Geoff Mulligan, at the time head of Secker & Warburg. On 18 July 2001 Coetzee wrote to Mulligan:

> Thanks for sending the flap copy for *Youth*. As it stands, however, this draft strikes me as on the one hand too detailed, on the other hand not informative enough about what is in the book. Could the author have another shot before I come in with suggestions?
>
> Let me spend a moment or two on *Boyhood*, *Youth*, and the question of genre. I have not been unhappy that *Boyhood* has floated in a rather indeterminate way between the classification Fiction and

the classification Biography & Memoirs. It was only when, reading the contract for *Youth*, I noticed that a work of biography seemed to carry a legal onus to tell no lies, that I became a little alarmed, and asked that, at least contractually, it be absolved of all pretensions to historical truth.

Now that *Youth* is legally a fiction, I'd be disappointed if it were to be marketed unambiguously as such — as *Youth: A novel*, for instance. And ditto, retrospectively, for *Boyhood*.

To this, Mulligan replies on 19 July 2001:

Thanks. We will have another look at the flap copy.

I appreciate what you say about the classification of *Boyhood* and *Youth*, and it seems to me to be right to preserve some sense of ambiguity. We will be obliged to refer to *Youth* as fiction or biography in the catalogue, and for bibliographic purposes, prize submissions and so on. Would you be happy for me to categorise the book as fiction, but try and maintain some ambiguity in the presentation and marketing?

In reply, Coetzee writes on 23 July 2001:

You write: 'We will be obliged to refer to *Youth* as fiction or biography in the catalogue, and for bibliographic purposes, prize submissions and so on. Would you be happy for me to categorise the book as fiction, but try and maintain some ambiguity in the presentation and marketing?'

Yes, if I absolutely have to choose between categorizing the book as fiction or as autobiography, I would go for the former; but the less absolute the categorization, from my point of view, the better.

VI

From his correspondence in the 1990s and the ever more frequent declining of flattering invitations to lecture at prestigious universities, one can deduce that Coetzee was gradually withdrawing from academia, wanting to concentrate on his creative work. Invitations to read from his work he still accepted, on condition that there would be no interviews or question-and-answer sessions. He was loath to prepare conference papers or—apart from the annual visits to the University of Chicago, which he still enjoyed—to lecture for long periods at other institutions.

In November 1996, however, Coetzee was invited by Bennington College to receive the biennial Stowe Award, comprising a medal and prize money of $50 000, and to deliver the Ben Belitt lecture, in honour of the celebrated American poet and translator of Neruda and Lorca. In his acceptance speech, published in the journal *Salmagundi*,[64] Coetzee spoke on the question 'What is realism?' He for the first time made use of the character Elizabeth Costello—a kind of alter ego for Coetzee, the author of nine novels, two volumes of poetry, a book on bird life and an extensive corpus of journalism. Australian by birth, Costello also lived for some years in England and France, and in the preceding decade or so—and here there is a clear allusion to Coetzee's own situation—'there has grown up around her a small critical industry; there is even an Elizabeth Costello Society, based in Albuquerque, New Mexico, which puts out a quarterly *Elizabeth Costello Newsletter.*[65] In this lecture Costello claims that the modern reader no longer has any faith in the truth of the text. 'Within the story, however,' writes Margaret Lenta in her discussion of *The Lives of Animals*,[66] 'texts are taken as "truth" of a kind: an interviewer speaks of a novel by Costello that questions the way in which women are portrayed by male writers, changing ways of understanding women for all responsive readers.'

The year after his visit to Bennington, in 1997, Coetzee accepted an invitation from Princeton to present the Tanner Lectures.[67] Instead of the conventional lecture, he presented his audience with a short novella, again using the world-famous fictitious Australian author, Elizabeth Costello, invited to address a prominent American university, Appleton College. Costello was celebrated for her pioneering feminist fiction, and known in particular for *The House on Eccles Street* (1969), a novel about Marion Bloom, the wife of Leopold Bloom in James Joyce's *Ulysses*. Instead of expounding on literature or discussing her own work, she devotes her two lectures to animal rights and the moral imperative for a vegetarian lifestyle. She does not hesitate to relate the humiliation, maltreatment and slaughter of animals to the Nazi atrocities against the Jews in the extermination camps. The resident poet laureate, Abraham Stern, finds her words so offensive that he refuses to attend the dinner in Costello's honour. In a note to her he says he finds her comparison of the murdered Jews with slaughtered cattle an insult to the memory of the dead of the Holocaust. Costello maintains that the matter is not in the first place a question of 'reason', but of human inability to understand and to recognise that animals are also creatures capable of suffering. By implication this is an admission that her position has not been adequately thought through, which prompts Nicholas Dawes to comment:

> There is no doubting the force of her vision, but she is hardly the most cogent advocate of animal rights. Her two lectures are rambling, tendentious and full of holes: the comparison with the Holocaust is dangerous and poorly thought out, and her attempt to describe the achievement of true sympathy with animals through an act of poetic imagination is attractive but unconvincing.[68]

On the front flap of the dust cover Coetzee's text is described in more detail in terms of the narrative framework:

> The idea of human cruelty to animals so consumes novelist Elizabeth Costello in her later years that she can no longer look another person in the eye: humans, especially meat-eating ones, seem to her to be conspirators in a crime of stupefying magnitude taking place on farms and in slaughterhouses, factories, and laboratories across the world.

Coetzee himself, a vegetarian of some 25 years' standing at the time of delivering the lectures, is nowhere visible during Elizabeth Costello's performance. Although he is delivering the Tanner Lectures, he is fully concealed by her, at one with the fictional writer he is introducing to his audience. When, after the first lecture, Costello firmly defends her vegetarian principles at an awkward dinner during which only three guests dare to order a fish dish, neither audience nor reader knows where Coetzee's own sympathies lie. In his review of *The Lives of Animals* David Attwell writes: 'We can assume the fictional mode facilitates a certain self-protective and ironic detachment',[69] a distancing that here results in a particularly complex form of postmodern metafiction, quite different from the ironic distance Coetzee achieves through the use of a third person in his autobiographies.

The texts of the two lectures were published in 1999 by Princeton University Press under the title *The Lives of Animals*, edited and introduced by the political philosopher Amy Gutmann. This edition also contains the responses of four experts on divergent subjects: the literary theorist Marjorie Garber, the moral philosopher Peter Singer, the theologian Wendy Doniger and the primatologist Barbara Smuts. In 2000 Coetzee's text was reprinted on its own by the London-based Profile books.

What is most striking about *The Lives of Animals* is the complexity of the literary design, and the relation between 'fiction' and 'reality', which here, even more than in other texts by Coetzee, assumes a novel form. Each of the two contributions, respectively titled 'The philosophers and the animals' and 'The poets and the animals', is in truth a lecture within a lecture, with the lecture as the fictive framework within which the larger non-fictive frame is subsumed — an instance, then, of Coetzee's boundary-shifting procedures, effacing once clear-cut distinctions between character and author.

The story opens on Costello's arrival in Waltham, where she is met by her son, John Bernard, associate professor in physics and astronomy at Appleton College. At first the narrative, although in the third person, is focalised through John. John's wife, a philosopher, has never really taken to her mother-in-law, and has scant sympathy with her vegetarian principles. At the close of the second lecture, Costello's authority as a dilettante philosopher, in Attwell's words, is undermined by the superior performance of the professional Thomas O'Hearne, her antagonist in the debate that constitutes her last obligation at Appleton. Her last impulse is to declare that she is morally isolated, the only one bearing witness to 'a crime of stupefying proportions'[70] that everyone around her commits every day. When her son takes her to the airport for her flight back, he says, 'There, there, it will soon be over.'[71] Attwell comments: 'An ambiguous remark, to say the least, as not only is she leaving to fly back to Australia, she is also near the end of her life. This works as a conclusion in *The Lives of Animals*, both because of its undeniable pathos and because we are made to share her precarious being.'[72]

But Costello was criticised also from other sources than Thomas O'Hearne in the fictive construct of the lecture; thus Steven Austad, Professor of Zoology at the University of Idaho,[73] directs his criticism past Costello at Coetzee:

> Probably a major reason I feel no compunctions about the human
> use of other species is that, as a biologist, I take distinctions between
> species seriously. I am keenly aware of the ubiquity of predation and
> parasitism in the natural world. Life lives on life, and whether or

not that life is photosynthetic strikes me as a capricious distinction. Are some animal species morally inferior to others because their digestive systems process meat?

I justify my meat eating by tradition. As Craig Stanford's book[74] makes abundantly clear, my ancestors have been killing and eating meat for more than 5 million years. What kind of egotism would it take to break a tradition like that?

VII

On 19 August 1995, before the publication of *Boyhood* and *The Lives of Animals*, Coetzee started work on a novel that was eventually to have the title *Disgrace*. In the final text, as published in 1999 by Secker & Warburg, the first two paragraphs of the first chapter read as follows:

> For a man of his age, fifty-two, divorced, he has, to his mind, solved the problem of sex rather well. On Thursday afternoons he drives to Green Point. Punctually at two p.m. he presses the buzzer at the entrance to Windsor Mansions, speaks his name, and enters. Waiting for him at the door of No. 113 is Soraya. He goes straight through to the bedroom, which is pleasant-smelling and softly lit, and undresses. Soraya emerges from the bathroom, drops her robe, slides into bed beside him. 'Have you missed me?' she asks. 'I miss you all the time,' he replies. He strokes her honey-brown body, unmarked by the sun; he stretches her out, kisses her breasts; they make love.
>
> Soraya is tall and slim, with long black hair and dark, liquid eyes. Technically he is old enough to be her father; but then, technically, one can be a father at twelve. He has been on her books for over a year; he finds her entirely satisfactory. In the desert of the week Thursday has become an oasis of *luxe et volupté*.[75]

That, however, is not how the opening of 19 August 1995 read, because Coetzee revised this opening no fewer than thirteen times. The first holograph, which would eventually number 386 pages, was written, like many other of Coetzee's manuscripts, in UCT exam books, and revised several times with a red pen before being transferred to the computer.

At the first attempt, on 19 August 1995, everything is said in a single paragraph:

> For someone of his age and temperament, he has solved the sexual business rather well. Every Wednesday afternoon he drives out to Green Point. At two p.m. exactly he rings the bell at 13 Windsor Court. The door is opened by Soraya, whose surname he thinks is Davids because the name on the letterbox downstairs is S. Davids. He goes to the bedroom, undresses, and gets into bed. The sheets are always fresh; it is a gesture that he approves of. Soraya enters, in a red bed robe. She drops the robe and gets into bed with him. She is a tall, slim woman in her thirties. He is sixty, old enough to be her father but not her grandfather. She has long black hair and dark liquid eyes. They have known each other for two years. He finds her, if not beautiful, then deeply attractive, deeply desirable. His desire for her, is there not only on Wednesday but throughout the week, as a pleasing tingle of anticipation.

Although this opening paragraph is competent, a comparison with the final text shows that Coetzee had not succeeded in ordering the information to his satisfaction. The focaliser, who for the duration of the novel will concentrate on the actions and thoughts of the central character, here speaks only of 'someone of his age'. It is only in later revisions that the reader is told that he is fifty-two and divorced. The 'temperament', too, of the central character, mentioned in the first sentence, remains obscure, because it is not elaborated on later. Also, the speculation about Soraya's surname on the letterbox is redundant to what is being offered here. In truth Soraya has an exclusively sexual function for him and is approached only on the level of that need, so that an indication of her outward appearance ('tall and slim', 'long black hair and dark liquid eyes') is enough. The word 'exactly' is eventually replaced with 'punctually', which conveys much more effectively the fixed, but also the virtually routine-determined and mechanical habits of the central character. The statement that he 'has solved the sexual business rather well' is later made provisional by inserting 'to his mind'. 'He has been visiting Soraya for two years' is replaced with 'He has been on her books for over a year', which brings back something of the clinical-commercial aspect of the sex act. 'A pleasing tingle of anticipation' eventually becomes '...in the desert of the week Thursday has become an oasis of *luxe et volupté*, the last words being a truncated quotation from one of the best-known French poems, Charles Baudelaire's 'L'invitation au voyage'[76] from his collection *Les fleurs du mal* (Flowers of Evil). In this context the French words establish the central character as educated and well-read.

A far-reaching change comes at the end of the first paragraph: 'He strokes her honey-brown body, unmarked by the sun, he stretches her out, kisses her breasts; they make love.' This casts Soraya as a mere object in the eyes of the focaliser. In contrast to earlier versions, when Soraya took the initiative, David Lurie is eventually the active one in the foreplay, as conveyed by the verbs 'strokes', 'stretches' and 'kisses'. His appreciation of her is limited to the physical, and 'he stretches her out' suggests a deliberate manipulation. The sex act is simply described as 'they make love', a 'hurried, euphemistic, contextually inappropriate phrasing', as Michael G. McDunnah puts it,[77] which conveys the absence of personal involvement.

What one gathers from the many rewritings of these two paragraphs, is the precision with which Coetzee, the meticulous craftsman, sketches a situation in a few words, creating his characters with extremely meagre resources and no redundant words. And what applies to the first two paragraphs, is true of the whole of *Disgrace*, a novel whose text has been stripped to essentials.

VIII

David Lurie, originally a professor of languages specialising in Romantic poetry, is already by the beginning of the novel obliged, by cuts and rationalisations at tertiary institutions, to teach communication skills at the Technical University of Cape Town. This is an assignment to which he dutifully resigns himself, but without any passion or interest. Fifty-two years old and divorced, he visits a prostitute in Green Point every Thursday afternoon to solve 'the problem of sex' conveniently, but also clinically and without emotional involvement.[78] When this prostitute is no longer available, he starts an impulsive relationship with Melanie Isaacs, one of his students, who lodges a complaint of sexual harassment against him. At the internal hearing Lurie acknowledges guilt, but refuses to apologise or to show remorse, on the grounds of his conviction that he has been a victim of the goddess of love. He will later say to his daughter Lucy: 'My case rests on the rights of desire, on the god who makes even the small birds quiver.'[79] He is consequently forced to vacate his position as lecturer. In Lurie's fall as a result of his distorted notion of romantic passion there is a trace of the protagonist's fall from grace in classical drama, though the comic moments prevent the events from attaining a truly tragic dimension. David Attwell points out an important and often disregarded aspect of this hearing, which is reminiscent of the hearings of the Truth and Reconciliation Commission chaired by Desmond Tutu:

> Perhaps the figure most neglected in the public criticism of the novel is Manas Mathabane, the Professor of Religious Studies who chairs the disciplinary inquiry following the charge of sexual harassment against David Lurie; Mathabane is not mentioned because he falls outside the stereotype the novel is taken to be peddling, since he reins in the more forensic of the inquisitors and insists that the hearing is not a trial. In his dedication to fairness and procedure, Mathabane is, in fact, the novel's true representative of the Enlightenment, and his generally forgiving stance echoes the presence of the clergy associated with the Truth and Reconciliation Commission.[80]

With this scandal hanging over him and in a state of disgrace, Lurie moves in with his unmarried daughter, Lucy, near Salem in the Eastern Cape, where she is running a farming business with a black man, Petrus, selling her produce regularly at a market in nearby Grahamstown. The change of setting introduces an element of the farm novel, as Coetzee practised it, among other writings, in *In the Heart of the Country*. Whereas Lurie in the Cape Town section of the novel comes across as a hard, unfeeling character with little compassion, he is now far more sympathetically drawn, especially when both he and his daughter become victims of violence, and he extends his concern to her welfare. He suffers serious burn wounds when he is locked up and set on fire, and she is repeatedly raped by three black men. This introduces a parallel into the novel: Lurie's taking advantage of Melanie Isaacs corresponds to the rape of Lucy. Also between Petrus and Lucy there is a parallel: the traditional roles of the old South Africa are reversed and Petrus becomes co-owner of the smallholding, whereas Lurie from time to time, in a further reversal of the earlier master-slave relationship, is in Petrus's employ and helps him to farm.

Lurie is aware of living in a state of disgrace. On his way back to the Eastern Cape, he visits Melanie's parents in George, and says to her father: 'I am sunk into a state of disgrace from which it will not be easy to lift myself. It is not a punishment I have refused. I do not murmur against it. On the contrary, I am living it out from day to day, trying to accept disgrace as my state of being.'[81]

The lives of both Lurie and his daughter are co-determined by the far-reaching changes in South Africa after the end of apartheid. What keeps him going is his ambition to write an opera about love and death, based on Lord Byron's relationship with the much younger Teresa Guiccioli, which he initiated in 1819 in Italy after virtually being banned from England when his relationship with his half-sister came to light.[82] Like Byron, Lurie has been forced to leave his home under a cloud and to seek refuge in a strange place (in Byron's case a foreign country). In his opera-in-progress Byron becomes the exponent of the disillusionment that Lurie also feels, and Lurie has visions of his daughter, like Byron's, begging him with arms extended to rescue her—much as Dostoevsky, in *The Master of Petersburg*, dreams of Pavel, the son whom he feels he abandoned, but now hopes to bring back to life. The opera, however, deals mainly with lost love and lost sexuality. The Teresa who rescues Lurie is, instead of Melanie, the unattractive Bev Shaw, a woman for whom he feels no great sexual desire.

The relation between Lurie and Lucy is a troubled one, the more so when it transpires that the rape has left her pregnant, but that she refuses to have an abortion or bring a charge against her assailants, opting instead to marry Petrus in exchange for his protection. She believes that the new South Africa is ruled by a new ethos, and that black people expect a certain sacrifice from her. Her last words in the novel are an allusion to the conclusion of Franz Kafka's *The Trial*:

> 'Yes, I agree, it is humiliating. But perhaps that is a good point to start from again. Perhaps that is what I must learn to accept. To start at ground level. With nothing. Not with nothing but. With nothing. No cards, no weapons, no property, no rights, no dignity.'
> 'Like a dog.'
> 'Yes, like a dog.'[83]

At the end of the novel Lurie devotes himself to the work at an animal clinic, where he euthanises unwanted and stray dogs, and where he becomes attached to a crippled dog who will never be claimed by an owner. In the closing scene, Lurie is about to give up on this dog and to take it, like a lamb to the slaughter, to the table in the consulting room for the fatal injection. Lurie thus, in a further reversal, takes on Petrus's function as the 'dog man'.

From Coetzee's notebook kept with the manuscript in filing boxes, it appears that he had originally entertained the notion of giving Lurie some aspects of the biblical Job, a man stripped of all respect, and that Lurie would at the end commit suicide. Another line of development, which he later abandoned completely, is a scene in which Melanie and her friend Ryan go to a club, but separate after a quarrel, after which she accepts a lift home from a strange man. When her body is found the next day, Ryan, to clear himself, places the blame on Lurie. Some vague trace of the Job figure does remain in Lurie, but the notes are interesting mainly as an indication of the different story lines that Coetzee considered before rejecting them relatively quickly.

As a very rare exception, and only because his agent Peter Lampack had forwarded it to him, Coetzee acceded to a request from John Mark Eberhardt, the books editor of *The Kansas City Star*, to answer a few questions on *Disgrace*. The novel had been chosen for discussion by a book club to which Eberhardt belonged, and the members were to be given a question-and-answer sheet. Coetzee's answers are dated 23 March 2001. As was his consistent policy as a writer, he did not answer any questions pertaining to the interpretation of his novel:

1. Some very unpleasant things happen in this book and yet *Disgrace* is not an oppressive reading experience. How did you manage to construct a book that delves into subject matter that can be quite grim — rape, racism, cruelty to animals etc. — and yet maintain the sort of lyrical flow the book displays? One early review of the book called it 'strangely exhilarating,' and I'd have to agree.

I write as well as I can. If the book has a lyrical flow, I'm glad. One doesn't need a theory of how to write well in order to write well.

2. Some readers have commented that David Lurie is a hard character to like. I beg to differ. His very refusal to turn away from his own shortcomings emerges as almost heroic. Did you intend for him to be an admirable character, even with his flaws?

The book took over two years to write. I couldn't have lived with DL for those two years if he had been an entirely unpleasant character.

3. Lurie, a professor, has a disastrous affair with one of his students. After that, though, the book takes some interesting and, to me, unexpected turns. How does one maintain such taut control over the material even when the story goes to places readers might not anticipate?

How do I maintain taut control? How does the high-wire artiste stay on the wire? By taking care not to fall off.

4. The academic gender politics of Lurie's affair are contrasted later in the novel with the brutal physical attack upon his daughter. But how much difference is there, really, between Lurie's acts and the acts of the three intruders? Certainly Lurie's student consented to sex—but could he be considered guilty of intellectual rape?

I'm not sure I know what intellectual rape is. Melanie Isaacs' ideas sound quite banal, barely worth getting excited about.

5. You still live in South Africa, although I understand you are moving. Have things changed much in the last couple of years, or is yours still a country in which these tensions will continue to unfold? What can South Africa do to heal its long history of racial discord? (It occurs to me that the question applies to America as well.)

I'm not a physician. If I were, the first words that would occur to me would be 'Physician, heal thyself.'

6. Perhaps I'm twisted, but I found the scenes dealing with cruelty to and neglect of animals perhaps even more harrowing to read than the depictions of the terrible things that happen to the human beings in this story. Why did you decide to include the way humans treat animals as a theme of this story?

There are many more animals in the world than there are human beings, so it isn't odd to pay attention to animals. I have written a book devoted entirely to the question of how humans treat animals: *The Lives of Animals*, published by Princeton University Press.

7. David Lurie says his sexual misadventure was driven by passion, but I wonder about that. Both parties in the affair, in fact, appear rather cavalier about it all, and in Lurie's case, there is certainly sexual desire, but even his desire seems suspect to me. Is David Lurie really just seeking a way out of an existence that had grown painful to him?

I don't know the answer. I don't know more about DL than what I wrote.

8. It's tempting to read Lurie's trysting with Bev, the animal clinic woman, as an example of some kind of spiritual growth (at least he's sleeping with a mature woman instead of his students). It's also tempting to read it as just another example of his womanizing. Which reading do you prefer, or does the truth of his relationship with Bev fall somewhere between those extremes?

I don't think it is a good idea for writers to set themselves up as authorities on how their books should be read.

9. David Lurie definitely could be described as arrogant as this tale begins. Perhaps some of that quality remains at the end, but if so, I didn't see it. Is there any way to be arrogant and be in disgrace simultaneously? Put another way, is David Lurie a Byronic hero? He certainly admires Byron's work, but is he at any time in this novel a Byronic character?

I'm not sure that one can be a Byronic character outside a Byronic drama. DL is a Byron scholar, he is writing an opera of a kind about Byron, doubtless Byron has had a formative effect on him, as all writers do whom we read deeply. Isn't that enough?

10. Is compassion more important than love?

Is it important to rank the virtues?[84]

IX

In their reviews of *Disgrace* South African critics tended to emphasise its disturbing quality. Gareth Cornwell posed some questions around the depressing, sombre, pessimistic cast of the novel: 'Is Lucy's response to her predicament a parable about the necessary expiation of white guilt in post-1994 South Africa? Is Coetzee suggesting that it is only through such gestures of self-abasement and radical self-refashioning that the binary logic of our societal impasse can be broken, that a genuine mutuality can insinuate itself into the race-torn fabric of the nation?'[85]

As against this, Ranti Williams, in the British *Times Literary Supplement* of 25 June 1999, declared 'filial relationship […] one of the most moving aspects of a moving book, as it unfolds against the author's favourite backdrop—the brutal beauty of the Southern African countryside'. Paul Bailey, in *The Independent* of 3 July 1999, expresses admiration for the novel's literary qualities: '*Disgrace* is a subtle, multi-layered story, as much concerned with politics as it is with the itch of male flesh. Coetzee's prose is chaste and lyrical without being self-conscious: it is a relief to encounter writing as quietly stylish as this.' Lucy Hughes-Hallett, in the London *Sunday Times*,[86] concentrates on the power of Coetzee's prose: 'With merciless integrity, Coetzee withholds consolations, but he offers the reader the excitement of a grand project, achieved without a falter. This is a harsh story, told in prose of spare, steely beauty and with an intelligent potency that makes it as exhilarating as it is grim. It confirms Coetzee's claim to be considered one of the best novelists alive.' Justin Cartwright writes in *The Daily Telegraph* of 22 September 1999: 'I would guess that in its bleak realism it is the product of Coetzee's deep unease about the dangerous superficiality of the philosophies underlying the new South Africa and that he was not prepared to risk misinterpretation by clothing his unease in his more familiar allegory.' Adam Mars-Jones writes in *The Observer* of 18 July 1999: 'Any novel set in South Africa is fated to be read as a political portrait, but the fascination of *Disgrace*—a somewhat perverse fascination, as some will feel—is the way it both encourages and contests such a reading by holding extreme alternatives in tension.' In *The New York Times* of 28 November 1999, Michael Gorra points out a thematic resemblance to Nadine Gordimer's 1998 novel,

The House Gun, set, like *Disgrace*, in the post-apartheid era.[87] He comments on the present-tense narration: '*Disgrace* is [...] written in the present tense, and its title denotes a continuing condition. Disgrace continues. And so do the characters' lives, which at the end of the book remain unresolved and unfinished, their problems and possibilities still open. This novel stands as one of the few I know in which the writer's use of the present tense is in itself enough to shape the structure and form of the book as a whole.' If *Disgrace* has a 'message' for the reader, writes Andrew O'Hehir in *Salon Reviews* of 5 November 1999, it is that political change can do virtually nothing to eradicate human misery — 'political and historical forces blow through the lives of individuals like nasty weather systems, bringing with them a destruction that is all the more cruel for being impersonal.'

Two of the most illuminating surveys of *Disgrace* are those by Elizabeth Lowry in the *London Review of Books* of 14 October 1999 and David Attwell in the *Journal of Southern African Studies* of December 2001. Lowry points out fascinating correspondences (and differences) between *Disgrace* and Coetzee's earlier *In the Heart of the Country*, in particular regarding the motif of the master-slave relation. '*Disgrace*,' she writes, 'is the best novel Coetzee has written. It is a chilling, spare book, the work of a mature writer who has refined his textual obsessions to produce an exact, effective prose and condensed his thematic concern with authority into a deceptively simple story.' She continues:

> *Disgrace* is about a society in the process of being overhauled, in which morality has been 'erased and reborn' and all the terms have changed. [...] The world being jettisoned is that of David Lurie and Mrs Curren, with its interest in Romantic poetry and the classics — a world whose humanist values have failed to resolve the conflict between coloniser and colonised. And yet these very values — a respect for the individual, sympathy, restraint — become the measure of what is missing, in human terms, in the revolution. The truth is that there are two patriarchs in *Disgrace*: that Petrus represents a force for oppression without pity as great, potentially, as David Lurie's. Lurie has made use of Soraya and Meláni, but there is a lethal symmetry in the fact that his own daughter is used in turn and becomes a chattel of the Petrus clan — a *bywoner*, without a voice. When the novel ends, news of her rape has for some time been bruited around the district by her rapists. The

point is that this is "not her story to spread but theirs: they are its owners". What *Disgrace* finally shows us is the promised victory of one expansionist force over another, with women as pawns, the objects of punitive violence. [...] The scenes of Petrus clearing his land, aided by Lurie, recall the passages in *Foe* in which Friday is set to work on the stone terraces, alongside his master. Petrus himself is recalcitrant, unyielding: he is the rock on which the future will be built. *Disgrace* is a deeply pessimistic book; [...] it will not win unqualified praise from Coetzee's more prescriptive critics in the South African literary establishment.

In his review David Attwell points out that there is indeed a clear linkage between certain historical events and their fictional manifestation in some of Coetzee's novels, but that this serves rather as a starting point for an aesthetic and ethical engagement, often in combination with each other. Against this background, says Attwell, one should beware of too soon reaching superficial conclusions about a novel in which the reader is confronted with the first treatment in Coetzee's oeuvre of post-apartheid South Africa, however much this period figures as the warp and weft of the novel. For Attwell Lurie is both victim and mediator of destruction. The Romantic era in which he used to specialise is no longer relevant to the world in which he finds himself. History has overtaken him, as is all too clear from the disciplinary hearing for sexual harassment to which he is subjected. Attwell comments that the hearing is just about the only time in the novel that public testimony is represented, with the Truth and Reconciliation Commission as the obvious frame of reference for the events. Attwell continues: 'Lurie's refusal to offer the desired tone of penitence, while admitting guilt, becomes the focus of attention in this passage, so one is drawn to the conclusion that an institutionally driven quest for confession and reconciliation is [...] in Lurie's terms another attack on the notion of a private life.'

Also in the attack on his daughter's farm, to which he has gone to recover from his humiliating experience in Cape Town, Lurie is overtaken by history:

Here an impulse toward allegory is most in evidence in the novel, since the farm novel is carefully positioned in the heart of the Eastern Cape, indeed Kaffraria, at Salem ('Peace') during the years of land reform, which makes *Disgrace* a reprisal of the farm novel tradition, which Coetzee himself has explored in *White Writing*, *In the Heart of the Country*, and *Life & Times of Michael K*. The two figures who carry most allegorical weight are the rural landowners who must negotiate a future together: Petrus [...], the former farm-hand who knows his time has arrived, and Lucy, heir of a settler history, attempting to live lightly, as a post-industrial-age hippie, on the simple routines and pleasures of rural life, but who cannot avoid becoming the representative of settlerdom's long history of appropriation. Lucy's rape is a case, however, of paying for the sins, not only of the fathers, but also of her own father, whose seduction of Melanie had a degree of coercion about it. When David's efforts to counsel Lucy are rejected, with Lucy using silence to recover a sense of her own agency and identity, one is made acutely aware that his position is deeply compromised, as a near-rapist himself, despite the aestheticisation of his passion.

The critical reception of *Disgrace*, both in theoretically informed academic commentary and in reviews, was overwhelmingly favourable and in general of a high quality. Few other contemporary novels have stimulated such critical attention. Apart from the contributions to *Encountering Disgrace*, edited by Bill McDonald,[88] there were special editions of *Scrutiny 2*, edited by Leon de Kock, and of *Interventions: The International Journal of Postcolonial Studies*, edited by Derek Attridge and Peter D. McDonald.

In the introduction to *Encountering Disgrace* Bill McDonald writes:

Disgrace's international reception confirmed Coetzee's place as a major novelist even as it inflamed the ongoing debate about his position in the culture and climate of his native South Africa. Though highly praised and prized, *Disgrace*'s implicit critique of the Truth and Reconciliation Commission, and its depiction of black assailants raping a white woman, drew heavy condemnation. Critics, including several prominent South African writers, accused Coetzee of deliberately arousing old racist fears and racial tensions just as the new, post-apartheid society was coming into being.[89]

X

Disgrace was eligible for the 1999 Booker Prize, which carried a cash component of £21 000. Other nominated novels were *Our Fathers* by the debut writer Andrew O'Hagan; *Fasting, Feasting* by the Indian-born British writer Anita Desai; *The Map of Love* by the Egyptian Ahdaf Soueif; Colm Tóibín's *The Blackwater Lightship*; and Michael Frayn's *Headlong*. There was unhappiness in some circles at the omission of Vikram Seth's *An Equal Music* and Salman Rushdie's *The Ground Beneath her Feet*. Gerald Kaufman, a Labour politician and chairman of the jury, tried to have Seth included, and another member of the jury, John Sutherland, exerted himself on Rushdie's behalf. The bookmakers fancied Michael Frayn's *Headlong*, but in the end it was *Disgrace* that won — the first time that the Booker had been awarded to an author for a second time. The other judges were the novelist Shena Mackay, John Sutherland, a professor in modern English literature, and two literary journalists, Boyd Tonkin and Natasha Walker. That there were misgivings about the choice of jury members was evident from a comment by Paul Levy, referring to them as members of 'the London metropolitan literary mob'.[90]

Announcing the contenders, Gerald Kaufman said: 'This shortlist is one of the strongest for years — and choosing one of the six to win the prize will be a really challenging task.' In a statement after the announcement of the prize, he called *Disgrace* 'the most beautifully written, most beautifully constructed novel' of the six on the shortlist. He described it as 'an allegory about what is happening to the human race in the post-colonial era' and continued: 'In a sense this is a millennial book, because it takes us through the 20th century into a new century into which the source of power is shifting away from Western Europe.'[91] Boyd Tonkin, one of the judges, called it in *The Independent* of 29 October 1999 'the first masterpiece to emerge from the new South Africa, J.M. Coetzee's *Disgrace* — perhaps the best novel to carry off the Booker in a decade.'

As with *Life & Times of Michael K*, Coetzee, who was conducting his annual course with Jonathan Lear at the University of Chicago, was not present at the award ceremony, and the prize was received on his behalf by Geoff Mulligan of Secker & Warburg. In a message read by Mulligan, Coetzee called the Booker 'the ultimate prize to win in the English-speaking world [...] and I am profoundly aware of the honour you have done to me'.

From the ranks of UCT there was great rejoicing at the award. Professor Wilmot James, the Dean of Arts, said it was 'another prestigious indication that he is a writer of global distinction.' The vice-chancellor, Dr Mamphela Ramphele, added: 'John Coetzee's Booker Prize reflects his brilliant contribution to South African literature.'[92] In her reaction Nadine Gordimer said: 'I am very delighted about John getting the Booker again. It is very good news. It is of more interest to me than South Africa winning the rugby match[93] and more significant for South African culture.'[94] André Brink added his voice to this: '*Disgrace* is pure grace, in terms of style and narrative line. Its astounding luminosity, its spareness, make it one of Coetzee's greatest achievements to date. He has always been great on endings [...] but nothing he has done so far can match the excruciating beauty of the last pages of *Disgrace*.'[95]

Apart from the Booker Prize, *Disgrace* also won the Commonwealth Writers' Prize for 2000, and in the same year the M-Net Award. Coetzee was not present at either of these ceremonies. In October 2006 *Disgrace* was chosen by *The Guardian* as the best British fiction—including the Commonwealth and Ireland—published between 1980 and 2005. Other contenders included writers like Julian Barnes, Salman Rushdie, A.S. Byatt and Ian McEwan.

It is understandable that in a country like South Africa, where before and after 1994 crimes like rape and all forms of assault were common, there should be divergent opinions on a novel like *Disgrace*, and that literary and political criteria should often get confused. One of the most vehement attacks on Coetzee came from the internationally known playwright Athol Fugard, who, in the London *Times*, admitted that he had not read *Disgrace*, but said that the whole theme depressed him, with its implication that we should accept the rape of a white woman on account of the evil deeds we had committed in the past. He declared it a lot of 'bloody bullshit' that a white woman would accept that being raped was a way of atoning for the deeds of the past.[96]

In reaction to Fugard's statement the poet Antjie Krog said: 'It is appalling that somebody should comment without first reading the book. It revives practices that we thought had long passed.' The philosopher Johann Rossouw pointed out that the title is *Disgrace*, not *Guilt*. Lurie's begging for forgiveness from the parents of the student with whom he had had an affair is, according to Rossouw, a personal act, far from the public eye. He thinks that Fugard's interpretation that white women will accept rape as a part of the burden of the past has no basis in the novel. Lucy's acceptance is based on a realisation that the order of things has changed in the country. It is thus not a question of capitulation, because she decides to stay on her plot of ground on her terms and in that way to become a part of Africa.[97]

The reaction of a number of writers tended to be ambivalent. Whereas she had expressed appreciation of Coetzee's reversal of the new political correctness in a personal letter, Nadine Gordimer diplomatically suppressed her true reservations about *Disgrace*. She mentions this in a letter to Philip Roth, whose novel *The Human Stain* also deals, amid increasing levels of political correctness, with an aging male professor. Gordimer writes: 'Now in this elegantly and powerfully written novel there is no deep feeling (except, maybe ... self-disgust), no love, until there is the need to put down a stray dog, the feeling for which is the sole life-affirmative emotion for anyone or anything in the professor.'[98] In a public statement in 2006 she said: 'In the novel *Disgrace* there is not one black person who is a real human being. I find it difficult to believe, indeed more than difficult, having lived here all my life and being part of everything that has happened here, that the black family protects the rapist because he's one of them. If that's the only truth he could find in the post-apartheid South Africa, I regretted this very much for him.'[99] Gordimer's view was echoed by Chris van Wyk, author of, among other books, *Shirley, Goodness and Mercy*, about his childhood in a coloured community. His sense is that *Disgrace* is a racist book: 'The white characters are fleshed out, the black evildoers are not.'[100] In *The Star* of 21 January 2000, the journalist Max du Preez objects to the way in which the professor and his daughter become symbols of white South Africa, whereas Petrus and the three rapists represent the black approach: 'If this is true, then the message of *Disgrace*, crudely put, is that black South Africans are revengeful of whites; that whites are not welcome in Africa unless they pay for it every day; that black and white attitudes and lifestyles are incompatible.' Salman Rushdie had problems with the 'bone-hard language' and the 'cold detachment' of *Disgrace*. It makes the book seem, according to him, 'heartless': 'all its intelligence cannot fill up the hole'.[101]

The novel was, though, defended by the South African novelist Damon Galgut: 'I suppose,' he writes, 'it was groundbreaking in the sense that there was something sacrosanct about the "new" South Africa, and he actually broke a taboo by speaking about it in those terms.' Though having certain reservations about the novel, he adds: 'some people here revere the book because they think it articulates exactly where we are now.' Homi Bhabha, professor of English at Harvard and a friend of Coetzee's, claimed that the power of the novel lay exactly in its capacity to confuse readers and lead them to uncertainty. *Disgrace*, he said in an interview, is 'a work of "open seams" rather than "suturing"' In a time of 'real social, historical, psychic crisis' Coetzee made his readers feel their anxiety and care instead of exorcising it 'in the way in which we as progressive liberals would want him to do'. Bhabha finds *Disgrace* a powerful novel because it 'allows people to project onto it some of their own most heartfelt but violent feelings'.[102]

In an oral submission to the Human Rights Commission's Hearings on Racism in the Media on 5 April 2000,[103] the ANC used *Disgrace* as an example of how racism still occurred among white South Africans. According to the submission, the novel projects an image of the black person as a 'faithless, immoral, uneducated, incapacitated primitive child', a vision that can be traced back to General J.B.M. Hertzog, the father of the so-called pure Afrikaner nationalism. In the submission, delivered by Jeff Radebe, minister of public enterprise, Lucy's shock at the personal viciousness of the attack is quoted, followed by her father's explanation that it was not personal, but 'history speaking through them'.[104] The ANC then, according to Radebe's submission, accuses Coetzee of depicting 'as brutally as he can' the white 'perception of the post-apartheid black man'. Apart from this, the subplot of the novel, where Lurie works in an animal shelter, is seen as a sign that the author is more concerned about the rights of animals than of humans. Less directly, Radebe goes on, with some allusion to Lucy's final words, to make a further claim:

> It is suggested that in these circumstances, it might be better that our white compatriots should emigrate because to be in post-apartheid South Africa it is to be in 'their territory', as a consequence of which the whites will lose their cars, their weapons, their property, their rights, their dignity. The white women would have to sleep with the barbaric black men.

Although Jeff Radebe's name appears on the ANC's submission, Smuts Ngonyama, spokesman for the presidency, makes the hard-to-believe statement that *A Marriage Made in Heaven,* in which the text appears, is 'not a book by the ANC'. In his article 'Race in *Disgrace*' in *Interventions,* IV: 3, 2002, David Attwell writes:

> However, the submission to the HRC hearings, which is included in the text, was indeed presented in the name of the ANC—it was read into the record by the then Minister of Public Enterprises, Jeff Radebe, acting as 'the vocal head of the policy department in the ANC'. [...]I have established, however, that neither the book nor the submission was widely discussed in any open forum of the ANC, certainly not in the National Executive Committee. An authoritative figure in the NEC, who would prefer not to be named, is reasonably sure that behind the collective lies the guiding hand of the President, Thabo Mbeki.[105]

Jakes Gerwel, former professor of Afrikaans and Dutch, and rector of the University of the Western Cape, and then director-general in the office of the president during Nelson Mandela's term of office, writes in an article in *Rapport* of 13 February 2000:

> J.M. Coetzee's recent award-winning novel has now for some time been nagging at one with the bleak view it projects of the social decline, moral disintegration and fraying of the national fabric of South Africa. How come that one of our most potent creative spirits—and undoubtedly one of the best-known internationally—would be inspired by such images in his fictional recreation of the country?
>
> Much (most, I would say) of what is interesting in the corpus of South African literature springs from the strange phenomenon of being-white-in-Africa. Coetzee's novelistic oeuvre makes up one of the most gripping contributions to that conversation. A sense of homelessness runs like a thread through many works in this genre. The question I am left with after Coetzee's prize-winning novel is: what does it say about the rest of us if the homelessness of the white-in-Africa is cast in these images?
>
> It is not just an existential homelessness of the white that becomes the metaphorical raw material of this picture. The near-barbaric post-colonial demands of black Africans and the exclusion of possibilities of civilised conciliation are the building blocks of

this tale. (Leaving out of the equation for the moment the coloured characters as whores, seducibles, plaintiffs and prosecutors-with-attitude.)[106]

That such racists exist, Gerwel concludes 'is no surprise; whether the nation can be typified by that, remains a question.'

The article by Gerwel appeared shortly after President Thabo Mbeki delivered his inaugural address on 4 February 2000, in which he concentrated on the battle against racism. Mbeki referred to an e-mail from an unnamed white engineer, from which he quoted the following:

Our girlfriends/wives are in constant threat of being brutally raped by some AIDS infected Kaffir (or gang of Kaffirs). [...] Everyday someone you know is either robbed, assaulted, hijacked or murdered. [...] Half these black bastards have bought their (drivers) licences from corrupt traffic cops. [...] All I am saying is that AIDS isn't working fast enough!!!

In his article '*Disgrace* effects', *Interventions*, IV: 3, 2002, in which he discusses the ANC's reaction to Coetzee's novel at some length, Peter D. McDonald writes that in the light of Mbeki's address Coetzee's presumed report on white racism in his novel does indeed sound dangerous and uncertain of implication. This is, however, to read *Disgrace* completely out of context.

According to McDonald the novel could survive the objections of the ANC and of Gerwel, if read in another way and from another angle. McDonald writes:

On the face of it nothing would change. Lurie would still be a white South African, Lucy would still be his daughter, and her attackers would still be black. The rape would also remain a disturbing pivotal moment in the story. At the same time, however, everything would change. In the first place, we would need to make sense of the characters, not as types in an allegory that constantly points beyond itself, but as complex individuals caught in an intricate network of evolving relationships that constitute the drama of the story. Yet we would also have to recognize that they are not absolutely singular. They are individuals whose identities are ineluctably shaped by ties based on gender, generation, sexuality, nationality, and ethnicity.

On this analysis, Lurie is not just white. He is always at the same time middle-aged, heterosexual, male, probably Jewish, etc. Likewise, Lucy's attackers are not just black. They are male, heterosexual, etc. Second, if we resist the strong temptation to read the novel as a story that bears witness to history, we would need to understand key events functionally, rather than expressively or mimetically. On this sort of reading the rape, for instance, would feature not as a sign of the 'realities of South African life'—however horrific its rape statistics may be—nor as a manifestation of 'white fears'. Its justification would lie primarily in its *narrative* function measured in part by its impact on the novel's central characters.

This view also informs Etienne Britz's take on the novel. For him, *Disgrace* is not just 'obsessed with South Africa':

> It is a book about a universal human type. The South African situation is used merely as an engrossing context for a typical human history of a fall from grace. An interest in South Africa is not even a prerequisite to being enthralled by *Disgrace*.[107]

As was to be expected, Coetzee did not respond in public to the ANC's attack on *Disgrace*. But he did have his private feelings on the matter. In a letter of 10 June 2000, he replies to a letter from Breyten Breytenbach: 'I saw selections from the document you mention—the ANC submission to the commission on racism in the media—and could make no sense of them, at least insofar as they related to my book. The sort of literary criticism that would get you an F in English I and maybe even in Matric.' And on 15 May 2002 he writes to David Attwell: 'I may have mentioned the remarks of Ronnie Kasrils on *Disgrace*. He and I were at a dinner party together in 2000 or so, and as we were all leaving he came up to me and said, "We had a good discussion of your book in Cabinet. You weren't without your defenders." He then named someone whose name I have forgotten, then a deputy minister, now an ambassador somewhere.'[108]

V

AUSTRALIA

(2002–)

CHAPTER 14

CHANGING PLACES

I

It is commonly believed that Coetzee's decision to leave South Africa for good in 2002 and settle in Australia was in direct reaction to the ANC's negative comments on *Disgrace*. Although this could have tipped the balance, it would be an over-simplification to ascribe his departure exclusively to that. Coetzee had often enough experienced incomprehension of and negative reactions to his work. During the State of Emergency of the 1980s, he said in a letter to Dick Penner that he would like to remain in South Africa as long as it was possible for him to do some good, in whatever way. 'As a writer,' he continued, 'I don't want to go into exile, if only because I have seen what exile does to writers.'¹ In any case, the preamble to his change of country and especially the chronology of events tell a different story.

As long ago as November 1989, Coetzee had been invited to act as writer-in-residence at the University of Queensland in Brisbane, Australia. This visit took place in 1990. Coetzee was accompanied by his partner, Dorothy Driver, and they used the opportunity to explore the country. In 1991 Dorothy was on an academic visit to Adelaide, and she was impressed with the city and the warmth with which she was received. In August 1991 they were in Australia again, this time as guests of the Department of English at the University of Melbourne, where they stayed in Ormond College. They travelled around, spent some time at the artists' colony on Arthur Boyd's former estate, took part in arts festivals, and visited Adelaide, whose setting and layout made a strong impression on Coetzee. On a later visit, Coetzee attended a writer's colloquium in Canberra, and in 1996 he and Dorothy visited Adelaide for a Writer's Week in which they both took part.

From his very first visit, Coetzee was charmed by Australia. '[F]rom the beginning, in a way that is hard to explain,' he said in August 2001 in an interview with Anne Susskind,² the South African-born Sydney literary critic, 'I have felt a strong pull toward the land and the landscape. I come from Africa, where the land tends to have a similarly mysterious, dwarfing power over people.' Although he had for many years lived in various cities in the US, he could never come to terms with the North American landscape. In his years in Texas he missed the empty earth and desolation of the Karoo, and elsewhere in America he always felt a bit of a stranger. He had felt just as ill at ease in the grey Surrey landscape when he was working as a programmer in England. The only other place where he could ever settle, he felt, was rural France, but then he would always be, although proficient in French, in a linguistically alien country.

Australia appealed so strongly to Coetzee on his repeated visits in the 1990s that he decided it might be an 'adventure' to settle there. The vast, barren landscape reminded him of the Karoo of his youth. The country had almost none of the crime of South Africa. In an e-mail to a friend he wrote that, sitting on a bench at Whale Beach in northern Sydney, he had to admire the idyllic scene before him: the families with their picnic baskets, the green bay with its orange sand and the absence of danger. Furthermore, as he said to Susskind in their interview, he was impressed with Australian egalitarianism, 'the way in which Australians relate to each other, spontaneously as far as I can see, as equals. You might say that anyone from South Africa, with its huge social and racial divisions, would have that reaction. But egalitarianism in Australia is, in my experience, quite unique in the world. Obviously it is a consequence of a particular social history. Nevertheless I find it profoundly admirable.'

On 29 March 1995, more than four years before the publication of *Disgrace*, Coetzee was asked by Robin McMullan of Canberrra to submit his CV to the Australian embassy for consideration. So he was already considering a move, with Adelaide as his preferred destination, and Melbourne as a second choice. It was, however, only in October 1999 that he approached various contacts to support his application for immigration, such as Nicolas Hasluck of the Australian Arts Council, Satendra Nandan of the Association of Commonwealth Literature Studies, and José Borghino of the Australian Society of Authors. On 13 December 1999 he appealed also to David Malouf, the prominent Australian author, to support his application. He writes that he is on the point of retiring from the University of Cape Town. 'This is a country,' he continues, 'in a deeply interesting phase of its historical evolution. But it is not a good place to grow old in. Ever since I first visited Australia in 1991 I have felt a tug toward the country and its landscape. My partner

Dorothy Driver feels much as I do. We would like to try living there. I don't envisage looking for another academic post; with my pension, my income from writing, and the proceeds of a two-month stint I spend annually at the University of Chicago, I should manage.'

By this time Coetzee had instructed a firm of attorneys in Sydney to deal with his and Dorothy's applications, while he was compiling a dossier of supporting material. Early in January 2001 somebody in the Australian embassy in South Africa informed them that they could expect a decision within the next month or two, and that this decision would be positive. Even before submitting their applications, Coetzee and Dorothy had arranged to be in Adelaide from February 2001, where Dorothy would be lecturing as a visiting professor. 'I am going along for the ride,' Coetzee wrote in a letter to David Attwell. He probably also wanted to have another look at Adelaide, where they intended to settle. Both were due to leave on 3 February, Coetzee to remain there until 7 March; Dorothy, until the end of April.

Since they had to have visas for this visit, and would have to show medical and police certificates at the border, Phil Lovering of the Australian embassy in Pretoria realised it would be simpler for all concerned if immigration visas could be issued immediately. On 1 February 2001 Coetzee wrote to Wayne Purcell, the Sydney attorney handling their immigration:

I have good news.

If I can get to the Australian High Commission in Pretoria before closing time tomorrow, Friday 2 February, bearing Dorothy's passport and my own, I can get immigration visas stamped into them. We will then catch a flight on Saturday 3 February and present ourselves to the immigration officials at Perth airport on Sunday 4 February, and we will be landed as immigrants.

I can't tell you how happy I am. Thank you for all you have done. [...] Phil Lovering at the High Commission has been helpful far beyond the call of duty.

Once they were in Adelaide, Coetzee received an e-mail from José Borghino of the Australian Society of Authors, informing him that their application for permanent residence had been approved. He was overjoyed that the wheels of bureaucracy had turned so smoothly. On 13 February Coetzee wrote to Borghino:

I had been meaning to write today to give you the good news and to thank you for all the trouble you went through on my behalf. In fact everything has come through in a rush. Ten days ago we were in South Africa wondering despondently how much longer we would have to wait for a decision. Then, just before we were due to fly to Adelaide, where my partner Dorothy Driver has a visiting appointment, we had a call from the High Commission to say that we were approved. I flew up to Pretoria to get the stamps in our passports, and a few hours later we were off. Dorothy will be here until the end of April. I have to return to South Africa in early March. From June until November we have commitments first in South Africa, then in the USA. So we won't be able to relocate properly until December. It looks like Adelaide will be where we will stay—we find it a congenial and manageable city.

Coetzee concludes by saying that he would like, as soon as he is eligible for it, to join the Australian Society of Authors.

Coetzee retired from the University of Cape Town in December 2001. On 28 December, when he was back in Cape Town after his annual visit to Chicago, the vice-chancellor, Njabulo Ndebele, hosted a farewell dinner for him. The plan was for Dorothy to keep her professorial position at UCT for the time being. She would commute between Cape Town and Adelaide, fulfilling her lecturing duties in Cape Town in the first semester of each year, joining Coetzee in the second semester.

Of the Australian literary scene, of which he was about to become a part, Coetzee said in his interview with Anne Susskind that he could not pretend to a thorough acquaintance:

I read the Australian modernists when I was young—Kenneth Slessor, A.D. Hope, Judith Wright—and thought they were better than anyone writing at home. Later I fell under the spell of Patrick White and read everything of his. I've read and admired Peter Carey, particularly the recent Ned Kelly book. Les Murray is a major poet by any standards. I like Peter Porter very much. I've read the younger writers in only a scattered way. I read Michael Meehan's first novel recently and was bowled over by it. Ditto for Raimond Gaita's childhood memoir.

In reply to Susskind's question on what he would miss about South Africa, he said:

> I am not sure what I am leaving behind. Or rather, I suspect I will find out what I leave behind only when I am in a position to look back. What will I miss? Living in a highly polyglot society, perhaps: walking down the street and hearing many different languages. And I will miss the University of Cape Town. [...]. Not as an institution but simply as an environment where one can move in a perfectly natural way among such handsome, happy, confident young people, of all races and backgrounds, with the world very much at their feet. It's a privilege not allowed to every aging person.

Early in March Coetzee returned to Cape Town. In May he and Dorothy travelled to Spain, where they cycled in a group from the French border in the Pyrenees to Santiago de Compostella, along the old pilgrim route, a distance of about 800 kilometres. Because they found the tempo a bit slow, they separated amicably from the rest of the group after about eight days and travelled south on their own. Both found it a wonderful holiday. After the cycling trip they visited Germany, Holland, France and the United Kingdom, before flying to Chicago for the annual series of lectures.

By early 2001 some newspapers were already referring to Coetzee's imminent departure, and journalists were trying to get confirmation from him of his intention and the reason for his move. He was, however, not willing to discuss his emigration with journalists intent on sensation. He did, on 21 March 2001, write to his London agent, Bruce Hunter, that he had decided to leave South Africa and to move to Australia as a self-employed writer, without seeking an academic position. The actual move, he wrote, would only be practicable by the end of 2001 or early in 2002. He saw no reason why his association with David Higham Associates, the agency to which Hunter was attached, should not continue as before. The story of his and Dorothy's imminent move had reached the Australian press the week before and had been taken over by the South African papers. 'My motives,' he writes, 'are what I would consider to be personal, and nobody's business but my own and those of a few people close to me; but of course journalists prefer to give the move a political spin. I have thought it best not to get drawn into a haggle.'

Geoff Mulligan of Random House (of which Secker & Warburg is a subsidiary) had been informed by Coetzee of their plans. In an e-mail of 21 March, Mulligan asked whether Coetzee could suggest what their representatives in South Africa should say when approached by the press for comment. Coetzee replied that he would appreciate an abrupt 'No Comment'. 'I think Random House Australia,' he continues in a lighter vein, 'has already been contacted. Whoever their spokesperson is said I had been contemplating the move for some time (which is true) and that I was much taken with the wallabies in the Hunter Valley (which is news to me).'

That Coetzee's decision to leave South Africa had not been lightly taken, is evident from his reply to a further question by Susskind:

> An interview is perhaps not the best medium in which to explore moral or intellectual complexities. And leaving a country is, in some respects, like the breakup of a marriage. It is an intimate matter.[3]

Although Coetzee nowhere commits himself as to the reasons for his emigration, it may be possible to draw certain conclusions from his life and his work. When he left South Africa at the end of 1961 and settled in England, he was appalled at the political course his country was steering with apartheid, and he intended never to return. When, in 1966, he was studying on a Fulbright Scholarship at the University of Texas, and later lecturing in Buffalo, he wanted to settle permanently in the US. However, his participation in Buffalo in a peaceful protest at the time of the Vietnam War against the presence of police on campus, and his arrest with 44 other members of staff, led to his visa not being renewed, even though he and his co-accused were acquitted at the subsequent trial. There was for a while the possibility of a permanent position in Canada or Hong Kong, but he preferred to return to South Africa, perhaps even felt intuitively that his real task as a writer and as a human being lay in the South Africa that he was trying to escape. Whatever the case, his decision to return led to a series of novels giving unique form to problems of the country and its people, while at the same time being prime contributions to contemporary literature.

With the dismantling of apartheid, the 'disgrace' that he had resisted in his own way, was considered something of the past, yet residues of conflict remained. In his acceptance speech for the Jerusalem Prize in 1987, Coetzee suggested that the racial conflict in South Africa usurped the writer's psyche to such an extent as to leave no scope for other themes. In the apartheid years he had not been a political activist; he would now still not want to intervene actively, but would continue to make his contribution of words, even from another country. Having for much of his life written books in which South Africa featured centrally, he realised that he had never really succeeded in escaping the country.[4] This was why he repeatedly told people that he had not left South Africa, but come to Australia.[5] It is, after all, a fact that a quarter of the world's people today live in countries other than the one in which their grandparents were born. Emigration is a worldwide phenomenon.[6] People do not necessarily leave a country because it has become intolerable to them: they may also be seeking greener pastures. And for Coetzee, as he grew older, Australia had become an attractive alternative. Compared with South Africa, with its large number of people under the age of 25, Australia has more people over the age of 50 and fewer under the age of 20. The economy and the healthcare in a country with a demographic tendency to an older age group are just better attuned to the needs of that group than in a country with a preponderance of young people. What strikes Coetzee about Australian politics is how trifling the issues are that are debated in parliament and elsewhere, especially compared with South Africa, where the big political themes involve meaningful national issues. In Australia the big issues are something of the past, and democracy has advanced to the point of a healthy cynicism about and contempt for politics and politicians.[7]

Not surprisingly, not all of Coetzee's South African admirers accepted his departure with equanimity. In a heartfelt letter of 29 December 2002 Mariana Swart made no secret of her feelings. She wrote:

> I have been thinking about writing this e-mail for several weeks. And now, with a glass of (cheap) sangria on hand (to give courage), and Boccherini in the background, I will take up my keyboard and say what I must say.
>
> Which is, that I am furious that you have left South Africa—yes, rage is in my heart and fury in my fingers (already the wine has taken effect—scrap the fury in my fingers part), and the sad result of all this will be, no doubt, a quick (albeit bemused) click on your Delete button to flush away my words. No doubt. But since you are (and have been for a very long time) my literary hero, I hope that you will shoulder the responsibility and read what I have to say before committing it to your electronic Refuse Bin (Recycle Bin would be a bit presumptuous, I guess). [...]

The fact of the matter is, simply put, that I derived a certain comfort from seeing you riding your bicycle in Rondebosch, or with your shopping basket in Checkers, or walking over Belmont bridge. For, I always thought, if this man, whom I consider a great thinker, and a great author, is still here, he must see a future, however dry and barren, in this country. [...]

I have often wondered how writers perceive us, their readers (if at all). [...] Do you realize that we [...] read your books and get something from it, maybe a sense of beauty, however austere, maybe just a passage, an idea, a thought—often we can't put into words what we 'get', because we lack the skill; or maybe the intellectual capacity. And yet we look at your words for wisdom and inspiration and the truth. [...] And we look not only at your words but also at your actions, however unfair and uncalled for that may be.

I ask myself: What are you doing in Adelaide, Australia? I just don't get it. I don't understand why you have left. [...] You should be settling down somewhere in the Karoo, and preparing yourself to write your last 2 or 3 (or whatever) books. Or is it maybe that you truly believe that whites have no place in Africa, and that you morally felt obliged to leave? But surely that can't be, because what are you doing in Australia then? It also has a colonial past of sorts, although not in the same sense as the African continent. And why did it take you so long?

No, it can be neither of these reasons; which leaves me with fear and cowardice. How can we (and I mean we in the broadest South African sense) make a go of it when people leave out of fear and disillusionment? And they do, in droves, it seems. And of course I am not oblivious to the fact that [...]I am afraid too, and a coward, for I know perfectly well that however much I believe that I must stay here in this country—our country—in spite of my fear, who knows what I will do should the opportunity to leave arise? [...]

Four of my best friends have left—departed to the States, the UK, New Zealand. And I am aware that this e-mail should probably have been addressed to them, but the fact remains that they are my very dear friends, and I would like to keep it that way. And you, I am afraid, have to bear the burden of my fury, which by now has dissipated and crumbled into a tiny heap of disappointment. And the fear of being abandoned in a country that I (the result of ten generations on African soil) still don't understand, yet love. [...]

You belong in South Africa—I believe that with all my heart. As I believe that you will only ever be able to write here. You need this landscape to feed you.

I am not very eloquent, I am afraid, and being Afrikaans probably makes it worse—much of what I wanted to say has been lost or come out wrong.

Despite my disappointment (do I care a damn, I hear you say), I will always admire your work, and always remain your reader.

II

The reason for Coetzee's choice of Adelaide, rather than for instance the much larger Sydney, is his preference for rural areas and small cities.[8] Adelaide, the capital of South Australia, with its wide roads, beautiful squares, right-angled, almost symmetrical city centre and its location on the Torrens River, was designed in 1836 by Colonel William Light. Although the city has both an Anglican and a Roman Catholic cathedral, South Australia has no dominant state religion. Its two cathedrals thus assume no central position, although the city with its 140 other churches of different denominations initially was known as the 'City of Churches'. Fortunately there were also 140 pubs to maintain a healthy balance.

Adelaide is the only city in the world separated from its suburbs and living areas by a belt of parks and gardens. Leaving the city, you are in rural Australia in no time at all. For Coetzee the advantage was that after visiting the centre of the city he could be in the countryside within thirty minutes by car and a little more by bicycle. He and Dorothy decided to have a house built in the suburb of Rostrevor, part of Adelaide Hills.[9] With his love of cycling, this area was ideal for him. 'Even in the driest summer months,' promises one of the guide books, 'the Adelaide Hills, a 30-minute drive from the city, offer crisper air, lush woodland shade and the delicious scent of eucalyptus from stands of gum trees. In autumn this is reinforced by the glorious colours of introduced deciduous trees, particularly in the wetter central area around Mt Lofty. Travelling along picturesque narrow roads you'll pass carts of fresh produce for sale, stone cottages, olive groves and vineyards. Locals wear grins from ear to ear, happy with the good life.'[10] Coetzee, though perhaps not grinning from ear to ear, was indeed happy with the attractive aspects of the city. In an interview with the academic journal *Lumen* he said: 'Adelaide seems to me a human-sized city, very attractive, very civilized, with a strong artistic community. There is also, for someone who enjoys cycling, the allure of the hills.'

Coetzee found the inhabitants of Adelaide extremely hospitable, making him and Dorothy feel at home very quickly. They made some good friends in a relatively short time. The climate suited him, and he liked the architecture. If Adelaide in comparison with more bustling cities was a trifle sluggish, that also was to his taste.

Upon settling in Australia, Coetzee became a research fellow in the Arts at the University of Adelaide—an honorary position carrying no remuneration and practically speaking no obligations. He sometimes acts as a supervisor to M.A. and Ph.D. students, or moderates honours exam scripts. He explained his involvement with the University of Adelaide as follows to *Lumen*:

When people at the University heard that I would be settling here, they very kindly contacted me and asked whether I would be interested in playing some role in academic life (I had been a fulltime academic from 1969 until my retirement in 2001), and I was happy to accept. I get a great deal out of the association: contact with likeminded people, an opportunity to keep a finger on the pulse of the next generation of Australian writers, freedom to use the University's research facilities. My involvement is also, frankly, a counter to the sense of isolation one might develop if one just sat at one's desk at home day after day.

On 20 December 2005 Coetzee received an honorary doctorate from the University of Adelaide. The vice-chancellor, Professor James McWha, said that the University of Adelaide was privileged to be associated with someone like Coetzee: 'Professor Coetzee is regarded as one of the world's finest writers and we are proud of our association with him. I am pleased that the University can show its support and appreciation for the contribution he has made in the field of literature by awarding him an honorary doctorate.'

When, in February 2004, Coetzee symbolically received the keys of the city from a cheering multitude of its citizens, he described Adelaide as a paradise on earth. He said that he was fortunate to spend half the year in Adelaide and the other half in the US as a visiting professor at the University of Chicago. 'I can't pretend,' he said, 'to have won this particular prize in the role of The Bard of Adelaide, and I probably won't live long enough to become the Bard of Adelaide.'[11]

For the 2004 Adelaide Writers' Week, thousands of people gathered on the lawns in the centre of the city to listen to their favourite writers, from Australia and elsewhere. An unusual guest that year was a writer straddling the divide: the South African John Coetzee, who had settled in South Australia. Taking his cue from 'At the Gate', the last section of his 2003 novel *Elizabeth Costello*, Coetzee read from an unpublished text, in characteristic tribute to the city of Adelaide:

> It was March, it was hot, but there were shaded walks to be had along the Torrens River, where black swans glided serenely.
>
> What kind of place is this, I asked myself—is this paradise on earth?
>
> What does one have to do to live here?
>
> Does one have to die first?

After signing a number of books for admirers, Coetzee vanished, happy to let his books speak on his behalf.

III

Most of the eight 'lessons' — specifically not 'lectures' — as the chapters are called in *Elizabeth Costello*, had previously appeared elsewhere, sometimes in a different form. 'Realism' and an earlier version of 'The problem of evil' were published in the journal *Salmagundi*, and 'The problem of evil' was presented in September 2001 in Chicago; 'The humanities in Africa' was delivered as a lecture at Stanford University and in Canberra, and afterwards collected in *The Best Australian Stories 2002* (edited by Peter Craven); 'The novel in Africa' was delivered at the Centro Historico in Mexico in March 1998, at the Writers' Festival in Sydney in May 2000 and afterwards at the University of California in Berkeley; both parts of 'The Lives of Animals' made up the text of Coetzee's Tanner Lectures at Princeton in 1998, and were also published in book form. From the manuscript of the novel, still in the author's possession, it appears that he wrote 'At the gate' in May 2001, during his visit to Stanford. The postscript in *Elizabeth Costello* is based on

'The letter of Lord Chandros' of Hugo von Hofmannsthal, as published in Von Hofmannsthal's *Selected Prose*, translated by Mary Hottinger and Tania and James Stern, New York, Pantheon Books, 1952.

From the chequered origins of these eight 'lessons' it is clear that the genesis of *Elizabeth Costello* differed markedly from that of Coetzee's other novels.[12] Thematically, too, it deviated from South African actualities and the colonial or post-colonial concerns of his earlier novels.[13] In con-struction, the eight lessons differ from most novels in having no clear plot or intrigue, and in that the characters of the protagonist and the secondary figures remain static. Elizabeth Costello, the Australian writer who at the beginning of the book is 67 years old, visits, sometimes accompanied by her son, John, different countries and cities where she has to appear as a speaker. To a greater or lesser extent, however, she is frequently misunderstood, leaving her discomfited and confused, asking herself what exactly she is trying to achieve by her lectures. In addition, her inability to achieve a certain level of intimacy with her son and her sister, or a measure of emotional rapport with fellow-writers, seems to testify to a spiritual emptiness in herself. Repeatedly, except in the last chapter, she is close to despair, feeling that she should rather not have come.

The subjects she confronts her audiences with are often the large issues that people of all ages have addressed: the true nature of evil,[14] responsibility, faith, love and desire, and the ways humans treat animals. Sometimes she pronounces on the task of the writer, for instance in 'The novel in Africa', in which the Nigerian writer Emmanuel Egudu opposes her, pointing out the specific problems facing a writer in a country that for lack of a tradition of reading is dependent on an oral culture, obliging him to seek a public in foreign countries. Her earthly peregrinations culminate in her arrival at the 'gate' in the last chapter, where she, now clearly posthumously, seeks entry:

> She has a vision of the gate, the far side of the gate, the side she is denied. At the foot of the gate, blocking the way, lies stretched out a dog, an old dog, his lion-coloured hide scarred from innumerable manglings. His eyes are closed, he is resting, snoozing. Beyond him is nothing but a desert of sand and stone, to infinity. It is her first vision in a long while, and she does not trust it, does not trust in particular the anagram GOD-DOG. *Too literary*, she thinks again. A curse on literature.[15]

Jane Poyner has written illuminatingly about this passage in *The African Review of Books*, demonstrating how Coetzee here enters into conversation with a variety of writers and texts:

> This passage invokes familiar Coetzean motifs: Samuel Beckett's absurd inversion of the Divine, for instance, and Kafka's tale which has been read by Jacques Derrida as an allegory of critical endeavour, the impossibility of locating 'correct' meanings in texts and a warning against reductive allegorical practices.[16]

That the unusual ensemble of *Elizabeth Costello* would elicit incomprehension and criticism from some readers was to be expected. In a review in the *Cape Times* of 19 September 2003 Justin Cartwright wrote:

> The first question which springs to mind is why did Coetzee use a fictional cover for his Tanner lectures? And then why did he publish this book, which brings together those lectures and other articles as a novel? [...] Maybe it was easier to make such points from the mouth of an invented character than from his own. But when you are invited to speak on ethical matters, it's something of a cop-out not to take all the blame yourself.

Cartwright's review was taken up by Michiel Heyns in the *Cape Times* of 23 September 2003. He takes Cartwright to task for the general 'shoddiness' and 'the apparent lack of care' in his review, and for the way in which he disconnectedly hops from one idea to the next. 'His one substantial point—that Elizabeth Costello is not a fully realised character—is all but obscured in the general fog of inchoate ideas.' Heyns himself wrote illuminatingly in *The Sunday Independent* of 5 October 2003 about 'the notion of embodying' as a central theme of the novel, and about the concluding section, 'At the gate', in which Elizabeth Costello arrives at the gate of the Hereafter, and as condition for entry has to declare her belief in something:

> Protesting, at first, that 'I am a writer, a trader in fictions ... I maintain beliefs only provisionally,' she nevertheless is brought to declare, after all, a belief, if only in the little frogs of the Dulgannon mudflats in Australia, which literally go underground in drought, to be revitalised by the rain 'and soon their voices resound again

in joyous exultation beneath the vault of the heavens'. In these frogs, presumably, Mrs Costello finds embodied most purely, unselfconsciously and unthinkingly the great binary of life and death, death and resurrection.

Most British critics reviewed *Elizabeth Costello* favourably, even though a few were unhappy with the 'odd' pairing of novel and academic treatise. D.J. Taylor writes in *The Independent* of 30 August 2003: '[...] the book, one of Coetzee's best, simply burns with creative passion.' Peter Parker in the British *Sunday Times* of 31 August 2003 finds it 'hugely enlightening and rewarding'. In the *London Review of Books* of 23 October 2003, James Wood refers to the complex way in which Coetzee refines the technique of the frame narrative, and offers fiction within fiction in such a way that it becomes far more complicated than a mere evasion of an own point of view on the part of the author:

> The paradox of the chosen form is that on the one hand Coetzee seems to be playing his usual withholding game: the famous ascetic, the pale undeliverer, the non-interviewee, who instead of tying himself to a series of propositions puts them in the mouth of a fictional creation and slips away behind her; yet, on the other hand, the ideas that Elizabeth Costello wants to propose in her lectures are so intense, so passionate and even at times irrational, that their extremity necessarily encourages us to follow them back to their recessed author, Coetzee himself. For if Coetzee were merely playing it safe by dramatising rather than propounding arguments, why make the arguments so violently unsafe?

In the US the critical response to *Elizabeth Costello* was extremely favourable, even though some of the reviewers questioned the strange form of the novel. In *The New York Times* of 26 October 2003 Judith Shulevitz says the novel 'is as haunting as anything Coetzee has written, because Elizabeth Costello is. It is a testament to Coetzee's ability to animate characters by economical means that within the narrow fictional frames that encase Costello's lectures he has created such a seductively contrary prophetess—a person profoundly compassionate in principle and chilly in practice, particularly with members of her own family.' In his long discussion in *The New York Review of Books*, the novelist and literary scholar David Lodge indicates how Coetzee blends and transcends generic conventions. Whereas on the publication of the Tanner Lectures there had emanated from some quarters the objection that Coetzee had adopted extreme, intolerant and judgemental arguments about animal rights and then had, through the device of Elizabeth Costello, evaded responsibility for 'his' point of view, the two lectures were no longer, within the greater context of the novel, open to this objection. At the same time, the novel confirmed the image readers had of Coetzee as a writer. He was never angling for popularity or fame. 'His books are always unsettling, unexpected, and uncomforting. He seems a rather aloof figure in the contemporary literary world.'

Coetzee received high praise in an e-mail from Wayne C. Booth, professor emeritus in English at the University of Chicago, one of the most prominent experts on fiction, and the author of, among other works, influential books like *The Rhetoric of Fiction* (1961) and *A Rhetoric of Irony* (1974). Booth writes: 'I've just completed Elizabeth C. and I'm once again immensely impressed. I would say that you've invented a new form of novel, one that some reviews have already complained about (as I don't have to tell you) but that a reader like me revels in. Thanks again.'

In South Africa the writer and literary scholar Marlene van Niekerk wrote enthusiastically and with great insight about *Elizabeth Costello*. She starts her review in *Rapport* of 30 November 2003 with the statement that the book is 'for many readers an unusual, cryptic, even baffling reading experience.' She continues:

> The reason for this is that it is not to be considered a novel in the usual sense of the word. But then, the overt self-presentation of the novel, as clearly stipulated in the subtitle, Eight Lessons, should act as a warning. Not that we need take the overtly stated absolutely at its word, especially not with a perverse and ironic and especially hyper-selfconscious writer like Coetzee.
>
> What we have here is a moving, indirect or pseudo-self portrait of J.M. Coetzee, a portrait of the artist as an old woman. If Boyhood and Youth were a form of autobiography of authorial origins, then I read this book as a kind of meta-autobiography of the writer as philosopher of the self, one who reflects on what being a writer—perhaps a last dubious manifestation of the divine and salvation—could mean in this era.
>
> These ideas and activities of self-interrogation we have up to now frequently encountered in the work of Coetzee. The latest

work is a culmination of what he himself somewhere calls *prose that thinks*, and, as always, here too, where ideas and representations are explicitly invoked, the prose is brutally clear, stripped and charged subcutaneously throughout with explosive irony and self-reflexive notation.

The main character, Elizabeth Costello, is 66 years old. An Australian writer, known in particular for her novel, The House on Eccles Street, in which she 'fleshed out' the character of Molly Bloom from James Joyce's Ulysses. She is a celebrated author, at the end of her career, travelling hither and yon on the face of the earth to receive awards, to present lectures, to be 'honoured'. But it is also a kind of via dolorosa or pilgrim's progress, literally to the gates of a deliberately clichéd Kafkaesque theatre of judgement, in which as scribe of the invisible [17] she has to account for her truth and convictions and defend them to her inquisitors.

Her life from suitcases, in bare hotel rooms and strange houses, in ever unfamiliar bathrooms and toilets, on ships and in planes, her physical alienation, displacement, loneliness and chronic exhaustion in these anonymous service areas, are evoked with searing precision and empathy. So too her reluctant and grumpy participation in the literary circuit, her impatience and irritation with the obtuse admirers and the vultures and poseurs of the literary world.

Costello is depicted as a kind of perishable meat offering which is fed upon cruelly or delicately by omnivorous literary scholars and biographers, also by critics who call into question the legitimacy of a life in writing. She is a woman delivered over to others, her fate the fate of people who want to be writers—being yourself for other people. In her navy-blue outfit with white shoes and not-always-clean hair, she looks to her dismayed son like Daisy Duck.

It is indeed a dubious dignity that Coetzee accords his alter ego. Her at times clumsy prophecies and preachings are not what her auditors want to hear. They want to be consoled, improved, warmed and affirmed (just like the readers of Coetzee's novels), but she keeps on doggedly making her bloody-minded points.

After outlining the eight 'lessons' of the book, with particular attention to Costello's visit to her sister, a Roman Catholic nun working in an AIDS hospital in Natal, Van Niekerk calls *Elizabeth Costello* from beginning to end 'a gripping, moving and seductive reading adventure, however unorthodox and genre-unspecific.' She continues:

> It is a book in which a fragile and passionate rationality is set up against the impoverished reason of self-assured science and dogmatic religiosity.
>
> It is a rationality that seeks to show the defenceless value of spirituality in the light of human mortality, a rationality that incorporates its own differences and internal contradictions by revelling and dissipating itself in the unstaunchable masquerade of fiction. That is why it can be a kind of 'confession' and 'testament' without once lapsing into a soggy soppiness, public sulking and scolding or a beating of the breast or simply the boring recounting of self-cherishing data. Local autobiographical authors with a tendency to the exhaustive and the exhausting and the perfect cadence could profit by following this example!
>
> *Elizabeth Costello* contains more of evocation, ideas, ingenuity, authorial good manners and chill brutality than many writers of 'ordinary' novels can scribble up in a lifetime. In fact: who wants to read an 'ordinary' novel if you can read this book?
>
> Coetzee is a writer's writer, but I have overheard even some highly sophisticated intellectuals and academics complain that his fiction is not 'lively', 'rich', 'human', 'warm', 'passionate' and 'picturesque' enough. I think that people who can say this about Coetzee, can't read. Furthermore: is the point not that the truly challenging writer would never previously have confronted the reader with speculations, questions and sensations (such as about and of 'humanity', its limits and its extreme capacities)? In any case, the critical voices show no sign of ceasing. There should be a J.M. Coetzee Chair at every South African university. It could just bring about a rebirth of the humanities.

IV

On 6 March 2006, on the opening day of the Adelaide Writers' Week, Coetzee officially received Australian citizenship at a special ceremony in a tent. The ceremony was conducted by Senator Amanda Vanstone, minister of immigration. In her short speech she said Australians should regard it as a compliment that somebody with Coetzee's status had decided to become one of them. Festival-goers watched the new citizen take his oath of allegiance to Australia and heard him address the crowd:

> In becoming a citizen one undertakes certain duties and responsibilities. One of the more intangible of those duties and responsibilities is, no matter what one's birth and background, to accept the historical past of the new country as one's own.

Coetzee, however, kept his South African nationality, and he reiterated the sentiment he had repeatedly expressed before:

> I did not so much leave South Africa, a country with which I retain strong emotional ties, but come to Australia. I came because from the time of my first visit in 1991, I was attracted by the free and generous spirit of the people, by the beauty of the land itself and—when I first saw Adelaide—by the grace of the city that I now have the honour of calling my home.[18]

CHAPTER 15

THE NOBEL PRIZE

I

A s early as in 1996, J.M. Coetzee's name had been mentioned in
relation to the Nobel Prize, but in that year the award went to Wislawa
Szymborska of Poland.[1] Again in 2000, there was some speculation
around the Prize: the Trinidad-born V.S. Naipaul, the Swedish poet
Tomas Tranströmer, the Belgian Hugo Claus or Coetzee. In the end,
however, the Prize went to the Chinese Gao Xingjian, a writer who was
not allowed to publish in his fatherland and had to emigrate to France.
In 2001 Anthony Fleischer, the president of the Swedish Academy,
personally nominated Coetzee, but V.S. Naipaul was the winner. In
2002, too, Fleischer recommended Coetzee.[2]

In all the years that his name had been mentioned in connection
with the Nobel Prize, Coetzee said in an interview,[3] he had not been
very interested in all the to-do around the award. He had been told that
any society or organisation of authors and any person holding a chair
at a university was entitled to nominate a writer for the Nobel Prize. He
was to find out only later that there were writers who kept their gazes
fixed on the Prize, got influential people to support their candidature,
and cultivated a certain repute in Scandinavian countries through translations and other means. How many writers were nominated annually
he did not know, he said in the interview, but it would not surprise him if
literally hundreds of names were submitted every year. He was unaware
of any propaganda made on his behalf for the award.

In September 2003 John and Dorothy left for the US for Coetzee's annual three-month stint at the University of Chicago, where he
was due to present a course on 'great books' with Jonathan Lear, and
Dorothy would lecture in the Department of English. After years as
Visiting Professor at Chicago, Coetzee had been promoted to the title of
'Distinguished Service Professor' in July 2003. On Wednesday evening,
1 October, John and Dorothy went for supper with Lear and his wife, and

554 J.M. Coetzee: A Life in Writing

had a relaxed evening of casual conversation.[4] On Thursday morning, just as Lear was about to leave for the university, his wife called him to the phone for a call from Sweden. The caller said that Coetzee had won the Nobel Prize for 2003, and asked for Coetzee's phone number to convey the news to him personally. Lear knew that Coetzee was using somebody else's phone and did not want the number to be publicly known, but in an unguarded moment, overwhelmed at the news, he supplied the number.

Within a few hours after the announcement of the prize, journalists from every corner of the globe descended upon Coetzee by telephone and by e-mail. Everybody wanted a statement on what the prize meant to him, and asked to arrange photo sessions; television networks and radio stations wanted to conduct interviews with him. All these requests were declined or ignored by Coetzee. He wrote to his friend Dianna Schwerdt in Adelaide on 3 October: 'I'm having a hard time at the moment with insomnia on the one hand and rude journalists on the other.' Some of the requests for interviews were addressed to the director of publicity at the University of Chicago, who passed the journalists' requests on to Lear. This obliged Coetzee to issue a statement on the university's website:

> I received the news in a phone call from Stockholm at 6 this morning. It came as a complete surprise—I was not even aware that the announcement was pending. I am particularly happy that the announcement has come during this autumn quarter, which is the time of year that I spend at the University of Chicago. The University of Chicago, and in particular the Committee on Social Thought, has been my intellectual home for the past seven years. Saul Bellow, my literary predecessor on the Committee, won the prize in 1976. This year I am teaching two courses with colleagues here—a course on Plato with the philosopher Jonathan Lear, and a course on Walt Whitman with the poet Mark Strand. And I am of course continuing with my own work. I am working on new fiction, and I have a book of translations of Dutch poets due out shortly.

Apparently at his wits' end with the ceaseless stream of calls, Coetzee asked his friend: 'Please, will you handle this?' Lear was willing, and all calls were redirected to him. When Coetzee and Lear turned up on Monday afternoon, 6 October, for their joint class on Plato, they were greeted by a horde of journalists wanting to take photos and conduct interviews. The students were obliged to intervene and literally force the journalists to leave, so that they could carry on with the class. Coetzee, amused at the whole situation, appreciated the spirit of the class.[5]

Coetzee was the second winner of the Nobel Prize for Literature from South Africa, after Nadine Gordimer in 1991, and the fourth from Africa, after the Nigerian Wole Soyinka (1986) and the Egyptian Naguib Mahfouz (1988). Horace Engdal, announcing Coetzee as the winner of the prize for 2003, said that that year's choice had been an easy one:

> We were very much convinced of the lasting value of his con-
> tribution to literature. I'm not speaking of the number of books,
> but the variety, and the very high average quality. I think he is a
> writer [...] who will continue to be discussed and analysed and we
> think he should belong to our literary heritage.

In their official report the Swedish Academy said that Coetzee'[portrays] in innumerable guises [...] the surprising involvement of the outsider'. His novels are characterised

> by their well-crafted composition, pregnant dialogue and analytical
> brilliance. But at the same time he is a scrupulous doubter, ruthless
> in his criticism of the cruel rationalism and cosmetic morality of
> Western civilisation. His intellectual honesty erodes all basis of
> consolation and distances itself from the tawdry drama of remorse
> and confession.

They conclude:

> There is a great wealth of variety in Coetzee's works. No two books
> ever follow the same recipe. Extensive reading reveals a recurring
> pattern, the downward spiralling journeys he considers necessary
> for the salvation of his characters. His protagonists are overwhelmed
> by the urge to sink but paradoxically derive strength from being
> stripped of all external dignity.

As a caution to journalists, and as a precaution to protect Coetzee's privacy, the Director of Publicity of the University of Chicago issued a statement that he did not expect the author to be available for interviews. He did, though, arrange for a number of colleagues to make statements about him. In his statement, Wayne C. Booth, Distinguished Service Professor Emeritus in English, said:

> Having read almost all of Coetzee's work I can honestly say that if I had been on the Nobel Prize Committee, he would have received it earlier. This enthusiasm springs from the ways in which he imagines himself sympathetically into characters of so many diverse kinds.[6]

Jonathan Lear, John U. Nef Distinguished Service Professor at the Committee on Social Thought, said:

> John Coetzee is one of the great writers of our times, but he is also one of the world's great teachers. In the tradition of the exemplar, and the witness, he teaches us all what is really involved in reading a great book. He has taught me to look with greater clarity at the human soul, and his remarks in and out of class are lifetime memories, reverberating away.

On the campus of the University of Texas at Austin, where Coetzee had studied in the 1960s and got his doctorate, the high tower of the central building with its 22 storeys was brightly lit in celebration of the Nobel Prize, a spectacle that ordinarily was reserved for great sports victories.[7] Congratulations poured in from all over, from friends, colleagues, publishers, agents and ex-students; and the vice-chancellors of the University of Adelaide and the University of Cape Town sent their good wishes, expressing their appreciation of his connection with their respective institutions.

Nic Stathakis, with whom he had been at school and with whom he remained life-long friends, informed him from Switzerland, where he had been living for years, 'If you still interact with mortals, a plate of beans and a bed (or two) are still at your disposal here.' Nadine Gordimer, who had won the Nobel Prize in 1991, said, 'I am delighted, he's a good friend and a great writer. I think it's great, I was the first and now he is the second. It is great for South Africa.'[8] Malvern van Wyk Smith, professor in English at Rhodes University, conveyed his congratulations, and told him that the *Eastern Province Herald* had hailed Dorothy in large print on their front page as 'The Driver Behind Coetzee.' From the poet Breyten Breytenbach Coetzee received an e-mail of which the subject line said 'Hêppie hêppie!' (a slang corruption of 'Happy

happy!' usually used at Christmas and New Year), and the message, in Afrikaans, read: 'Heartiest congratulations on the big prize! We are glad and proud of you. You deserve it through and through. And all the best for the windy days ahead.' André Brink, too, was bowled over: 'I'm still too overwhelmed by the wonderful news to think of anything original to say. You have done us all proud. And I cannot think of anyone else in the world who deserved it more than you do, right now.' The historian Hermann Giliomee wrote in an e-mail: 'John! You brick. [...] I'm over the moon about your prize. As it happens I heard the news while we were on a Van Wyk Louw-themed tour, travelling through the barren Koue Bokkeveld. There is a grandeur of desolation about the land and the will of the people to survive nevertheless that reminded me of you and your work. Your prize means an immense amount to everybody grappling with this vast and sorrowful land.' In a later e-mail Giliomee wrote: 'The Afrikaans press is calling you an Afrikaner. Is that true?' Coetzee replied: 'About group identity I've always said: you can't just pick and choose, you also have to be picked and chosen. If they want me, they can have me.' To which Giliomee replied: 'We really want you. You'll just have to decide: a hybrid Afrikaner (Athol Fugard), an ordinary Afrikaner or a dyed-in-the-wool Afrikaner. I myself am an otherwise Afrikaner.' Coetzee's response to this was: 'A doubtful Afrikaner, perhaps.'[9]

Among Coetzee's close friends the only cautionary comment came from his former student friend and colleague Geoffrey Haresnape, who in a predominantly sympathetic article in *Pen News* of December 2003 asked whether it was wise to accept the Nobel Prize, in the light of the fact that this Swedish multimillionaire had made his fortune from explosives. Jonty Driver's laconic response was: 'If Tutu can accept a Nobel Prize, I reckon one can take one's chances with the morality!'[10]

A few days before the announcement of the prize, an article appeared in the *Lifestyle* supplement of the Johannesburg *Sunday Times*, written by Colin Bower of Juta's publishing house. He called Coetzee's style wooden and lifeless and his characters linguistic contrivances; his novels, according to Bower, fail to represent real emotions and experiences. 'Coetzee is a charlatan,' is the provocative opening sentence of an article taking up a whole page, without backing up its claims with any evidence. Among other gripes he complains about the emptiness of Coetzee's artistic vision. 'I have searched in vain,' he writes, 'for evidence of literary craftsmanship in Coetzee, the kind of craftsmanship that might justify a Booker or two. In fact, I find the opposite: writing that is disengaged, [...] which makes the task of specific demonstration invidious.'[11]

This rash article soon elicited a vehement reaction. On 5 October 2003 Henk Rossouw wrote in the *Sunday Times:* 'Colin Bower's prose is like the tea they serve in nursing homes: milky, weak, saccharine. [...] Criticism of J.M. Coetzee deserves space in *Lifestyle*, but it has to be written with authority and confidence.' Among the responses published on 19 October 2003 in the *Sunday Times* was a letter from G.W. Bairstow, clearly someone who had been to school with Coetzee:

> Colin Bower is an idiot. How any newspaper could publish the article you did beats me. John Maxwell Coetzee has now won the Nobel Prize.
>
> Surely those who judge the Man Booker Prize and the Nobel Prize are qualified far and away above Bower?
>
> John M. Coetzee was always brilliant. He was a whiz kid in every subject he touched from an early age. Those of us who attended school with him knew this then and accept that it is so now. He was also a reasonable sportsman and always a gentleman.
>
> Just because he shuns the limelight, which he did as a teenager, why should he be castigated, especially by a nonentity?

In a tribute to Coetzee in *Rapport* of 5 October 2003 André Brink wrote:

> With piquant timing the *Sunday Times* a week ago published one of the most vicious and pigheaded onslaughts ever published. That it was written by a publisher, one Colin Bower, makes it all the more unpalatable. But now the Swedish Academy has with a single stroke exposed that pain in the arse of an article in all its miserable myopia.[12]

In spite of such stout responses to Bower's article, South Africans did not exactly take to the streets in song and dance upon the announcement of Coetzee's achievement. The French newspaper *Le Monde* wrote on the occasion that Coetzee was a novelist but little read and understood in his native land. Christopher Hope commented:

> What lies behind the puzzlement, the derision, is the feeling that 'they', that is 'the west' or 'the north' in new South African

speak—meaning much the same place as 'the outside world' in old South African speak—are ganging up on 'us', by rewarding writers who run the country down. For what is under attack is not Coetzee's writing but his attitude to life, liberation, and the new South Africa. He is a seditious, cerebral novelist, obsessed by questions of loneliness, liberty and guilt. And that is politically worrying, and un-South African. Coetzee, wrote one commentator, was a 'western' writer who happened to live in Africa—for 'western' read 'white'.[13]

Hope's commentary was probably conditioned by the ANC's response to *Disgrace*, of recent memory, which clearly reminded him of the apartheid regime's fierce reaction to the dissident black writers of the 1960s, and of the vehement campaign against the *Sestigers*, who had dared to violate the taboos of Afrikanerdom.[14]

Even so, President Thabo Mbeki, who in 1999 had vilified Coetzee as a racist, was now prepared to congratulate him on a prize that he called a triumph for the South African nation and for the whole African continent. In his declaration on behalf of the president, Bheki Khumalo said: 'We take off our hats to and salute our latest Nobel Laureate and bask with him in the glory radiating from this singular recognition.' This did not mean that the ANC was prepared to recant its previous condemnation of Coetzee, as requested by the Democratic Alliance. According to Smuts Ngonyama, spokesman for the ANC, the ANC stood by its submission to the Human Rights Commission, and saw no contradiction between the branding of Coetzee as an ideologue of racism and the congratulations on the award.

After Mbeki's paean, Coetzee received congratulations from another unexpected source, the South African Communist Party. 'The South African Communist Party (SACP),' runs the statement, 'joins South Africa and the rest of the literary world to congratulate John Maxwell Coetzee for being awarded the 2003 Nobel Literature Award. The SACP salutes Coetzee for his consistent and penetrating analysis and critique of social injustice.'

Several leading articles noted the award of the Nobel Prize to Coetzee. The most insightful commentary came from the *Mail & Guardian* in their edition of 3–9 October 2003:

(N)ot since Samuel Beckett (one of Coetzee's key influences) got the prize in 1969 has it gone to an author so unattached to any cause, so pessimistic about the possibility of redemption, so sceptical about humanity's progress and its capacity for ethical action. In the mid-1980s in South Africa, as this country seemed locked in a terrible war between oppressors and liberators, Coetzee refused to allow his protagonist Michael K to join the freedom fighters. Unlike Nadine Gordimer's characters, who usually opted (though not without deep inner struggle) to join the forces of liberation, whatever their failures, Michael K decided instead to look after his vegetables. It is as though a novel such as *Life & Times of Michael K* operates in the gap of doubt present in Gordimer — the gap she closes but Coetzee leaves open, even widens. He took a lot of flak for that.

Likewise, Coetzee's most famous novel, *Disgrace*, and his first to be set explicitly in post-apartheid South Africa, is not a hopeful or comforting book. It seems to argue, via the shape of its narrative, that the promise of a new dispensation in South Africa — the promise of a new ethical space — is unfulfilled. It drew cries of baffled outrage from some of the less sophisticated readers in the African National Congress.

But Coetzee's relentless deconstruction of our self-delusions, including our pretensions to knowledge and mastery, rediscovers the fundamentals of our humanity in the quality of empathy. For that reason, and because he writes with such cold beauty, the award to him should be widely hailed in South Africa.

Pity he's an Australian now. We still need his limpid gaze.

Within hours of the announcement there was not a single book of Coetzee's available in the Akademibokhandeln in Stockholm, with the same trend discernible in the large bookstores of London and New York. With Coetzee now squarely in the spotlight, his books sold very well in bookstores in South Africa, according to a report in *Rapport*. A spokesperson for Random House said that the demand for his books had doubled since the announcement of the prize.

II

There was wide speculation whether the intensely private Coetzee, who had not shown up for either of his Booker Prizes, would travel to Stockholm to receive the Nobel Prize in person. In *Elizabeth Costello*, which as it happened was published at this time, the protagonist, after all, says: 'I should have asked them to forget the ceremony and send the cheque in the mail.'[15]

There was, however, no cause for concern. Before John and Dorothy left the US for the award ceremony, he gave, in November 2003, a public reading of his work in New York at Lincoln Center. People trampled each other underfoot for tickets, and touts sold black-market tickets outside the Public Library.[16]

While still in Chicago, Coetzee received a letter from Ingrid Wetterqvist of the Swedish ministry of foreign affairs. The Nobel Foundation, she told Coetzee, had appointed her to assist him during his visit to Sweden and to make everything as easy for him as possible, and ensure the smooth running of events. In her letter she outlines the obligations attendant upon a Nobel laureate, and mentions other optional activities: 'The awards,' she writes, 'generate a lot of interest, and I know that you must have been approached directly by a large number of interested individuals and organisations. I have also understood that you wish to be restrictive. Being the gatekeeper is one of my functions, another is to coordinate and respond on your behalf.' Mindful of the kind of reporting to which he was likely to be subjected, he asked her to keep journalists at bay. He would grant one interview, but that would be with David Attwell, whom he knew and trusted. The only problem that cropped up on the visit was that Coetzee initially wanted to reserve copyright in his Nobel acceptance address. The problem was resolved when he agreed that the lecture might be disseminated as widely as possible, but that he would reserve the right to use it in his fiction in future.

Upon John and Dorothy's arrival in Stockholm, the weather was freezing, with the first snowstorm of the year. They were accommodated in the imposing Grand Hotel in the city centre. On Sunday evening, 7 December, the guests assembled in a hall with glittering chandeliers to hear Coetzee's Nobel Lecture.[17] He was introduced by Horace Engdahl, fulltime secretary of the Swedish Academy, who did not mention Coetzee's illustrious career, merely saying that the award winner would use his lecture to shed light on the insignificance of the writer as a human being.

Coetzee, with his neatly cut grey-white hair and beard, dressed in a dark-grey suit with a white shirt and tie, took up his place at the lectern, carefully removed his glasses and replaced them in leisurely fashion with reading glasses, a routine he would repeat several times in the course of Nobel Week, almost as if to take a moment to forget about the world about him and to focus on the words before him. He started reading his text in a low voice, but with manifest authority. He told how as a nine-year-old he had in his imagination entered into the experiences of the shipwrecked Robinson Crusoe and his servant Man Friday, and how confusing he had found the name Daniel Defoe on the title page. He had gone to check in the *Children's Encyclopaedia*, and decided that Defoe must be a pen name for Robinson Crusoe. Under the title 'He and his man' he then delivered his lecture, an appealing tale about Crusoe who at first has to work under the incessant chattering of his wife, and later, as a widower, inhabits a room on the waterfront of Bristol, with little more than his faded umbrella and a dead parrot for company. He receives reports on ducks and on deaths in a plague-tormented London, written by an agile man with a brisk step who looks as if he might be Defoe and has worked for eleven years as a secret agent and political reporter. Coetzee thus switches the roles of Crusoe and Defoe, but this man could also be Friday. Questions are raised about the ownership of stories, the complexity of narratives and the relative nature of allegorical interpretation. Ultimately it transpires that Coetzee's lecture is not just about fictional characters. The third-person narrative is as little removed from his own experience as that in *Boyhood* and *Youth*.

On Monday afternoon, 8 December, Coetzee was in the Akademibok-handeln to sign copies of his books. An hour before the appointed time the line of people waiting for him stretched out of the bookstore into the street. He signed in silence, and responded at most with a 'thank you' to compliments. A few hours later he was in the Royal Theatre to read three passages from *Boyhood*: a section on his experiences as a Boy Scout, and how he had declared himself a Roman Catholic in Worcester on the grounds of his admiration for the Romans. The preponderantly Swedish audience laughed and applauded so enthusiastically that Coetzee had to remain on stage for longer than planned.

On Tuesday, 9 December, the South African Embassy hosted an official lunch for Coetzee. Journalists were surprised to hear from the ambassador, Gladys Sonto-Kudjoe, that she had had an enjoyable conversation with Coetzee. She said he was a humble, down-to-earth person who was willing to answer questions patiently. The lunch was attended by the Swedish minister of cultural affairs, representatives of the Swedish Academy, and members of the diplomatic corps. Coetzee's cordiality at this meal was in strong contrast to his behaviour towards journalists, who had not been able to get a word out of him. The Reuters journalist managed to elicit only four words: 'I am not sure.'

Shortly after four o' clock on Wednesday, 10 December, the Nobel laureates were congratulated by their families, friends and admirers on the stage of the concert hall. The stage was decorated with 6 000 red, yellow and purple flowers from the Italian village of San Remo, where Alfred Nobel had spent his last years. Like the other laureates, Coetzee, dressed in a dress suit with tailcoat, received his Nobel Prize from King Carl XVI Gustaf. After the awards the Stockholm Philharmonic played the third movement of Beethoven's Eighth Symphony. Proceedings then moved to Stockholm's Town Hall, where about 500 torches in front of the building ushered in the 1 300 guests from the icy darkness. In the Blue Hall the tables were laden with cutlery and glasses, and a royal meal was served, devised by the winner of that year's Swedish chef-of-the-year contest. Upon Coetzee's return to Adelaide, Lisa Garmack asked him whether the Swedes had served him good vegetarian food, and told how Isaac B. Singer, the Nobel winner in 1978, had to wait half an hour for his meal, until he left the table, to be found later in the kitchen with a cup of tea. Coetzee assured her that the meals were excellent at the two banquets during their visit. 'And the Academy's chef produced a 14-course vegan Chinese meal on our evening there. Finally, we located an excellent vegetarian restaurant not far from the Grand Hotel. So we have no complaints about food.'

After a week of preserving a near-universal silence, he surprised the guests with the most personal after-dinner speech of all the laureates:

Your Majesties, Your Royal Highnesses, Ladies and Gentlemen; Distinguished Guests, Friends

The other day, suddenly, out of the blue, while we were talking about something completely different, my partner Dorothy burst out as follows: 'On the other hand,' she said, *on the other hand*, how proud your mother would have been! What a pity she isn't still alive! And your father too! How proud they would have been of you!'

'Even prouder than of my son the doctor?' I said. 'Even prouder than of my son the professor?'

'Even prouder.'

'If my mother were still alive,' I said, 'she would be ninety-nine and a half. She would probably have senile dementia. She would not know what was going on around her.'

But of course I missed the point. Dorothy was right. My mother would have been bursting with pride. *My son the Nobel Prize winner.* And for whom, anyway, do we do the things that lead to Nobel Prizes if not for our mothers?

'*Mommy, Mommy, I won a prize.*'

'*That's wonderful, my dear. Now eat your carrots before they get cold.*'

'Why must our mothers be ninety-nine and long in the grave before we can come running home with the prize that will make up for all the trouble we have been to them?

To Alfred Nobel, 107 years in the grave, and to the Foundation that so faithfully administers his will and that has created this magnificent evening for us, my heartfelt gratitude. To my parents, how sorry I am that you cannot be here.

Thank you.

For the Swedish daily *Dagens Nyheter* Coetzee granted an interview to David Attwell.[18] When asked how he saw the significance of the award, both personally and in more general terms, Coetzee replied: 'In its conception the literature prize belongs to days when a writer could still be thought of as, by virtue of his or her occupation, a sage, someone with no institutional affiliations who could offer an authoritative word on our times as well as on our moral life. (It has always struck me as strange, by the way, that Alfred Nobel did not institute a philosophy prize, or for that matter that he instituted a physics prize but not a mathematics prize, to say nothing of a music prize — music is, after all, more universal than literature, which is bound to a particular language.) The idea of a writer as sage is pretty much dead today. I would certainly feel very uncomfortable in the role.'

To the question what the future had in store for the 2003 winner of the Nobel Prize, Coetzee replied, bringing to mind his increasing reluctance to deliver papers at conferences or to act the public figure: 'Already he is being peppered with invitations to travel far and wide to give lectures. That has always seemed to me one of the stranger aspects of literary fame: you prove your competence as a writer and an inventor of stories, and then people clamour for you to make speeches and tell them what you think about the world.' When Attwell asked him how he saw his relation to South Africa, as manifested in his work, Coetzee's reply once again indicated his awareness of the complex historical position from which he writes: 'Seen from the outside as an historical specimen,

I am a late representative of the vast movement of European expansion that took place from the sixteenth century to the mid twentieth century of the Christian era, a movement that more or less achieved its purpose of conquest and settlement in the Americas and Australasia, but failed totally in Asia and almost totally in Africa. I say that I represent this movement because my intellectual allegiances are clearly European, not African.'

And when asked, in conclusion, to comment on the function of the ending of *Elizabeth Costello*, based on a text by Hugo von Hofmannsthal, Coetzee's reply reaffirmed a principle he has maintained consistently ever since *Dusklands*: 'I tend to resist invitations to interpret my own fiction. If there were a better, clearer, shorter way of saying what the fiction says, then why not scrap the fiction? Elizabeth, Lady C, claims to be writing at the limits of language. Would it not be insulting to her if I were diligently to follow after her, explaining what she means but is not smart enough to say?'

III

After the cold and snow of Stockholm, Coetzee and Dorothy were pleased to be back in the more amenable climate of Adelaide. Did he perhaps, on his homecoming, think of the short, epigrammatic poem, 'Kroonjaar', [Prize Year] by the Dutch poet A. Roland Holst?

> Hollowly homaged
> He returns to his house
> Many-multiplied
> To a mouse.[19]

He wrote to Jane Palfreyman of Random House in Australia, possibly a trifle dyspeptically: 'Stockholm was fun for everyone except the laureates.' Ingrid Wetterqvist of the Swedish ministry of foreign affairs, tasked with helping them during the visit, had had a bad case of flu for the duration of their visit, but had nevertheless meticulously executed her brief. Unfortunately the nasty virus had migrated to John and Dorothy, and they had returned to Adelaide the worse for it. Although they had admired their receptionist's perseverance during their visit, they now, with their running noses, wished she had rather stayed at home in bed.[20]

Both John and Dorothy had arranged, before the award of the Nobel Prize, to pay an academic visit to Stanford University in the US from 27 March to June 2004. Coetzee now felt, however, that he wanted to be entirely free of academic commitments and concentrate on his writing. He wrote to Susan Welch on 25 January 2004 that he had terminated his agreement with the University of Chicago to lecture there for three months a year. He did not have the stomach, he says in this letter, for the bureaucratic red tape around the application for a US visa, and having to fill in countless forms to effect payment of his emolument. 'You probably know,' he writes to Welch, 'though only in an abstract way, what a time-consuming, expensive, and humiliating business it has become to get a US visa. Another reason for staying at home.'

But more important than his impatience with red tape was his resistance to delivering public lectures and continuing to perform as an academic. After the Nobel Prize he was bombarded from near and far with requests for lectures, invitations that he now declined with the excuse that he was a bad lecturer — an excuse cropping up in numerous e-mails, manifestly contradicted by the testimony of generations of appreciative students. When, for instance, he was invited to appear at La Trobe University, he wrote to Peter Rose on 5 February 2004:

As you must know, it is the fate of Nobel prize-winners to cease being writers and become itinerant lecturers. It is a fate I am determined to avoid. In the past three months I have had more invitations than I can shake a stick at — invitations to lecture, to contribute essays, to endorse books, to sign petitions, etc etc.

The only lecturing invitations I have accepted were from the Nobel people themselves and from the *New York Review*, and what I offered there were pieces of fiction rather than lectures in any conventional sense.

Writing fiction is a solution I have resorted to before — I detest lecturing and do it badly — but the problem is that these pieces take months to write, far more time than a conventional lecture, and more time than I can afford at present.

So I don't see a way in which I can accept the invitation from La Trobe. I could offer a reading, but I doubt very much that that would do. I'm sorry.

The invitation of Professor Li to visit the Tinghua University in China was also declined in an e-mail of 17 April 2004:

> I am grateful to you for the invitation to visit Tinghua University and speak there during the 2004–5 academic year. Your university has a world-wide reputation.
>
> I regret, however, that I am unable to accept. Since the award of the Nobel Prize I have received more invitations than I can accommodate. I am concerned to avoid the fate of so many writers who have won the Nobel Prize in the past—the fate of neglecting their own writing while they travel the globe giving speeches.
>
> I thank you for the honour of the invitation and ask you to excuse me for not accepting.

Increasingly, too, Coetzee shied away from demands made on him, though he was still prepared to help writers where he could. He wrote to Barbara Wiesner of the writers' centre of South Australia that he would rather not deliver a lecture, but that he was prepared to help the writers at this centre on a one-on-one basis with their creative work. He also promoted, by putting his name to petitions and appeals, the cause of writers oppressed by dictatorial regimes. When, however, he was asked to sign a petition asking for an academic boycott of Israel, he answered firmly: 'I am afraid I am not a supporter of academic boycotts, in Israel or elsewhere.'

As before, so after the Nobel Prize, most reporters could not get an interview from Coetzee. As a gesture of goodwill to the University of Adelaide he did grant a written interview to Ben Osborne for the April edition of the journal *Lumen*. Asked what effects the award of the Nobel Prize had had on him and his writing, whether it inhibited or enlivened him, Coetzee replied:

> During the course of the Nobel ceremonies I had the pleasure of being a dinner guest at the Swedish Academy. The Swedish Academy is responsible for deciding the prize for literature. The members of the Academy struck me as intelligent, learned, and sensitive human beings, but not gods. Nor did they pretend to be gods. The Academy has made many wise choices in the past, and now and then a not-so-wise choice. To none of us is it yet clear whether the choice they made in 2003 was a wise choice or not. The point of these remarks is the following. It would be exceedingly foolish of me to think that

> I am all of a sudden a better writer now than I was a year ago. In
> other words, I had better keep my feet on the ground and my head
> out of the clouds.

In a few cases, mostly out of friendship with the person approaching
him, he allowed one of the reporters to submit a few questions to him
by e-mail. Even then, his impatience with the often naive questions put
to him was all too clear from his replies. This was the case with Didier
Jacob, who in May 2004 conducted an e-mail interview with him for
Le Nouvel Observateur. When Jacob comments that Coetzee is known
to speak to the press very rarely, and asks whether Coetzee prefers
silence, music or words, he replies: 'Do I like silence? I prefer silence to
chatter, certainly. I like music, but then I prefer to give the music my full
attention. I do not write with music in the background, since it disturbs
the rhythms of my prose.' In reply to the observation that there is a lot
of violence in his books and to the question of which moments in his
life he remembers as the most violent, Coetzee replies blandly: 'I have
lived a quiet, even sedate life.' When the journalist refers to Beckett's
asocial life and asks if Coetzee is attempting something similar, he
replies: 'Is it true that Beckett lived a non-social life? Beckett had friends,
Beckett worked actively in the theatre. I have friends, I have taught in
universities for thirty years. My students will be surprised to hear that
they do not constitute part of society.' When Jacob asks him if, in spite of
his reluctance to grant interviews, he nevertheless. through the media.
remains abreast of current affairs, his answer is quite brusque: 'Yes, of
course I keep myself informed of events.' A question as to whether he is
pessimistic about the future of literature elicits an abrupt 'No'.

The questions raised as to what one can learn from his books and
who he is trying to reach through his books remain unanswered. When
Jacob asks him whether the Nobel Prize has changed his life, he replies:
'Not in its essentials. Nobel Prizes are almost always awarded to people
in the twilight of their years, when their habits are fixed.' About his life
in Adelaide he can say only that he leads 'an exemplary bourgeois' life.
In conclusion Jacob asks him: 'Would you please describe precisely the
room where you write?' To which Coetzee conscientiously provides his
most complete but sardonically deadpan answer:

> My study is on the second floor, facing west, overlooking a stony
> creek overshadowed by tall pine trees. I write at a table facing a

blank wall. Behind me are bookshelves. To my right is the desk I used when I was at school; in its drawers I keep stationery.

IV

So Coetzee, on his return from Stockholm, wanted above all to devote himself to his writing and disprove the popular notion that a writer after winning the Nobel Prize never again produced anything of worth.

Coetzee's first publication since the prize appeared as early as December 2003, though the manuscript must have been in preparation long before the announcement of the award. This was *Landscape with Rowers*, a selection from the work of a number of prominent Dutch poets, with the translation of each poem printed facing its original, which was published by Princeton University Press. The collection, Coetzee writes on 17 December 2003 to his Dutch publisher Eva Cossée, 'is simply a collection of translations of poems that I have come across and liked. They are in no way a representative selection, or a cross-section of modern Dutch poetry.' The poets from whose work he included examples were Gerrit Achterberg, whose *Ballade van de Gasfitter* he had translated in the 1960s while studying at the University of Texas,[21] Sybren Polet, Hugo Claus, Cees Nooteboom, Hans Faverey (whose work provided the title for the collection) and Rutger Kopland. What is striking about this selection is that Coetzee did not include examples from the classical canon, from Gorter and Leopold to Nijhoff and Marsman, but concentrated on poets who, though divergent in nature and style, were to a large extent innovative, broadening the scope of Dutch poetry. Some of the examples he selected are complex texts, requiring for a full comprehension a thorough knowledge of Dutch—an indication of the extent to which Coetzee keeps his finger on the pulse of the language and its latest literary utterances.[22]

Coetzee's London agent, Bruce Hunter, told him on 14 January 2004 that a private publisher, Rees & O'Neill, had expressed interest in publishing his Nobel lecture in a de luxe edition. Coetzee agreed to this, but pointed out that Penguin was also going to publish a hardcover version and that Eva Cossée wanted to publish a Dutch translation. In the event all three were published in de luxe editions—the Rees & O'Neill edition, in particular, being beautifully produced as regards typography, typesetting and binding. Eva Cossée had already over the

2002/3 new year published a bilingual limited gift edition of 1500 copies of Coetzee's short story 'A house in Spain' for her friends and acquaintances[23]—another token of the cordial relations between Coetzee and his Dutch publisher.

In *The New York Review of Books* of 15 January 2004, Coetzee published an Elizabeth Costello story titled 'As a woman grows older', which had not formed part of the 2003 novel. Eva Cossée published this in 2008 in a Dutch translation by Peter Bergsma as *Als een vrouw ouder wordt*, together with 'Aan de poort', the Dutch version of 'At the gate', the last section of Elizabeth Costello.

Coetzee had continued to write his illuminating essays on writers and books for *The New York Review of Books*. A selection of the pieces written from 2000 to 2005, together with essays published elsewhere, was collected in *Inner Workings* (2007) and introduced by Derek Attridge.

In his introduction Attridge points out that Coetzee often, and increasingly in his later work, blends fiction and non-fiction, in particular through the use of the fictitious Australian writer Elizabeth Costello, who addresses current events. While this strategy reckons all pronouncements to the account of his character, Coetzee is himself the speaker in his literary essays, casting a creative eye on other writers and yet, in a kind of meta-gaze, betraying something of his own convictions, opinions and beliefs.

The most important subjects that Coetzee addresses in his essays, according to Attridge, are the relation between art and politics, the continuum between the aesthetic and the erotic, the responsibility of the writer, the ethical potential of fiction, and the place and purpose of literature, with the attendant joys and challenges for the writer. Attridge points out that Coetzee's novels and autobiographies enact the same themes, testifying to the 'wholeness and persistence of his understanding of the artist's vocation'.[24] There is no dualism between Coetzee the fiction writer and Coetzee the critic: both activities are prompted by the same impulse.

Writers in whom Coetzee has shown particular interest are figures such as Italo Svevo, Robert Walser, Robert Musil, Walter Benjamin, Bruno Schulz, Joseph Roth and Sándor Márai. They are writers who experienced the suffering of two world wars, some of whom died in the Nazi camps. Attridge writes: 'What emerges from this group of essays is a Europe in painful transition, and a series of literary works whose originality is seen as the artist's necessary response to far-reaching change.'[25] Everywhere in these essays the reader is taken by surprise by Coetzee's acute insights and astounding power of formulation. Thus he notes that echoes of Robert Walser's prose appear in Kafka, for instance in the 'lucid syntactic layout, its casual juxtapositions of the elevated with the banal, and its eerily convincing logic of paradox'.[26] These are elements that are to be found in Coetzee's work as well. In Robert Musil and his response to his time there may also be something of Coetzee's own relation to the despicable apartheid regime, under which he spent most of his life: 'Musil's work, from beginning to end, is of a piece: the evolving record of a confrontation between a man of supreme intelligent sensibility and the times that gave birth to him, times he would bitterly but justly call "accursed"'.[27] Coetzee's interest in the task of the translator is once again evident from his comments apropos of Michael Hofmann's too-British translation of Joseph Roth, using words and expressions that would puzzle an American reader; Coetzee delivers a plea for a more neutral translation: 'Just as there is a case to be made for translating into the dialect of English that the translator commands most vividly, there is a contrary case to be made for using as linguistically neutral, as mid-Atlantic, a dialect as possible.'[28]

In the work of a second group of writers who appear in *Inner Workings* from the aftermath of the two wars—figures like Paul Celan, Günter Grass, W.G. Sebald and Hugo Claus—it is, according to Attridge, more difficult to discern a fixed pattern, although Europe's recent dark history provides a constantly recurring frame of reference. In the work of W.G. Sebald Coetzee traces 'the crossing and indeed trampling of boundaries between fiction and nonfiction',[29] which is increasingly the tendency of Coetzee's own fiction. By contrast with his reservations about Joseph Roth's British translator, he finds Paul Celan's translations of the Russian poet Osip Mandelstam 'an extraordinary act of inhabiting another poet',[30] a judgement which is equally applicable to Coetzee's own fine revised translation of Achterberg's *Ballade van de Gasfitter*.

In the second half of the book Coetzee concentrates in the main on English and American authors, such as Graham Greene, Samuel Beckett, Walt Whitman, William Faulkner, Henry Miller and Philip Roth. In his discussion of Saul Bellow Coetzee comments that some of his novels give no indication of which characters are entitled to the reader's sympathy, who is the victim and who the persecutor. The absence of any 'authorial guidance'[31] is something Coetzee's work has in common with Bellow, just as the interplay of fiction and reality that he finds in Philip Roth's

The Plot Against America forms the warp and weft of his own *Summertime*.
Writing about Samuel Beckett's shorter prose, Coetzee characterises it
in terms that are largely, if not completely, true also of works like *In
the Heart of the Country* and *Life & Times of Michael K* : 'It is a world of
confined spaces or else bleak wastes, inhabited by asocial and indeed
misanthropic monologuers helpless to terminate their monologue,
tramps with failing bodies and never-sleeping minds condemned to a
purgatorial treadmill on which they rehearse again and again the great
themes of Western philosophy.'[32] Coetzee mentions the 'haunting
verbal beauty' of Beckett's prose and then describes Beckett in terms
that could be applied almost verbatim to his own works, except for some
of the later novels (for instance *Elizabeth Costello* and *Diary of a Bad Year*),
in which there is a gradual move towards metaphysical awareness:

> Beckett was an artist possessed by a vision of life without
> consolation or dignity or promise of grace, in the face of which
> our only duty—inexplicable and futile of attainment, but a duty
> nonetheless—is not to lie to ourselves. It was a vision to which he
> gave expression in language of a virile strength and intellectual
> subtlety that marks him as one of the great prose stylists of the
> twentieth century.[33]

The collection concludes on a consideration of specific works by three
winners of the Nobel Prize: Nadine Gordimer, Gabriel García Márquez and V.S. Naipaul.[34] Like Coetzee, Naipaul was one of those who
arrived in England from the colonies with a 'colonial education that
was comically old-fashioned by metropolitan standards. That very
education, however, made of them trustees of a culture that had
decayed in the "mother" country.'[35] Naipaul, Coetzee continues, maintains that he is not blessed with fantasy and could draw only on his
childhood in Port of Spain. Only after years of writing did he come
to the Proustian realisation that his subject was himself, a 'colonial'
brought up in a culture, so he was told, that did not belong to him and
without, as he was also told, a history.[36] Thus ill-equipped he had to
make his way through the world.

Coetzee writes about Nadine Gordimer's novel *The Pickup* (2001), in
which the character Julie Summers leaves South Africa to join her Arab
lover in the Middle East: 'Most of all [...] Julie is tired of South Africa in
a way that, while it may be hard to find credible in someone so young,

is all too easy to believe in someone of Gordimer's generation—tired of the daily demands that a country with a centuries-long history of exploitation and violence and disheartening contrasts of poverty and affluence makes upon the moral conscience.'[37] Coetzee wonders what historical context is available for a writer like Gordimer born into a late-colonial community and having to function as a writer. His reply constitutes both an implicit criticism of Gordimer, and a tacit reflection on his own situation:

> The ethical framework for her own life's work was laid in the 1950s, as the iron curtain of apartheid was descending, when she first read Jean-Paul Sartre and the Algerian-born Albert Camus. Under the influence of that reading she adopted the role of witness to the fate of South Africa. 'The function of the writer,' wrote Sartre, 'is to act in such a way that nobody can be ignorant of the world and that nobody may say that he is innocent of what it is all about.' The stories and novels Gordimer wrote in the next three decades are populated with characters, mainly white South Africans, living in the Sartrean bad faith, pretending to themselves that they do not know what it is all about; her self-ordained task was to bring to bear on them the evidence of the real in order to crack their lie. [...] At the heart of the novel of realism is the theme of disillusionment. At the end of *Don Quixote*, Alonso Quixana, who has set out to right the wrongs of the world, comes home sadly aware not only that he is no hero but that in the world as it has become there can be no more heroes. As stripper-away of convenient illusions and unmasker of colonial bad faith, Gordimer is an heir of the tradition of realism that Cervantes inaugurates. Within that tradition she was able to work quite satisfactorily until the late 1970s, when she was made to realise that to black South Africans, the people to whose struggle she bore historical witness, the name Zola, to say nothing of the name Proust, carried no resonance—that she was too European to matter to the people who mattered most to her. Her essays of the period show her struggling inconclusively in the toils of the question of what it means to write *for* a people—to write for their sake and on their behalf, as well as to be read by them. [...] With the end of apartheid and the relaxation of the ideological imperatives that under apartheid had overshadowed all cultural affairs, Gordimer was liberated from such self-laceration.

574 J.M. Coetzee: A Life in Writing

The fiction she has published in the new century shows a welcome readiness to pursue new avenues and a new sense of the world. If the writing tends to be somewhat bodiless, somewhat sketchy by comparison with the writing of her major period, if the devotion to the texture of the real that characterises her best work is now only intermittent, if she is sometimes content to gesture toward what she means rather than pinning it down exactly in words, that is, one senses, because she feels she has already proved herself, does not need to perform those Herculean labours anew.[38]

CHAPTER 16

THE 'AUSTRALIAN' NOVELS

I

In the years after the 2003 Nobel Prize, J.M. Coetzee still often travelled on invitation to Europe and other parts of the world. By accommodating several invitations in a single journey, avoiding repeated long-haul flights from Australia, he guarded against unduly fragmenting his time. In April and May 2004 he and Dorothy visited Stanford in the US, where Dorothy presented lectures and John gave guidance to creative-writing students. In June and July they travelled to Italy to attend a literary conference, and afterwards undertook a cycle tour in France. In March 2005 he read from his work at the Galway Cúirt in Ireland; he and Dorothy had planned to meet Gisela in the French countryside for a holiday, but she was involved in a serious accident and could not join them. In November 2005 they travelled to Tasmania, where Coetzee read from his work on several campuses, and they saw a fair amount of the island. In December 2007 they visited Japan as guests of the Japan Foundation, and in January 2011 they travelled to India as guests at the Jaipur Literary Festival. In June 2011 he read from unpublished work in the Central Hall of the University of York at the first Festival of Ideas, which included a conference on Samuel Beckett. He also attended the Kingston Writers Fest in Canada in September 2011.

In June 2006 he visited York, where David Attwell had been appointed as a colleague of Derek Attridge, whose book, *J.M. Coetzee and the Ethics of Reading,* appeared early in 2005. Later that month he signed copies in Warsaw for his many readers and admirers in Poland, and read from his work in the Palace of Culture and Science in Warsaw, which the former Soviet Union had donated to its neighbour. He wrote to Angela Bowne: 'Poland was very interesting. I did two book-signings, so got to speak to scores and scores of Poles, though only for fifteen seconds each. I find them very attractive people, particularly the women. I also managed to visit the village where my great-grandfather [Balthazar du Biel] was born in 1844 (he became an Evangelical missionary, which is how he ended up in Africa).' The rest of June he and Dorothy devoted to a cycle tour in France, overnighting in his daughter's house in Gaja-la-Selve, about 50 kilometres from Carcassonne.

Coetzee remained active in literary life, defending the rights of authors and helping young writers by promoting their work at the request of publishers. Along with fourteen other Nobel laureates he signed a petition in April 2004 calling for the release of imprisoned Burmese writers, and in August 2007 he lent his support to a call from the Peter Weiss Foundation to break the silence surrounding the crimes against humanity in Zimbabwe. He also signed a petition from the same foundation to the president of China about abuses of human rights in that country. He acted as a judge for the South African PEN Literary Award, selecting a number of short stories published in 2005, with an introduction by him, as *African Compass — New Writing from Southern Africa*. For a similar anthology in 2006, under the title *African Road*, he was once again asked to judge the finalists. In 2008 he was one of the selectors for the Jan Rabie/*Rapport* Prize for innovative Afrikaans prose, an indication that he had kept his interest in Afrikaans literature. Also in 2008, he was the final judge of a new SA PEN Literary Prize for short stories in English. In a statement he said: 'Having experienced myself how helpful and encouraging it is to a writer to have one's work recognised in the form of literary awards, I'm delighted to be able to play a part in assisting other authors.'

In 2009 Coetzee was a judge for the John Button Prize, a prize worth 20 000 Australian dollars in memory of a former minister of industry, awarded for the best non-fiction work published in the preceding year on politics or public policy. When Harold Pinter was awarded the Nobel Prize in 2005, Coetzee expressed, on invitation, his appreciation of Pinter's work: 'Harold Pinter has taught us how to listen to the silences between the words, the silences that hold so much meaning and some-times so much menace. His influence on the dialogue we hear in con-temporary theatre and cinema is as incalculable as it is invisible. The award of the Nobel Prize is entirely appropriate.'

In December 2004 Coetzee was elected to the Australian Academy of the Humanities, and in South Africa on 27 September he was honoured with the National Order of Mapungubwe (Gold) for his exceptional contribution to literature, placing South Africa on the world map of writing. Coetzee travelled from Adelaide to Pretoria to receive the award personally from President Thabo Mbeki. It was by all accounts a graceful and gracious ceremony.

In 2007 Coetzee collaborated with other prominent writers on 'The First Chapter Series', published by the Oak Tree Press as rare de luxe editions in aid of South African children suffering from AIDS. In 2008 Coetzee and Gordimer were two of the writers defending the Czech author Milan Kundera against accusations of aiding the Czechoslovakian police during the time of the communist regime. His continuing interest in South Africa was evident from his support for a petition of writers against the proposed media legislation that the ANC government wanted to pilot through parliament in spite of the opposition of its ally, COSATU (Congress of South African Trade Unions).

By now Coetzee was turning down many of the invitations that were flooding in — not only to lecture at overseas universities, but also to appear at literary festivals, deliver papers, or to write, as he had done in the past, introductions to particular editions. On this score, he did, though, make exceptions. He accepted an invitation from Grove Press to write an introduction to the fourth and last volume of a collected edition of the works of Samuel Beckett. He also wrote an introduction to the letters of Hendrik Witbooi published in French.[1] But when approached by Penguin to write an introduction to one of D.H. Lawrence's novels, he declined, writing to Laura Barber at Penguin on 7 January 2004:

> Since the Nobel announcement I have had, as you can imagine, all kinds of invitations to give lectures, compose blurbs, give interviews, provide introductions, write columns, etc. The danger I run is of dissipating myself on a multiplicity of little projects that, in the long run, don't count.
>
> I don't class the proposed Lawrence introduction among these little projects. Furthermore, we were discussing it before the Nobel business came up. Nevertheless, I think I must decline. It would entail an amount of reading and research that I can't afford. I hope you will understand.

Also in 2004, in May of that year, he declined the prestigious invitation, direct from the President of Mexico, to take part in the Festival Internacional. Even the more tempting invitation, from Christoph Buchwald, the husband of Eva Cossée, to choose his hundred best-loved Dutch poems for an anthology, was turned down: 'The idea is an attractive one, but I think I must decline. Knowing my obsessive temperament, I would not regard the task as properly done until I had read the entire body of Low Country poetry from the Middle Ages to the present day, and I just don't have the time to do that.'

At the end of 2003 Coetzee terminated his cherished connection with the University of Chicago and his collaboration with Jonathan Lear. He wrote to his Serbian translator, Arijana Božović, with whom he had built up a close connection, on 8 November 2004: 'After seven years, I have, with some regret, broken the link with Chicago. I liked the university, I was fond of my colleagues, but there were too many counterbalancing considerations: my dislike of big cities, the fact that I no longer need the money, the political setup in the US.' In fact, the 'political setup' under George W. Bush, along with the long and exhausting journey from Adelaide to New York, was in these years cropping up in more than one of his refusals. Although he appreciated the attempts of PEN to broaden the horizons of American readers, he was not prepared to visit New York City as their guest in April 2005. He writes:

> To get to New York from Adelaide, where I live, involves some thirty hours of air travel. I am getting on for 65. I never sleep on airplanes. I contemplate the 30-hour journey, the few days in New York trying to function ten or eleven hours out of phase, then the thirty-hour journey back, and my heart quails. The organism won't take that kind of battering any more.
>
> I feel I ought also to say that the prospect of all the bureaucratic bloodymindedness that one has to subject oneself to in order to get into Fortress America nowadays is not appealing.

A strong indication of his feelings about the political situation in the US was the fact that, after accepting an invitation from Stanford University for the spring term (April and May) of 2005, he informed them that he would not be coming if George W. Bush was re-elected for a second term in November 2004. He responded in similar fashion to an invitation from the San Jose State University to consider a position there in the autumn of 2005–6. He would, he said, give it his serious consideration if an immediate decision was not expected of him. He adds, however:

I must tell you candidly that my decision will hinge in part on what happens in the November presidential election and what policy changes, if any, occur after that election. I am not sure I want to return to a United States still under Bush and Cheney.[2] This is not at all a matter of making some kind of political statement. It is about the folly of choosing to reside in a country where the rule of law no longer applies, particularly to foreigners.

It was in particular the uncovering of the physical and psychological abuse and sexual humiliation of prisoners by military police in the Abu Ghraib prison in Iraq that appalled Coetzee. On 14 June 2004, after his visit to Stanford, he writes to Julia Kristeva:

I have just spent two months in the USA, at Stanford University. I found the visit disturbing. To begin with, America is becoming more and more like a jealously guarded fortress. And then the mood of almost everyone with whom I came in contact was gloomy and, after the Abu Ghraib scandal broke, full of shame.

It seems to me that a real crisis will face all of us—not just Americans—in November. If George Bush and the men around him are re-elected by the American voters, there is every reason to fear they will use the next four years to try to change the face of the world. But how does one reach those Americans who do not share these fears, or do not share them profoundly enough to come out and vote?

When he received an invitation to visit Dartmouth College in 2007 or 2008, he declined it in January 2006:

Allow me to explain why—I hope you will understand. My links with the United States extend back over four decades. I have spent some eleven years of my life there; much of my intellectual formation took place in American universities. I have too much affection for the country not to find the United States under its present administration a disturbing and depressing place to be.

I live in hope that in 2008 the electorate will mandate a change in direction. If that happens, and if you care to repeat your offer after 2008, be assured I will give it my most careful attention.

Coetzee, having experienced the structural violence on the part of the South African government in the 1970s and 1980s, did not hesitate to express himself strongly against the intended anti-terrorist legislation of the Australian prime minister, John Howard.[3] At a reading from his work at the National Library in Canberra, Coetzee said: 'I used to think that the people who created [South Africa's] laws that effectively suspended the rule of law were moral barbarians. Now I know they were just pioneers ahead of their time.' On behalf of PEN in Sydney he wrote a letter of protest on 10 April 2006 to the executive director of the Australian Legal Reform Commission:

> Whether the suicide bombings and other murderous acts being plotted and committed nowadays in the name of Islam add up to a threat to the security of the West or merely a threat to the personal safety of citizens, only the verdict of history will tell. What we can say with more certainty is that the response of Western states, notably the United States and its closest allies, a response that has included the suspension of certain civil liberties and certain aspects of the rule of law, has been carried out so hastily and with so little public debate as to be a source of national shame for years to come.
>
> New laws [...] criminalize acts of expression on the basis of the ideas they advance or are interpreted as advancing. [...] but the history of censorship shows again and again that, once laws are on the books, ingenious and unexpected new uses are found for them. [...]
>
> Those entrusted with the review of the new security legislation should take the time to consider whether it is truly in the long-term interest of the nation to create a breach between the state and the intelligentsia on fundamental issues of liberal democracy.

So strongly did Coetzee feel about the political events in the US that he took the extreme step of turning down an honorary doctorate from Harvard. On 26 July 2004 he wrote to Professor Lawrence H. Summers, the president of Harvard:

> Thank you for your letter of June 22 informing me that the Governing Boards have voted to confer on me the honorary degree of Doctor of Letters. The University does me a great honor.
>
> You ask me to confirm that I will be able to participate in the Commencement ceremonies of June 9, 2005.

I regret that I am not at present in a position to do so, and will not be until November. To be candid—and this is not easy to say—I have decided that I will not be returning to the United States until there has been a change of regime and a return to the rule of law.

It pains me to inconvenience you and to involve Harvard University, with which I have had a rewarding relationship dating back to 1991, and where I have many good friends, in a matter which is in no sense the fault of the University.

Not all refusals were politically motivated. When, about a year later, the University of Brussels wanted to award Coetzee an honorary doctorate, he declined on the grounds of the exhaustion and inconvenience of a long flight from Australia to Europe, especially for just a short visit and that in the European winter.

In some instances, Coetzee allowed himself to turn down invitations to deliver lectures simply because, after a long career in academia, he was enjoying retirement too much to forfeit its benefits. An invitation from the local University of Adelaide to present a lecture as part of a series was turned down in October 2005, this time on the (manifestly inaccurate) grounds that he had never been good at lecturing: 'When I retired from academic life in 2002, I promised myself I would never give another lecture, and thus far I have kept my promise. I have no gifts as a lecturer, and—unlike natural-born lecturers—mistrust everything I say almost as soon as I have said it. So could I ask you to excuse me?'

Another recurring motif in Coetzee's refusals is his simple dislike of journalists. When an Australian journalist, embarked on an article on 'concepts of self-denial', asked Coetzee for an interview on the subject, his response was to the point if cryptic: 'Sorry, I don't have any thoughts about self-denial that would be worth immortalizing in print.' Asked in 2005 for a tribute to Nelson Mandela in case of the statesman's death, reflecting on the spirit and impact of this remarkable public life, he was equally terse: 'Writing an obituary of a person who is still alive—and whom I wish a long life—is something I am not prepared to do.' A documentary film on his life, too, was turned down: 'Thanks for the offer to put together a documentary about me and my work,' he wrote, 'but I couldn't think of anything more painful than participating in such a project. I'm not a good subject, I'm afraid. My life has been entirely uneventful, and I have absolutely no presence or competence as an actor.' His life in Adelaide was so tranquil that he wrote to Arijana

Božović, his Serbian translator: 'Do I have any news? I lead such a quiet life that I scratch my head trying to think of anything that might qualify. I went to a Christmas party last night where I met a woman, an immigrant from Germany, who said she had taught German in Australian schools but had given it up and wild horses would not drag her back. Australian children have no interest in learning foreign languages, she said, they are too far from anything foreign.'

Now and then he was prepared to answer a journalist's questions, such as those posed by e-mail by Adeeb Kamal for *Nizwa*, the leading cultural quarterly in Arabic. It was the first ever interview conducted with Coetzee in Arabic. He did, though, caution Kamal beforehand: 'In responding to your questions—and I hope you will forgive me for saying so—I have followed the principle that as much thought and effort should go into formulating the answer as went into formulating the question:'

1. What are the significant, deep moments in your life that encourage you to write?—I merely wish to write well and to do justice to my subject.

2. Why do you write?—This is not a question I ask myself.

3. Are you satisfied with your success or isolation?—I am not isolated. I suspect I have become more successful—that is to say, better known—than I deserve to be.

4. In a world full of conflict, what do you think is the writer's responsibility?—There are many kinds of writers. There is no single responsibility shared by all of them except to write as well as they can.

5. You don't enjoy fame; why?—Fame is for the future to decide. All that the present can offer is celebrity.

6. At the moment of hearing that you had been awarded the Nobel Prize, what were your thoughts and feelings?—I was incredulous.

7. You are living now in Adelaide; why? Is it a kind of exile?—I live in Adelaide because I like the city. Living in Adelaide is not a form of exile. Adelaide is my home.

8. What are the important books that have affected your life and your creative writing, especially the books that you read in your childhood?—I have outgrown the books that I read in my childhood. For thirty years, before I retired from academic life, I was a professor of literature. Many of the books that I read and studied

and discussed with students and wrote about—more books than I can name—have fed into my own writing.

9. What are the Arabic books that you love?—I regret to say I know nothing of Arabic literature beyond the novels of Naguib Mahfouz and the poems of Adonis.

10. Author Rian Malan describes you as: 'a man of almost monkish self-discipline and dedication. He does not drink, smoke or eat meat. He cycles vast distances to keep fit and spends at least an hour at his writing desk each morning, seven days a week. A colleague who has worked with him for more than a decade claims to have seen him laugh just once.' Is this an exaggeration?—I have met Rian Malan only once in my life. He does not know me and is not qualified to talk about my character.

11. What is your advice to the translators who want to translate your novels, especially Arabic translators?—Pay attention to the words on the page and to the shape of the sentences.

II

One day in November 2002, during his annual visit to Chicago, Coetzee was cycling next to the lake that borders the university campus for kilometres. It was bitterly cold, the lake was partly frozen, and the strong wind blew some of the water onto the road. The bicycle skidded, and Coetzee fell and broke his collar-bone. For a few months every movement was painful, and he wore his arm in a sling for more than a month. In January 2003 he wrote to a friend that the collar-bone was slowly on the mend, but that he still did not have the full use of his left arm. Everything, including writing, happened more slowly than before and he could write letters only with one hand by computer.[4]

Whether this incident was the direct inspiration for *Slow Man*, the first novel Coetzee undertook after settling in Adelaide, is difficult to say, but it must have had some impact on him. He started working on it on 13 July 2004 and completed the final text in December 2004, quite a short time span for him, even considering that he now, after his retirement as an academic and with his declining of invitations, had more time to devote to his creative work. That he must have worked exceptionally hard is clear from the fact that the manuscript[5] comprises no fewer than 25 versions of the text. Asked what he meant by the title, he replied on 4 February 2005: 'Besides the primary meaning of slow (as in to ride slowly), I had the following connotations in mind: (1) slow as in 'slow on the uptake,' 'slow to get the message,' not very perceptive; (2) slow as a euphemism for not very clever, stupid; the virtuous side of slowness, as in (3) Nietzsche, 'I am a teacher of slow reading'.

The opening of the novel is extremely dramatic. Paul Rayment—originally an immigrant from France, divorced, a retired photographer who has collected some valuable old photographs of Australian miners—is thrown from his bicycle by an approaching car in Magill Road in Adelaide:

> The blow catches him from the right, sharp and surprising and painful, like a bolt of electricity, lifting him up off the bicycle. *Relax!* he tells himself as he flies through the air (*flies through the air with the greatest of ease!*), and indeed he can feel his limbs go obediently slack. *Like a cat* he tells himself: *roll, then spring to your feet, ready for what comes next.* The unusual word *limber* or *limbre* is on the horizon too.[6]

Rayment suffers serious injuries, and his right leg has to be amputated above the knee. He recovers, but needs home care in his flat after the hospitalisation. The first nurse irritates him so insufferably with her references to the bedpan as the 'potty' and his penis as his 'willy' that he asks for a substitute. That he, who in the past could lead an independent existence, is now dependent on other people, makes him painfully aware of the tribulations and loneliness of age, the fragility of the body, and the limits of medical care. He finds it difficult to lead his diminished life; a prosthesis he finds abhorrent, in spite of the strong recommendations of his doctor and nurses.

After another few failed attempts, Rayment acquires the services of Marijana Jokić, a Croatian immigrant, who can dress his wound professionally, treat him like an adult, and help him to the toilet without embarrassing him. One day Marijana brings along her youngest daughter, Ljuba. Later she tells him about her son, Drago, who even though they can't afford it, wants to study at the imposing Wellington College in Canberra to gain admission to the Australian Defence Force. Because she fears that Drago, who has been given a motorbike by his father, will, with the recklessness of youth, risk his life, she arranges for him to visit so that Rayment can talk to him, show him what the cycle looks like after the accident, and make him aware of the dangers of a motorbike. The visits of Marijana's children bring home to Rayment his own childlessness. His concern for the Jokić family, and his growing love for Marijana, which he confesses to her, prompt him to offer to pay for Drago's training. He does not withdraw this offer when the boy steals one of his valuable sets of historic photos and replaces it with a bad imitation. He is also prepared to intercede when Blanka, the other Jokić daughter, is accused of shoplifting.[7]

To represent this dualism between Rayment's 'unsuitable' love for a married woman and his unselfish concern for the children, Coetzee employs a metaphor from Plato. The human being is represented by Plato as a chariot drawn by two horses: a white one and a black one, representing respectively reason and passion. Rayment remembers this depiction from the cover of a book he used to own:

> It showed a chariot drawn by two steeds, a black steed with flashing eyes and distended nostrils representing the base appetites, and a white steed of calmer mien, representing the less easily identifiable nobler passions. Standing in the chariot, gripping the reins, was a young man with a half-bared torso and a Grecian nose and a fillet around his brow, representing presumably the self, that which calls itself *I*.[8]

When Marijana becomes aware of his feelings for her, she at first stays away from Rayment's flat. At this point, at the beginning of Chapter 13, he is visited by Elizabeth Costello, the Australian novelist who in Coetzee's previous novel was invited to deliver a series of lectures on divergent subjects. She moves into his flat. It soon transpires that she knows the history of both Rayment and the Jokić family; her omniscience has the quality of a Greek chorus. With her 'pursuit of intuitions'[9] she is partly a manipulator (as in bringing the blind Marianna to his bed), and partly a fairy godmother: even though she at times irritates Rayment with her nosiness and her knowledge of his personal life and past, he sees her as 'a kind of life-force, guardian angel, or ministering Madonna'.[10] Christopher Hope calls her both 'mentor' and 'tormentor'; Shaun de Waal says Coetzee 'is in his element here, not only in handling the tensions of Rayment's "unsuitable passion" for Marijana, but in detailing the complications and psychological difficulties of a burden of care that often produces love as its consequence without a relation of love as its cause.'[11] De Waal also points out the fascinating variation on the master-servant relation that has been a dominant motif in Coetzee's fiction from his earliest novels, though the roles are reversed here.

Though many reviewers were of the opinion that the first part of *Slow Man* was exceptionally satisfying, showing Coetzee at his best, many found that the intrusion of Elizabeth Costello suspended the gripping realism of the opening and got the novel bogged down in philosophical speculation. According to Anita Brookner,[12] Elizabeth Costello breaks into Rayment's story, destroying the fiction of events by creating a new fictional situation. By repeating (with the change of a single word) the first sentence of the novel, she in effect becomes the author of Paul's tale, with the implication that he is no more than a character in her novel-in-progress. She is the unflattering mask of old age, companion to his own decrepitude. 'Costello,' Shaun de Waal writes, 'is a muse in reverse: rather than the object of beauty that inspires the artist, she is rather a subject of disgust and irritation, the artist who enters the text to urge her subject into a more assertive and exciting life.'[13] Adam Kirsch, in his review[14] of the book, is outspokenly critical; he finds Elizabeth Costello's questions 'laboriously posed' and less engaging than the relationship between Paul and Marijana in the first part of the novel. 'All Mr Coetzee finally accomplishes in *Slow Man,*' he writes, 'is to run a promising novel off the rails.' The tale of Rayment's tribulations in the first twelve chapters, however, is so gripping, simultaneously intelligent and amusing, that one gladly buys into his fictionality. Coetzee's language in this novel has acquired a new rhythm, a rich blend of the 'typically' Australian ('no worries') and, in Rayment's French-inflected diction, something more formal. But what is particulary striking is the speech of the Croatian Marijana: 'a rapid, approximate Australian-English with Slavic liquids and an uncertain command of *a* and *the*'.[15] These linguistic habits produce some hilarious moments, as when with evident pride she talks about her husband, who was famous in Croatia for his expertise, but who in Australia has been reduced to a mere mechanic:

'In Croatia, you know, Mr Rayment, my husband was famous man, sort of. You don't believe me? In all newspapers photographs of him. Miroslav Jokić and mechanical duck. On television'—with two fingers she makes walking motions in the air—'pictures of mechanical duck. Only man who can make mechanical duck walk, make noise like how you say *kwaak*, eat'—she pats her bosom—'other things too. Old, old duck. Come from Sweden. Come to Dubrovnik 1680, from Sweden. Nobody know how to fix it. Then Miroslav Jokić fix it perfect. One week, two week he is famous man in Croatia. But here'—she casts her eyes up to the heavens—'who cares? In Australia nobody hear of mechanical duck. Don't know what is it. Miroslav Jokić, nobody hear of him. Just auto worker. Is nothing, auto worker.'[16]

The often negative reception in the newspapers was balanced by more thoughtful essays on *Slow Man* by scholars such as Mike Marais, C. Kenneth Pellow, Derek Attridge and David Attwell. For Attwell the novel is in the first place about physical frailty and ageing, with caring as a sub-theme, but also very much about the relation between an author and his creations. 'Paul Rayment,' he writes, 'is being written into being by Elizabeth Costello, but he also resists her; in fact, her insistence that he take responsibility for the action, by acting on his desires and by "pushing the mortal envelope," as she puts it, would seem to allegorize the kind of negative capability on which a successful narrative would depend. Elizabeth is both predator and parasite, but she insists on Paul's taking charge.'[17] A further sub-theme of the novel, pointed out by Donald Powers, is the emigrant experience, in the case of both Marijana and Rayment, and the connection between emigration and writing.[18]

Personal responses from friends and associates were also on the whole favourable. Per Wastberg of the Swedish Academy congratulated Coetzee, in a letter of 11 February 2005, on the imminent novel that, according to his information, would be appearing in Swedish translation almost simultaneously with the British edition. He finds the news 'most exciting—also a relief that you do not belong to the ancient breed that took the Nobel Prize so seriously that they fell into lifelong silence'. Jonathan Lear wrote in an e-mail of 28 October 2005 that he was 'delighted and moved' by the book: 'Caritas, incarnation, redemption, the reality of those with whom we must live inside and outside—in the human situation, without an ounce of sentimentality.'

Slow Man was nominated for the Booker Prize for 2005, but it did not get onto the shortlist. It was, however, named by *The Globe and Mail* as one of the best books of 2005. Besides, sales in Britain and the US and the Netherlands were good.

III

A matter of public import in which Coetzee took an interest from the outset in Australia was animal rights. He associated himself with the Australian Association of Humane Research, and with the Oxford Centre for Animal Ethics in Britain.[19] He was also particularly active in Voiceless, an Australian organisation initiated by Brian Sherman, who invited Coetzee to take office in 2004. Voiceless works for the respectful and compassionate treatment of animals, and for public awareness of the conditions inflicted on animals. Where necessary, it also intervenes to alleviate suffering.

On 22 February 2007 an art exhibition was opened in the Sherman Gallery in Sydney entitled 'Voiceless: I feel therefore I am'. For this occasion Coetzee wrote a speech containing echoes of Elizabeth Costello's lectures in *The Lives of Animals*. He starts by pointing out that there is something badly amiss in the relations between humans and other animals. This dysfunctional relationship has in the last century or so taken the shape of the industrialisaton of animal farming. The food industry has reduced living animals to products for human consumption. Voiceless applies its energies mainly to combating this large-scale industrialisation, without ignoring other practices that could be deemed cruel—such as the use of animals in laboratory experiments, and the trade in wild animals or furs. There are people who know exactly what is happening on the factory farms, but who maintain that these practices are justified and that it is not necessary to effect any changes. And then there are people who are horrified when they contemplate the treatment of animals on the farms and at the abattoirs, but who arrange their lives so as to be buffered against thinking about it, and who leave their children in the dark about the slaughter. This large-scale slaughter is, according to Coetzee, a relatively recent phenomenon, and, like Elizabeth Costello, he does not scruple to relate it to the atrocities of the Second World War:

> The transformation of animals into production units dates back to
> the late nineteenth century, and since that time we have already
> had one warning on the grandest scale that there is something
> deeply, cosmically wrong with regarding and treating fellow beings

as mere units of any kind. This warning came to us so loud and clear that you would have thought it was impossible to ignore it. It came when in the middle of the twentieth century a group of powerful men in Germany had the bright idea of adapting the methods of the industrial stockyard, as pioneered and perfected in Chicago,[20] to the slaughter—or what they preferred to call the *processing*—of human beings.

Of course we cried out in horror when we found out about this. We cried: *What a terrible crime, to treat human beings like cattle! If we had only known beforehand!* But our cry should more accurately have been: *What a terrible crime, to treat human beings like units in an industrial process!* And that cry should have had a postscript: *What a terrible crime, come to think of it, to treat any living being like a unit in an industrial process!*

Voiceless, Coetzee continues, strives for the improvement of conditions in which animals must spend their lives, and in the long run for the elimination of factories on farms in which animals are destroyed. '[I]ts persuasive efforts,' he says, 'are directed at the vast majority of the public who know and don't know that there is something bad going on, something that stinks to high heaven. What is going on stinks so badly that most people don't really require a lot of persuading. The problem is to persuade people enough for them to take action in the way they run their lives.'

In the years after he joined Voiceless, Coetzee contributed, especially through interviews, public declarations and publications, to the struggle for animal rights. In *The Death of the Animal* (2009) he participated with, among others, Matthew Calarco, Harlain B. Miller and Cary Wolfe, in a dialogue led by Paola Calarco, the editor of the book, who in her introduction extends the notion of the non-human to such an extent as to render the somewhat belittling category of 'the animal' meaningless.[21]

In an interview with Anne Susskind in May 2004 for *The Bulletin*, Coetzee expressed himself vigorously on the mechanical processing of animals into food. Asked whether he was a vegetarian, he replied: 'Of course I don't (eat meat). It's a repulsive habit. I gave it up thirty years ago. God knows why it took me so long. I suppose I thought it was normal human behaviour.' Asked whether animals could have feelings, he reacted with some vehemence: 'I am impatient with questions that imply that creatures have to pass some kind of test concocted in a philosophy department before they can be permitted to live.' The modern economy, he said, is based on the mechanisation of the food supply. 'If that food supply includes what are euphemistically called animal products (as if pigs and cows sat diligently at the controls of the sausage machine) then the procedures for turning animals into food must be mechanized. In fact, to the extent that it is possible, not only the deaths of animals but their lives as well, from conception onwards, must be mechanized.' Asked what was wrong with the industry, Coetzee replied:

> The answer: everything. To begin with, it is obscene. No decent person wants to be associated with it. If you ask for proof, consider the fact that by tacit agreement we camouflage slaughterhouses and deny access to the public. Consider also the taboo on the word 'death' within the industry. Even though we are no longer a religious society, the aura of pollution is not quite dead and pollution certainly attaches to people who make a living spilling blood.
>
> As for vegetarianism, it is hard to understand why people should want to chew dead flesh, but then it is equally hard to understand why they should want to suck burning weeds. Yet they do. In both cases we confront a habit and even a craving. You can't ban it without causing a revolution.

A complete revolution in human attitudes would not, however, bring a magical solution:

> If I withdraw myself from the carnivore population, all that happens is that the industry makes a minuscule adjustment and 'produces' six chickens fewer per annum, and half a turkey, and two lambs, and so forth. That is to say, six fewer chickens are allowed to be born and to live their rather wretched six-week cycle and then to have their heads chopped off. Is the world a better place if those particular six chickens are never born? Do the six chickens, looking back over their brief lives, conclude that life has been a blessing or a curse? There is no way of answering these questions, there is not even a way of posing them without sounding ludicrous.
>
> The collective human decision to domesticate animals with an eye to slaughter has led to a warping of population sizes for which

there is now no remedy. If by some miracle the whole of mankind were suddenly to turn vegetarian, we would be left with billions of animals on our hands which were due to be slaughtered, animals which no 'farmer' would have a rational incentive for taking care of, and which we would as a matter of urgency have to sterilize to prevent them from producing yet more unwanted generations. That is the kind of bad world we have created around ourselves.

When Coetzee was invited to become one of the presidents of the British Royal Society for the Prevention of Cruelty to Animals, he declined:

> Your invitation does me honour, but I am afraid I must decline. As you may know, I do involve myself in animal causes. But it seems to me best that I spend my energies in assisting organizations and pressure groups whose goals I wholeheartedly support; also organizations and groups nearer home.
>
> For myself (and please do not take this as a criticism of the RSPCA, whose achievements I laud), I believe that our first goal ought to be to put a stop to, or at least raise doubts in people's minds about, practices of raising animals in order to kill them in the pride of life.

Coetzee was asked once whether he was a strict vegetarian, or a vegan. His reply betrays his usual impatience with labels:

> No, I'm not a vegan. In fact I'm not enamoured of the terms 'vegetarian' and 'vegan', which sounds like the names of faiths or philosophies. I don't eat dead animals but I do eat eggs (though less and less) and cheese, and wear leather. I can't produce a rationale for my behaviour, but I'm also suspicious of making reason the measure of all conduct.

When a journalist asked whether he fasted from time to time, Coetzee replied: 'I have never fasted voluntarily, but I do find the less I eat the better I feel. A sensation of airness.' And when asked why he should want to help animals, he gave a sharp, humorous reply: 'They were here on earth before we were. We are their guests. I'd like to persuade human beings to behave like good guests.'

IV

Coetzee's next novel, *Diary of a Bad Year*, was published in 2007: as usual, first in the Dutch translation (under the title *Dagboek van een slecht jaar*), before being issued several months later in London in the original English by Harvill Secker, the new imprint name of Secker & Warburg.

The central figure is a 72-year-old, internationally venerated, much-awarded writer, a sufferer from Parkinson's disease, and known only by his initials J.C. He was born in South Africa, but has been settled for years in a ground-floor flat in Sydney, Australia. There he is occupied in writing a contribution for a German publisher (Mittwoch Verlag in Berlin) to a collection of 'strong opinions', to which six eminent writers from all over the world will contribute their opinions on controversial topics of their choice, and lament all that is wrong in the modern world. J.C.'s contribution comprises thirty essays of varying length, dealing with subjects such as the origin of the state, democracy, terrorism (in particular 'Islamist terrorism' and the reactions of George W. Bush and Tony Blair to this) and controversial detention camps, such as the one at Guantánamo Bay. J.C. writes scathingly about the torture and humiliation suffered by inmates of this facility:

> Someone should put together a ballet under the title *Guantanamo, Guantanamo!* A corps of prisoners, their ankles shackled together, thick felt mittens on their hands, muffs over their ears, black hoods over their heads, do the dances of the persecuted and desperate. Around them, guards in olive-green uniforms prance with demonic energy and glee, cattle prods and billy-clubs at the ready. They touch the prisoners with the prods and the prisoners leap; they wrestle prisoners to the ground and shove the clubs up their anuses and the prisoners go into spasms. In a corner, a man on stilts in a Donald Rumsfeld mask alternately writes at his lectern and dances ecstatic little jigs.[22]

J.C. has strong opinions, too, on political life in Australia (with a sharp glance at John Howard, the prime minister at the time), and on the national feeling of shame at everything that can go awry in the modern state. The latter subject leads him straight to South Africa: 'The generation of white South Africans to which I belong, and the next generation, and perhaps the generation after that too, will go bowed under the shame of the crimes that were committed in their name.'[23]

But other matters too pass under J.C.'s critical scrutiny, such as the degeneration of universities into business ventures under the pressure of rationalisation; paedophilia, with reference to the Stanley Kubrick film *Lolita*; the slaughter of animals to provide food for humans; and divergent topics such as competition, mathematical problems, probability, invasions and plunder, Harold Pinter, music, tourism, authority in fiction and — as conclusion — life in the hereafter.

The reader familiar with Coetzee's life and works and the points of view he adopted in the preceding decade and more on burning issues, will be tempted to find points of contact with the J.C. of *Diary of a Bad Year*. Like *Boyhood* (1997) and *Youth* (2002), *Diary of a Bad Year* seems intended to be read autobiographically. Some details in the novel do accord with what we know of Coetzee's life, but by no means all. The protagonist is, like Coetzee, the author of *Waiting for the Barbarians* and of a book on censorship,[24] but he lives in Sydney, not Adelaide, and was born in 1934, not 1940 like Coetzee.

Furthermore, the essays J.C. writes are skilfully placed within a fictional narrative frame that orders the whole into a novel, albeit a novel deviating from the normal expectations of most novel readers. In the block in which J.C. lives, he one day comes across Anya, a young woman of Philippine descent, who shares a flat on the top floor with her friend, Alan, a financial adviser. From their first meeting J.C. is fascinated by this woman, who, apart from being very attractive, assumes that he is from South America and addresses him as Señor C:

My first glimpse of her was in the laundry room. It was mid-morning on a quiet spring day and I was sitting, watching the washing go around, when this quite startling young woman walked in. Startling because the last thing I was expecting was such an apparition; also because the tomato-red shift she wore was so startling in its brevity.[25]

That the coquettish Anya, who wiggles her behind provocatively for him, charms J.C. from the start, is evident from his description of her 'white slacks that showed off a derrière so near perfect as to be angelic' and his prayer: 'God, grant me one wish before I die, I whispered; but then was overtaken with shame at the specificity of the wish, and withdrew it.'[26]

Because Señor C's Parkinsonism prevents him from typing, he hires Anya at a highly lucrative rate to transcribe his 'strong opinions' for the German publisher, which he writes down with a shaky hand or otherwise reads into a dictaphone. As in *Elizabeth Costello* and *Slow Man*, then, the protagonist is debilitated by age and disease, and starting to lose his grip on things. As Elizabeth Costello is assisted by her son and Paul Rayment by Marijana, J.C. is sustained in his loneliness and illness by Anya, who apart from the transcriptions also at times tidies the flat. In many respects the novel provides no flattering self-portrait of its main character. Like Rayment in *Slow Man* and David Lurie in *Disgrace*, J.C. is enthralled by a younger woman, although there is in his case never any possibility of an intimate relationship.

The evolving intrigue is further complicated by Alan's many objections to Anya's work and his suspicion that the author is merely using the project as a cover for his erotic ambitions. Alan, however, is clearly something of a white-collar thug, as he proves by loading software onto Senor C's computer to enable him to access his investments for his own profit. This scheme ultimately causes a breakdown in Alan's relationship with Anya, expedited by Alan's drunken and insulting behaviour during a disastrous dinner in J.C.'s flat.

Contrary to expectations aroused by the title, *Diary of a Bad Year* has nothing in common with an ordinary diary, or even with literary diaries like Defoe's *A Journal of the Plague Year* or Gogol's *Diary of a Madman*. The intrigue of the book is instead a free variation on familiar clichés in literature: the eternal romantic triangle as the basis of a conflict; the fascination of an older man with a younger woman; the underhand scheming of the younger man to do the older man out of his money; and the deathbed confession at the end, complete with an allusion in the novel's last sentence to Horatio's closing speech in *Hamlet*: 'Good night, sweet Prince, / And flights of angels sing thee to thy rest!'[27] The unusual construction of the book, however, presents these well-worn situations in a novel way. Each page contains two, later three, different texts or layers typographically separated from each other by horizontal lines, at times subtly interconnecting. In the top section the reader is given JC's essays, underneath which is a section in which he is speaking in his own person or talking to Anya. Later Anya joins the text in the third layer, sometimes in conversation with Alan. Anya is often responsible for comic effects in the tale, and is at times critical of the writings of Señor C. At her prompting he follows the series of 'strong opinions' with a 'Second Diary' in which he expresses milder opinions and talks more gently or more personally about, among other things, his father, 'mass emotion', 'the hurly-burly of politics', 'the erotic life', 'idea for a story', 'the classics', 'the writing life' and 'boredom'. The series ends on tributes to Bach and Dostoevsky.

Whereas the book at first seems like a gallimaufry of opinions on all sorts of topical and other issues, it becomes, through the interweaving of the texts and by the over-arching structure, a gripping tale. Basically *Diary of a Bad Year* is a hybrid of essay and fiction. Elements of the traditional novel, such as character, background and plot, are subordinated to a metafictional approach. In so far as there is a plot, it is located in Anya's reactions to her employer and especially in Alan's designs on Señor C's money. The design is such that the reader cannot remain passive and must decide how to read the book from page to page with its different voices and layers. As in *Elizabeth Costello*, but then in a very different way, Coetzee here adopts the technique of embedding non-fictional content in fictional form. The ageing writer confesses to Anya that he no longer has the perseverance to write a novel: 'To write a novel you have to be like Atlas, holding up a whole world on your shoulders and supporting it there for months and years while its affairs work themselves out. It is too much for me as I am today.'[28] In one of the second group of essays Señor C writes that earlier, when he was still a professor of literature, he had imagined that he was a novelist, not a lecturer. Now the critics want to persuade him that he's actually never been a novelist, but 'a pedant who dabbles in fiction'.[29] He continues, in terms that irresistibly link JC with John Coetzee, for all the self-evident differences:

> In public life the role I play nowadays is that of distinguished figure (distinguished for what no one can quite recall), the kind of notable who is taken out of storage and dusted off to say a few words at a cultural event (the opening of a new hall in the art gallery; the prize-giving at an eisteddfod) and then put back in the cupboard. An appropriately comic and provincial fate for a man who half a century ago shook the dust of the provinces off his feet and sallied forth into the great world.[30]

In his review of *Diary of a Bad Year* James Wood says that the novel assumes a 'daring form'. 'Señor C's essays,' he continues, 'occupy the bulk of each page, more or less, but running beneath them, like the news crawl on a TV screen, are what read like short entries by Señor C and by Anya, which offer a running commentary on the developing relationship of employer and employee, and which convey the plot of the novel, such as it is.'[31] From the manuscript, still in possession of the author, it appears that Coetzee initially wrote only the 'essays' ('Strong opinions' and 'Second Diary') and only then the lower sections.[32] The general typographical layout bears some resemblance to the novel *Menuet* (1948) by the Flemish writer Louis Paul Boon, in which the consecutive narratives of the three narrators are accompanied by a series of newspaper reports appearing at the foot of each page and relating intertextually to the main text.[33] Eric Paul Meljac relates *Diary of a Bad Year* to a short story by Gabriel Josipovici, 'Mobius the stripper: A topological exercise'. In this story Josipovici also makes use of horizontal lines to divide up the pages: in the upper section the tale of the 'stripper' is told, while the lower section deals with the writer conveying the tale of Mobius.[34] Another fictional parallel is suggested by Jeff Simon, who compares Coetzee's novel with Nabokov's complex *Pale Fire*, on which Coetzee wrote an essay early in his career: 'Just as *Pale Fire* is a long "fictional" poem by fictional poet John Shade and then gloriously lunatic academic commentary by a fiction-within-a-fiction-within-a-fiction named Charles Kinbote, *Diary of a Bad Year* is a counterpoint of voices on every page.'[35]

Despite reviewers who were obviously unhappy with the direction of Coetzee's novels since *Elizabeth Costello, Diary of a Bad Year* received a predominantly favourable press. Christopher Tayler in *The Guardian* of 1 September 2007 expressed admiration for the humour and the masterly technical control: 'Funnier than anything else he's written, if sometimes in a rather donnish way, it eventually becomes unexpectedly moving, offering surprises while avoiding a final thunderclap with the restraint that Coetzee's readers have learned to expect.' Justin Cartwright, in *The Independent on Sunday* of 2 September 2007, is full of praise for the book, though he may perhaps draw too direct a line from the fictional events to the writer's life: 'It is a revealing book, a wonderful book of essays, a subtle and touching near love story, and an autobiography, an extraordinary account of John Coetzee's deepest preoccupations and beliefs. In the gradually revealed loyalty and decency of Anya, Coetzee seems to suggest rather regretfully that he has neglected love and warmth in his own life.'

In the *Chicago Sun-Times* of 23 December 2007, Vikram Johri writes: 'What is rather fascinating about the idea of three strands running on one page is that it allows us to appreciate Coetzee's genius better. On the top is a truly academic enterprise, lofty in its studied concern. At the center is the lonely rambling of a writer who is losing his gifts. And at the bottom, the rushed monologue of youth, gravid with its concomitant impertinence.' He continues: 'It must therefore be asked: What is Coetzee's métier? Why does he write? The disaffected nature of his prose gives us clues to a will for silence, a preponderant instinct for quietude. Yet, *Diary of a Bad Year* is a loud book, filled with both verve for life and the enervating prospect of death. It's one of his more approachable reads, and it is a mark of Coetzee's talent that he is able to enmesh the philistine with the profound with such enviable ease.' Claire Messud, in *The Boston Globe* of 30 December 2007, is particularly taken with the novel's conclusion, in which Anya transcends her initial superficiality and grows into a complex and compassionate individual: 'The strange peace that she and J.C. are able to reach together is perhaps a first for Coetzee: It may not be funny, but it is generous, and loving, and comes suspiciously close to a happy ending.' David Marcus in *Dissent* of Winter 2009 calls *Diary of a Bad Year* Coetzee's most explicitly political novel: 'Coetzee is not only capturing the anxious discontent of his own "late" style but that of many of his contemporary intellectuals. This is an era overwhelmed by political failure—one in which "the outrage and the shame is so great," writes John C, "that all calculation, all prudence, is overwhelmed and one must act, that is to say, speak"—and if this novel comes to us as overwrought and, on occasion, exhausting, then it is a consequence of our own alienating, polemical selves.'

In June 2008 it was announced that *Diary of a Bad Year* had been awarded the M-Net Literary Award for English fiction. Apparently the jury was initially not unanimous in this decision, judging by an article by Michael Titlestad in *Safundi: The Journal of South African and American Studies*, 10: 4, October 2009. What bothered some members of the jury was whether the novel could be judged independently of Coetzee's whole oeuvre, and whether Coetzee, as an Australian citizen (though he had retained his South African passport) was eligible for the award. There was also the question whether *Diary of a Bad Year*, with its Australian setting and problematics, could really be regarded as a 'South African' novel.

These considerations, which are strictly speaking irrelevant to a purely literary estimate of the novel, were, however, just a smokescreen for personal animosity ('But he is so cold!'). Titlestad writes:

> The reasons for this dislike are difficult to fathom (he is, after all, South Africa's greatest literary asset). His emigration is probably the dominant cause of the hostility. South Africans are quick to feel betrayed. I have heard the opinion expressed often enough that one who has capitalized (symbolically, economically, and politically) on the wretchedness of South African history should at least stay the course. [...] Another reason for the animosity is that Coetzee has famously refused to participate in anything resembling literary celebrity culture. [...] He is, in fact, a sponsor's nightmare: his absence from award ceremonies, no matter how philosophically or psychologically motivated, presents as a critique of the entire economy of prestige.

Nevertheless, with some persuasion from Titlestad, who could not countenance the neglect of an important work on such unliterary grounds, *Diary of a Bad Year* was duly awarded the M-Net Prize. Coetzee did not, however, travel to South Africa to receive the prize money. On the evening of the ceremony it was handed to the South African representative of his American publisher.

CHAPTER 17

'THE DANCE OF THE PEN'

I

After retiring from UCT and settling in Adelaide, John Coetzee became a far more relaxed person. At UCT he had often been embroiled in petty departmental squabbles that drained his energy. He at times had to attend departmental meetings that clashed with his practice of devoting the early hours of the day to creative labour. In Adelaide he could stick to his routine and rhythm, even though, judging by the volume of his e-mails—sometimes 60 per day—which he conscientiously replied to, he was not cut off from other people and the literary world. Although he increasingly turned down invitations to deliver lectures or make a public appearance, he was still prepared to advise younger writers and to assist publishers by writing a recommendation as cover copy for a new publication.

In Cape Town he had disliked gardening and for recreation preferred, apart from cycling, walking on Table Mountain or attending big sporting events (cricket and rugby). On the plot in Adelaide Hills, where he and Dorothy settled, he developed into a dedicated and obsessive gardener, and enjoyed sweeping up the bluegum bark in the afternoons. Like his characters Cruso and Friday in *Foe*, he undertook projects like building small terraces and making plantings. Dorothy could notice a change in John since his arrival in Australia. At dinners and parties he joked and jested. He was a happy man, visibly so to all who came into contact with him.[1]

Yet there was still, so many years after the terrible events of April 1989, an undercurrent of grief over the death of his son, Nicolas. An added concern was the situation and health of his daughter, Gisela, who had remained in Cape Town and was living in a house in Observatory. At UCT, where she was enrolled as a B.A. student from 1988 to 1990, she had generally fared well, passing with distinctions in English and in African Literature. After a year overseas she completed her B.A.

Honours in English in 1992 with an aggregate of 72 per cent.[2] Both she and John saw to it that she did not follow any of his courses, but Dorothy Driver, at the time also a professor in the Department of English, found Gisela to be one of the most talented and brilliant students she had ever had. Gisela, however, lacked the discipline of her father and at times lost control of her affairs. She also had something fatalistic in her make-up. At an early age she had wished that she had never been born. Later she thought that she should really have died, rather than Nicolas, whose death had shattered her. In a strange way she felt responsible for the death of her mother and her brother: her mother because during her last illness she had not given her enough attention and had been absent from her deathbed, her brother because at the time of his death she had had a bad relationship with him. In a letter of 15 June 1992, John Coetzee wrote to his friend Howard Wolf in Buffalo that Gisela was wondering why she was bothering to study literature. 'I have the delicate task of reassuring her,' he writes,

> freeing her (if that is possible) from the feeling that she is under an obligation to emulate me, that she is at liberty to do with her life whatever she wishes, without at the same time tipping the balance the other way and insisting that what I have staked out as my territory is mine alone, and she must not trespass on it. Her boyfriend dropped by the other day to have a heart-to-heart talk with me, something he has never done before. He told me Gisela tells him she is the one who should have died. Nicolas was smarter, more ambitious, etc. Subtext: there is a weight of expectation on her which she can't fulfil. What nonsense. Children find it so hard to accept that they are loved absolutely and unconditionally. (Not only children!) Or do we kid ourselves when we claim to love absolutely and unconditionally?

In her twenties Gisela only briefly had permanent employment—at Exclusive Books, first in Hillbrow in Johannesburg and later in Claremont, Cape Town. She developed epilepsy in her early thirties, which proved difficult to control and was now the victim of the same ailment that plagued Coetzee's much-admired Dostoevsky all his life.

Gisela's epilepsy gave rise to agoraphobia,[3] which led her to a hermit's existence. On 16 November 2004 Coetzee wrote to Catherine Lauga du Plessis: '[Gisela] is not flourishing. She is suffering from severe agoraphobia and does not leave the house. Admittedly there are many people in South Africa too frightened to leave the safety of the house, but I believe her condition is clinical.' The epileptic seizures persisted. During one seizure in April 2004 she broke a leg. In another seizure shortly afterwards she broke the other leg, so badly that she had to be operated on and had to spend a long time in the orthopaedic section of the hospital. It was established that she had a very fragile bone structure as a consequence of osteoporosis, a disease common in older people but rarely afflicting a person in her thirties. The second bad break crippled her, making it very difficult for her to get by without a wheelchair or walking frame. On top of all this, she found that when she tried to walk she lost her balance, a symptom of the epileptic condition and its treatment, not a consequence of the fall. To walk, she now had to use both a stick and a walking frame. She also developed a problem with her vision: she had lost the capacity to judge distances, making it very difficult for her to cross a street, not being able to tell how far an approaching car was from her.[4] John wrote to his friend Jonathan Lear: '2005 was a bit of a nightmare for [Gisela]. She spent three spells in hospital, two for a compound fracture of her left leg, the third after trauma caused during an epileptic seizure. Her life is complicated by a destructive home life (with a man with whom she fights) and alcohol.' If she could be persuaded to come and spend some time with him in Adelaide, her condition might improve: 'I can't hope to bring her health, but I can at least feed her properly for a while and introduce a little placidity into her life.'

As with Nicolas, who had also been mixed up with drink and drugs, Gisela's circumstances deteriorated, and she had to be admitted to a rehabilitation centre for alcoholics. Did the two Coetzee children perhaps inherit genes from their parents making them vulnerable to alcohol abuse? At one stage Jack Coetzee, John's father, had regularly over-indulged in alcohol, and Cecil Jubber, Philippa's brother, was an alcoholic.[5] With Nicolas dead and Gisela in such straits, the conclusion of *Waiting for the Barbarians*, with its playing children presaging a certain hope for the future, becomes doubly devastating.

John Coetzee visited Cape Town in October 2005 to assess the situation for himself. On 7 October 2005 he wrote to Arijana Božović: 'I have just arrived back from South Africa. I was there on a one-week visit, mainly to see my daughter and try to persuade her there is at least one person in the world who cares whether she lives or dies. She is in a bad state, not helped by a bad "marriage", but is beginning to walk again, albeit tentatively.' On 10 October he writes to her again:

> I got back from Cape Town only a few days ago, where I spent much of my time with Gisela. She is in a bad way, physically and psychologically. She has been either on her back or in a wheelchair for nearly six months, and there has been a lot of muscle wasting. She can take a few tottering steps at a time, but her balance is not good and the pressure soon gets to be painful. She is also flailing around rather helplessly with all the medications that have been prescribed, which she feels obscurely are not good for her. But she doesn't have the expertise to come off medication, particularly medication that affects her neurological state, successfully. She is also in a state of childish rebellion against her doctors. She had various medical appointments to which I was going to ferry her, but then she had a freak accident at home, resulting in a huge and unsightly cut across her face, and cancelled everything. So I don't think I did much good.

And on 21 November 2005 he reports another accident:

> Bad news from Cape Town. While alone at home, Gisela had a severe epileptic seizure and began to vomit blood. She also fell, smashing her face (four teeth lost) and breaking a collar-bone. She is still in hospital. She is very weak, suffering from cirrhosis of the liver and undergoing alcohol withdrawal symptoms. She needs two different kinds of care: post-operative nursing and controlled rehabilitation from alcohol dependency. No one I am aware of offers this combination and she makes everything more difficult by fighting against the second.' John wrote to Jonathan Lear: 'I'm hoping to bring Gisela out on a visit to Adelaide later this month.'

Gisela visited Adelaide for about a month, but after her return had to be admitted for care to an institution in Wynberg. With her strong will to independence, she returned to her home in Observatory, in the face of her father's opposition, with a carer who visited her only a few days a week. On Monday, 6 July 2006, while alone at home, she suffered another epileptic seizure and incurred serious head injuries. She was found only a day later, and taken in an unconscious state to the intensive care unit of Groote Schuur Hospital. Two operations were done on her, but the doctors were initially not able to stop the bleeding. A third operation had to be performed, with complications that prolonged the critical condition. She emerged from the coma only a fortnight later, able to follow movement with her eyes and react with a light pressure of her hand when asked to do so. She was still disoriented and in a very weakened state, connected to a ventilator.[6] On 13 August John Coetzee, who had flown to Cape Town immediately to assist her, wrote in an e-mail:

> Gisela is still in Groote Schuur, in the neurology ward, but she is out of danger. At one stage it seemed she might be paralysed, but fortunately that is not so.
>
> It is not yet clear how much brain damage she has suffered. She is able to speak, but her mental state seemed confused.[7]

Since then Gisela's condition has improved miraculously. She was placed in an institution in Mowbray where she received the care she needed. Fortunately there was no permanent brain damage, and at the beginning of January 2011 she was able to move back to her home in Observatory, with a carer coming in from time to time to help her.

II

Apart from the worry and concern about Gisela's condition, John Coetzee started to experience health problems of his own. In 2007 — the 'bad year' of the title of his second 'Australian' novel — he was treated for prostate cancer. In 2010 he received radiation, which relieved the condition.[8]

The anxiety over his state of health was compounded in February 2009 when John Coetzee learnt that his brother David, who was living in Washington with his wife and two sons, and with whom he had a close relationship, had been diagnosed with a mesothelioma, an extremely aggressive cancer attacking the pleura. Because the disease had been discovered at a late stage, the prognosis was very bad. David received radiation and then intense chemotherapy, but he had little energy and was in constant pain. He was given morphine for the pain, which meant that he was fully conscious only part of the time. Despite his condition, he maintained his cheerful demeanour and humour. John visited his brother in May 2009, but David's condition was hopeless, and he died on 19 January 2010, at home, with his wife, Akwe Amosu, and his two sons, Sam and Corin, by his bedside. When it became clear the end was near, John flew to Washington again to say goodbye to his brother, who died shortly after John caught the plane back to Adelaide.[9] In the first stanza of the poem 'Descent' from her collection *Not Goodbye* Akwe Amosu alludes to the last meeting of the two brothers:

> Two days before, your brother
> read your gaunt reflection
> and said you looked handsome
> but you were changing by the hour,
> shedding everything you didn't
> need any more, like your face.[10]

Although prostate cancer is incurable, with proper care the patient can live for years. The diagnosis of 2007 and the medical treatment did make a difference to John Coetzee's life, but his energy levels and industriousness have not been affected. He is still able to keep to his rigorous daily programme, and devotes at least a few hours every morning to his writing. There is no quenching his creative drive. 'I follow the dance of the pen,'[11] he wrote in 1994 in *The Master of Petersburg*. And the dance carries on.

III

In the novels that Coetzee published since settling in Australia, the protagonist in all three cases is an elderly person beset with age-related ailments and infirmities. Elizabeth Costello is sixty-six, and has with the years become a bit frail, incapable of undertaking the demanding lecturing trips all over the world without the help of her son. Paul Rayment in *Slow Man* is on the eve of a comfortable retirement when he is run down on his bicycle by a young man in a car. Losing one leg as a result, he henceforth has to lead the life of an invalid, dependent on the care of others. In *Diary of a Bad Year* the central character suffers from Parkinson's disease, and is reliant on the services of Anya to transcribe his writings.

The progression of debilitation in this series of characters is striking. Coetzee takes these 'intimations of mortality' even further in *Summertime* (2009). The central figure is the late author J.M. Coetzee, whose biography an English biographer, one Vincent, wants to write. He intends to concentrate on the period 1972–1975, the years when the late John, having had to leave the US under a cloud, is living with his father in a dilapidated house in Tokai, trying to make a living by giving private lessons in English to strangers. To flesh out his biography, Vincent interviews various people whom John knew at this stage of his life: Julia, a psychotherapist now living in Ontario but at the time his neighbour and occasional lover; Margot, a cousin who was often on the family farm, Voëlfontein, and for whom he developed a certain affection; Adriana, a Brazilian dancer he was in love with, though she initially suspected him of harbouring more than schoolmasterly feelings for her daughter, to whom he was giving English lessons; Martin, who had been a fellow-candidate for a lectureship at UCT, but who shortly afterwards left South Africa permanently; and Sophie, a colleague in the French department at UCT, with whom John co-taught a course in African literature—he in anglophone writers, she in francophone.

The biographer is thus concentrating on a phase of John's youth when he settled in Cape Town after a period of study and lecturing in the US. In the subtitle *Summertime* is described as *Scenes from Provincial Life*, marking it as part of a trilogy with *Boyhood* and *Youth*. A conspicuous feature of *Summertime* is the concatenation of different narrative techniques. Whereas the linear narratives of *Boyhood* and *Youth* are entrusted to a single voice, the biographer in *Summertime* is seldom the speaker, his task being shouldered mainly by his interviewees. The first part of the novel, 'Notebooks 1972–5', and the last are made up of fragments from a diary kept by the dead author. In the first section all the entries are dated, whereas the five entries in the concluding section are undated. The entries are frequently interrupted with italicised phrases such as '*To be expanded*', '*Avoid pushing*', '*Theme to carry further*', etc., suggesting that the author had intended to use the diary fragments as building blocks for some future creative project. This is confirmed when the biographer, in reply to Julia's question as to the meaning and authorship of the italicised sections, replies: 'Coetzee wrote them himself. They are memos to himself, written in 1999 or 2000, when he was thinking of adapting those particular entries for a book.'[12] What at first would seem to be mere notes from a diary, then, are transformed by later additions into pointers towards later expansion by the dead writer, and thus a rough copy, a text-in-the-making betraying a certain provisionality and incompleteness. The incompleteness is deceptive, because what the reader gets—paradoxically—is a complete text of which the apparent provisionality is part of the whole.

Also in the interviews the reader is at times faced with a complex chain of narrative methods. What he finds on paper is not always an exact copy of what the informant told the prospective biographer, because in his transcriptions the biographer sometimes takes such liberties as to verge on distortion and misrepresentation, to be indignantly rejected by the informants. Thus the whole interview with Margot, as the biographer confesses at the beginning of this section, is a rewriting as much as a transcription, with the aim of turning it into an unbroken narrative, at times by adding 'fictitious' dialogue. The discrepancy between what Margot really told Vincent and what he transcribed conceals the 'real' events. The relation between events and distortions, facts and fiction, truth and lies, becomes a central factor in the structure of the novel.

Summertime thus differs radically from *Boyhood* and *Youth* in that here there is no direct narrative, only a complexity of voices all simultaneously telling the story of John at this time of his life. In his review of *Summertime* Patrick Denman Flanery writes:

> Rather, it is an assemblage of texts: dated and undated fragments from the fictional Coetzee's notebooks; and five interviews with people who knew him in that period, conducted by a young English biographer, known only as Mr Vincent. Vincent has assembled the fragments and transcripts but not rendered them into a final, fixed narrative form; *Summertime* must thus be described as a fictional biography in the process of becoming—one focused on the years in which its fictionalized subject was himself becoming a writer. Through the notebook fragments and interviews, we see John struggle with two major obstacles: how to reconcile his cultural, intellectual and ethical attitudes with the reality of living in apartheid-era South Africa, a country that seems emphatically philistine and ideologically bankrupt; and how to have meaningful intimate relationships with women. [...]
>
> *Summertime*'s shifty position between biography and fiction becomes a powerful analogy for Coetzee's difficulties positioning himself in the world; it is as we struggle to get to grips with its

mixture of disclosure and secretiveness that we come closest to him. And precisely as we fail to pin him down, we feel sure that this trilogy has earned its place at the heart of contemporary literature.[13] The relation between fact and fiction in *Summertime* touches upon the whole question of what truth value the novel may be taken to have, and what application it has to the life of the actual writer J.M. Coetzee. An important key to the character of the fictional dead author, but also to the form that autobiography assumes in *Summertime*, is to be found in the biographer's words to Sophie: 'What Coetzee writes there cannot be trusted, not as a factual record—not because he was a liar but because he was a fictioneer. In his letters he is making up a fiction of himself for his correspondents; in his diaries he is doing much the same for his own eyes, or perhaps for posterity. As documents they are valuable, of course; but if you want the truth you have to go behind the fictions they elaborate and hear from people who know him directly, in the flesh.'[14]

Although *Summertime* forms part of an autobiographical trilogy, it becomes, more extremely than either *Boyhood* or *Youth,* a subversion of the genre, in that the narrative strategies and content shift generic boundaries. The reader simply cannot accept the information supplied about the late John at face value, and anybody who reads it as 'truth' will have been gulled. For instance, Coetzee did after his return to South Africa live in Tokai for a while, but—contrary to what the novel would have us believe—with his wife, Philippa, and their two children, never with his father. His father was not in 1972–1975 a widower, but married to Vera, who only died in 1985. Coetzee did as a young student at UCT teach struggling scholars to supplement his income, but in mathematics, not in English as the Adriana section would have it. He was indeed in 1971 a candidate for a vacant lectureship in English at UCT, along with Jonathan Crewe, upon whom the character of Martin is vaguely modelled, and who in 1974 wrote an important essay on *Dusklands* in *Contrast*; but contrary to *Summertime*'s account, both were appointed, not just Martin. The cousin called Margot in *Summertime*, but by her real name, Agnes, in *Boyhood*, never spent a night in a bakkie in the Koup near Voëlfontein with Coetzee, and he never intended to buy his father a house in Merweville.[15] And, of course, John Coetzee is not dead, but, in spite of advancing years, still labouring energetically in his house in Adelaide, Australia.

The title of the novel recalls George Gershwin's Broadway hit of 1935 from *Porgy and Bess*. The first two verses of the song go as follows:

> Summertime,
> And the livin' is easy
> Fish are jumpin'
> And the cotton is high
>
> Your daddy's rich
> And your mamma's good lookin'
> So hush little baby
> Don't you cry ...[16]

Any possible allusion to the Gershwin song must have been ironically intended, as this phase in John's life, as represented in the novel, was hardly a time of carefree youth. The solitary John of *Summertime* reminds one rather of Willem Temeer, the main character in Marcellus Emants's *Een nagelaten bekentenis* that Coetzee translated as *A Posthumous Confession*. In *Summertime* we are given a negative self-portrait, a stripping bare of the self, an attempt through a variety of perspectives to explain why the late John made such a cold-blooded impression on people. The interviews take place in different contexts, but ultimately the subject remains unexplained and unsolved, his essential self never revealed. Literature has seldom known such an example of authorial self-disgust as this embodiment of the person of J.M. Coetzee.

Apart from the near-brutal honesty with which the protagonist is presented here,[17] the reader is enthralled by the essentially unknowable subject that the biographer tries in vain to capture — also an unambiguous warning to any real-life biographer who might want to trace the life of J.M. Coetzee.

Summertime contains some of the finest prose and often also of the most hilarious situations in Coetzee's oeuvre. As in his other works, Coetzee makes liberal use of literary references and allusions, such as to John Keats's 'Ode to a nightingale' ('My heart aches, and a drowsy numbness pains / My sense, as though of hemlock I had drunk');[18] Samuel Beckett's *Waiting for Godot* ('Given the existence of a personal God ...');[19] and Robert Herrick's 'Upon Julia's clothes':[20]

When as in silks my Julia goes,
Then, then, methinks, how sweetly flowes
That liquefaction of her clothes.

Next, when I cast mine eyes and see
That brave vibration each way free;
O how that glittering taketh me![21]

The playful approach seems to lend a certain hilarity to the whole representation, but it could also be, as Thomas Jones has suggested, 'an elegant request that the sum of Coetzee's existence as a public figure should be looked for only in his writing, and ample evidence, once again, why that request should be honoured'.[22] Two reviewers traced interesting literary and historical connections to *Summertime*. Geordie Williamson wrote: 'Like Philip Larkin, whose poem "Posterity" is written from the posthumous viewpoint of a creative artist imagining his biographer at work, and who takes the opportunity to mockingly construct his own epitaph, Coetzee's death frees him from the old constraints. Not only does Coetzee dose himself with self-ridicule, he also permits his self-construction some naked displays of emotion.'[23] James Meek suggested: 'One way of reading *Summertime* is as a confession, an acknowledgment to women Coetzee has loved [...] The Byron in John pulls him towards women and engagement in worthy causes, the Jesus in him pulls him away. "His life project was to be gentle," says Julia of John, but goes on to say that this was why she couldn't stay with him.'[24]

In his review Tim Parks writes:

It is a teasing and surprisingly funny book, at once as elaborately elusive and determinedly confessional as ever autobiography could be. If *Boyhood* and *Youth* were remarkable for Coetzee's use of the third person (the author declining to identify with his younger self) and the present tense (a narrative device more commonly associated with fiction than memoir), *Summertime* takes both distancing and novelizing a step further. Despite our seeing Coetzee's name on the cover and hence assuming the author alive and well, we are soon asked to believe that he is now dead, the book being made up of five interviews conducted by [a ...] biographer who is speaking to people he presumes were important to the writer during the years 1972–1975.[25]

André Brink found it one of Coetzee's 'unforgettable works': 'This book would in its own right have been worthy of a Nobel Prize.'[26]

Summertime was shortlisted for the Booker Prize in 2009 and for the Commonwealth Prize in 2010, but won neither award. It did receive, in Australia, the Queensland Premier's Literary Award and the Christina Stead Prize, the latter worth around £19 000. And in 2011 Coetzee's autobiographical trilogy was published in a single volume by Harvill Secker as *Scenes from Provincial Life: I Boyhood II Youth III Summertime*.

IV

In the years since being awarded the Nobel Prize, John Coetzee has kept up his contributions to *The New York Review of Books*—with reviews, for instance, of Norman Mailer's *The Castle in the Forest* (February 2007) and *The Dogs & the Wolves* by Irène Némirovsky (November 2008). Apart from his lucid prose, which could serve as an example to many contemporary critics, with their feeble grasp of their medium and their jargon-encumbered utterances, his essays are notable for their incisive judgements.

He also revisited Afrikaans poetry, in a translation, published in *Poetry: The Translation Issue*, 190: 1, April 2007, of Ina Rousseau's 'Eden', the opening poem in her collection *Die verlate tuin* (1954):

> Somewhere in Eden, after all this time,
> does there still stand, abandoned, like
> a ruined city, gates sealed with grisly nails,
> the luckless garden?
>
> Is sultry day still followed there
> by sultry dusk, sultry night,
> where on the branches sallow and purple
> the fruit hangs rotting?
>
> Is there still, underground,
> spreading like lace among the rocks
> a network of unexploited lodes,
> onyx and gold?

Through the lush greenery
their wash echoing afar
do there still flow the four glassy streams
of which no mortal drinks?
Somewhere in Eden, after all this time,
does there still stand, like a city in ruins,
forsaken, doomed to slow decay,
the failed garden?

Whereas most commentators in the past had read this poem purely in terms of the age-old Judaeo-Christian myth of the Lost Paradise, Coetzee also related it, in the short discussion accompanying the translation, to the garden that the first Dutch settlers at the Cape established as refreshment post for the ships en route to the East. His interpretation thus connects with motifs that he developed in *White Writing*, reading the poem as Rousseau's deeply pessimistic consideration of a failed enterprise: 'the failed garden, the failed colony, seen in backward view from some unspecific future date when it not only lies abandoned but has almost receded into the mists of the past, contradicts absolutely the vision of a white Christian South Africa enduring far into the future that was being trumpeted around her.' For the New South Africa, born in such hope in 1994, this is a dismaying reading.

One of the important projects to which Coetzee had to attend in these years was the filming of his novel *Disgrace*, on which several filmmakers had taken out options. From the start Coetzee was wary lest his novel be taken advantage of for political purposes by a filmmaker and possible South African collaborators. In an e-mail of 21 February 2004 he mentioned his concern to his agent, Peter Lampack:

Disgrace has become somewhat of a political football in South Africa. Anyone who makes a film of *Disgrace* is thus entering a charged field, particularly if the film is shot in South Africa with local South African advisors. If it is a big-budget production, there will be interest in it from the beginning, including interest from political quarters. There will inevitably be an awareness that the film could influence the way in which South Africa is viewed abroad.

The reason why I want script approval is to ensure that the production is not influenced by people in South Africa with political interests of their own, whether on the left or on the right, and given a slant that the book does not have. I regard this as a real danger because the people making the film, as outsiders, will have no sense of the political nuances that even small, innocent-seeming details can hold for insiders; also, frankly, because as outsiders it may not matter much to them what political fallout the film may have in South Africa.

Eventually the rights to *Disgrace* were awarded to the Australian married couple Steve Jacobs and Anna-Maria Monticelli, who managed to get the Oscar-winning American actor John Malkovich for the role of David Lurie, with the South African Jessica Haines as Lucy. In October 2008 the film was awarded the Black Pearl Award in Abu Dhabi for the best entry at the Middle East International Film Festival, and in Toronto it won the International Critics' Prize. Although the film was shot partly in Cape Town and the Cederberg, the filmmakers did not manage to raise a cent of funding in South Africa. The film was shown worldwide in 2010.[27]

The possible exploitation of his novel for political motives was also the reason for Coetzee's refusal of a request for an Afrikaans translation of *Disgrace*, after initially granting it. In January 2004 Dan Roodt of Praag Uitgewers, a man with right-wing (even extreme right-wing) political convictions, applied to Coetzee's agents, David Higham Associates, to have the novel translated and to publish it, even though it would have a relatively small market in Afrikaans. Coetzee agreed to this request, but Roodt missed the 18-month deadline for publication and did not inform the agents of any delay. In a letter of 18 October 2005, Coetzee wrote to his agents that he had not received any manuscript for inspection, as the agreement stipulated, and that as far as he knew, no translation had been published. 'Since April 2004,' he continues, 'I have found out certain facts about Praag and its owner Dan Roodt, and have no wish to be publicly associated with its activities. Therefore I would like to ask for your opinion about terminating the contract, as I believe we are now entitled to do.' In spite of Roodt's protests, the contract was cancelled. *Disgrace* eventually appeared in Afrikaans as *In Oneer*, translated by the poet Fanie Olivier and published by Umuzi, an imprint of Random House Struik in Cape Town.

The year 2010 was a special one in John Coetzee's life, because he turned seventy on 9 February. On 5 May 2010 he was the guest of his American alma mater, the University of Texas at Austin, where in a lecture he recollected his student days there, and spoke about his experiences with censorship against the social and political background of the 1970s in South Africa. With quotations from the reports on three of his books that had been submitted for vetting, and that had been unearthed by Hermann Wittenberg in the archives of the Publications Control Board and also mentioned by Peter McDonald in *The Literature Police*, he had the audience roaring with laughter at the obtuseness displayed by the censors. Later in May he repeated this lecture in the French capital and received an honorary doctorate from the American University of Paris. On 22 June 2010 he read from his work in the Norwich Playhouse in Britain with fellow-writers from South Africa—Jonty Driver, Zoë Wicomb and Gabeba Baderoon. For this occasion he chose a twenty-minute-long short story, which, with its humorous take on the Karoo world of his youth, had the audience at his feet.

But the greatest honour accorded Coetzee was in Amsterdam, where his Dutch publisher, Eva Cossée, with the participation of the cultural centre De Balie, presented a three-day festival from 13 to 16 May 2010, under the title 'Is dit J.M. Coetzee?' Elleke Boehmer conducted an interview with David Attwell on the making of *Doubling the Point*, and a Festschrift was presented to the jubilarian. Under the direction of Lotte van den Berg the play *Braakland* by Compagnie Dakar was performed on a patch of vacant earth on the outskirts of Amsterdam. Coetzee was knighted as *Ridder van de Nederlandse Leeuw*, a royal distinction very rarely conferred upon foreigners. In her speech the acting Amsterdam mayor, Carolien Gehrels, praised Coetzee for his role in connecting South African and Dutch literature, his translations from Dutch into English, his essays on Dutch writers, and the special bond between him and his Dutch publisher, which had caused every new novel of Coetzee's since 2002 to be published first in Dutch translation before being released in English. In response Coetzee commenced his word of thanks in Dutch:

> Before I begin I want to thank from the bottom of my heart the many fellow-artists, fellow-writers, fellow-readers who took part in the events of the last three days. I have found the last three evenings a very moving experience. I have never written for a specific reading public or for specific readers, but always somewhat blindly for the future and the people of the future. It is thus with a certain measure of surprise, even with a certain shock or tremor, that I meet real reading people who have actually read my books.

I have found these three evenings in Amsterdam of personal interest, because here I am read in a language in which I feel myself to be a somewhat more humorous writer than in the original English.[28]

After this, Coetzee read an unpublished story about Elizabeth Costello, who, at the end of her life, is living in a small mountain village in Castille, in Spain, sharing her house with a multitude of cats and the village idiot, Pablo. Her son, John, visits her from the US. The text is the distillate of their conversations and discussions, in which he tries to establish why on earth she has chosen to settle in this godforsaken place at the back of beyond with the cats and the idiot. As in the later Coetzee, this, once again, is a tale of withdrawal and unconditional sympathy, but it is also truly hilarious.

In her introduction at the beginning of the festival, Eva Cossée jokingly referred to Coetzee as '*het feestvarkentje*', the party animal. Throughout the proceedings Coetzee kept quiet, speaking his words of thanks only at the very end. When Cossée had brought him to the train for departure, he hugged her tightly and said: 'It was fun!'[29]

Coetzee, by now, is not only a writer whose work has been honoured in many ways, amongst others by means of prestigious awards for literature, he is also an author whose books are read widely, in many languages, by an increasing number of readers. The sales figures of some titles are counted in the hundreds of thousands, and continue to rise steadily.

Tributes continue to be showered upon Coetzee. In March 2011, in the South Australian Art gallery in Adelaide, a series of Protea coins bearing Coetzee's head was launched by the South African Mint. Such a series is struck to commemorate an event from South Africa's history or to honour an extraordinary South African. Three hundred silver coins were struck: this is the first time that a South African writer has been honoured in this way.

EPILOGUE

John Coetzee started work on *Summertime* in April 2005. He revised the final manuscript twice, in the light of comments from his British and American editors, in February 2009 and again in March 2009. He corrected the proofs from Harvill Secker soon afterwards and returned them on 1 June 2009. The Dutch translation, *Zomertijd*, was published in July 2009 by Eva Cossée in Amsterdam, and the original English about two months later by Harvill Secker in London.[1]

My letter of 9 June 2008 to John Coetzee, in which I asked his permission to undertake his biography, must have reached him while he was still writing away at *Summertime*. My request may have raised a smile. Here he had been since April 2005 in Adelaide writing about a fictional English biographer, Mr Vincent, engaged in the preliminaries for a biography of the dead author J.M. Coetzee. And here appears a real biographer applying to write a real biography. This biographer does not, as one would expect, emerge from the ranks of the English literary world, but from the much smaller province of Afrikaans literature. Perhaps the very fact that the request was coming from outside the sphere of English literature may have appealed to Coetzee, with his contrarian take on things.

When I was in Adelaide in March 2009 to conduct interviews with John Coetzee, he was on his second revision of *Summertime*. He answered all my questions meticulously, and impressed me as a man of integrity. From the manuscripts that I perused in his office in the second week of my stay, I also got the impression of an incredibly hard worker who had spared no effort to develop and deploy his talent. The various versions, up to fourteen, that had been produced of *Disgrace* provide some measure of the demands Coetzee makes of himself as a writer. A student interested in the genesis of his novels would find wonderful material here.

In the course of our conversations I also developed a certain compassion with this intensely private and reserved man. Even on highly sensitive topics he kept strictly to the facts. Only when he spoke of the illness of his daughter, Gisela, was there a measure of emotion, and, at first, reticence. On this topic I got the impression—for the only time in our conversations—that he was withholding certain information from me (which he later provided). Add to this the sorrow he experienced at his father's dishonesty and alcoholism, the life and death of Nicolas, and the death from cancer of Philippa, and one stands amazed that someone could experience so much unhappiness and yet sustain himself and continue his work.

Forty years before writing *Summertime*, in which the fictional author, John Coetzee, is laid to rest, J.M. Coetzee wrote his first novel, *Dusklands*. He and his family were then, after their return from the US, temporarily settled in a vacant house at Maraisdal near the family farm Voëlfontein in the heart of his beloved Karoo. In *Dusklands* Jacobus Coetzee imagines his own death in the following terms:

> … if the worst comes you will find that I am not irrevocably attached to life. I know my lessons. I too can retreat before a beckoning finger through the infinite corridors of my self. I too can attain and inhabit a point of view from which […] I can be seen to be superfluous. At present I do not care to inhabit such a point of view; but when the day comes you will find that whether I am alive or dead, whether I ever lived or never was born, has never been of real concern to me. I have other things to think about.[2]

Shortly after my visit to Adelaide in 2009 I reached the age of seventy; not long afterwards John Coetzee reached the same age and there were festive celebrations in Amsterdam and elsewhere. We are thus both in our eighth decade, having reached our biblical allotment of years. I would be satisfied to contemplate the future with the equanimity that is so finely expressed in J.M. Coetzee's lucid prose.

EDITOR'S NOTE

John Kannemeyer died on 25 December 2011, soon after completing the manuscript on the life and work of J.M. Coetzee.

He had made corrections and alterations to the manuscript based on reader's reports by David Attwell, Derek Attridge and myself. He acknowledged this assistance in the preface.

A comprehensive reader's report by Lars Engle had not been read by John Kannemeyer before his unexpected death. In the editing of the manuscript, recommendations from this report were of great help, along with futher comments by David Attwell, Johan Bruwer, Eva Cossée and Michiel Heyns.

Hannes van Zyl

Translator's note

Compared with, say, a complex novel, a work of non-fiction presents relatively few obstacles to the translator: facts translate into facts more smoothly than flights of the poetic imagination. Still, language being the multifarious thing it is, no translation is entirely without its pitfalls, and this book has been no exception. In particular the narrative tense has proved intractable at times. In Afrikaans, narratives, even non-fiction narratives, are almost invariably conducted in the present tense, and John Kannemeyer has consistently adopted this convention in his biography. I have almost as consistently converted this to the usual (though no longer invariable) English narrative tense, the simple past. There is, however, a contrary convention, namely that citations from published works are discussed as if happening in the present. I have at times, but only at times, adopted this convention, to bring greater immediacy to discussions of quoted extracts. The test has been ease of reading rather than strict consistency. Readers irritated with the inconsistency will know, at any rate, that it was not unintentional.

There are many quotations from Afrikaans and Dutch in this biography. I have generally translated these myself, indicating my intervention in brackets or footnotes. This signalling is purely to safeguard the authors of the originals, where I may have translated incorrectly or clumsily.

ENDNOTES

FOREWORD

1 The first of these studies to appear in book form was that of Teresa Dovey, *The Novels of J.M. Coetzee* (1988). Of the most prominent studies in book form (excluding the many university dissertations) are: Dick Penner, *Countries of the Mind* (1989); Kevin Goddard and John Read, ed., *J.M. Coetzee: A Bibliography* (1990); Susan Van Zanten Gallagher, *A Story of South Africa* (1991); David Attwell, *J.M. Coetzee: South Africa and the Politics of Writing* (1993); Dominic Head, *J.M. Coetzee* (1997); Michael Valdez Moses, Graham Huggan and Stephen Watson, eds, *Critical Perspectives on J.M. Coetzee* (1996); Rosemary Jane Jolly, *Colonization, Violence and Narration in White South African Writing: André Brink, Breyten Breytenbach and J.M. Coetzee* (1996); Sue Kossew, *Pen and Power: A Post-colonial Reading of the Novels of J.M. Coetzee and André Brink* (1997); Sue Kossew, ed., *Critical Essays on J.M. Coetzee* (1998); T. Kai Norris Easton, *Textuality and the Land* (2000); Derek Attridge, *J.M. Coetzee and the Ethics of Reading* (2005); Jane Poyner, ed., *J.M. Coetzee and the Idea of the Public Intellectual* (2006); Liliana Sikorska, ed., *A Universe of (Hi)stories* (2006); Manfred Loimeier, *J.M. Coetzee: Edition & Kritik* (2008); Bill McDonald, ed., *Encountering Disgrace* (2009);Dominic Head, *The Cambridge Introduction to J.M. Coetzee* (2009); Carrol Clarkson, *J.M. Coetzee: Countervoices* (2009); Patrick Hayes, *J.M. Coetzee and the Novel* (2010); Andrew van der Vlies, *J.M. Coetzee's Disgrace* (2010); Anton Leist & Peter Singer, eds, *J.M. Coetzee and Ethics* (2010).

2 Since the completion of the manuscript of this biography, J.M. Coetzee has reached an agreement with the University of Texas to lodge his manuscripts and documents in perpetuity in the Harry Ransom Center in Austin. A first consignment, which would include the Harvard documents, was to be transferred late in 2011, with further instalments to follow in 2012 and 2013. (Information from J.M. Coetzee in an e-mail to me on 3.8.2011.)

3 *J.M. Coetzee: A Bibliography*, compiled by Kevin Goddard and John Read and introduced by Teresa Dovey, Grahamstown, NELM, 1990, p. 12.

4 David Attwell, *J.M. Coetzee: South Africa and the Politics of Writing*, Berkeley, University of California Press / Cape Town, David Philip, 1993, p. 6.

5 Derek Attridge, *J.M. Coetzee and the Ethics of Reading*, Chicago, University of Chicago Press / Scottsville, University of KwaZulu-Natal Press, 2005, p. 139.

6 J.M. Coetzee, *Truth in Autobiography*, Cape Town, University of Cape Town, 1984.

7 J.M. Coetzee, *Doubling the Point: Essays and Interviews*, edited by David Attwell, Cambridge, Massachusetts / London, Harvard University Press, 1992, p. 18.

8 Ibid., p. 391.

9 Martin van Amerongen, *Mijn leven zijn leven*, Amsterdam, Stichting Collectieve Propaganda van het Nederlandse Boek, 1993, p. 9.

10 James Olney, ed., *Autobiography: Essays Theoretical and Critical*, Princeton, Princeton University Press, 1980, p. 11.

11 *Summertime*, p. 225.

12 J.M. Coetzee, 'Dostoevsky: The miraculous years', *Stranger Shores: Essays 1986–1999*, London, Secker & Warburg, 2001, p. 144.

13 Roland Barthes, *Image-Music-Text*, a selection from his essays translated by Stephen Heath, Glasgow, Fontana / Collins, 1977, p. 148.

14 Wim Hazeu, *Vestdijk: Een biografie*, Amsterdam, De Bezige Bij, 2005, p. 242. [Translation M.H.]

CHAPTER 1

1 J.M. Coetzee, *Elizabeth Costello*, London, Secker & Warburg, 2003, p1.

2 Thus we are told that he is a descendant of Dutch colonists who settled at the Cape in the seventeenth century, that his parents were Afrikaners without any British blood, that they preferred to raise their children in English, and that Coetzee is therefore an Afrikaner writing in English. In the *Pen Nieuwsbrief* of May 2004 Robert Dorsman writes that Coetzee was born into an Afrikaans family, but asked his parents to send him to an English secondary school, a request they granted. According to an article by Susan van Zanten Gallagher in the *Cyclopedia of World Authors*, he grew up on 'his father's isolated sheep farm in the stony semi-desert of the Karroo'. (*Cyclopedia of World Authors*, fourth revised edition, 2004.) He received his schooling in English, even though, according to Regina Janes, the 'Boer nationalists' in power 'demanded that Afrikaner children not learn English'. (Regina Janes, ' "Writing without authority": J.M. Coetzee and his fictions', *Salmagundi*, 114, 115, Spring / Summer 1997.) In her version, he left South Africa in the 1960s to study linguistics in Britain. (Ibid.) Coetzee's son, according to Wikipedia, died in 1989 at the age of twenty-three in a car accident. His father, writes Laban Carrick Hill in a synoptic account, ('J.M. Coetzee', *British Writers, Supplement VI*, ed. Jay Parini, New York, Charles Scribner's Sons, 2001.) was an attorney but never practised law. All these accounts are fallacious or only partly true.

3 This information is uncritically reproduced in articles — as in those by Laban Carrick Hill, (Ibid.), Allan Riding (*The New York Times*, 3.10.2003.) and Jeroen Vullings (Jeroen Vullings, 'J.M. Coetzee laat zich niet kennen', *Vrij Nederland*, 30.7.2005.) — and even finds its way into *World Literature Today* of January–April 2004, an edition containing several articles devoted to Coetzee after he received the Nobel Prize for Literature in 2003.

4 Thus Laban Carrick Hill mentions that the K in Coetzee's *Life & Times of Michael K* has been linked by commentators with Franz Kafka's *Der Proze* (*The Trial*), but he claims that the C in Coetzee is often interchangeable with a K, and that Coetzee's middle name is Michael.

5 J.M. Coetzee, *White Writing: On the Culture of Letters in South Africa*, New Haven / London, Yale University Press, 1988, p. 1.

6 The spelling Couché seems to indicate French origins, but all details and documents relating to earlier generations, apart from the names of the parents, have been lost in the murk of many wars. Genealogical particulars regarding the progenitors and later generations of Coetzees at the Cape can be found in N.A. Coetzee's *Die stamouers Coetzee en nageslagte*, Pretoria, Perskor, 1979 and *Die onbekende toekoms: Coetzees in Suid-Afrika en Namibië*, privately published by the author, Hannes Coetzee, Boordfontein, 2005. Hannes Coetzee, however, does not provide any particulars after the third generation of the J.M. Coetzee line of the family. For further details the interested reader has to rely on *Suid-Afrikaanse geslagsregisters / South African genealogies*, part I, compiled by J.A. Heese and R.T.J. Lombard, Pretoria, HSRC, 1986. Condensed information regarding the progenitors is provided by C. Pama in *Die groot Afrikaanse familienaamboek*, Cape Town, Human & Rousseau, 1983, p. 81. An important unpublished source, available from the

Genealogical Institute of South Africa, is the three-part *Coetzee-familie in Suid-Afrika* by I. Groesbeek, S. Veltkamp-Visser and L. Zöllner, Pretoria, HSRC, 1991.

7 The parents of this patriarch were Gerard Couché and Margaretha Claasdochter, citizens of the city of Kampen. Dirk Couché was born in 1655 in Kampen. Before his departure for the Cape he married Sara van der Schulp, born in Amsterdam in 1654. They sailed from Texel on the *Asia* and landed at the Cape on 8 May 1679. In their first years at the Cape the couple lived in a house in Papendorp (the present Woodstock), and it seems probable that he was already supplying farm produce to passing ships of the VOC. In 1682 Governor Simon van der Stel granted him a farm in Stellenbosch that would later be known as Coetzenburg—today the site of the sports centre of the University of Stellenbosch. He kept the house in Papendorp, and in 1721 the couple moved back there on account of the wife's poor health. (N.A. Coetzee, op. cit., p. 92.)

8 Jan Visagie, 'Historiese Coetzenburg-plaas van bekende baanbrekers', *Die Burger*, 12.8.2000.

9 Although, with such progenitors, J.M. Coetzee is certainly of Dutch descent, the possibility of English ancestry on the matriarchal side cannot be excluded. Jacob, the father of the progenitress, Sara van der Schulp, married one Maria (or Mary?) Elison, a surname suggesting English descent. This would have been perfectly possible in the Amsterdam of the seventeenth century, which, like the other great trading cities of Europe at the time, was home to a significant contingent of English tradespeople.

10 Gerrit Coetzee, baptised in 1729, married his first wife, Johanna Elizabeth Romond, in 1766. Her father was from Zuthpen in the Netherlands, but, judging by the surname Romond, he was probably a French fugitive who on account of his Protestant faith had fled to the Netherlands and afterwards to

the Cape; even though he settled at the Cape earlier than the French Huguenots of 1688. Such immigrants, who had had to abandon their possessions in France, were usually destitute and immigration to the Cape, with the assurance of a VOC appointment or with initial financial aid from the Company for farming, was often a godsend.

Gerrit and Johanna's son, Gerrit Coetzee, born in 1775, in 1801 married Johanna Hendrina Buitendag, baptised in 1778. Their son Gerrit, born in 1811, in turn married, in 1837, Elizabeth Jacoba Hess, born in 1807 and baptised in the Lutheran Church in Cape Town. This Gerrit was, according to the Cape Almanac of 1869, a blacksmith, a trade he practised from premises at 67 Dorp Street, Cape Town, later assisted by his son Gerrit.

Through the marriage to Buitendag (German spelling Buitendach), a German strain had entered the Coetzee line, and this was reinforced by the marriage of Gerrit Coetzee of the fifth generation to the daughter of Frederik Laurens Hess and Aletta Elizabeth Delport. This marriage was also the reason for the deviation, after the sixth generation, from the customary first name of Gerrit for the first-born son, the son of Gerrit and Aletta being given the names of his German grandfather, Frederik Laurens, with the addition of Johannes. Johannes could be a reversion to one of the sons of the patriarch, but it seems more likely that it is the masculine form of the name of both his maternal grandmother and great-grandmother.

Frederik, who was born on the West Coast and would later settle in the town of Ceres, married, in 1865 in Cape Town, Elizabeth Agnes Mills, whose mother was from Hamilton in Scotland. Like his father, Frederik was a blacksmith, but in the 1880s he suffered a major setback when he went bankrupt and his property in town was sold, with his furniture, to settle his debts.

The marriage between Frederik Laurens Johannes and Elizabeth Agnes Mills brought the first known introduction of British influence and culture into the Coetzee family. They were the great-grandparents of the writer. J.M. Coetzee seems not to have been aware of these ancestors when, in one of his interviews with David Attwell in 1992, he stated that although, on account of his English home language, no Afrikaner would regard him as an Afrikaner, he did not, strictly speaking, qualify as an English-speaking South African either, because of his lack of British ancestors. (J.M. Coetzee, *Doubling the Point: Essays and Interviews*, ed. David Attwell, Cambridge, Massachusetts / London, Harvard University Press, 1992, pp. 341–342.) It also seems likely that in 1992 he was unaware of his German ancestry in the Coetzee line, and even the possibility of French ancestry. (Information on Gerrit Coetzee, born 1775, and Gerrit Frederick Coetzee was supplied by e-mail, dated 19 May 2010, from Professor Gerhard Geldehuys.) References to German and British 'blood' are purely metaphorical, without any suggestion of the medically nonsensical notions of 'pure' blood or 'racial purity'. It is a matter of cultural formation, which with the different schools, churches, etc., was of some interest in the South Africa of the time.

11 Some sources, like the *South African Biographical Dictionary*, part II, eds W.J. de Kock and D.W. Krüger, Cape Town, Tafelberg, cite her surname as Paling.
12 J.M. Coetzee, *White Writing*, p. 1.
13 In the *South African Biographical Dictionary* there are by mistake two lemmata devoted to Jacobus Coetsé: in part II by N.A. Coetzee, eds W.J. de Kock and D.W. Krüger, Cape Town, Tafelberg, 1972, pp. 136–137; and in part V by E.J. Prins, eds C.J. Beyers and J.L. Basson, Pretoria, HSRC, 1987, pp. 146–147. Apart from the already-mentioned books by N.A. Coetzee and Hannes Coetzee, a chapter is devoted to Jacobus Coetsé in M.H.D. Smith's

Boerepioniers van die Sandveld, edited and supplemented by R.T.J. Lombard, Pretoria, HSRC, 1985, pp. 29–39.
14 Karel Schoeman has written about the travels of Jacobus Coetsé and Hendrik Hop in Chapter 9 of *Cape Lives of the Eighteenth Century* (Pretoria, Protea Boekehuis, 2011). Schoeman also provides fascinating information on the turbulent lives of some of the sons of the patriarchs.
15 J.M. Coetzee, *Dusklands*, Johannesburg, Ravan Press, 1974, p. 115.
16 Ibid., p. 114.
17 The progenitor of the De Beers in South Africa was Matthys Andries de Beer, originally from the Netherlands. His son Zacharias (1719–1777) was a burgher in Stellenbosch, but in 1762 Governor Ryk Tulbagh granted him permission to settle on the farm Queeckvalleij, later written Kweekvallei, at the foot of the Great Swartberg. His son Samuel de Beer (circa 1762–after 1809) was the ninth of Zacharias's fifteen children, and the eldest from his third marriage, to Dina Margaretha van Dyk. He grew up in the Drakenstein, near Franschhoek, a well-read, cultured man with a good knowledge of world affairs. He married Anna Eleanora de Villiers in 1783. From 1794, a year before the British occupation of the Cape, he lived on the farm granted to his father, on which the town of Prince Albert, named for the consort of Queen Victoria, would be established in 1842. Samuel de Beer irrigated his gardens and vineyards from a spring against the hill behind his house, and delivered butter and dried fruit to the Cape Town market, as well as good quality wine, comparable with the highly regarded Constantia wines.
18 Hinrich Lichtenstein, *Travels in Southern Africa II*, translated from the German by Anne Plumptre, London, B. Clarke, 1815, pp. 69–71. Lichtenstein's visit is also described by Lawrence Green, *Karoo*, Cape Town, Howard Timmins, reprinted 1975, pp. 110–111. It is interesting that Lichtenstein, through Samuel de Beer,

should comment on the laziness of the indigenous people, a motif that J.M. Coetzee was to examine in his essay 'Idleness in South Africa' in *White Writing*, pp. 12–35.

19 Patricia Storrar, *A Colossus of Roads*, Cape Town, Murray & Roberts / Concor, 1984. The information about the silver spoon that Bain gave to Lenie was derived from a letter from Mrs Sylvia Coetzee to me, 20.11.2008.

20 Information in an e-mail from Paul Kloppers, a cousin of J.M. Coetzee's, 1.6.2009.

21 This fragment was given to me on 1.6.2009 by Paul Kloppers.

22 This information was supplied by Professor Gerhard Geldenhuys of Stellenbosch, who put at my disposal the manuscript of an unpublished article ('Vermoedens oor die voorname van die skrywer J.M. Coetzee') and an ancestral chart of the author.

23 Some of the information about Gerrit Maxwell Coetzee and his family contained here was compiled on 26.2.2009 by Pieter Hugo, and made available to me by Stefan Wehmeyer, second cousin of J.M. Coetzee.

24 Information from the article by Professor Gerhard Geldenhuys mentioned above.

25 M.O. Kritzinger, *Driekwarteeufees-gedenkboek van die Ned. Geref. Kerk, Laingsburg 1882–1957*, Cape Town (Elsiesrivier), National Commercial Printers, 1957, p. 148.

26 One of the matches arranged by Logan in which Gert played forms the subject of an affidavit, because the result verges on the incredible. During the early stages of the Boer War, Logan arranged a match, to be played at Prince Albert Road, between the members of the British garrison at Prince Albert and a local team. The military were the first to bat. W.A. Brown Rowan launched a bowling attack, and in the first innings took three British wickets for not a single run. Gert Coetzee took over the bowling and took two more wickets for no runs. When Rowan resumed bowling, he took the rest

of the wickets, without any of the batsmen scoring a single run. There was, though, one leg bye scored from Coetzee's bowling, even though the batsman was almost run out, with one more run from a no-ball. The British team thus scored a total of two runs in its entire innings. Much later, on 5 March 1935, Gert Coetzee and two other participants signed a declaration in the magistrate's office in Prince Albert to confirm the result in writing. It was later reported in the *Cape Argus*. (The details of this match were provided by Paul Kloppers in an e-mail, with the affidavit attached.)

27 M.F. Erasmus, *Halfeeufees-gedenkboek Ned. Geref. Gemeente Merweville, K.P.1904–1954*, Cape Town, National Commercial Printers, 1954, p. 41.

28 Information by letter from Mrs Sylvia Coetzee, 20.11.2008.

29 Information received from Lydia Barrella of the Fransie Pienaar Museum in Prince Albert in a letter of 4.3.2009. Gert's wife Lenie was chairwoman of the Women's Agricultural Union of Prince Albert. Gert died in 1946, but Lenie survived him by many years, and was known to the grandchildren as 'Mum' Coetzee. A photo of her hangs in the Fransie Pienaar Museum.

30 J.M. Coetzee, *Boyhood*, London, Secker & Warburg, 1997, p. 97.

31 J.M. Coetzee, *Summertime*, London, Harvill Secker, 2009, p.106. The memory is here given to Carol.

32 Information by Mrs Sylvia Coetzee in a letter of June 2010.

33 *Boyhood*, p. 128.

34 Ibid., p. 127.

35 *Summertime*, pp. 106–7.

36 'A *slap gat*: a rectum, an anus, over which one has less than complete control. Hence *slapgat*: slack, spineless.' *Summertime*, p. 116.

37 *Summertime*, p. 116. (*Gesellig*: companionable.) This is all put into the mouth of the character Margot, in her interview with the fictional biographer. However, in real life Gert Coetzee was, according to Mrs Sylvia Coetzee in her letter to me of June 2010, not as

much of a bully as the novel suggests. Three of his sons farmed in the Koup and the Northern Cape. According to Mrs Coetzee, farmers who can keep up their courage there and make a success of their farming can't be *slapgatte*. The youngest son and daughter, too, were upstanding citizens.

38 Information from Gerald Coetzee, owner of Voëlfontein and cousin of J.M. Coetzee, in a personal interview, 23.5.2009.

39 Thanks to the research of Stefan Wehmeyer, a second cousin of J.M. Coetzee's, the German ancestors of the family, all from the working class with trades like miller and tailor, can be traced back to the seventeenth century. The ancestors of the South African Wehmeyers lived in the village of Quakenbrück, already established in 1235, north of Osnabrück in Lower Saxony. The name Quackenbrück sounds as if it should refer to a frog-filled brook, but has no such meaning. A 'Brück' is a bridge, and 'Quacken' has the same root as the English word 'quake'; the word thus means a bridge over a marshy, unstable territory. The first recorded Wehmeyer was Johann Gerd Wehmeyer (1666–1705), followed by two generations sharing the same name: Berend Hinrich Wehmeyer (1701–1788 and 1736–1788 respectively).

The patriarch who came to the Cape in 1789, one of the last immigrants to arrive in the service of the Dutch East India Company, was Gottlieb Wilhelm Bernard Wehmeyer (1763–1803), who in 1791 married Catherina Elizabeth Zondagh (1772–1809). He had probably left the verdant little city on the banks of the Hasen River on account of the lack of jobs in Germany at the time. It is also possible that he was lured by the adventure of a new and uncharted land, just as his uncle had left the small-town family stronghold to become a ship's doctor on the high seas.

Gottlieb's son Bernard Mathys (1794–1850) was in 1823 to marry his own cousin, Martha Maria Zondagh

(1806–1858) from the Langkloof in the Southern Cape. He was a field cornet, and in the 1830s bought land near Avontuur. Unlike his father, who died at a relatively early age in the Cape, he settled in the Southern Cape, because his grandfather Zondagh lived in that part of the world. By 1839 Bernard had subdivided part of his farm at Avontuur into plots, rented these out to coloured people at an annual tariff, and invited missionaries from Pacaltsdorp to do missionary work among them.

Bernard's son Gottlieb Wilhem Bernard (1826–1901) was born in Port Elizabeth in the Eastern Cape and was known for his fluency in Dutch and English. His farm was Oude Wolwekraal in what was to become the Uniondale district. In 1852 he was elected as a member of the Cape Parliament, representing George, a position he held up to 1858. After his retirement he campaigned for the building of a church in Uniondale and a proper road along the mountain pass between this town and Knysna, which was eventually completed by Thomas Bain, to be known as the Prince Albert Pass.

Gottlieb's son was Petrus Hendrik (Piet) Wehmeyer (1864–1931). He married Louisa Amelia du Biel (1873–1928) in 1859, and inherited his father's farm, Oude Wolwekraal. Piet and Amelia were the maternal grandparents of John Coetzee. Since they both died before his birth, he could at most have heard of them through recollections of his mother and other family members. Besides, the Wehmeyers lived far away from J.M. Coetzee's childhood places like Cape Town, Worcester and the Karoo farm Voëlfontein. What he did learn from his mother, as reported by the distanced John in *Boyhood*, is that when ostrich feathers were in demand worldwide and fetching astronomical prices on the London market, his grandfather Piet was persuaded by two feather buyers to start farming ostriches rather than sheep. (*Boyhood*, p. 22.) When the price of feathers plunged owing to over-production and the outbreak of World War I in 1914, the buyers who had encouraged him to switch were nowhere to be found, and Piet Wehmeyer and his son Roland, who farmed with him, went bankrupt and lost their farm, like many others in the Little Karoo.

After their years on Wolwekraal, Piet and Louisa settled in Uniondale. After the death of his wife, Piet lived with one of his daughters in Stellenbosch, where he died. (Stefan Wehmeyer, 'Terug: 'n Reis na Quackenbrück, Niedersächse, Duitsland', *Cape Librarian*, July—August 2007.)

40 E-mail to me, 27.10.2008.

41 Dalene Matthee, *Fiela se kind*, Cape Town, Tafelberg, 1985, p. 15. [Translation M.H.]

42 *Summertime*, p. 99.

43 The linguist Abel Coetzee (1906–1975) did make some contributions in the field of anthropology, but as a literary critic his judgement was unreliable, and his aggressive rashness cost him the favour of most of the writers of his time. The interweaving of pseudo-documentation with authentic sources in the novel *Op soek na generaal Mannetjies Mentz* (*In Search of General Mannetjies Mentz*) (1998) by Christoffel Coetzee (1945–1999), bears some resemblance to *Dusklands* (1974), J.M. Coetzee's first novel. The literary critic Ampie Coetzee (1939–) has since the 1960s been a prominent commentator on the 'Sestigers' and on the poet Breyten Breytenbach.

44 The original German manuscript of the diary is kept in the C.S. van Wyk Collection, Document Centre, J.S. Gericke Library, University of Stellenbosch. The Afrikaans text of *'n Ewebeeld en stroom musiek* forms part of the same collection.

45 *Boyhood*, p. 118.

46 Ibid., p.120.

47 Ibid., p. 118.

48 Kay Redfield Jamison, *Touched with Fire: Manic-depressive Illness and the Artistic Temperament*, New York, Simon and Schuster, 1993.

49 The books of Albert du Biel are:

Getrou (Faithful), written as a serial for *Die Huisgenoot* in 1914, and published in book form in 1921; *Die misdade van die vaders* (The crimes of the fathers) (1919); *Kain* (Cain) (1922); the series of tales and sketches *Oor berg en vlakte* (Over mountain and plain) (1922–1925); *Die verraaier* (The traitor) (1931); *Die eenoog-verkenner* (The one-eyed scout) (1932); and *Bloudoorns* (Bluethorn) (1944).

50 Advertisement for this series in the back of the first edition of *Kain* (1922).

51 P.C. Schoonees, *Die prosa van die Tweede Afrikaanse Beweging*, third revised edition, Pretoria, J.H. du Bussy / Cape Town, HAUM, 1939, p. 131.

52 Albert du Biel, *Die verraaier*, Paarl, Die Specialiteite-Maatskappy, 1931, p. 72.

53 *Boyhood*, p. 120. Coetzee cites the title of Du Biel's novel incorrectly as *Die sondes van die vaders*, that is, *The Sins of the Fathers* rather than *The Crimes of the Fathers*.

54 *White Writing*, p. 143.

55 Ibid., p. 136.

56 *Dusklands*, pp. 49 and 51.

CHAPTER 2

1 Interview with Gerald Coetzee, 23.5.2009.

2 Ibid.

3 The information about Jack Coetzee's being struck from the roll and all relevant documentation are available under motion 547 of 1941 of the Cape Division of the Supreme Court and are kept in the Cape Archives.

4 Interview with J.M. Coetzee, 16.3.2009.

5 Ibid.

6 J.M. Coetzee, *Boyhood*, London, Secker & Warburg, 1997, p. 35.

7 Ibid., p. 30.

8 Ibid., p. 80.

9 Ibid., p. 81.

10 J.M. Coetzee, *Age of Iron*, London, Secker & Warburg, 1990, p. 85.

11 *Boyhood*, p. 31.

12 This is how Coetzee renders the

attitude of Vera's mother-in-law in *Boyhood*, p. 37. In an interview with me on 24.10.2008, Sylvia Coetzee, John's aunt and the widow of his father's brother Son, said that Lenie Coetzee was a very hospitable and compassionate person and that such an interpretation is definitely based on an erroneous impression. In reply to my question during an interview with Coetzee on 16.3.2009 as to whether he had here deviated from the actual situation in order to isolate the John character in *Boyhood*, he said: 'I am just going on what my mother said and she said she wasn't welcome.' It is also possible that Gert Coetzee's health at this stage was not good, and that Lenie Coetzee for that reason preferred not to have house guests. Already by 26 September 1941, when Jack Coetzee's malpractices were brought to court, the firm of attorneys Stegmann & Able of Johannesburg requested the Johannesburg Law Society not to make their proceedings available to the press: 'Respondent's father is an old and delicate man, and we trust that you and Counsel will be able to arrange for the press to omit any report of the matter at this stage.' The letter from Stegmann & Able is kept in the Cape Archives as part of the documents under motion 547 of 1941 of the Cape Division of the Supreme Court.

13 Interview with J.M. Coetzee 16.3.2009.

14 *Age of Iron*, p.15. In the manuscript of *Boyhood*, which he started writing on 20 March 1987, Coetzee writes about a night that Vera spent as a child under an ox wagon on the Swartberg Pass. This part, that is kept with the *Boyhood* manuscript in the Harry Ransom Center at Texas, differs from the extract in the completed text of *Age of Iron* in that it is written in the first person and addressed to the mother:

It is night, it is night on the Swartberg Mountains, it is deep in the night, and you are lying in the darkness under the belly of a wagon, by the roadside, wrapped in a blanket that smells of babies, among other sleepers of whom you alone are awake. If you crept out from under the wagon, you could see the stars, thousands of stars in the clear sky, and the horses and oxen, tethered, moving softly. But you do not creep out, you wrap yourself tight in the blanket, you close your eyes and breathe in the smells of the earth, the smells of the wagon, tar, grease, leather, above you.

On this cold night high in the mountains the only wind that blows seems to blow high in the night sky, between the stars, keeping the spaces between them clear and black. On earth it is still, and you are safe under the wagon with all your family sleeping around you. If the wagon were to move, if the wheels were to slip and turn, the bed creak, the wagon to roll, you would be left exposed to the sky and the brilliance of the stars, or you would even be crushed by a wheel passing over you, a huge iron-shod wheel as tall as yourself. But the wheels are stopped with rocks, the wagon does not roll, you are safe, soon you will be asleep again. You are safe and I am safe. That is how it always is when I say by myself, How did it begin? When I ask, How did it begin? it is always to you I recur, to the little girl under the wagon in the night on the mountain pass, under the wagon that might have begun to roll but did not, that stood firm and still between her and the stars, sheltering her, when it might have failed. Nothing failed, from beginning to end. Nothing failed, and therefore you were, and therefore I am.

15 *Boyhood*, p. 39.

16 Ibid., p. 48.

17 The cumbersome syntax and some of the images recall Wordsworth, whose poetry Jack was familiar with, but it is also possible that he knew Wilfred Owen's bitter First World War poems. In 'the echoing thunder of the guns' there is perhaps a memory of 'the monstrous anger of the guns' in Owen's 'Anthem for Doomed Youth'. Jack's poem is entitled 'Lines written after burying a friend', and time and place are indicated as 'In the Field, October 1944':

Take Thou Thy toll, grim Death;
Let not our sorrow stay Thy scythe.
Here in these cloud-clad mountains
cold,
That with their rock-bound trails and
icy blasts,
With raging torrents and with looming
cliffs
Darkly conspire with the vengeful foe
To stem our onward surge,
Take Thy full tribute of proud Youth.
Demand Thy measure to the brim
From these the sons of distant lands
Who, knowing well the price,
Dared here with Thee to shake the
dice.
But when Thou dost exact Thy toll,
And we amid the echoing thunder of
the guns,
In slushy graves lay to their final rest
Those who with laughter gay and
helpful hands
Did cheer our easeless way,
Think not then in our sorrow
weakness lies.
Tis then that we anew are made aware
That not alone by battles won and
glory gained,
Nor vapourings vague of years of peace,
Nor charters signed by them that rule,
Shall that be gained for which we
suffer now.
Tis then that we renew the pledge
That not by other efforts but our own,
Thou shalt ne'er again with visage grim,
Reap Thy harvest from the fields of War.
(Text in possession of J.M. Coetzee.)

18 *Boyhood*, p. 41.
19 Ibid.:'When he asks his mother
what the Ossewabrandwag is, she
says it is just nonsense, people who
marched in the streets with torches.'
The Ossewabrandwag ('Oxwagon
Sentinels') was an anti-British, pro-
German organisation opposed to South
African participation in Word War II.
20 Ibid., p. 43.
21 Ibid.
22 Interview with Sylvia Coetzee,
24.10.2008.
23 *Boyhood*, p. 35.
24 Ibid., p. 12.
25 Telephone conversation on
25.1.2009 with Agnes Heinrich,

a cousin of J.M. Coetzee and the
daughter of Joubert Olivier.
26 E-mail from J.M. Coetzee, 12.2.2009.
27 *Boyhood*, p. 67.
28 Ibid., p. 73
29 Ibid., p. 74
30 Ibid., p. 75.
31 Ibid., p. 77. *Jou moer!*: Bugger you!
32 Information from the video *Passages*
directed by Henion Han and Cheryl
Tuckett, made for SABC 3, 1997.
33 Interview with J.M. Coetzee,
16.3.2009.
34 E-mail to me, 27.10.2008.
35 *Boyhood*, p. 106.
36 C.J. Driver, *Patrick Duncan: South
African and Pan-African*, London,
Heinemann, 1980, p. 61.
37 J.M. Coetzee, *White Writing: On the
Culture of Letters in South Africa*, New
Haven and London, Yale University
Press, 1988, p. 137.
38 *Boyhood*, p. 67. In an unpublished
article entitled 'The NP victory and
English civil servants', Hermann
Giliomee writes: 'Undoubtedly there
were individual cases where people
of merit had been unjustly denied
promotion, but if the government
had done this on a large scale it would
have come up against the powerful
Civil Service Commission, which could
and did block irregular promotions
and dismissals.'
39 *Boyhood*, p. 1.
40 Akwe Amosu, *Not Goodbye*, Plumstead,
Snail Press, 2010, p. 34.
41 *Boyhood* , p. 3.
42 Ibid., p. 4.
43 Ibid., p. 22.
44 J.M. Coetzee, *Summertime*, London,
Harvill Secker, 2009, p. 108.
45 *Boyhood*, p. 9.
46 Ibid., p. 82.
47 Ibid., pp. 82–83.
48 Ibid., p. 83.
49 See Coetzee on this topic in one of
his interviews in *Doubling the Point:
Essays and Interviews*, ed. David Attwell,
Cambridge, Massachusetts / London,
Harvard University Press, 1992, p. 20.
50 Coloureds form a minority group
within South Africa, however they are
the predominant population group in

the Western Cape. The definition of
law makers in the apartheid period was
a negative one: a coloured was a person
obviously neither white nor African.
Coloured people were formed by their
exclusion from the white dominant
group, particularly in the church and
schools, and by the identification
of most with Western culture and
Christian faith. Coloureds are generally
bilingual, yet subsets within the group
are exclusively Afrikaans speakers.
Their ancestry may include European
settlers, indigenous Khoisan and Xhosa
people, and slaves imported from the
Dutch East Indies, or a combination
of all. Coloureds are traditionally
associated with the erstwhile Cape
Province. Under segregation policies
they enjoyed more rights and privileges
than Black Africans.

51 *Boyhood*, p. 84.
52 Ibid., p. 85.
53 Ibid., p. 85.
54 Ibid., p. 86.
55 Ibid., p. 87.
56 Ibid., p. 87.
57 Ibid., p. 90. A bulala lamp is a bright
    miner's lamp strapped to the head or
    miner's helmet.
58 Ibid., p. 91.
59 Ibid., p.98.
60 Ibid., p.101.
61 Ibid., pp. 101–102.
62 Ibid., p. 93.
63 Ibid., p 95.
64 Ibid., p. 96.
65 Ibid., p. 80.
66 Ibid., p. 97. This wish returns in
    Summertime, p. 108.
67 Ibid., p. 79.
68 Ibid., p. 100.
69 Ibid.
70 This letter is in possession of Mrs
    Coetzee.
71 This is a reference to a temporary
    sojourn by J.M. Coetzee and his wife
    and two children in 1971, after his
    return from the US, on a farm near
    Leeu-Gamka and Voëlfontein. That
    he also highly valued his aunt Sylvia
    Coetzee, is evident from an e-mail
    to me, dated 10.10.2008: 'She was
    always my favourite aunt, and knew

me from about the time I was six,
which was when she married my
father's older brother and moved to
Voëlfontein. [...] She was fond of my
mother—generally my mother was not
popular with my father's family.'
72 *Boyhood*, p. 93.
73 Ibid., pp. 94–95.
74 *Boyhood*, p. 81 '*Volksmond*': demotic
    speech.
75 *Boyhood*, p. 125.
76 Ibid., p. 124.
77 Ibid., p. 66.
78 *Age of Iron*, p. 47.
79 *Boyhood*, pp. 108–109
80 *Die Burger*, 1.6.1950.
81 *Boyhood*, p. 109.
82 Ibid., p. 5.
83 Ibid., p. 122.
84 Ibid., p. 28.
85 Ibid., p. 9, 13.
86 Ibid., p. 10.
87 Ibid., p. 49.
88 Coetzee himself would later mature
    into a competent batsman.
89 Ibid., pp. 50–51.
90 Ibid., p. 29.
91 Ibid., p. 29.
92 Ibid., p. 18–19.
93 Upon enquiry during my interviews
    in March 2009, Coetzee was not able to
    provide the author or title of this series.
94 *Boyhood*, p. 26.
95 Ibid., p. 27.
96 Ibid., p. 55.
97 Ibid., p. 55.
98 Ibid., p. 16–17.
99 Ibid., p. 54.
100 Ibid., p. 36.
101 Ibid., p. 72.
102 Ibid., pp. 45–46.
103 Ibid., p. 103.
104 Ibid., p. 104.
105 Ibid., p. 106.
106 Ibid., p. 104.
107 Ibid., p. 105.
108 Ibid., pp. 105–106.
109 Ibid., pp. 106–107.
110 Ibid., pp. 56–57.
111 Interview with Jennifer Crwys-
    Williams, *Sunday Times*, 4.12.1983.
112 *Doubling the Point*, p. 393.
113 This comment occurs in an
    attachment to an e-mail sent to me by

J.M. Coetzee on 27.10.2008.

114 *Boyhood*, p. 106.

115 Ibid., p. 124.

116 E-mail from J.M. Coetzee to me, 27.10.2008.

117 *Doubling the Point*, p. 29.

118 The information regarding Jack Coetzee's re-admission to the attorney's roll and all documentation pertaining to it are available under motion 445 of 1950 of the Cape Division of the Supreme Court and are kept in the Cape Archives.

CHAPTER 3

1 J.M. Coetzee, *Boyhood*, London, Secker & Warburg, 1997, p. 133.

2 Ibid., p. 134.

3 Interview with J.M. Coetzee, 17.3.2009.

4 *Boyhood*, p. 144.

5 Interview with J.M. Coetzee, 17.3.2009.

6 E-mail from Nic Stathakis, 6.9.2009.

7 J.M. Coetzee, *Slow Man*, London, Secker & Warburg, 2005, p. 65.

8 *Boyhood*, p. 135. These schools are not identified, but could well have been SACS (the South African College School) and the Diocesan College (Bishops), although the Coetzees might not have been able to afford the high fees of the latter.

9 Ibid., p. 136.

10 Ibid., p. 137.

11 Information on the history of St Joseph's Marist College was derived from an interview with Hugh Fynn, the current principal of the school, on 10.2.2009; a pamphlet, 'A brief history of St Joseph's Marist College', obtainable from the school; and '*Opvoeding van 91 jaar gevier*' ['Education of 91 years celebrated'], an article in *Die Burger*, 2.3.2009.

12 Interview with J.M. Coetzee, 17.3.2009.

13 *Boyhood*, p. 137.

14 J.M. Coetzee, *Youth*, London, Vintage Books, 2002, pp. 38–39.

15 The facts do not support Coetzee's statement in *Boyhood* that '[t]he boys from Diocesan College [...] do not condescend even to play rugby or cricket against St Joseph's' (p. 136), because in the school's annual for 1956 results are published of matches against Diocesan College.

16 Collected in J.M. Coetzee, *Inner Workings: Essays 2000–2005*, London, Vintage Books, 2007, p. 30.

17 *St Joseph's College Magazine*, December 1953.

18 Personal e-mail, 27.10.2008.

19 E-mail of 16.2.2007 from Helmut Losken to Jackie Dent, who kindly put it at my disposal.

20 A well-known book by Th H. van de Velde, originally written in Dutch, and translated into many languages.

21 *Boyhood*, p. 147.

22 According to an e-mail from Stannard Silcock, a teacher of J.M. Coetzee at St Joseph's, to Jackie Dent, 16.2.2007, Theo Stravropoulos is a pseudonym. His real name is Anthony Lykiardopulos. He has since died.

23 *Boyhood*, p. 148.

24 Ibid.

25 Ibid., p. 143.

26 J.M. Coetzee, *Doubling the Point: Essays and Interviews*, edited by David Attwell, Cambridge, Massachusetts / London, Harvard University Press, 1992, pp. 393–394.

27 Ibid., p. 394.

28 *Boyhood*, p. 140. The references are to Charles Stewart Parnell, the nineteenth-century agitator and land reformer, and to Roger David Casement, who had entered into negotiations with Germany on the eve of the Easter Risings in 1916, and was later executed.

29 Brother Augustine, Stannard Silcock, was appointed to one of the training colleges in Natal at the end of John's matriculation year, but returned to St Joseph's in 1962 as principal. He left Cape Town again in 1967, to establish another Marist school in Natal. In 1971 he went to London to study for a degree in theology, but then left the Marist order and started teaching at a teacher's training college in Warwickshire. In 1983 he was

appointed as principal of the Marian College, Linmeyer, Johannesburg, where he established one of the first multi-racial schools in South Africa. In 1991 he returned to England, where he is living in Bridge Court, Weybridge, Surrey.

30 E-mail from Stannard Silcock, 17.3.2009.

31 Telephonic interview with Billy Steele, former classmate of J.M. Coetzee, 14.2.2009.

32 Telephonic interview with Billy Steele, 14.2.2009.

33 T. Tyfield and K.R. Nicol, eds, *The Living Tradition*, Cape Town, Maskew Miller, third edition, 1954, p. iii.

34 J.M. Coetzee, *Diary of a Bad Year*, London, Harvill Secker, 2007, pp. 217–218.

35 *Boyhood*, pp. 139–40.

36 J.M. Coetzee made this statement in writing in reply to a series of questions put to him by Shauna Westcott in a letter of 6.5.1981. It is not clear whether Westcott published her question-and-answer conversation with Coetzee, or used it as the basis of an article. The letter containing the questions and answers is in Coetzee's possession. NELM has no record of a publication by Westcott on Coetzee.

37 E-mail to me, 27.10.2008.

38 E-mail to me.

39 *Youth*, p. 21.

40 Ibid.

41 Invisible blackness filled the absent air,
Darkness that would have wrung the heavy tears
Of hopelessness from human eyes, had they
Been there to be dissolved and weakly crushed
Into the fatal gloom. A sickly sea
Of matter oozed aimless everywhere.
This was the Universe, devoid of shape
And life, encircled by perpetual night.
To this the shapeless Chaos roused himself.
A million years he lay, while on and on
The septic sore of space poured forth its filth,

And on and on the stream of matter rolled
Lightly touching each, he left
To all infinity. Eternity
And more he lay, as slow was born into
His darksome mind a dream of light, of pure
And undefiled brilliance. Then, as was
The thought created, came the light, a stream
Of liquid white without an origin,
As blinding as the savage lightning flash.
It flickered off, as though depending on
The wavering will of Chaos, lying blind
And stunned before his miracle. He blinked,
His ancient eyes grew round in childlike awe
And wonderment. For all his age, there was
In him yet of th'eternal child. Then rose
He, and with bursting pride surveyed his works.
The sluggish streams of matter still sweep on,
But from their surface shimmered sequined points
Of flashing, dancing light, while glancing beams
Did send the shadows slyly slinking to
The farthest corners of his vast domain.
A formless creature stirred nearby and rose
In all its shrouded age and hideousness.
Nyx, who for all eternity had lied
A living death and never woken, looked around.
All light seemed drawn into her gloomy form,
So that there shone a wall of solid black
Around her, against which the striving beams
Did vainly press. Yet as she crouched under
Her shroud of dark, their secret stole into
Her mind the same benign and glorious
Emotion which the ancient Chaos first
Had felt when he beheld the mighty All.
Then from her form the clouds of blackness slipped,
And gentle drops of liquid light caressed
Her old and haggard face. Bemused the pair

Looked on, he at his domain and she
At him.
Then suddenly the gloomy veil
Of darkness fell again, and all was black,
For hideous Erebus had woken to
The hateful light, which at his presence
    paled,
Grew dim, and faded everywhere. Hate,
    born
Within his breast, welled up, directed
    'gainst
His father, who had dared create both
    Light
And Erebus. With fierce and raging blows
He battered Chaos, toppling him from
    his
High vantage point into the cataracts
Below. While welkin mocked his dying
    shouts,
In inborn evil Erebus took for
Himself as wife the ancient Nyx.
And yet,
Their sinful and adulterous union
    brought
About a glorious event, for from
The aged Nyx there sprung the glitt'ring
    pair
Who were for evermore to banish gloom –
The twin Aether, the Light, and Hemera,
The Day, Light's complement. Their
    flashing and
Tumultuous natures, pitiless in strength
And merciless in brilliance, suited
    more
To rule than to obedience, rebelled
Against a living death. The welkin once
Again reverberated to the clash
Of strife divine, till pinion'd Erebus
Lay shrivelled by the sear of alien light.
His ashes stirred, as though a faint spring
    breeze
Were passing o'er that barren spot, and in
Their dust a smooth body writhed and
    turned,
Till vaguely could be seen the figure of
A cherub, from whom all the while arose
The fragrance of a flowery morn, of
    dew
On roses, and of daisies nodding in
The sun. This was the child of Light and
    Day,
A child of youth eternal, Eros, love's
Sweet herald, whose ambrosial arrows
    charm

The human race and make life
    purposeful.
The great work of creation then began.
The cataracts were dammed, and weight
    imposed.
As sluggishly the streams of matter took
On gluey weight and sensed constricting
    bands
Of gravity, they squelched in vain
    transports
Of rage, and pond'rously protested
    'gainst
Their ordered and eternal journey
    round
And round each other.
 Naught availed the groans
Of tortured elements, and silently
The crisscross tracery across the skies
Began of stars and planets, meteors,
    moons,
And their celestial entourage. Yet all
Was cold and dead. Upon the surface of
Each planet whipped an icy wind that
    sent
The dry dust scurrying before it like
The spirits of the dead before the spells
And incantations of a sorcerer,
Whilst gloomy peaks surveyed the
    darkened view.
The cherub Eros saw this as he winged
His flight over his vast domain. A chill
Dismay descended on him as he watched
The worlds revolve, rotate, remorselessly.
He hovered o'er the planet Gaea while
To his mind there came the thought of
    trees,
Of sunlight weaving patterns with the
    shade,
Of water bubbling over rounded stones
And dropping limpid to a ferny pool;
Of shell-blue skies, of soft bird-calls at
    dusk,
Of laughter rippling through the
    woods—he snatched
The quiver from his back, the bowstring
    bent,
And arrows cleaved their spiteful way into
The barren rock.
 While Eros clapped his hands
In youthful glee, the boulders crumbled to
A rich, dark loam, from which there
    straightway sprang
Fresh grass, while saplings fast took root
    and shot

632 J.M. COETZEE: A LIFE IN WRITING

Upright, like soldiers on parade all clad
In green, with arms and trappings
   brown. There was
The sound of water swirling 'gainst the
   rocks,
While brooklets babbled round the elm-
   trees' roots.
As though amused by the nonsense of
   the stream,
The skies laughed back and gained a
   lighter hue,
So that the distant angry stars grew dim,
Then faded, leaving one great Sun to
   smile
Benignly on the Earth, which waved to it
The scent of rose, of shrinking violet,
Of much-lamented narcissus, and all
The sweet array of her bouquet.
   Afar
Young Eros heard a novel sound, unlike
The water's dainty haste, unlike the call
Of bird or animal. A startled doe
Rushed through a verdant glade, and
   frightened birds
Flew squawking by. Into the glade there
   stepped
A noble youth, and by his side a maid
As fair as dawn upon a misty morn
And dainty as a dewdrop trembling on
A rosebud.
The lovers in the wood, and winged his
   way
From worlds of mortals to the gods'
   abode.

As the subtitle indicates, Coetzee
employs Greek and Roman creation
myths, specifically in the area of
cosmogony, in which the universe
moves from a chaotic and vague pre-
past to a more distinct ordering of
primordial matter.
   Coetzee's version of the creation
myth deviates from Hesiod's account,
the primary source of the Greek
creation myth. Hesiod describes the
creation as follows:
   Verily at the first Chaos came to
   be, but next wide-bosomed Earth,
   the ever-sure foundation of all the
   deathless ones who hold the peaks of
   snowy Olympus, and dim Tartarus in
   the depth of the wide-pathed Earth,
   and Eros (Love), fairest among the

deathless gods, who unnerves the
limbs and overcomes the mind and
wise counsels of all gods and all men
within them. From Chaos came forth
Erebus and black Night; but of Night
were born Aether and Day, whom
she conceived and bare from union
in love with Erebus. And Earth first
bare starry Heaven, equal to herself,
to cover her on every side, and to be
an ever-sure abiding-place for the
blessed gods. (Hesiod, *The Homeric
Hymns, and Homerica*, with an English
translation by Hugh G. Evelyn-White,
London, Heinemann / Cambridge,
Massachusetts, Harvard University
Press, 1959, pp. 87–89.)
   In Part I of *The Greek Myths*, of which
the first edition appeared in 1955
and which could thus have provided
a source for Coetzee, Robert Graves
distinguishes four different creation
myths: 'The Pelasgian Creation Myth,
the Homeric and Orphic Creation
Myths, The Olympian Creation Myth
and Two Philosophical Creation Myths.'
(Robert Graves, *The Greeks Myths I*,
Harmondsworth, Penguin, 1955 and
1960, unpaginated table of contents.)
Coetzee's rendering contains some part
of the fourth version, the philosophical
creation myths. Graves sums up the
relevant parts as follows:
   Some say that Darkness was first, and
   from Darkness sprang Chaos. From a
   union between Darkness and Chaos
   sprang Night, Day, Erebus, and the Air.
   [...] From a union between Air and
   Day sprang Mother Earth, Sky, and the
   other Titans, Tartarus, and the Three
   Erinnyes, or Furies. (Ibid., pp. 33–34.)
   Upon these meagre elements
Coetzee improvised freely. Whereas
in the original version Darkness gives
birth to Chaos, in Coetzee's version
both Darkness (the female Nyx) and
the male Erebus (also the symbol of
darkness) are born of Chaos. Even
so, Coetzee creates the impression
that light already inheres in Chaos.
Although it is not stated explicitly, one
gets the impression that he regards
Nyx as the wife of Chaos, rather than
his sister. Nyx falls under the spell

of the rays of light, Erebus resists violently and obtrudes himself upon her sexually. From this coupling, according to John's version that is not found in the original myth, Air and Day are born. In their turn, according to him, they are the parents of Eros, an account that deviates completely from the Greek myth. According to Hesiod, Eros is a son of Chaos, whereas in later mythologies he is a son of Aphrodite by Zeus, Ares or Hermes. (John Warrington, Everyman's Classical Dictionary, London, J.M. Dent / New York, E.P. Dutton, 1961, p. 221.) Thus even at this early stage of his development Coetzee demonstrates a readiness to depart from his source and forge a new direction.

What makes this poem such an exceptional achievement for a sixteen-year-old boy? Unlike the vast majority of his predecessors in English literature, he does not make use of the Genesis version, as John Milton did in *Paradise Lost*, but of Greek and Roman myths. There are examples in eighteenth- and nineteenth-century English literature of poets exploring cosmogony and shaping it into poetry, but through his deviations from the mythological data and the originality of his own interpretations, Coetzee demonstrates an independence distinguishing him from possible models. As for poems more broadly, not to say long-windedly, conceived, of those his prescribed anthology, *The Living Tradition*, furnished examples, such as Milton's great elegy 'Lycidas' and Pope's 'The Rape of the Lock'; but Coetzee's poem ranges much more widely than a few prescribed examples. From information furnished in the manuscript of *Boyhood*, it appears that he had already read Milton's *Samson Agonistes* and large parts of his *Paradise Lost*; in the latter he was particularly impressed with Lucifer's monologue after his fall.

Coetzee's poem is very rich linguistically, even where he inverts normal syntax, as in 'Then rose / He and with bursting pride surveyed his

works', 'against which the striving beams / Did vainly press', 'there secret stole into / Her mind the same benign and glorious / Emotion', 'Then from her form the clouds of blackness slipped.' Apart from the rather ceremonious archaism of such inversions, he also adopts an archaic type of poetic licence with unusual contractions and the omission of syllables, as in ''gainst', 'glitt'ring', 'pinion'd' and 'pond'rously'. There are no signs of metrical collapse or of dull patches; the text displays a sensitivity to the sound value of words with the many ringing alliterations ('sickly sea', 'surface shimmered sequined points', 'fragrance of a flowery morn' and 'brooklets babbled'), and the ingenious internal rhymes ('infinity—Eternity, a dream of light—a stream / Of liquid white, dancing—glancing') confirm his statement in *Youth* that at school he had experienced a short-lived enthusiasm for Gerard Manley Hopkins. (*Youth*, p. 20.) He also reactivates words designated by the dictionary as poetic and obsolete, such as 'welkin' for the sky, heavens or firmament. There are some surprising images, such as 'gentle drops of liquid light', 'shrouded age', combining a suggestion of mysterious concealment with funereal solemnity, and 'gloomy form', with its melancholy overtones.

It could be objected that the image of young trees as 'soldiers on parade all clad / In green, with arms and trappings brown' is at odds with the imaginative sphere of the poem. There is also something amiss, both syntactically and semantically, in the closing lines: 'The lovers in the wood and winged his way / From worlds of mortals to the gods' abode.' Does 'winged his way' refer to the 'noble youth' appearing at the conclusion, or to the flying Eros? If the latter (which seems the more likely), why the shift to the departing god of love from the youthful couple, who should by rights now enjoy the limelight? Or is there perhaps a printing error in the magazine? It is possible that the concluding lines should read: '[Eros

634 J.M. Coetzee: A Life in Writing

greeted] the lovers in the wood, and winged his way / From worlds of mortals to the gods' abode,' in which case, of course, the criticism would be invalidated.

42 *Youth*, pp. 15–16.

43 E-mail to me.

44 It is virtually certain that this Tony is the friend of Coetzee's youth who in *Boyhood* is referred to under the pseudonym of Theo Stavropoulos. His real name is Anthony Lykiardopulos.

45 The lecture is collected in J.M. Coetzee, *Stranger Shores: Essays 1986–1999*, London, Secker & Warburg, 2001, pp. 1–19.

46 Ibid., pp. 10–11.

47 *Doubling the Point*, p. 24.

48 Ibid., p. 393.

49 *Boyhood*, p. 154.

50 Ibid., pp. 155–156.

51 The information regarding Jack Coetzee's second striking from the roll of attorneys and all documentation pertaining to it are available under motion 815 of 1960 of the Cape Division of the Supreme Court, and are kept in the Cape Archives. Although the striking was only enacted in 1960, it is clear that the whole business had had a long gestation and that the family had been since 1956 in a financial and—on account of the disgrace—social quandary.

52 *Boyhood*, p. 160.

CHAPTER 4

1 Information on the founding history of the university is available in Howard Phillips, *The University of Cape Town 1918–1948*, Cape Town, UCT Press, 1993, pp. 1–10.

2 J.M. Coetzee, *Youth*, London, Vintage Books, 2002, p. 1.

3 Early in the 1960s the South African monetary unit was changed from British pounds, shillings and pence to a decimal system with rands and cents. Originally R2 was worth £1.

4 J.M. Coetzee, *Youth*, p. 1.

5 A guinea was equivalent to £1.1.0.

6 In the Adriana section of his novel *Summertime* (London, Harvill Secker, 2009, p. 155 ff.), Coetzee sketches a situation in which he tutors a Brazilian schoolgirl in English. Given the delicate interplay of fiction and reality in *Summertime*, we can assume that this situation is entirely fictional. As a student he gave extra tuition only in mathematics, not in English. The suggestion that in 1971, after his return from the US, in the period in which this part of the novel is set, he was still tutoring, does not accord with the fact that at the time Coetzee was a lecturer in English at the University of Cape Town.

7 Personal e-mail from John Kensch, 5.5.2009.

8 *Youth*, p. 2 and letter from H.M. Batson to Coetzee, 24.11.1958.

9 At this time the subject sociology had the status of a faculty. It was downgraded in the late 1960s to a department in the Faculty of Arts.

10 Letter of 2.12.1958 from L.E. Taylor, acting university librarian, to J.M. Coetzee.

11 Letter from the secretary of this college to Coetzee, 2.3.1960.

12 *Youth*, p. 2.

13 Interview with J.M. Coetzee, 18.3.2009.

14 *Youth*, pp. 89–90.

15 Ibid., p. 3.

16 Ibid., p. 18.

17 J.M. Coetzee, *Boyhood*, London, Secker & Warburg, 1997, p. 165.

18 Ibid., p. 166. The death and burial of Aunt Annie are described at the end of *Boyhood*, creating the impression that this happened during the John character's high school years. But this is an instance where Coetzee takes liberties with time, because Aunt Annie only died in 1958, when Coetzee was a second-year student at UCT.

19 *Youth*, p. 3.

20 J.M. Coetzee, *Doubling the Point: Essays and Interviews*, edited by David Attwell, Cambridge, Massachusetts / London, Harvard University Press, 1992, p. 29.

21 Information from Daniel Hutchinson in an e-mail to me, March 2010.

22 *Youth*, pp. 32–35.

23 Ibid., p. 10.

24 The word 'distilled' is derived from the Dutch poet H. Marsman's characterisation of the poet as a transformer and the creation of poetry as a distillation process: 'The grain of living is distilled into the jenever of poetry.' (H. Marsman, *Verzameld werk*, Amsterdam, Querido, 1960, p. 596).

25 T.S. Eliot, 'Tradition and the individual talent', *Selected Essays*, London, Faber and Faber, third expanded edition, 1958, p. 21.

26 *Youth*, p. 11: ' ... he wrestled with words and rhymes...'.

27 T.S. Eliot, *Collected Poems 1909–1962*, London, Faber and Faber, 1963, pp. 198 and 202–203.

28 Eliot, 'Hamlet', *Selected Essays*, p. 145.

29 *The Open Universities in South Africa*, Johannesburg, Witwatersrand University Press, 1957, p. 10.

30 Ibid., pp. 6–7.

31 Mark Gevisser, *The Dream Deferred: Thabo Mbeki*, Johannesburg and Cape Town, Jonathan Ball Publishers, 2007, p. 112.

32 Hermann Giliomee, *Die Afrikaners: 'n Biografie*, Cape Town, Tafelberg, 2004, p. 472 and Tom Lodge, *Sharpville: An Apartheid Massacre and its Consequences*, Oxford University Press, 2011.

33 *Die Burger*, 22.3.1960. This poem, which was read by President Nelson Mandela in 1994 in his first offical address, has been translated into English. The full title is 'The child who was shot dead by soldiers at Nyanga'.

34 *Youth*, p. 37.

35 *Die Burger*, 31.3.1960.

36 C.J. Driver, *Patrick Duncan: South African and Pan-African*, London, Heinemann, 1980, p. 180.

37 *Youth*, p. 37.

38 Ibid., p. 38.

39 Ibid., p. 39.

40 In the trial of several student activists, Leftwich supplied the police with the names of all his friends, became state witness and went scot-free. He left the country after the trial and settled overseas. See in this regard Hugh Lewin, *Stones against the Mirror*, Cape Town, Umuzi, 2011.

41 C.J. Driver, 'Used to be great friends', *Granta* 80, Winter 2002.

42 *Doubling the Point*, p. 394.

43 *Youth*, p. 22.

44 J.M. Coetzee, *Slow Man*, London, Secker & Warburg, 2005, p. 195.

45 In an interview with me on 19.3.2009, Coetzee said: 'I am deeply interested in music, but I am not a particularly visual person and have only an amateur's interest in art.'

46 Henri Poincaré, 'Mathematical creation', Brewster Ghiselin, ed., *The Creative Process*, fourth impression, New York, Mentor, 1959, p. 33.

47 P.J. Browne, W.N. Everitt and I.W. Knowles, 'Douglas Barker Sears: His work in differential equations', *Quaestiones Mathematicae*, 22, 1999, pp. 1–6.

48 Information from *MathSciNet* and 'The principal features of his character were vanity', *Proceedings of the London Mathematical Society*, 3: 5, 1955, pp. 48–70, and letter to me from Prof. G.C.L. Brümmer, 15.2.2010.

49 Interview with Joanna Scott, 'Voice and trajectory', *Salmagundi*, 114, 115, Spring / Summer 1997.

50 J.M. Coetzee, *Diary of a Bad Year*, London, Harvill Secker, 2007, pp. 87–96.

51 *Notices of the American Mathematical Society*, 56: 8, September 2009.

52 *Youth*, p. 23.

53 Ibid., p. 24.

54 Information from the *UCT Calendar*, 1957–1960.

55 Phillips, *The University of Cape Town 1918–1948*, p. 265.

56 Ibid., p. 265.

57 Ibid.

58 Ibid., p. 264.

59 Ibid.

60 J.M. Coetzee, 'Great teachers: Robert Guy Howarth, *Conference & Common Room*, 32: 1, Spring 1995.

61 Personal interview with J.M. Coetzee, 16.3.2009.

62 This and subsequent information in the following paragraphs is substantially based on my interview with Coetzee on 16.3.2009.

63 *Youth*, p. 26.

64 J.M. Coetzee, 'Great teachers: Robert Guy Howarth', *Conference & Common Room*, 32: 1, Spring 1995.

65 *Youth*, p. 27.

66 J.M. Coetzee, 'Great teachers: Robert Guy Howarth', *Conference & Common Room*, 32: 1, Spring 1995.

67 Information on Howarth based on my interview with Coetzee, 16.3.2009.

68 Quoted by A.L. Mcleod, *R.G. Howarth: Australian Man of Letters*, New Delhi, New Dawn Press, 2005, p. 120.

69 Ibid., p. 135.

70 Ibid., p. 139. On his return to Australia Howarth did not have a long career. A.L. Mcleod writes: 'Howarth was hit in Sydney by a motor bike in the early hours of 31 December 1973. He was taken to Sydney Hospital where he did not recover lucid consciousness again and died on the 22nd of January 1974. He left the home of friends and continued by train. It seemed that all of his injuries did not come from the motor-bike accident and it is likely that he was 'done over', his wallet and keys taken and that he eventually lurched out from Town Hall station on to the road.' (ibid., p. 151.)

71 J.M. Coetzee, 'Great teachers: Robert Guy Howarth', *Conference & Common Room*, 32: 1, Spring 1995. In a leading article in the *Cape Times* of 26.1.1974 Howarth is praised for his 'unobtrusive kindness to numbers of young people'.

72 *Youth*, p. 75.

73 Ibid., p. 76.

74 Ibid., p. 25.

75 *The Letters of Ezra Pound*, London, Faber and Faber, 1951, p. 91.

76 T.S. Eliot, 'John Dryden', *Selected Essays*, pp. 305-316.

77 G. Haresnape, 'Coetzee has just left the building', *Pen News*, December 2003.

78 This quotation and the information in the following paragraphs are from a series of e-mails to me from Jonty Driver, April and May 2009.

79 Letter to me.

80 'The oracular voice', collected by Robert L. Ross, ed., *International Literature in English: Essays on the Major Writers*, Chicago / London, St James, 1991, pp. 637-646.

81 *Youth*, p. 69.

82 Interview with J.M. Coetzee, 16.3.2009.

83 E-mail to me from Daniel Hutchinson, March 2010.

84 Ibid.

85 *Youth*, pp. 28-29.

86 Personal letter to me.

87 Letter from the registrar to J.M. Coetzee, 8.4.1960.

88 *Youth*, p. 40.

89 J.M. Coetzee, 'Remembering Texas', *Doubling the Point*, p. 50.

90 *Youth*, p. 62.

91 *Summertime*, p.5.

92 *Youth*, p. 41.

CHAPTER 5

1 J.M. Coetzee, *Doubling the Point*, ed. David Attwell, Cambridge, Massachusetts / London, Harvard University Press, 1992, p. 394.

2 J.M. Coetzee, *Diary of a Bad Year*, London, Harvill Secker, 2007, p. 191.

3 J.M. Coetzee, *The Master of Petersburg*, London, Secker & Warburg, 1994, p. 15.

4 Dominic Sandbrook, *White Heat: A History of Britain in the Swinging Sixties*, London, Little, Brown, 2006, p. xiv.

5 Ibid., p. xv.

6 'You can walk it on the grass', *Time*, 15.4.1966.

7 J.M. Coetzee, *Youth*, London, Vintage Books, 2002, pp. 71-72.

8 Ibid., p. 90.

9 J.M. Coetzee, *Elizabeth Costello*, London, Secker & Warburg, 2003, p. 30.

10 *Youth*, pp. 84-86.

11 *Doubling the Point*, p. 96.

12 *Youth*, pp. 86-87. Coetzee's version would seem to imply that the expulsion from the Commonwealth was directed by Britain. In fact, it was initiated by Jawaharlal Nehru, the Indian prime minister, with the support of the other Afro-Asian members of the Commonwealth and John Diefenbaker of Canada.

13 Ibid., pp. 100-101.

14 Quoted by Mark Gevisser, *The Dream Deferred: Thabo Mbeki*, Johannesburg

and Cape Town, Jonathan Ball Publishers, 2007, p. 156.

15 Ibid., p. 203.

16 'Waiting for Mandela', *New York Review of Books*, 8.5.1986.

17 *Youth*, p. 116.

18 Ibid., p. 137.

19 Ibid., pp. 42–43.

20 Ibid., p. 48.

21 Ibid., p. 49.

22 Ibid., p. 91.

23 Ibid., pp. 92–93.

24 Ibid., p. 58.

25 Hugh Kenner, *The Poetry of Ezra Pound*, London, Faber and Faber, 1951, p. 61, quoted from *Spirit of Romance*, p. 5.

26 *Youth*, p. 50.

27 Willem Kuipers, 'Kaartje naar Londen', *De Volkskrant*, 8.3.2002.

28 *Youth*, pp. 56–57.

29 Ibid., p. 53.

30 Ibid., p. 65.

31 Joanna Scott, 'Voice and trajectory: An interview with J.M. Coetzee', *Salmagundi*, 114, 115, Spring / Summer 1997.

32 Quoted by Fernando de Lima Paulo, *Imagining the Unimaginal: A Reading of J.M. Coetzee's* Foe, Universidade Federal de Minas Gerais, 2002, pp. 4–5.

33 Biographical details provided by David's wife, Akwe Amosu, to J.M. Coetzee, who made it available to me.

34 Information from an interview with J.M. Coetzee, 17.03.2009.

35 Fernando de Lima Paulo, op. cit.

36 *Youth*, pp. 62–63.

37 The cutting is in Coetzee's possession, but lacks a date of publication.

38 Geoffrey Haresnape, 'The writers' circle', *Personality*, 1.2.1968. Ed.: David Attwell pointed out that Stephen Gray too wrote an unpublished short story in which a character based on John Coetzee is portrayed satirically. This story is lodged with other manuscripts of Gray in the Harry Ransom Humanities Research Centre in Austin.

39 J.M. Coetzee, *The works of Ford Madox Ford with particular reference to the novels*, unpublished M.A.thesis, University of Cape Town, 1963.

40 *Youth*, p. 83.

41 Ibid., p. 122.

42 Ibid., p. 140.

43 *Doubling the Point*, pp. 18 and 17.

44 Interview with me, 20.3.2009.

45 Coetzee's return to South Africa and the fact that he survived without an income for the rest of 1963, lead one to suspect that he must after all have been able to save some money in his time in London. He had always, from childhood, been able to live frugally. It seems likely, then, that he could save more from his salary than the £10 per month he mentions in *Youth*.

46 T.S. Eliot, *Murder in the Cathedral*, *Collected Plays*, London, Faber and Faber, 1962, p. 30.

47 *Youth*, pp. 164–165.

48 *Doubling the Point*, pp. 51–52.

49 In reply to a series of questions Shauna Westcott put to him in a letter of 6.5.1981.

50 Fernando de Lima Paulo, *Imagining the Unimaginal: A Reading of J.M. Coetzee's* Foe, Universidade Federal de Minas Gerais, 2002, p. 4.

51 *Youth*, p. 166.

52 It is noteworthy that Coetzee never published an independent essay on Ford Madox Ford, as he could easily have done by lifting an extract from his M.A. dissertation. Was he later disillusioned in the writer in whom he had become interested because of Ezra Pound's enthusiasm? *Youth* makes clear that parts of Ford's oeuvre bored him, and that he never stumbled upon an undiscovered masterpiece.

53 Interview with me, 19.3.2009.

54 N.P. van Wyk Louw, *Tristia*, Cape Town, Human & Rousseau, 1962, p. 36. [Translation M.H.]

55 Ibid., p. 14. [Translation M.H.]

56 *Youth*, p. 117.

57 E-mail from Lionel Knight, 12.5.2009.

58 In fact it was to Austin, Texas.

59 Back to South Africa.

60 This must have been the Ganapathy who figures in *Youth*.

61 E-mail to me, 14.5.2009.

62 In reply to a series of questions Shauna Westcott put to him in a letter of 6.5.1981.

Chapter 6

1 J.M. Coetzee, *Doubling the Point: Essays and interviews*, edited by David Attwell, Cambridge, Massachusetts / London, Harvard University Press, 1992, pp. 25–26.
2 J.M. Coetzee, 'Samuel Beckett, the short fiction', *Inner Workings: Essays 2000–2005*, London, Vintage, 2007, p. 169.
3 J.M. Coetzee, *Youth*, London, Vintage, 2002, p. 155.
4 In one of his interviews with David Attwell, Coetzee says, for instance: 'My academic record wasn't good enough to open major fellowships to me' (*Doubling the Point*, p. 26). Coetzee's study record in English at UCT was excellent, and this statement simply does not accord with the facts.
5 In 'Remembering Texas' (*Doubling the Point*, p. 50), an essay dating from 1984, Coetzee writes that he was paid $2 100 for the year. This amount, though, is given as $2 300 in the letter of 26.7.1966 from the University of Texas .
6 Written interview with Shauna Westcott, 6.5.1981. The text is in J.M. Coetzee's possession, but apparently was never published.
7 Information from *Encyclopaedia Britannica*, part 2, London / Chicago / Genève / Sydney / Toronto, William Benton Publisher, 1964, pp. 773–774.
8 This formulation is reminiscent of Coetzee's reflections on the graves of coloured people on Voëlfontein in *Boyhood* (London, Secker & Warburg, 1997, p. 97): 'Whatever dies here, dies firmly and finally: its flesh is picked off by the ants, its bones are bleached by the sun, and that is that. [...] From the earth comes a deep silence, so deep that it could almost be a hum.'
9 J.M. Coetzee, 'Meat country', *Granta*, 52, Winter 1995.
10 *Doubling the Point*, p. 57.
11 *Youth*, p. 77.
12 Ibid. This pronouncement is given to the alienated John, wandering aimlessly in the streets of London, and is based, at this stage, on an extremely limited

acquaintance with Dutch poetry. Commentators have on occasion read this out of context as if it were J.M. Coetzee's own judgement and condemnation of Dutch poetry. But in *Youth* this harsh judgement reinforces the central character's isolation.
13 Coetzee refers to her as 'Rosamund' (*Doubling the Point*, p. 50). Other sources call her 'Ruth'.
14 *Doubling the Point*, p. 50.
15 Ibid., p. 24.
16 Ibid., pp. 52–53.
17 Ibid., p. 53.
18 In the text in J.M. Coetzee's possession, this interview is dated as 25.2.1983, but it never appeared in *Fair Lady*.
19 J.M. Coetzee, 'Idleness in South Africa', *White Writing*, New Haven / London, Yale University Press, 1988, pp. 12–35.
20 *Doubling the Point*, p. 51.
21 Ibid., p. 51.
22 Rae Nadler-Olenick, 'Cape Town to Stockholm, with a layover in Austin', *The Alcade*, January / February 2004.
23 *Doubling the Point*, p. 51.
24 One of Beckett's better students later characterised his manner of teaching as follows: 'He was a very impersonal lecturer. He said what he had to say and then left the lecture room ... I believe he considered himself a bad lecturer and that makes me sad because he was so good ... Many of his students would, unfortunately, agree with him.' This judgement is cited by Coetzee in his discussion of the first volume of *The Letters of Samuel Beckett*. It appeared under the title 'The making of Samuel Beckett' in *The New York Review of Books*, 30 April 2009.
25 *Doubling the Point*, p. 25.
26 J.M. Coetzee, *Inner workings: Essays 2000–2005*, London, Vintage, 2007, pp. 169–170.
27 Ibid., pp. 172–173.
28 *Doubling the Point*, p. 25.
29 *UCT Studies in English*, 9, 1979. In this discussion of Bair's biography Coetzee makes a comment that in the light of what was later to be said about him by journalists, and parroted by more than

one commentator, is applicable to him as well: 'The Beckett legend concocted by journalists, turning to their own advantage Beckett's notorious reclusiveness and the iconography of "genius" displayed in the photographs (the "piercing"stare, the "devastated" looks, etc.) has been a pop-existentialist stereotype of the explorer of the abyss, the Lazarus who has seen it all and come back to tell his tale.'

30 *Doubling the Point*, p. 39.

31 Samuel Beckett, *Watt*, edited by C.J. Ackerley, London, Faber and Faber, 2009, p. viii.

32 Ibid., pp. vii–viii.

33 *Doubling the Point*, p. 22.

34 J.M. Coetzee, *The English Fiction of Samuel Beckett: An Essay in Stylistic Analysis*, Ph.D dissertation, University of Texas at Austin, January 1969, pp. 159–160.

35 Rae Nadler-Olenick, 'Cape Town to Stockholm, with a layover in Austin', *The Alcade*, January / February 2004. About twenty years before Coetzee's stylo-statistical study, a reading method was developed at the Gemeentelijke Universiteit van Amsterdam, under the direction of Prof. W.G. Hellinga, that examined linguistic values in relation to a particular instance of usage. This method, that came to be known as stylistics on a linguistic base, was adopted in South Africa by several exponents who used and expanded it in their doctoral dissertations. This form of stylistics, like stylo-statitistics, was at most a demonstration and thus a cul-de-sac; exponents eventually abandoned the method for alternative approaches. It is nevertheless true that in the 1950s the method provided an important corrective to the predominantly impressionistic approaches.

36 *The Alcade*, January / February 2004.

37 J.M. Coetzee, 'Meat country', *Granta* 52, Winter 1995.

38 Ibid.

39 *The Alcade*, January / February 2004.

40 Coetzee, *White Writing*, pp. 38–39.

41 *Doubling the Point*, p. 52.

42 J.M. Coetzee, *Diary of a Bad Year*, London, Harvill Secker, 2007, p. 133.

43 J.M. Coetzee, *Dusklands*, Johannesburg, Ravan Press, 1974, pp. 6 and 31.

44 Ibid., pp. 6–7 and 14.

45 Cape Town, Cape Times Limited, 1928.

46 John Barrow, *An account of Travels into the Interior of Southern Africa in the Years 1797 and 1798*, London, A. Strachan, 1801, p. 81.

47 Henry Lichtenstein, *Travels in South Africa*, Cape Town, Van Riebeeck Society, 1928, pp. 124–125.

48 *The Journals of Hendrik Jacob Wikar (1779)* with an English Translation by A.W. van der Horst and *The Journals of Jacobus Coetsé Janz (1760) and Willem van Reenen (1791)* with an English Translation by Dr E.E. Mossop, Cape Town, Van Riebeeck Society, 1935.

49 Peter Temple, 'The private world of a major new S.A. talent', *The Star*, 14.6.1974.

50 Breyten Breytenbach, *Ysterkoei-blues: Versamelde gedigte 1964–1975*, Cape Town, Human & Rousseau, 2001, pp. 289–290. [Translation M.H.]

51 *The Alcade*, January / February 2004.

52 The National Liberation Front (against South Vietnam).

53 The cutting of this letter is part of the material in J.M. Coetzee's possession that he made available to me. There is no date of publication on it.

54 Ilias Venezis, 'The seagulls', translated by Mauna Coetzee, *Contrast* 31, VIII: 3.7.1973.

55 *Doubling the Point*, p. 20.

56 Ibid., p. 103.

57 Information from *Time*, 12.8.1966, Wikipedia (Charles Whitman) and *The Summer Texan*, 2.8.1966.

58 Interview with J.M. Coetzee, 18.3.2009.

59 Much later, on 23.4.2006, Coetzee told a journalist on the *Texas Monthly* by e-mail about one of the most upsetting aspects of the events: 'One of the things I heard that rather shocked me was that while Whitman was at work some students had raced back to their fraternities to get their guns to join in the gun battle. I hadn't fully

comprehended that lots of people around me in Austin not only owned guns but had them close at hand and regarded themselves as free to use them.' He continues: 'I didn't then and don't now regard Whitman's killing spree as uniquely American—madmen like that crop up all over the place—but I did regard the rush to be part of the gunfight as particularly Texan.'

60 *Doubling the Point*, p. 53.

CHAPTER 7

1 J.M. Coetzee, *Youth*, London, Vintage Books, 2003, p. 152.
2 Richard A. Siggelkow, *Dissent and Disruption and a University under Siege*, Buffalo, New York, Prometheus Books, 1991, p. 53.
3 Ibid., p. 63.
4 Ibid., quoted, p. 65.
5 Ibid., p. 90.
6 J.M. Coetzee, *Dusklands*, Johannesburg, Ravan Press, 1974, unpaginated, and *Can We Win in Vietnam?: The American Dilemma*, with contributions by Frank E. Armbruster, Raymond D. Gastil, Herman Kahn, William Pfaff and Edmund Stillman, second publication in the Hudson Institute Series, London, Pall Mall Press, 1968, p. 10.
7 *Can We Win in Vietnam?*, p. 10, my italics.
8 Ibid., p. 9, my italics.
9 Interview with J.M. Coetzee, 18.3.2009.
10 Siggelkow, op. cit., p. 20.
11 This is the figure cited by *Time*, 12.1.1968. *Newsweek* of 30.3.1970, however, put the number at 16 000.
12 Personal interview with J.M. Coetzee, 18.3.2009. Much of the information in this paragraph is derived from this interview.
13 Siggelkow, op. cit., p. 21 cited.
14 The abbreviation for 'Alternating current / Direct current' here refers to people with both critical and creative abilities.
15 In reply to a series of questions she put to him by letter on 6.5.1981.
16 MFW: Mondays, Fridays, Wednesdays;

TT: Tuesdays, Thursdays.
17 J.M. Coetzee, *Doubling the Point: Essays and Interviews*, edited by David Attwell, Cambridge, Massachusetts, Harvard University Press, 1992, p. 336.
18 Ibid.
19 Collected in *Doubling the Point*, pp. 344–360.
20 Ibid., p. 336.
21 Ibid., p. 337.
22 J.M. Coetzee, *Summertime*, London, Harvill Secker, 2009, p. 232.
23 These notes are kept as part of the Coetzee documents at NELM, Grahamstown. Letters, exam papers, notices and bibliographies pertaining to Coetzee's work at UB are in his personal possession.
24 J.M. Coetzee, *Landscape with rowers: Poetry from the Netherlands*, Princeton / Oxford, Princeton University Press, 2004, pp. 2–29.
25 Ibid., p. viii.
26 Buber (*I and Thou*, translated by Ronald Gregor Smith, Edinburgh, T & T Clark, ninth impression, 1957, pp. 14–15) writes: 'Love does not cling to the *I* in such a way as to have the *Thou* only for its "content," its object; but love is *between I* and *Thou*. The man who does not know this, with his very being know this, does not know love; even though he ascribes to it the feelings he lives through, experiences, enjoys, and expresses. […] Love is responsibility of an *I* for a *Thou*'.
27 *Doubling the Point*, pp. 86–87.
28 Ibid., p. 90.
29 Ibid., p. 88.
30 *Landscape with Rowers*, p. 8.
31 Ibid., p. 9.
32 *Doubling the Point*, p. 73.
33 *Landscape with Rowers*, p. 7.
34 J.M. Coetzee, *In the Heart of the Country*, Johannesburg, Ravan Press, 1976, p. 41.
35 J.M. Coetzee, *Stranger Shores: Essays 1986–1999*, London, Secker & Warburg, 2001, p. 43.
36 Marcellus Emants, *Een nagelaten bekentenis*, introduced by Etienne Britz, Pretoria / Cape Town, Academica, 1980, p. 21. [Translation M.H.]
37 *Stranger Shores*, p. 43.

38 Ibid., p. 45.
39 Personal letter to me.
40 *Dusklands*, p. 51.
41 Marcellus Emants, *A Posthumous Confession*, translated and introduced by J.M. Coetzee, London /Melbourne / New York, Quartet Encounters, 1986, p. 13.
42 *Stranger Shores*, p. 44.
43 *A Posthumous Confession*, p. 7.
44 Information from a personal interview with J.M. Coetzee, 18.03.2009.
45 Stanley Karnow, *Vietnam: A History*, revised and expanded edition, London, Pimloco, 1991, pp. 541–542.
46 Ibid., pp. 472–473.
47 *Spectrum*, 27.4.1970.
48 Siggelkow, op. cit., pp. 154–155.
49 Ibid., p. 187.
50 Rae Nadler-Olenick, 'Cape Town to Stockholm with a layover in Austin', *The Alcade*, January—February 2004.
51 Siggelkow, op. cit., p. 207.
52 Ibid., pp. 207–210.
53 *Spectrum*, 20.4.1970.
54 Siggelkow, op. cit., p. 214.
55 Ibid., p. 215.
56 *Spectrum*, 3.4.1970.
57 *Newsweek*, 30.3.1970.
58 Here there follows a list of the officials, among them Peter Regan, the acting president.
59 *Summertime*, p. 227.
60 Information from a personal interview with J.M. Coetzee, 18.3.2009.
61 Siggelkow, op. cit., p. 219.
62 Joanna Scott: 'Voice and trajectory: An interview with J.M. Coetzee', *Salmagundi*, 114, 115, Spring / Summer 1997.
63 I quote from the typescript in Coetzee's possession.
64 *Youth*, p. 137.
65 Ibid., p. 139.

CHAPTER 8

1 Quoted by Susan van Zanten Gallagher, *A Story of South Africa: J.M. Coetzee's Fiction in Context*, Cambridge, Massachusetts / London, Harvard University Press, 1991, p. 53.
2 *Cape Argus*, 19.6.1974.
3 Dick Penner, *Countries of the Mind: The Fiction of J.M. Coetzee*, New York / Westport, Connecticut / London, Greenwood Press, 1989, p. 3 quoted.
4 Ibid., p. 20 quoted.
5 J.M. Coetzee, *Age of Iron*, London, Secker & Warburg, 1990, p. 25.
6 David Attwell, *J.M. Coetzee: South Africa and the Politics of Writing*, Berkeley / Los Angeles / Oxford, University of California Press / Cape Town / Johannesburg, David Philip, 1993, pp. 28–29.
7 For this formulation, see Coetzee on 'Robert Musil's *Diaries*', *Stranger Shores: Essays 1986–1999*, London, Secker & Warburg, 2001, p. 104.
8 Since 21 August 1972 fell on a Monday, 20 August is probably intended here. In that issue, though, there in no report on an attack in Francistown, and also not in other issues of the *Sunday Times* in the same month.
9 J.M. Coetzee, *Summertime*, London, Harvill Secker, 2009, p. 4.
10 Dick Penner refers to this on p. 20 of *Countries of the Mind*. Coetzee provided more information on this event in an e-mail of 12.8.2009.
11 In 1979 a bullet was fired through the front door of Colin Eglin's flat in Sea Point. Eglin was another prominent member of the Progressive Party and was Slabbert's predecessor as leader of this party. Apparently the government, to clear itself, blamed the incident on members of the Beelders gang, who were later prosecuted. Eglin writes about this in his autobiography (*Crossing the Borders of Power*, Johannesburg / Cape Town, Jonathan Ball, 2007, pp. 186 and 191–192).
12 My transcription of the DVD. It was published in a Dutch translation in Wim Kayzer, *Van de schoonheid en de troost*, Amsterdam, Contact, 2000, pp. 310–311.
13 J.M. Coetzee, *White Writing: On the Culture of Letters in South Africa*, New Haven / London, Yale University Press, 1988, p. 7.
14 Ibid., p. 9.
15 J.M. Coetzee, *Doubling the Point: Essays*

and Interviews, edited by David Attwell, Cambridge, Massachusetts / London, Harvard University Press, 1992, p. 115.

16 Eugène N. Marais, *Die volledige versamelde gedigte,* edited by Marissa Baard, J.C. Kannemeyer, Kristèl Roets, Nicol Stassen and Marni Viviers, Pretoria, Protea Boekhuis, 2005, p. 85. [Translation M.H.] This vision of the relentless cruelty of nature recurs frequently in the oeuvre of Marais. In his internationally known work *Die siel van die mier* (1934) [*The Soul of the White Ant,* translated 1937] he posits the absence of love as the central tenet of nature and the avoidance of pain as the primary condition for the survival of all life. In nature a constant relentless cruelty and lack of feeling rules supreme: 'Never have its pitiless eyes misted over with brimming tears, never has it reached out a protective or caressing hand to the loveliest and most guileless of its creatures.' (Eugène N. Marais, *Die siel van die mier,* edited by S. Francine Honing, J.C. Kannemeyer, Annie Klopper, LiMari Louw and Mia Oosthuizen, Pretoria, Protea Boekhuis, 2007, p. 74.) [Translation M.H.]

17 *Doubling the Point,* p. 117.

18 J.M. Coetzee, *In the Heart of the Country,* Johannesburg, Ravan Press, 1977, p. 138.

19 J.M. Coetzee, *Age of Iron,* London, Secker & Warburg, 1990, p. 16.

20 Teresa Dovey, *The Novels of J.M. Coetzee,* Craighall, Ad Donker, 1988, p. 55, quoted.

21 Information in a letter from Mrs Sylvia Coetzee to me, 2.12.2008.

22 *Summertime,* p. 89.

23 Personal interview with Gerald Coetzee, 23.5.2009.

24 Personal interview with Gisela Coetzee, 7.4.2010.

25 The text of this article was kindly lent to me by Mrs Sylvia Coetzee.

26 Interview with Chris Perold, 11.3.2010.

27 's-Gravenhage, Martinus Nijhoff.

28 Cape Town, Van Riebeeck Society, 1935.

29 In her book *Digging through Darkness: Chronicles of an Archaeologist,* Johannesburg, Witwatersrand University Press, 1995, p. 6, Carmel Schrire writes: 'Coetzee seems to challenge the informed reader to spot the seams when he tranforms the actual Van Riebeeck Society into the fictional Van Plettenberg Society, and the well-known Cape Archives, into the unknown South African National Archives. His teasing is light, but his message is profound. Attribution is moot because historic documents that seek to alter the truth are more fictional than inventions.'

30 J.M. Coetzee, *Dusklands,* Johannesburg, Ravan Press, 1974, p. 115.

31 Derek Attridge, *J.M. Coetzee and the Ethics of Reading,* Scottsville, University of KwaZulu-Natal Press, 2005, p. 15.

32 In the manuscript the paragraph on p. 125, starting with the words 'The Namaqua were a people of medium stature', contains many more details than in the published text. I transcribe that part of the manuscript, without addition of all the corrections and rewritings:

They were a people of medium stature. The men were slender, the women plump. Their skins were yellowish-brown in color. I employ the preterite because the Namaqua have been much bastardized, particularly the Little Namaqua living south of the Orange River. Their hair was short and curly like the wool of lambs. Their foreheads wrinkled early as a result of much squinting. Their eyes were black, their vision piercing like that of the Bushmen. Bleek, recording the legends of the Dawn's Heart and the Dawn's Heart Child, suggests that Bushmen had discerned the satellites of Jupiter with the naked eye long before Galileo. Their teeth were as white as ivory and did not decay, but were ground down by the passing of time, so that old men had mouths full of stumps. Their hands and feet were elegantly small. Their buttocks, and particularly the buttocks of mature women, protruded unpleasantly. Boys were taught to force their testicles back into the body cavity

when these descended. With empty
scrota they were noted for fleetness of
foot. Like the women of ancient Egypt,
their females suffered from a peculiar
conformation / deformation of the
labia minora, which in some cases
protruded to a length of three inches
and in most extended as an elliptical
tube an inch or so in length. While
the women of Egypt considered such
elongation a defect and were prepared
to undergo the pains of cautery the
Hottentots accepted it as natural.
Doubtless they had no reason to
think otherwise, for the women of the
Bushmen had the same conformation /
deformation and females among the
colonists were, one need hardly say,
too delicate to expose themselves /
their pudenda / shame to the gaze
of savages. The breasts of mature /
full-grown Namaqua women were long
enough to be tossed over their shoulders
to the children carried on their backs.
The flaccidity of their breasts should
be attributed to the habit of suckling
children up to the age of three.

33 *Doubling the Point*, p. 90.
34 Gallagher, *A Story of South Africa*, p. 74.
35 T. Kai Norris Easton, *Textuality and the Land: Reading* White Writing *and the Fiction of J.M. Coetzee*, unpublished D.Phil. dissertation, University of London, 2000, p. 63.
36 Gallagher, *A Story of South Africa* , p. 79.
37 Peter Knox-Shaw, '*Dusklands:* A metaphysics of violence', *Contrast*, XIV: 1, 1982.
38 Attwell, *J.M. Coetzee: South Africa and the Politics of Writing*, pp. 46–47.
39 The words 'but he is also pictured' have been deleted in the manuscript and replaced with 'but from our ivory towers we have also indulgently smiled at (him as)'. The last two words have been deleted again.
40 The words 'an illiterate boer' are replaced with 'the credulous hunter.'
41 Originally 'white'.
42 Later 'dwelling'.
43 Later 'that'.
44 The words 'loss of so many good men on the' have been struck through and replaced with 'fruitless'.

45 The date 1761 was later changed to 1761–62.
46 Easton, op. cit., p. 58.
47 *Dusklands*, p. 116.
48 Ibid., p. 104.
49 Information from a personal interview with J.M. Coetzee, 17.3.2009.
50 *Summertime*, pp. 206–207.
51 Daniel Hutchinson in an e-mail to me, March 2010.
52 J.M. Coetzee, 'Great teachers: Robert Guy Howarth', *Conference & Common Room*, 32: 1, Spring 1995.
53 Personal e-mail to me, March 2010.
54 Ibid.
55 E-mail from Jonathan Crewe, 26.4.2009.
56 Ian Glenn, 'Nadine Gordimer, J.M. Coetzee and the politics of interpretation', *The South African Atlantic Quarterly*, 93: 1, Winter 1994.
57 Daniel Hutchinson in an e-mail of March 2010.
58 Personal e-mail from Lesley Marx, 10.5.2009.
59 T.S. Eliot, 'The metaphysical poets', *Selected Essays*, London, Faber and Faber, 1951, p. 287.
60 Collected in *Doubling the Point*, p. 344.
61 The review of *Local Colour* appeared in *Beeld*, 24.11.1975; that of *The Orange Earth* in *Rapport*, 6.8.1978.
62 Collected in *Research in African Literature*, XI: 2, 1980.
63 At the time of their occupation houses in this area had no street numbers.
64 *Summertime*, p. 7.
65 C.P. Cavafy, *Collected Poems*, Trans. Edmund Keeley & Philip Sherrard, ed. George Savidis, Princeton University Press, 1992.
66 Hermann Wittenberg, 'J.M. Coetzee and Ravan Press: Towards an archaeology of *Dusklands*', Carol Clarkson, ed., *J.M. Coetzee and the Aesthetics of Place*, Cape Town, UCT Press, 2012.
67 Less than 1 per cent of the books in African bookstores are indigenous works published locally in indigenous languages. This has important implications for the writer's voice, as many African writers consciously bear in mind their metropolitan readers,

and avoid writing for and from their communities. This is a problem that Coetzee was to return to later in the second 'lesson' of his *Elizabeth Costello* (London, Secker & Warburg, 2003), 'The Novel in Africa'. The strongest indigenous book industry in Africa was and remains the Afrikaans publishing industry. The difference between Afrikaans and Dutch was so great that Afrikaans authors could not publish their books in Amsterdam in untranslated form. They were dependent on the local industry. The growth of Afrikaans as a language to a large extent went hand-in-hand with a growth in Afrikaner nationalism. With support from the government, through the establishment of good Afrikaans schools and universities and public amenites, a strong Afrikaans literature was founded. English and black authors in South Africa were to a large extent subjected to the same metropolitan pressure as writers in the rest of Africa. Even though the English literary industry was more viable in South Africa than in the rest of Africa, it was not as strong as its Afrikaans counterpart. It is only now, almost two decades after the change of government, that a strong indigenous English literary industry is developing.

68 Andrew van der Vlies, *South African Textual Cultures*, Manchester and New York, Manchester University Press, 2007, p. 136.

69 Wittenberg, op. cit.

70 Ibid., op. cit.

71 Wittenberg, op. cit.

72 Alan Lennox-Short, ed., *English and South Africa*, Cape Town, Nasou, 1973.

73 Easton, op. cit., p. 53. Coetzee wrote the different stages of the holograph of 'The Vietnam Project' in UCT exam books, then still in folio format.

74 Gallagher's assertion in *A Story of South Africa* (p. 51) that Coetzee completed both stories in the USA is thus patently inaccurate.

75 *Dusklands*, p. 3.

76 Ibid., p. 3.

77 Ibid., p. 23.

78 Ibid., pp. 18–19.

79 Ibid., p. 39.

80 David Attwell, *J.M. Coetzee: South Africa and the Politics of Writing*, p. 49.

81 Joanna Scott, 'Voice and trajectory: An interview with J.M. Coetzee', *Salmagundi*, 114, 115, Spring / Summer 1997.

82 Sue Kossew, *Pen and power: A post-colonial reading of J.M. Coetzee and André P. Brink*, Amsterdam, Rodopi, 1996, p. 34.

83 *Dusklands*, p. 33.

84 Pascal Carré, *John Maxwell Coetzee: Power and the Individual Consciousness*, Université de Liege, 1984–1985, p. 9.

85 Pierre Macherey uses the concept 'thematic ancestor' in *A Theory of Literary Production*, translated by Geoffrey Wall, London, Routledge and Kegan Paul, 1978, pp. 240–248. It is quoted by Allan Gardiner in 'J.M. Coetzee's *Dusklands*: Colonial encounters of the Robinsonian kind', *World Literature Written in English*, 27: 2, Fall 1987.

86 Since the relation between master and servant or slave occurs as a dominant motif in several of Coetzee's novels, it is necessary to explicate Hegel's pronouncements in this regard and to show what forms this relation assumes in the literature of the twentieth century. George Steiner (*The New Yorker*, 12.7.1982) provides a clear exposition:

The most famous of all modern political allegories is that which Hegel called 'The Master and the Servant'. Hegel sees the human condition as quintessentially polemic. There is a sense in which a man can establish his full identity, can come into full possession of his own consciousness, only by destroying his equal. With eloquent intensity, Hegel argues that the opaquely challenging and resistant presence of 'the other man'—of *l'autre*, as the existentialists will call him—must be overcome if we are to be integrally ourselves. Even Goethe, a spirit more serene than Hegel, asks, 'Do I truly live if another is alive?' But an immediate logical objection springs to mind. The mortal duel of opposed egos must end either in mutual destruction — as happens to Creon and Antigone in the play that Hegel placed at the very summit of human invention — or in the elimination of the adversary. In which case, however, there will be no counter-presence, no witness, left to mirror, to validate, the claims of the victorious self. To remain sole victor is to be trapped in a mute emptiness.

Hence the parable of master and servant. Rather than expose their lives to agonistic encounter and likely destruction, most men relinquish the status of the heroic. They evade the threatening ordeal of mastery. They are prepared to serve. In any society, Hegel contends, an élite of masters, potentially in internecine conflict, will dominate a much larger class of servants. Those who are not prepared to put their own existence to the test of ultimate spiritual-psychic combat must and will serve those who are. The master sees in the eyes of his servant the constant acknowledgement of his own sacrificial, menaced individuality. It is at this point that Hegel's dialectical model reveals an unrivalled political and psychological acumen. At first, it would appear that the relation between the suprematists of the ego and their helots is one of static subjection. This is not so. The master *needs* the servant — intimately, compellingly. It is only the servant who can underwrite the master's self-recognition. Moreover, in economic and technical terms the master grows less and less productive, less and less independent precisely to the degree that he relies on the servant. It is the servant, not the master, who embodies the positive impulses and capacities for renewal in the community. Becoming more and more aware of his indispensability (more self-aware), the servant will seek with other servants bonds of solidarity which masters, in their tragic autism, cannot entertain. It is, in consequence, the servant who is the carrier of historical evolution and the explorer of new modes of human interaction.

It is not difficult to see that this Hegelian parable is central to the conflictual models of history and of society in Marxism; or that it plays a seminal role in such exemplary modern fables as Brecht's *Pultila and His Servant*, Beckett's *Waiting for Godot* and Genet's *The Maids*. But if Hegel's paradigm has been used, and used brilliantly, to dramatize confrontations between the sexes, between social classes, between dominant and obeisant sensibilities in a given milieu and society, it has been equally suggestive with regard to racial conflicts and the politics of colonialism. The novels of Conrad (*Nostromo* in particular), the tales of Kipling, Faulkner's chronicles of masters and sometime slaves in Yoknapatawpha Country exemplify Hegel's precise, somber reading of the doomed symbiosis between ruler and subject — doomed because it contains within its brutal yet intricate dynamics the end of the heroic caste. Masters die in the arms of their compassionately mocking servants.

87 Dick Penner, *Countries of the Mind: The Fiction of J.M. Coetzee*, New York / Westport, Connecticut / London, Greenwood Press, 1989, p. 21.

88 Attridge, *J.M. Coetzee and the Ethics of Reading*, p. 15.

89 *Dusklands*, p. 5.

90 Ibid.

91 Ibid., pp. 6–7.

92 Ibid., p. 33.

93 Ibid., p. 30.

94 Easton, op. cit., p. 55.

95 From this one gathers that Coetzee had at the time of writing to Cope not yet submitted the manuscript to Ad Donker.

96 Personal e-mail from Jonathan Crewe, 26.4.2009.

97 The name Ravan was proposed by Van Zyl: *Ra* for Randall, *va* for Van Zyl and *n* for Naudé.

98 Peter Randall, 'The beginnings of

Ravan Press: a memoir', *Ravan: Twenty-five Years (1972–1997)*, edited by G.E. de Villiers, Randburg, Ravan Press, 1997. In the same volume Glenn Moss writes about the later course of Ravan Press's publications, and in another contribution Albert Grundlingh concentrates on the publications in the field of history.

99 J.M. Coetzee in a personal interview of 8.5.1999 with Peter McDonald, *The Literature Police*, Oxford, Oxford University Press, 2009, p. 137.

100 Wittenberg, op. cit.

101 Coetzee means 'PROJECT'.

102 The correspondence between Coetzee and Ravan Press is held in photocopy form at the National English Literary Museum in Grahamstown, in the Spro-Cas collection in the Cullen Library of the University of the Witwatersrand and with Macmillan Press in Johannesburg, which took over from Hodder & Stoughton, which had taken over from Ravan Press. (See on this Wittenberg, op. cit.) The original letters of the larger part of this collection are still in possession of J.M. Coetzee.

103 Wittenberg, op. cit.

104 By the early 1980s it was extremely difficult to get hold of this edition from antiquarian booksellers, and by 1985 merchants in the US were paying $250 per copy. In a report in the *Saturday Argus* of 1.7.2000 William Pretorius stated that the first printing of *Dusklands* was fetching $500 (R3 400).

105 Wittenberg, op.cit.

106 Ibid.

107 Personal interview with J.M. Coetzee, 20.3.2009.

108 In Crewe's manuscript the original words after 'and' have been so struck through that they are no longer legible. He wrote over this 'it is not overshadowed by the latter work'. Apparently, mindful of Cope's caution, he rewrote this part in such a way as to forestall scepticism as regards the comparison of Coetzee and Conrad.

109 Translation M.H.

110 André P. Brink, 'Master of the human condition', *Sunday Times*, 7.12.2003.

111 On the page in question Crewe writes the following, inter alia: 'The *trompe l'oeil* consistency of the traditional novel is deliberately eschewed in *Dusklands*. The disclosure of the stage machinery in a magic-show transforms miracle into elementary mechanics, and the magician into an operator (in more than one sense of the word). Similarly, when the conjuring trick — the phrase is used advisedly — of the traditional novel is deliberately exposed; when the 'autonomous reality' of the work of art is reduced, after all, to the exigencies of novel writing (the suffering heroine dies in chapter XX because the novelist has miscalculated the number of instalments needed to fulfil his contract) then the magical potency of the artefact is dispelled. The artificer stands caught in the act of pulling the levers; no longer a vatic "medium" through whom the gods communicate their ineffable truths to men.'

112 In her review of *In the Heart of the Country* Jean Marquard would later (*Oggendblad*, 28.4.1978) write: 'At the time [of the publication of *Dusklands*] Coetzee's publishers received anxious telephone calls from readers who thought it might be advisable for Ravan Press to change their proof-readers.'

113 There were also further repercussions after the publication of *Dusklands*. In a letter of 2 June 1974 Coetzee writes that his colleague Philip Birkinshaw had told him that the SABC would definitely not have *Dusklands* reviewed — not because they had anything against the book, but because they did not want (clearly for political reasons) to give the publisher any publicity. In his reply Randall says that the whole matter makes him furious, but that he will take it up with the head of the English Service of the SABC, without mentioning Birkinshaw's name. In a letter of 25 June 1974 to the head of the English Service Randall asks formally, in the light of the great literary interest of the novel, that it be reviewed. He enclosed a copy of the book with his

letter. It would be incomprehensible, he says, if the SABC were to ignore such a 'major new South African work of literature'. According to a letter of 10 October 1974 from Coetzee to Randall there was indeed a broadcast of a review on 27 September.

114 Peter Knox-Shaw, '*Dusklands*: A metaphysics of violence', *Contrast*, 4:1, 1982, pp. 26–38.

115 Gallagher, *A Story of South Africa*, p. 67.

116 http://eprints.soas.ac.uk/9804/1/EASTON.pdf

117 *John M. Coetzee: Passages*, edited by Henion Han, produced by Cheryl Tuckett, videocassette, 52 minutes, London, Dizzy Ink, 1999; my transcription of Abrahams's words.

118 Ibid.; as in the case of Abrahams, my transcription of Marx. That *Dusklands* was indeed to prove a 'seedbed' for later writers is true especially of Afrikaans writers, like André Brink who in *'n Oomblik in die wind* (1975) [*An Instant in the Wind*] also makes use of the illusion of historical factuality and authenticity by relying on archival sources. In his review of *Dusklands* (*Rapport*, 19.5.1974) Brink writes of 'The narrative of Jacobus Coetzee': 'It is a shocking, convincing and in places even brilliant piece of work. I say this in spite of the fact that I started reading with a grudge in my heart (for an entirely subjective reason: if you've been labouring away yourself for a year-and-a-half at a novel with an eighteenth-century travel journal set in the Cape interior as background, you can't help feeling grumpy when someone else gets there first!') [Translation M.H.]

119 Stephen Watson, 'Colonialism & the novels of J.M. Coetzee', *Selected Essays 1980–1990*, Cape Town, The Carrefour Press, 1990, p. 37.

120 Michael Vaughan, 'Literature and politics: Current South African writing in the seventies', *Journal of Southern African Studies* 9, October 1982.

121 Peter Knox-Shaw, '*Dusklands*: A metaphysics of violence', *Contrast* XIV: 1, 1982.

122 Sue Kossew, *Pen and Power: A Post-Colonial Reading of J.M. Coetzee and André P. Brink*, p. 3.

123 Alastair Bruce, *Aspects of time and narrative in the novels of JM Coetzee*, MA thesis, University of Cape Town, 1997.

124 Penner, op. cit., p. xiii.

125 *The Star*, 8.2.1977.

126 Gordimer's championing of *Dusklands* is mentioned in footnote 17 of Andrew van der Vlies's article 'Farming stories II: J.M. Coetzee and the (heart of a) country', *South African Textual Cultures*, p. 50.

CHAPTER 9

1 In 1991 Coetzee was to publish an article on 'Apartheid thinking', which he later collected in the volume *Giving Offense: Essays on Censorship*, Chicago and London, University of Chicago Press, 1996. In this essay he analyses Cronjé's crude notions of racial purity and miscegenation, leading him to see the 'Coloured' as a degenerate human being, with his 'impure blood' a 'more cunning impostor' in the white community than the black man. Such ideas prompt Coetzee ultimately to brand Cronjé as 'crazy' (*Giving Offense*, p. 183).

2 For this formulation, see André Brink, 'Die konteks van Sestig: Herkoms en situasie', *Literatuur in die strydperk*, Cape Town, Human & Rousseau, 1985, p. 60.

3 Peter D. McDonald, *The Literature Police: Apartheid, Censorship and its Cultural Consequences*, Oxford, Oxford University Press, 2009, p. 39.

4 Ibid., pp. 26–27.

5 Brink, 'Die konteks van Sestig: Herkoms en situasie', *Literatuur in die strydperk*, p. 59. [Translation M.H.]

6 'Etienne Leroux in gesprek met F.I.J. van Rensburg', *Gesprekke met skrywers 1*, Cape Town, Tafelberg, 1971, p. 59.

7 Brink, op. cit., p. 60.

8 Translation M.H.

9 Cited in *Rapport*, 27.11.1977. [Translation M.H.]

10 *Giving Offense*, p. 213.

11 Ibid.

12 J.M. Coetzee, *Doubling the Point*,

edited by David Attwell, Cambridge, Massachusetts / London, Harvard University Press, 1992, p. 298.

13 Ibid., pp. 299–300.

14 *Giving Offense*, p. 10.

15 Ibid., p. 9.

16 McDonald here errs on the date. It was early in 1975.

17 *The Literature Police*, p. 63.

18 Personal interview with JM Coetzee, 19.03.2009.

19 In all probability Coetzee here erred on the date, writing 1976 instead of 1975.

20 An example of how radically Coetzee was to amend the text with repeated revisions and adaptation, abbreviating it to its essence, is the numbered section 33. In the manuscript it runs as follows:

The woman is lying just as I left her, on her side with her knees drawn up to her chin. If I am not careful she will harden in that position and I will have difficulty moving her. Her hair has fallen forward over her face in a gluey, dark-red wing which fortunately threatens to harden over a face I do not want to see. (When I have time to think, I will find that her eyes are screwed shut, her lips drawn back, her teeth clenched, and I will wonder what it was, in my hatchet-blow perhaps, that froze her in this particular rictus.) ~~The man~~My father, however, has moved, therefore must have been living even after the endless pounding I gave him through the blanket. Man, like most of the carnivores, is tenacious of life. The very last experience of my father's life must have been an unsatisfactory one, a sobbing and scrabbling with dull muscles toward an illusory zone of safety. Here he lies with his head and arms over the edge of the bed, black with contusions and the weight of blood trying to pour out. Should he not rather have done as I did when I was drowning: try to follow the gentle ghost as far as you can in the passage out, close the eyes on an image of a balloon skipping, riding, rising free?

The final text, as published in London by Secker & Warburg, 1977 (in 1999 published paperback by Vintage and in Johannesburg by Ravan Press, 1978) reads as follows:

The woman lies on her side with her knees drawn up to her chin. If I do not hurry she will set in that position. Her hair falls over her face in a sticky dark-red wing. Though her last act was to flinch from the terrific axe, screwing her eyes shut, clenching her teeth, the face has now relaxed. But the man, tenacious of life, has moved. His final experience must have been an unsatisfactory one, a groping with dulled muscles toward an illusory zone of safety. He lies head and arms over the edge of the bed, black with his heavy blood. It would have been better for him to have yielded the gentle ghost, following it as far as he could on its passage out, closing his eyes on the image of a swallow swooping, rising, riding.

21 Since the pagination varies in the British, American and Ravan editions, the reference in the text is to the numbered sections, not to the pages.

22 J.M. Coetzee, *White Writing*, New Haven / London, Yale University Press, 1988, pp. 5–6.

23 Jerzy Koch and Pawel Zajas point out in their article 'Uit de donkere dagen van voor linguistic turn oftewel wat J.M. Coetzee in de bekentenis van Willem Termeer zag en wat hij daarmee deed' (*Tydskrif vir Letterkunde* nr 1, 2011) that *In the Heart of the Country* allies itself through its title with the tradition of the near-endemic use of the word 'land' in the novels and publications of many South Africans, such as those by Karel Schoeman, F.A. Venter, Alan Paton and Thomas Boydell. It also harks back to Conrad's *Heart of Darkness*. Koch and Zajas point out resemblances between Emants's Willem Termeer, the main character in *Een nagelaten bekentenis*, and Magda in *In the Heart of the Country*, but also between Emants and Termeer and between Magda and Coetzee. However, they proceed from the mistaken assumption that Coetzee was working on the Emants translation at the same time as on the novel. In fact

he had started the translation in 1968 in Buffalo, and completed it before his return to South Africa in 1971. He completed 'The Narrative of Jacobus Coetzee' early in 1972. He submitted the translation for publication at the same time as the novel.

24 David Attwell, *J.M. Coetzee: South Africa and the Politics of Writing*, Berkeley / Los Angeles / Oxford, University of California Press /Cape Town / Johannesburg, David Philip, 1993, p. 57.

25 Susan van Zanten Gallagher (*A Story of South Africa: J.M. Coetzee's Fiction in Context*, Cambridge, Massachusetts / London, Harvard University Press, 1991, p. 83) thinks that the novel is set in the period from about 1870 to 1960, but the year 1960 is questionable.

26 Joanna Scott, 'Voice and trajectory: An interview with J.M. Coetzee', *Salmagundi*, 114, 115, Spring / Summer, 1997.

27 *Doubling the Point*, p. 60.

28 See, on this, David Attwell, op. cit., pp. 57–58.

29 In the manuscript of *In the Heart of the Country* there is an important change in the names of the characters. Initially the wife of Hendrik was named Katrina and the old domestic servant was Lena; later both names are changed to Anna, and Hendrik's wife, at Magda's suggestion, then becomes Klein-Anna.

30 Dick Penner, *Countries of the Mind*, New York / Westport, Connecticut / London, Greenwood Press, 1989, p. 57 quoted.

31 Attwell, op. cit., p. 67, interprets this as a series of rapes, but Derek Attridge sees it, rightly to my mind, as only one (Derek Attridge, *J.M. Coetzee and the Ethics of Reading*, Scottsville, University of KwaZulu-Natal Press / Chicago and London, University of Chicago Press, 2005, footnote on p. 26).

32 Gallagher, op. cit., p. 100.

33 Folke Rhedin, interview with J.M. Coetzee, *Kunapipi*, VI: 1, 1984.

34 Derek Attridge, op. cit., pp. 28–29.

35 Gallagher, op. cit., p.84.

36 *White Writing*, pp. 6–7.

37 Ibid., pp. 71–72.

38 Attridge, op. cit., p. 29.

39 The reference is to Ian Glenn, 'Game hunting in *In the Heart of the Country*', *Critical Perspectives on J.M.Coetzee*, edited by Graham Huggan and Stephen Watson, London, Macmillan, 1996, p. 125.

40 Dominic Head, *J.M. Coetzee*, Cambridge, Cambridge University Press, 1997, p. 59.

41 Attridge, op. cit., pp. 30–31.

42 *Giving Offense*, pp. 35–36.

43 Ibid., p. 38.

44 In 1975 André Brink's novel *'n Oomblik in die wind* was published in a limited and signed edition of 1 000 copies by Taurus, a small publishing firm opposed to all forms of censorship that was run by three lecturers at the University of the Witwatersrand. The publisher had canvassed subscribers to the edition in advance. Upon publication, practically all copies had been sold, and were available only from booksellers who were prepared to buy copies despite the danger of a banning. In the event, *'n Oomblik in die wind* and its English translation (*An Instant in the Wind*) were not banned.

45 These words next to the colophon were later to lead to a misunderstanding, because in the uncorrected proofs they were amended to 'English version prepared by the author from the original Afrikaans', an extension taken over by Harper & Row for the American edition. In a letter to Corona Machemer of this firm, dated 17 August 1977, Coetzee writes: 'The original was *not* written in Afrikaans, but in English with the dialogue in Afrikaans. What I fear is that reviewers are going to pick up the notion that I am some kind of voice from within the Afrikaner laager (which is about as false as one can get), and then construct a reading around this error.'

46 Hermann Wittenberg, 'The taint of the censor: J.M. Coetzee and the making of *In the heart of the country*', *English in Africa*, 35:2, October 2008.

47 Peter Randall, 'The beginnings of Ravan Press: A memoir', G.E. de Villiers, ed., *Ravan: Twenty-five Years (1972–1997)*, Randburg, Ravan Press, 1997, p. 9.

48 Peter McDonald, op. cit., p. 108.

49 Wittenberg, op. cit.

50 Ibid.

51 *Giving Offense*, p. 38. Hermann Wittenberg also quotes this passage in his article on the printing history of *In the Heart of the Country*.

52 McDonald, op. cit., p. 315. McDonald writes more comprehensively about how the censors treated Coetzee in an article entitled ' "Not undesirable": How J.M. Coetzee escaped the censor', *Times Literary Supplement*, 19.5.2000.

53 Wittenberg, op. cit.

54 Wittenberg, op. cit.

55 Coetzee writes about the founding and function of *Staffrider* in *African Book Publishing Record*, 5: 4, October 1979. He also explains the title: 'A staffrider, in the parlance of the Johannesburg townships, is someone who rides the crowded city trains by climbing perilously on to the roofs of the carriages or standing on the steps.' Coetzee expresses appreciation for the contribution of an established journal like *Contrast*, which does excellent work in terms of its liberal, non-racial credo. With quality as its criterion, however, according to Coetzee, there are certain things that cannot be said in liberal white journals, 'not because their editors see themselves as exercising the censor's function', but 'because in terms of their own ethos these quarterly literary journals are not the appropriate forum for overtly "political" and "raw" reportage'. A magazine like *Staffrider*, he believes, creates the space for literature to extend into radical new directions.

56 *Doubling the Point*, p. 375.

57 J.M. Coetzee, *Summertime*, London, Harvill Secker, 2009, pp. 8–9.

58 Wittenberg, op. cit.

59 The extract from *In the Heart of the Country* in *Standpunte* comprised sections 85–94.

60 Translation of Brink's review and article by M.H.

61 Stephen Watson, 'Colonialism & the novels of J.M. Coetzee', *Selected Essays 1980–1990*, Cape Town, The Carrefour Press, 1990, p. 45.

62 Translation of Anna M. Louw's review by M.H.

63 *John M. Coetzee: Passages*, directed by Henion Han, produced by Cheryl Tuckett, videocassette, 52 minutes, London, Dizzy Ink, 1999; my transcription of Marx's words.

64 Josephine Dodd, 'Naming and framing: Naturalization and colonization in J.M. Coetzee's *In the Heart of the Country*,' *World Literature in English*, 27: 2, 1987.

65 Reported in *Pretoria News* and *Die Burger*, both 19.4.1978.

66 Telephone conversation with Marilyn Honikman, 14.12.2009.

67 Coetzee, *Summertime*, p. 246.

68 In reply to a query from Levinson about which part of the Karoo he had had in mind with the writing of *In the Heart of the Country*, Coetzee replied on 1 July 1980: 'You might explore the Prince Albert—Klaarstroom area (turn off the N1 at Kruidfontein). The whole of the region is very dry at the moment, and many of the farms are run by absentee owners.'

69 In his interview with Joanna Scott ('Voice and trajectory: An interview with J.M. Coetzee', *Salmagundi*, 114, 115, Spring / Summer, 1997) Coetzee says: 'I know of at least one woman who took the story to heart to the extent of reading it as a retelling, in other terms, of her own life story. And took it to heart to the extent of wanting to make it her own by doing a film of the book, which she eventually brought off. […] It wasn't as though the events of Magda's life recalled the events of her life. It is rather that there was something in the voice that she took as her own.'

70 Obvious spelling errors have been corrected in these quotations. Marion Hänsel's mother tongue was French and her English was by no means faultless.

71 Quoted in an interview in *The Star*, 29.4.1983. On 8 April 1983 there was also a stage production of *In the Heart of the Country* in Cape Town, producd by Bobby Dibble, a project initiated by Community Arts.

72 *The New York Times*, 29.11.2009.

73 Details compiled by Akwe Amosu and made available to me by J.M. Coetzee.

74 Telephone interview with Agnes Heinrich, 25.1.2009.

75 Nellis du Biel in an e-mail of 5.9.2009 to Stefan Wehmeyer, who kindly made it available to me.

76 Telephone interview with Carol Goosen, 17.1.2009.

77 Interview with Gerald Coetzee, 23.5.2009.

78 Interview with J.M. Coetzee, 23.3.2009.

79 Interview with Chris and Sandra Perold, 11.3.2010.

80 E-mail from Jonty Driver, 1.5.2009.

81 J.M. Coetzee, *Slow Man*, London, Secker & Warburg, 2005, p. 230.

82 Ibid., p. 231.

83 The Black Sash was a non-violent white women's resistance organisation founded in 1955. Their striking black sashes were worn as a mark of mourning and to protest against the succession of unjust laws. Apart from regular street demonstrations and political meetings Black Sash volunteers also spent many hours in the monitoring of courts and pass offices.

84 Interview with Catherine Lauga du Plessis, 27.11.2009.

85 Interview with Gisela Coetzee, 7.4.2010.

86 Interview with Chris and Sandra Perold, 11.3.2010.

87 Interview with Lisa Perold, 25.5.2009.

88 E-mail from Daniel Hutchinson, March 2010.

89 Interview with Catherine Lauga du Plessis, 27.11.2009.

90 E-mail from Daniel Hutchinson, March 2010.

91 *Doubling the Point*, p. 337.

92 Interview with Chris and Sandra Perold, 11.3.2010.

93 Ibid., 11.3.2010.

94 Interview with Dorothy Driver,

95 Personal interview with J.M. Coetzee, 20.3.2009.

96 Interview with Gisela Coetzee, 7.4.2010.

CHAPTER 10

1 J.M. Coetzee, *Youth*, London, Vintage Books, 2002, p.62.

2 Allister Sparks, *The Mind of South Africa*, London, Heinemann, 1990, p. 219.

3 Mary Benson, *Nelson Mandela: The Man and the Movement*, New York, Norton, 1986, p. 90.

4 Ibid., p. 222.

5 Hermann Giliomee, *The Afrikaners*, Cape Town, Tafelberg, 2003, pp. 580, 648 and 652.

6 Rykie van Reenen, *Op die randakker*, Cape Town, Tafelberg, 1980, p. 87. Translation M.H.

7 Jacques Pauw, *Into the Heart of Darkness*, Johannesburg, Jonathan Ball Publishers, 1997, p. 188.

8 J.M. Coetzee, *Doubling the Point: Essays and Interviews*, edited by David Attwell, Cambridge, Massachusetts / London, Harvard University Press, 1992, pp. 361–368.

9 J.M. Coetzee, *Giving Offense: Essays on censorship*, Chicago / London, University of Chicago Press, 1996, pp. 215–232.

10 Christopher van Wyk, *It is Time to Go Home*, Johannesburg, Ad Donker, 1979, p. 45.

11 *Doubling the Point*, p. 364.

12 Ibid.

13 For this formulation, see Sparks, op. cit., p. 220.

14 Breyten Breytenbach, *The True Confessions of an Albino Terrorist*, Emmarentia, Taurus, 1984, pp. 311–312.

15 Breyten Breytenbach, *Skryt: Om 'n sinkende skip blou te verf*, Amsterdam, Meulenhoff, 1972, p. 27. [Translation M.H.]

16 *Giving Offense*, p. 218.

17 *Doubling the Point*, p. 366.

18 J.M. Coetzee, *Waiting for the Barbarians*, Johannesburg, Ravan Press, 1981, p. 6.

The British edition appeared in 1980 from Secker & Warburg.

19 *Waiting for the Barbarians*, p. 5.

20 Ibid., p. 12.

21 Ibid., p. 126.

22 *Doubling the Point*, p. 141.

23 Review with Joanna Scott, 'Voice and trajectory: An interview with J.M. Coetzee', *Salmagundi*, 114, 115, Spring / Summer, 1997.

24 *Doubling the Point*, p. 142.

25 In his interview with Joanna Scott, however, Coetzee makes the cautionary remark: 'I've always been slightly bemused by the description of me as an allegorist, but maybe I know less than other people do.'

26 Bernard Levin, *London Sunday Times*, 23.11.1980.

27 *Waiting for the Barbarians*, p. 135.

28 Gallagher points out a further resemblance: 'A still more dominant presence, however, is Kafka, evident in the brutal scene in which a line of barbarian prisoners are flogged. The word "ENEMY" is written on their backs in charcoal, and they are thrashed until the word is effaced (WB, 104–106). Through his allusions, as well as specifically in this scene, Coetzee investigates an association between torture, identity and writing. The specific reference is to Kafka's story "In the Penal Colony", the influence of which extends beyond the one scene in *Waiting for the Barbarians*.' (*A Story of South Africa*, p. 76.)

29 *The Collected Poems of C.P. Cavafy*, translated by Evangelos Sachperoglou, Oxford, 2007, p.17.

30 *Waiting for the Barbarians*, p. 79. These words recur almost verbatim in Coetzee's essay 'Into the dark chamber', *Doubling the Point*, p. 361.

31 *Waiting for the Barbarians*, p. 94.

32 Derek Attridge, *J.M. Coetzee & the Ethics of Reading*, Scottsville, University of KwaZulu-Natal Press, 2005, p. 70.

33 *Waiting for the Barbarians*, p. 104.

34 Ibid., p. 114.

35 Ibid., p. 133.

36 Ibid., p. 138.

37 Ibid., pp. 110–112.

38 Ibid., p. 112.

39 Ibid., p. 155.

40 Ibid., pp. 155–156.

41 Gallagher, *A story of South Africa*, p. 137.

42 Levin here omits the word 'he' before 'the truth' in his quotation, but it does provide for an interesting variation, with application to the magistrate's understanding of his role in the Empire.

43 Peter D. McDonald, *The Literature Police*, Oxford, Oxford University Press, 2009, pp. 312–313.

44 In his interview with Joanna Scott ('Voice and trajectory: An interview with J.M. Coetzee', *Salmagundi*, 114, 115, Spring / Summer, 1997) Coetzee elaborates on the way in which the censorship process worked in practice in South Africa: 'It's not as though my books slipped through the net without being read by the censors. […] One has to remember the way in which the system operated. There were so-called reading committees, on which there would typically be clergymen, retired teachers, custodians of culture—that kind of sector of Afrikaans society. These reading committees were set up more or less according to the convenience of the members of the committee, and were assigned books—at least novels—more or less at random to read. So there was always something a little hit-or-miss about the system. To put it another way, it was not a system of censorship such as you would set up in an ideal dystopia. Some books got bad committees, some books got good committees. Some books that were by any reckoning innocuous got banned. Probably I was the other side of the coin.'

45 It is unknown in which journal or newspaper Jean Marquard's review was published. NELM does possess a photocopy of the original published review, with no mention of the source or the date of publication. A search through various indexes and source guides turned up nothing.

46 David Stuart Hull informed Coetzee on 1 April 1981 that after a ten-year-long association with James Brown

Associates he had decided to join Peter Lampack Agency, and to take his clients with him. There would be no problem in representing Coetzee at this firm in conjunction with Murray Pollinger in London. Coetzee went along with this and moved to the new agency along with Hull.

47 Baumann is referring to Jaap Marais, leader of the extreme right-wing Herstigte Nasionale Party [Regrouped National Party] and Eugene Terre'Blanche, leader of the badly organised paramilitary Afrikaner-Weerstandsbeweging (AWB) [Afrikaner Resistance Movement].

48 Translation of Dutch reviews by M.H.

49 Quoted by Gallagher, *A Story of South Africa*, p. 135.

50 This address was published in its totality in *Die Vaderland*, 1.5.1981.

51 N.P. van Wyk Louw, *Berigte te velde*, Cape Town, Nasionale Boekhandel, second impression, 1959, pp. 10 and 12–13, collected in *Versamelde prosa*, Cape Town, Tafelberg, 1986, pp. 6, 8–9.

52 'Towards a true materialism', *New Contrast*, 13, December 1981, collected in Sue Kossew, ed, *Critical Essays on J.M. Coetzee*, New York, G.K. Hall, 1998.

53 Telephonic information from Wilma Stockenström, 17.11.2008.

54 *English in Africa*, 9: 2, October 1982.

55 *English in Africa*, 12: 1, May 1985, collected in *Doubling the Point*.

56 Coetzee's review was published in *Die Suid-Afrikaan*, Summer 1985, and collected in Willie Burger and Helize van Vuuren, eds, *Sluiswagter by die dam van stemme*, Pretoria, Protea Boekhuis, 2002, pp. 140–142.

57 *Weekly Mail*, 26.12.1985.

58 J.M. Coetzee, *White Writing*, New Haven / London, Yale University Press, 1989, p. 11.

59 Ibid., p. 2.

60 Ibid.

61 Ibid., p. 65.

62 Ibid., p. 54.

63 J.M. Coetzee, *Stranger Shores*, London, Secker & Warburg, 2001, p. 254.

64 *White Writing*, p. 167.

65 Ibid., p. 165.

66 Ibid., p. 8.

67 Ibid., p. 167.

68 A translation of Peter Blum, *Steenbok tot poolsee*, Cape Town, Nasionale Boekhandel, 1955, p. 7.

69 Coetzee, *White Writing*, p. 168.

70 Roy Campbell, *Collected Works* I, edited by Peter Alexander, Michael Chapman and Marcia Leveson, Craighall, Johannesburg, Ad Donker, 1985, p. 124.

71 Coetzee, *White Writing*, p. 177.

72 Helize van Vuuren, *Die Suid-Afrikaan*, December 1988; Cherry Clayton, *Times Literary Supplement*, 23–29.9.1989; and Hennie Aucamp, *Die Burger*, 15.9.1988.

73 To the question why he did not in *White Writing* write much, for instance, about Roy Campbell and William Plomer, Coetzee replied, in an interview with me on 19.03.2009, that he was not much interested in them. To the question why he did not attend, for instance, to the poetry of N.P. van Wyk Louw and D.J. Opperman, he replied 'When I went to America, I spoke Afrikaans to no one and did not read Afrikaans literature. When I really started exploring that avenue in Texas, it was with Dutch literature. So until I came back to South Africa in the 1970s I knew very little of Afrikaans literature. When I started reading then, it was what was currently published in the 1970s, not Van Wyk Louw or Opperman: Brink, Stockenström, Anna Louw and that. Van Wyk Louw was simply not on my radar-screen. I know poems of Opperman, but did not read a single volume of his.'

74 These articles appeared as 'The white tribe' in *Vogue*, March 1986; 'Tales of Afrikaners', *New York Times Magazine*, 9.3.1986, reprinted in *Reader's Digest*, August 1986 and in *Fair Lady*, 28.5.1986.

75 *Doubling the Point*, p. 104.

76 Cambridge University Press, 1966.

77 Interview with Dorothy Driver, 3.4.2009.

78 At a mature age, Gillham divorced his wife and married a young student of his, in spite of her parents'

resistance, the difference in age causing some comment among his colleagues. A report in the *Sunday Times* of 12 October 2003 alleged that Gillham was the model for Coetzee's character of David Lurie in *Disgrace*, a Cape Town professor who has an affair with one of his students. But Lurie does not resemble Gillham in a single respect, except in the relationship with the student, as Coetzee stressed in an interview. (Interview with J.M. Coetzee, 17.3.2009.) In any case, the relationship between an older man and a young woman is one of the familiar archetypes of literature.

79 Interview with J.M. Coetzee, 17.3.2009.
80 Interview with J.M. Coetzee, 23.3.2009.
81 These details and what follows are based largely on information that Dorothy Driver provided in an interview on 3.4.2009. She also made available to me a curriculum vitae. She wrote about her years at what was to become NELM in 'Memories of NELM', *NELM News, Anniversary Edition.*

Chapter 11

1 David Welsh, *The Rise and Fall of Apartheid*, Johannesburg & Cape Town, Jonathan Ball, 2009, p. 273.
2 Nadine Gordimer, *The Essential Gesture: Writing, Politics and Places*, London, Penguin, 1989, pp. 262–263.
3 David Welsh, op. cit., p. 245.
4 Ibid., p. 250.
5 See on this Ampie Coetzee and James Polley, eds, *Crossing Borders: Writers Meet the ANC*, Bramley, Taurus, 1990.
6 J.M. Coetzee, *Giving Offense*, Chicago and London, University of Chicago Press, 1996, p. 165.
7 J.M. Coetzee, *Doubling the Point*, ed. David Attwell, Cambridge, Massachusetts / London, Harvard University Press, 1992, p. 209.
8 'Waiting for Mandela', *New York Review of Books*, 8 May 1986.
9 *The New Republic*, 13.6.1988.
10 J.M. Coetzee, *Age of Iron*, London,

Secker & Warburg, 1990, p. 16.
11 Interview with Stephen Watson, *Speak*, May / June 1978.
12 Interview with Edwin Hart, *The Star*, 25.2.1981.
13 Personal interview, 20.3.2009.
14 Joanna Scott, 'Voice and trajectory: An interview with J.M. Coetzee', *Salmagundi*, 114, 115, Spring / Summer, 1997.
15 Ibid.
16 Dick Penner in *Countries of the Mind*, New York / Westport, Connecticut / London, Greenwood Press, 1989, p. 94 provides the following information on the particular form of this omniscient narrator: 'In the writer's workshop which Coetzee conducted on 6 March 1984, in Lexington, one of the participants observed that the primary narrator of *Michael K* employs "a very odd kind of omniscience, as if it were rooted in the individual's [Michael's] character." Coetzee responded: "It's a mixture. It's a fluctuation in and out. There is — if I can use an oxymoron — a limited omniscient point of view operating in part I of that book. That is to say, there is someone who is telling the story about Michael K, who looks like an omniscient narrator, but he doesn't actually tell you very much. And ... there is no guarantee that he knows very much."'
17 Tony Morphet, 'An interview with J.M. Coetzee', *Social Dynamics*, 10: 1, 1984, reprinted in *TriQuarterly*, Spring / Summer 1987.
18 Dominic Head, *J.M. Coetzee*, Cambridge, Cambridge University Press, 1997, p. 93.
19 Nevertheless, Coetzee said in his interview with Tony Morphet: 'I don't believe Kafka has an exclusive right to the letter K. Nor is Prague the centre of the universe.' And in her discussion of the novel in *The New York Review of Books* of 27 February 1984, Nadine Gordimer says: 'the initial probably stands for Kotze or Koekemoer and has no reference, nor need it have, to Kafka.' Gordimer's review is collected in *Telling Times*, London / Berlin / New

York, Bloomsbury, 2010, pp. 396–403.

20 An indication of the plush lifestyle of the Buhrmanns and other white couples, as Helene Müller has shown in *Standpunte* 38: 1, February 1985, are the exotic names of these blocks of flats (*Côte d'or, Malibu Heights, Copacabana*), almost as if the inhabitants have relocated to some other part of the world.

21 J.M. Coetzee, *Life &Times of Michael K*, Johannesburg, Ravan Press, 1983, pp. 63–64.

22 Ibid., p. 135.

23 Ibid., p. 84.

24 Ibid., pp. 125–126.

25 Ibid., p. 200. My italics.

26 Ibid., p. 220.

27 'I will show you fear in a handful of dust' from 'The Burial of the Dead' in *The Waste Land*, T.S. Eliot, *The Complete Poems and Plays*, London, Faber and Faber, 1969, p. 61.

28 David Ward, *Chronicles of Darkness*, London / New York, Routledge, 1989, p. 167.

29 Allister Sparks, *The Star*, 2.11.1983. In an interview with me Coetzee could not confirm this information.

30 *Life & Times of Michael K*, p. 249.

31 Ibid., pp. 249–250.

32 Stephen Watson, 'Speaking: J.M. Coetzee', *Speak*, 1: 3, May / June 1978.

33 Commentators have pointed out the kinship between *Life & Times of Michael K* and Pauline Smith's short story 'Desolation', in which Alie van Staden returns, with her orphaned grandson, to the town of her childhood—even though the similarity is mainly confined to the journey through a barren landscape. Teresa Dovey has pointed out the recurring attempt in South African literature to articulate the experiences and tribulations of a (mainly) black victim of the system, citing *Die Swerfjare van Poppie Nongena* (The Long Journey of Poppie Nongena) by Elsa Joubert as an example. She could also have mentioned Alan Paton's *Cry the Beloved Country*, F.A. Venter's *Swart Pelgrim* (Dark Pilgrim), Adam Small's *Kanna hy kô hystoe* (Kanna's Coming Home),

Karel Schoeman's *Na die geliefde land* (Towards the Beloved Country) and Nadine Gordimer's *July's People*. (Teresa Dovey, *The Novels of J.M. Coetzee*, Craighall, Ad Donker, 1988, pp. 265–267.)

34 Interview with Hugh Roberton, *Pretoria News*, 18.8.1983.

35 Dovey, op. cit., p. 267.

36 Gallagher here omits Kafka!

37 Susan van Zanten Gallagher, *A Story of South Africa: J.M. Coetzee's Fiction in Context*, Cambridge, Massachusetts / London, Harvard University Press, 1991, p. 45.

38 David Stuart Hull.

39 Murray Pollinger.

40 In Joseph Conrad's *Heart of Darkness*.

41 Viking Penguin did indeed publish the novel in the US, but only in 1984, later, then, than the Secker & Warburg edition in Britain.

42 Nevertheless Coetzee said in an interview with Erik van Ees in the *Haagse Post*, 12.11.1983: 'What does remain unclear at the end, and I did that deliberately, is whether Michael K lives on or not.' [Translation M.H.]

43 In *Doubling the Point*, however, Coetzee says: 'As a writer I am not worthy to loose the latchet on Kafka's shoe. But I have no regrets about the use of the letter K in *Michael K*, *hubris* though it may seem. There is no monopoly on the letter K; or, to put it another way, it is as much possible to center the universe on the town of Prince Albert in the Cape Province as on Prague' (p. 199).

44 I am quoting from the Reader's Report in terms of the Publications Act of 1974, series number P83 / 10 / 168. The submission of *Life & Times of Michael K* to the censors is discussed by Peter D. McDonald, *The Literature Police*, Oxford, Oxford University Press, 2009, pp. 314–315.

45 *Life & Times of Michael K*, pp. 243–244.

46 *Pretoria News*, 13.10.1983.

47 It is hardly credible that David Gillham, could, in an attempt to assert his authority, have made such an absurd demand so late in their

relationship. It is not known where the radio station concerned got hold of this 'information'.

48   *Weekend Post*, 29.10.1983.

49   W.L. Webb, 'Coetzee first under the bridge', *The Bookseller*, 29.10.1983 and T. Kai Norris Easton, *Textuality and the land*, Ph D-dissertation, University of London, 2000, p. 215.

50   Interview with Jennifer Crwys-Williams, *Sunday Times*, 4.12.1983.

51   *John M. Coetzee: Passages*, edited by Henion Han, produced by Cheryl Tuckett, videocassette, 52 minutes, London, Dizzy Ink, 1999. My transcription of Marx's words.

52   Translation M.H.

53   This article appeared under the title 'The Great South African Novel' in *Leadership SA*, 2: 4, 1983. Internationally, Coetzee writes, there has been great interest in South African writers, probably because they have access to a subject of compelling interest: the South African situation. People who want to know the truth about South Africa turn to Nadine Gordimer and André Brink, but there is also a demand for new and, more specifically, black voices. People are also prepared to get to know more about that strange species, the Afrikaner, 'who from the outside look as though they are sleepwalking into the grave'. The impression one has, he continues, is that people go to Brink for the exotic and sensational elements in his work. Nadine Gordimer's reputation is very high, but South Africans are not always aware of this, and the white reading public has developed an oddly ambivalent relationship with her. If a great South African novel is ever written, it will probably come from her pen. She is probably on the list of the twenty-five most important novelists writing today, and *The Conservationist* and *Burger's Daughter* in particular are supreme examples of her work. 'Brink, it seems to me, has for a long time been writing below his potential'—a questionable judgement. 'He is a man of formidable intellect and talent, and clearly the most gifted critic in South Africa today. [...] As for writers like Etienne Leroux and myself who in our different ways work in modes less committedly realistic than Gordimer or Brink, I think [...] that our products are less likely to fall into the Great Novel class.' He selects, as his examples of respectable South African novels, *'n Droë wit seisoen* [*A Dry White Season*] (Brink), *Cry, the Beloved Country* (Paton), *Bart Nel* (Van Melle), *Laat vrugte* (Van den Heever) and *Story of an African Farm* (Schreiner). Since publication of his article, Coetzee could have added quite a number of contemporary novels, both in English and Afrikaans, by younger authors.

54   In this respect it is very illuminating to note the ideas on the Great Afrikaans Novel of Karel Schoeman, of whose novel *'n Ander land* [*Another Country*] Coetzee wrote very appreciatively in *Die Suid-Afrikaan* of Summer 1985. In the same issue of *Die Suid-Afrikaan* in which Coetzee's review appeared, Schoeman pronounces extremely cynically on the possibility of a truly great Afrikaans novel. The reason for his cynicism is in the first place—and here his thoughts show some similarity to Coetzee's—'that there is in present South African society no nutrient medium for greatness of this nature, and in the second place that if a truly great work were to appear, it would find no sounding board in the Afrikaans cultural milieu.'[Translation M.H.] The urban Afrikaner, according to him, has not succeeded in establishing an urban culture to replace the former farming culture. In addition, the average member of the Afrikaans community attaches little value to the rules, structure and possibilities of his language.

55   Translation M.H.

56   This article is collected in Sue Kossew, ed., *Critical Essays on J.M. Coetzee*, New York, G.K. Hall, 1998, and in Nadine Gordimer, *Telling Times: Writing and Living 1954–2008*, London, Bloomsbury, 2010.

57   Patrick Hayes, *J.M. Coetzee and the*

Novel, Oxford, Oxford University Press, 2010, p. 74.

58 J.M. Coetzee, *Stranger Shores: Essays 1986–1999*, London, Secker & Warburg, 2001, p. 295, quoted.

59 Quoted by Penner, *Countries of the Mind*, p. 75.

60 *Doubling the Point*, pp. 206–208.

61 Gallagher, *A Story of South Africa: J.M. Coetzee's Fiction in Context*, p. 170.

62 Reprinted in *Stranger Shores*, p. 20.

63 J.M. Coetzee, *Boyhood*, London, Secker & Warburg, 1997, p. 45.

64 Elleke Boehmer, *Colonial and Postcolonial Literature: Migrant Metaphors*, Oxford, Oxford University Press, 1995, p. 17.

65 *Stranger Shores*, p. 21.

66 Daniel Defoe, *The Life and Adventures of Robinson Crusoe*, edited with an introduction by Angus Ross, London, Penguin, reprinted 1985, p. 25.

67 *Stranger Shores*, p. 22.

68 J.M. Coetzee, *Foe*, London, Secker & Warburg, 1986, p. 40.

69 Ibid., p. 118.

70 Ibid., p. 143.

71 Ibid., pp. 143–144. The poem of Gezelle's alluded to here is 'Het schrijverke'. That Coetzee was aware of this poem is evident from an e-mail that he sent on 27 February 2002 to Kris Phillipps: 'There is a poem about the water skipper by the 19th-century Dutch poet Guido Gezelle. When I can lay my hands on it, I'll translate it for you.' In *Foe* Coetzee traces back the movement of the waterskater spelling the name of God to an Arabic origin. In reply to a query from André Brink, he wrote on 16 April 2004: 'my understanding is that [it] is a commonplace of Arabic lore that the waterskater writes the name of Allah. Whether it comes to Gezelle directly from the Arabs I don't know.'
Some lines relevant to *Foe* run as follows: (Guido Gezelle, *Dichtwerken* I, edited by Fr Baur, Amsterdam, L.J. Veen, s.j., pp. 42–43):
The Waterfly
O crinkling weltering waterfly
  with a black little coat on your back,
I like to see often your dear little head
  that writes many lines in its track!
[...]
O tell me, you dear little waterflies
  because you are twenty or more,
there must be a fellow in your midst
  who can tell me your ancient lore.
[...]
'We write', so it spoke, 'and we write in our track
  what told us our Master to write,
when He shaped us and teached us, long time ago,
  one lesson, never to hide:
we write what every wise man can read,
  and why can't you read the lot?
We are writing and writing again and again
  the holy Name of God!'
[translation: H.Reuvers, <<http: www.petericepudding.com / gezelle.htm>>]

72 Penner, *Countries of the Mind*, p. 113.

73 *Foe*, p. 33.

74 Coetzee's *now* refers to the 1980s, when, amid great political turmoil, he was working on *Foe*. He sees the problem in a wider context than that of the African urge to find an own voice after years of colonisation.

75 Coetzee made this note on 1 December 1983. Easton also refers to it on p. 297 of *Textuality and the Land*.

76 *Foe*, p. 21.

77 Ibid., p. 23.

78 Toril Moi, editor, *The Kristeva Reader*, New York, Columbia University Press, 1986, p. 37.

79 Sheila Roberts, 'Post-colonialism, or the House of Friday—J.M. Coetzee's *Foe*', *World Literature Written in English*, 31:1, 1991.

80 For the explication that follows, I am drawing verbatim on Richard Begam's exemplary article, 'Silence and mut(e)ilation: White writing in J.M. Coetzee's *Foe*', Michael Valdez Moses, ed., *The Writings of J.M. Coetzee, The South Atlantic Quarterly*, 93: 1, Winter 1994.

81 *Foe*, p. 157.

82 Patrick Hayes, *J.M. Coetzee and the Novel*, Oxford, Oxford University Press, 2010, p. 109.

83 Later Michael Chapman, in a discussion of Teresa Dovey's *The Novels of J.M. Coetzee: Lacanian Allegories*,

Journal of Literary Studies 4: 3, 1988, was to dismiss the novel as irrelevant in a yet more vehement criticism: 'In our knowledge of the human suffering on our own doorstep of thousands of detainees who are denied recourse to the rule of law, *Foe* does not so much speak to Africa as provide a kind of masturbatory release, in this country, for the Europeanising dreams of an intellectual coterie,' quoted by Michael Marais, 'Death and the space of the response to the other in J.M. Coetzee's *The Master of Petersburg*', Jane Poyner, ed., *J.M. Coetzee and the Idea of the Public Intellectual*, Athens, Ohio University Press, 2006, p. 84. Marais comments: 'It goes without saying that such assessments accuse Coetzee not only of bad politics, but also of bad ethics.' In *South African Review of Books*, April / May 1989, Stephen Watson and Douglas Reid Skinner reacted to Chapman's view of the novel as set out in the *South African Review of Books*, December 1988 and January 1989.

84 Translation M.H.
85 *Doubling the Point*, pp. 96–99.
86 *The New York Times*, 11.4.1987.
87 Gallagher, op. cit., pp. 166–167.
88 Text of the citation, by permission of Dr Anne Cameron, from the Strathclyde University Archives, OS 89 / 21: Honorary Graduates: Presenters' speeches, 1985: John Maxwell Coetzee (Professor Derek Attridge).
89 The cancelled visit of Salman Rushdie to South Africa is referred to by Peter D. McDonald, *The Literature Police: Apartheid, Censorship and its Cultural Consequences*, Oxford, Oxford University Press, 2009, pp. 211–214; Ronald Suresh Roberts, *No Cold Kitchen: A Biography of Nadine Gordimer*, Johannesburg, STE Publishers, 2005, pp. 493–495; and David Attwell, 'The life and times of Elizabeth Costello', *J.M. Coetzee and the Ideal of the Public Intellectual*, Jane Poyner, ed., Athens, Ohio University Press, 2006, pp. 26–27.
90 Ian Glenn, 'Nadine Gordimer, J.M. Coetzee, and the politics of interpretation', Michael Valdez Moses,

ed., *The South Atlantic Quarterly*, 93: 1, Winter 1994.
91 The complete text of Coetzee's speech is as follows:

For this, the Friday session of the Book Week, the organizers sold some four hundred tickets. If the original plan had been gone through with, the evening would have consisted of a discussion between Mr Rushdie and myself, compèred by David Bunn and Jane Taylor. We had intended to discuss: cultural relations between the so-called peripheries of the world, like Southern Africa, like the Indian subcontinent, and the Euro-American metropoles, the question of who owns so-called world languages; problems of writing from the position of exile, or in general from a displaced position; and so forth—questions, broadly speaking, of the politics of writing in a postcolonial world. No doubt the particular pathology of South Africa would have been at the centre of our discussions.

What happened, of course, was that we were overtaken by the politics of writing in an ugly, violent and unexpected form. On Wednesday the organizers had the unhappy task of announcing that the man around whose presence the week had been structured would not be appearing, for reasons outside their control. There was a scramble behind the scenes to put together a substitute performance. Nadine Gordimer flew in from Johannesburg to help out. There were plans to pipe in the voice of Mr Rushdie as the voice of Mongane Serote had been piped in on Monday evening. These plans fell through.

So Salman Rushdie is not here in any form. The question for me is: what am I doing here on the platform at the Weekly Mail Book Week? I appeared last year and agreed to appear this year, not because I enjoy speeches or public debates (I don't), but (a) because I am sympathetic to certain of the things the *Weekly Mail* stands for (freedom of information, freedom of the press) and generally in favour of the underdog; and (b) because I think that hearing intelligent voices from abroad, Jonty Driver's last year and Salman Rushdie's this year, is a good thing for us in South Africa.

Now Mr Rushdie has been disinvited, and as for the *Weekly Mail* my sense is that it comes out of the affair more than a little embarrassed. In fact, a whole segment of the South African intellectual community, in which I include myself, comes out of the affair looking pretty stupid. Since no one before David Bunn has seemed in a hurry to talk publicly about the affair, there are certain things that I would like to say in a fraternal spirit, though not wholly.

Explaining the cancellation of Mr Rushdie's visit, the Weekly Mail issued a statement making it clear that it had itself not disinvited him. The Congress of South African Writers, the Writers' Union, had done so by withdrawing its co-sponsoring of the invitation. That, in effect, was the end of that, though the Weekly Mail noted that it was saddened by the decision. What is lacking from the statement, it seems to me, what will perhaps be supplied at a future date, is an explanation of how the Weekly Mail ever landed in a position in which its invitation to Mr Rushdie was subject to veto from the Writers' Union. The Writers' Union issued its own statement on the cancellation. Exercising its veto it advised the Weekly Mail to withdraw its invitation, or its co-invitation, to Mr Rushdie on the grounds that the Writers' Union cannot guarantee his safety in South Africa.

I accept without question that the threats of violence against Mr Rushdie himself and subsequently against the organizers of the conference, the sponsors, their families, the participants and even the audience, that is yourselves, were seriously meant. The people who did the threatening, were, I have no doubt, terrorists, real terrorists, and facing them was, I am sure, a terrifying

experience. I will also accept that the Writers' Union was unaware that in diplomatic code it is a calculated snub to withdraw an invitation to a guest on the grounds that one is unable to guarantee his safety. I will accept that, whoever the writer was who worded the statement, he simply did not think of saying "There have been threats against your life which we take very seriously. If you decide not to come, we will understand fully. If, despite the threats, you still decide to come, we will do everything in our power, our limited power, to ensure your safety. You understand that we cannot call on the assistance of the police."

What I will not accept, is that the Writers' Union has given us the full story. I believe, and will continue to believe, until I am otherwise convinced, that some kind of trade-off took place in a smoke-filled room, some kind of calling in of debt, some kind of compromise or bargain or settlement in which the Rushdie visit was given up for the sake of unity of the anti-apartheid alliance and in particular for the sake of not making life too difficult for Muslims in the alliance.

So, what am I doing here, speaking, doing my bit to keep the show on the road for the *Weekly Mail* which stands for the principle of free speech, but finds that it can live with the fact of free speech for selected persons only; for the sponsoring booksellers who opposed a telephone call to Mr Rushdie tonight on the grounds that it might alienate certain of their staff and customers; for the Congress of South African Writers, which is dedicated to the freedom of speech as long as freedom of speech does not threaten the unity of the struggle? Why involve myself any further in this sorry spectacle from which no one emerges looking good except Mr Rushdie himself, who in the face of a massive campaign of hatred organized against him by Muslim reactionaries, a campaign of which the South African end is only a tiny part, was prepared to the last to come here, to face the music, to go through with his commitment?

I am here for three reasons. The first is to register publicly my protest against the silencing of Mr Rushdie's voice, in the first place by the Muslim Right and then for their own hypocritical reasons by the South African censors. It is a protest which many people here tonight will, I am sure, want to support, though because of the critical role they have been playing it will not be easy for some to associate themselves wholeheartedly with it. Here I think principally of the Congress of South African Writers, though I do not exempt the organizers and sponsors of the Book Week.

The second reason is that I want to say something about Islamic fundamentalism which no one else seems in a hurry to say. Islamic fundamentalism in its activist manifestation is bad news. Religious fundamentalism in general is bad news. We know about religious fundamentalism in South Africa. Calvinist fundamentalism has been an unmitigated force of benightedness in our history. Lebanon, Israel, Ireland, South Africa, wherever there is a bleeding sore on the body of the world, the same hard-eyed, narrow-minded fanatics are busy, indifferent to life, in love with death. And behind them always come the mullahs, the rabbis, the predikante, chanting their blessings. I do not exclude Cambodia from the list, I do not exclude the madness of the secular apocalyptics.

These words are addressed particularly to the Congress of South African Writers. Don't get involved with such people; don't get into alliances with them. There is nothing more inimical to writing than the spirit of fundamentalism. Fundamentalism abhors the play of signs, the endlessness of writing. Fundamentalism means nothing more or less than going back to an origin and staying there. It stands for the one founding Book and after

that no more books. As the various books of the various fundamentalisms, each claiming to be the one true book, phantasize themselves to be signed in fire or engraved in stone, so they aspire to strike dead every rival book, petrifying the sinuous, Protean, forward-gliding life of the letters on their pages, turning them into physical objects to be anathematised, things of horror not to be touched, not be looked upon. This is what Salman Rushdie wrote about in *The Satanic Verses* and this is why the fundamentalists of Islam want him dead. Rushdie blasphemously presents the Prophet not as author but as writer. The fundamentalists want Rushdie dead for asserting being-a-writer against being-an-authority, for asserting himself as an equal and rival to the Prophet, for denying the authority of the originary writing. *The Satanic Verses* strikes at the foundations of the structure of authority of Islam and it does so in the name of writing. A bold act indeed to publish such a book. The Congress of South African Writers ought to decide where it stands on the central question: the question of the right of Mr Rushdie to write against authority. And it ought then to act in accordance with its decision.

The third and final reason why I am on the platform here is that I am as much part of this defeat as anyone else. I am here with my tail between my legs, like the rest of the participants, like the organizers too. That loose and fragile alliance of people, those who believe in freedom of speech and those who believe in freedom of speech for some people—we have suffered a crushing defeat. There are smiles in the mosques, there are chuckles in the corridors of Pretoria where they issued the troublemaker Rushdie with an entry visa and then watched as we proceeded to self-destruct. We are so demoralized, afraid even to pick up a telephone and dial Mr Rushdie's London number for fear that someone will throw a bomb at us, that we have no sense of whether the Rushdie affair will in a year's time have vanished from people's memories or, on the contrary, will go down in history as a moment after which people simply got tired of pretending that there was any place for the liberal shibboleths, freedom of speech, freedom of association and the rest, in the anti-apartheid struggle.

(On an enquiry from me Coetzee replied that he no longer had the text of the address in his possession. A cassette recording of the speech was, however, put at my disposal by Jane Smith, with the help of Marilyn Honikman (formerly Kirkwood). I transcribed the text and asked Coetzee to check the transcription.)

92 *Doubling the Point*, p. 298.

CHAPTER 12

1 One of the informants of the fictive biographer in the partly autobio-graphical *Summertime* (London, Harvill Secker, 2009) provides a description that does Coetzee less than justice: 'In appearance he was not what most people would call attractive. He was scrawny, he had a beard, he wore horn-rimmed glasses and sandals. He looked out of place, like a bird, one of those flightless birds; or like an abstracted scientist who had wandered by mistake out of his laboratory. There was an air of seediness about him too, an air of failure.' (p.21)

2 *The Observer*, 30.10.1983.

3 Rian Malan, *Resident Alien*, Johannesburg / Cape Town, Jonathan Ball, 2009, p. 95.

4 Ibid.

5 Ibid., p. 97.

6 Ibid., p. 95.

7 Reprinted, among other places, in the *Sunday Times*, 7.10.1990.

8 J.M. Coetzee, *Doubling the Point*, edited by David Attwell, Cambridge, Massachusetts / London, England, Harvard University Press, 1992, p. 65. This pronouncement does prompt the question whether a writer can ever

claim not to be a public figure. Simply by publishing, he willy-nilly enters the public domain.

9 Ibid. This statement provides Carrol Clarkson with the radiant nucleus of her interesting study *Countervoices*, Hampshire, Palgrave Macmillan, 2009.

10 Personal e-mail to me, May 2009.

11 Personal interview, 20.3.2009.

12 Personal interview with J.M. Coetzee, 19.3.2009.

13 Personal e-mail from Daniel Hutchinson, March 2010.

14 Personal e-mail from Howard Wolf, March 2010.

15 J.M. Coetzee, 'Playing total(itarian) rugby', *Die Suid-Afrikaan*, August 1988.

16 Personal interview with J.M. Coetzee, 19.3.2009.

17 J.M. Coetzee, *Diary of a Bad Year*, London, Harvill Secker, 2007, pp. 141–142.

18 'De Nobelprijswinnaar houdt van fietsen', *De Muur*, 31, January 2011, pp. 213–214. This special edition appeared under the title *Slipstroom*.

19 'Te midden der kampioenen', *De Muur*, 31, January 2011, pp. 221–222. [Translation M.H.]

20 My transcription of the DVD. It was published in a Dutch translation in Wim Kayzer, *Van de schoonheid en de troost*, Amsterdam, Contact, 2000, pp. 310–311.

21 J.C. Kannemeyer, *Leipoldt: 'n Lewensverhaal*, Cape Town, Tafelberg, 1999, p. 654, quoted.

22 Compare the pronouncement by Deirdre Bair in *Samuel Beckett: A Biography*, London, Jonathan Cape, 1978, p. 640: 'In all of this century, it would be difficult to come upon another writer who has so lived through his art that it has become the substance of his life. Beckett himself insists that his life is "dull and without interest. The professors know more about it than I do." He abhors the interest in his person and insists with intense sincerity that "nothing matters but the writing. There has been nothing else worthwhile."'

23 Allister Sparks, *The Star*, 2.11.1983.

24 Kayser, op. cit.

25 *Doubling the Point*, p. 246.
26 Alex Smith, *Drinking from the Dragon's Well*, Cape Town, Umuzi, Random House Struik, 2008, p. 20.
27 Telephone conversation with Marina le Roux, 25.1.2009.
28 *The Alcade*, January / February 2004.
29 Ibid.
30 J.M. Coetzee, *Truth in Autobiography*, Cape Town, University of Cape Town 1985, p. 4.
31 Dick Penner, *Countries of the Mind: The Fiction of J.M. Coetzee*, New York / Westport, Connecticut / London, Greenwood Press, 1989, p. 19.
32 At this time there was also the prospect that the Cape Town film-maker Cliff Bestall would film *The Life & Times of Michael K* for British television, but this came to nothing.
33 E-mail from Howard Wolf, April 2009 and a letter of 1.5.2009.
34 *Doubling the Point*, p. 24.
35 Personal interview, 20.3.2009.
36 In 1993 Coetzee was also 'writer in residence' at Yale, and in 1994 he once again spent time at the University of Texas. In 1997 he visited both the University of Texas at Houston and the University of California at Berkeley.
37 Letter from Dorothy Driver to Douglas Reid Skinner, 25.10.1991.
38 Personal e-mail from Manju Jaidka, 2.5.2009.
39 Information from a personal interview with J.M. Coetzee, 16.3.2009.
40 *Summertime*, pp. 245–247.
41 Ibid., pp. 256–258.
42 J.M. Coetzee, *Boyhood*, London, Secker & Warburg, 1997, p. 35.
43 Personal information to me from Stefan Wehmeyer, 2010.
44 Personal interview with Gisela Coetzee, 7.4.2010.
45 Interview with Catherine Lauga du Plessis, 27.11.2009.
46 J.M. Coetzee, *Age of Iron*, London, Secker & Warburg, 1990, p. 15.
47 Ibid., p. 110.
48 Ibid., p. 57.
49 From the information in the Harry Ransom Center at Texas it appears that Coetzee worked on the manuscript over a period of four years, from August 1987 to March 1990. There are twelve versions of the novel. Originally Vercueil was called Pratt and in certain sections he acted as first-person narrator.
50 The thoroughness of Coetzee's preparation for this aspect of the novel is apparent from a letter he wrote on 6 July 1989 to Dr Christine Dare of the St Luke's Hospice, 92 Harfield Road, Kenilworth:
I am writing a novel in which one of the characters, a woman in her sixties, has cancer. In the interests of detail, I need to know the names (brand-names) of the pain-killing drugs that would ordinarily be prescribed at two different stages of her disease.
In the first stage, some time after what had seemed a successful mastectomy, a metastasis has been detected in the hipbone. She decides against being hospitalized. She still leads a life of limited activity. At this stage, she needs an analgesic to *get by* and to sleep.
At the second and more advanced stage she is in continual pain, is for the most part bedridden, and can move only with difficulty.

I realize that no doctor would prescribe drugs on the basis of such a sketchy description. But, fortunately, we are talking about a fictional patient.
It is not known how the doctor reacted to this request. With the manuscript of *Age of Iron* at Texas there are copies of a number of brochures on the care of a cancer patient: *The Care of the Cancer Patient* by L.G. Capra, London, William Heinemann Medical Books Ltd, 1972; *Cancer Care Nursing* by Marileen Ivers Donovan and Sandra Girton Pierce, New York, Appleton-Century Crofts, 1976; *A Short Textbook of Clinical Oncology* by R.D. Rubens and R.K. Knight, London, Hodder and Stoughton, 1980; and *The Management of Terminal Malignant Disease* edited by Dame Cecily Saunders, Edward Arnold, 1984.
51 *Age of Iron*, p. 120.
52 Ibid., p. 23.
53 Although Philippa's name does not appear in the dedication to *Age of Iron*,

her imminent death was a reality for Coetzee while writing the novel in the late 1980s.

54 For instance on pp. 107 and 132.

55 D.A. Robinson, *The confessional novel in South Africa: A study of J.M. Coetzee's Age of Iron (1990) and Menán du Plessis's A State of Fear (1983)*, M.A., University of Natal, Durban, 1992, p. 58.

56 Leonard Thompson, *A History of South Africa*, New Haven, Yale University Press, 1990, p. 235.

57 *Age of Iron*, p. 49.

58 Ibid., p. 148.

59 David Attwell, *J.M. Coetzee: South Africa and the Politics of Writing*, Berkeley, University of California Press / Cape Town, David Philip, 1993, p. 119.

60 *Age of Iron*, p. 149.

61 Ibid., p. 36.

62 Ibid., p. 148.

63 Derek Attridge, *J.M. Coetzee & the Ethics of Reading: Literature in the Event*, Scottsville, University of KwaZulu-Natal Press, 2005, p. 110.

64 Ibid.

65 It is striking that Florence repeatedly expresses disapproval at the presence of Vercueil on the premises (e.g. on p. 34 of *Age of Iron*), ultimately branding him as 'rubbish' (p. 44). This evokes a protest from Mrs Curren: 'He is not a rubbish person. There are no rubbish people. We are all people together' (p. 44). In the manuscript, Coetzee here added a passage not included in the final text:

'Florence,' I said, 'there is a writer who lives in Johannesburg, called Nadine Gordimer, who writes about people like us. She writes about people who talk like us. It is a very humiliating experience to read about oneself in her books. We must try not to be like people in the books Mrs. Gordimer writes.'

'She writes about us, all the time. She gives us different names, but she writes about us. She writes about us because there are so many of us, all over the country, talking together like we do. Florence, it's no good. We must try to talk in a different way. We

must put this Mrs. Gordimer behind us. Florence, you mustn't pretend that you don't know what I'm talking about. You know very well what I'm talking about.'

Florence laughed. For a moment, when she raised her eyes to the sky and laughed, she allowed intelligence and amusement and — yes — appreciation of my words to appear in her features […] for a moment, purely as a demonstration, I felt, I felt, purely as a demonstration that they were there, behind the face she chose to present to me.

'This Mrs. Gordimer is an interesting writer,' she said. 'I must read her books one day. I must look in the bookshop, in CNA.'

66 *Age of Iron*, p. 181.

67 Ibid., p. 181. Attridge writes: 'he finally murders her' (op.cit., p. 102). Perhaps it may euphemistically be described as euthanasia.

68 James McCorkle, 'Gender, Text and Space in J.M. Coetzee's fiction', *Space and Crossings: Essays on Literature and Culture in Africa and Beyond*, edited by Rita Wilson and Carlotta von Maltzan, Frankfurt, Peter Lang, 2001, p. 109.

69 Nellis du Biel in an e-mail of 5.9.2009 to Stefan Wehmeyer, who kindly put it at my disposal.

70 Patrick Hayes, *J.M. Coetzee and the Novel: Writing and Politics after Beckett*, Oxford, Oxford University Press, 2010, p. 144.

71 Ibid., pp. 145–146.

72 Translation M.H.

73 Translation of Olivier and Lindenberg by M.H.

74 Lionel Abrahams (1928–2004) was an important figure in South African literature, both as poet, polemicist, apologist for the mainly banned Soweto poets and as editor (among others of the work of Herman Charles Bosman). Although there is no doubting Coetzee's appreciation of the review of *Age of Iron*, his letter may also have been prompted by the fact that Abrahams was severely disabled by spastic paralysis, making any act of reading or writing a major exertion.

75 Interview with Dorothy Driver, 3.4.2009.

76 In a discussion of *Youth* in *The Sunday Independent* of 16.6.2002, Ronald Suresh Roberts refers explicitly to Nicolas's 'suicide'. In a telephone conversation with me on 27.1.2009, Roberts would neither confirm or deny that this pronouncement was based on documentary evidence.

77 The information in this and the following nine paragraphs is, unless otherwise stated, based on a personal interview with J.M. Coetzee, 20.3.2009.

78 Information from an interview with Lisa Perold, 25.5.2009.

79 Interview with Dorothy Driver, 3.4.2009.

80 Ibid.

81 Information about Nicolas's results was obtained from the student centre of the University of Cape Town.

82 *Forgive the Father* is a memoir by Howard Wolf.

83 Information from Lisa Perold in the aforementioned interview.

84 'Register of deaths, state mortuary', Johannesburg, Mortuary number 883 / 04 / 1989.

85 This and further information, unless otherwise stated, from Dorothy Driver, interview 3.4.2009.

86 Personal interview, 7.4.2010.

87 In my interview with Gisela Coetzee, she alleged that there had been no autopsy. If this were the case, it would be highly irregular, but it is contradicted by the information contained in the 'Register of deaths state mortuary'.

88 Telephonic interview with Marilyn Honikman, formerly Kirkwood, 14.12.2009.

89 Interview with Chris Perold, 11.3.2010.

90 E-mail from Howard Wolf, May 2009.

91 Sue Kossew, 'The anxiety of authorship: J.M. Coetzee's *The Master of Petersburg* (1994) and André Brink's *On the Contrary* (1993)', *English in Africa*, 23: 1, May 1996.

92 The titles *Falling Man* by Don DeLillo and *Falling Out of Time* by O.R. Melling were also still commercially available.

93 In the single-volume edition of his comprehensive biography of Dostoevsky (*Dostoevsky: A Writer in his Time*, Princeton / Oxford, Princeton University Press, 2010), Joseph Frank writes: 'This totally unscrupulous agitator with a will of iron composed a *Catechism of a Revolutionary* whose utilitarian approval of any means to obtain presumably beneficial social ends makes Machiavelli look like a choirboy' (p. xvi).

94 A.J. Wiggers and others, *Grote Winkler Prins Encyclopedie*, part 14, Amsterdam, Elsevier, 1972, p. 80.

95 J.M. Coetzee, *The Master of Petersburg*, London, Secker & Warburg, 1994, p. 121.

96 Ibid., pp. 43–44.

97 In one of the unpublished notes that form part of the manuscript of the novel, Coetzee writes:

Anna Dostoevskaya presents an un-attractive picture of Pavel. He is of course her rival in age. FMD abandons him in favour of her. After 1867 he constantly emphasizes good fatherhood—a reaction against a guilty conscience?
  On his side, Pavel regards AD, a girl of his own age, as belonging to his camp, as 'his'. AD: 'He says his father is too old to begin a new life.' When Pavel delivers this message to D—recalling him to his duty—D has a fit of (guilty?) rage, calls him 'pompous, moralizing,' and throws him out of his study.
  Words of Pavel to FMD: 'If I have any criticism, it is that you left your son alone when he needed a guiding hand …' Kafka and his father: Pavel is the one who ought to be writing the long letter.

98 The original biography was published in five volumes, which makes it the most comprehensive work of this nature in the history of biographies of a literary personality. In his collection *Stranger Shores* Coetzee devoted a penetrating essay to this biography.

99 Reprinted in the *Cape Times*, 5.3.1994.

100 Joseph Frank, 'The rebel', *The New Republic*, 213: 16.

101 Interview with Joanna Scott, 'Voice and trajectory', *Salmagundi*, 114, 115, Spring / Summer 1997.

102 In an address to the *Weekly Mail* Book Week in 1987 in the Baxter Theatre in Cape Town, published as 'The novel today', *Upstream*, 6, 1988.

103 J.M. Coetzee, *Stranger Shores: Essays 1986–1999*, London, Secker & Warburg, 2001, p. 295, cited.

104 Monica Popescu, 'Waiting for the Russians: Coetzee's *The Master of Petersburg* and the Logic of Late Postcolonialism', Michael Chapman, ed., *Postcolonialism: South African Perspectives*, Newcastle, U.K., Cambridge Scholars Publishing, 2008.

105 The comparison could also be extended to the systems of censorship in the two countries.

106 *The Master of Petersburg*, pp. 137–138.

107 Ibid., p. 112.

108 It does, however, return in modified form when Anya hands Dostoevsky a telegram in his study 'and pronounced the words that even tonight beat in his head like dull bells, each pealing with its full and final weight: "Fedya, *Pavel is dead!*"' (*The Master of Petersburg*, pp. 123–124).

109 Ibid., pp. 15 and 26–27.

110 Ibid., p. 26.

111 Ibid., p. 33.

112 Ibid., p. 77.

113 Ibid., pp. 20–21 and 105.

114 J.M. Coetzee, *Landscape with Rowers: Poetry from the Netherlands*, Princeton / Oxford, Princeton University Press, 2004, p. viii.

115 Gerrit Achterberg, *Verzamelde gedichten*, tenth impression, Amsterdam, Querido, 1988, pp. 258–259. Translation M.H., with help from and thanks to Siegfried Huigen.

116 My italics.

117 *The Master of Petersburg*, p. 5.

118 Ibid., pp. 221–222.

119 Ibid., p. 235.

120 Ibid., p. 236.

121 Stephen Watson, *New Contrast*, XXII: 4, December 1994.

122 These words refer back to the words of Matryona to Nechaev on p. 157: 'They pay him thousands of roubles to write books', words uttered to her by Pavel.

123 *The Master of Petersburg*, p. 250.

124 Quoted in *The Herald* (Zimbabwe), 24.7.1995.

125 When asked by the *Times Literary Supplement* to select his best book of the year, Brink chose, in the edition of 2 December 1994, Julia Blackburn's *Daisy Bates in the Desert* and Coetzee's *The Master of Petersburg*. He writes about Coetzee's novel : 'Stylistically and imaginatively, J.M. Coetzee's *The Master of Petersburg* is a match for Daisy Bates. Hard, clean, stripped and bright, his narrative reinvents the Dostoevsky we know from literary history and from the novels. But this is history from the inside, imagining the creative mind in its secret workings, as it draws on bitter experience, on loss and deprivation, and above all on the imagination, in its attempts to remake the world and to reconcile the individual vision with the vagaries and vulgarities of politics. Despite the deceptively lucid narrative, this novel may be less accessible than others in Coetzee's *oeuvre*, but in some ways it may be his finest, and certainly his most intensely moving.'

CHAPTER 13

1 Personal interview, 20.3.2009.

2 *Sunday Times*, 7.10.1990.

3 Hermann Giliomee, *Die Afrikaners: 'n Biografie*, Cape Town, Tafelberg, 2004, p. 586. [Translation M.H.]

4 Among other stipulations the eventually approved constitution states: 'We the people of South Africa, Recognise the injustices of our past; Honour those who suffered for justice and freedom in our land; Respect those who have worked to build and develop our country; and Believe that South Africa belongs to all who live in it, united in our diversity. We therefore, through our freely elected representatives, adopt this Constitution as the supreme law of the

Republic so as to
Heal the divisions of the past and
establish a society based on democratic
values, social justice and fundamental
human rights;
Lay the foundations for a democratic
and open society in which government
is based on the will of the people and
every citizen is equally protected by law;
Improve the quality of life of all
citizens and free the potential of
each person; and
Build a united and democratic
South Africa able to take its rightful
place as a sovereign state in the
family of nations.
http:// www.info.gov.za / documents /
constitution/1996/96preamble.htm.

5 Nelson Mandela, *Long Road to Freedom*,
   Randburg, Macdonald Purnell, 1994,
   p. 612.
6 Hermann Giliomee and Bernard
   Mbenga, eds, *Nuwe geskiedenis van Suid-
   Afrika*, Cape Town, Tafelberg, 2007,
   p. 413.
7 J.M. Coetzee, *Diary of a Bad Year*,
   Londen, Harvill Secker, 2007, p. 117.
8 Patti Waldmeir, *Anatomy of a Miracle*,
   New York, W.W. Norton, 1997, p. 287.
9 In *Disgrace* he writes, referring to David
   Lurie: 'Because he has no respect for
   the material he teaches, he makes no
   impression on his students. They look
   through him when he speaks, forget
   his name. Their indifference galls him
   more than he will admit. Nevertheless
   he fulfils to the letter his obligations
   toward them, their parents and the state.
   Month after month he sets, collects,
   reads, and annotates their assignments,
   correcting lapses in punctuation,
   spelling and usage, interrogating weak
   arguments, appending to each paper a
   brief, considered critique.
      He continues to teach because it
   provides him with a livelihood; also
   because it teaches him humility, brings
   home to him who he is in the world.
   The irony does not escape him: that
   the one who comes to teach learns the
   keenest of lessons, while those who
   come to learn learn nothing.' (J.M.
   Coetzee, *Disgrace*, London, Secker &
   Warburg, 1999, pp. 4–5.)

10 PEN hhtp: // ht.ly / 3TkQ1.
11 André Brink, 'My buurman John', *By*,
    6.2.2010. [Translation M.H.]
12 J.M. Coetzee, *Doubling the Point: Essays
    and Interviews*, edited by David Attwell,
    Cambridge, Massachusetts / London,
    Harvard University Press, 1992, p. 341.
13 Schonstein's books have since been
    published in Britain by Harper Collins
    and have been translated into Dutch
    and Swedish.
14 J.M. Coetzee, 'Critic and citizen:
    A response', *Pretexts: Literary and
    Cultural Studies*, IX: 1, 2000. On
    18.1.1999, for instance, Coetzee
    wrote to Jonathan Crewe about the
    fate of Dutch in South Africa: 'The
    UCT department of what used to be
    Nederlands en Afrikaans first renamed
    itself Netherlandic Studies and then
    amalgamated with African Languages.
    I would imagine that there isn't much
    Vondel read under their auspices
    nowadays.'
15 *Diary of a Bad Year*, p. 35.
16 In the same interview Coetzee
    expressed reservations about the new
    literary 'show business': 'The spectacle
    of writers being used to market their
    own books, particularly younger
    writers, is dismaying and depressing,
    and it doesn't even work particularly
    well. I rarely find that a writer has
    much of interest to say about his or
    her own work, and there is a good
    reason for that. When you have
    completed a book you move on to
    other concerns, you have no interest
    in going back to what you have written
    in an exploratory frame of mind.'
17 An amusing instance is the interview
    that Philip R. Wood conducted with
    Coetzee in 1994 for a special edition
    of the *South Atlantic Quarterly*. Wood's
    questions extend over almost thirteen
    pages, and Coetzee's replies hardly
    more than a page.
18 In two cases in these years Coetzee
    allowed himself to be persuaded
    to appear in video recordings. In
    September 1997 Henion Han and
    Cheryl Tuckett produced a 52-minute
    film on Coetzee for SABC-TV, a
    combination of a documentary

and an autobiography. It consists of interviews with a number of Coetzee experts—Lesley Marx, David Attwell, Rita Barnard, Lionel Abrahams and Ashraf Jamal—commenting on his work, and of readings by Coetzee from his novels, during which he does not appear, but scenes are shown of the Cape landscape, the Swartberg Pass that figures in *Life & Times of Michael K*, the Rondebosch common, and scenes at the University of Cape Town. From time to time Coetzee himself makes brief appearances for flashbacks to his youth. The distinctive quality of the documentary is the insight of the producer, Cheryl Tuckett, who found a way of focusing on the novels, rather than on Coetzee's presence. She had him read voice-over, and filled the screen with appropriately evocative images. This avoids the journalistic errors that Coetzee dislikes so much. Roger Thompson of the BBC said about the film: 'This is a very bold, uncompromising piece of work', and Zakes Mda wrote in *The Star*: 'This unusual documentary about a great artist is a piece of art itself—and rarely does a television programme qualify as art ... a valuable contribution to our understanding of this great writer.' At the invitation of the Dutchman Wim Kayzer, Coetzee also participated, along with some twenty internationally known intellectuals, in a series in which an interview of an hour and a half was conducted with each on the topics 'beauty' and 'consolation'. For the whole of his interview Coetzee speaks haltingly, hesitantly, with many pauses and silences, searching for the correct words to convey exactly what he wants to say. He took Kayser to Dias Beach near Cape Point, which to him embodied the unspoilt beauty of the African landscape, more or less as it must have been in 1486 when the Portuguese explorers passed here. Coetzee found 'beauty' a complex word with both an original and an extended meaning. In Dutch the text of Coetzee's interview was published in Wim Kayzer, *Het boek van de schoonheid en de troost*, Amsterdam / Antwerpen,

Uitgeverij Contact, 2000.
19 The information in this section is based largely on a personal interview with Jonathan Lear in Chicago, 20.4.2010.
20 Jonathan Lear, 'The aims of educations address 2009', *The Aims of Education: Selected Essays*, Chicago, University of Chicago, 2009.
21 J.M. Coetzee, *Elizabeth Costello*, London, Secker & Warburg, 2003, p. 125.
22 In 2001 Coetzee's name was again mentioned in relation to the Nobel Prize for Literature, but it went to V.S. Naipaul. When Sandy Blanton in a letter of 24.10.2001 alluded to the possibility of Coetzee's winning the Nobel Prize, he replied: 'You mention the Nobel Prize and my chances of getting it. In my case, writing in English and coming from the same country as a recent prizewinner are strikes against me. So I wouldn't hold my breath if I were you.'
23 Documentation regarding the honorary doctorate to Coetzee was provided by William Offhaus, Special Collections, University Archives, Buffalo.
24 Letter from J.M. Coetzee to Howard Wolf, 2.6.1989.
25 J.M. Coetzee, *Doubling the Point: Essays and Interviews*, edited by David Attwell, Cambridge, Massachusetts / London, Harvard University Press, 1992, p. 18.
26 The account was published as 'Doubling the writer: David Attwell in his textual dialogue with J.M. Coetzee', *Wasafiri*, 63 (2010). It appeared under the name of Elleke Boehmer, who had conducted the interview with Attwell. In the Netherlands it appeared as 'David Attwell en Elleke Boehmer: *Schrijversdubbel*, *J.M. Coetzee: Persoon en personage*, Amsterdam, Cossee, 2010, pp. 61–79.
27 This article appeared in *Meanjin: New Writing in Australia*, 64: 4, 2005, and was reprinted in the *Weekend Australian*, 28–29.1.2006. I am here being led by the details provided by Coetzee.
28 There has been some speculation as to whether Coetzee's special

relationship with his Dutch publisher has anything to do with the similarity in sound of their surnames, or whether there may even be a family connection. Eva Cossée's ancestors were religious refugees who fled France to settle in Holland. The patriarch of the Coetzee family in South Africa, with the first name Dirk, originally spelt his surname Couché, but changed it to Coetsé at the Cape. The spelling Couché suggests French origins, but any details and documents pertaining to earlier generations were lost in the annals of countless wars. It is, however, not wholly improbable that some family connection may exist between Coetzee and his Dutch publisher.

29 There were several reviews that Coetzee never reprinted in any of his collections, among others his appreciative short assessment of Sydney Clouts's *Collected Poems*, a poet who he thinks will be remembered for ten or twenty short poems dating mainly from his early middle years. He refers to Anthony Delius's pronouncement that Clouts was 'the most original poet South Africa has ever produced', a judgement that Coetzee shares, as far as English-language South African poetry is concerned.

30 J.M. Coetzee, *Stranger Shores: Essays 1986–1999*, London, Secker & Warburg, 2001, p. 48.

31 Ibid., p. 73.

32 Ibid., p. 83.

33 *Doubling the Point*, p. 90.

34 *Elizabeth Costello*, p. 121.

35 *Stranger Shores*, p. 92.

36 T.S. Eliot, *On Poetry and Poets*, London, Faber and Faber, 1957, p. 68.

37 *Stranger shores*, pp. 3–5.

38 Ibid., p. 7.

39 Ibid., pp. 6–7.

40 Ibid., p. 19.

41 Ibid., p. 240.

42 Ibid., p. 243.

43 Ibid., p. 245.

44 Ibid., pp. 271–272.

45 J.M. Coetzee, *Giving Offense*, Chicago / London, University of Chicago Press, 1996, pp. 204–214.

46 *Doubling the Point*, p. 341.

47 *Stranger Shores*, p. 306.

48 Ibid., pp. 311–312.

49 J.M. Coetzee, *Boyhood*, London, Secker & Warburg, 1997, p. 87.

50 *Stranger Shores*, p. 312.

51 J.M. Coetzee, *Truth in Autobiography*, Cape Town, University of Cape Town, 1984, p. 1.

52 Ibid., p. 3. Coetzee writes: 'We can equally well see the confessional enterprise as one of *finding* the truth as of *telling* the truth.'

53 *Doubling the Point*, pp. 391–392.

54 Derek Attridge, *J.M. Coetzee and the Ethics of Reading*, Scottsville, University of KwaZulu-Natal Press, 2005, p. 149.

55 L.N. Tolstoy, *Childhood Boyhood Youth*, translated and introduced by Rosemary Edmonds, Harmondsworth, Penguin, 1964, pp. 7–8.

56 On the question of truth in autobiography Coetzee writes in an e-mail of 16.3.2004 to Tim Guest:

Autobiography, and to a lesser extent memoir, seem to me to involve an undertaking to tell the truth, and to tell the truth in quite an exacting sense, which would include not making up anything.

There has always seemed to me to be something wrong with such a criterion. How can one vouch for the truth of feelings recalled at a distance of decades? How can one even vouch for the truth of memories that are shared with no one else? How can one prevent either from being coloured by invention?

I have accordingly written two books of the memoir genre for which I claim no historical truthfulness and in which invention has been used freely, rather than being kept at bay.

You ask how the personages mentioned in the books have reacted. Some are dead by now, many have not read the books, some never existed in the real world, some have suffered name changes, some have had acts attributed to them that must have surprised them. One that I know of has ceased to communicate with me, one has, from the depths of the English countryside, written to me.

57 The manuscript of *Youth* is in possession of the author, with whose permission I was able to consult it in March 2009.

58 In the British edition *Youth* was published without a subtitle, but in the American edition, in accordance with *Boyhood, Scenes from Provincial Life II* is added to the title page.

59 In reply to a number of e-mail questions from David Attwell in July 2002 after the publication of *Youth*, and following up on statements made ten years earlier in *Doubling the Point*, Coetzee replied at length in an e-mail that in edited form later appeared as J.M. Coetzee and David Attwell, 'All autobiography is *autre*-biography', *Selves in question: Interviews on Southern African auto / biography*, J. Lütge Coullie, S. Meyer, T. Ngwenya and T. Olver, eds, Honolulu, University of Hawaii Press, 2006:

If we accept, for the moment, that all writing is autobiography, then the statement that all writing is autobiography is itself autobiography, a moment in the autobiographical enterprise. Which is a roundabout way of saying that the remarks you refer to, published in *Doubling the Point*, do not exist outside of time and outside of my life-story.

I would still say that all writing is autobiography; but whether, when I say so today, I mean quite the same as what I meant when I said so ten or twelve years ago, is a matter of memory, fallible and unverifiable memory. What I do know for a fact is that between then and now I have published two books, *Boyhood* and *Youth*, which are in some sense autobiographical. I have also, at the University of Chicago, run seminars on Wordsworth's *Prelude* and Roland Barthes' *Roland Barthes* and other texts that lead one to think hard about what autobiography is. I cannot believe that my thinking about autobiography has not been deepened to an extent by these reading and writing experiences. So perhaps we should distinguish: I cannot intend quite the same as I originally intended, though the two statements, then and now, may mean the same.

You ask about genres and about the, to some extent, legitimate demand of readers that they be told what genre territory they are being asked to enter. But genre is not, to my mind, a refined concept. Genre definitions—at least those definitions employed by ordinary readers—are quite crude. What if the writer wants to trouble the boundaries of the genre? Does the autobiographical pact between writer and reader—the pact that says that, at the very least, the reader will be told no outright, deliberate lies—trump the disquiet one may feel about the quite crude definition of lying that many readers may hold?

60 The examples from Defoe, Brontë and Dickens are cited by Anna Cichoń in her essay on '*Boyhood*: *Scenes from provincial life* and *Youth*—J.M. Coetzee's autobiographies', Liliana Sikorska, ed., *A Universe of (Hi)stories: Essays on J.M. Coetzee*, Frankfurt am Main, Peter Lang, 2006, p.59.

61 Ibid., p. 63.

62 Matthew Cheney, *The Quarterly Conversation*, 7.12.2009.

63 In 2008 the Dutch filmmaker Ben van Lieshout based *De muze* on *Youth*, a film about a character named John who wanders around in solitude in a Dutch harbour town in search of love and literature. The film, about 72 minutes long, consists of images of wandering characters, with virtually no dialogue.

64 *Salmagundi*, 114–115, 1997, reprinted in *Best American Essays 1998*, ed. Cynthia Ozick, Boston, Houghton Mifflin, 1998, and later collected in *Elizabeth Costello*, London, Secker & Warburg, 2003.

65 *Elizabeth Costello*, pp. 1–2.

66 *The Sunday Independent*, 18.5.2003.

67 The Tanner Lectures on human values, in which several universities collaborate and which change venue

annually, were instituted in 1978 by
the American intellectual Obert Clark
Tanner. In his foundation lecture
Tanner said: 'I hope these lectures
will contribute to the intellectual
and moral life of mankind. I see
them simply as a search for a better
understanding of human behavior and
human values. This understanding
may be pursued for its own intrinsic
worth, but it may also eventually have
practical consequences for the quality
of personal and social life.'

68 *Sunday Times*, 28.9.2003. Nicolas
Dawes's review deals with *Elizabeth
Costello*, in which *The Lives of Animals* is
reprinted.

69 *The Sunday Independent*, 12.12.1999.

70 J.M. Coetzee, *The Lives of Animals*,
Princeton, Princeton University Press,
1999, p. 69.

71 Ibid., p. 69. When the BBC in 2002
wanted to adapt *The Lives of Animals*
for television, Coetzee objected to the
script. In a letter to Jess Cleverly of the
BBC, he writes on 19 January 2002:
'Before I respond to your specific
questions, let me say that in my eyes
the fundamental weakness of the script
is a lack of feel for the characters.
This is not something that can be set
right via a few technical adjustments.
Whether you want to make a really
good film or merely a passable film is
up to you. My opinion is that to make
a good film you would need a new
scriptwriter. To make a passable film
it may or may not be enough to patch
up the present draft.' Coetzee then
attends specifically to the character of
Elizabeth Costello, giving some idea
of how he had conceptualised the
character for himself: 'Elizabeth is a
forceful personality used to having
her own way. Norma is an intelligent
if rather narrow academic type who
is (justifiably) frustrated at having to
live the life of a jobless and rather
penurious academic wife. To an extent
she is taking out her frustrations on
her husband by making his mother's
visit as difficult for him as she can;
but she also has viable philosophical
objections to the position Elizabeth

takes on animals. She would hold
these opinions whether or not
Elizabeth came visiting. John is not
the weak, evasive, and false person
he emerges as in the script, merely
a youngish man (mid-thirties) who
would like to get back to his own
work but who has resigned himself to
devoting these few days to his mother's
visit and who would above all like to
keep the peace between his wife and
his mother.'

72 *The Sunday Independent*, 12.12.1999.

73 *Natural Selections*, 6, 1999.

74 *The Hunting Apes: Meat Eating and the
Origins of Human Behavior*, Princeton,
Princeton University Press, 1999.

75 The manuscript of *Disgrace* is in the
possession of the author, who during
my visit to Adelaide, Australia, in
March 2009 kindly granted me access
to it.

76 'There, all is but measure and beauty,
Luxury, calm and sensual delight.'
Baudelaire: Selected Verse, with prose trans-
lations by Francis Scarfe, Harmonds-
worth, Penguin, 1961, p. 107. My thanks
to Catherine Lauga du Plessis, Coetzee's
French translator, who brought the
Baudelaire allusion to my attention.

77 Michael G. McDunnah, '"We are
not asked to condemn": Sympathy,
subjectivity and the narration
of *Disgrace*', Bill McDonald, ed.,
Encountering Disgrace, New York,
Camden House, 2009, p. 19.

78 *Disgrace*, p. 1.

79 Ibid., p. 89.

80 David Attwell, 'Race in *Disgrace*',
Interventions, IV: 3, 2002.

81 *Disgrace*, p. 172.

82 Fiona MacCarthy, *Byron: Life and
Legend*, London, John Murray, 2002,
pp. 353–373.

83 *Disgrace*, p. 205.

84 Eberhardt followed up Coetzee's
concise replies with a request for a
slightly more comprehensive response.
Coetzee's reply, on 24 March 2001,
was if anything more terse: 'I'm
sorry you find my responses to your
questions unsatisfactory. I don't
normally respond to journalists'
questions — I believe books should

make their own way. I made an exception in this case as a favor to Peter. Let's leave it at that.'

85 *The English Academy Review*, XVI: 1999.

86 Reprinted in the *Saturday Argus*, 7.8.1999.

87 In *The New York Times* of 14 November 1999, Rachel L. Swarns also points out the kinship between the two novels, emerging as it were from the watershed of two eras. In Afrikaans literature this theme had already been explored in Karel Schoeman's *Afskeid en vertrek* (1990), with its painful realisation of the passing of a whole way of life and a segment of civilisation; and in his *Verkenning* (1996), in which the violence on the Eastern Cape border of the early nineteenth century shows some resemblance to the contemporary unrest and uncertainty in the new South Africa. Related themes are also present in novels by André Brink, Etienne van Heerden and Eben Venter.

88 Bill McDonald, *Encountering Disgrace*, New York, Camden House, 2009.

89 Ibid., pp. 5–6. When in 2001 *Disgrace* was prescribed as a set text for about 6 000 matriculants at independent schools, some parents complained on grounds of racism, sexism and explicit sexual scenes in the novel. According to Tom Waspe, an official of the Department of Education in charge of prescribed books for Gauteng matriculants, *Disgrace* will probably also be considered as a set text in the province. 'We will not,' said Waspe, 'avoid books that deal with racial issues, metaphorically or even if racist behaviour is depicted. We are not just looking for rosy, feel-good books that do not deal with the realities of life.' (*Business Day*, 8.11. 2001.) In the series *Literature Guides* for school use a guide to *Disgrace* appeared in 2007 (Northlands, Macmillan). Another introduction to the novel is Andrew van der Vlies's *Disgrace*, London / New York, Continuum, 2010.

90 Merritt Moseley, 'The Booker prize for 1999', *Sewanee Review*, 108: 4, Fall 2000.

91 Sarah Lyall, 'South African writer wins top British prize for second time',

The New York Times, 26.10.1999.

92 *UCT News*, December 1999.

93 Against England in the same year.

94 In a personal letter of 22.11.1999, Nadine Gordimer wrote to Coetzee: 'Your novel is wonderfully disturbing—which I believe fiction should be, and only the very best is. People may argue about your "intention", what your novel is "about"; it will never be understood that we writers—a writer is the medium, in the sense of possessed (without the mystification implied) of what is happening in our society, transformed by the imagination from the general to the particular: the people we invent.' Gordimer then asks why the student (Isaacs) and the professor (Lurie) have Jewish names. Coetzee replied on 9.12.1999 that he found it difficult to talk about his own work: 'One of the reasons why I dodge interviews is that I find myself continually pushed or dragged into what feel like betrayals of the people I have created—into giving interpretations of them when their motives are as mysterious to me as the motives of "real" people around me.' He points out that Isaacs is a very common name among coloured people. As for Lurie, he did not realise that it was an exclusively Jewish name. He associated it with 'lorey', the bird name, 'lori' in French.

95 Maureen Isaacson, 'J.M. Coetzee receives Booker prize with characteristic coolness', *The Sunday Independent*, 31.10.1999.

96 Reported in *Beeld*, 18.1.2000.

97 Ibid.

98 Quoted in Ronald Suresh Roberts, *No Cold Kitchen: A Biography of Nadine Gordimer*, Johannesburg, STE Publishers, 2005, pp. 551.

99 Quoted by Rachel Donadio, *The New York Times*, 16.12.2007.

100 Ibid.

101 *The Independent*, 7.5.2000.

102 Galgut and Bhabha's assessments are quoted by Rachel Donadio, *The New York Times*, 16.12.2007.

103 'Statement of the ANC at the Human Rights Commission Hearings

on Racism in the Media, 5 April 2000', collected as an epilogue to the book *A Marriage made in Heaven*, Johannesburg, Skotaville, 2001.

104 *Disgrace*, p. 156.

105 The *Sunday Times* of 5 October 2003 reported on this as follows: 'Piquantly, Mbeki was believed to have ghostwritten an ANC minister's vitriolic denunciation of *Disgrace* in 2000. One newspaper, the *Mail & Guardian*, claimed to have traced the speech to Mbeki's computer. The president was reportedly enraged by the book's description of a gang rape of a white woman by black men and its theme of the violent eviction of white farmers from their land by squatters.' With reference to the ANC's accusation that *Disgrace* deployed racist stereotypes, Mike Marais in the *Mail & Guardian* of 28 April—4 May 2000 points to the parallel between the rape of the student Melanie by Lurie and the rape of Lucy by three black men. It is a parallel that clearly illustrates that the violence that the novel depicts in post-apartheid society is endemic to the whole society, not restricted to a single group or race. 'Accordingly,' Marais writes, 'this is a novel that could and should speak to South Africans about their present, their past and their possible futures. Sadly, though, the paradigms that inform our reading habits are, it seems, coextensive with the ways in which we see the world in general. So, although perverse, it is understandable that this novel now stands accused of being a symptom of that which it so obviously seeks to address.' In a conversation with Hettie Scholtz in *Insig* of June 2000 on the ANC's charge of racism in the novel, Marlene van Niekerk replies: 'It's bullshit, of course, and only demonstrates the lack of intellectual refinement and, more, what thick-skinned insouciance prevails with them as the image that they are prepared to transmit to the world. It makes one think of the Nats of old. It's the same bullnecked obstinacy that one used to see in their propaganda. Subtlety in fiction wasn't exacty high up either, on their list of national priorities.'

106 Translation M.H.

107 Etienne Britz, 'Coetzee se *Disgrace*. Van skande tot skoonheid', *Die Burger*, 6.9.1999. [Translation M.H.]

108 On 14.4.2011 Ronnie Kasrils wrote to Hermann Giliomee, who at my request had enquired from him about the matter: 'The novel of course was not on the agenda. It came up tangentially—a light digression of a few minutes. I respect JM and was most impressed with *The Barbarians* but spoke critically about *Disgrace*. Lindiwe Sisulu was very defensive of the novel and disagreed with me—and possibly others. I found it too pessimistic. The Chair, President Mbeki, soon brought us back to order.' Lindiwe Sisulu, however, did not later become an ambassador.

CHAPTER 14

1 Dick Penner, *Countries of the Mind: The Fiction of J.M. Coetzee*, New York / Westport, Connecticut / London, Greenwood Press, 1989, p. 19 quoted.

2 *The Bulletin Review*, 5.9.2001.

3 According to a report in *The Herald* of 20.10.2006, Coetzee reiterated this sentiment in a rare interview with Australian television. It was also repeated in *The Sunday Independent*, 27.10.2002.

4 I am drawing here and in the rest of the paragraph on a personal interview with J.M. Coetzee, 23.3.2009.

5 In the *Mail & Guardian* of 14.6.2007 this 'profound announcement' of Coetzee's is reproduced as follows: 'I did not so much leave South Africa, a country with which I retain strong emotional ties, as come to Australia.'

6 In an interview with Luke Slattery of *The Australian*, Coetzee said: 'I don't regard the move as a matter of breaking shackles at all. I have been visiting Australia on and off for the past ten years, and am strongly attracted by the country—by the landscape, by the people, by other features harder to define. I am moving *to* Australia, not moving *away from* South Africa. [...]

But I have not lost my sympathy for South Africans, not at all. [...] One should remember that we live in a world of migration on a scale hitherto unknown in history. One person in four world-wide does not live in the country in which his or her grandparents were born. It is not an extraordinary step to change residence.'

7 This formulation is based on one of the ideas expressed by the 72-year-old Australian writer in Coetzee's novel *Diary of a Bad Year* (London, Harvill Secker, 2007, p. 15).

8 Personal interview with J.M. Coetzee, 23.3.2009.

9 Unfortunately Coetzee and Dorothy's new architect-designed home in Adelaide Hills took a while longer to complete than envisaged. As a result of a financial dispute between the builder and one of the subcontractors, which had to be resolved in the magistrate's court in 2002, completion was temporarily delayed (*The Weekend Australian*, 13–14.12.2003). Because Coetzee was named as the second respondent in the case, some papers drew the erroneous conclusion that he had not been prepared to pay.

10 Susannah Farfor, George Dunford, Jill Kirby, *Adelaide & South Australia*, Victoria, Lonely Planet, third edition, 2005, p. 87.

11 *Cape Times*, 20.2.2004.

12 There are considerable differences between the text of the diptych in *The Lives of Animals* and as reprinted in *Elizabeth Costello*. Patrick Denman Flanery has written about this in '(Re-) marking Coetzee & Costello: The [textual] *Lives of animals*', *English Studies in Africa*, 47: 1, 2004.

13 In spite of the Russian material and setting of *The Master of Petersburg*, there are aspects of the resistance to Czarist tyranny that form a parallel to the revolt against apartheid in the 1980s and '90s.

14 In 'The problem of evil' Elizabeth Costello refers to an actual writer, Paul West, author of a novel with the title *The Very Rich Hours of Count von Stauffenberg*, about the attempt

upon the life of Adolf Hitler. In 'The novelist and the hangman' in *Harper's Magazine* of July 2004, Paul West reacted to this.

15 J.M. Coetzee, *Elizabeth Costello*, London, Secker & Warburg, 2003, pp. 224–225.

16 That such an intertextual game could not satisfy all readers is evident from an assessment by Rosellen Brown in *The New Leader*, 86: 6, November / December 2003: 'the novel consists of skips, of interrupted narrative, and endless, if uncomfortable, performance, both literal (poor Elizabeth is forever in the spotlight) and figurative (the author assembling a new text out of many old ones).'

17 On p. 199 of *Elizabeth Costello* the protagonist says, upon her arrival at one of the gates: 'I am a writer, and what I write is what I hear. I am a secretary of the invisible, one of the many secretaries over the ages.' Coetzee is here making use of the poem 'Secretaries' by the Polish poet Czesław Miłos. In English translation the poem runs as follows:
I am no more than a secretary of the invisible thing
That is dictated to me and a few others.
Secretaries, mutually unknown, we walk the earth
Without much comprehension.
Beginning a phrase in the middle
Or ending it with a comma. And how it all looks when completed
Is not up to us to inquire, we won't read it anyway.
(Czesław Miłos, *Selected Poems*, Kraków, Wydawnictwo Literackie, 1996, p. 249, translated by Czesław Miłos and Robert Hass.)

18 *Cape Argus*, 6.3.2006.

CHAPTER 15

1 It was reported in *The Star* of 2.10.1999 that, according to Swedish sources, both Coetzee and André Brink were contenders for the 1999 Nobel Prize. It was, however, awarded to the German Günter Grass.

2 *PEN News*, July 2004.
3 Personal interview with J.M. Coetzee, 20. 3.2009.
4 The information in this and the following paragraphs is gleaned from an interview with Jonathan Lear, Chicago, 20.4.2010.
5   In his article on Coetzee in *The Daily Telegraph*, 29.11.2003 Rian Malan portrayed the South African author as 'reclusive and secretive'. Susan Dunn wrote a letter in reply to the same paper. During his visit to Stanford, said Susan Dunn, Coetzee lunched every afternoon with students and colleagues, took part in seminars and discussion groups, and in general fulfilled his social duties. For recreation he went cycling with friends in the hills around Stanford. In the preceding five years he had delivered more than fifty public lectures in eleven countries on five continents. According to her, this is not the behaviour of a recluse. 'Is it possible,' she asks, 'that what Malan calls reclusiveness may be no more than a dislike for journalists?' On 17.12.2003 Gay Baines added her voice to that of Dunn: 'I was privileged to take a writing seminar from Coetzee at SUNY-Buffalo 15 years ago, and I have never forgotten it. Neither have my friends! When the prize was announced, everyone was calling me up, e-mailing me. The thing that I remember most about him is his humor. Why does everyone say he never laughs? He laughed a great deal when we chatted before or during class, and his comments during the seminars were full of subtle wit. I've never met a more courteous man, let alone a person even more shy than myself.'
6 On 2 October 2003, the day of the announcement, Wayne Booth wrote to Coetzee in an e-mail: 'What a surprise and pleasure this morning to have three telephone calls from various journalists asking me to be interviewed about you. Usually when the Nobel is awarded I have some doubts, and often I have to confess that I've never read the author's work. It's wonderful to have the prize go to an author I would myself have awarded it to—one whose works have almost all been read by me. [...] Congratulations—and I hope that the prize doesn't destroy your life with too many interruptions like this one.'
7 The respect that Texas still accords Coetzee is evident from an e–mail that Bernth Lindfors sent David Attwell on 13 September 2011: 'The University still remembers him. That was demonstrated during a timeout at the football game against Rice the Saturday before last when UT was bragging on a loudspeaker about all its international awardees. When the Nobel was mentioned, a photo of JM's face against a background of the University tower was projected on the jumbotron. That brought cheers from the crowd.'
8 *Cape Times*, 3.10.2003.
9 The whole of the exchange with Giliomee is in Afrikaans. Translation M.H.
10 In an e-mail to me, 9.5.2009.
11 Colin Bower, 'The art and artifice of J.M. Coetzee', *Sunday Times*, 28.9.2003.
12 [Translation M.H.] Bower's article was taken over from the journal *Scrutiny 2*, of which Leon de Kock was the editor. In *Rapport* of 12 October 2003 De Kock defended the publication of this article as the airing of an opinion that, even though taking a negative view of Coetzee's oeuvre, was entitled to a hearing. He did not defend the substance of the article.
13 Ibid.
14 Breyten Breytenbach wrote an e-mail on 2.10.2003 to Jakes Gerwel about his criticism of *Disgrace* in his *Rapport* article, and what he regarded as Gerwel's complicity in Coetzee's departure to Australia: 'I'm sure we are all very pleased with the Nobel accorded to John Coetzee. (I'm certainly happy.) But I cannot help but remembering that devastating article you wrote about *Disgrace*, when poor John could not produce the moral *stroop* [unction] of political prostitution to find favour in the eyes of the masters, and how that article then was recycled (probably by Thabo himself), submissioned to the HRC

(presided over by the Honourable Honest Pityana) on racism, and how this must have been one of the contributing factors why Coetzee left the country. *Hoe voel jou boude nou?* [So is your backside smarting now?]'

15 J.M. Coetzee, *Elizabeth Costello*, London, Secker & Warburg, 2003, p. 3.

16 *This Day*, 23–24.1.2004.

17 What follows here and in subsequent chapters on the proceedings in Stockholm derives largely, at times verbatim, from Theresa Biberauer's excellent reportage in *Die Burger* and *Beeld* of 8.12.2003. A few facts, however, were added from other sources.

18 It was published in the edition of 8.12.2003.

19 A. Roland Holst, *Gedichten 1911–1976*, compiled, edited and introduced by Jan van der Vegt, Amsterdam / Antwerpen, Meulenhoff / Manteau, 2004, p. 538. [Translation M.H.]

20 E-mail to Shaun Irlam, 24.12.2003.

21 Coetzee extensively revised his translation of *Ballade van de Gasfitter* for publication. He wrote to Catherine Lauga du Plessis, his French translator, on 19.3.2005: 'In the early 1970s I spent months working on a translation of a sonnet sequence by the Dutch poet Gerrit Achterberg. The translation was published in the mid-1970s: I thought it was absolutely the best I could do. In 2002 I started to assemble and revise my various translations of Dutch poets for a collection. I started to fiddle with the Achterberg translation, got more and more involved, and in the end threw it out and translated the whole sequence de novo; and when I was finished I thought it was again absolutely the best I could do. The lesson: a translation is not just uniquely the translator's work, it is uniquely the translator's as he /she is at some particular time of life.'

22 In the preface to *Landscape with Rowers* (Princeton / Oxford, Princeton University Press, 2004, p. vii) Coetzee states that, whereas Dutch literature, although of

European stature, 'does not often pretend to eminence', its Afrikaans counterpart 'has not been shy to flaunt its modest achievements'. Coetzee's statement is probably a reaction to an exaggerated literary nationalism which he discerns in the uncritical adulation of some literary scholars. Even so, he repeatedly writes with insight and appreciation about some of these 'modest achievements'. He is, in fact, the English literary scholar who can pronounce, with more authority than any of his colleagues, on Afrikaans literature.

23 Asked whether he owned a house in Spain, Coetzee replied by e-mail: 'In fact no "house in Spain". There is a house in France which belongs to my daughter.'

24 Derek Attridge, Introduction to J.M. Coetzee, *Inner Workings*, London, Vintage Books, 2007, p. x.

25 Ibid., p. xi.

26 Ibid., p. 19.

27 Ibid., p. 39.

28 Ibid., p. 93.

29 Ibid., p. 145.

30 Ibid., p. 122.

31 Ibid., p. 217.

32 Ibid., p. 169.

33 Ibid., pp. 172–173.

34 A separate section is devoted to the essay on the filming of *The Misfits* by Arthur Miller. Attridge comments on this: 'One senses Coetzee's commitment both to art and to ethics when he offers, at the end of the chapter on *The Misfits*, a telling comment on the difference between the photographic image and the literary representation: the wild horses being rounded up in the movie were *really* traumatized.' (Introduction, p. xii.)

35 Ibid., p. 283.

36 Ibid., p. 287.

37 Ibid., p. 246.

38 Ibid., pp. 255–256.

CHAPTER 16

1 Hendrik Witbooi. '*Votre paix sera la mort de ma nation*': *Lettres de guerre d'Henrik*

Witbooi, capitaine du Grand Namaqua-land, edited and translated by Dominique Bellec and Jocelynd Nayrand, with a foreword by J. M. Coetzee (pp. 9–18), published by Le Passagier Clandestin, Le Pre Saint-Gervais, 2011.

2   Dick Cheney, vice-president in the George W. Bush presidency.

3   This critique is elaborated on through the persona of a seventy-two-year-old Australian writer in J.M. Coetzee's novel *Diary of a Bad Year*, London, Harvill Secker, 2007.

4   Details of this incident are derived from several e-mails from Coetzee and an interview with Jonathan Lear in Chicago, 20.4.2010.

5   The manuscript is in the possession of the author, who in March 2008 kindly gave me access to it.

6   J.M. Coetzee, *Slow Man*, London, Secker & Warburg, 2005, p. 1.

7   Coetzee's thorough preparation for this novel is demonstrated by his enquiry to an Australian lawyer whether a shop owner in Rundle Mall in central Adelaide would be within his rights if he reported a 14-year-old girl caught shoplifting to the police. Also as regards Drago's forgery, he writes to his friend Sharon Zwi in Sydney, on 3 February 2004: 'I wonder if I might ask you for some specialist information. I am writing a novel, set in Australia, in which forgery of an old photograph figures. The original photograph dates from the mid-19th century and is worth quite a lot of money. It is stolen, copied, and the copy returned in place of the original. The forgery is done by a person with some expertise, but the owner detects the forgery when he inspects and handles the copy. My question has two parts. (1) What sort of thing might the forger do to make the copy look like an old photograph? (2) What sort of thing would give away even a fairly expert forgery?' Zwi replied: 'I know what I would do to make a photograph look old, but I think I'd be found out quite quickly. I don't know how much of an expert forger your character is. For

an amateur I would use sepia toner when processing, which bleaches out the black and replaces it with sepia colouring. Today's papers are mostly plastic coated for quick processing and drying, but professionals and serious art work is still done on fibre based papers. I'd use fibre based paper for a forgery.' She continues: 'Some of the ways you'd recognise a 19th century photograph would be: 1. The fineness of detail in things such as lacework or other details on clothing. The silver used was a lot finer than it is today. 2. 19th century papers would definitely be on fibre based paper, not plastic coated as most commercial papers are today. 3. There was no hardener in the gelatin to stabilise it, and as a result it would have bits of the image wash away if wet, or stored in humid conditions where it swelled. It also tended to turn yellow and collect bits of dirt as a result of the softer gelatin.' She refers him to three books on the subject: 1. *The Keepers of the Light — 19th Century Photographic Techniques: A History and Working Guide to Early Photographic Processes* by William Crawford, published by Morgan and Morgan, New York, 1979. 2. *Kodak: Care and Identification of 19th Century Photographic Prints* by James M. Reilly, published by Eastman Kodak in 1986. 3. *Kodak: Conservation of Photographs*, Eastman Kodak, 1985.

8   *Slow Man*, p. 53.

9   Ibid., p. 85.

10   Christopher Hope, *The Guardian*, 17.9.2005.

11   Shaun de Waal, *Mail & Guardian*, 23.9.2005.

12   *The Spectator*, 12.9.2005.

13   Ibid.

14   Adam Kirsch, *The New York Sun*, 14.9.2005.

15   *Slow Man*, p.27.

16   Ibid., pp. 91–92.

17   David Attwell, 'Coetzee's estrange-ment', unpublished paper delivered at 'A Dialog Conference on J M Coetzee: South African Nobel Prize Winner' (Paris, Universität Salzburg, 2006).

18   Donald Powers, 'Emigration, photography, and writing in J.M.

Coetzee's *Slow Man*', *Postamble*, 5: 2, 2010.

19 Personal interview with J.M. Coetzee, 23.3.2009.

20 In *The Lives of Animals* Elizabeth Costello says that the Nazis learnt their methods of extermination in the stockyards of Chicago. In reply to a question about this, Coetzee wrote in an e-mail 21.12.2005: 'The idea for the automobile assembly line came from the practices of the Chicago stockyards, where the carcases of slaughtered animals were moved by means of an overhead conveyor from one station to the next, each station being tasked with a particular operation on the carcase. The Detroit assembly line was copied in the Volkswagen assembly line; during the war the Volkswagen assembly line, modified with the Chicago stockyard in mind, was used as a model for dealing with prisoners destined for extinction. I can't give you chapter and verse. The book *Eternal Treblinka* probably contains the relevant documentation, also the prizewinning book on Chicago by someone with a name like Croton.'

21 Paola Cavalieri, ed., *The Death of the Animal*, New York, Columbia University Press, 2009. In *The Wounded Animal* (Princeton, Princeton University Press, 2009) Stephen Mulhall published a many-levelled study of the novel *Elizabeth Costello*.In *J.M. Coetzee and Ethics*, edited by Anton Leist and Peter Singer (New York, Columbia University Press, 2010), a number of essays on Coetzee are collected, among others on 'Humans, animals, and morality'.

22 *Diary of a Bad Year*, p. 37.

23 Ibid., p. 44.

24 Ibid., p. 22, 171.

25 Ibid., p. 3.

26 Ibid., p. 8.

27 William Shakespeare, *Hamlet*, V: 2, edited by T.J.B. Spencer, introduced by Anne Barton, Harmondsworth, Penguin, 1980, p. 202.

28 *Diary of a Bad Year*, p. 54. In his own voice Señor C writes: 'Of late, sketching stories seems to have become a substitute for writing them' (ibid., p. 185).

29 Ibid., p. 191.

30 Ibid., p. 191.

31 James Wood, 'Squall lines', *The New Yorker*, 24.12.2007.

32 Coetzee wrote the 'Strong opinions' section from 12 September 2005 to 31 May 2006. 'Second diary' is not dated in the manuscript. On 7 June 2011 he replied by e-mail to an enquiry of mine: 'I supplied the publishers with 23 computer files and a set of instructions for how these files should be combined. Files X_1, X_2,..., X_9 made up the top stream of the page. Files Y_1,...Y_5, Y_8, Y_9 made up the middle stream. Files Z_2... Z_5, Z_7-Z_9 made up the bottom stream.'

33 In his review of the Dutch translation of Coetzee's novel (*Spectrum*, 11.8.2007), Jaap Goedegebuure pointed out the correspondences with *Menuet*, conjecturing that Coetzee must have read Boon's novel. In an interview on 20.3.2009 Coetzee confirmed that he knew Boon's *De kapellekensbaan*, but not *Menuet*.

34 Eric Paul Meljac, 'Seductive lines: The use of horizontal bars of Josipovici and Coetzee, and the art of seduction', *Journal of Modern Literature*, 33: 1, 2010.

35 Jeff Simon, *The Buffalo News*, 30.12.2007.

CHAPTER 17

1 Personal interview with Dorothy Driver, 3.4.2009.

2 Information from the administrative office of the University of Cape Town, by courtesy of Professor Guillaume Brümmer.

3 Agoraphobia: the fear of squares or open places.

4 The information on Gisela's medical condition is derived largely from two personal interviews with J.M. Coetzee, 16 and 25.3.2009.

5 Whereas earlier researchers believed that genetic factors played no significant role, new research, among others that of Donald Goodwin, has shown persuasively that the 'increased rate of alcoholism in the descendants of alcoholics appears to correlate

with alcohol abuse in heredity, not in environment' (George E. Vaillant, *The Natural History of Alcoholism*, Cambridge, Massachusetts, Harvard University Press, 1983, p. 64). See also Michael D. Köhnke, 'Approach to the genetics of alcoholism: A review based on pathophysiology', *Biochemical Pharmacology* 75, 2008.

6 Information from a telephone conversation with Lynette Märki, a cousin of J.M. Coetzee, on 9.7.2009.

7 Personal e-mail to me, 13.8.2009.

8 The information in this paragraph is based largely on two interviews with Dorothy Driver, 3.4.2009 and 8.4.2010.

9 Information from a personal e-mail from J.M. Coetzee, 25.1.2010.

10 Akwe Amosu, *Not Goodbye*, Plumstead, Snailpress, 2010, p. 40.

11 J.M. Coetzee, *The Master of Petersburg*, London, Secker & Warburg, 1994, p. 236.

12 J.M. Coetzee, *Summertime*, London, Harvill Secker, 2009, p. 20.

13 Patrick Denman Flanery, 'J.M. Coetzee's autre-biography', *Times Literary Supplement*, 9.9.2009.

14 *Summertime*, pp. 225–226.

15 Athough I knew the answer in advance, to make quite sure I phoned John Coetzee's cousin, Agnes Heinrich, on 28 July 2009 in Monte Vista. She has no recollection of a joint visit to Merweville or of John's wanting to buy a house there. She definitely never spent a night with him in a bakkie near Voëlfontein. After his return from America she once, at one of the family gatherings on the farm, said to him: 'You know, John, I actually don't know you at all.' She added

that when as children they visited the Coetzees in Worcester, John and his brother David took to their heels.

16 Quoted as introduction to Eben Venter's review of *Summertime*, *Rapport*, 4.10.2009.

17 Nashen Moodley, *Mail & Guardian*, 23–29.7.2010.

18 *Summertime*, p. 158.

19 Ibid., p. 112; compare Samuel Beckett, *Waiting for Godot*, London, Faber and Faber, n.d., pp. 42–43.

20 *Summertime*, p. 33.

21 *The Poetical Works of Robert Herrick*, Oxford, Clarendon Press, 1956, p. 261.

22 Thomas Jones, *The Observer*, 6.9.2009.

23 Geordie Williamson, 'Dissection of the self', *The Australian*, 5.9.2009.

24 James Meek, 'Heart of the writer', *The Guardian*, 12.9.2009.

25 Tim Park, 'The education of 'John Coetzee', *The New York Review of Books*, 11 February 2010.

26 André Brink, 'My buurman John', *By*, 6.2.2010.

27 In 'Alle eer aan *Disgrace*', collected in *Brouhaha* (Cape Town, Tafelberg, 2010, pp. 113–117), Eben Venter published an interview with Steve Jacobs and wrote about the genesis of the film.

28 Translation M.H.

29 Personal e-mail from Eva Cossée, 21.5.2010.

Epilogue

1 Information from a personal e-mail from J.M. Coetzee, 7.6.2011.

2 J.M. Coetzee, *Dusklands*, Johannesburg, Ravan Press, 1974, p. 114.

INDICES

CHRONOLOGICAL LIST OF WORKS
BY J.M. COETZEE

1974 *Dusklands*, published by Ravan Press (Johannesburg) 8, 11, 21, 33, 156, 159, 160, 167, 203, 207, 217, 218, 221, 234, 235, 237–59, 274, 283, 287, 288, 290, 292, 302, 306, 310, 323, 335, 353, 354, 374, 429, 506, 565, 607, 616

1977 *In the Heart of the Country*, published by Secker & Warburg (London) and as *From the Heart of the Country* by Harper (New York) —won the CNA and Mofolo-Plomer prizes 8, 71, 181, 214, 260, 274–8, 282–318, 334, 335, 340, 342, 344, 346, 352, 353, 359, 373, 388, 411, 435, 445, 477, 489, 517, 523, 525, 572

1980 *Waiting for the Barbarians*, published by Secker & Warburg (London) —won the Geoffrey Faber, James Tait Black and CNA prizes 154, 307, 308, 326, 332, 334–59, 362, 368, 380, 381, 388, 404, 412, 416, 443, 445, 449, 453, 457, 458, 459, 462, 474, 477, 489, 494, 495, 498, 593, 601

1983 *Life & Times of Michael K*, published by Secker & Warburg (London) —won the Booker and CAN prizes 203, 379, 381–400, 415, 445, 458, 461, 462, 477, 525, 526, 560, 572

1986 *Foe*, published by Secker & Warburg (London) 175, 239, 276, 401–11, 415, 422, 423, 446, 458, 462, 489, 495, 508, 524, 599

1986 *A Land Apart*, anthology with an introduction by J.M. Coetzee and André Brink, published by Faber & Faber (London) 360

1988 *White Writing: On the Culture of Letters in South Africa*, published by Yale University Press (New Haven, Cape Town and London) 17, 19, 33, 43, 148, 212, 275, 281, 282, 313, 362, 363, 365, 382, 386, 394, 405, 448, 492, 496, 504, 611

1990 *Age of Iron*, published by Secker & Warburg (London) —won the British Sunday Express Book of the Year Award 37, 52, 208, 214, 379, 441, 443–52, 458, 464, 489, 504

1992 *Doubling the Point: Essays and Interviews*, edited by David Attwell and published by Harvard University Press (Cambridge, Massachusetts / London) 86, 130, 150, 162, 176, 179, 212, 275, 310, 323, 329, 330, 332, 335, 365, 411, 423, 434, 490, 492–4, 497, 504, 507, 613

1994 *The Master of Petersburg*, published by Secker & Warburg (London) 111, 437, 452, 458, 460–64, 467–9, 489, 504, 518, 604

1996 *Giving Offense: Essays on Censorship*, published by University of Chicago Press (Chicago) 265, 285, 298, 329–31, 436, 496

1997 *Boyhood: Scenes from Provincial Life*, published by Secker & Warburg (London) 8, 9, 12, 31, 32, 36–40, 43, 44, 45, 47–51, 53, 55, 64, 66, 67, 71, 86, 112, 182, 215, 218, 382, 383, 401, 428, 441, 443, 444, 481, 503–10, 514, 549, 562, 593, 605–7, 609, 610

1999 *Disgrace*, published by Secker & Warburg (London) —won the Booker Prize 33, 147, 158, 214, 471, 473, 474, 477, 491, 503, 514, 516, 519, 522–32, 535, 536, 559, 560, 594, 611, 612, 615

1999 *The Lives of Animals*, published by Princeton University Press (Princeton) 471, 511, 512–14, 521, 545, 588

INDEX OF PROPER NAMES

Coetsé, Johannes Hendrik 19, 20
Coetzee (née Wehmeyer), Vera Hildred
   17, 28, 29, 34, 36–41, 44, 49, 53, 59,
   62, 63, 75, 80, 123, 319, 320, 439,
   440, 441, 443, 448, 458, 607
Coetzee, Agnes Elizabeth 28
Coetzee, Alan Hubert 28
Coetzee, Alfred Kenneth (Bubbles) 28
Coetzee, Ampie 30
Coetzee, Christoffel 30
Coetzee, Constance (Connie) 28
Coetzee, Corin 28, 319, 603
Coetzee, David Keith 34, 136, 319, 603
Coetzee, Dirk 376
Coetzee, Dr S.J. 21
Coetzee, Frederik Laurens Johannes 21, 23
Coetzee, Gerald (cousin of the author
   and owner of the family farm
   Voëlfontein) 12, 25, 35, 215, 320
Coetzee, Gerald Zacharias (Son or
   Sonny) 11, 26, 28, 44, 52, 215
Coetzee, Gerrit (baptised 1683) 18
Coetzee, Gerrit (Gert) Maxwell 12, 13,
   21, 22, 23, 26
Coetzee, Gisela Gabrièle 8, 11, 173, 215,
   320, 321, 324, 340, 422, 426, 434,
   439, 441, 442, 453, 454, 456, 457,
   575, 599–603, 616
Coetzee, Irene Linda (1899–1990) 22,
   26
Coetzee, Jack see Coetzee, Zacharias
Coetzee, Jacobus (character in 'The
   Narrative of Jacobus Coetzee' in
   Dusklands) 8, 21, 30, 159, 160, 204,
   217, 219–24, 234–41, 243, 244,
   246–8, 250–54, 275, 353, 445, 616
Coetzee, James Mills 28
Coetzee, Janet Agnes (Girlie) 28, 34, 35,
   45, 76
Coetzee, Joy 28
Coetzee, Lenie 22–6, 28, 37
Coetzee, Leonore (Lynne) 28
Coetzee, Nicolas Guy Talbot 7, 12, 162,
   173, 215, 217, 267, 320–22, 324, 340,
   422, 439, 452–9, 465, 466, 469, 486,
   599, 600, 601, 616
Coetzee, Philippa see Jubber, Philippa
Coetzee, Prof. Abel 261
Coetzee, Samuel (Sam) 319, 603

Coetzee, Son/Sonny see Coetzee, Gerald
   Zacharias
Coetzee, Stanley Maxwell Buller (1901–
   1985) 22
Coetzee, Sylvia 11, 49, 50, 215, 217, 457
Coetzee, Zacharias (Zach or Jack) 12, 17,
   28, 29, 34–40, 43–4, 49, 57, 59–62,
   75, 76, 319, 320, 439, 440, 443, 448,
   601
Connolly, Thomas E. 172, 201
Conrad, Joseph 90, 96, 126, 127, 249,
   250, 305, 337, 353, 495
Cook, Albert 172
Cooper, William 505
Coover, Robert 269
Cope, Jack 164, 177, 208, 240, 242, 249,
   258, 310
Costello, Elizabeth (fictional author) 17,
   113, 483, 495, 498, 511–13, 546–50,
   570, 585–8, 594, 604, 614
Couché (later spelled Coetsé), Dirk 18
Couché, Gerard 18
Court, Kathryn 346, 347, 388
Couzens, Tim 492
Cowley, Abraham 97
Craven, Peter 545
Creeley, Robert 172
Crewe, Jonathan V. 13, 225, 226, 242,
   243, 246, 247, 249, 250, 253, 351, 607
Cronin, A.J. 57
Cronjé, Prof. Geoff 260, 377
Crusoe, Robinson (fictional character)
   175, 239, 401, 402, 404, 405, 409,
   489, 491, 562
Crwys-Williams, Jennifer 203, 392

Dapper, Olfert 158
Dawn, Eugene (protagonist in 'The
   Vietnam Project' in Dusklands) 8, 33,
   157, 236–40, 251, 252, 323, 383
De Beer (later Coetzee), Magdalena
   Catherina (Lenie) 22, 23, 24, 25, 26
De Beer, Zacharias (Zaag) Johannes
   Hendricus (born 1858) 23
De Gaulle, Charles 113
De Klerk, F.W. 471, 472, 474
De Kock, Eugene 376
De Kock, Leon 525
De Maupassant, Guy 96

GENERAL INDEX